THE

SUNDAY

2018

PEOPLE'S EDITION

WITH THE NEW TRANSLATION OF THE MASS

Sundays Year B

From First Sunday of Advent 2017
to Christ the King 2018

Texts approved for use
in England and Wales, Scotland, and Ireland.

CATHOLIC TRUTH SOCIETY

Catholic Truth Society
40-46 Harleyford Road, London, SE11 5AY

First Published 2017

ISBN

The CTS New Sunday Missal 2018 (RM25): 978 1 78469 179 0

Cover design, compilation and typographical design and layout
© 2017 Catholic Truth Society

Concordat cum originali: Paul Moynihan

Imprimatur: ✠ Peter Smith, Archbishop of Southwark, 6th June 2017.

Acknowledgements:

The CTS is grateful for the help of the Association for Latin in the Liturgy in the preparation of this volume.

Extracts from scripture (excepting Psalm texts) from the Jerusalem Bible © 1966 Darton Longman and Todd and Doubleday & Company Inc.

The English translation of the Gospel Readings for the Palm Sunday Procession from the Catholic Edition of the Revised Standard Version of the Bible © 1965, 1966 by the Division of Christian Education of the National Council of the Churches of Christ in the United States of America. Used by permission. All rights reserved.

Psalm texts from the Grail Psalms © 1963 The Grail (England).

New English Translation 2010, granted *recognitio* by the Congregation for Divine Worship and the Discipline of the Sacraments, for the dioceses of the Bishops' Conferences of England and Wales (Prot. N. 915/06/L, 28 March 2010), and Scotland, (Prot. N. 1021/07/L, 23 June 2010), and Ireland (Prot. N. 516/05/L, 18 June 2010).

The English translation and chants of The Roman Missal © 2010, International Commission on English in the Liturgy Corporation. All rights reserved.

Latin text of Missale Romanum: Libreria Editrice Vaticana omnia sibi vindicat iura. Sine eiusdem licentia scripto data nemini liceat hunc Missale denuo imprimere aut in aliam linguam vertere © 2008, Libreria Editrice Vaticana.

Papal Magisterium used for introductions to feasts and seasons © Libreria Editrice Vaticana, Vatican City State.

Rite of Eucharistic Exposition and Benediction taken from *Holy Communion and Worship of the Eucharist Outside Mass* (The Roman Ritual) Vol. 1, Approved by the Bishops' Conference of England and Wales, Ireland and Scotland and confirmed by decree of the Sacred Congregation for the Sacraments and Divine Worship 29 May 1976.

Rosary Meditations and material for Preparation for Mass and Thanksgiving after Mass taken from *Eucharistic Adoration* D667 first published CTS, 2004.

TABLE OF CONTENTS

PREPARATION FOR MASS

| Prayer of Saint Ambrose | Oratio S. Ambrosii |

Prayer of Saint Ambrose

I draw near, loving Lord Jesus Christ,
to the table of your most
    delightful banquet
in fear and trembling,
a sinner, presuming not
    upon my own merits,
but trusting rather in your
    goodness and mercy.
I have a heart and body
    defiled by my many offences,
a mind and tongue
over which I have kept no good watch.
Therefore, O loving God,
    O awesome Majesty,
I turn in my misery, caught in snares,
to you the fountain of mercy,
hastening to you for healing,
flying to you for protection;
and while I do not look forward
    to having you as Judge,
I long to have you as Saviour.
To you, O Lord, I display my wounds,
to you I uncover my shame.
I am aware of my many and great sins,
for which I fear,
but I hope in your mercies,
which are without number.
Look upon me, then,
    with eyes of mercy,
Lord Jesus Christ, eternal King,
God and Man, crucified for mankind.
Listen to me,
    as I place my hope in you,
have pity on me, full of miseries
    and sins,
you, who will never cease
to let the fountain of compassion flow.
Hail, O Saving Victim,

Oratio S. Ambrosii

Ad mensam dulcissimi convivii tui,
    pie Domine Iesu Christe,
ego peccator de propriis meis
    meritis nihil præsumens,
sed de tua confidens misericordia
    et bonitate,
accedere vereor et contremisco.
Nam cor et corpus habeo multis
    criminibus maculatum,
mentem et linguam non
    caute custoditam.

Ergo, o pia Deitas,
    o tremenda maiestas,
ego miser,
    inter angustias deprehensus,
ad te fontem misericordiæ recurro,
ad te festino sanandus,
sub tuam protectionem fugio;
et, quem Iudicem sustinere nequeo,
Salvatorem habere suspiro.
Tibi, Domine, plagas meas ostendo,
tibi verecundiam meam detego.
Scio peccata mea multa
    et magna, pro quibus timeo:
spero in misericordias tuas,
    quarum non est numerus.
Respice ergo in me oculis
    misericordiæ tuæ,
Domine Iesu Christe, Rex æterne,
    Deus et homo,
crucifixus propter hominem.
Exaudi me sperantem in te:
miserere mei pleni miseriis
    et peccatis,
tu qui fontem miserationis
numquam manare cessabis.
Salve, salutaris victima,

offered for me and
for the whole human race
on the wood of the Cross.
Hail, O noble and precious Blood,
flowing from the wounds
of Jesus Christ, my crucified Lord,
and washing away the sins
of all the world.
Remember, Lord, your creature,
whom you redeemed by your Blood.
I am repentant of my sins,
I desire to put right what I have done.
Take from me, therefore, most
merciful Father,
all my iniquities and sins,
so that, purified in mind and body,
I may worthily taste the Holy of Holies.
And grant that this sacred foretaste
of your Body and Blood
which I, though unworthy,
intend to receive,
may be the remission of my sins,
the perfect cleansing of my faults,
the banishment of shameful thoughts,
and the rebirth of right sentiments;
and may it encourage
a wholesome and
effective performance
of deeds pleasing to you
and be a most firm defence
of body and soul
against the snares of my enemies.
Amen.

Prayer of Saint Thomas Aquinas

Almighty eternal God,
behold, I come to the Sacrament
of your Only Begotten Son,
our Lord Jesus Christ,
as one sick to the physician of life,
as one unclean to

pro me et omni humano genere
in patibulo Crucis oblata.

Salve, nobilis et pretiose Sanguis,
de vulneribus crucifixi Domini mei
Iesu Christi profluens,
et peccata totius mundi abluens.

Recordare, Domine, creaturæ tuæ,
quam tuo Sanguine redemisti.
Pænitet me peccasse,
cupio emendare quod feci.
Aufer ergo a me, clementissime Pater,
omnes iniquitates et peccata mea,
ut, purificatus mente et corpore,
digne degustare merear
Sancta sanctorum.
Et concede, ut hæc sancta
prælibatio Corporis
et Sanguinis tui,
quam ego indignus
sumere intendo,
sit peccatorum meorum remissio,
sit delictorum perfecta purgatio,
sit turpium cogitationum effugatio
ac bonorum sensuum regeneratio,
operumque tibi placentium
salubris efficacia,
animæ quoque et corporis
contra inimicorum meorum
insidias firmissima tuitio.
Amen.

Oratio S. Thomæ Aquinatis

Omnipotens sempiterne Deus,
ecce accedo ad sacramentum
Unigeniti Filii tui,
Domini nostri Iesu Christi,
accedo tamquam infirmus
ad medicum vitæ

the fountain of mercy,
as one blind to the light
    of eternal brightness,
as one poor and needy to
    the Lord of heaven and earth.
I ask, therefore, for the abundance
    of your immense generosity,
that you may graciously cure
    my sickness,
wash away my defilement,
give light to my blindness,
enrich my poverty,
clothe my nakedness,
so that I may receive
    the bread of Angels,
the King of kings and Lord of lords,
with such reverence and humility,
such contrition and devotion,
such purity and faith,
such purpose and intention
as are conducive to the salvation of
    my soul.
Grant, I pray, that I may receive
not only the Sacrament
    of the Lord's Body and Blood,
but also the reality and power
    of that Sacrament.
O most gentle God,
grant that I may so receive
the Body of your Only Begotten
    Son our Lord Jesus Christ,
which he took from
    the Virgin Mary,
that I may be made worthy
    to be incorporated into his
    Mystical Body
and to be counted among
    its members.
O most loving Father,
grant that I may at last gaze for ever
upon the unveiled face

immundus ad
    fontem misericordiæ,
cæcus ad lumen claritatis æternæ,
pauper et egenus ad
    Dominum cæli et terræ.
Rogo ergo immensæ largitatis
    tuæ abundantiam,
quatenus meam curare
    digneris infirmitatem,
lavare fœditatem,
    illuminare cæcitatem,
ditare paupertatem,
    vestire nuditatem,
ut panem Angelorum,
    Regem regum
    et Dominum dominantium,
tanta suscipiam reverentia
    et humilitate,
tanta contritione et devotione,
    tanta puritate et fide,
tali proposito et intentione,
sicut expedit saluti animæ meæ.
Da mihi, quæso,
    dominici Corporis et Sanguinis
non solum suscipere sacramentum,
sed etiam rem
    et virtutem sacramenti.
O mitissime Deus,
da mihi Corpus Unigeniti Filii tui,
Domini nostri Iesu Christi,
quod traxit de Virgine Maria,
    sic suscipere,
ut corpori suo mystico
merear incorporari
et inter eius membra connumerari.

O amantissime Pater,
    concede mihi dilectum
    Filium tuum,

of your beloved Son,
whom I, a wayfarer,
propose to receive now veiled
    under these species:
Who lives and reigns with you
    for ever and ever.
Amen.

quem nunc velatum
    in via suscipere propono,
revelata tandem facie
    perpetuo contemplari:
Qui tecum vivit et regnat
in sæcula sæculorum.
Amen.

PRAYER BEFORE MASS

O God, to whom every heart is open, every desire known and from whom no secrets are hidden; purify the thoughts of our hearts by the inspiration of your Holy Spirit, that we may perfectly love you, and worthily praise your holy name. Amen.

Before Holy Communion

Prayer for Help

O God, help me to make a good Communion. Mary, my dearest mother, pray to Jesus for me. My dear Angel Guardian, lead me to the Altar of God.

Act of Faith

O God, because you have said it, I believe that I shall receive the Sacred Body of Jesus Christ to eat, and his Precious Blood to drink. My God, I believe this with all my heart.

Act of Humility

My God, I confess that I am a poor sinner; I am not worthy to receive the Body and Blood of Jesus, on account of my sins. Lord, I am not worthy to receive you under my roof; but only say the word, and my soul will be healed.

Act of Sorrow

My God, I detest all the sins of my life. I am sorry for them, because they have offended you, my God, you who are so good. I resolve never to commit sin any more. My good God, pity me, have mercy on me, forgive me.

Act of Adoration

O Jesus, great God, present on the Altar, I bow down before you.
I adore you.

Act of Love and Desire

Jesus, I love you. I desire with all my heart to receive you. Jesus, come into my poor soul, and give me your Flesh to eat and your Blood to drink.

Give me your whole Self, Body, Blood, Soul and Divinity, that I may live for ever with you.

THE ORDER OF MASS

ORDO MISSÆ CUM POPULO

THE INTRODUCTORY RITES

Before Mass begins, the people gather in a spirit of recollection, preparing for their participation in the Mass.

All stand during the entrance procession.

SIGN OF THE CROSS

After the Entrance Chant, the Priest and the faithful sign themselves with the Sign of the Cross:

Priest: In nómine Patris, et Fílii, et Spíritus Sancti.

A-men.

Response: **Amen.**

GREETING

The Priest greets the people, with one of the following:

1. Pr. Grátia Dómini nostri Iesu Christi,
   et cáritas Dei,
   et communicátio Sancti Spíritus
   sit cum ómnibus vobis.

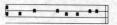

Et cum spí-ri-tu tu-o.

   R. **Et cum spíritu tuo.**

2. Pr. Grátia vobis et pax a Deo Patre nostro
   et Dómino Iesu Christo.
   R. **Et cum spíritu tuo.**

3. Pr. Dóminus vobíscum.
   R. **Et cum spíritu tuo.**

The Priest, or a Deacon, or another minister, may very briefly introduce the faithful to the Mass of the day.

THE ORDER OF MASS WITH A CONGREGATION

THE INTRODUCTORY RITES

Before Mass begins, the people gather in a spirit of recollection, preparing for their participation in the Mass.

All stand during the entrance procession.

SIGN OF THE CROSS

After the Entrance Chant, the Priest and the faithful sign themselves with the Sign of the Cross:

Priest: In the name of the Father, and of the Son, and of the Holy Spirit.

A-men.

Response: Amen.

GREETING

The Priest greets the people, with one of the following:

1. Pr. The grace of our Lord Jesus Christ,
   and the love of God,
   and the communion of the Holy Spirit
   be with you all.

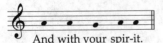

And with your spir-it.

R. **And with your spirit.**

2. Pr. Grace to you and peace from God our Father
   and the Lord Jesus Christ.
   R. **And with your spirit.**

3. Pr. The Lord be with you.
   R. **And with your spirit.**

The Priest, or a Deacon, or another minister, may very briefly introduce the faithful to the Mass of the day.

PENITENTIAL ACT*

There are three forms of the Penitential Act which may be chosen from as appropriate. Each Penitential Act begins with the invitation to the faithful by the Priest:

Pr. Fratres, agnoscámus peccáta nostra,
ut apti simus ad sacra mystéria celebránda.

A brief pause for silence follows.

Then one of the following forms is used:

---

1. Confíteor Deo omnipoténti et vobis, fratres,
quia peccávi nimis
cogitatióne, verbo, ópere et omissióne:

(and, striking their breast, they say:)

mea culpa, mea culpa, mea máxima culpa.
Ideo precor beátam Mariám semper Vírginem,
omnes Angelos et Sanctos,
et vos, fratres, oráre pro me
ad Dóminum Deum nostrum.

---

2. **Pr.** Miserére nostri, Dómine.

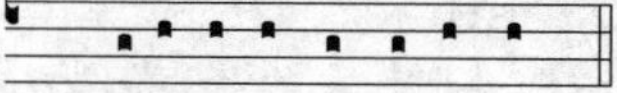

Qui- a peccá- vi- mus ti- bi.

R. Quia peccávimus tibi.

Pr. Osténde nobis, Dómine, misericórdiam tuam.

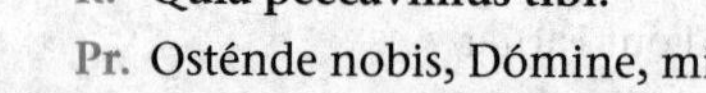

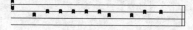

Et sa- lu- tá- re tu- um da no- bis.

R. Et salutáre tuum da nobis.

---

* From time to time on Sundays, especially in Easter Time, instead of the customary Penitential Act, the blessing and sprinkling of water may take place (as in pp.16-21) as a reminder of Baptism.

PENITENTIAL ACT*

There are three forms of the Penitential Act which may be chosen from as appropriate.
Each Penitential Act begins with the invitation to the faithful by the Priest:

Pr. Brethren (brothers and sisters),
  let us acknowledge our sins,
 and so prepare ourselves to celebrate the sacred mysteries.

A brief pause for silence follows.

Then one of the following forms is used:

---

1. I confess to almighty God
and to you, my brothers and sisters,
that I have greatly sinned,
in my thoughts and in my words,
in what I have done and in what I have failed to do,

(and, striking their breast, they say:)

through my fault, through my fault,
through my most grievous fault;
therefore I ask blessed Mary ever-Virgin,
all the Angels and Saints,
and you, my brothers and sisters,
to pray for me to the Lord our God.

---

2. **Pr.** Have mercy on us, O Lord.

For we have sinned a-gainst you.

 R. **For we have sinned against you.**

 Pr. Show us, O Lord, your mercy.

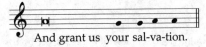

And grant us your sal-va-tion.

 R. **And grant us your salvation.**

---

* From time to time on Sundays, especially in Easter Time, instead of the customary Penitential
Act, the blessing and sprinkling of water may take place (as in pp. 16-21) as a reminder of Baptism.

Invocations naming the gracious works of the Lord may be made, as in the example below:

3. Pr. Qui missus es sanáre contrítos corde:
    Kýrie, eléison.

Ký- ri- e,   e- lé- i- son.

R. Kýrie, eléison.

Pr. Qui peccatóres vocáre venísti:
    Christe, eléison.

Chri- ste,   e- lé- i- son.

R. Christe, eléison.

Pr. Qui ad déxteram Patris sedes, ad interpellándum pro nobis:
    Kýrie, eléison.

Ký- ri- e,   e- lé- i- son.

R. Kýrie, eléison.

The absolution by the Priest follows:

Pr. Misereátur nostri omnípotens Deus
    et, dimíssis peccátis nostris,
    perdúcat nos ad vitam ætérnam.

A-men.

R. Amen.

The Kýrie, eléison (Lord, have mercy) invocations follow, unless they have just occurred.

Pr. Kýrie, eléison.

y-ri-e,   e-lé- i-son.

Invocations naming the gracious works of the Lord may be made, as in the example below:

3. Pr. You were sent to heal the contrite of heart:
   Lord, have mercy. Or: Kýrie, eléison.

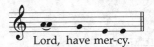
Lord, have mer-cy.   Or: repeat music/words from Latin, p.14.

   R. Lord, have mercy.

   Pr. You came to call sinners:
   Christ, have mercy. Or: Christe, eléison.

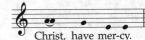
Christ, have mer-cy.   Or: repeat music/words from Latin, p.14.

   R. Christ, have mercy.

   Pr. You are seated at the right hand of the Father to intercede for us:
   Lord, have mercy. Or: Kýrie, eléison.

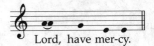
Lord, have mer-cy.   Or: repeat music/words from Latin, p.14.

   R. Lord, have mercy.

The absolution by the Priest follows:

Pr. May almighty God have mercy on us,
   forgive us our sins,
   and bring us to everlasting life.

A-men.

R. Amen.

The Kýrie, eléison (Lord, have mercy) invocations follow, unless they have just occurred.

   Pr. Lord, have mercy.

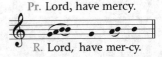
R. Lord, have mer-cy.

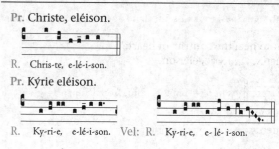

Pr. Christe, eléison.

R.   Chris-te, e-lé-i-son.

Pr. Kýrie eléison.

R.   Ky-ri-e, e-lé-i-son.   Vel: R.   Ky-ri-e, e-lé-i-son.

RITE FOR THE BLESSING AND SPRINKLING OF WATER

If this rite is celebrated during Mass, it takes the place of the usual Penitential Act at the beginning of Mass. After the greeting, the Priest calls upon the people to pray in these or similar words:

Dominum Deum nostrum, fratres carissimi,
suppliciter deprecemur,
ut hanc creaturam aquæ benedicere dignetur,
super nos aspergendam in nostri memoriam baptismi.
Ipse autem nos adiuvare dignetur,
ut fideles Spiritui, quem accepimus, maneamus.

And after a brief pause for silence, he continues with hands joined:

Omnipotens sempiterne Deus, qui voluisti ut per aquam,
fontem vitæ ac purificationis principium,
etiam animæ mundarentur
æternæque vitæ munus exciperent,
dignare, quæsumus, hanc aquam ✠ benedicere,
qua volumus hac die tua, Domine, communiri.
Fontem vivum in nobis tuæ gratiæ renovari
et ab omni malo spiritus et corporis
per ipsam nos defendi concedas,
ut mundis tibi cordibus propinquare
tuamque digne salutem valeamus accipere.
Per Christum Dominum nostrum.
R. Amen.

Pr. Christ, have mercy.

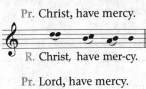

R. Christ, have mer-cy.

Pr. Lord, have mercy.

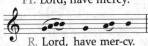

R. Lord, have mer-cy.

RITE FOR THE BLESSING AND SPRINKLING OF WATER

If this rite is celebrated during Mass, it takes the place of the usual Penitential Act at
the beginning of Mass. After the greeting, the Priest calls upon the people to pray
in these or similar words:

Dear brethren (brothers and sisters),
let us humbly beseech the Lord our God
to bless this water he has created,
which will be sprinkled on us
as a memorial of our Baptism.
May he help us by his grace
to remain faithful to the Spirit we have received.

And after a brief pause for silence, he continues with hands joined:

Almighty ever-living God,
who willed that through water,
the fountain of life and the source of purification,
even souls should be cleansed
and receive the gift of eternal life;
be pleased, we pray, to ✠ bless this water,
by which we seek protection on this your day, O Lord.
Renew the living spring of your grace within us
and grant that by this water we may be defended
from all ills of spirit and body,
and so approach you with hearts made clean
and worthily receive your salvation.
Through Christ our Lord.
R. Amen.

Or:

Domine Deus omnipotens,
qui es totius vitæ corporis et animæ fons et origo,
hanc aquam, te quæsumus, ✠ benedicas,
qua fidenter utimur
ad nostrorum implorandam veniam peccatorum
et adversus omnes morbos inimicique insidias
tuæ defensionem gratiæ consequendam.
Præsta, Domine, ut, misericordia tua interveniente,
aquæ vivæ semper nobis saliant in salutem,
ut mundo tibi corde appropinquare possimus,
et omnia corporis animæque pericula devitemus.
Per Christum Dominum nostrum.
R. Amen.

Or, during Easter Time:

Domine Deus omnipotens,
precibus populi tui adesto propitius;
et nobis, mirabile nostræ creationis opus,
sed et redemptionis nostræ mirabilius, memorantibus,
hanc aquam ✠ benedicere tu dignare.
Ipsam enim tu fecisti,
ut et arva fecunditate donaret,
et levamen corporibus nostris munditiamque præberet.
Aquam etiam tuæ ministram misericordiæ condidisti;
nam per ipsam solvisti tui populi servitutem,
illiusque sitim in deserto sedasti;
per ipsam novum foedus nuntiaverunt prophetæ,
quod eras cum hominibus initurus;
per ipsam denique, quam Christus in Iordane sacravit,
corruptam naturæ nostræ substantiam
in regenerationis lavacro renovasti.
Sit igitur hæc aqua nobis suscepti baptismatis memoria,
et cum fratribus nostris, qui sunt in Paschate baptizati,
gaudia nos tribuas sociare.
Per Christum Dominum nostrum.
R. Amen.

Or:

Almighty Lord and God,
who are the source and origin of all life,
whether of body or soul,
we ask you to ✠ bless this water,
which we use in confidence
to implore forgiveness for our sins
and to obtain the protection of your grace
against all illness and every snare of the enemy.
Grant, O Lord, in your mercy,
that living waters may always spring up for our salvation,
and so may we approach you with a pure heart
and avoid all danger to body and soul.
Through Christ our Lord.
R. Amen.

Or, during Easter Time:

Lord our God,
in your mercy be present to your people's prayers,
and, for us who recall the wondrous work of our creation
and the still greater work of our redemption,
graciously ✠ bless this water.
For you created water to make the fields fruitful
and to refresh and cleanse our bodies.
You also made water the instrument of your mercy:
for through water you freed your people from slavery
and quenched their thirst in the desert;
through water the Prophets proclaimed the new covenant
you were to enter upon with the human race;
and last of all,
through water, which Christ made holy in the Jordan,
you have renewed our corrupted nature
in the bath of regeneration.
Therefore, may this water be for us
a memorial of the Baptism we have received,
and grant that we may share
in the gladness of our brothers and sisters
who at Easter have received their Baptism.
Through Christ our Lord.
R. Amen.

Where the circumstances of the place or the custom of the people suggest that the mixing of salt be preserved in the blessing of water, the Priest may bless salt, saying:

Supplices te rogamus, omnipotens Deus,
ut hanc creaturam salis
benedicere ✠ tua pietate digneris,
qui per Eliseum prophetam in aquam mitti eam iussisti,
ut sanaretur sterilitas aquæ.
Præsta, Domine, quæsumus,
ut, ubicumque hæc salis et aquæ commixtio
fuerit aspersa,
omni impugnatione inimici depulsa,
præsentia Sancti tui Spiritus nos iugiter custodiat.
Per Christum Dominum nostrum.
R. Amen.

Then he pours the salt into the water, without saying anything.

Afterward, taking the aspergillum, the Priest sprinkles himself and the ministers, then the clergy and people, moving through the church, if appropriate.

Meanwhile, one of the following chants, or another appropriate chant is sung.

Outside Easter Time

Antiphon   Ps 50:9

Asperges me, Domine, hyssopo et mundabor:
lavabis me, et super nivem dealbabor.

During Easter Time

Antiphon   Cf. Ez 47:1-2,9

Vidi aquam egredientem de templo,
a latere dextro, alleluia;
et omnes, ad quos pervenit aqua ista, salvi facti sunt,
et dicent: alleluia, alleluia.

When he returns to his chair and the singing is over, the Priest stands facing the people and, with hands joined, says:

Deus omnipotens nos a peccatis purificet,
et per huius Eucharistiæ celebrationem dignos nos reddat,
qui mensæ regni sui participes efficiamur.
R. Amen.

Then, when it is prescribed, the hymn Gloria in excelsis (Glory to God in the highest) is sung or said.

Where the circumstances of the place or the custom of the people suggest that the mixing of salt be preserved in the blessing of water, the Priest may bless salt, saying:

We humbly ask you, almighty God:
be pleased in your faithful love to bless ✠ this salt
you have created,
for it was you who commanded the prophet Elisha
to cast salt into water,
that impure water might be purified.
Grant, O Lord, we pray,
that, wherever this mixture of salt and water is sprinkled,
every attack of the enemy may be repulsed
and your Holy Spirit may be present
to keep us safe at all times.
Through Christ our Lord.
R. Amen.

Then he pours the salt into the water, without saying anything.
Afterward, taking the aspergillum, the Priest sprinkles himself and the ministers, then the clergy and people, moving through the church, if appropriate.
Meanwhile, one of the following chants, or another appropriate chant is sung.

Outside Easter Time

Antiphon   Ps 50:9
Sprinkle me with hyssop, O Lord, and I shall be cleansed;
wash me and I shall be whiter than snow.

During Easter Time

Antiphon   Cf. Ez 47:1-2,9
I saw water flowing from the Temple,
from its right-hand side, alleluia:
and all to whom this water came
were saved and shall say: alleluia, alleluia.

When he returns to his chair and the singing is over, the Priest stands facing the people and, with hands joined, says:

May almighty God cleanse us of our sins,
and through the celebration of this Eucharist
make us worthy to share at the table of his Kingdom.
R. Amen.

Then, when it is prescribed, the hymn Gloria in excelsis (Glory to God in the highest) is sung or said.

THE GLORIA

On Sundays (outside Advent and Lent), Solemnities and Feast Days, this hymn is
either sung or said:

G ló-ri-a in ex-cél-sis De- o.   Et in ter-ra pax ho-mí-ni-bus   bo-næ

vol-un-tá-tis.   Lau-dá- mus te.   Be-ne-dí-ci-mus te   Ado-rá-

mus te.   Glo-ri-fi-cámus te.   Grá-ti- as á-gi-mus ti-bi   prop-ter

mag-nam gló-ri-am tu-am.   Dó-mi-ne De- us, Rex cæ-léstis,   De-us

Pa-ter om-ní-po-tens. Dómi-ne Fí-li uni-gé-ni-te,   Ie-su Christe.

Dó-mi-ne De-us, Agnus De-i,   Fí-li-us Pa-tris,   Qui tollis peccáta

mun- di,   mi-se-ré- re nobis.   Qui tollis peccáta mundi,   súscipe de-

pre-ca-ti-ó-nem no- stram.   Qui sedes ad déxteram Patris,   mi-seré-

THE GLORIA

On Sundays (outside Advent and Lent), Solemnities and Feast Days, this hymn is either sung or said:

Glo-ry to God in the high-est,

and on earth peace to peo-ple of good will.

We praise you, we bless you, we a-dore you, we glo-ri-fy you,

we give you thanks for your great glo-ry,

Lord God, heav-en-ly King, O God, al-might-y Fa-ther.

Lord Je-sus Christ, On-ly Be-got-ten Son,

Lord God, Lamb of God, Son of the Fa-ther,

you take a-way the sins of the world, have mer-cy on us;

you take a-way the sins of the world, re-ceive our prayer;

you are seat-ed at the right hand of the Fa-ther, have mer-cy on us.

re nobis. Quóni-am tu solus Sanctus.   Tu solus Dó-mi-nus   Tu solus Al-tíssimus, Ie-su Christe. Cum Sancto Spí-ri-tu,   in gló-ri-a
De- i Pa- tris.   A-   men.

Glória in excélsis Deo
et in terra pax homínibus bonæ voluntátis.

Laudámus te,
benedícimus te,
adorámus te,
glorificámus te,
grátias ágimus tibi propter magnam glóriam tuam,
Dómine Deus, Rex cæléstis,
Deus Pater omnípotens.

Dómine Fili Unigénite, Iesu Christe,
Dómine Deus, Agnus Dei, Fílius Patris,
qui tollis peccáta mundi, miserére nobis;
qui tollis peccáta mundi, súscipe deprecatiónem nostram.
Qui sedes ad déxteram Patris, miserére nobis.

Quóniam tu solus Sanctus, tu solus Dóminus, tu solus Altíssimus,
Iesu Christe, cum Sancto Spíritu: in glória Dei Patris.
Amen.

When this hymn is concluded, the Priest, says: **Pr. Orémus.**
And all pray in silence. Then the Priest says the Collect prayer, which ends:
R. Amen.

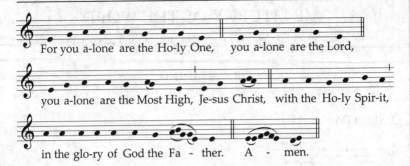

For you a-lone are the Ho-ly One,   you a-lone are the Lord,

you a-lone are the Most High, Je-sus Christ,   with the Ho-ly Spir-it,

in the glo-ry of God the Fa - ther.   A - men.

Glory to God in the highest,
and on earth peace to people of good will.

We praise you,
we bless you,
we adore you,
we glorify you,
we give you thanks for your great glory,
Lord God, heavenly King,
O God, almighty Father.

Lord Jesus Christ, Only Begotten Son,
Lord God, Lamb of God, Son of the Father,
you take away the sins of the world, have mercy on us;
you take away the sins of the world, receive our prayer;
you are seated at the right hand of the Father,
have mercy on us.

For you alone are the Holy One,
you alone are the Lord,
you alone are the Most High,
Jesus Christ,
with the Holy Spirit,
in the glory of God the Father.
Amen.

When this hymn is concluded, the Priest, says: **Pr. Let us pray.**
And all pray in silence. Then the Priest says the Collect prayer, which ends:
R. Amen.

THE LITURGY OF THE WORD

By hearing the word proclaimed in worship, the faithful again enter into the unending dialogue between God and the covenant people.

FIRST READING

The reader goes to the ambo and proclaims the First Reading, while all sit and listen. The reader ends:

Verbum Dómini.

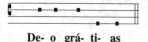

De- o grá- ti- as

R. **Deo grátias.**

It is appropriate to have a brief time of quiet between readings as those present take the word of God to heart.

PSALM

The psalmist or cantor sings or says the Psalm, with the people making the response.

SECOND READING

On Sundays and certain other days there is a second reading. The reader ends:

Verbum Dómini.

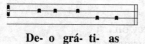

De- o grá- ti- as

R. **Deo grátias.**

GOSPEL

The assembly stands for the Gospel Acclamation. Except during Lent the Acclamation is:

R. **Allelúia!**

During Lent the following forms may be used or another similar phrase:

R. **Laus tibi, Christe, Rex ætérnæ glóriæ!** Or:

R. **Laus et honor tibi, Dómine Iesu!** Or:

R. **Glória et laus tibi, Christe!** Or:

R. **Glória tibi, Christe, Verbo Dei!**

THE LITURGY OF THE WORD

By hearing the word proclaimed in worship, the faithful again enter into the unending dialogue between God and the covenant people.

FIRST READING

The reader goes to the ambo and proclaims the First Reading, while all sit and listen. The reader ends:

The word of the Lord.

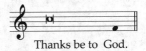

Thanks be to God.

R. **Thanks be to God.**

It is appropriate to have a brief time of quiet between readings as those present take the word of God to heart.

PSALM

The psalmist or cantor sings or says the Psalm, with the people making the response.

SECOND READING

On Sundays and certain other days there is a second reading. The reader ends:

The word of the Lord.

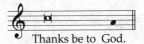

Thanks be to God.

R. **Thanks be to God.**

GOSPEL

The assembly stands for the Gospel Acclamation. Except during Lent the Acclamation is:

R. **Alleluia!**

During Lent the following forms may be used or another similar phrase:

R. **Praise to you, O Christ, king of eternal glory!** Or:

R. **Praise and honour to you, Lord Jesus!** Or:

R. **Glory and praise to you, O Christ!** Or:

R. **Glory to you, O Christ, you are the Word of God!**

At the ambo the Deacon, or the Priest says:

Pr. Dóminus vobíscum.

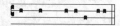

Et cum spíritu tuo.

R. **Et cum spíritu tuo.**

Pr. Léctio sancti Evangélii secúndum N.

He makes the Sign of the Cross on the book and, together with the people, on his forehead, lips, and breast.

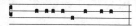

Glória tibi Dómine.

R. **Glória tibi, Dómine.**

At the end of the Gospel:

Pr. Verbum Dómini.

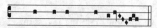

Laus ti-bi, Christe.

R. **Laus tibi, Christe.**

THE HOMILY

Then follows the Homily, which is preached by a Priest or Deacon on all Sundays and Holydays of Obligation. After a brief silence all stand.

THE CREED

On Sundays and Solemnities, the Profession of Faith will follow. Especially during Lent and Easter Time, the Apostles' Creed may be used.

THE NICENO-CONSTANTINOPOLITAN CREED

Credo in unum De- um,   Patrem omni-poténtem factó-rem cæli et

terræ, vi-sibili-um óm-nium et invi-si-bí- lium.   Et in unum Dó-

At the ambo the Deacon, or the Priest says:

Pr. The Lord be with you.

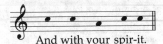

And with your spir-it.

R. **And with your spirit.**

Pr. A reading from the holy Gospel according to N.

He makes the Sign of the Cross on the book and, together with the people, on his forehead, lips, and breast.

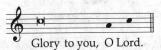

Glory to you, O Lord.

R. **Glory to you, O Lord.**

At the end of the Gospel:

Pr. The Gospel of the Lord.

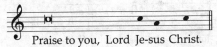

Praise to you, Lord Je-sus Christ.

R. **Praise to you, Lord Jesus Christ.**

THE HOMILY

Then follows the Homily, which is preached by a Priest or Deacon on all Sundays and Holydays of Obligation. After a brief silence all stand.

THE CREED

On Sundays and Solemnities, the Profession of Faith will follow. Especially during Lent and Easter Time, the Apostles' Creed may be used.

THE NICENO-CONSTANTINOPOLITAN CREED

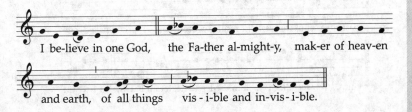

I be-lieve in one God, the Fa-ther al-might-y, mak-er of heav-en and earth, of all things vis-i-ble and in-vis-i-ble.

minum Iesum Christum, Fí-lium De-i uni-gé-ni-tum. Et ex Pa-

tre na- tum ante ómni-a sæ- cu-la. De-um de De-o, lumen de

lumine, De-um verum de De-o vero. Géni-tum, non fac-tum, con-

substanti-á-lem Patri: per quem ómni-a facta sunt. Qui propter nos

At the words

homines et propter nostram sa-lútem descéndit de cæ-lis. Et in-

that follow, up to and including **et homo factus est**, all bow.

carná-tus est de Spí-ri-tu Sancto ex Ma-rí-a Vírgi-ne, et homo

factus est. Cru-ci-fí- xus é-ti-am pro nobis sub Pónti-o Pi-lá-to,

passus et sepúl- tus est. Et resurré-xit térti-a di-e, secúndum Scrip-

turas, Et ascéndit in cæ- lum, sedet ad déxteram Patris. Et í-terum

I be-lieve in one Lord   Je-sus Christ,   the Only Be - got-ten Son

of God,   born of the Father be - fore all a-ges.   God from God,

Light from Light,   true God from true God,   be-got-ten, not made,

con-sub-stan-tial with the Fa-ther;   through him all things were

made.   For us men and for our sal-va-tion   he came down from

At the words that follow, up to and including and became man, all bow.

heav-en,   and by the Ho-ly Spir-it was in-car-nate   of the Vir-gin

Mar-y,   and be-came man.

For our sake he was cru-ci-fied   un-der Pon-tius Pi-late,   he

suffered death and was bur-ied,   and rose a-gain on the third day

in accordance with the Scrip-tures. He as-cend-ed in-to heav-en

ventúrus est cum gló-ri-a,   iudicá-re vivos et mórtu-os, cu-ius reg-

ni non e-rit fi-nis.   Et in Spí-ri-tum Sanctum, Dóminum   et vi-vi-

fi-cántem: qui ex Patre Fi-li-óque pro-cédit.   Qui cum Patre et Fí-

li-o   simul adorá-tur et conglo-ri-ficá-tur: qui locú-tus est per

prophé-tas.   Et unam, sanctam, cathó-li-cam et apostó-li-cam Ec-

clé-si-am. Confí-te-or unum baptísma   in remissi - ónem pec-ca

tó-rum. Et exspécto resurrecti-ó-nem mortu-ó-rum.   Et vi-tam ven-

túri sæ-cu-li.   A-   men

and is seated at the right hand of the Fa-ther.   He will come a-gain

in glo-ry   to judge the living and the dead   and his kingdom will

have no end.

I be-lieve in the Ho-ly Spir-it,   the Lord, the giv-er of life,   who

pro-ceeds from the Father and the Son,   who with the Fa-ther and

the Son   is adored and glo-ri-fied,   who has spoken through the

proph-ets.   I be-lieve in one, ho-ly, ca-tho-lic   and a-pos-tol-ic

Church.   I con-fess one Bap-tism   for the for - give-ness of sins

and I look for-ward to the res-ur-rec-tion of the dead   and the life

of the world to come.   A - men.

Credo in unum Deum,
Patrem omnipoténtem,
factórem cæli et terræ,
visibílium ómnium et invisibílium.

Et in unum Dóminum Iesum Christum,
Fílium Dei Unigénitum,
et ex Patre natum ante ómnia sǽcula.
Deum de Deo, lumen de lúmine,
    Deum verum de Deo vero,
génitum, non factum, consubstantiálem Patri:
per quem ómnia facta sunt.
Qui propter nos hómines et propter nostram salútem
descéndit de cælis.

(all bow)

Et incarnátus est de Spíritu Sancto
ex María Vírgine, et homo factus est.

Crucifíxus étiam pro nobis sub Póntio Piláto;
passus et sepúltus est,
et resurréxit tértia die, secúndum Scriptúras,
et ascéndit in cælum, sedet ad déxteram Patris.

Et íterum ventúrus est cum glória,
    iudicáre vivos et mórtuos,
cuius regni non erit finis.

Et in Spíritum Sanctum, Dóminum et vivificántem:
qui ex Patre Filióque procédit.
Qui cum Patre et Fílio simul adorátur et conglorificátur:
qui locútus est per prophétas.

Et unam, sanctam, cathólicam et apostólicam Ecclésiam.
Confíteor unum baptísma in remissiónem peccatórum.
Et exspécto resurrectiónem mortuórum,
et vitam ventúri sǽculi. Amen.

I believe in one God,
the Father almighty,
maker of heaven and earth,
of all things visible and invisible.

I believe in one Lord Jesus Christ,
the Only Begotten Son of God,
born of the Father before all ages.
God from God, Light from Light,
true God from true God,
begotten, not made, consubstantial with the Father;
through him all things were made.
For us men and for our salvation
he came down from heaven,

(all bow)

and by the Holy Spirit was incarnate of the Virgin Mary,
and became man.

For our sake he was crucified under Pontius Pilate,
he suffered death and was buried,
and rose again on the third day
in accordance with the Scriptures.
He ascended into heaven
and is seated at the right hand of the Father.
He will come again in glory
to judge the living and the dead
and his kingdom will have no end.

I believe in the Holy Spirit, the Lord, the giver of life,
who proceeds from the Father and the Son,
who with the Father and the Son is adored and glorified,
who has spoken through the prophets.

I believe in one, holy, catholic and apostolic Church.
I confess one Baptism for the forgiveness of sins
and I look forward to the resurrection of the dead
and the life of the world to come. Amen.

THE APOSTLES' CREED

Credo in Deum, Patrem omnipoténtem,
Creatórem cæli et terræ,
et in Iesum Christum, Fílium eius únicum,
Dóminum nostrum,

at the words that follow up to and including **Maria Virgine**, all bow.

qui concéptus est de Spíritu Sancto,
natus ex María Vírgine,
passus sub Póntio Piláto,
crucifíxus, mórtuus, et sepúltus,
descéndit ad ínferos,
tértia die resurréxit a mórtuis,
ascéndit ad cælos,
sedet ad déxteram Dei Patris omnipoténtis,
inde ventúrus est iudicáre vivos et mórtuos.

Credo in Spíritum Sanctum,
sanctam Ecclésiam cathólicam,
Sanctórum communiónem,
remissiónem peccatórum,
carnis resurrectiónem,
vitam ætérnam. Amen.

THE PRAYER OF THE FAITHFUL (BIDDING PRAYERS)

Intentions will normally be for the Church; for the world; for those in particular need; and for the local community. After each there is time for silent prayer, followed by the next intention, or concluded with a sung phrase such as Christe audi nos, or Christe exaudi nos, or by a responsory such as:

R.   **Præsta, ætérne omnípotens Deus.** Or:
R.   **Te rogámus audi nos.** Or:
R.   **Kýrie, eléison.**

The Priest concludes the Prayer with a collect.

THE APOSTLES' CREED

I believe in God,
the Father almighty
Creator of heaven and earth,
and in Jesus Christ, his only Son, our Lord,

at the words that follow up to and including the Virgin Mary, all bow.

who was conceived by the Holy Spirit,
born of the Virgin Mary,
suffered under Pontius Pilate,
was crucified, died and was buried;
he descended into hell;
on the third day he rose again from the dead;
he ascended into heaven,
and is seated at the right hand of God
    the Father almighty;
from there he will come to judge the living and the dead.

I believe in the Holy Spirit,
the holy catholic Church,
the communion of saints,
the forgiveness of sins,
the resurrection of the body,
and life everlasting. Amen.

THE PRAYER OF THE FAITHFUL (BIDDING PRAYERS)

Intentions will normally be for the Church; for the world; for those in particular
need; and for the local community. After each there is time for silent prayer,
followed by the next intention, or concluded with a sung phrase such as Christ,
hear us, or Christ graciously hear us, or by a responsory such as:

Let us pray to the Lord.
R. **Grant this, almighty God.** Or:
R. **Lord, have mercy.** Or:
R. **Kýrie, eléison.**

The Priest concludes the Prayer with a collect.

THE LITURGY OF THE EUCHARIST

For Catholics, the Eucharist is the source and summit of the whole Christian life.

After the Liturgy of the Word, the people sit and the Offertory Chant begins. The faithful express their participation by making an offering, bringing forward bread and wine for the celebration of the Eucharist and perhaps other gifts to relieve the needs of the Church and of the poor.

PREPARATORY PRAYERS

Standing at the altar, the Priest takes the paten with the bread and holds it slightly raised above the altar with both hands, saying:

Pr. Benedíctus es, Dómine, Deus univérsi,
quia de tua largitáte accépimus panem,
quem tibi offérimus,
fructum terræ et óperis mánuum hóminum:
ex quo nobis fiet panis vitæ.

R. **Benedíctus Deus in sǽcula.**

The Priest then takes the chalice and holds it slightly raised above the altar with both hands, saying:

Pr. Benedíctus es, Dómine, Deus univérsi,
quia de tua largitáte accépimus vinum,
quod tibi offérimus,
fructum vitis et óperis mánuum hóminum,
ex quo nobis fiet potus spiritális.

R. **Benedíctus Deus in sǽcula.**

The Priest completes additional personal preparatory rites, and the people rise as he says:

Pr. Oráte, fratres:
ut meum ac vestrum sacrifícium
acceptábile fiat apud Deum Patrem omnipoténtem.

R. **Suscípiat Dóminus sacrifícium de mánibus tuis**
ad laudem et glóriam nóminis sui,
ad utilitátem quoque nostram
totiúsque Ecclésiæ suæ sanctæ.

PRAYER OVER THE OFFERINGS

The Priest says the Prayer over the Offerings, at the end of which the people acclaim:

R. **Amen.**

THE LITURGY OF THE EUCHARIST

For Catholics, the Eucharist is the source and summit of the whole Christian life.

After the Liturgy of the Word, the people sit and the Offertory Chant begins. The faithful express their participation by making an offering, bringing forward bread and wine for the celebration of the Eucharist and perhaps other gifts to relieve the needs of the Church and of the poor.

PREPARATORY PRAYERS

Standing at the altar, the Priest takes the paten with the bread and holds it slightly raised above the altar with both hands, saying:

Pr. Blessed are you, Lord God of all creation,
for through your goodness we have received
the bread we offer you:
fruit of the earth and work of human hands,
it will become for us the bread of life.

R. **Blessed be God for ever.**

The Priest then takes the chalice and holds it slightly raised above the altar with both hands, saying:

Pr. Blessed are you, Lord God of all creation,
for through your goodness we have received
the wine we offer you:
fruit of the vine and work of human hands,
it will become our spiritual drink.

R. **Blessed be God for ever.**

The Priest completes additional personal preparatory rites, and the people rise as he says:

Pr. Pray, brethren (brothers and sisters),
that my sacrifice and yours
may be acceptable to God,
the almighty Father.

R. **May the Lord accept the sacrifice at your hands**
for the praise and glory of his name,
for our good
and the good of all his holy Church.

PRAYER OVER THE OFFERINGS

The Priest says the Prayer over the Offerings, at the end of which the people acclaim:

R. **Amen.**

THE EUCHARISTIC PRAYER

Extending his hands, the Priest says:

Pr. Dóminus vobíscum.

Et cum spí-ri-tu tu-o.

R. **Et cum spíritu tuo.**

Pr. Sursum corda.

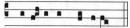

Habémus ad Dóminum.

R. **Habémus ad Dóminum.**

Pr. Grátias agámus Dómino Deo nostro.

Dignum et iustum est.

R. **Dignum et iustum est.**

The Priest continues with the Preface appropriate to the Season or Feast at the end of which all sing or say:

anc-tus, * Sanc-tus, Sanc-tus Dó-mi-nus De-us Sá-ba-oth. Ple-ni

sunt cæ-li et ter-ra gló-ri-a tu-a. Ho-sán-na in ex-cél-sis. Be-ne-díc-

tus qui ve-nit in nómine Dómini.   Ho-sán-na in excél-sis.

THE EUCHARISTIC PRAYER

Extending his hands, the Priest says:

Pr. The Lord be with you.

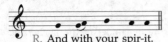

R. And with your spir-it.

R. And with your spirit.

Pr. Lift up your hearts.

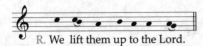

R. We lift them up to the Lord.

R. We lift them up to the Lord.

Pr. Let us give thanks to the Lord our God.

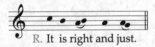

R. It is right and just.

R. It is right and just.

The Priest continues with the Preface appropriate to the Season or Feast at the end of which all sing or say:

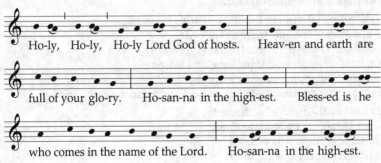

Ho-ly, Ho-ly, Ho-ly Lord God of hosts. Heav-en and earth are full of your glo-ry. Ho-san-na in the high-est. Bless-ed is he who comes in the name of the Lord. Ho-san-na in the high-est.

Sanctus, Sanctus, Sanctus Dóminus Deus Sábaoth.
Pleni sunt cæli et terra glória tua.
Hosánna in excélsis.
Benedíctus qui venit in nómine Dómini.
Hosánna in excélsis.

After the Sanctus the congregation kneels for the remainder of the Eucharistic
Prayer. (Texts for the four principal Eucharistic Prayers follow: Eucharistic Prayer I at
p.80, II at p.92, III at p.100, IV at p.110.)

PREFACES

ADVENT

PRÆFATIO I DE ADVENTU

De duobus adventibus Christi

In Missis de tempore a prima dominica Adventus usque ad diem 16 decembris

Vere dignum et iustum est, æquum et salutare,
nos tibi semper et ubique gratias agere:
Domine, sancte Pater, omnipotens æterne Deus:
per Christum Dominum nostrum.

Qui, primo adventu in humilitate carnis assumptæ,
dispositionis antiquæ munus implevit,
nobisque salutis perpetuæ tramitem reseravit:
ut, cum secundo venerit in suæ gloria maiestatis,
manifesto demum munere capiamus,
quod vigilantes nunc audemus exspectare promissum.

Et ideo cum Angelis et Archangelis,
cum Thronis et Dominationibus,
cumque omni militia cælestis exercitus,
hymnum gloriæ tuæ canimus,
sine fine dicentes:

Sanctus, Sanctus, Sanctus Dominus Deus Sabaoth. . .

Holy, Holy, Holy Lord God of hosts.
Heaven and earth are full of your glory.
Hosanna in the highest.
Blessed is he who comes in the name of the Lord.
Hosanna in the highest.

After the Sanctus the congregation kneels for the remainder of the Eucharistic Prayer. (Texts for the four principal Eucharistic Prayers follow: Eucharistic Prayer I at p.81, II at p.93, III at p.101, IV at p.111.)

PREFACES

ADVENT

PREFACE I OF ADVENT

The two comings of Christ

From the First Sunday of Advent until 16 December

It is truly right and just, our duty and our salvation,
always and everywhere to give you thanks,
Lord, holy Father, almighty and eternal God,
through Christ our Lord.

For he assumed at his first coming
the lowliness of human flesh,
and so fulfilled the design you formed long ago,
and opened for us the way to eternal salvation,
that, when he comes again in glory and majesty
and all is at last made manifest,
we who watch for that day
may inherit the great promise
in which now we dare to hope.

And so, with Angels and Archangels,
with Thrones and Dominions,
and with all the hosts and Powers of heaven,
we sing the hymn of your glory,
as without end we acclaim:

Holy, Holy, Holy Lord God of hosts. . .

PRÆFATIO II DE ADVENTU

De duplici exspectatione Christi

17 decembris-24 decembris

Vere dignum et iustum est, æquum et salutare,
nos tibi semper et ubique gratias agere:
Domine, sancte Pater, omnipotens æterne Deus:
per Christum Dominum nostrum.

Quem prædixerunt cunctorum præconia prophetarum,
Virgo Mater ineffabili dilectione sustinuit,
Ioannes cecinit affuturum et adesse monstravit.
Qui suæ nativitatis mysterium
tribuit nos prævenire gaudentes,
ut et in oratione pervigiles
et in suis inveniat laudibus exsultantes.

Et ideo cum Angelis et Archangelis,
cum Thronis et Dominationibus,
cumque omni militia cælestis exercitus,
hymnum gloriæ tuæ canimus,
sine fine dicentes:
Sanctus, Sanctus, Sanctus Dominus Deus Sabaoth. . .

CHRISTMAS

PRÆFATIO I DE NATIVITATE DOMINI

De Christo luce

Vere dignum et iustum est, æquum et salutare,
nos tibi semper et ubique gratias agere:
Domine, sancte Pater, omnipotens æterne Deus:

Quia per incarnati Verbi mysterium
nova mentis nostræ oculis lux tuæ claritatis infulsit:
ut, dum visibiliter Deum cognoscimus,
per hunc in invisibilium amorem rapiamur.

Et ideo cum Angelis et Archangelis,
cum Thronis et Dominationibus,
cumque omni militia cælestis exercitus,
hymnum gloriæ tuæ canimus, sine fine dicentes:
Sanctus, Sanctus, Sanctus Dominus Deus Sabaoth. . .

PREFACE II OF ADVENT

The twofold expectation of Christ

17 December-24 December

It is truly right and just, our duty and our salvation,
always and everywhere to give you thanks,
Lord, holy Father, almighty and eternal God,
through Christ our Lord.

For all the oracles of the prophets foretold him,
the Virgin Mother longed for him
with love beyond all telling,
John the Baptist sang of his coming
and proclaimed his presence when he came.

It is by his gift that already we rejoice
at the mystery of his Nativity,
so that he may find us watchful in prayer
and exultant in his praise.

And so, with Angels and Archangels,
with Thrones and Dominions,
and with all the hosts and Powers of heaven,
we sing the hymn of your glory,
as without end we acclaim:

Holy, Holy, Holy Lord God of hosts. . .

CHRISTMAS

PREFACE I OF THE NATIVITY OF THE LORD

Christ the Light

It is truly right and just, our duty and our salvation,
always and everywhere to give you thanks,
Lord, holy Father, almighty and eternal God.

For in the mystery of the Word made flesh
a new light of your glory has shone upon the eyes of our mind,
so that, as we recognise in him God made visible,
we may be caught up through him in love of things invisible.

And so, with Angels and Archangels,
with Thrones and Dominions,
and with all the hosts and Powers of heaven,
we sing the hymn of your glory,
as without end we acclaim:

Holy, Holy, Holy Lord God of hosts. . .

PRÆFATIO II DE NATIVITATE DOMINI

De restauratione universa in Incarnatione

Vere dignum et iustum est, æquum et salutare,
nos tibi semper et ubique gratias agere:
Domine, sancte Pater, omnipotens æterne Deus:
per Christum Dominum nostrum.

Qui, in huius venerandi festivitate mysterii,
invisibilis in suis, visibilis in nostris apparuit,
et ante tempora genitus esse cœpit in tempore;
ut, in se erigens cuncta deiecta,
in integrum restitueret universa,
et hominem perditum ad cælestia regna revocaret.

Unde et nos, cum omnibus Angelis te laudamus,
iucunda celebratione clamantes:

Sanctus, Sanctus, Sanctus Dominus Deus Sabaoth. . .

PRÆFATIO III DE NATIVITATE DOMINI

De commercio in Incarnatione Verbi

Vere dignum et iustum est, æquum et salutare,
nos tibi semper et ubique gratias agere:
Domine, sancte Pater, omnipotens æterne Deus:
per Christum Dominum nostrum.

Per quem hodie commercium nostræ reparationis effulsit,
quia, dum nostra fragilitas a tuo Verbo suscipitur,
humana mortalitas non solum
in perpetuum transit honorem,
sed nos quoque, mirando consortio, reddit æternos.

Et ideo, choris angelicis sociati,
te laudamus in gaudio confitentes:

Sanctus, Sanctus, Sanctus Dominus Deus Sabaoth. . .

PREFACE II OF THE NATIVITY OF THE LORD

The restoration of all things in the Incarnation

It is truly right and just, our duty and our salvation,
always and everywhere to give you thanks,
Lord, holy Father, almighty and eternal God,
through Christ our Lord.

For on the feast of this awe-filled mystery,
though invisible in his own divine nature,
he has appeared visibly in ours;
and begotten before all ages,
he has begun to exist in time;
so that, raising up in himself all that was cast down,
he might restore unity to all creation
and call straying humanity back to the heavenly Kingdom.

And so, with all the Angels, we praise you,
as in joyful celebration we acclaim:

Holy, Holy, Holy Lord God of hosts. . .

PREFACE III OF THE NATIVITY OF THE LORD

The exchange in the Incarnation of the Word

It is truly right and just, our duty and our salvation,
always and everywhere to give you thanks,
Lord, holy Father, almighty and eternal God,
through Christ our Lord.

For through him the holy exchange that restores our life
has shone forth today in splendour:
when our frailty is assumed by your Word
not only does human mortality receive unending honour
but by this wondrous union we, too, are made eternal.

And so, in company with the choirs of Angels,
we praise you, and with joy we proclaim:

Holy, Holy, Holy Lord God of hosts. . .

PRÆFATIO DE EPIPHANIA DOMINI

De Christo lumine gentium

Vere dignum et iustum est, æquum et salutare,
nos tibi semper et ubique gratias agere:
Domine, sancte Pater, omnipotens æterne Deus:

Quia ipsum in Christo salutis nostræ mysterium
hodie ad lumen gentium revelasti,
et, cum in substantia nostræ mortalitatis apparuit,
nova nos immortalitatis eius gloria reparasti.

Et ideo cum Angelis et Archangelis,
cum Thronis et Dominationibus,
cumque omni militia cælestis exercitus,
hymnum gloriæ tuæ canimus,
sine fine dicentes:

Sanctus, Sanctus, Sanctus Dominus Deus Sabaoth. . .

LENT
PRÆFATIO I DE QUADRAGESIMA

De spiritali significatione Quadregesimæ

Vere dignum et iustum est, æquum et salutare,
nos tibi semper et ubique gratias agere:
Domine, sancte Pater, omnipotens æterne Deus:
per Christum Dominum nostrum.

Quia fidelibus tuis dignanter concedis
quotannis paschalia sacramenta
in gaudio purificatis mentibus exspectare:
ut, pietatis officia et opera caritatis propensius exsequentes,
frequentatione mysteriorum, quibus renati sunt,
ad gratiæ filiorum plenitudinem perducantur.

Et ideo cum Angelis et Archangelis,
cum Thronis et Dominationibus,
cumque omni militia cælestis exercitus,
hymnum gloriæ tuæ canimus,
sine fine dicentes:

Sanctus, Sanctus, Sanctus Dominus Deus Sabaoth. . .

PREFACE OF THE EPIPHANY OF THE LORD
Christ the light of the nations

It is truly right and just, our duty and our salvation,
always and everywhere to give you thanks,
Lord, holy Father, almighty and eternal God.

For today you have revealed the mystery
of our salvation in Christ
as a light for the nations,
and, when he appeared in our mortal nature,
you made us new by the glory of his immortal nature.

And so, with Angels and Archangels,
with Thrones and Dominions,
and with all the hosts and Powers of heaven,
we sing the hymn of your glory,
as without end we acclaim:

Holy, Holy, Holy Lord God of hosts. . .

LENT
PREFACE I OF LENT
The spiritual meaning of Lent

It is truly right and just, our duty and our salvation,
always and everywhere to give you thanks,
Lord, holy Father, almighty and eternal God,
through Christ our Lord.

For by your gracious gift each year
your faithful await the sacred paschal feasts
with the joy of minds made pure,
so that, more eagerly intent on prayer
and on the works of charity,
and participating in the mysteries
by which they have been reborn,
they may be led to the fullness of grace
that you bestow on your sons and daughters.

And so, with Angels and Archangels,
with Thrones and Dominions,
and with all the hosts and Powers of heaven,
we sing the hymn of your glory,
as without end we acclaim:

Holy, Holy, Holy Lord God of hosts. . .

PRÆFATIO II DE QUADRAGESIMA

De spiritali pænitentia

Vere dignum et iustum est, æquum et salutare,
nos tibi semper et ubique gratias agere:
Domine, sancte Pater, omnipotens æterne Deus:

Qui filiis tuis ad reparandam mentium puritatem,
tempus præcipuum salubriter statuisti,
quo, mente ab inordinatis affectibus expedita,
sic incumberent transituris
ut rebus potius perpetuis inhærerent.

Et ideo, cum Sanctis et Angelis universis,
te collaudamus, sine fine dicentes:

Sanctus, Sanctus, Sanctus Dominus Deus Sabaoth. . .

PRÆFATIO III DE QUADRAGESIMA

De fructibus abstinentiæ

Vere dignum et iustum est, æquum et salutare,
nos tibi semper et ubique gratias agere:
Domine, sancte Pater, omnipotens æterne Deus:

Qui nos per abstinentiam tibi gratias referre voluisti,
ut ipsa et nos peccatores ab insolentia mitigaret,
et, egentium proficiens alimento,
imitatores tuæ benignitatis efficeret.

Et ideo, cum innumeris Angelis,
una te magnificamus laudis voce dicentes:

Sanctus, Sanctus, Sanctus Dominus Deus Sabaoth. . .

PRÆFATIO IV DE QUADRAGESIMA

De fructibus ieiunii

Vere dignum et iustum est, æquum et salutare,
nos tibi semper et ubique gratias agere:
Domine, sancte Pater, omnipotens æterne Deus:

Qui corporali ieiunio vitia comprimis, mentem elevas,
virtutem largiris et præmia:
per Christum Dominum nostrum.

PREFACE II OF LENT
Spiritual penance

It is truly right and just, our duty and our salvation,
always and everywhere to give you thanks,
Lord, holy Father, almighty and eternal God.

For you have given your children a sacred time
for the renewing and purifying of their hearts,
that, freed from disordered affections,
they may so deal with the things of this passing world
as to hold rather to the things that eternally endure.

And so, with all the Angels and Saints,
we praise you, as without end we acclaim:

Holy, Holy, Holy Lord God of hosts. . .

PREFACE III OF LENT
The fruits of abstinence

It is truly right and just, our duty and our salvation,
always and everywhere to give you thanks,
Lord, holy Father, almighty and eternal God.

For you will that our self-denial should give you thanks,
humble our sinful pride,
contribute to the feeding of the poor,
and so help us imitate you in your kindness.

And so we glorify you with countless Angels,
as with one voice of praise we acclaim:

Holy, Holy, Holy Lord God of hosts. . .

PREFACE IV OF LENT
The fruits of fasting

It is truly right and just, our duty and our salvation,
always and everywhere to give you thanks,
Lord, holy Father, almighty and eternal God.

For through bodily fasting you restrain our faults,
raise up our minds,
and bestow both virtue and its rewards,
through Christ our Lord.

Per quem maiestatem tuam laudant Angeli,
adorant Dominationes, tremunt Potestates.
Cæli cælorumque Virtutes, ac beata Seraphim,
socia exsultatione concelebrant.

Cum quibus et nostras voces ut admitti iubeas, deprecamur,
supplici confessione dicentes:

Sanctus, Sanctus, Sanctus Dominus Deus Sabaoth. . .

PRÆFATIO I DE PASSIONE DOMINI

De virtute Crucis

Vere dignum et iustum est, æquum et salutare,
nos tibi semper et ubique gratias agere:
Domine, sancte Pater, omnipotens æterne Deus:

Quia per Filii tui salutiferam passionem
sensum confitendæ tuæ maiestatis totus mundus accepit,
dum ineffabili crucis potentia
iudicium mundi et potestas emicat Crucifixi.

Unde et nos, Domine, cum Angelis et Sanctis universis,
tibi confitemur, in exsultatione dicentes:

Sanctus, Sanctus, Sanctus Dominus Deus Sabaoth. . .

EASTER

PRÆFATIO PASCHALIS I

De mysterio paschali

Vere dignum et iustum est, æquum et salutare:
Te quidem, Domine, omni tempore confiteri,
sed in hac potissimum nocte (die) gloriosius prædicare,
(sed in hoc potissimum gloriosius prædicare,)
cum Pascha nostrum immolatus est Christus.

Ipse enim verus est Agnus
qui abstulit peccata mundi.
Qui mortem nostram moriendo destruxit,
et vitam resurgendo reparavit.

Quapropter, profusis paschalibus gaudiis,
totus in orbe terrarum mundus exsultat.

Through him the Angels praise your majesty,
Dominions adore and Powers tremble before you.
Heaven and the Virtues of heaven and the blessed Seraphim
worship together with exultation.
May our voices, we pray, join with theirs
in humble praise, as we acclaim:

Holy, Holy, Holy Lord God of hosts. . .

PREFACE I OF THE PASSION OF THE LORD

The power of the Cross

It is truly right and just, our duty and our salvation,
always and everywhere to give you thanks,
Lord, holy Father, almighty and eternal God.

For through the saving Passion of your Son
the whole world has received a heart
to confess the infinite power of your majesty,
since by the wondrous power of the Cross
your judgement on the world is now revealed
and the authority of Christ crucified.

And so, Lord, with all the Angels and Saints,
we, too, give you thanks, as in exultation we acclaim:

Holy, Holy, Holy Lord God of hosts. . .

EASTER

PREFACE I OF EASTER

The Paschal Mystery

It is truly right and just, our duty and our salvation,
at all times to acclaim you, O Lord,
but (on this night / on this day / in this time) above all
to laud you yet more gloriously,
when Christ our Passover has been sacrificed.

For he is the true Lamb
who has taken away the sins of the world;
by dying he has destroyed our death,
and by rising, restored our life.

Therefore, overcome with paschal joy,
every land, every people exults in your praise

Sed et supernæ virtutes atque angelicæ potestates
hymnum gloriæ tuæ concinunt, sine fine dicentes:

Sanctus, Sanctus, Sanctus Dominus Deus Sabaoth. . .

PRÆFATIO PASCHALIS II

De vita nova in Christo

Vere dignum et iustum est, æquum et salutare:
Te quidem, Domine, omni tempore confiteri,
sed in hoc potissimum gloriosius prædicare,
cum Pascha nostrum immolatus est Christus.

Per quem in æternam vitam filii lucis oriuntur,
et regni cælestis atria fidelibus reserantur.
Quia mors nostra est eius morte redempta,
et in eius resurrectione vita omnium resurrexit.

Quapropter, profusis paschalibus gaudiis,
totus in orbe terrarum mundus exsultat.
Sed et supernæ virtutes atque angelicæ potestates
hymnum gloriæ tuæ concinunt, sine fine dicentes:

Sanctus, Sanctus, Sanctus Dominus Deus Sabaoth. . .

PRÆFATIO PASCHALIS III

De Christo vivente et semper interpellante pro nobis

Vere dignum et iustum est, æquum et salutare:
Te quidem, Domine, omni tempore confiteri,
sed in hoc potissimum gloriosius prædicare,
cum Pascha nostrum immolatus est Christus.

Qui se pro nobis offerre non desinit,
nosque apud te perenni advocatione defendit;
qui immolatus iam non moritur,
sed semper vivit occisus.

Quapropter, profusis paschalibus gaudiis,
totus in orbe terrarum mundus exsultat.
Sed et supernæ virtutes atque angelicæ potestates
hymnum gloriæ tuæ concinunt, sine fine dicentes:

Sanctus, Sanctus, Sanctus Dominus Deus Sabaoth. . .

and even the heavenly Powers, with the angelic hosts,
sing together the unending hymn of your glory,
as they acclaim:

Holy, Holy, Holy Lord God of hosts. . .

PREFACE II OF EASTER

New life in Christ

It is truly right and just, our duty and our salvation,
at all times to acclaim you, O Lord,
but in this time above all to laud you yet more gloriously,
when Christ our Passover has been sacrificed.

Through him the children of light rise to eternal life
and the halls of the heavenly Kingdom
are thrown open to the faithful;
for his Death is our ransom from death,
and in his rising the life of all has risen.

Therefore, overcome with paschal joy,
every land, every people exults in your praise
and even the heavenly Powers, with the angelic hosts,
sing together the unending hymn of your glory,
as they acclaim:

Holy, Holy, Holy Lord God of hosts. . .

PREFACE III OF EASTER

Christ living and always interceding for us

It is truly right and just, our duty and our salvation,
at all times to acclaim you, O Lord,
but in this time above all to laud you yet more gloriously,
when Christ our Passover has been sacrificed.

He never ceases to offer himself for us
but defends us and ever pleads our cause before you:
he is the sacrificial Victim who dies no more,
the Lamb, once slain, who lives for ever.

Therefore, overcome with paschal joy,
every land, every people exults in your praise
and even the heavenly Powers, with the angelic hosts,
sing together the unending hymn of your glory,
as they acclaim:

Holy, Holy, Holy Lord God of hosts. . .

PRÆFATIO PASCHALIS IV

De restauratione universi per mysterium paschale

Vere dignum et iustum est, æquum et salutare:
Te quidem, Domine, omni tempore confiteri,
sed in hoc potissimum gloriosius prædicare,
cum Pascha nostrum immolatus est Christus.

Quia, vetustate destructa, renovantur universa deiecta,
et vitæ nobis in Christo reparatur integritas.

Quapropter, profusis paschalibus gaudiis,
totus in orbe terrarum mundus exsultat.
Sed et supernæ virtutes atque angelicæ potestates
hymnum gloriæ tuæ concinunt, sine fine dicentes:

Sanctus, Sanctus, Sanctus Dominus Deus Sabaoth. . .

PRÆFATIO PASCHALIS V

De Christo sacerdote et victima

Vere dignum et iustum est, æquum et salutare:
Te quidem, Domine, omni tempore confiteri,
sed in hoc potissimum gloriosius prædicare,
cum Pascha nostrum immolatus est Christus.

Qui, oblatione corporis sui,
antiqua sacrificia in crucis veritate perfecit,
et, seipsum tibi pro nostra salute commendans,
idem sacerdos, altare et agnus exhibuit.

Quapropter, profusis paschalibus gaudiis,
totus in orbe terrarum mundus exsultat.
Sed et supernæ virtutes atque angelicæ potestates
hymnum gloriæ tuæ concinunt, sine fine dicentes:

Sanctus, Sanctus, Sanctus Dominus Deus Sabaoth. . .

PREFACE IV OF EASTER

The restoration of the universe through the Paschal Mystery

It is truly right and just, our duty and our salvation,
at all times to acclaim you, O Lord,
but in this time above all to laud you yet more gloriously,
when Christ our Passover has been sacrificed.

For, with the old order destroyed,
a universe cast down is renewed,
and integrity of life is restored to us in Christ.

Therefore, overcome with paschal joy,
every land, every people exults in your praise
and even the heavenly Powers, with the angelic hosts,
sing together the unending hymn of your glory,
as they acclaim:

Holy, Holy, Holy Lord God of hosts. . .

PREFACE V OF EASTER

Christ, Priest and Victim

It is truly right and just, our duty and our salvation,
at all times to acclaim you, O Lord,
but in this time above all to laud you yet more gloriously,
when Christ our Passover has been sacrificed.

By the oblation of his Body,
he brought the sacrifices of old to fulfilment
in the reality of the Cross
and, by commending himself to you for our salvation,
showed himself the Priest, the Altar, and the Lamb of sacrifice.

Therefore, overcome with paschal joy,
every land, every people exults in your praise
and even the heavenly Powers, with the angelic hosts,
sing together the unending hymn of your glory,
as they acclaim:

Holy, Holy, Holy Lord God of hosts. . .

PRÆFATIO I DE ASCENSIONE DOMINI

De mysterio Ascensionis

Vere dignum et iustum est, æquum et salutare,
nos tibi semper et ubique gratias agere:
Domine, sancte Pater, omnipotens æterne Deus:

Quia Dominus Iesus, Rex gloriæ,
peccati triumphator et mortis,
mirantibus Angelis, ascendit (hodie) summa cælorum,
Mediator Dei et hominum,
Iudex mundi Dominusque virtutum;
non ut a nostra humilitate discederet,
sed ut illuc confideremus, sua membra, nos subsequi
quo ipse, caput nostrum principiumque, præcessit.

Quapropter, profusis paschalibus gaudiis,
totus in orbe terrarum mundus exsultat.
Sed et supernæ virtutes atque angelicæ potestates
hymnum gloriæ tuæ concinunt, sine fine dicentes:
Sanctus, Sanctus, Sanctus Dominus Deus Sabaoth. . .

PRÆFATIO II DE ASCENSIONE DOMINI

De mysterio Ascensionis

Vere dignum et iustum est, æquum et salutare,
nos tibi semper et ubique gratias agere:
Domine, sancte Pater, omnipotens æterne Deus:
per Christum Dominum nostrum.

Qui post resurrectionem suam
omnibus discipulis suis manifestus apparuit,
et ipsis cernentibus est elevatus in cælum,
ut nos divinitatis suæ tribueret esse participes.

Quapropter, profusis paschalibus gaudiis,
totus in orbe terrarum mundus exsultat.
Sed et supernæ virtutes atque angelicæ potestates
hymnum gloriæ tuæ concinunt, sine fine dicentes:

Sanctus, Sanctus, Sanctus Dominus Deus Sabaoth. . .

PREFACE I OF THE ASCENSION OF THE LORD

The mystery of the Ascension

It is truly right and just, our duty and our salvation,
always and everywhere to give you thanks,
Lord, holy Father, almighty and eternal God.

For the Lord Jesus, the King of glory,
conqueror of sin and death,
ascended (today) to the highest heavens,
as the Angels gazed in wonder.

Mediator between God and man,
judge of the world and Lord of hosts,
he ascended, not to distance himself from our lowly state
but that we, his members, might be confident of following
where he, our Head and Founder, has gone before.

Therefore, overcome with paschal joy,
every land, every people exults in your praise
and even the heavenly Powers, with the angelic hosts,
sing together the unending hymn of your glory,
as they acclaim:

Holy, Holy, Holy Lord God of hosts. . .

PREFACE II OF THE ASCENSION OF THE LORD

The mystery of the Ascension

It is truly right and just, our duty and our salvation,
always and everywhere to give you thanks,
Lord, holy Father, almighty and eternal God,
through Christ our Lord.

For after his Resurrection
he plainly appeared to all his disciples
and was taken up to heaven in their sight,
that he might make us sharers in his divinity.

Therefore, overcome with paschal joy,
every land, every people exults in your praise
and even the heavenly Powers, with the angelic hosts,
sing together the unending hymn of your glory,
as they acclaim:

Holy, Holy, Holy Lord God of hosts. . .

PRÆFATIO I DE DOMINICIS « PER ANNUM »

De mysterio paschali et de populo Dei

Vere dignum et iustum est, æquum et salutare,
nos tibi semper et ubique gratias agere:
Domine, sancte Pater, omnipotens æterne Deus:
per Christum Dominum nostrum.

Cuius hoc mirificum fuit opus per paschale mysterium,
ut de peccato et mortis iugo ad hanc gloriam vocaremur,
qua nunc genus electum, regale sacerdotium,
gens sancta et acquisitionis populus diceremur,
et tuas annuntiaremus ubique virtutes,
qui nos de tenebris ad tuum admirabile lumen vocasti.

Et ideo cum Angelis et Archangelis,
cum Thronis et Dominationibus,
cumque omni militia cælestis exercitus,
hymnum gloriæ tuæ canimus,
sine fine dicentes:

Sanctus, Sanctus, Sanctus Dominus Deus Sabaoth. . .

PRÆFATIO II DE DOMINICIS « PER ANNUM »

De mysterio salutis

Vere dignum et iustum est, æquum et salutare,
nos tibi semper et ubique gratias agere:
Domine, sancte Pater, omnipotens æterne Deus:
per Christum Dominum nostrum.

Qui, humanis miseratus erroribus,
de Virgine nasci dignatus est.
Qui, crucem passus, a perpetua morte nos liberavit
et, a mortuis resurgens, vitam nobis donavit æternam.

Et ideo cum Angelis et Archangelis,
cum Thronis et Dominationibus,
cumque omni militia cælestis exercitus,
hymnum gloriæ tuæ canimus,
sine fine dicentes:

Sanctus, Sanctus, Sanctus Dominus Deus Sabaoth. . .

PREFACE I OF THE SUNDAYS IN ORDINARY TIME

The Paschal Mystery and the People of God

It is truly right and just, our duty and our salvation,
always and everywhere to give you thanks,
Lord, holy Father, almighty and eternal God,
through Christ our Lord.

For through his Paschal Mystery,
he accomplished the marvellous deed,
by which he has freed us from the yoke of sin and death,
summoning us to the glory of being now called
a chosen race, a royal priesthood,
a holy nation, a people for your own possession,
to proclaim everywhere your mighty works,
for you have called us out of darkness
into your own wonderful light.

And so, with Angels and Archangels,
with Thrones and Dominions,
and with all the hosts and Powers of heaven,
we sing the hymn of your glory,
as without end we acclaim:

Holy, Holy, Holy Lord God of hosts. . .

PREFACE II OF THE SUNDAYS IN ORDINARY TIME

The mystery of salvation

It is truly right and just, our duty and our salvation,
always and everywhere to give you thanks,
Lord, holy Father, almighty and eternal God,
through Christ our Lord.

For out of compassion for the waywardness that is ours,
he humbled himself and was born of the Virgin;
by the passion of the Cross he freed us from unending death,
and by rising from the dead he gave us life eternal.

And so, with Angels and Archangels,
with Thrones and Dominions,
and with all the hosts and Powers of heaven,
we sing the hymn of your glory,
as without end we acclaim:

Holy, Holy, Holy Lord God of hosts. . .

PRÆFATIO III DE DOMINICIS « PER ANNUM »

De salvatione hominis per hominem

Vere dignum et iustum est, æquum et salutare,
nos tibi semper et ubique gratias agere:
Domine, sancte Pater, omnipotens æterne Deus:

Ad cuius immensam gloriam pertinere cognoscimus
ut mortalibus tua deitate succurreres;
sed et nobis provideres de ipsa
mortalitate nostra remedium,
et perditos quosque unde perierant, inde salvares,
per Christum Dominum nostrum.

Per quem maiestatem tuam adorat exercitus Angelorum,
ante conspectum tuum in æternitate lætantium.

Cum quibus et nostras voces ut admitti iubeas, deprecamur,
socia exsultatione dicentes:

Sanctus, Sanctus, Sanctus Dominus Deus Sabaoth. . .

PRÆFATIO IV DE DOMINICIS « PER ANNUM »

De historia salutis

Vere dignum et iustum est, æquum et salutare,
nos tibi semper et ubique gratias agere:
Domine, sancte Pater, omnipotens æterne Deus:
per Christum Dominum nostrum.

Ipse enim nascendo vetustatem hominum renovavit,
patiendo delevit nostra peccata,
æternæ vitæ aditum præstitit a mortuis resurgendo,
ad te Patrem ascendendo cælestes ianuas reseravit.

Et ideo, cum Angelorum atque Sanctorum turba,
hymnum laudis tibi canimus, sine fine dicentes:
Sanctus, Sanctus, Sanctus Dominus Deus Sabaoth. . .

PREFACE III OF THE SUNDAYS IN ORDINARY TIME

The salvation of man by a man

It is truly right and just, our duty and our salvation,
always and everywhere to give you thanks,
Lord, holy Father, almighty and eternal God.

For we know it belongs to your boundless glory,
that you came to the aid of mortal beings with your divinity
and even fashioned for us a remedy out of mortality itself,
that the cause of our downfall
might become the means of our salvation,
through Christ our Lord.

Through him the host of Angels adores your majesty
and rejoices in your presence for ever.
May our voices, we pray, join with theirs
in one chorus of exultant praise, as we acclaim:

Holy, Holy, Holy Lord God of hosts. . .

PREFACE IV OF THE SUNDAYS IN ORDINARY TIME

The history of salvation

It is truly right and just, our duty and our salvation,
always and everywhere to give you thanks,
Lord, holy Father, almighty and eternal God,
through Christ our Lord.

For by his birth he brought renewal
to humanity's fallen state,
and by his suffering cancelled out our sins;
by his rising from the dead
he has opened the way to eternal life,
and by ascending to you, O Father,
he has unlocked the gates of heaven.

And so, with the company of Angels and Saints,
we sing the hymn of your praise,
as without end we acclaim:

Holy, Holy, Holy Lord God of hosts. . .

PRÆFATIO V DE DOMINICIS « PER ANNUM »

De creatione

Vere dignum et iustum est, æquum et salutare,
nos tibi semper et ubique gratias agere:
Domine, sancte Pater, omnipotens æterne Deus:

Qui omnia mundi elementa fecisti,
et vices disposuisti temporum variari;
hominem vero formasti ad imaginem tuam,
et rerum ei subiecisti universa miracula,
ut vicario munere dominaretur omnibus quæ creasti,
et in operum tuorum magnalibus iugiter te laudaret,
per Christum Dominum nostrum.

Unde et nos cum omnibus Angelis te laudamus,
iucunda celebratione clamantes:

Sanctus, Sanctus, Sanctus Dominus Deus Sabaoth. . .

PRÆFATIO VI DE DOMINICIS « PER ANNUM »

De pignore æterni Paschatis

Vere dignum et iustum est, æquum et salutare,
nos tibi semper et ubique gratias agere:
Domine, sancte Pater, omnipotens æterne Deus:

In quo vivimus, movemur et sumus,
atque in hoc corpore constituti
non solum pietatis tuæ cotidianos experimur effectus,
sed æternitatis etiam pignora iam tenemus.
Primitias enim Spiritus habentes,
per quem suscitasti Iesum a mortuis,
paschale mysterium speramus nobis esse perpetuum.

Unde et nos cum omnibus Angelis te laudamus,
iucunda celebratione clamantes:

Sanctus, Sanctus, Sanctus Dominus Deus Sabaoth. . .

PREFACE V OF THE SUNDAYS IN ORDINARY TIME

Creation

It is truly right and just, our duty and our salvation,
always and everywhere to give you thanks,
Lord, holy Father, almighty and eternal God.

For you laid the foundations of the world
and have arranged the changing of times and seasons;
you formed man in your own image
and set humanity over the whole world in all its wonder,
to rule in your name over all you have made
and for ever praise you in your mighty works,
through Christ our Lord.

And so, with all the Angels, we praise you,
as in joyful celebration we acclaim:

Holy, Holy, Holy Lord God of hosts. . .

PREFACE VI OF THE SUNDAYS IN ORDINARY TIME

The pledge of the eternal Passover

It is truly right and just, our duty and our salvation,
always and everywhere to give you thanks,
Lord, holy Father, almighty and eternal God.

For in you we live and move and have our being,
and while in this body
we not only experience the daily effects of your care,
but even now possess the pledge of life eternal.

For, having received the first fruits of the Spirit,
through whom you raised up Jesus from the dead,
we hope for an everlasting share in the Paschal Mystery.

And so, with all the Angels, we praise you,
as in joyful celebration we acclaim:

Holy, Holy, Holy Lord God of hosts. . .

PRÆFATIO VII DE DOMINICIS « PER ANNUM »

De salute per obœdientiam Christi

Vere dignum et iustum est, æquum et salutare,
nos tibi semper et ubique gratias agere:
Domine, sancte Pater, omnipotens æterne Deus:

Quia sic mundum misericorditer dilexisti,
ut ipsum nobis mitteres Redemptorem,
quem absque peccato
in nostra voluisti similitudine conversari,
ut amares in nobis quod diligebas in Filio,
cuius obœdientia sumus ad tua dona reparati,
quæ per inobœdientiam amiseramus peccando.

Unde et nos, Domine, cum Angelis et Sanctis universis
tibi confitemur, in exsultatione dicentes:

Sanctus, Sanctus, Sanctus Dominus Deus Sabaoth. . .

PRÆFATIO VIII DE DOMINICIS « PER ANNUM »

De Ecclesia adunata ex unitate Trinitatis

Vere dignum et iustum est, æquum et salutare,
nos tibi semper et ubique gratias agere:
Domine, sancte Pater, omnipotens æterne Deus:

Quia filios, quos longe peccati crimen abstulerat,
per sanguinem Filii tui Spiritusque virtute,
in unum ad te denuo congregare voluisti:
ut plebs, de unitate Trinitatis adunata,
in tuæ laudem sapientiæ multiformis
Christi corpus templumque Spiritus nosceretur Ecclesia.

Et ideo, choris angelicis sociati,
te laudamus in gaudio confitentes:

Sanctus, Sanctus, Sanctus Dominus Deus Sabaoth. . .

PREFACE VII OF THE SUNDAYS IN ORDINARY TIME

Salvation through the obedience of Christ

It is truly right and just, our duty and our salvation,
always and everywhere to give you thanks,
Lord, holy Father, almighty and eternal God.

For you so loved the world
that in your mercy you sent us the Redeemer,
to live like us in all things but sin,
so that you might love in us what you loved in your Son,
by whose obedience we have been restored to those gifts of yours
that, by sinning, we had lost in disobedience.

And so, Lord, with all the Angels and Saints,
we, too, give you thanks, as in exultation we acclaim:

Holy, Holy, Holy Lord God of hosts. . .

PREFACE VIII OF THE SUNDAYS IN ORDINARY TIME

The Church united by the unity of the Trinity

It is truly right and just, our duty and our salvation,
always and everywhere to give you thanks,
Lord, holy Father, almighty and eternal God.

For, when your children were scattered afar by sin,
through the Blood of your Son and the power of the Spirit,
you gathered them again to yourself,
that a people, formed as one by the unity of the Trinity,
made the body of Christ and the temple of the Holy Spirit,
might, to the praise of your manifold wisdom,
be manifest as the Church.

And so, in company with the choirs of Angels,
we praise you, and with joy we proclaim:

Holy, Holy, Holy Lord God of hosts. . .

PRÆFATIO I DE SS.MA EUCHARISTIA

De sacrificio et de sacramento Christi

Vere dignum et iustum est, æquum et salutare,
nos tibi semper et ubique gratias agere:
Domine, sancte Pater, omnipotens æterne Deus:
per Christum Dominum nostrum.

Qui, verus æternusque Sacerdos,
formam sacrificii perennis instituens,
hostiam tibi se primus obtulit salutarem,
et nos, in sui memoriam, præcepit offerre.
Cuius carnem pro nobis immolatam
dum sumimus, roboramur,
et fusum pro nobis sanguinem dum potamus, abluimur.

Et ideo cum Angelis et Archangelis,
cum Thronis et Dominationibus,
cumque omni militia cælestis exercitus,
hymnum gloriæ tuæ canimus,
sine fine dicentes:

Sanctus, Sanctus, Sanctus Dominus Deus Sabaoth. . .

PRÆFATIO II DE SS.MA EUCHARISTIA

De fructibus Sanctissimæ Eucharistiæ

Vere dignum et iustum est, æquum et salutare,
nos tibi semper et ubique gratias agere:
Domine, sancte Pater, omnipotens æterne Deus:
per Christum Dominum nostrum.

Qui cum Apostolis suis in novissima cena convescens,
salutiferam crucis memoriam prosecuturus in sæcula,
Agnum sine macula se tibi obtulit,
perfectæ laudis munus acceptum.

Quo venerabili mysterio fideles tuos alendo sanctificas,
ut humanum genus, quod continet unus orbis,
una fides illuminet, caritas una coniungat.

Ad mensam igitur accedimus tam mirabilis sacramenti,
ut, gratiæ tuæ suavitate perfusi,
ad cælestis formæ imaginem transeamus.

PREFACE I OF THE MOST HOLY EUCHARIST

The Sacrifice and the Sacrament of Christ

It is truly right and just, our duty and our salvation,
always and everywhere to give you thanks,
Lord, holy Father, almighty and eternal God,
through Christ our Lord.

For he is the true and eternal Priest,
who instituted the pattern of an everlasting sacrifice,
and was the first to offer himself as the saving Victim,
commanding us to make this offering as his memorial.
As we eat his flesh that was sacrificed for us,
we are made strong,
and, as we drink his Blood that was poured out for us,
we are washed clean.

And so, with Angels and Archangels,
with Thrones and Dominions,
and with all the hosts and Powers of heaven,
we sing the hymn of your glory,
as without end we acclaim:

Holy, Holy, Holy Lord God of hosts. . .

PREFACE II OF THE MOST HOLY EUCHARIST

The fruits of the Most Holy Eucharist

It is truly right and just, our duty and our salvation,
always and everywhere to give you thanks,
Lord, holy Father, almighty and eternal God,
through Christ our Lord.

For at the Last Supper with his Apostles,
establishing for the ages to come the saving memorial of the Cross,
he offered himself to you as the unblemished Lamb,
the acceptable gift of perfect praise.

Nourishing your faithful by this sacred mystery,
you make them holy, so that the human race,
bounded by one world,
may be enlightened by one faith
and united by one bond of charity.

And so, we approach the table of this wondrous Sacrament,
so that, bathed in the sweetness of your grace,
we may pass over to the heavenly realities here foreshadowed.

Propter quod cælestia tibi atque terrestria
canticum novum concinunt adorando,
et nos cum omni exercitu Angelorum proclamamus,
sine fine dicentes:

Sanctus, Sanctus, Sanctus Dominus Deus Sabaoth. . .

PRÆFATIO I DE APOSTOLIS

De Apostolis pastoribus populi Dei

Vere dignum et iustum est, æquum et salutare,
nos tibi semper et ubique gratias agere:
Domine, sancte Pater, omnipotens æterne Deus:

Qui gregem tuum, Pastor æterne, non deseris,
sed per beatos Apostolos continua protectione custodis,
ut iisdem rectoribus gubernetur,
quos Filii tui vicarios eidem contulisti præesse pastores.

Et ideo cum Angelis et Archangelis,
cum Thronis et Dominationibus,
cumque omni militia cælestis exercitus,
hymnum gloriæ tuæ canimus,
sine fine dicentes:

Sanctus, Sanctus, Sanctus Dominus Deus Sabaoth. . .

PRÆFATIO II DE APOSTOLIS

De apostolico fundamento et testimonio

Vere dignum et iustum est, æquum et salutare,
nos tibi semper et ubique gratias agere:
Domine, sancte Pater, omnipotens æterne Deus:
per Christum Dominum nostrum.

Quoniam Ecclesiam tuam
in apostolicis tribuisti consistere fundamentis,
ut signum sanctitatis tuæ in terris maneret ipsa perpetuum,
et cælestia præberet cunctis hominibus documenta.

Quapropter nunc et usque in sæculum
cum omni militia Angelorum
devota tibi mente concinimus,
clamantes atque dicentes:

Sanctus, Sanctus, Sanctus Dominus Deus Sabaoth. . .

Therefore, all creatures of heaven and earth
sing a new song in adoration,
and we, with all the host of Angels,
cry out, and without end we acclaim:

Holy, Holy, Holy Lord God of hosts. . .

PREFACE I OF APOSTLES

The Apostles, shepherds of God's people

It is truly right and just, our duty and our salvation,
always and everywhere to give you thanks,
Lord, holy Father, almighty and eternal God.

For you, eternal Shepherd, do not desert your flock,
but through the blessed Apostles
watch over it and protect it always,
so that it may be governed
by those you have appointed shepherds
to lead it in the name of your Son.

And so, with Angels and Archangels,
with Thrones and Dominions,
and with all the hosts and Powers of heaven,
we sing the hymn of your glory,
as without end we acclaim:

Holy, Holy, Holy Lord God of hosts. . .

PREFACE II OF APOSTLES

The apostolic foundation and witness

It is truly right and just, our duty and our salvation,
always and everywhere to give you thanks,
Lord, holy Father, almighty and eternal God,
through Christ our Lord.

For you have built your Church
to stand firm on apostolic foundations,
to be a lasting sign of your holiness on earth
and offer all humanity your heavenly teaching.

Therefore, now and for ages unending,
with all the host of Angels,
we sing to you with all our hearts,
crying out as we acclaim:

Holy, Holy, Holy Lord God of hosts. . .

PRÆFATIO I DE SANCTIS MARTYRIBUS
De signo et exemplo martyrii

Vere dignum et iustum est, æquum et salutare,
nos tibi semper et ubique gratias agere:
Domine, sancte Pater, omnipotens æterne Deus:

Quoniam beati martyris N. pro confessione nominis tui,
ad imitationem Christi,
sanguis effusus tua mirabilia manifestat,
quibus perficis in fragilitate virtutem,
et vires infirmas ad testimonium roboras,
per Christum Dominum nostrum.

Et ideo, cum cælorum Virtutibus,
in terris te iugiter celebramus,
maiestati tuæ sine fine clamantes:

Sanctus, Sanctus, Sanctus Dominus Deus Sabaoth. . .

PRÆFATIO II DE SANCTIS MARTYRIBUS
De mirabilibus Dei in martyrum victoria

Vere dignum et iustum est, æquum et salutare,
nos tibi semper et ubique gratias agere:
Domine, sancte Pater, omnipotens æterne Deus:

Quoniam tu magnificaris in tuorum laude Sanctorum,
et quidquid ad eorum pertinet passionem,
tuæ sunt opera miranda potentiæ:
qui huius fidei tribuis clementer ardorem,
qui suggeris perseverantiæ firmitatem,
qui largiris in agone victoriam,
per Christum Dominum nostrum.

Propter quod cælestia tibi atque terrestria
canticum novum concinunt adorando,
et nos cum omni exercitu Angelorum
proclamamus, sine fine dicentes:

Sanctus, Sanctus, Sanctus Dominus Deus Sabaoth. . .

PREFACE I OF HOLY MARTYRS

The sign and example of martyrdom

It is truly right and just, our duty and our salvation,
always and everywhere to give you thanks,
Lord, holy Father, almighty and eternal God.

For the blood of your blessed Martyr N.,
poured out like Christ's to glorify your name,
shows forth your marvellous works,
by which in our weakness you perfect your power
and on the feeble bestow strength to bear you witness,
through Christ our Lord.

And so, with the Powers of heaven,
we worship you constantly on earth,
and before your majesty
without end we acclaim:

Holy, Holy, Holy Lord God of hosts. . .

PREFACE II OF HOLY MARTYRS

The wonders of God in the victory of the Martyrs

It is truly right and just, our duty and our salvation,
always and everywhere to give you thanks,
Lord, holy Father, almighty and eternal God.

For you are glorified when your Saints are praised;
their very sufferings are but wonders of your might:
in your mercy you give ardour to their faith,
to their endurance you grant firm resolve,
and in their struggle the victory is yours,
through Christ our Lord.

Therefore, all creatures of heaven and earth
sing a new song in adoration,
and we, with all the host of Angels,
cry out, and without end we acclaim:

Holy, Holy, Holy Lord God of hosts. . .

PRÆFATIO I DE DEFUNCTIS

De spe resurrectionis in Christo

Vere dignum et iustum est, æquum et salutare,
nos tibi semper et ubique gratias agere:
Domine, sancte Pater, omnipotens æterne Deus:
per Christum Dominum nostrum.

In quo nobis spes beatæ resurrectionis effulsit,
ut, quos contristat certa moriendi condicio,
eosdem consoletur futuræ immortalitatis promissio.
Tuis enim fidelibus, Domine, vita mutatur, non tollitur,
et, dissoluta terrestris huius incolatus domo,
æterna in cælis habitatio comparatur.

Et ideo cum Angelis et Archangelis,
cum Thronis et Dominationibus,
cumque omni militia cælestis exercitus,
hymnum gloriæ tuæ canimus,
sine fine dicentes:

Sanctus, Sanctus, Sanctus Dominus Deus Sabaoth. . .

PRÆFATIO II DE DEFUNCTIS

Christus mortuus est pro vita nostra

Vere dignum et iustum est, æquum et salutare,
nos tibi semper et ubique gratias agere:
Domine, sancte Pater, omnipotens æterne Deus:
per Christum Dominum nostrum.

Ipse enim mortem unus accepit,
ne omnes nos moreremur;
immo unus mori dignatus est,
ut omnes tibi perpetuo viveremus.

Et ideo, choris angelicis sociati,
te laudamus in gaudio confitentes:

Sanctus, Sanctus, Sanctus Dominus Deus Sabaoth. . .

PREFACE I FOR THE DEAD

The hope of resurrection in Christ

It is truly right and just, our duty and our salvation,
always and everywhere to give you thanks,
Lord, holy Father, almighty and eternal God,
through Christ our Lord.

In him the hope of blessed resurrection has dawned,
that those saddened by the certainty of dying
might be consoled by the promise of immortality to come.
Indeed for your faithful, Lord,
life is changed not ended,
and, when this earthly dwelling turns to dust,
an eternal dwelling is made ready for them in heaven.

And so, with Angels and Archangels,
with Thrones and Dominions,
and with all the hosts and Powers of heaven,
we sing the hymn of your glory,
as without end we acclaim:

Holy, Holy, Holy Lord God of hosts. . .

PREFACE II FOR THE DEAD

Christ died so that we might live

It is truly right and just, our duty and our salvation,
always and everywhere to give you thanks,
Lord, holy Father, almighty and eternal God,
through Christ our Lord.

For as one alone he accepted death,
so that we might all escape from dying;
as one man he chose to die,
so that in your sight we all might live for ever.

And so, in company with the choirs of Angels,
we praise you, and with joy we proclaim:

Holy, Holy, Holy Lord God of hosts. . .

PRÆFATIO III DE DEFUNCTIS

Christus, salus et vita

Vere dignum et iustum est, æquum et salutare,
nos tibi semper et ubique gratias agere:
Domine, sancte Pater, omnipotens æterne Deus:
per Christum Dominum nostrum:

Qui est salus mundi, vita hominum, resurrectio mortuorum.

Per quem maiestatem tuam adorat exercitus Angelorum,
ante conspectum tuum in æternitate lætantium.
Cum quibus et nostras voces ut admitti iubeas, deprecamur,
socia exsultatione dicentes:

Sanctus, Sanctus, Sanctus Dominus Deus Sabaoth. . .

PRÆFATIO IV DE DEFUNCTIS

De vita terrena ad gloriam cælestem

Vere dignum et iustum est, æquum et salutare,
nos tibi semper et ubique gratias agere:
Domine, sancte Pater, omnipotens æterne Deus:

Cuius imperio nascimur, cuius arbitrio regimur,
cuius præcepto in terra, de qua sumpti sumus,
peccati lege absolvimur.
Et, qui per mortem Filii tui redempti sumus,
ad ipsius resurrectionis gloriam
tuo nutu excitamur.

Et ideo, cum Angelorum atque Sanctorum turba,
hymnum laudis tibi canimus, sine fine dicentes:

Sanctus, Sanctus, Sanctus Dominus Deus Sabaoth. . .

PREFACE III FOR THE DEAD

Christ, the salvation and the life

It is truly right and just, our duty and our salvation,
always and everywhere to give you thanks,
Lord, holy Father, almighty and eternal God,
through Christ our Lord.

For he is the salvation of the world,
the life of the human race,
the resurrection of the dead.

Through him the host of Angels adores your majesty
and rejoices in your presence for ever.
May our voices, we pray, join with theirs
in one chorus of exultant praise, as we acclaim:

Holy, Holy, Holy Lord God of hosts. . .

PREFACE IV FOR THE DEAD

From earthly life to heavenly glory

It is truly right and just, our duty and our salvation,
always and everywhere to give you thanks,
Lord, holy Father, almighty and eternal God.

For it is at your summons that we come to birth,
by your will that we are governed,
and at your command that we return,
on account of sin,
to that earth from which we came.

And when you give the sign,
we who have been redeemed by the Death of your Son,
shall be raised up to the glory of his Resurrection.

And so, with the company of Angels and Saints,
we sing the hymn of your praise,
as without end we acclaim:

Holy, Holy, Holy Lord God of hosts. . .

PRÆFATIO V DE DEFUNCTIS

De resurrectione nostra per victoriam Christi

Vere dignum et iustum est, æquum et salutare,
nos tibi semper et ubique gratias agere:
Domine, sancte Pater, omnipotens æterne Deus:

Quia, etsi nostri est meriti quod perimus,
tuæ tamen est pietatis et gratiæ
quod, pro peccato morte consumpti,
per Christi victoriam redempti,
cum ipso revocamur ad vitam.

Et ideo, cum cælorum Virtutibus,
in terris te iugiter celebramus,
maiestati tuæ sine fine clamantes:

Sanctus, Sanctus, Sanctus Dominus Deus Sabaoth. . .

PREFACE V FOR THE DEAD

Our resurrection through the victory of Christ

It is truly right and just, our duty and our salvation,
always and everywhere to give you thanks,
Lord, holy Father, almighty and eternal God.

For even though by our own fault we perish,
yet by your compassion and your grace,
when seized by death according to our sins,
we are redeemed through Christ's great victory,
and with him called back into life.

And so, with the Powers of heaven,
we worship you constantly on earth,
and before your majesty
without end we acclaim:

Holy, Holy, Holy Lord God of hosts. . .

EUCHARISTIC PRAYER I
(THE ROMAN CANON)

Pr.Te ígitur, clementíssime Pater,
per Iesum Christum, Fílium tuum,
Dóminum nostrum,
súpplices rogámus ac pétimus,
uti accépta hábeas
et benedícas ✠ hæc dona, hæc múnera,
hæc sancta sacrifícia illibáta,
in primis, quæ tibi offérimus
pro Ecclésia tua sancta cathólica:
quam pacificáre, custodíre, adunáre
et régere dignéris toto orbe terrárum:
una cum fámulo tuo Papa nostro N.
et Antístite nostro N*.
et ómnibus orthodóxis atque cathólicæ
et apostólicæ fídei cultóribus.

Commemoration of the Living.
Meménto, Dómine,
famulórum famularúmque tuárum N. et N.
et ómnium circumstántium,
quorum tibi fides cógnita est et nota devótio,
pro quibus tibi offérimus:
vel qui tibi ófferunt hoc sacrifícium laudis,
pro se suísque ómnibus:
pro redemptióne animarúm suárum,
pro spe salútis et incolumitátis suæ:
tibíque reddunt vota sua
ætérno Deo, vivo et vero.

Within the Action
Communicántes,
et memóriam venerántes,
in primis gloriósæ semper Vírginis Maríæ,
Genetrícis Dei et Dómini nostri Iesu Christi:
† sed et béati Ioseph, eiúsdem Vírginis Sponsi,
et beatórum Apostolórum ac Mártyrum tuórum,
Petri et Pauli, Andréæ,
(Iacóbi, Ioánnis,
Thomæ, Iacóbi, Philíppi,

---

*Mention may be made here of the Coadjutor Bishop or Auxiliary Bishops.

EUCHARISTIC PRAYER I
(THE ROMAN CANON)

Pr. To you, therefore, most merciful Father,
we make humble prayer and petition
through Jesus Christ, your Son, our Lord:
that you accept
and bless ✠ these gifts, these offerings,
these holy and unblemished sacrifices,
which we offer you firstly
for your holy catholic Church.
Be pleased to grant her peace,
to guard, unite and govern her
throughout the whole world,
together with your servant N. our Pope
and N. our Bishop,*
and all those who, holding to the truth,
hand on the catholic and apostolic faith.

Commemoration of the Living.
Remember, Lord, your servants N. and N.
and all gathered here,
whose faith and devotion are known to you.
For them, we offer you this sacrifice of praise
or they offer it for themselves
and all who are dear to them:
for the redemption of their souls,
in hope of health and well-being,
and paying their homage to you,
the eternal God, living and true.

Within the Action
In communion with those whose memory we venerate,
especially the glorious ever-Virgin Mary,
Mother of our God and Lord, Jesus Christ,
† and blessed Joseph, her Spouse,
your blessed Apostles and Martyrs,
Peter and Paul, Andrew,
(James, John,
Thomas, James, Philip,

---

* Mention may be made here of the Coadjutor Bishop or Auxiliary Bishops.

Bartholomǽi, Matthǽi,
Simónis et Thaddǽi:
Lini, Cleti, Cleméntis, Xysti,
Cornélii, Cypriáni,
Lauréntii, Chrysógoni,
Ioánnis et Pauli,
Cosmæ et Damiáni)
et ómnium Sanctórum tuórum;
quorum méritis precibúsque concédas,
ut in ómnibus protectiónis tuæ muniámur auxílio.
(Per Christum Dóminum nostrum. Amen.)

PROPER FORMS OF THE COMMUNICANTES

On the Nativity of the Lord and throughout the Octave

Communicántes,
et (noctem sacratíssimam) diem sacratíssimum celebrántes,
(qua) quo beátæ Maríæ intemeráta virgínitas
huic mundo édidit Salvatórem:
sed et memóriam venerántes,
in primis eiúsdem gloriósæ semper Vírginis Maríæ,
Genetrícis eiúsdem Dei et Dómini nostri Iesu Christi: †

On the Epiphany of the Lord

Communicántes,
et diem sacratíssimum celebrántes,
quo Unigénitus tuus, in tua tecum glória coætérnus,
in veritáte carnis nostræ visibíliter corporális appáruit:
sed et memóriam venerántes,
in primis gloriósæ semper Vírginis Maríæ,
Genetrícis eiúsdem Dei et Dómini nostri Iesu Christi: †

From the Mass of the Easter Vigil until the Second Sunday of Easter

Communicántes,
et (noctem sacratíssimam) diem sacratíssimum celebrántes
Resurrectiónis Dómini nostri Iesu Christi secúndum carnem:
sed et memóriam venerántes,
in primis gloriósæ semper Vírginis Maríæ,
Genetrícis eiúsdem Dei et Dómini nostri Iesu Christi: †

Bartholomew, Matthew,
Simon and Jude;
Linus, Cletus, Clement, Sixtus,
Cornelius, Cyprian,
Lawrence, Chrysogonus,
John and Paul,
Cosmas and Damian)
and all your Saints;
we ask that through their merits and prayers,
in all things we may be defended
by your protecting help.
(Through Christ our Lord. Amen.)

PROPER FORMS OF THE COMMUNICANTES

On the Nativity of the Lord and throughout the Octave

Celebrating the most sacred night (day)
on which blessed Mary the immaculate Virgin
brought forth the Saviour for this world,
and in communion with those whose memory we venerate,
especially the glorious ever-Virgin Mary,
Mother of our God and Lord, Jesus Christ, †

On the Epiphany of the Lord

Celebrating the most sacred day
on which your Only Begotten Son,
eternal with you in your glory,
appeared in a human body, truly sharing our flesh,
and in communion with those whose memory we venerate,
especially the glorious ever-Virgin Mary,
Mother of our God and Lord, Jesus Christ, †

From the Mass of the Easter Vigil until the Second Sunday of Easter

Celebrating the most sacred night (day)
of the Resurrection of our Lord Jesus Christ in the flesh,
and in communion with those whose memory we venerate,
especially the glorious ever-Virgin Mary,
Mother of our God and Lord, Jesus Christ, †

On the Ascension of the Lord

Communicántes,
et diem sacratíssimum celebrántes,
quo Dóminus noster, Unigénitus Fílius tuus,
unítam sibi fragilitátis nostræ substántiam
in glóriæ tuæ déxtera collocávit:
sed et memóriam venerántes,
in primis gloriósæ semper Vírginis Maríæ,
Genetrícis eiúsdem Dei et Dómini nostri Iesu Christi: †

On Pentecost Sunday

Communicántes,
et diem sacratíssimum Pentecóstes celebrántes,
quo Spíritus Sanctus
Apóstolis in ígneis linguis appáruit:
sed et memóriam venerántes,
in primis gloriósæ semper Vírginis Maríæ,
Genetrícis Dei et Dómini nostri Iesu Christi: †

Hanc ígitur oblatiónem servitútis nostræ,
sed et cunctæ famíliæ tuæ,
quǽsumus, Dómine, ut placátus accípias:
diésque nostros in tua pace dispónas,
atque ab ætérna damnatióne nos éripi
et in electórum tuórum iúbeas grege numerári.
(Per Christum Dóminum nostrum. Amen.)

From the Mass of the Easter Vigil until the Second Sunday of Easter

Hanc ígitur oblatiónem servitútis nostræ,
sed et cunctæ famíliæ tuæ,
quam tibi offérimus
pro his quoque, quos regeneráre dignátus es ex aqua et Spíritu Sancto,
tríbuens eis remissiónem ómnium peccatórum,
quǽsumus, Dómine, ut placátus accípias:
diésque nostros in tua pace dispónas,
atque ab ætérna damnatióne nos éripi
et in electórum tuórum iúbeas grege numerári.
(Per Christum Dóminum nostrum. Amen.)

On the Ascension of the Lord

> Celebrating the most sacred day
> on which your Only Begotten Son, our Lord,
> placed at the right hand of your glory
> our weak human nature,
> which he had united to himself,
> and in communion with those whose memory we venerate,
> especially the glorious ever-Virgin Mary,
> Mother of our God and Lord, Jesus Christ, †

On Pentecost Sunday

> Celebrating the most sacred day of Pentecost,
> on which the Holy Spirit
> appeared to the Apostles in tongues of fire,
> and in communion with those whose memory we venerate,
> especially the glorious ever-Virgin Mary,
> Mother of our God and Lord, Jesus Christ, †

Therefore, Lord, we pray:
graciously accept this oblation of our service,
that of your whole family;
order our days in your peace,
and command that we be delivered from eternal damnation
and counted among the flock of those you have chosen.
(Through Christ Our Lord. Amen.)

From the Mass of the Easter Vigil until the Second Sunday of Easter

> Therefore, Lord, we pray:
> graciously accept this oblation of our service,
> that of your whole family,
> which we make to you
> also for those to whom you have been pleased to give
> the new birth of water and the Holy Spirit,
> granting them forgiveness of all their sins;
> order our days in your peace,
> and command that we be delivered from eternal damnation
> and counted among the flock of those you have chosen.
> (Through Christ our Lord. Amen.)

Quam oblatiónem tu, Deus, in ómnibus, quǽsumus,
benedíctam, adscríptam, ratam,
rationábilem, acceptabilémque fácere dignéris:
ut nobis Corpus et Sanguis fiat dilectíssimi Fílii tui,
Dómini nostri Iesu Christi.

Qui, prídie quam paterétur,
accépit panem in sanctas ac venerábiles manus suas,
et elevátis óculis in cælum
ad te Deum Patrem suum omnipoténtem,
tibi grátias agens benedíxit,
fregit,
dedítque discípulis suis, dicens:

Accípite et manducáte ex hoc omnes:
hoc est enim Corpus meum,
quod pro vobis tradétur.

Símili modo, postquam cenátum est,
accípiens et hunc præclárum cálicem
in sanctas ac venerábiles manus suas,
item tibi grátias agens benedíxit,
dedítque discípulis suis dicens:

Accípite et bíbite ex eo omnes:
hic est enim calix Sánguinis mei
novi et ætérni testaménti,
qui pro vobis et pro multis effundétur
in remissiónem peccatórum.
Hoc fácite in meam commemoratiónem.

Be pleased, O God, we pray,
to bless, acknowledge,
and approve this offering in every respect;
make it spiritual and acceptable,
so that it may become for us
the Body and Blood of your most beloved Son,
our Lord Jesus Christ.

On the day before he was to suffer,
he took bread in his holy and venerable hands,
and with eyes raised to heaven
to you, O God, his almighty Father,
giving you thanks, he said the blessing,
broke the bread
and gave it to his disciples, saying:

TAKE THIS, ALL OF YOU, AND EAT OF IT,
FOR THIS IS MY BODY,
WHICH WILL BE GIVEN UP FOR YOU.

In a similar way, when supper was ended,
he took this precious chalice
in his holy and venerable hands,
and once more giving you thanks, he said the blessing
and gave the chalice to his disciples, saying:

TAKE THIS, ALL OF YOU, AND DRINK FROM IT,
FOR THIS IS THE CHALICE OF MY BLOOD,
THE BLOOD OF THE NEW AND ETERNAL COVENANT,
WHICH WILL BE POURED OUT FOR YOU AND FOR MANY
FOR THE FORGIVENESS OF SINS.

DO THIS IN MEMORY OF ME.

Pr. Mystérium fídei.

The people continue, acclaiming one of the following:

Mortem tu-am annunti-ámus, Dómi-ne,   et tu-am resurrecti-ó-

nem confi-témur, do-nec vé-ni-as.

1. **Mortem tuam annuntiámus, Dómine,**
et tuam resurrectiónem confitémur, donec vénias.

Quoti-escúmque manducámus panem hunc   et cálicem bíbimus,

mortem tu-am annunti-ámus, Dómine, donec vé- ni-as.

2. **Quotiescúmque manducámus panem hunc**
et cálicem bíbimus,
mortem tuam annuntiámus, Dómine, donec vénias.

Salvátor mundi, salva nos, qui per crucem et resurrecti-ónem tu-am

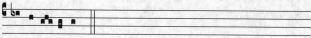

li-be-rá- sti nos.

3. **Salvátor mundi, salva nos,**
qui per crucem et resurrectiónem tuam liberásti nos.

Pr. The mystery of faith.

The people continue, acclaiming one of the following:

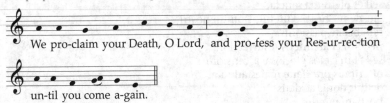

We pro-claim your Death, O Lord, and pro-fess your Res-ur-rec-tion un-til you come a-gain.

1. **We proclaim your Death, O Lord,**
and profess your Resurrection
until you come again.

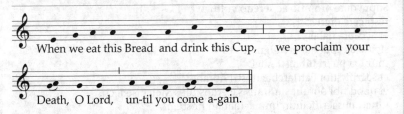

When we eat this Bread and drink this Cup, we pro-claim your Death, O Lord, un-til you come a-gain.

2. **When we eat this Bread and drink this Cup,**
we proclaim your Death, O Lord,
until you come again.

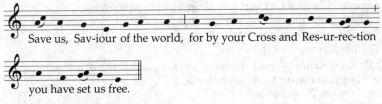

Save us, Sav-iour of the world, for by your Cross and Res-ur-rec-tion you have set us free.

3. **Save us, Saviour of the world,**
for by your Cross and Resurrection
you have set us free.

Only in Ireland: 4. **My Lord and my God.**

Pr. Unde et mémores, Dómine,
nos servi tui,
sed et plebs tua sancta,
eiúsdem Christi, Fílii tui, Dómini nostri,
tam beátæ passiónis,
necnon et ab ínferis resurrectiónis,
sed et in cælos gloriósæ ascensiónis:
offérimus præclárae maiestáti tuæ
de tuis donis ac datis
hóstiam puram,
hóstiam sanctam,
hóstiam immaculátam,
Panem sanctum vitæ ætérnæ
et Cálicem salútis perpétuæ.

Supra quæ propítio ac seréno vultu
respícere dignéris:
et accépta habére,
sícuti accépta habére dignátus es
múnera púeri tui iusti Abel,
et sacrifícium Patriárchæ nostri Abrahæ,
et quod tibi óbtulit summus sacérdos tuus Melchísedech,
sanctum sacrifícium, immaculátam hóstiam.

Súpplices te rogámus, omnípotens Deus:
iube hæc perférri per manus sancti Angeli tui
in sublíme altáre tuum,
in conspéctu divínæ maiestátis tuæ;
ut, quotquot ex hac altáris participatióne
sacrosánctum Fílii tui Corpus et Sánguinem sumpsérimus,
omni benedictióne cælésti et grátia repleámur
(Per Christum Dóminum nostrum. Amen.)

Commemoration of the Dead.

Meménto étiam, Dómine, famulórum famularúmque tuárum N. et N.,
qui nos præcessérunt cum signo fídei,
et dórmiunt in somno pacis.
Ipsis, Dómine, et ómnibus in Christo quiescéntibus,
locum refrigérii, lucis et pacis,
ut indúlgeas, deprecámur.
(Per Christum Dóminum nostrum. Amen.)

Nobis quoque peccatóribus fámulis tuis,
de multitúdine miseratiónum tuárum sperántibus,

Pr. Therefore, O Lord,
as we celebrate the memorial of the blessed Passion,
the Resurrection from the dead,
and the glorious Ascension into heaven
of Christ, your Son, our Lord,
we, your servants and your holy people,
offer to your glorious majesty
from the gifts that you have given us,
this pure victim,
this holy victim,
this spotless victim,
the holy Bread of eternal life
and the Chalice of everlasting salvation.

Be pleased to look upon these offerings
with a serene and kindly countenance,
and to accept them,
as once you were pleased to accept
the gifts of your servant Abel the just,
the sacrifice of Abraham, our father in faith,
and the offering of your high priest Melchizedek,
a holy sacrifice, a spotless victim.

In humble prayer we ask you, almighty God:
command that these gifts be borne
by the hands of your holy Angel
to your altar on high
in the sight of your divine majesty,
so that all of us, who through this participation at the altar
receive the most holy Body and Blood of your Son,
may be filled with every grace and heavenly blessing.
(Through Christ our Lord. Amen.)

Commemoration of the Dead.

Remember also, Lord, your servants N. and N.,
who have gone before us with the sign of faith
and rest in the sleep of peace.
Grant them, O Lord, we pray,
and all who sleep in Christ,
a place of refreshment, light and peace.
(Through Christ our Lord. Amen.)

To us, also, your servants, who, though sinners,
hope in your abundant mercies,

partem áliquam et societátem donáre dignéris
cum tuis sanctis Apóstolis et Martýribus:
cum Ioánne, Stéphano,
Matthía, Bárnaba,
(Ignátio, Alexándro,
Marcellíno, Petro,
Felicitáte, Perpétua,
Agatha, Lúcia,
Agnéte, Cæcília, Anastásia)
et ómnibus Sanctis tuis:
intra quorum nos consórtium,
non æstimátor mériti,
sed véniæ, quæsumus, largítor admítte.
Per Christum Dóminum nostrum.

Per quem hæc ómnia, Dómine,
semper bona creas, sanctíficas, vivíficas, benedícis,
et præstas nobis.

Pr. Per ipsum, et cum ipso, et in ipso,
est tibi Deo Patri omnipoténti,
in unitáte Spíritus Sancti,
omnis honor et glória
per ómnia sǽcula sæculórum.

   A-men.
R.   **Amen.**

Then follows the Communion Rite, p.120.

EUCHARISTIC PRAYER II

Pr. Dóminus vóbiscum.
R.   **Et cum spíritu tuo.**
Pr. Sursum corda.
R.   **Habémus ad Dóminum.**
Pr. Grátias agámus Dómino Deo nostro.
R.   **Dignum et iustum est.**
Pr. Vere dignum et iustum est, æquum et salutáre, nos tibi, sancte Pater,

graciously grant some share
and fellowship with your holy Apostles and Martyrs:
with John the Baptist, Stephen,
Matthias, Barnabas,
(Ignatius, Alexander,
Marcellinus, Peter,
Felicity, Perpetua,
Agatha, Lucy,
Agnes, Cecilia, Anastasia)
and all your Saints;
admit us, we beseech you,
into their company,
not weighing our merits,
but granting us your pardon,
through Christ our Lord.

Through whom
you continue to make all these good things, O Lord;
you sanctify them, fill them with life,
bless them, and bestow them upon us.

Pr. Through him, and with him, and in him,
O God, almighty Father,
in the unity of the Holy Spirit,
all glory and honour is yours,
for ever and ever.

A-men.

R. **Amen.**

Then follows the Communion Rite, p.121.

EUCHARISTIC PRAYER II

Pr. The Lord be with you.
R. **And with your spirit.**
Pr. Lift up your hearts.
R. **We lift them up to the Lord.**
Pr. Let us give thanks to the Lord our God.
R. **It is right and just.**
Pr. It is truly right and just, our duty and our salvation,

semper et ubíque grátias ágere
per Fílium dilectiónis tuæ Iesum Christum,
Verbum tuum per quod cuncta fecísti:
quem misísti nobis Salvatórem et Redemptórem,
incarnátum de Spíritu Sancto et ex Vírgine natum.

Qui voluntátem tuam adímplens
et pópulum tibi sanctum acquírens
exténdit manus cum paterétur,
ut mortem sólveret et resurrectiónem manifestáret.

Et ídeo cum Angelis et ómnibus Sanctis
glóriam tuam prædicámus, una voce dicéntes:

The people sing or say aloud the Sanctus.

Sanctus, * Sanc-tus, Sanc-tus Dó-mi-nus De-us Sá-ba-oth. Ple-ni
sunt cæ-li et ter-ra gló-ri-a tu-a. Ho-sán-na in ex-cél-sis. Be-ne-díc-
tus qui ve-nit in nómine Dómini.   Ho-sán-na in excél-sis.

Sanctus, Sanctus, Sanctus Dóminus Deus Sábaoth.
Pleni sunt cæli et terra glória tua.
Hosánna in excélsis.
Benedíctus qui venit in nómine Dómini.
Hosánna in excélsis.

Pr. Vere Sanctus es, Dómine, fons omnis sanctitátis.

Hæc ergo dona, quǽsumus,
Spíritus tui rore sanctífica,
ut nobis Corpus et ✠ Sanguis fiant
Dómini nostri Iesu Christi.

always and everywhere to give you thanks, Father most holy,
through your beloved Son, Jesus Christ,
your Word through whom you made all things,
whom you sent as our Saviour and Redeemer,
incarnate by the Holy Spirit and born of the Virgin.

Fulfilling your will and gaining for you a holy people,
he stretched out his hands as he endured his Passion,
so as to break the bonds of death and manifest the resurrection.

And so, with the Angels and all the Saints
we declare your glory,
as with one voice we acclaim:

The people sing or say aloud the Sanctus.

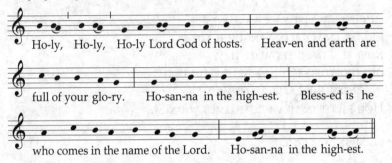

Ho-ly, Ho-ly, Ho-ly Lord God of hosts. Heav-en and earth are full of your glo-ry. Ho-san-na in the high-est. Bless-ed is he who comes in the name of the Lord. Ho-san-na in the high-est.

Holy, Holy, Holy Lord God of hosts.
Heaven and earth are full of your glory.
Hosanna in the highest.
Blessed is he who comes in the name of the Lord.
Hosanna in the highest.

Pr. You are indeed Holy, O Lord,
the fount of all holiness.

Make holy, therefore, these gifts, we pray,
by sending down your Spirit upon them like the dewfall,
so that they may become for us
the Body and ✠ Blood of our Lord Jesus Christ.

Qui cum Passióni voluntárie traderétur,
accépit panem et grátias agens fregit,
dedítque discípulis suis, dicens:

Accípite et manducáte ex hoc omnes:
hoc est enim Corpus meum,
quod pro vobis tradétur.

Símili modo, postquam cenátum est,
accípiens et cálicem,
íterum grátias agens dedit discípulis suis, dicens:

Accípite et bíbite ex eo omnes:
hic est enim calix Sánguinis mei
novi et ætérni testaménti,
qui pro vobis et pro multis effundétur
in remissiónem peccatórum.
Hoc fácite in meam commemoratiónem.

Pr. Mystérium fídei.

The people continue, acclaiming one of the following:

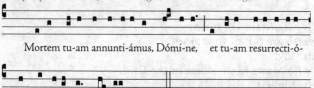

Mortem tu-am annunti-ámus, Dómi-ne,   et tu-am resurrecti-ó-

nem confi-témur, do-nec vé-ni-as.

1. **Mortem tuam annuntiámus, Dómine,**
et tuam resurrectiónem confitémur, donec vénias.

At the time he was betrayed
and entered willingly into his Passion,
he took bread and, giving thanks, broke it,
and gave it to his disciples, saying:

TAKE THIS, ALL OF YOU, AND EAT OF IT,
FOR THIS IS MY BODY,
WHICH WILL BE GIVEN UP FOR YOU.

In a similar way, when supper was ended,
he took the chalice
and, once more giving thanks,
he gave it to his disciples, saying:

TAKE THIS, ALL OF YOU, AND DRINK FROM IT,
FOR THIS IS THE CHALICE OF MY BLOOD,
THE BLOOD OF THE NEW AND ETERNAL COVENANT,
WHICH WILL BE POURED OUT FOR YOU AND FOR MANY
FOR THE FORGIVENESS OF SINS.
DO THIS IN MEMORY OF ME.

Pr. The mystery of faith.

The people continue, acclaiming one of the following:

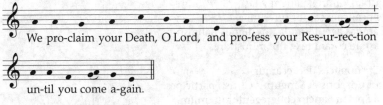

We pro-claim your Death, O Lord, and pro-fess your Res-ur-rec-tion un-til you come a-gain.

1. We proclaim your Death, O Lord,
and profess your Resurrection
until you come again.

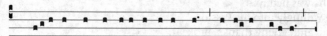

Quoti-escúmque manducámus panem hunc   et cálicem bíbimus,

mortem tu-am annunti-ámus, Dómine, donec vé- ni-as.

2. **Quotiescúmque manducámus panem hunc
et cálicem bíbimus,
mortem tuam annuntiámus, Dómine, donec vénias.**

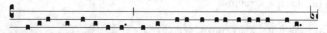

Salvátor mundi, salva nos, qui per crucem et resurrecti-ónem tu-am

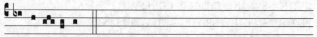

li-be-rá- sti nos.

3. **Salvátor mundi, salva nos,
qui per crucem et resurrectiónem tuam liberásti nos.**

Pr. Mémores ígitur mortis et resurrectiónis eius,
tibi, Dómine, panem vitæ
et cálicem salútis offérimus,
grátias agéntes quia nos dignos habuísti
astáre coram te et tibi ministráre.

Et súpplices deprecámur
ut Córporis et Sánguinis Christi partícipes
a Spíritu Sancto congregémur in unum.

Recordáre, Dómine, Ecclésiæ tuæ toto orbe diffúsæ,
ut eam in caritáte perfícias
una cum Papa nostro N. et Epíscopo nostro N.*
et univérso clero.

---

*Mention may be made here of the Coadjutor Bishop or Auxiliary Bishops.

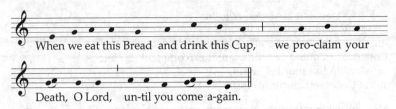

When we eat this Bread and drink this Cup, we pro-claim your Death, O Lord, un-til you come a-gain.

2. **When we eat this Bread and drink this Cup,**
we proclaim your Death, O Lord,
until you come again.

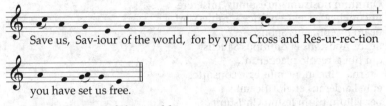

Save us, Sav-iour of the world, for by your Cross and Res-ur-rec-tion you have set us free.

3. **Save us, Saviour of the world,**
for by your Cross and Resurrection
you have set us free.

Only in Ireland: 4. **My Lord and my God.**

Pr. Therefore, as we celebrate
the memorial of his Death and Resurrection,
we offer you, Lord,
the Bread of life and the Chalice of salvation,
giving thanks that you have held us worthy
to be in your presence and minister to you.

Humbly we pray
that, partaking of the Body and Blood of Christ,
we may be gathered into one by the Holy Spirit.

Remember, Lord, your Church,
spread throughout the world,
and bring her to the fullness of charity,
together with N. our Pope and N. our Bishop*
and all the clergy.

---

*Mention may be made here of the Coadjutor Bishop or Auxiliary Bishops.

In Masses for the Dead, the following may be added:

Meménto fámuli tui (fámulæ tuæ) N.,
quem (quam) (hódie) ad te ex hoc mundo vocásti.
Concéde, ut, qui (quæ) complantátus (complantáta) fuit
    similitúdini mortis Fílii tui,
simul fiat et resurrectiónis ipsíus.

Meménto étiam fratrum nostrórum,
qui in spe resurrectiónis dormiérunt,
omniúmque in tua miseratióne defunctórum,
et eos in lumen vultus tui admítte.
Omnium nostrum, quǽsumus, miserére,
ut cum beáta Dei Genetríce Vírgine María,
beáto Ioseph, eius Sponso,
beátis Apostólis et ómnibus Sanctis,
qui tibi a sǽculo placuérunt,
ætérnæ vitæ mereámur esse consórtes,
et te laudémus et glorificémus
per Fílium tuum Iesum Christum.

Per ipsum, et cum ipso, et in ipso,
est tibi Deo Patri omnipoténti,
in unitáte Spíritus Sancti,
omnis honor et glória
per ómnia sǽcula sæculórum.

A-men.
R. **Amen.**

Then follows the Communion Rite, p.120.

EUCHARISTIC PRAYER III

Pr. Vere Sanctus es, Dómine,
et mérito te laudat omnis a te cóndita creatúra,
quia per Fílium tuum,
Dóminum nostrum Iesum Christum,
Spíritus Sancti operánte virtúte,
vivíficas et sanctíficas univérsa,
et pópulum tibi congregáre non désinis,

In Masses for the Dead, the following may be added:

Remember your servant N.,
whom you have called (today)
from this world to yourself.
Grant that he (she) who was united with your Son in a death like his,
may also be one with him in his Resurrection.

Remember also our brothers and sisters
who have fallen asleep in the hope of the resurrection,
and all who have died in your mercy:
welcome them into the light of your face.
Have mercy on us all, we pray,
that with the Blessed Virgin Mary, Mother of God,
with blessed Joseph, her Spouse,
with the blessed Apostles,
and all the Saints who have pleased you throughout the ages,
we may merit to be coheirs to eternal life,
and may praise and glorify you
through your Son, Jesus Christ.

Through him, and with him, and in him,
O God, almighty Father,
in the unity of the Holy Spirit,
all glory and honour is yours,
for ever and ever.

A-men.

R. **Amen.**

Then follows the Communion Rite, p.121.

EUCHARISTIC PRAYER III

Pr. You are indeed Holy, O Lord,
and all you have created
rightly gives you praise,
for through your Son our Lord Jesus Christ,
by the power and working of the Holy Spirit,
you give life to all things and make them holy,
and you never cease to gather a people to yourself,

ut a solis ortu usque ad occásum
oblátio munda offerátur nómini tuo.

Súpplices ergo te, Dómine, deprecámur,
ut hæc múnera, quæ tibi sacránda detúlimus,
eódem Spíritu sanctificáre dignéris,
ut Corpus et ✠ Sanguis fiant
Fílii tui Dómini nostri Iesu Christi,
cuius mandáto hæc mystéria celebrámus.

Ipse enim in qua nocte tradebátur
accépit panem
et tibi grátias agens benedíxit,
fregit, dedítque discípulis suis, dicens:

ACCÍPITE ET MANDUCÁTE EX HOC OMNES:
HOC EST ENIM CORPUS MEUM,
QUOD PRO VOBIS TRADÉTUR.

Símili modo, postquam cenátum est,
accípiens cálicem,
et tibi grátias agens benedíxit,
dedítque discípulis suis, dicens:

ACCÍPITE ET BÍBITE EX EO OMNES:
HIC EST ENIM CALIX SÁNGUINIS MEI
NOVI ET ÆTÉRNI TESTAMÉNTI,
QUI PRO VOBIS ET PRO MULTIS EFFUNDÉTUR
IN REMISSIÓNEM PECCATÓRUM.
HOC FÁCITE IN MEAM COMMEMORATIÓNEM.

so that from the rising of the sun to its setting
a pure sacrifice may be offered to your name.

Therefore, O Lord, we humbly implore you:
by the same Spirit graciously make holy
these gifts we have brought to you for consecration,
that they may become the Body and ✠ Blood
of your Son our Lord Jesus Christ,
at whose command we celebrate these mysteries.

For on the night he was betrayed
he himself took bread,
and, giving you thanks, he said the blessing,
broke the bread and gave it to his disciples, saying:

TAKE THIS, ALL OF YOU, AND EAT OF IT,
FOR THIS IS MY BODY,
WHICH WILL BE GIVEN UP FOR YOU.

In a similar way, when supper was ended,
he took the chalice,
and, giving you thanks, he said the blessing,
and gave the chalice to his disciples, saying:

TAKE THIS, ALL OF YOU, AND DRINK FROM IT,
FOR THIS IS THE CHALICE OF MY BLOOD,
THE BLOOD OF THE NEW AND ETERNAL COVENANT,
WHICH WILL BE POURED OUT FOR YOU AND FOR MANY
FOR THE FORGIVENESS OF SINS.
DO THIS IN MEMORY OF ME.

Pr. Mystérium fídei.

The people continue, acclaiming one of the following:

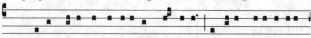

Mortem tu-am annunti-ámus, Dómi-ne, et tu-am resurrecti-ó-

nem confi-témur, do-nec vé-ni-as.

1. Mortem tuam annuntiámus, Dómine,
et tuam resurrectiónem confitémur, donec vénias.

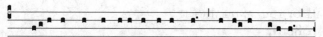

Quoti-escúmque manducámus panem hunc et cálicem bíbimus,

mortem tu-am annunti-ámus, Dómine, donec vé- ni-as.

2. Quotiescúmque manducámus panem hunc
et cálicem bíbimus,
mortem tuam annuntiámus, Dómine, donec vénias.

Salvátor mundi, salva nos, qui per crucem et resurrecti-ónem tu-am

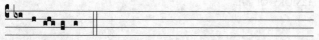

li-be-rá- sti nos.

3. Salvátor mundi, salva nos,
qui per crucem et resurrectiónem tuam liberásti nos.

Pr. The mystery of faith.

The people continue, acclaiming one of the following:

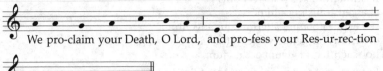

We pro-claim your Death, O Lord, and pro-fess your Res-ur-rec-tion un-til you come a-gain.

1. We proclaim your Death, O Lord,
and profess your Resurrection
until you come again.

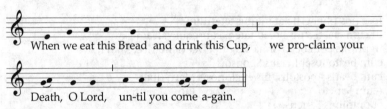

When we eat this Bread and drink this Cup, we pro-claim your Death, O Lord, un-til you come a-gain.

2. When we eat this Bread and drink this Cup,
we proclaim your Death, O Lord,
until you come again.

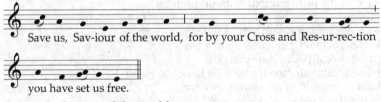

Save us, Sav-iour of the world, for by your Cross and Res-ur-rec-tion you have set us free.

3. Save us, Saviour of the world,
for by your Cross and Resurrection
you have set us free.

Only in Ireland: **4.** **My Lord and my God.**

Pr. Mémores ígitur, Dómine,
eiúsdem Fílii tui salutíferæ passiónis
necnon mirábilis resurrectiónis
et ascensiónis in cælum,
sed et præstolántes álterum eius advéntum,
offérimus tibi, grátias reteréntes,
hoc sacrifícium vivum et sanctum.

Réspice, quæsumus, in oblatiónem Ecclésiæ tuæ
et, agnóscens Hóstiam,
cuius voluísti immolatióne placári,
concéde, ut qui Córpore et Sánguine Fílii tui refícimur,
Spíritu eius Sancto repléti,
unum corpus et unus spíritus inveniámur in Christo.

Ipse nos tibi perfíciat munus ætérnum,
ut cum eléctis tuis hereditátem cónsequi valeámus,
in primis cum beátissima Vírgine, Dei Genetríce, María,
cum beáto Ioseph, eius Sponso,
cum beátis Apóstolis tuis et gloriósis Martýribus
(cum Sancto N.: the saint of the day or Patron Saint)
et ómnibus Sanctis,
quorum intercessióne
perpétuo apud te confídimus adiuvári.

Hæc Hóstia nostræ reconciliatiónis profíciat,
quæsumus, Dómine,
ad totíus mundi pacem atque salútem.
Ecclésiam tuam, peregrinántem in terra,
in fide et caritáte firmáre dignéris
cum fámulo tuo Papa nostro N. et Epíscopo nostro N.*,
cum episcopáli órdine et univérso clero
et omni pópulo acquisitiónis tuæ.

Votis huius famíliæ, quam tibi astáre voluísti,
adésto propítius.
Omnes fílios tuos ubíque dispérsos
tibi, clemens Pater, miserátus coniúnge.

---

*Mention may be made here of the Coadjutor Bishop or Auxiliary Bishops.

Pr. Therefore, O Lord, as we celebrate the memorial
of the saving Passion of your Son,
his wondrous Resurrection
and Ascension into heaven,
and as we look forward to his second coming,
we offer you in thanksgiving
this holy and living sacrifice.

Look, we pray, upon the oblation of your Church
and, recognising the sacrificial Victim by whose death
you willed to reconcile us to yourself,
grant that we, who are nourished
by the Body and Blood of your Son
and filled with his Holy Spirit,
may become one body, one spirit in Christ.

May he make of us
an eternal offering to you,
so that we may obtain an inheritance with your elect,
especially with the most Blessed Virgin Mary, Mother of God,
with blessed Joseph, her Spouse,
with your blessed Apostles and glorious Martyrs
(**with Saint N.:** the Saint of the day or Patron Saint)
and with all the Saints,
on whose constant intercession in your presence
we rely for unfailing help.

May this Sacrifice of our reconciliation,
we pray, O Lord,
advance the peace and salvation of all the world.
Be pleased to confirm in faith and charity
your pilgrim Church on earth,
with your servant **N.** our Pope and **N.** our Bishop*,
the Order of Bishops, all the clergy,
and the entire people you have gained for your own.

Listen graciously to the prayers of this family,
whom you have summoned before you:
in your compassion, O merciful Father,
gather to yourself all your children
scattered throughout the world.

---

*Mention may be made here of the Coadjutor Bishop or Auxiliary Bishops.

† Fratres nostros defúnctos
et omnes qui, tibi placéntes, ex hoc sǽculo transiérunt,
in regnum tuum benígnus admítte,
ubi fore sperámus,
ut simul glória tua perénniter satiémur,
per Christum Dóminum nostrum,
per quem mundo bona cuncta largíris. †

Per ipsum, et cum ipso, et in ipso,
est tibi Deo Patri omnipoténti,
in unitáte Spíritus Sancti,
omnis honor et glória
per ómnia sǽcula sæculórum.

A-men.
R. **Amen.**

Then follows the Communion Rite, p.120.

When this Eucharistic Prayer is used in Masses for the Dead, the following may be said:
† Meménto fámuli tui (fámulæ tuæ) N.,
quem (quam) (hódie) ad te ex hoc mundo vocásti.
Concéde, ut, qui (quæ) complantátus (complantáta)
    fuit símilitúdini mortis Fílii tui,
simul fiat et resurrectiónis ipsíus,
quando mórtuos suscitábit in carne de terra
et corpus humilitátis nostræ
configurábit córpori claritátis suæ.
Sed et fratres nostros defúnctos,
et omnes qui, tibi placéntes, ex hoc sǽculo transiérunt,
in regnum tuum benígnus admítte,
ubi fore sperámus,
ut simul glória tua perénniter satiémur,
quando omnem lácrimam abstérges ab óculis nostris,
quia te, sícuti es, Deum nostrum vidéntes,
tibi símiles érimus cuncta per sǽcula,
et te sine fine laudábimus,
per Christum Dóminum nostrum,
per quem mundo bona cuncta largíris. †

† To our departed brothers and sisters
and to all who were pleasing to you
at their passing from this life,
give kind admittance to your kingdom.
There we hope to enjoy for ever the fullness of your glory
through Christ our Lord,
through whom you bestow on the world all that is good. †

Through him, and with him, and in him,
O God, almighty Father,
in the unity of the Holy Spirit,
all glory and honour is yours,
for ever and ever.

A-men.

R. **Amen.**

Then follows the Communion Rite, p.121.

When this Eucharistic Prayer is used in Masses for the Dead, the following may be said:

† Remember your servant N.
whom you have called (today)
from this world to yourself.
Grant that he (she) who was united with your Son in a death like his,
may also be one with him in his Resurrection,
when from the earth
he will raise up in the flesh those who have died,
and transform our lowly body
after the pattern of his own glorious body.
To our departed brothers and sisters, too,
and to all who were pleasing to you
at their passing from this life,
give kind admittance to your kingdom.
There we hope to enjoy for ever the fullness of your glory,
when you will wipe away every tear from our eyes.
For seeing you, our God, as you are,
we shall be like you for all the ages
and praise you without end,
through Christ our Lord,
through whom you bestow on the world all that is good. †

EUCHARISTIC PRAYER IV

Pr. Dóminus vóbiscum.

R. **Et cum spíritu tuo.**

Pr. Sursum corda.

R. **Habémus ad Dóminum.**

Pr. Grátias agámus Dómino Deo nostro.

R. **Dignum et iustum est.**

Pr. Vere dignum est tibi grátias ágere,
vere iustum est te glorificáre, Pater sancte,
quia unus es Deus vivus et verus,
qui es ante sǽcula et pérmanes in ætérnum,
inaccessíbilem lucem inhábitans;
sed et qui unus bonus atque fons vitæ cuncta fecísti,
ut creatúras tuas benedictiónibus adimpléres
multásque lætificáres tui lúminis claritáte.

Et ídeo coram te innúmeræ astant turbæ Angelórum,
qui die ac nocte sérviunt tibi
et, vultus tui glóriam contemplántes,
te incessánter gloríficant.

Cum quibus et nos et, per nostram vocem,
omnis quæ sub cælo est creatúra
nomen tuum in exsultatióne confitémur, canéntes:

The people sing or say aloud the Sanctus.

S anc-tus, * Sanc-tus, Sanc-tus Dó-mi-nus De-us Sá-ba-oth. Plé-ni

sunt cæ-li et ter-ra gló-ri-a tu-a. Ho-sán-na in ex-cél-sis. Be-ne-díc-

tus qui ve-nit in nómine Dómini. Ho-sán-na in excél-sis.

EUCHARISTIC PRAYER IV

Pr. The Lord be with you.

R. **And with your spirit.**

Pr. Lift up your hearts.

R. **We lift them up to the Lord.**

Pr. Let us give thanks to the Lord our God.

R. **It is right and just.**

Pr. It is truly right to give you thanks,
truly just to give you glory, Father most holy,
for you are the one God living and true,
existing before all ages and abiding for all eternity,
dwelling in unapproachable light;
yet you, who alone are good, the source of life,
have made all that is,
so that you might fill your creatures with blessings
and bring joy to many of them by the glory of your light.

And so, in your presence are countless hosts of Angels,
who serve you day and night
and, gazing upon the glory of your face,
glorify you without ceasing.

With them we, too, confess your name in exultation,
giving voice to every creature under heaven,
as we acclaim:

The people sing or say aloud the Sanctus.

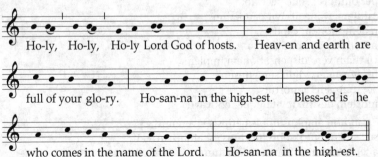

Ho-ly, Ho-ly, Ho-ly Lord God of hosts. Heav-en and earth are
full of your glo-ry. Ho-san-na in the high-est. Bless-ed is he
who comes in the name of the Lord. Ho-san-na in the high-est.

Sanctus, Sanctus, Sanctus Dóminus Deus Sábaoth.
Pleni sunt cæli et terra glória tua.
Hosánna in excélsis.
Benedíctus qui venit in nómine Dómini.
Hosánna in excélsis.

Pr. Confitémur tibi, Pater sancte,
quia magnus es et ómnia ópera tua
in sapiéntia et caritáte fecísti.
Hóminem ad tuam imáginem condidísti,
eíque commisísti mundi curam univérsi,
ut, tibi soli Creatóri sérviens,
creatúris ómnibus imperáret.
Et cum amicítiam tuam, non obœdiens, amisísset,
non eum dereliquísti in mortis império.
Omnibus enim misericórditer subvenísti,
ut te quæréntes invenírent.
Sed et fœdera plúries homínibus obtulísti
eósque per prophétas erudísti in exspectatióne salútis.

Et sic, Pater sancte, mundum dilexísti,
ut, compléta plenitúdine témporum,
Unigénitum tuum nobis mítteres Salvatórem.
Qui, incarnátus de Spíritu Sancto
et natus ex María Vírgine,
in nostra condiciónis forma est conversátus
per ómnia absque peccáto;
salútem evangelizávit paupéribus,
redemptiónem captívis,
mæstis corde lætítiam.
Ut tuam vero dispensatiónem impléret,
in mortem trádidit semetípsum
ac, resúrgens a mórtuis,
mortem destrúxit vitámque renovávit.

Et, ut non ámplius nobismetípsis viverémus,
sed sibi qui pro nobis mórtuus est atque surréxit,
a te, Pater, misit Spíritum Sanctum
primítias credéntibus,

Holy, Holy, Holy Lord God of hosts.
Heaven and earth are full of your glory.
Hosanna in the highest.
Blessed is he who comes in the name of the Lord.
Hosanna in the highest.

Pr. We give you praise, Father most holy,
for you are great
and you have fashioned all your works
in wisdom and in love.
You formed man in your own image
and entrusted the whole world to his care,
so that in serving you alone, the Creator,
he might have dominion over all creatures.
And when through disobedience he had lost your friendship,
you did not abandon him to the domain of death.
For you came in mercy to the aid of all,
so that those who seek might find you.
Time and again you offered them covenants
and through the prophets
taught them to look forward to salvation.

And you so loved the world, Father most holy,
that in the fullness of time
you sent your Only Begotten Son to be our Saviour.
Made incarnate by the Holy Spirit
and born of the Virgin Mary,
he shared our human nature
in all things but sin.
To the poor he proclaimed the good news of salvation,
to prisoners, freedom,
and to the sorrowful of heart, joy.
To accomplish your plan,
he gave himself up to death,
and, rising from the dead,
he destroyed death and restored life.

And that we might live no longer for ourselves
but for him who died and rose again for us,
he sent the Holy Spirit from you, Father,

qui, opus suum in mundo perfíciens,
omnem sanctificatiónem compléret.

Quǽsumus ígitur, Dómine,
ut idem Spíritus Sanctus
hæc múnera sanctificáre dignétur,
ut Corpus et ✠ Sanguis fiant
Dómini nostri Iesu Christi
ad hoc magnum mystérium celebrándum,
quod ipse nobis relíquit in fœdus ætérnum.

Ipse enim, cum hora venísset
ut glorificarétur a te, Pater sancte,
ac dilexísset suos qui erant in mundo,
in finem diléxit eos:
et cenántibus illis
accépit panem, benedíxit ac fregit,
dedítque discípulis suis, dicens:

Accípite et manducáte ex hoc omnes:
hoc est enim Corpus meum,
quod pro vobis tradétur.

Símili modo
accípiens cálicem, ex genímine vitis replétum,
grátias egit, dedítque discípulis suis, dicens:

Accípite et bíbite ex eo omnes:
hic est enim calix Sánguinis mei
novi et ætérni testaménti,
qui pro vobis et pro multis effundétur
in remissiónem peccatórum.
Hoc fácite in meam commemoratiónem.

Pr. Mystérium fídei.

The people continue, acclaiming one of the following:

as the first fruits for those who believe,
so that, bringing to perfection his work in the world,
he might sanctify creation to the full.

Therefore, O Lord, we pray:
may this same Holy Spirit
graciously sanctify these offerings,
that they may become
the Body and ✠ Blood of our Lord Jesus Christ
for the celebration of this great mystery,
which he himself left us
as an eternal covenant.

For when the hour had come
for him to be glorified by you, Father most holy,
having loved his own who were in the world,
he loved them to the end:
and while they were at supper,
he took bread, blessed and broke it,
and gave it to his disciples, saying:

TAKE THIS, ALL OF YOU, AND EAT OF IT,
FOR THIS IS MY BODY,
WHICH WILL BE GIVEN UP FOR YOU.

In a similar way,
taking the chalice filled with the fruit of the vine,
he gave thanks,
and gave the chalice to his disciples, saying:

TAKE THIS, ALL OF YOU, AND DRINK FROM IT,
FOR THIS IS THE CHALICE OF MY BLOOD,
THE BLOOD OF THE NEW AND ETERNAL COVENANT,
WHICH WILL BE POURED OUT FOR YOU AND FOR MANY
FOR THE FORGIVENESS OF SINS.
DO THIS IN MEMORY OF ME.

Pr. The mystery of faith.

The people continue, acclaiming one of the following:

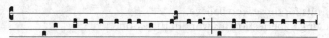

Mortem tu-am annunti-ámus, Dómi-ne,   et tu-am resurrecti-ó-

nem confi-témur, do-nec vé-ni-as.

1. **Mortem tuam annuntiámus, Dómine,**
et tuam resurrectiónem confitémur, donec vénias.

Quoti-escúmque manducámus panem hunc   et cálicem bíbimus,

mortem tu-am annunti-ámus, Dómine, donec vé- ni-as.

2. **Quotiescúmque manducámus panem hunc**
et cálicem bíbimus,
mortem tuam annuntiámus, Dómine, donec vénias.

Salvátor mundi, salva nos, qui per crucem et resurrecti-ónem tu-am

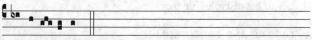

li-be-rá- sti nos.

3. **Salvátor mundi, salva nos,**
qui per crucem et resurrectiónem tuam liberásti nos.

Pr. Unde et nos, Dómine, redemptiónis nostræ memoriále nunc celebrántes, mortem Christi
eiúsque descénsum ad ínferos recólimus,
eius resurrectiónem
et ascensiónem ad tuam déxteram profitémur,

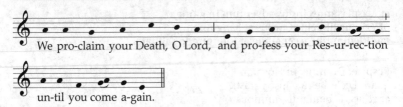

We pro-claim your Death, O Lord, and pro-fess your Res-ur-rec-tion un-ti you come a-gain.

1. **We proclaim your Death, O Lord,**
and profess your Resurrection
until you come again.

When we eat this Bread and drink this Cup, we pro-claim your Death, O Lord, un-til you come a-gain.

2. **When we eat this Bread and drink this Cup,**
we proclaim your Death, O Lord,
until you come again.

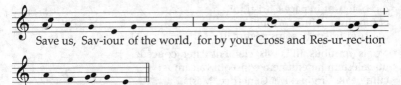

Save us, Sav-iour of the world, for by your Cross and Res-ur-rec-tion you have set us free.

3. **Save us, Saviour of the world,**
for by your Cross and Resurrection
you have set us free.

Only in Ireland: 4. **My Lord and my God.**

Pr. Therefore, O Lord,
as we now celebrate the memorial of our redemption,
we remember Christ's Death
and his descent to the realm of the dead,
we proclaim his Resurrection
and his Ascension to your right hand,

et, exspectántes ipsíus advéntum in glória,
offérimus tibi eius Corpus et Sánguinem,
sacrifícium tibi acceptábile et toti mundo salutáre.

Réspice, Dómine, in Hóstiam,
quam Ecclésiæ tuæ ipse parásti,
et concéde benígnus ómnibus
qui ex hoc uno pane participábunt et cálice,
ut, in unum corpus a Sancto Spíritu congregáti,
in Christo hóstia viva perficiántur,
ad laudem glóriæ tuæ.

Nunc ergo, Dómine, ómnium recordáre,
pro quibus tibi hanc oblatiónem offérimus:
in primis fámuli tui, Papæ nostri N.,
Epíscopi nostri N.*, et Episcopórum órdinis univérsi,
sed et totíus cleri, et offeréntium,
et circumstántium,
et cuncti pópuli tui,
et ómnium, qui te quærunt corde sincéro.

Meménto étiam illórum,
qui obiérunt in pace Christi tui,
et ómnium defunctórum,
quorum fidem tu solus cognovísti.

Nobis ómnibus, fíliis tuis, clemens Pater, concéde,
ut cæléstem hereditátem cónsequi valeámus
cum beáta Vírgine, Dei Genetríce, María,
cum beáto Ioseph, eius Sponso,
cum Apóstolis et Sanctis tuis
in regno tuo, ubi cum univérsa creatúra,
a corruptióne peccáti et mortis liberáta,
te glorificémus per Christum Dóminum nostrum,
per quem mundo bona cuncta largíris.

Per ipsum, et cum ipso, et in ipso,
est tibi Deo Patri omnipoténti,
in unitáte Spíritus Sancti,
omnis honor et glória
per ómnia sæcula sæculórum.

---

* Mention may be made here of the Coadjutor Bishop or Auxiliary Bishops.

and, as we await his coming in glory,
we offer you his Body and Blood,
the sacrifice acceptable to you
which brings salvation to the whole world.

Look, O Lord, upon the Sacrifice
which you yourself have provided for your Church,
and grant in your loving kindness
to all who partake of this one Bread and one Chalice
that, gathered into one body by the Holy Spirit,
they may truly become a living sacrifice in Christ
to the praise of your glory.

Therefore, Lord, remember now
all for whom we offer this sacrifice:
especially your servant N. our Pope,
N. our Bishop,* and the whole Order of Bishops,
all the clergy,
those who take part in this offering,
those gathered here before you,
your entire people,
and all who seek you with a sincere heart.

Remember also
those who have died in the peace of your Christ
and all the dead,
whose faith you alone have known.

To all of us, your children,
grant, O merciful Father,
that we may enter into a heavenly inheritance
with the Blessed Virgin Mary, Mother of God,
with blessed Joseph, her Spouse,
and with your Apostles and Saints in your kingdom.
There, with the whole of creation,
freed from the corruption of sin and death,
may we glorify you through Christ our Lord,
through whom you bestow on the world all that is good.

Through him, and with him, and in him,
O God, almighty Father,
in the unity of the Holy Spirit,
all glory and honour is yours,
for ever and ever.

---

* Mention may be made here of the Coadjutor Bishop or Auxiliary Bishops.

A-men.

R. **Amen.**

Then follows the Communion Rite.

THE COMMUNION RITE

The eating and drinking together of the Lord's Body and Blood in a Paschal meal is the culmination of the Eucharist

THE LORD'S PRAYER

After the chalice and paten have been set down, the congregation stands and the Priest says:

Pr. Præcéptis salutáribus móniti,
et divína institutióne formáti,
audémus dícere:

Together with the people, he continues:

Pater noster, qui es in cæ-lis: sancti-fi-cé-tur nomen tu-um; advéni-at regnum tu-um; fi-at volúntas tu-a, sic-ut in cæ-lo, et in terra. Panem nostrum coti-di-ánum da nobis hódi-e; et dimítte nobis débi-ta nostra, sicut et nos dimíttimus de-bi-tó-ribus nostris; et ne nos indúcas in tenta-ti-ó-nem; sed líbera nos a ma-lo.

A-men.

R. Amen.

Then follows the Communion Rite.

THE COMMUNION RITE

The eating and drinking together of the Lord's Body and Blood in a Paschal meal is the culmination of the Eucharist

THE LORD'S PRAYER

After the chalice and paten have been set down, the congregation stands and the Priest says:

Pr. At the Saviour's command
and formed by divine teaching,
we dare to say:

Together with the people, he continues:

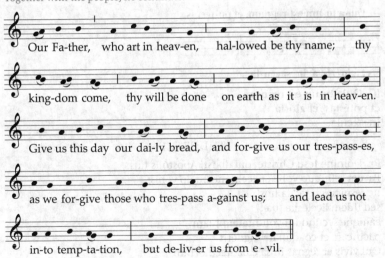

Our Fa-ther, who art in heav-en, hal-lowed be thy name; thy king-dom come, thy will be done on earth as it is in heav-en. Give us this day our dai-ly bread, and for-give us our tres-pass-es, as we for-give those who tres-pass a-gainst us; and lead us not in-to temp-ta-tion, but de-liv-er us from e-vil.

R. **Pater noster, qui es in cælis:**
sanctificétur nomen tuum;
advéniat regnum tuum;
fiat volúntas tua, sicut in cælo, et in terra.
Panem nostrum cotidiánum da nobis hódie;
et dimítte nobis debíta nostra,
sicut et nos dimíttimus debitóribus nostris;
et ne nos indúcas in tentatiónem;
sed líbera nos a malo.

Pr. Líbera nos, quǽsumus, Dómine, ab ómnibus malis,
da propítius pacem in diébus nostris,
ut, ope misericórdiæ tuæ adiúti,
et a peccáto simus semper líberi
et ab omni perturbatióne secúri:
exspectántes beátam spem
et advéntum Salvatóris nostri Iesu Christi.

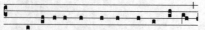

Qui-a tu-um est regnum, et po-téstas,

et gló- ri- a in saecu-la.

R. **Quia tuum est regnum,**
et potéstas, et glória
in sǽcula.

THE PEACE

Pr. Dómine Iesu Christe, qui dixísti Apostólis tuis:
Pacem relínquo vobis, pacem meam do vobis:
ne respícias peccáta nostra,
sed fidem Ecclésiæ tuæ;
eámque secúndum voluntátem tuam
pacificáre et coadunáre dignéris.
Qui vivis et regnas in sǽcula sæculórum.

R. **Amen.**

R. **Our Father, who art in heaven,**
hallowed be thy name;
thy kingdom come,
thy will be done
on earth as it is in heaven.
Give us this day our daily bread,
and forgive us our trespasses,
as we forgive those who trespass against us;
and lead us not into temptation,
but deliver us from evil.

Pr. Deliver us, Lord, we pray, from every evil,
graciously grant peace in our days,
that, by the help of your mercy,
we may be always free from sin
and safe from all distress,
as we await the blessed hope
and the coming of our Saviour, Jesus Christ.

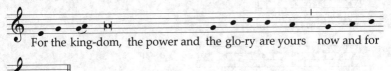

For the king-dom, the power and the glo-ry are yours   now and for ev-er.

R. **For the kingdom,**
the power and the glory are yours
now and for ever.

THE PEACE

Pr. Lord Jesus Christ,
who said to your Apostles:
Peace I leave you, my peace I give you;
look not on our sins,
but on the faith of your Church,
and graciously grant her peace and unity
in accordance with your will.
Who live and reign for ever and ever.
R. **Amen.**

Pr. Pax Dómini sit semper vobíscum.

Et cum spí-ri- tu tu- o.

R. Et cum spíritu tuo.

Then, if appropriate, the Deacon, or the Priest, adds:

Pr. Offérte vobis pacem.

And all offer one another the customary sign of peace.

BREAKING OF THE BREAD

Then the Priest takes the host, breaks it over the paten, and places a small piece in the chalice. Meanwhile the following is sung or said:

A g-nus De-i, * qui tol-lis pec-cá-ta mundi:

mi-se-ré-re no-bis.

Ag-nus De-i, * qui tol-lis pec-cá-ta mundi:

mi-se-ré-re no-bis.

Ag-nus De-i, * qui tol-lis pec-cá-ta mun-di:

do-na no-bis pa-cem.

Pr. The peace of the Lord be with you always.

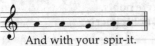

And with your spir-it.

R. **And with your spirit.**

Then, if appropriate, the Deacon, or the Priest, adds:

Pr. Let us offer each other the sign of peace.

And all offer one another the customary sign of peace.

BREAKING OF THE BREAD

Then the Priest takes the host, breaks it over the paten, and places a small piece in the chalice. Meanwhile the following is sung or said:

Lamb of God, * you take a-way the sins of the world,

have mer-cy on us.

Lamb of God, * you take a-way the sins of the world,

have mer-cy on us.

Lamb of God, * you take a-way the sins of the world,

grant us peace.

The invocation may even be repeated several times if the fraction is prolonged. Only the final time, however, is grant us peace said.

Agnus Dei, qui tollis peccáta mundi: miserére nobis.
Agnus Dei, qui tollis peccáta mundi: miserére nobis.
Agnus Dei, qui tollis peccáta mundi: dona nobis pacem.

Then the Priest, with hands joined, says quietly:

Domine Iesu Christe, Fili Dei vivi,
qui ex voluntate Patris,
cooperante Spiritu Sancto,
per mortem tuam mundum vivificasti:
libera me per hoc sacrosanctum Corpus et Sanguinem tuum
ab omnibus iniquitatibus meis et universis malis:
et fac me tuis semper inhærere mandatis,
et a te numquam separari permittas.

Or:

Perceptio Corporis et Sanguinis tui, Domine Iesu Christe,
non mihi proveniat in iudicium et condemnationem:
sed pro tua pietate prosit mihi
ad tutamentum mentis et corporis,
et ad medelam percipiendam.

INVITATION TO COMMUNION

All kneel. The Priest genuflects, takes the host and, holding it slightly raised above the paten or above the chalice says aloud:

Pr. Ecce Agnus Dei, ecce qui tollit peccáta mundi.
    Beáti qui ad cenam Agni vocáti sunt.
R. **Dómine, non sum dignus, ut intres sub tectum meum,**
    sed tantum dic verbo, et sanábitur ánima mea.

While the Priest is receiving the Body of Christ, the Communion Chant begins.

COMMUNION PROCESSION

After the priest has reverently consumed the Body and Blood of Christ he takes the paten or ciborium and approaches the communicants.

The Priest raises the host slightly and shows it to each of the communicants, saying:

Pr. Corpus Christi.
R. **Amen.**

Lamb of God, you take away the sins of the world, have mercy on us.
Lamb of God, you take away the sins of the world, have mercy on us.
Lamb of God, you take away the sins of the world, grant us peace.

Then the Priest, with hands joined, says quietly:

Lord Jesus Christ, Son of the living God,
who, by the will of the Father
and the work of the Holy Spirit,
through your Death gave life to the world,
free me by this, your most holy Body and Blood,
from all my sins and from every evil;
keep me always faithful to your commandments,
and never let me be parted from you.

Or:

May the receiving of your Body and Blood,
Lord Jesus Christ,
not bring me to judgement and condemnation,
but through your loving mercy
be for me protection in mind and body
and a healing remedy.

INVITATION TO COMMUNION

All kneel. The Priest genuflects, takes the host and, holding it slightly raised above
the paten or above the chalice says aloud:

Pr. Behold the Lamb of God,
    behold him who takes away the sins of the world.
    Blessed are those called to the supper of the Lamb.

R. **Lord, I am not worthy**
    that you should enter under my roof,
    but only say the word
    and my soul shall be healed.

While the Priest is receiving the Body of Christ, the Communion Chant begins.

COMMUNION PROCESSION

After the priest has reverently consumed the Body and Blood of Christ he takes the
paten or ciborium and approaches the communicants.

The Priest raises the host slightly and shows it to each of the communicants, saying:

Pr. The Body of Christ.

R. **Amen.**

When Communion is ministered from the chalice:

Pr. Sanguis Christi.

R. Amen.

After the distribution of Communion, if appropriate, a sacred silence may be observed for a while, or a psalm or other canticle of praise or a hymn may be sung.

PRAYER AFTER COMMUNION

Then, the Priest says:

Pr. Orémus.

All stand and pray in silence for a while, unless silence has just been observed. Then the Priest says the Prayer after Communion, at the end of which the people acclaim:

R. Amen.

THE CONCLUDING RITES

The Mass closes, sending the people forth to put what they have celebrated into effect in their daily lives.

Any brief announcements follow here. Then the dismissal takes place.

Pr. Dóminus vóbiscum.

Et cum spí-ri-tu tu-o.

R. Et cum spíritu tuo.

The Priest blesses the people, saying:

Pr. Benedícat vos omnípotens Deus,
    Pater, et Fílius, ✠ et Spíritus Sanctus.

A-men.

R. Amen.

When Communion is ministered from the chalice:

Pr. The Blood of Christ.

R. **Amen.**

After the distribution of Communion, if appropriate, a sacred silence may be observed for a while, or a psalm or other canticle of praise or a hymn may be sung.

PRAYER AFTER COMMUNION

Then, the Priest says:

Pr. Let us pray.

All stand and pray in silence for a while, unless silence has just been observed. Then the Priest says the Prayer after Communion, at the end of which the people acclaim:

R. **Amen.**

THE CONCLUDING RITES

The Mass closes, sending the people forth to put what they have celebrated into effect in their daily lives.

Any brief announcements follow here. Then the dismissal takes place.

Pr. The Lord be with you.

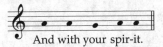

And with your spir-it.

R. **And with your spirit.**

The Priest blesses the people, saying:

Pr. May almighty God bless you,
the Father, and the Son, ✠ and the Holy Spirit.

A-men.

R. **Amen.**

Then the Deacon, or the Priest himself says the Dismissal:

Pr. Ite, missa est.

Or:

Pr. Ite, ad Evangélium Dómini annuntiándum.

Or:

Pr. Ite in pace, glorificándo vita vestra Dóminum.

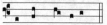

De- o grá- ti-as.

R. **Deo grátias.**

Or:

Pr. Ite in pace.

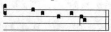

De- o grá- ti- as.

R. **Deo grátias.**

Then the Priest venerates the altar as at the beginning. After making a profound bow with the ministers, he withdraws.

Then the Deacon, or the Priest himself says the Dismissal:

Pr. Go forth, the Mass is ended.

Or:

Pr. Go and announce the Gospel of the Lord.

Or:

Pr. Go in peace, glorifying the Lord by your life.

R. Thanks be to God.

R. Thanks be to God.

Or:

Pr. Go in peace.

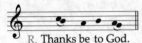

R. Thanks be to God.

R. Thanks be to God.

Then the Priest venerates the altar as at the beginning. After making a profound bow with the ministers, he withdraws.

SOLEMN BLESSINGS

The following blessings may be used, at the discretion of the Priest, at the end of the celebration of Mass, or of a Liturgy of the Word, or of the Office, or of the Sacraments.

The Deacon or, in his absence, the Priest himself, says the invitation: *Inclinate vos ad benedictionem.* Then the Priest, with hands extended over the people, says the blessing, with all responding: Amen.

I. For Celebrations in the Different Liturgical Times

1. In Adventu

Omnipotens et misericors Deus, cuius Unigeniti adventum
et præteritum creditis, et futurum exspectatis,
eiusdem adventus vos illustratione sanctificet
et sua benedictione locupletet.
R. Amen.

In præsentis vitæ stadio reddat vos in fide stabiles,
spe gaudentes, et in caritate efficaces.
R. Amen.

Ut, qui de adventu Redemptoris nostri
secundum carnem devota mente lætamini,
in secundo, cum in maiestate sua venerit,
præmiis æternæ vitæ ditemini.
R. Amen.

Et benedictio Dei omnipotentis,
Patris, et Filii, ✠ et Spiritus Sancti,
descendat super vos et maneat semper.
R. Amen.

2. In Nativitate Domini

Deus infinitæ bonitatis,
qui incarnatione Filii sui mundi tenebras effugavit,
et eius gloriosa nativitate
hanc noctem (diem) sacratissimam irradiavit,
effuget a vobis tenebras vitiorum,
et irradiet corda vestra luce virtutum.
R. Amen.

Quique eius salutiferæ nativitatis gaudium magnum
pastoribus ab Angelo voluit nuntiari,
ipse mentes vestras suo gaudio impleat,
et vos Evangelii sui nuntios efficiat.
R. Amen.

SOLEMN BLESSINGS

The following blessings may be used, at the discretion of the Priest, at the end of the celebration of Mass, or of a Liturgy of the Word, or of the Office, or of the Sacraments.

The Deacon or, in his absence, the Priest himself, says the invitation: Bow down for the blessing. Then the Priest, with hands extended over the people, says the blessing, with all responding: Amen.

I. For Celebrations in the Different Liturgical Times

1. Advent

May the almighty and merciful God,
by whose grace you have placed your faith
in the First Coming of his Only Begotten Son
and yearn for his coming again,
sanctify you by the radiance of Christ's Advent
and enrich you with his blessing.
R. Amen.

As you run the race of this present life,
may he make you firm in faith,
joyful in hope and active in charity.
R. Amen.

So that, rejoicing now with devotion
at the Redeemer's coming in the flesh,
you may be endowed with the rich reward of eternal life
when he comes again in majesty.
R. Amen.

And may the blessing of almighty God,
the Father, and the Son, ✠ and the Holy Spirit,
come down on you and remain with you for ever.
R. Amen.

2. The Nativity of the Lord

May the God of infinite goodness,
who by the Incarnation of his Son has driven darkness from the world
and by that glorious Birth has illumined this most holy night (day),
drive far from you the darkness of vice
and illumine your hearts with the light of virtue.
R. Amen.

May God, who willed that the great joy
of his Son's saving Birth
be announced to shepherds by the Angel,
fill your minds with the gladness he gives
and make you heralds of his Gospel.
R. Amen.

Et, qui per eius incarnationem terrena cælestibus sociavit,
dono vos suæ pacis et bonæ repleat voluntatis,
et vos faciat Ecclesiæ consortes esse cælestis.
R. Amen.

Et benedictio Dei omnipotentis,
Patris, et Filii, ✠ et Spiritus Sancti,
descendat super vos et maneat semper.
R. Amen.

3. Initio anni

Deus, fons et origo totius benedictionis,
gratiam vobis concedat,
benedictionis suæ largitatem infundat,
atque per totum annum vos salvos et incolumes protegat.
R. Amen.

Custodiat fidei vobis integritatem,
tribuat spei longanimitatem,
perseverantem usque ad finem
cum sancta patientia caritatem.
R. Amen.

Dies et actus vestros in sua pace disponat,
preces hic et ubique exaudiat,
et ad vitam æternam feliciter vos perducat.
R. Amen.

Et benedictio Dei omnipotentis,
Patris, et Filii, ✠ et Spiritus Sancti,
descendat super vos et maneat semper.
R. Amen.

4. In Epiphania Domini

Deus, qui vos de tenebris vocavit in admirabile lumen suum,
suam vobis benedictionem benignus infundat,
et corda vestra fide, spe et caritate stabiliat.
R. Amen.

Et quia Christum sequimini confidenter,
qui hodie mundo apparuit lux relucens in tenebris,
faciat et vos lucem esse fratribus vestris.
R. Amen.

And may God, who by the Incarnation
brought together the earthly and heavenly realm,
fill you with the gift of his peace and favour
and make you sharers with the Church in heaven.
R. Amen.

And may the blessing of almighty God,
the Father, and the Son, ✠ and the Holy Spirit,
come down on you and remain with you for ever.
R. Amen.

3. The Beginning of the Year

May God, the source and origin of all blessing,
grant you grace,
pour out his blessing in abundance,
and keep you safe from harm throughout the year.
R. Amen.

May he give you integrity in the faith,
endurance in hope,
and perseverance in charity
with holy patience to the end.
R. Amen.

May he order your days and your deeds in his peace,
grant your prayers in this and in every place,
and lead you happily to eternal life.
R. Amen.

And may the blessing of almighty God,
the Father, and the Son, ✠ and the Holy Spirit,
come down on you and remain with you for ever.
R. Amen.

4. The Epiphany of the Lord

May God, who has called you
out of darkness into his wonderful light,
pour out in kindness his blessing upon you
and make your hearts firm
in faith, hope and charity.
R. Amen.

And since in all confidence you follow Christ,
who today appeared in the world
as a light shining in darkness,
may God make you, too,
a light for your brothers and sisters.
R. Amen.

Quatenus, peregrinatione peracta,
perveniatis ad eum, quem magi stella prævia quæsierunt,
et gaudio magno, lucem de luce,
Christum Dominum invenerunt.
R. Amen.

Et benedictio Dei omnipotentis,
Patris, et Filii, ✠ et Spiritus Sancti,
descendat super vos et maneat semper.
R. Amen.

5. De Passione Domini

Deus, Pater misericordiarum, qui Unigeniti sui passione
tribuit vobis caritatis exemplum,
præstet ut, per servitium Dei et hominum,
percipiatis suæ benedictionis ineffabile donum.
R. Amen.

Ut ab eo sempiternæ vitæ munus obtineatis,
per cuius temporalem mortem, æternam vos evadere creditis.
R. Amen.

Quatenus, cuius humilitatis sequimini documenta,
eius resurrectionis possideatis consortia.
R. Amen.

Et benedictio Dei omnipotentis,
Patris, et Filii, ✠ et Spiritus Sancti,
descendat super vos et maneat semper.
R. Amen.

6. Tempore paschali

Deus, qui per resurrectionem Unigeniti sui
dignatus est vobis bonum redemptionis
adoptionisque conferre,
sua benedictione vos tribuat congaudere.
R. Amen.

And so when your pilgrimage is ended,
may you come to him
whom the Magi sought as they followed the star
and whom they found with great joy, the Light from Light,
who is Christ the Lord.
R. Amen.

And may the blessing of almighty God,
the Father, and the Son, ✠ and the Holy Spirit,
come down on you and remain with you for ever.
R. Amen.

5. The Passion of the Lord

May God, the Father of mercies,
who has given you an example of love
in the Passion of his Only Begotten Son,
grant that, by serving God and your neighbour,
you may lay hold of the wondrous gift of his blessing.
R. Amen.

So that you may receive the reward of everlasting life from him,
through whose earthly Death
you believe that you escape eternal death.
R. Amen.

And by following the example of his self-abasement,
may you possess a share in his Resurrection.
R. Amen.

And may the blessing of almighty God,
the Father, and the Son, ✠ and the Holy Spirit,
come down on you and remain with you for ever.
R. Amen.

6. Easter Time

May God, who by the Resurrection of his Only Begotten Son
was pleased to confer on you
the gift of redemption and of adoption,
give you gladness by his blessing.
R. Amen.

Et quo redimente percepistis donum perpetuæ libertatis,
eo largiente hereditatis æternæ consortes effici valeatis.
R. Amen.

Et cui resurrexistis in baptismate iam credendo,
adiungi mereamini in patria cælesti nunc recte vivendo.
R. Amen.

Et benedictio Dei omnipotentis,
Patris, et Filii, ✠ et Spiritus Sancti,
descendat super vos et maneat semper.
R. Amen.

7. In Ascensione Domini
Benedicat vos omnipotens Deus,
cuius Unigenitus hodierna die cælorum alta penetravit,
et vobis, ubi est ipse, ascendendi aditum reservavit.
R. Amen.

Concedat ut, sicut Christus post resurrectionem suam
visus est discipulis manifestus,
ita vobis in iudicium veniens
appareat pro æternitate placatus.
R. Amen.

Et qui eum consedere Patri in sua creditis maiestate,
ipsum usque in finem sæculi vobiscum permanere
secundum eius promissionem læti valeatis experire.
R. Amen.

Et benedictio Dei omnipotentis,
Patris, et Filii, ✠ et Spiritus Sancti,
descendat super vos et maneat semper.
R. Amen.

8. De Spiritu Sancto
Deus, Pater luminum, qui discipulorum mentes
Spiritus Paracliti infusione dignatus est illustrare,
sua vos faciat benedictione gaudere,
et perpetuo donis eiusdem Spiritus abundare.
R. Amen.

May he, by whose redeeming work
you have received the gift of everlasting freedom,
make you heirs to an eternal inheritance.
R. Amen.

And may you, who have already risen with Christ
in Baptism through faith,
by living in a right manner on this earth,
be united with him in the homeland of heaven.
R. Amen.

And may the blessing of almighty God,
the Father, and the Son, ✠ and the Holy Spirit,
come down on you and remain with you for ever.
R. Amen.

7. The Ascension of the Lord

May almighty God bless you,
for on this very day his Only Begotten Son
pierced the heights of heaven
and unlocked for you the way
to ascend to where he is.
R. Amen.

May he grant that,
as Christ after his Resurrection
was seen plainly by his disciples,
so when he comes as Judge
he may show himself merciful to you for all eternity.
R. Amen.

And may you, who believe he is seated
with the Father in his majesty,
know with joy the fulfilment of his promise
to stay with you until the end of time.
R. Amen.

And may the blessing of almighty God,
the Father, and the Son, ✠ and the Holy Spirit,
come down on you and remain with you for ever.
R. Amen.

8. The Holy Spirit

May God, the Father of lights,
who was pleased to enlighten the disciples' minds
by the outpouring of the Spirit, the Paraclete,
grant you gladness by his blessing
and make you always abound with the gifts of the same Spirit.
R. Amen.

Ignis ille, qui super discipulos mirandus apparuit,
corda vestra ab omni malo potenter expurget,
et sui luminis infusione perlustret.
R. Amen.

Quique dignatus est in unius fidei confessione
diversitatem adunare linguarum,
in eadem fide perseverare vos faciat,
et per illam a spe ad speciem pervenire concedat.
R. Amen.

Et benedictio Dei omnipotentis,
Patris, et Filii, ✠ et Spiritus Sancti,
descendat super vos et maneat semper.
R. Amen.

9. Per annum, I
Benedicat vobis Dominus, et custodiat vos.
R. Amen.

Illuminet faciem suam super vos, et misereatur vestri.
R. Amen.

Convertat vultum suum ad vos, et donet vobis suam pacem.
R. Amen.

Et benedictio Dei omnipotentis,
Patris, et Filii, ✠ et Spiritus Sancti,
descendat super vos et maneat semper.
R. Amen.

10. Per annum, II
Pax Dei, quæ exsuperat omnem sensum,
custodiat corda vestra et intellegentias vestras
in scientia et caritate Dei,
et Filii sui, Domini nostri Iesu Christi.
R. Amen.

Et benedictio Dei omnipotentis,
Patris, et Filii, ✠ et Spiritus Sancti,
descendat super vos et maneat semper.
R. Amen.

11. Per annum, III
Omnipotens Deus sua vos clementia benedicat,
et sensum in vobis sapientiæ salutaris infundat.
R. Amen.

May the wondrous flame that appeared above the disciples,
powerfully cleanse your hearts from every evil
and pervade them with its purifying light.

R. Amen.

And may God, who has been pleased to unite many tongues
in the profession of one faith,
give you perseverance in that same faith
and, by believing, may you journey from hope to clear vision.

R. Amen.

And may the blessing of almighty God,
the Father, and the Son, ✠ and the Holy Spirit,
come down on you and remain with you for ever.

R. Amen.

9. Ordinary Time I

May the Lord bless you and keep you.

R. Amen.

May he let his face shine upon you
and show you his mercy.

R. Amen.

May he turn his countenance towards you
and give you his peace.

R. Amen.

And may the blessing of almighty God,
the Father, and the Son, ✠ and the Holy Spirit,
come down on you and remain with you for ever.

R. Amen.

10. Ordinary Time II

May the peace of God,
which surpasses all understanding,
keep your hearts and minds
in the knowledge and love of God,
and of his Son, our Lord Jesus Christ.

R. Amen.

And may the blessing of almighty God,
the Father, and the Son, ✠ and the Holy Spirit,
come down on you and remain with you for ever.

R. Amen.

11. Ordinary Time III

May almighty God bless you in his kindness
and pour out saving wisdom upon you.

R. Amen.

Fidei documentis vos semper enutriat,
et in sanctis operibus, ut perseveretis, efficiat.
R. Amen.

Gressus vestros ad se convertat,
et viam vobis pacis et caritatis ostendat.
R. Amen.

Et benedictio Dei omnipotentis,
Patris, et Filii, ✠ et Spiritus Sancti,
descendat super vos et maneat semper.
R. Amen.

12. Per annum, IV

Deus totius consolationis dies vestros in sua pace disponat,
et suæ vobis benedictionis dona concedat.
R. Amen.

Ab omni semper perturbatione vos liberet,
et corda vestra in suo amore confirmet.
R. Amen.

Quatenus donis spei, fidei et caritatis divites,
et præsentem vitam transigatis in opere efficaces,
et possitis ad æternam pervenire felices.
R. Amen.

Et benedictio Dei omnipotentis,
Patris, et Filii, ✠ et Spiritus Sancti,
descendat super vos et maneat semper.
R. Amen.

13. Per annum, V

Omnipotens Deus universa a vobis adversa semper excludat,
et suæ super vos benedictionis dona propitiatus infundat.
R. Amen.

Corda vestra efficiat divinis intenta eloquiis,
ut repleri possint gaudiis sempiternis.
R. Amen.

Quatenus, quæ bona et recta intellegentes,
viam mandatorum Dei inveniamini semper currentes,
et civium supernorum efficiamini coheredes.
R. Amen.

Et benedictio Dei omnipotentis,
Patris, et Filii, ✠ et Spiritus Sancti,
descendat super vos et maneat semper.
R. Amen.

May he nourish you always with the teachings of the faith
and make you persevere in holy deeds.
R. Amen.

May he turn your steps towards himself
and show you the path of charity and peace.
R. Amen.

And may the blessing of almighty God,
the Father, and the Son, ✠ and the Holy Spirit,
come down on you and remain with you for ever.
R. Amen.

12. Ordinary Time IV

May the God of all consolation order your days in his peace
and grant you the gifts of his blessing.
R. Amen.

May he free you always from every distress
and confirm your hearts in his love.
R. Amen.

So that on this life's journey
you may be effective in good works,
rich in the gifts of hope, faith and charity,
and may come happily to eternal life.
R. Amen.

And may the blessing of almighty God,
the Father, and the Son, ✠ and the Holy Spirit,
come down on you and remain with you for ever.
R. Amen.

13. Ordinary Time V

May almighty God always keep every adversity far from you
and in his kindness pour out upon you the gifts of his blessing.
R. Amen.

May God keep your hearts attentive to his words,
that they may be filled with everlasting gladness.
R. Amen.

And so, may you always understand what is good and right,
and be found ever hastening along
in the path of God's commands,
made coheirs with the citizens of heaven.
R. Amen.

And may the blessing of almighty God,
the Father, and the Son, ✠ and the Holy Spirit,
come down on you and remain with you for ever.
R. Amen.

14. Per annum, VI

Benedicat vos Deus omni benedictione cælesti,
sanctosque vos et puros
in conspectu suo semper efficiat;
divitias gloriæ suæ in vos abundanter effundat,
verbis veritatis instruat, Evangelio salutis erudiat,
et caritate fraterna semper locupletet.
Per Christum Dominum nostrum.
R. Amen.

Et benedictio Dei omnipotentis,
Patris, et Filii, ✠ et Spiritus Sancti,
descendat super vos et maneat semper.
R. Amen.

II. For Celebrations of the Saints

15. De beata Maria Virgine

Deus, qui per beatæ Mariæ Virginis partum
genus humanum sua voluit benignitate redimere,
sua vos dignetur benedictione ditare.
R. Amen.

Eiusque semper et ubique patrocinia sentiatis,
per quam auctorem vitæ suscipere meruistis.
R. Amen.

Et qui hodierna die devotis mentibus convenistis,
spiritalium gaudiorum cælestiumque præmiorum
vobiscum munera reportetis.
R. Amen.

Et benedictio Dei omnipotentis,
Patris, et Filii, ✠ et Spiritus Sancti,
descendat super vos et maneat semper.
R. Amen.

16. De sanctis Petro et Paulo

Benedicat vos omnipotens Deus,
qui in beati Petri confessione vos saluberrima stabilivit,
et per eam in Ecclesiæ soliditate fidei fundavit.
R. Amen.

Et quos beati Pauli instruxit indefessa prædicatione,
suo semper exemplo doceat Christo fratres lucrifacere.
R. Amen.

14. Ordinary Time VI

May God bless you with every heavenly blessing,
make you always holy and pure in his sight,
pour out in abundance upon you the riches of his glory,
and teach you with the words of truth;
may he instruct you in the Gospel of salvation,
and ever endow you with fraternal charity.
Through Christ our Lord.
R. Amen.

And may the blessing of almighty God,
the Father, and the Son, ✠ and the Holy Spirit,
come down on you and remain with you for ever.
R. Amen.

II. For Celebrations of the Saints

15. The Blessed Virgin Mary

May God, who through the childbearing of the Blessed Virgin Mary
willed in his great kindness to redeem the human race,
be pleased to enrich you with his blessing.
R. Amen.

May you know always and everywhere
the protection of her,
through whom you have been found worthy to receive
the author of life.
R. Amen.

May you, who have devoutly gathered on this day,
carry away with you the gifts of spiritual joys and heavenly rewards.
R. Amen.

And may the blessing of almighty God,
the Father, and the Son, ✠ and the Holy Spirit,
come down on you and remain with you for ever.
R. Amen.

16. Saints Peter and Paul, Apostles

May almighty God bless you,
for he has made you steadfast in Saint Peter's saving confession
and through it has set you on the solid rock of the Church's faith.
R. Amen.

And having instructed you
by the tireless preaching of Saint Paul,
may God teach you constantly by his example
to win brothers and sisters for Christ.
R. Amen.

Ut Petrus clave, Paulus verbo,
ope intercessionis uterque
in illam patriam nos certent inducere,
ad quam meruerunt illi, alter cruce, alter gladio,
feliciter pervenire.
R. Amen.

Et benedictio Dei omnipotentis,
Patris, et Filii, ✠ et Spiritus Sancti,
descendat super vos et maneat semper.
R. Amen.

17. De Apostolis

Deus, qui vos in apostolicis tribuit consistere fundamentis,
benedicere vobis dignetur
beatorum Apostolorum N. et N. (beati Apostoli N.)
meritis intercedentibus gloriosis.
R. Amen.

Et apostolicis præsidiis vos pro cunctis faciat testes veritatis,
qui vos eorum munerari documentis voluit et exemplis.
R. Amen.

Ut eorum intercessione
ad æternæ patriæ hereditatem pervenire possitis,
per quorum doctrinam fidei firmitatem possidetis.
R. Amen.

Et benedictio Dei omnipotentis,
Patris, et Filii, ✠ et Spiritus Sancti,
descendat super vos et maneat semper.
R. Amen.

18. De omnibus Sanctis

Deus, gloria et exsultatio Sanctorum,
benedicat vos benedictione perpetua,
qui vobis tribuit eximiis suffragiis roborari.
R. Amen.

Eorum intercessione a præsentibus malis liberati,
et exemplis sanctæ conversationis instructi,
in servitio Dei fratrumque inveniamini semper intenti.
R. Amen.

So that by the keys of St Peter and the words of St Paul,
and by the support of their intercession,
God may bring us happily to that homeland
that Peter attained on a cross
and Paul by the blade of a sword.
R. Amen.

And may the blessing of almighty God,
the Father, and the Son, ✠ and the Holy Spirit,
come down on you and remain with you for ever.
R. Amen.

17. The Apostles

May God, who has granted you
to stand firm on apostolic foundations,
graciously bless you through the glorious merits
of the holy Apostles N. and N. (the holy Apostle N.).
R. Amen.

And may he, who endowed you
with the teaching and example of the Apostles,
make you, under their protection,
witnesses to the truth before all.
R. Amen.

So that through the intercession of the Apostles,
you may inherit the eternal homeland,
for by their teaching you possess firmness of faith.
R. Amen.

And may the blessing of almighty God,
the Father, and the Son, ✠ and the Holy Spirit,
come down on you and remain with you for ever.
R. Amen.

18. All Saints

May God, the glory and joy of the Saints,
who has caused you to be strengthened
by means of their outstanding prayers,
bless you with unending blessings.
R. Amen.

Freed through their intercession from present ills
and formed by the example of their holy way of life,
may you be ever devoted
to serving God and your neighbour.
R. Amen.

Quatenus cum iis omnibus
valeatis illius patriæ vos gaudia possidere,
in qua filios suos supernis coniungi civibus
in pace perpetua sancta lætatur Ecclesia.
R. Amen.

Et benedictio Dei omnipotentis,
Patris, et Filii, ✠ et Spiritus Sancti,
descendat super vos et maneat semper.
R. Amen.

III. Other Blessings

19. In dedicatione ecclesiæ

Deus, Dominus cæli et terræ,
qui vos hodie ad huius domus dedicationem adunavit,
ipse vos cælesti benedictione faciat abundare.
R. Amen.

Concedatque vobis fieri templum suum
et habitaculum Spiritus Sancti,
qui omnes filios dispersos voluit in Filio suo congregari.
R. Amen.

Quatenus feliciter emundati,
habitatorem Deum in vobismetipsis possitis habere,
et æternæ beatitudinis hereditatem
cum omnibus Sanctis possidere.
R. Amen.

Et benedictio Dei omnipotentis,
Patris, et Filii, ✠ et Spiritus Sancti,
descendat super vos et maneat semper.
R. Amen.

20. In celebrationibus pro defunctis

Benedicat vos Deus totius consolationis,
qui hominem ineffabili bonitate creavit,
et in resurrectione Unigeniti sui
spem credentibus resurgendi concessit.
R. Amen.

Nobis, qui vivimus, veniam tribuat pro peccatis,
et omnibus defunctis locum concedat lucis et pacis.
R. Amen.

So that, together with all,
you may possess the joys of the homeland,
where Holy Church rejoices
that her children are admitted in perpetual peace
to the company of the citizens of heaven.
R. Amen.

And may the blessing of almighty God,
the Father, and the Son, ✠ and the Holy Spirit,
come down on you and remain with you for ever.
R. Amen.

III. Other Blessings

19. For the Dedication of a Church

May God, the Lord of heaven and earth,
who has gathered you today for the dedication of this church,
make you abound in heavenly blessings.
R. Amen.

And may he, who has willed that all his scattered children
should be gathered together in his Son,
grant that you may become his temple
and the dwelling place of the Holy Spirit.
R. Amen.

And so, when you are thoroughly cleansed,
may God dwell within you
and grant you to possess with all the Saints
the inheritance of eternal happiness.
R. Amen.

And may the blessing of almighty God,
the Father, and the Son, ✠ and the Holy Spirit,
come down on you and remain with you for ever.
R. Amen.

20. In Celebrations for the Dead

May the God of all consolation bless you,
for in his unfathomable goodness he created the human race,
and in the Resurrection of his Only Begotten Son
he has given believers the hope of rising again.
R. Amen.

To us who are alive, may God grant pardon for our sins,
and to all the dead, a place of light and peace.
R. Amen.

Ut omnes cum Christo sine fine feliciter vivamus,
quem resurrexisse a mortuis veraciter credimus.
R. Amen.

Et benedictio Dei omnipotentis,
Patris, et Filii, ✠ et Spiritus Sancti,
descendat super vos et maneat semper.
R. Amen.

So may we all live happily for ever with Christ,
whom we believe truly rose from the dead.
R. Amen.

And may the blessing of almighty God,
the Father, and the Son, ✠ and the Holy Spirit,
come down on you and remain with you for ever.
R. Amen.

THANKSGIVING AFTER MASS

Prayer of Saint Thomas Aquinas

I give you thanks,
Lord, holy Father,
    almighty and eternal God,
who have been pleased
    to nourish me,
a sinner and your
    unworthy servant,
with the precious Body and Blood
of your Son, our Lord Jesus Christ:
this through no merits of mine,
but due solely to
    the graciousness of your mercy.

And I pray that this
    Holy Communion
may not be for me an offence
    to be punished,
but a saving plea for forgiveness.
May it be for me the armour of faith,
and the shield of good will.
May it cancel my faults,
destroy concupiscence
    and carnal passion,
increase charity and patience,
    humility and obedience
and all the virtues,
may it be a firm defence against
    the snares of all my enemies,
both visible and invisible,
the complete calming of
    my impulses,
both of the flesh and of the spirit,
a firm adherence to you,
    the one true God,
and the joyful completion of my
    life's course.

Oratio S. Thomas Aquinatis

Gratias tibi ago, Domine,
sancte Pater,
    omnipotens æterne Deus,
qui me peccatorem,
    indignum famulum tuum,
nullis meis meritis, sed sola
    dignatione misericordiæ tuæ
satiare dignatus es pretioso Corpore
    et Sanguine Filii tui,
Domini nostri Iesu Christi.

Et precor,
    ut hæc sancta communio
non sit mihi reatus ad pœnam,
sed intercessio salutaris ad veniam.
Sit mihi armatura fidei,
    et scutum bonæ voluntatis.
Sit vitiorum meorum evacuatio,
concupiscentiæ
    et libidinis exterminatio,
caritatis et patientiæ,
    humilitatis et obœdientiæ,
omniumque virtutum
    augmentatio:
contra insidias
    inimicorum omnium
tam visibilium quam invisibilium,
    firma defensio:
motuum meorum, tam carnalium
    quam spiritalium,
perfecta quietatio:
in te uno ac vero Deo
    firma adhæsio,
atque finis mei felix consummatio.

And I beseech you to lead me,
    a sinner,
to that banquet beyond all telling,
where with your Son and the
    Holy Spirit
you are the true light of
    your Saints,
fullness of satisfied desire,
    eternal gladness,
consummate delight and
    perfect happiness.
Through Christ our Lord.
Amen.

Et precor te,
    ut ad illud ineffabile convivium
me peccatorem perducere digneris,
ubi tu, cum Filio tuo et
    Spiritu Sancto,
Sanctis tuis es lux vera,
    satietas plena,
gaudium sempiternum,
iucunditas consummata et
    felicitas perfecta.
Per Christum Dominum nostrum.
Amen.

Prayer to the Most Holy Redeemer

Soul of Christ, sanctify me.
Body of Christ, save me.
Blood of Christ, embolden me.
Water from the side of Christ,
    wash me.

Passion of Christ, strengthen me.
O good Jesus, hear me.
Within your wounds hide me.
Never permit me to be parted
    from you.

From the evil Enemy defend me.
At the hour of my death call me
and bid me come to you,
that with your Saints
    I may praise you
for age upon age.
Amen.

Aspirationes ad Ss.mum Redemptorem

Anima Christi, sanctifica me.
Corpus Christi, salva me.
Sanguis Christi, inebria me.
Aqua lateris Christi, lava me.

Passio Christi, conforta me.
O bone Iesu, exaudi me.
Intra tua vulnera absconde me.
Ne permittas me separari a te.

Ab hoste maligno defende me.
In hora mortis meæ voca me.
Et iube me venire ad te,
ut cum Sanctis tuis laudem te
in sæcula sæculorum.

Amen.

Prayer of Self-Offering

Receive, Lord, my entire freedom.
Accept the whole of my memory,
my intellect and my will.

Oblatio sui

Suscipe, Domine,
    universam meam libertatem.
Accipe memoriam, intellectum
    atque voluntatem omnem.

Whatever I have or possess,
it was you who gave it to me;
I restore it to you in full,
and I surrender it completely
to the guidance of your will.
Give me only love of you
together with your grace,
and I am rich enough
and ask for nothing more.
Amen.

Quidquid habeo vel possideo,
    mihi largitus es:
id tibi totum restituo,
ac tuæ prorsus voluntati
    trado gubernandum.
Amorem tui solum cum gratia tua
    mihi dones,
et dives sum satis, nec aliud
    quidquam ultra posco.
Amen.

Prayer to Our Lord Jesus Christ Crucified

Oratio ad Dominum nostrum Iesum Christum Crucifixum

Behold, O good and loving Jesus,
that I cast myself on my knees
    before you
and, with the greatest fervour
    of spirit,
I pray and beseech you to instill
    into my heart
ardent sentiments of faith,
    hope and charity,
with true repentance for my sins
and a most firm purpose
    of amendment.
With deep affection and sorrow
I ponder intimately
and contemplate in my mind
    your five wounds,
having before my eyes what
    the prophet David
had already put in your mouth
    about yourself, O good Jesus:
They have pierced my hands and
    my feet;
they have numbered all my bones
    (Ps 21:17-18).

En ego, o bone et dulcissime Iesu,
ante conspectum tuum genibus
    me provolvo,
ac maximo animi ardore te oro
    atque obtestor,
ut meum in cor vividos fidei,
    spei et caritatis sensus,
atque veram peccatorum
    meorum pœnitentiam,
eaque emendandi firmissimam
    voluntatem velis imprimere;

dum magno animi affectu et dolore
tua quinque vulnera mecum
    ipse considero
ac mente contemplor,
illud præ oculis habens,
quod iam in ore ponebat tuo David
    propheta de te, o bone Iesu:

Foderunt manus meas
    et pedes meos:
dinumeraverunt omnia ossa mea
    (Ps 21:17-18).

The Universal Prayer Attributed to Pope Clement XI

I believe, O Lord,
  but may I believe more firmly;
I hope,
  but may I hope more securely;
I love,
  but may I love more ardently;
I sorrow,
   but may I sorrow more deeply.

I adore you as my first beginning;
I long for you as my last end;
I praise you as my
   constant benefactor;
I invoke you as my
   gracious protector.

By your wisdom direct me,
by your righteousness restrain me,
by your indulgence console me,
by your power protect me.

I offer you, Lord, my thoughts to
   be directed to you,
my words, to be about you,
my deeds, to respect your will,
my trials, to be endured for you.

I will whatever you will,
I will it because you will it,
I will it in the way you will it,
I will it for as long as you will it.

Lord, enlighten my understanding,
   I pray:
arouse my will,
cleanse my heart,
sanctify my soul.

Oratio universalis sub nomine Clementis Pp. XI vulgata

Credo, Domine,
   sed credam firmius;
spero, sed sperem securius;
amo, sed amem ardentius;
doleo, sed doleam vehementius.

Adoro te ut primum principium;
desidero ut finem ultimum;
laudo ut benefactorem perpetuum;
invoco ut defensorem propitium.

Tua me sapientia dirige,
iustitia contine,
clementia solare,
potentia protege.

Offero tibi, Domine, cogitanda,
   ut sint ad te;
dicenda, ut sint de te;
facienda, ut sint secundum te;
ferenda, ut sint propter te.

Volo quidquid vis,
volo quia vis,
volo quomodo vis,
volo quamdiu vis.

Oro, Domine:
   intellectum illumines,
voluntatem inflammes,
cor emundes,
animam sanctifices.

May I weep for past sins,
repel future temptations,
correct evil inclinations,
nurture appropriate virtues.

Defleam præteritas iniquitates,
repellam futuras tentationes,
corrigam vitiosas propensiones,
excolam idoneas virtutes.

Give me, good God,
love for you, hatred for myself,
zeal for my neighbour,
contempt for the world.

Tribue mihi, bone Deus,
amorem tui, odium mei,
zelum proximi,
contemptum mundi.

May I strive to obey superiors,
to help those dependent on me,
to have care for my friends,
forgiveness for my enemies.

Studeam superioribus obœdire,
inferioribus subvenire,
amicis consulere,
inimicis parcere.

May I conquer sensuality
    by austerity,
avarice by generosity,
anger by gentleness,
lukewarmness by fervour.

Vincam voluptatem austeritate,
avaritiam largitate,
iracundiam lenitate,
tepiditatem fervore.

Render me prudent in planning,
steadfast in dangers,
patient in adversity,
humble in prosperity.

Redde me prudentem in consiliis,
constantem in periculis,
patientem in adversis,
humilem in prosperis.

Make me, O Lord, attentive at prayer,
moderate at meals,
diligent in work,
steadfast in intent.

Fac, Domine,
    ut sim in oratione attentus,
in epulis sobrius,
in munere sedulus,
in proposito firmus.

May I be careful to maintain
    interior innocence,
outward modesty,
exemplary behaviour,
a regular life.

Curem habere innocentiam
    interiorem,
modestiam exteriorem,
conversationem exemplarem,
vitam regularem.

May I be always watchful in
    subduing nature,
in nourishing grace,
in observing your law,
in winning salvation.

Assidue invigilem naturæ
    domandæ,
gratiæ fovendæ,
legi servandæ,
saluti promerendæ.

May I learn from you
how precarious are earthly things,
how great divine things,
how fleeting is time,
how lasting things eternal.

Grant that I may prepare for death,
fear judgement,
flee hell,
gain paradise.
Through Christ our Lord.
Amen.

Discam a te quam tenue quod
terrenum,
quam grande quod divinum,
quam breve quod temporaneum,
quam durabile quod æternum.

Da, ut mortem præveniam,
iudicium pertimeam,
infernum effugiam,
paradisum obtineam.
Per Christum Dominum nostrum.
Amen.

Prayers to the Blessed Virgin Mary | Orationes ad B. Mariam Virginem

O Mary, Virgin and
Mother most holy,
behold, I have received your
most dear Son,
whom you conceived in
your immaculate womb,
brought forth, nursed and
embraced most tenderly.
Behold him at whose sight
you used to rejoice and be filled
with all delight;
him whom, humbly and lovingly,
once again I present
and offer him to you
to be clasped in your arms,
to be loved by your heart,
and to be offered up to
the Most Holy Trinity
as the supreme worship of adoration,
for your own honour and glory
and for my needs and for those of
the whole world.
I ask you therefore,
most loving Mother:

O Maria, Virgo
et Mater sanctissima,
ecce suscepi dilectissimum
Filium tuum,
quem immaculato utero
tuo concepisti,
genuisti, lactasti atque suavissimis
amplexibus strinxisti.
Ecce, cuius aspectu lætabaris
et omnibus deliciis replebaris,
illum ipsum tibi humiliter
et amanter repræsento et offero,

tuis bracchiis constringendum,
tuo corde amandum,

sanctissimæque Trinitati in
supremum latriæ cultum,
pro tui ipsius honore et gloria
et pro meis totiusque mundi
necessitatibus, offerendum.
Rogo ergo te, piissima Mater,

entreat for me the forgiveness
    of all my sins
and, in abundant measure,
    the grace
of serving him in the future
    more faithfully,
and at the last, final grace,
so that with you I may praise him
for all the ages of ages.
Amen.

impetra mihi veniam omnium
    peccatorum meorum,
uberemque gratiam ipsi deinceps
    fidelius serviendi,
ac denique gratiam finalem,
ut eum tecum laudare possim
per omnia sæcula sæculorum.

Amen.

Hail, Mary, full of grace, the Lord is
    with thee;
blessed art thou amongst women,
and blessed is the fruit of thy
    womb, Jesus.
Holy Mary, Mother of God,
pray for us sinners
now and at the hour of our death.
Amen.

Ave Maria, gratia plena, Dominus
    tecum;
benedicta tu in mulieribus,
et benedictus fructus ventris tui,
    Iesus.
Sancta Maria, Mater Dei,
ora pro nobis peccatoribus
nunc et in hora mortis nostræ.
Amen.

AFTER HOLY COMMUNION

Act of Faith

O Jesus, I believe that I have received your Flesh to eat and your Blood to drink, because you have said it, and your word is true. All that I have and all that I am are your gift and now you have given me yourself.

Act of Adoration

O Jesus, my God, my Creator, I adore you, because from your hands I came and with you I am to be happy for ever.

Act of Humility

O Jesus, I am not worthy to receive you, and yet you have come to me that my poor heart may learn of you to be meek and humble.

Act of Love

Jesus, I love you; I love you with all my heart. You know that I love you, and wish to love you daily more and more.

Act of Thanksgiving

My good Jesus, I thank you with all my heart. How good, how kind you are to me. Blessed be Jesus in the most holy Sacrament of the Altar.

Act of Offering

O Jesus, receive my poor offering.
Jesus, you have given yourself to me,
and now let me give myself to you:
I give you my body, that I may be chaste and pure.
I give you my soul, that I may be free from sin.
I give you my heart, that I may always love you.
I give you my every breath that I shall breathe,
and especially my last.
I give you myself in life and in death,
that I may be yours for ever and ever.

For Yourself

O Jesus, wash away my sins with your Precious Blood.

O Jesus, the struggle against temptation is not yet finished. My Jesus, when temptation comes near me, make me strong against it. In the moment of temptation may I always say: "My Jesus, mercy! Mary, help!"

O Jesus, may I lead a good life; may I die a happy death. May I receive you before I die. May I say when I am dying: "Jesus, Mary and Joseph, I give you my heart and my soul".

Listen now for a moment to Jesus Christ; perhaps he has something to say to you. Answer Jesus in your heart, and tell him all your troubles. Then say:

For Perseverance

Jesus, I am going away for a time, but, I trust, not without you. You are with me by your grace. I resolve never to leave you by mortal sin. Although I am so weak I have such hope in you. Give me grace to persevere. Amen.

IF I CAN'T GET TO MASS

Spiritual Communion

Spiritual Communion is the heartfelt desire to receive Our Lord, even when we are unable because of the distance or for some other reason. This desire to receive him through spiritual Communion is an act of love which prolongs our thanksgiving even when we are not in the Eucharistic presence of Our Lord. The wish to live constantly in his presence can be fuelled by acts of love and desire to be united with him and is a means of drawing more deeply from the life of the Holy Spirit dwelling within our souls in the state of grace. 'The effects of a sacrament can be received by desire. Although in such a case the sacrament is not received physically . . . nevertheless the actual reception of the sacrament itself brings with it fuller effect than receiving it through desire alone' (St Thomas Aquinas). The writings of the saints reveal many formulae for making a spiritual Communion:

Acts of Spiritual Communion

My Jesus, I believe that You are truly present in the Most Holy Sacrament. I love You above all things, and I desire to receive You into my soul. Since I cannot at this moment receive You sacramentally, come at least spiritually into my heart. I embrace You as being already there and unite myself wholly to You. Never permit me to be separated from You. Amen.

(St Alphonsus Liguori)

I wish, my Lord, to receive You with the purity, humility and devotion with which your Most Holy Mother received You, with the spirit and fervour of the saints. Come, Lord Jesus.

Give me, good Lord, a longing to be with You ... give me warmth, delight and quickness in thinking upon You. And give me Your grace to long for Your holy sacraments, and specially to rejoice in the presence of Your very blessed Body, Sweet Saviour Christ, in the Holy Sacrament of the altar.

(St Thomas More)

30 November

In Scotland

SAINT ANDREW, APOSTLE AND MARTYR, PATRON OF SCOTLAND

The lesson of the grain of wheat that dies in order to bear fruit also has a parallel in the life of Saint Andrew. Tradition tells us that he followed the fate of his Lord and Master, ending his days in Patras, Greece. Like Peter, he endured martyrdom on a cross, the diagonal cross that we venerate today as the cross of Saint Andrew. From his example we learn that the path of each single Christian, like that of the Church as a whole, leads to new life, to eternal life, through the imitation of Christ and the experience of his cross.

(Pope Benedict XVI)

Solemnity

Entrance Antiphon Cf. Mt 4:18-19	Ant. ad introitum
BESIDE the Sea of Galilee, the Lord saw two brothers, Peter and Andrew, and he said to them: Come after me and I will make you fishers of men.	DOMINUS secus mare Galilææ vidit duos fratres, Petrum et Andream, et vocavit eos: Venite post me, faciam vos fieri piscatores hominum.

The Gloria in excelsis (Glory to God in the highest) is said.

Collect	Collecta
We humbly implore your majesty, O Lord, that, just as the blessed Apostle Andrew was for your Church a preacher and pastor, so he may be for us a constant intercessor before you. Through our Lord Jesus Christ, your Son, who lives and reigns with you in the unity of the Holy Spirit, one God, for ever and ever.	Maiestatem tuam, Domine, suppliciter exoramus, ut, sicut Ecclesiæ tuæ beatus Andreas apostolus exstitit prædicator et rector, ita apud te sit pro nobis perpetuus intercessor. Per Dominum nostrum Iesum Christum Filium tuum, qui tecum vivit et regnat in unitate Spiritus Sancti, Deus, per omnia sæcula sæculorum.

FIRST READING

A reading from the book of Wisdom   3:1-9

He accepted them as a holocaust.

The souls of the virtuous are in the hands of God,
no torment shall ever touch them.
In the eyes of the unwise, they did appear to die,
their going looked like a disaster,
their leaving us, like annihilation;
but they are in peace.
If they experienced punishment as men see it,
their hope was rich with immortality;
slight was their affliction, great will their blessings be.
God has put them to the test
and proved them worthy to be with him;
he has tested them like gold in a furnace,
and accepted them as a holocaust.
When the time comes for his visitation they will shine out;
as sparks run through the stubble, so will they.
They shall judge nations, rule over peoples,
and the Lord will be their king for ever.
They who trust in him will understand the truth,
those who are faithful will live with him in love;
for grace and mercy await those he has chosen.

  The word of the Lord.

Responsorial Psalm   Ps 30:3-4,6,8,17,21. R. v.6

R. **Into your hands, O Lord,**
   I commend my spirit.

   Be a rock of refuge for me,
   a mighty stronghold to save me,
   for you are my rock, my stronghold.
   For your name's sake, lead me and guide me. R.

   Into your hands I commend my spirit.
   It is you who will redeem me, Lord.
   As for me, I trust in the Lord:
   let me be glad and rejoice in your love. R.

   Let your face shine on your servant.
   Save me in your love.

You hide them in the shelter of your presence
from the plotting of men. R.

SECOND READING

A reading from the letter of St Paul to the Romans   10:9-18

*Faith comes from what is preached, and what is preached comes from the word
of Christ.*

If your lips confess that Jesus is Lord and if you believe in your heart that
God raised him from the dead, then you will be saved. By believing from
the heart you are made righteous; by confessing with your lips you are
saved. When scripture says: those who believe in him will have no cause
for shame, it makes no distinction between Jew and Greek: all belong to the
same Lord who is rich enough, however many ask his help, for everyone
who calls on the name of the Lord will be saved.

But they will not ask his help unless they believe in him, and they will
not believe in him unless they have heard him, and they will not hear
him unless they get a preacher, and they will never have a preacher unless
one is sent, but as scripture says: The footsteps of those who bring good
news are a welcome sound. Not everyone, of course, listens to the Good
News. As Isaiah says: Lord, how many believe what we proclaimed? So
faith comes from what is preached, and what is preached comes from the
word of Christ.

Let me put the question: is it possible that they did not hear? Indeed
they did; in the words of the psalm, their voice has gone out through all
the earth, and their message to the ends of the world.

The word of the Lord.

Gospel Acclamation   2 Ch 7:16
R. **Alleluia, alleluia!**
Follow me, says the Lord,
and I will make you fishers of men.
R. **Alleluia!**

GOSPEL

A reading from the holy Gospel according to Matthew   4:18-22

And they left their nets at once and followed him.

As Jesus was walking by the Sea of Galilee he saw two brothers, Simon,
who was called Peter, and his brother Andrew; they were making a cast
in the lake with their net, for they were fishermen. And he said to them,
'Follow me and I will make you fishers of men.' And they left their nets at
once and followed him.

Going on from there he saw another pair of brothers, James son of Zebedee and his brother John; they were in their boat with their father Zebedee, mending their nets, and he called them. At once, leaving the boat and their father, they followed him.

The Gospel of the Lord.

The Creed is said.

Prayer over the Offerings

Grant us, almighty God,
    that through these offerings,
which we bring on the feast day
    of Saint Andrew,
we may please you by what
    we have brought
and be given life by what
    you have accepted.
Through Christ our Lord.

Preface of the Apostles, pp.70-71.

Super oblata

Concede nobis, omnipotens Deus,
ut his muneribus,
    quæ in beati Andreæ festivitate
      deferimus,
et tibi placeamus exhibitis, et
    vivificemur acceptis.
Per Christum Dominum nostrum.

Communion Antiphon Cf. Jn 1:41-42

Andrew told his brother Simon:
We have found the Messiah,
    the Christ,
and he brought him to Jesus.

Ant. ad communionem

Dixit Andreas Simoni fratri suo:
Invenimus Messiam,
    qui dicitur Christus.
Et adduxit eum ad Iesum.

Prayer after Communion

May communion in your Sacrament
    strengthen us, O Lord,
so that by the example of the
    blessed Apostle Andrew
we, who carry in our body
    the Death of Christ,
may merit to live with him in glory.
Who lives and reigns
    for ever and ever.

Post communionem

Roboret nos, Domine,
    sacramenti tui communio,
ut, exemplo beati Andreæ apostoli,
Christi mortificationem ferentes,
cum ipso vivere mereamur
    in gloria.
Qui vivit et regnat
    in sæcula sæculorum.

A formula of Solemn Blessing, pp.146-147, may be used.

3 December

FIRST SUNDAY OF ADVENT

Today, on the First Sunday of Advent, we begin a new liturgical year; that is, a new journey of the People of God with Jesus Christ, our Shepherd, who guides us through history toward the fulfilment of the Kingdom of God....This journey never comes to an end. Just as in each of our lives we always need to begin again, to get up again, to rediscover the meaning of the goal of our lives, so also for the great human family it is always necessary to rediscover the common horizon toward which we are journeying. The horizon of hope! This is the horizon that makes for a good journey. The season of Advent restores this horizon of hope, a hope which does not disappoint for it is founded on God's Word. A hope which does not disappoint, simply because the Lord never disappoints! He is faithful!

(Pope Francis)

Entrance Antiphon   Cf. Ps 24:1-3

To you, I lift up my soul,
O my God.
In you, I have trusted; let me not be
put to shame.
Nor let my enemies exult over me;
and let none who hope in you
be put to shame.

Ant. ad introitum

Ad te levavi animam meam,
Deus meus, in te confido,
non erubescam.
Neque irrideant me inimici mei,
etenim universi qui te exspectant
non confundentur.

The Gloria in excelsis (Glory to God in the highest) is not said.

Collect

Grant your faithful, we pray,
almighty God,
the resolve to run forth to meet
your Christ
with righteous deeds at his coming,
so that, gathered at his right hand,
they may be worthy to possess
the heavenly Kingdom.
Through our Lord Jesus Christ,
your Son,
who lives and reigns with you
in the unity of the Holy Spirit,
one God, for ever and ever.

Collecta

Da, quæsumus, omnipotens Deus,
hanc tuis fidelibus voluntatem,
ut, Christo tuo venienti iustis
operibus occurrentes,
eius dexteræ sociati, regnum
mereantur possidere cæleste.
Per Dominum nostrum Iesum
Christum Filium tuum,
qui tecum vivit et regnat
in unitate Spiritus Sancti,
Deus, per omnia sæcula sæculorum.

FIRST READING

A reading from the prophet Isaiah   63:16-17; 64:1,3-8

Oh, that you would tear the heavens open and come down.

You, Lord, yourself are our Father,
Our Redeemer is your ancient name.
Why, Lord, leave us to stray from your ways
and harden our hearts against fearing you?
Return, for the sake of your servants,
the tribes of your inheritance.
Oh, that you would tear the heavens open and come down
– at your Presence the mountains would melt.
No ear has heard,
no eye has seen
any god but you act like this
for those who trust him.
You guide those who act with integrity
and keep your ways in mind.
You were angry when we were sinners;
we had long been rebels against you.
We were all like men unclean,
all that integrity of ours like filthy clothing.
We have all withered like leaves
and our sins blew us away like the wind.
No one invoked your name
or roused himself to catch hold of you.
For you hid your face from us
and gave us up to the power of our sins.
And yet, Lord, you are our Father;
we the clay, you the potter,
we are all the work of your hand.

The word of the Lord.

Responsial Psalm   Ps 79:2-3,15-16,18-19. R. v.4

R. **God of hosts, bring us back;**
   let your face shine on us and we shall be saved.

   O shepherd of Israel, hear us,
   shine forth from your cherubim throne.
   O Lord, rouse up your might,
   O Lord, come to our help. R.

God of hosts, turn again, we implore,
look down from heaven and see.
Visit this vine and protect it,
the vine your right hand has planted. R.

May your hand be on the man you have chosen,
the man you have given your strength.
And we shall never forsake you again:
give us life that we may call upon your name. R.

SECOND READING

A reading from the first letter of St Paul to the Corinthians   1:3-9
We are waiting for our Lord Jesus Christ to be revealed.

May God our Father and the Lord Jesus Christ send you grace and peace.

I never stop thanking God for all the graces you have received through Jesus Christ. I thank him that you have been enriched in so many ways, especially in your teachers and preachers; the witness to Christ has indeed been strong among you so that you will not be without any of the gifts of the Spirit while you are waiting for our Lord Jesus Christ to be revealed; and he will keep you steady and without blame until the last day, the day of our Lord Jesus Christ, because God by calling you has joined you to his Son, Jesus Christ; and God is faithful.

The word of the Lord.

Gospel Acclamation   Ps 84:8

R. **Alleluia, alleluia!**
Let us see, O Lord, your mercy
and give us your saving help.
R. **Alleluia!**

GOSPEL

A reading from the holy Gospel according to Mark   13:33-37
Stay awake, because you do not know when the master of the house is coming.

Jesus said to his disciples: 'Be on your guard, stay awake, because you never know when the time will come. It is like a man travelling abroad: he has gone from home, and left his servants in charge, each with his own task; and he has told the doorkeeper to stay awake. So stay awake, because you do not know when the master of the house is coming, evening, midnight, cockcrow, dawn; if he comes unexpectedly, he must not find you asleep. And what I say to you I say to all: Stay awake!'

The Gospel of the Lord.

The Creed is said.

Prayer over the Offerings | Super oblata

Accept, we pray, O Lord,
   these offerings we make,
gathered from among your gifts to us,
and may what you grant us to
   celebrate devoutly here below,
gain for us the prize
   of eternal redemption.
Through Christ our Lord.

Suscipe, quæsumus,
   Domine, munera
quæ de tuis offerimus
   collata beneficiis,
et, quod nostræ devotioni concedis
   effici temporali,
tuæ nobis fiat præmium
   redemptionis æternæ.
Per Christum Dominum nostrum.

Preface I of Advent, pp.42-43.

Communion Antiphon   Ps 84:13 | Ant. ad communionem

The Lord will bestow his bounty,
   and our earth shall yield
   its increase.

Dominus dabit benignitatem,
et terra nostra dabit fructum suum.

Prayer after Communion | Post communionem

May these mysteries, O Lord,
in which we have participated,
profit us, we pray,
for even now,
   as we walk amid passing things,
you teach us by them to love
   the things of heaven
and hold fast to what endures.
Through Christ our Lord.

Prosint nobis, quæsumus, Domine,
   frequentata mysteria,
quibus nos,
   inter prætereuntia ambulantes,
iam nunc instituis amare cælestia
   et inhærere mansuris.
Per Christum Dominum nostrum.

A formula of Solemn Blessing, pp.132-133, may be used.

8 December

THE IMMACULATE CONCEPTION
OF THE BLESSED VIRGIN MARY

Mary responds to God's proposal by saying: "Behold, I am the handmaid of the Lord". She does not say: "Well, this time I will do God's will; I will make myself available, then I will see…". No. Hers is a full, total "yes", for her entire life, without conditions…For each of us too, there is a history of salvation made up of "yeses" and "noes". Sometimes, though, we are experts in the half-hearted "yes": we are good at pretending not to understand what God wants and what our conscience suggests… Every "yes" to God gives rise to stories of salvation for us and for others. In this Advent journey, God wishes to visit us and awaits our "yes".

(Pope Francis)

Solemnity

Entrance Antiphon   Is 61:10

I REJOICE heartily in the Lord,
in my God is the joy of my soul;
for he has clothed me with a robe
    of salvation,
and wrapped me in a mantle
    of justice,
like a bride adorned with her jewels.

Ant. ad introitum

G AUDENS gaudebo in Domino,
et exsultabit anima mea
    in Deo meo;
quia induit me vestimentis salutis,
et indumento iustitiæ
    circumdedit me,
quasi sponsam ornatam
    monilibus suis.

The Gloria in excelsis (Glory to God in the highest) is said.

Collect

O God, who by the Immaculate
    Conception of the Blessed Virgin
prepared a worthy dwelling
    for your Son,
grant, we pray,
that, as you preserved her
    from every stain
by virtue of the Death of your Son,
    which you foresaw,

Collecta

Deus, qui per immaculatam
    Virginis Conceptionem
dignum Filio tuo
    habitaculum præparasti,
quæsumus, ut, qui ex morte
    eiusdem Filii tui prævisa,
eam ab omni labe præservasti,
nos quoque mundos,

so, through her intercession,
we, too, may be cleansed
    and admitted to your presence.
Through our Lord Jesus Christ,
    your Son,
who lives and reigns with you
    in the unity of the Holy Spirit,
one God, for ever and ever.

eius intercessione,
ad te pervenire concedas.
Per Dominum nostrum Iesum
    Christum Filium tuum,
qui tecum vivit et regnat
    in unitate Spiritus Sancti,
Deus, per omnia sæcula sæculorum.

FIRST READING

A reading from the book of Genesis   3:9-15,20

I will make you enemies of each other; your offspring and her offspring.

After Adam had eaten of the tree, the Lord God called to him, 'Where are you?' he asked. 'I heard the sound of you in the garden,' he replied. 'I was afraid because I was naked, so I hid.' 'Who told you that you were naked?' he asked. 'Have you been eating of the tree I forbade you to eat?' The man replied, 'It was the woman you put with me; she gave me the fruit, and I ate it.' Then the Lord God asked the woman, 'What is this you have done?' The woman replied, 'The serpent tempted me and I ate.'

Then the Lord God said to the serpent, 'Because you have done this,
'Be accursed beyond all cattle,
all wild beasts.
You shall crawl on your belly and eat dust
every day of your life.
I will make you enemies of each other:
you and the woman,
your offspring and her offspring.
It will crush your head
and you will strike its heel.'

The man named his wife 'Eve' because she was the mother of all those who live.

The word of the Lord.

Responsional Psalm   Ps 97:1-4. R. v.1

R. **Sing a new song to the Lord
for he has worked wonders.**

Sing a new song to the Lord
for he has worked wonders.
His right hand and his holy arm
have brought salvation. R.

The Lord has made known his salvation;
has shown his justice to the nations.
He has remembered his truth and love
for the house of Israel. R.

All the ends of the earth have seen
the salvation of our God.
Shout to the Lord all the earth,
ring out your joy. R.

SECOND READING

A reading from the letter of St Paul to the Ephesians   1:3-6,11-12
Before the world was made, God chose us in Christ.

Blessed be God the Father of our Lord Jesus Christ,
who has blessed us with all the spiritual blessings of heaven in Christ.
Before the world was made, he chose us, chose us in Christ,
to be holy and spotless, and to live through love in his presence,
determining that we should become his adopted sons,
    through Jesus Christ
for his own kind purposes,
to make us praise the glory of his grace,
his free gift to us in the Beloved.
And it is in him that we were claimed as God's own,
chosen from the beginning,
under the predetermined plan of the one who guides all things
as he decides by his own will;
chosen to be,
for his greater glory,
the people who would put their hopes in Christ before he came.

The word of the Lord.

Gospel Acclamation   Cf. Lk 1:28

R. **Alleluia, alleluia!**
Hail, Mary, full of grace; the Lord is with thee!
Blessed art thou among women.
R. **Alleluia!**

GOSPEL

A reading from the holy Gospel according to Luke   1:26-38
Rejoice, so highly favoured! The Lord is with you.

The angel Gabriel was sent by God to a town in Galilee called Nazareth, to a virgin betrothed to a man named Joseph, of the house of David; and the virgin's name was Mary. He went in and said to her, 'Rejoice, so highly favoured! The Lord is with you.' She was deeply disturbed by these words and asked herself what this greeting could mean, but the angel said to her, 'Mary, do not be afraid; you have won God's favour. Listen! You are to conceive and bear a son, and you must name him Jesus. He will be great and will be called Son of the Most High. The Lord God will give him the throne of his ancestor David; he will rule over the House of Jacob for ever and his reign will have no end.' Mary said to the angel, 'But how can this come about, since I am a virgin?' 'The Holy Spirit will come upon you' the angel answered, 'and the power of the Most High will cover you with its shadow. And so the child will be holy and will be called Son of God. Know this too: your kinswoman Elizabeth has, in her old age, herself conceived a son, and she whom people called barren is now in her sixth month, for nothing is impossible to God.' 'I am the handmaid of the Lord,' said Mary, 'let what you have said be done to me.' And the angel left her.

    The Gospel of the Lord.

The Creed is said.

Prayer over the Offerings	Super oblata
Graciously accept the saving sacrifice which we offer you, O Lord, on the Solemnity of the Immaculate Conception of the Blessed Virgin Mary, and grant that, as we profess her,	Salutarem hostiam, quam in sollemnitate immaculatæ Conceptionis beatæ Virginis Mariæ tibi, Domine, offerimus, suscipe dignanter, et præsta,

on account of your prevenient grace,
to be untouched by any stain of sin,
so, through her intercession,
we may be delivered from all
    our faults.
Through Christ our Lord.

ut, sicut illam tua gratia præveniente
ab omni labe
profitemur immunem,
ita, eius intercessione, a culpis
    omnibus liberemur.
Per Christum Dominum nostrum.

Preface: The Mystery of Mary
and the Church.

Præfatio: De mysterio Mariæ
et Ecclesiæ.

It is truly right and just,
    our duty and our salvation,
always and everywhere
    to give you thanks,
Lord, holy Father,
    almighty and eternal God.

Vere dignum et iustum est,
    æquum et salutare,
nos tibi semper et ubique
    gratias agere:
Domine, sancte Pater,
    omnipotens æterne Deus:

For you preserved the most Blessed
    Virgin Mary
from all stain of original sin,
so that in her, endowed with
    the rich fullness of your grace,
you might prepare a worthy
    Mother for your Son
and signify the beginning
    of the Church,
his beautiful Bride without spot
    or wrinkle.

Qui beatissimam Virginem Mariam
ab omni originalis culpæ
    labe præservasti,
ut in ea,
    gratiæ tuæ plenitudine ditata,
dignam Filio tuo
    Genetricem præparares
et Sponsæ eius Ecclesiæ,
sine ruga vel macula formosæ,
    signares exordium.

She, the most pure Virgin,
    was to bring forth a Son,
the innocent Lamb who would
    wipe away our offences;
you placed her above all others
to be for your people an advocate
    of grace
and a model of holiness.

Filium enim erat purissima
    Virgo datura,
qui crimina nostra Agnus
    innocens aboleret;
et ipsam præ omnibus tuo
    populo disponebas
advocatam gratiæ
    et sanctitatis exemplar.

And so, in company with the choirs
of Angels,
we praise you, and with joy
we proclaim:

Holy, Holy, Holy Lord God of hosts...

Et ideo, choris angelicis sociati,
te laudamus in gaudio confitentes:

Sanctus, Sanctus, Sanctus. . .

Communion Antiphon

Glorious things are spoken of you,
O Mary,
for from you arose the sun of justice,
Christ our God.

Ant. ad communionem

Gloriosa dicta sunt de te, Maria,
quia ex te ortus est sol iustitiæ,
Christus Deus noster.

Prayer after Communion

May the Sacrament we have received,
O Lord our God,
heal in us the wounds of that fault
from which in a singular way
you preserved Blessed Mary in her
Immaculate Conception.
Through Christ our Lord.

Post communionem

Sacramenta quæ sumpsimus,
Domine Deus noster,
illius in nobis culpæ
vulnera reparent,
a qua immaculatam beatæ
Mariæ Conceptionem
singulariter præservasti.
Per Christum Dominum nostrum.

A formula of Solemn Blessing, pp.144-145, may be used.

10 December

SECOND SUNDAY OF ADVENT

On this second Sunday of Advent, the Liturgy places us in the school of John the Baptist, who preached "a baptism of repentance for the forgiveness of sins". Perhaps we ask ourselves, "Why do we have to convert? Conversion is about an atheist who becomes a believer or a sinner who becomes just. But we don't need it. We are already Christians. So we are okay". But this isn't true. In thinking like this, we don't realise that it is precisely because of this presumption that we must convert...But let us ask ourselves: is it true that in the various situations and circumstances of life, we have within us the same feelings that Jesus has? We're not all right. We must always convert and have the sentiments that Jesus had.

(Pope Francis)

Entrance Antiphon   Cf. Is 30:19,30

O PEOPLE of Sion, behold,
the Lord will come to save
the nations,
and the Lord will make the glory
of his voice heard
in the joy of your heart.

Ant. ad introitum

P OPULUS Sion, ecce Dominus
veniet ad salvandas gentes;
et auditam faciet Dominus gloriam
vocis suæ
in lætitia cordis vestri.

The Gloria in excelsis (Glory to God in the highest) is not said.

Collect

Almighty and merciful God,
may no earthly undertaking
hinder those
who set out in haste to meet
your Son,
but may our learning
of heavenly wisdom
gain us admittance to his company.
Who lives and reigns with you
in the unity of the Holy Spirit,
one God, for ever and ever.

Collecta

Omnipotens et misericors Deus,
in tui occursum Filii festinantes
nulla opera terreni actus impediant,
sed sapientiæ cælestis eruditio nos
faciat eius esse consortes.
Qui tecum vivit et regnat
in unitate Spiritus Sancti,
Deus, per omnia sæcula sæculorum.

FIRST READING

A reading from prophet Isaiah   40:1-5,9-11

Prepare a way for the Lord.

'Console my people, console them'
says your God.
'Speak to the heart of Jerusalem
and call to her
that her time of service is ended,
that her sin is atoned for,
that she has received from the hand of the Lord
double punishment for all her crimes.'

A voice cries, 'Prepare in the wilderness
a way for the Lord.
Make a straight highway for our God
across the desert.
Let every valley be filled in,
every mountain and hill be laid low,
let every cliff become a plain,
and the ridges a valley;
then the glory of the Lord shall be revealed
and all mankind shall see it;
for the mouth of the Lord has spoken.'

Go up on a high mountain,
joyful messenger to Zion.
Shout with a loud voice,
joyful messenger to Jerusalem.
Shout without fear,
say to the towns of Judah,
'Here is your God.'

Here is the Lord coming with power,
his arm subduing all things to him.
The prize of his victory is with him,
his trophies all go before him.
He is like a shepherd feeding his flock,
gathering lambs in his arms,
holding them against his breast
and leading to their rest the mother ewes.

   The word of the Lord.

Responsorial Psalm   Ps 84:9-14. R. v.8

R. **Let us see, O Lord, your mercy
   and give us your saving help.**

> I will hear what the Lord God has to say,
> a voice that speaks of peace,
> peace for his people.
> His help is near for those who fear him
> and his glory will dwell in our land. R.

> Mercy and faithfulness have met;
> justice and peace have embraced.
> Faithfulness shall spring from the earth
> and justice look down from heaven. R.

> The Lord will make us prosper
> and our earth shall yield its fruit.
> Justice shall march before him
> and peace shall follow his steps. R.

SECOND READING

A reading from the second letter of St Peter   3:8-14

We are waiting for the new heavens and new earth.

There is one thing, my friends, that you must never forget: that with the Lord, 'a day' can mean a thousand years, and a thousand years is like a day. The Lord is not being slow to carry out his promises, as anybody else might be called slow; but he is being patient with you all, wanting nobody to be lost and everybody to be brought to change his ways. The Day of the Lord will come like a thief, and then with a roar the sky will vanish, the elements will catch fire and fall apart, the earth and all that it contains will be burnt up.

Since everything is coming to an end like this, you should be living holy and saintly lives while you wait and long for the Day of God to come, when the sky will dissolve in flames and the elements melt in the heat. What we are waiting for is what he promised: the new heavens and new earth, the place where righteousness will be at home. So then, my friends, while you are waiting, do your best to live lives without spot or stain so that he will find you at peace.

The word of the Lord.

Gospel Acclamation   Lk 3:4,6

R. **Alleluia, alleluia!**
Prepare a way for the Lord,
make his paths straight,
and all mankind shall see the salvation of God.
R. **Alleluia!**

GOSPEL

A reading from the holy Gospel according to Mark   1:1-8
Make his paths straight.

The beginning of the Good News about Jesus Christ, the Son of God. It is
written in the book of the prophet Isaiah:

> Look, I am going to send my messenger before you;
> he will prepare your way.
> A voice cries in the wilderness:
> Prepare a way for the Lord,
> make his paths straight,

and so it was that John the Baptist appeared in the wilderness, proclaiming
a baptism of repentance for the forgiveness of sins. All Judaea and all the
people of Jerusalem made their way to him, and as they were baptised by him
in the river Jordan they confessed their sins. John wore a garment of camel-
skin, and he lived on locusts and wild honey. In the course of his preaching
he said, 'Someone is following me, someone who is more powerful than I
am, and I am not fit to kneel down and undo the strap of his sandals. I have
baptised you with water, but he will baptise you with the Holy Spirit.'

The Gospel of the Lord.

The Creed is said.

Prayer over the Offerings	Super oblata
Be pleased, O Lord, with our humble prayers and offerings, and, since we have no merits to plead our cause, come, we pray, to our rescue with the protection of your mercy. Through Christ our Lord.	Placare, Domine, quæsumus, nostræ precibus humilitatis et hostiis, et, ubi nulla suppetunt suffragia meritorum, tuæ nobis indulgentiæ succurre præsidiis. Per Christum Dominum nostrum.

Preface I of Advent, pp.42-43.

Communion Antiphon Ba 5:5;4:36 | Ant. ad communionem

| Jerusalem, arise and stand upon the heights, and behold the joy which comes to you from God. | Ierusalem, surge et sta in excelso, et vide iucunditatem, quæ veniet tibi a Deo tuo. |

Prayer after Communion | Post communionem

| Replenished by the food of spiritual nourishment, we humbly beseech you, O Lord, that, through our partaking in this mystery, you may teach us to judge wisely the things of earth and hold firm to the things of heaven. Through Christ our Lord. | Repleti cibo spiritalis alimoniæ, supplices te, Domine, deprecamur, ut, huius participatione mysterii, doceas nos terrena sapienter perpendere, et cælestibus inhærere. Per Christum Dominum nostrum. |

A formula of Solemn Blessing, pp.132-133, may be used.

17 December

THIRD SUNDAY OF ADVENT

This Third Sunday of Advent helps us to rediscover a special dimension of repentance: joy. Whoever repents and approaches the Lord, feels joy. The prophet Zephaniah says to us today: "Sing aloud, O daughter of Zion!"; and the apostle Paul exhorts the Christians of Philippi: "Rejoice in the Lord always". Today, it takes courage to speak of joy, which, above all, requires faith! The world is beset by many problems, the future is burdened by uncertainties and fears. Yet, Christians are a joyful people, and their joy is not something superficial and ephemeral, but deep and stable, because it is a gift from the Lord that fills life. Our joy comes from the certainty that "the Lord is at hand": he is close with his tenderness, his mercy, his forgiveness and his love.

(Pope Francis)

Entrance Antiphon Ph 4:4-5	Ant. ad introitum
REJOICE in the Lord always; again I say, rejoice. Indeed, the Lord is near.	GAUDETE in Domino semper: iterum dico, gaudete. Dominus enim prope est.

The Gloria in excelsis (Glory to God in the highest) is not said.

Collect	Collecta
O God, who see how your people faithfully await the feast of the Lord's Nativity, enable us, we pray, to attain the joys of so great a salvation and to celebrate them always with solemn worship and glad rejoicing. Through our Lord Jesus Christ, your Son, who lives and reigns with you in the unity of the Holy Spirit, one God, for ever and ever.	Deus, qui conspicis populum tuum nativitatis dominicæ festivitatem fideliter exspectare, præsta, quæsumus, ut valeamus ad tantæ salutis gaudia pervenire, et ea votis sollemnibus alacri semper lætitia celebrare. Per Dominum nostrum Iesum Christum Filium tuum, qui tecum vivit et regnat in unitate Spiritus Sancti, Deus, per omnia sæcula sæculorum.

FIRST READING

A reading from the prophet Isaiah   61:1-2,10-11
I exult for joy in the Lord.

The spirit of the Lord has been given to me,
for the Lord has anointed me.
He has sent me to bring good news to the poor,
to bind up hearts that are broken;

to proclaim liberty to captives,
freedom to those in prison;
to proclaim a year of favour from the Lord.

'I exult for joy in the Lord,
my soul rejoices in my God,
for he has clothed me in the garments of salvation,
he has wrapped me in the cloak of integrity,
like a bridegroom wearing his wreath,
like a bride adorned in her jewels.

'For as the earth makes fresh things grow,
as a garden makes seeds spring up,
so will the Lord make both integrity and praise
spring up in the sight of the nations.'

The word of the Lord.

Responsorial Psalm   Lk 1:46-50,53-54. R. Is 61:10

R. **My soul rejoices in my God.**

My soul glorifies the Lord,
my spirit rejoices in God, my Saviour.
He looks on his servant in her nothingness;
henceforth all ages will call me blessed. R.

The Almighty works marvels for me.
Holy his name!
His mercy is from age to age,
on those who fear him. R.

He fills the starving with good things,
sends the rich away empty.
He protects Israel, his servant,
remembering his mercy. R.

SECOND READING

A reading from the first letter of St Paul to the Thessalonians   5:16-24

May you all be kept safe, spirit, soul and body, for the coming of the Lord.

Be happy at all times; pray constantly; and for all things give thanks to God, because this is what God expects you to do in Christ Jesus.

Never try to suppress the Spirit or treat the gift of prophecy with contempt; think before you do anything – hold on to what is good and avoid every form of evil.

May the God of peace make you perfect and holy; and may you all be kept safe and blameless, spirit, soul and body, for the coming of our Lord Jesus Christ. God has called you and he will not fail you.

The word of the Lord.

Gospel Acclamation   Is 61:1 (Lk 4:18)

R. **Alleluia, alleluia!**
The Spirit of the Lord has been given to me.
He has sent me to bring good news to the poor.
R. **Alleluia!**

GOSPEL

A reading from the holy Gospel according to John   1:6-8,19-28

There stands among you – unknown to you – the one who is coming after me.

A man came, sent by God.
His name was John.
He came as a witness,
as a witness to speak for the light,
so that everyone might believe through him.
He was not the light,
only a witness to speak for the light.

This is how John appeared as a witness. When the Jews sent priests and Levites from Jerusalem to ask him, 'Who are you?' he not only declared, but he declared quite openly, 'I am not the Christ.' 'Well then,' they asked 'are you Elijah?' 'I am not' he said. 'Are you the Prophet?' He answered, 'No.' So they said to him, 'Who are you? We must take back an answer to those who sent us. What have you to say about yourself?' So John said, 'I am, as Isaiah prophesied:

a voice that cries in the wilderness:
Make a straight way for the Lord.'

Now these men had been sent by the Pharisees, and they put this further question to him, 'Why are you baptising if you are not the Christ, and not Elijah, and not the prophet?' John replied, 'I baptise with water, but there stands among you – unknown to you – the one who is coming after me; and I am not fit to undo his sandal-strap.' This happened at Bethany, on the far side of the Jordan, where John was baptising.

The Gospel of the Lord.

The Creed is said.

Prayer over the Offerings	Super oblata
May the sacrifice of our worship, Lord, we pray, be offered to you unceasingly, to complete what was begun in sacred mystery and powerfully accomplish for us your saving work. Through Christ our Lord.	Devotionis nostræ tibi, Domine, quæsumus, hostia iugiter immoletur, quæ et sacri peragat instituta mysterii et salutare tuum nobis potenter operetur. Per Christum Dominum nostrum.

Preface II of Advent, pp.44-45.

Communion Antiphon Cf. Is 35:4	Ant. ad communionem
Say to the faint of heart: Be strong and do not fear. Behold, our God will come, and he will save us.	Dicite: Pusillanimes, confortamini et nolite timere: ecce Deus noster veniet et salvabit nos.

Prayer after Communion	Post communionem
We implore your mercy, Lord, that this divine sustenance may cleanse us of our faults and prepare us for the coming feasts. Through Christ our Lord.	Tuam, Domine, clementiam imploramus, ut hæc divina subsidia, a vitiis expiatos, ad festa ventura nos præparent. Per Christum Dominum nostrum.

A formula of Solemn Blessing, pp.132-133, may be used.

24 December

FOURTH SUNDAY OF ADVENT

The Gospel for this Sunday of Advent highlights the figure of Mary...The Gospel says: "she entered the house of Zechariah and greeted Elizabeth". After this greeting, Elizabeth feels enveloped in great astonishment...To celebrate Christmas in a fruitful manner, we are called to pause in "places" of astonishment. The first place is the other, in whom we recognise a brother or sister, because since the birth of Jesus occurred, every face is marked with a semblance to the Son of God.

(Pope Francis)

Entrance Antiphon   Cf. Is 45:8

DROP down dew from above,
   you heavens,
and let the clouds rain down
   the Just One;
let the earth be opened
   and bring forth a Saviour.

Ant. ad introitum

RORATE, cæli, desuper,
   et nubes pluant iustum;
aperiatur terra
   et germinet Salvatorem.

The Gloria in excelsis (Glory to God in the highest) is not said.

Collect

Pour forth, we beseech you, O Lord,
your grace into our hearts,
that we, to whom the Incarnation
   of Christ your Son
was made known by the message
   of an Angel,
may by his Passion and Cross
be brought to the glory
   of his Resurrection.
Who lives and reigns with you
   in the unity of the Holy Spirit,
one God, for ever and ever.

Collecta

Gratiam tuam,
   quæsumus, Domine,
mentibus nostris infunde,
   ut qui, Angelo nuntiante,
Christi Filii tui
   incarnationem cognovimus,
per passionem eius et crucem
ad resurrectionis gloriam perducamur.
Per Dominum nostrum Iesum
   Christum Filium tuum,
qui tecum vivit et regnat
   in unitate Spiritus Sancti,
Deus, per omnia sæcula sæculorum.

FIRST READING

A reading from the second book of Samuel   7:1-5,8-12,14,16

The kingdom of David will always stand secure before the Lord.

Once David had settled into his house and the Lord had given him rest from all the enemies surrounding him, the king said to the prophet Nathan, 'Look, I am living in a house of cedar while the ark of God dwells in a tent.' Nathan said to the king, 'Go and do all that is in your mind, for the Lord is with you.'

But that very night the word of the Lord came to Nathan:

'Go and tell my servant David, "Thus the Lord speaks: Are you the man to build me a house to dwell in? I took you from the pasture, from following the sheep, to be leader of my people Israel; I have been with you on all your expeditions; I have cut off all your enemies before you. I will give you fame as great as the fame of the greatest on earth. I will provide a place for my people Israel; I will plant them there and they shall dwell in that place and never be disturbed again; nor shall the wicked continue to oppress them as they did, in the days when I appointed judges over my people Israel; I will give them rest from all their enemies. The Lord will make you great; the Lord will make you a House. And when your days are ended and you are laid to rest with your ancestors, I will preserve the offspring of your body after you and make his sovereignty secure. I will be a father to him and he a son to me. Your House and your sovereignty will always stand secure before me and your throne be established for ever."'

The word of the Lord.

Responsorial Psalm   Ps 88:2-5,27,29. R. Cf. v.2

R. **I will sing for ever of your love, O Lord.**

I will sing for ever of your love, O Lord;
through all ages my mouth will proclaim your truth.
Of this I am sure, that your love lasts for ever,
that your truth is firmly established as the heavens. R.

'I have made a covenant with my chosen one;
I have sworn to David my servant:
I will establish your dynasty for ever
and set up your throne through all ages.' R.

He will say to me: 'You are my father,
my God, the rock who saves me.'
I will keep my love for him always;
for him my covenant shall endure. R.

SECOND READING

A reading from the letter of St Paul to the Romans   16:25-27

The mystery, which was kept secret for endless ages, is now made clear.

Glory to him who is able to give you the strength to live according to the
Good News I preach, and in which I proclaim Jesus Christ, the revelation
of a mystery kept secret for endless ages, but now so clear that it must be
broadcast to pagans everywhere to bring them to the obedience of faith.
This is only what scripture has predicted, and it is all part of the way the
eternal God wants things to be. He alone is wisdom; give glory therefore to
him through Jesus Christ for ever and ever. Amen.

The word of the Lord.

Gospel Acclamation   Lk 1:38
R. **Alleluia, alleluia!**
I am the handmaid of the Lord:
let what you have said be done to me.
R. **Alleluia!**

GOSPEL

A reading from the holy Gospel according to Luke   1:26-38

Listen! You are to conceive and bear a son.

The angel Gabriel was sent by God to a town in Galilee called Nazareth,
to a virgin betrothed to a man named Joseph, of the house of David; and
the virgin's name was Mary. He went in and said to her, 'Rejoice, so highly
favoured! The Lord is with you.' She was deeply disturbed by these words
and asked herself what this greeting could mean, but the angel said to her,
'Mary, do not be afraid; you have won God's favour. Listen! You are to
conceive and bear a son, and you must name him Jesus. He will be great
and will be called Son of the Most High. The Lord God will give him the
throne of his ancestor David; he will rule over the House of Jacob for ever
and his reign will have no end.' Mary said to the angel, 'But how can this
come about, since I am a virgin?' 'The Holy Spirit will come upon you', the
angel answered, 'and the power of the Most High will cover you with its
shadow. And so the child will be holy and will be called Son of God. Know
this too: your kinswoman Elizabeth has, in her old age, conceived a son,
and she whom people called barren is now in her sixth month, for nothing
is impossible to God.' 'I am the handmaid of the Lord,' said Mary, 'let what
you have said be done to me.' And the angel left her.

The Gospel of the Lord.

The Creed is said.

Prayer over the Offerings

May the Holy Spirit, O Lord,
sanctify these gifts laid upon
    your altar,
just as he filled with his power the
    womb of the Blessed Virgin Mary.
Through Christ our Lord.

Preface II of Advent, pp.44-45.

Super oblata

Altari tuo, Domine,
    superposita munera
Spiritus ille sanctificet,
qui beatæ Mariæ viscera
    sua virtute replevit.
Per Christum Dominum nostrum.

Communion Antiphon   Is 7:14

Behold, a Virgin shall conceive
    and bear a son;
and his name will be called
    Emmanuel.

Ant. ad communionem

Ecce Virgo concipiet,
    et pariet filium;
et vocabitur nomen eius
    Emmanuel.

Prayer after Communion

Having received this pledge
    of eternal redemption,
we pray, almighty God,
that, as the feast day of our
    salvation draws ever nearer,
so we may press forward
    all the more eagerly
to the worthy celebration of the
    mystery of your Son's Nativity.
Who lives and reigns
    for ever and ever.

Post communionem

Sumpto pignore
    redemptionis æternæ,
quæsumus, omnipotens Deus,
ut quanto magis dies salutiferæ
    festivitatis accedit,
tanto devotius proficiamus
ad Filii tui digne nativitatis
    mysterium celebrandum.
Qui vivit et regnat
    in sæcula sæculorum.

A formula of Solemn Blessing, pp.132-133, may be used.

25 December

THE NATIVITY OF THE LORD

Solemnity

At the Vigil Mass

Yet Christmas has above all a taste of hope because, for all the darkness in our lives, God's light shines forth. His gentle light does not frighten us. God, who is in love with us, draws us to himself with his tenderness, by being born poor and frail in our midst, as one of us. He is born in Bethlehem, which means "house of bread". In this way, he seems to tell us that he is born as bread for us; he enters our life to give us his life; he comes into our world to give us his love. He does not come to devour or to lord it over us, but instead to feed and serve us.

(Pope Francis)

24 December

This Mass is used on the evening of 24 December, either before or after First Vespers (Evening Prayer I) of the Nativity.

Entrance Antiphon Cf. Ex 16:6-7	Ant. ad introitum
TODAY you will know that the Lord will come, and he will save us, and in the morning you will see his glory.	HODIE scietis, quia veniet Dominus, et salvabit nos, et mane videbitis gloriam eius.

The Gloria in excelsis (Glory to God in the highest) is said.

Collect	Collecta

O God, who gladden us year by year as we wait in hope for our redemption, grant that, just as we joyfully welcome your Only Begotten Son
   as our Redeemer,
we may also merit to face
   him confidently
when he comes again as our Judge.
Who lives and reigns with you
   in the unity of the Holy Spirit,
one God, for ever and ever.
	Deus, qui nos redemptionis nostræ annua exspectatione lætificas, præsta, ut Unigenitum tuum, quem læti suscipimus Redemptorem, venientem quoque Iudicem securi
	   videre mereamur,
	Dominum nostrum,
	   Iesum Christum.
	Qui tecum vivit et regnat
	   in unitate Spiritus Sancti,
	Deus, per omnia sæcula sæculorum.

FIRST READING

A reading from the prophet Isaiah   62:1-5

The Lord takes delight in you.

About Zion I will not be silent,
about Jerusalem I will not grow weary,
until her integrity shines out like the dawn
and her salvation flames like a torch.
The nations then will see your integrity,
all the kings your glory,
and you will be called by a new name,
one which the mouth of the Lord will confer.
You are to be a crown of splendour in the hand of the Lord,
a princely diadem in the hand of your God;
no longer are you to be named 'Forsaken'
nor your land 'Abandoned',
but you shall be called 'My Delight'
and your land 'The Wedded';
for the Lord takes delight in you
and your land will have its wedding.
Like a young man marrying a virgin,
so will the one who built you wed you,
and as the bridegroom rejoices in his bride,
so will your God rejoice in you.

   The word of the Lord.

Responsorial Psalm   Ps 88:4-5,16-17,27,29. R. Cf. v.2

R. **I will sing for ever of your love, O Lord.**

'I have made a covenant with my chosen one;
I have sworn to David my servant:
I will establish your dynasty for ever
and set up your throne through all ages.' R.

Happy the people who acclaim such a king,
who walk, O Lord, in the light of your face,
who find their joy every day in your name,
who make your justice the source of their bliss. R.

'He will say to me: "You are my father,
my God, the rock who saves me."
I will keep my love for him always;
for him my covenant shall endure.' R.

SECOND READING

A reading from the Acts of the Apostles   13:16-17,22-25
Paul's witness to Christ, the son of David.

When Paul reached Antioch in Pisidia, he stood up in the synagogue, held
up a hand for silence and began to speak:

'Men of Israel, and fearers of God, listen! The God of our nation Israel
chose our ancestors, and made our people great when they were living as
foreigners in Egypt; then by divine power he led them out.

'Then he made David their king, of whom he approved in these words,
"I have selected David son of Jesse, a man after my own heart, who will
carry out my whole purpose." To keep his promise, God has raised up for
Israel one of David's descendants, Jesus, as Saviour, whose coming was
heralded by John when he proclaimed a baptism of repentance for the
whole people of Israel. Before John ended his career he said, "I am not the
one you imagine me to be; that one is coming after me and I am not fit to
undo his sandal."'

The word of the Lord.

Gospel Acclamation

R. **Alleluia, alleluia!**
Tomorrow there will be an end to the sin of the world
and the saviour of the world will be our king.
R. **Alleluia!**

GOSPEL

A reading from the holy Gospel according to Matthew   1:1-25

The ancestry of Jesus Christ, the son of David.

A genealogy of Jesus Christ, the son of David, son of Abraham:

Abraham was the father of Isaac,
Isaac the father of Jacob,
Jacob the father of Judah and his brothers,
Judah the father of Perez and Zerah, Tamar being their mother,
Perez the father of Hezron,
Hezron the father of Ram,
Ram the father of Amminadab,
Amminadab the father of Nahshon,
Nahshon the father of Salmon,
Salmon was the father of Boaz, Rahab being his mother,
Boaz the father of Obed, Ruth being his mother,
Obed was the father of Jesse;
and Jesse was the father of King David.

David was the father of Solomon, whose mother had been Uriah's wife,
Solomon was the father of Rehoboam,
Rehoboam the father of Abijah,
Abijah the father of Asa,
Asa was the father of Jehoshaphat,
Jehoshaphat the father of Joram,
Joram the father of Azariah,
Azariah was the father of Jotham,
Jotham the father of Ahaz,
Ahaz the father of Hezekiah,
Hezekiah was the father of Manasseh,
Manasseh the father of Amon,
Amon the father of Josiah;
and Josiah was the father of Jechoniah and his brothers.
Then the deportation to Babylon took place.

After the deportation to Babylon:
Jechoniah was the father of Shealtiel,
Shealtiel the father of Zerubbabel,
Zerubbabel was the father of Abiud,
Abiud the father of Eliakim,
Eliakim the father of Azor,
Azor was the father of Zadok,
Zadok the father of Achim,
Achim the father of Eliud,

Eliud was the father of Eleazar,
Eleazar the father of Matthan,
Matthan the father of Jacob,
and Jacob was the father of Joseph the husband of Mary; of her was born
Jesus who is called Christ.

The sum of generations is therefore: fourteen from Abraham to David;
fourteen from David to the Babylonian deportation; and fourteen from
the Babylonian deportation to Christ.

[This is how Jesus Christ came to be born. His mother Mary was
betrothed to Joseph; but before they came to live together she was found
to be with child through the Holy Spirit. Her husband Joseph, being a
man of honour and wanting to spare her publicity, decided to divorce her
informally. He had made up his mind to do this when the angel of the Lord
appeared to him in a dream and said, 'Joseph son of David, do not be afraid
to take Mary home as your wife, because she has conceived what is in her by
the Holy Spirit. She will give birth to a son and you must name him Jesus,
because he is the one who is to save his people from their sins.' Now all this
took place to fulfil the words spoken by the Lord through the prophet:

The Virgin will conceive and give birth to a son
and they will call him Emmanuel,

a name which means 'God-is-with-us'. When Joseph woke up he did what
the angel of the Lord had told him to do: he took his wife to his home and,
though he had not had intercourse with her, she gave birth to a son; and
he named him Jesus.

The Gospel of the Lord.]

Shorter Form, verses 18-25. Read between [ ]
The Creed is said.
All kneel at the words **and by the Holy Spirit was incarnate**.

Prayer over the Offerings	Super oblata
As we look forward, O Lord, to the coming festivities, may we serve you all the more eagerly for knowing that in them you make manifest the beginnings of our redemption. Through Christ our Lord.	Tanto nos, Domine, quæsumus, promptiore servitio hæc præcurrere concede sollemnia, quanto in his constare principium nostræ redemptionis ostendis. Per Christum Dominum nostrum.

Preface I, II or III of the Nativity of the Lord, pp.44-47.

Communion Antiphon Cf. Is 40:5	Ant. ad communionem

The glory of the Lord
    will be revealed,
and all flesh will see the salvation
    of our God.
	Revelabitur gloria Domini,
	et videbit omnis caro salutare
	    Dei nostri.

Prayer after Communion	Post communionem

Grant, O Lord, we pray,
that we may draw new vigour
from celebrating the Nativity
    of your Only Begotten Son,
by whose heavenly mystery
    we receive both food and drink.
Who lives and reigns
    for ever and ever.
	Da nobis, quæsumus, Domine,
	Unigeniti Filii tui recensita
	    nativitate vegetari,
	cuius cælesti mysterio pascimur
	    et potamur.
	Qui vivit et regnat
	    in sæcula sæculorum.

A formula of Solemn Blessing, pp.132-135, may be used.

At the Mass during the Night

25 December

If we want to celebrate Christmas authentically, we need to contemplate this sign: the frail simplicity of a tiny newborn child...That is where God is. With this sign, the Gospel reveals a paradox. It speaks of the emperor, the governor, the high and mighty of those times, yet God does not make himself present there. He appears not in the splendour of a royal palace, but in the poverty of a stable; not in pomp and show, but in simplicity of life; not in power, but in astonishing smallness. In order to meet him, we need to go where he is. We need to bow down, to humble ourselves, to make ourselves small.

(Pope Francis)

On the Nativity of the Lord all Priests may celebrate or concelebrate three Masses, provided the Masses are celebrated at their proper times.

Entrance Antiphon Ps 2:7	Ant. ad introitum

THE Lord said to me:
   You are my Son.
It is I who have begotten you this day.

DOMINUS dixit ad me:
   Filius meus es tu,
ego hodie genui te.

Or:

Vel:

Let us all rejoice in the Lord,
   for our Saviour has been born
   in the world.
Today true peace has come down
   to us from heaven.

Gaudeamus omnes in Domino,
quia Salvator noster natus
   est in mundo.
Hodie nobis de cælo pax
   vera descendit.

The Gloria in excelsis (Glory to God in the highest) is said.

Collect

O God, who have made
   this most sacred night
radiant with the splendour
   of the true light,
grant, we pray, that we,
   who have known the mysteries
   of his light on earth,
may also delight in his gladness
   in heaven.
Who lives and reigns with you
   in the unity of the Holy Spirit,
one God, for ever and ever.

Collecta

Deus, qui hanc sacratissimam
   noctem
veri luminis fecisti
   illustratione clarescere,
da, quæsumus, ut, cuius in terra
   mysteria lucis agnovimus,
eius quoque gaudiis perfruamur
   in cælo.
Qui tecum vivit et regnat
   in unitate Spiritus Sancti,
Deus, per omnia sæcula sæculorum.

FIRST READING

A reading from the prophet Isaiah   9:1-7

A Son is given to us.

The people that walked in darkness
has seen a great light;
on those who live in a land of deep shadow
a light has shone.
You have made their gladness greater,
you have made their joy increase;
they rejoice in your presence
as men rejoice at harvest time,
as men are happy when they are dividing the spoils.
For the yoke that was weighing on him,

the bar across his shoulders,
the rod of his oppressor,
these you break as on the day of Midian.
For all the footgear of battle,
every cloak rolled in blood,
is burnt,
and consumed by fire.
For there is a child born for us,
a son given to us
and dominion is laid on his shoulders;
and this is the name they give him:
Wonder-Counsellor, Mighty-God,
Eternal-Father, Prince-of-Peace.
Wide is his dominion
in a peace that has no end,
for the throne of David
and for his royal power,
which he establishes and makes secure
in justice and integrity.
From this time onwards and for ever,
the jealous love of the Lord of hosts will do this.

   The word of the Lord.

Responsorial Psalm   Ps 95:1-3,11-13. R. Lk 2:11

R. **Today a saviour has been born to us;**
   he is Christ the Lord.

   O sing a new song to the Lord,
   sing to the Lord all the earth.
   O sing to the Lord, bless his name. R.

   Proclaim his help day by day,
   tell among the nations his glory
   and his wonders among all the peoples. R.

   Let the heavens rejoice and earth be glad,
   let the sea and all within it thunder praise,
   let the land and all it bears rejoice,
   all the trees of the wood shout for joy
   at the presence of the Lord for he comes,
   he comes to rule the earth. R.

   With justice he will rule the world,

he will judge the peoples with his truth. R.

R. **Today a saviour has been born to us;**
   he is Christ the Lord.

SECOND READING

A reading from the letter of St Paul to Titus   2:11-14
God's grace has been revealed to the whole human race.

God's grace has been revealed, and it has made salvation possible for
the whole human race and taught us that what we have to do is to give
up everything that does not lead to God, and all our worldly ambitions;
we must be self-restrained and live good and religious lives here in this
present world, while we are waiting in hope for the blessing which will
come with the Appearing of the glory of our great God and saviour Christ
Jesus. He sacrificed himself for us in order to set us free from all wickedness
and to purify a people so that it could be his very own and would have no
ambition except to do good.

   The word of the Lord.

Gospel Acclamation   Lk 2:10-11

R. **Alleluia, alleluia!**
I bring you news of great joy:
today a saviour has been born to us, Christ the Lord.
R. **Alleluia!**

GOSPEL

A reading from the holy Gospel according to Luke   2:1-14
Today a saviour has been born to you.

Caesar Augustus issued a decree for a census of the whole world to be
taken. This census – the first – took place while Quirinius was governor
of Syria, and everyone went to his own town to be registered. So Joseph
set out from the town of Nazareth in Galilee and travelled up to Judaea, to
the town of David called Bethlehem, since he was of David's House and
line, in order to be registered together with Mary, his betrothed, who was
with child. While they were there the time came for her to have her child,
and she gave birth to a son, her first-born. She wrapped him in swaddling
clothes, and laid him in a manger because there was no room for them at
the inn. In the countryside close by there were shepherds who lived in the
fields and took it in turns to watch their flocks during the night. The angel
of the Lord appeared to them and the glory of the Lord shone round them.

They were terrified, but the angel said, 'Do not be afraid. Listen, I bring you news of great joy, a joy to be shared by the whole people. Today in the town of David a saviour has been born to you; he is Christ the Lord. And here is a sign for you: you will find a baby wrapped in swaddling clothes and lying in a manger.' And suddenly with the angel there was a great throng of the heavenly host, praising God and singing:

> 'Glory to God in the highest heaven,
> and peace to men who enjoy his favour'.

The Gospel of the Lord.

The Creed is said. All kneel at the words **and by the Holy Spirit was incarnate**.

Prayer over the Offerings | Super oblata

May the oblation of this day's feast be pleasing to you, O Lord, we pray, that through this most holy exchange we may be found in the likeness of Christ, in whom our nature is united to you. Who lives and reigns for ever and ever.	Grata tibi sit, Domine, quæsumus, hodiernæ festivitatis oblatio, ut, per hæc sacrosancta commercia, in illius inveniamur forma, in quo tecum est nostra substantia. Qui vivit et regnat in sæcula sæculorum.

Preface I, II or III of the Nativity of the Lord, pp.44-47.

Communion Antiphon Jn 1:14 | Ant. ad communionem

The Word became flesh, and we have seen his glory.	Verbum caro factum est, et vidimus gloriam eius.

Prayer after Communion | Post communionem

Grant us, we pray, O Lord our God, that we, who are gladdened by participation in the feast of our Redeemer's Nativity, may through an honourable way of life become worthy of union with him. Who lives and reigns for ever and ever.	Da nobis, quæsumus, Domine Deus noster, ut, qui nativitatem Redemptoris nostri frequentare gaudemus, dignis conversationibus ad eius mereamur pervenire consortium. Per Christum Dominum nostrum.

A formula of Solemn Blessing, pp.132-135, may be used.

At the Mass at Dawn

There is a straight line between the manger and the cross where Jesus will become bread that is broken. It is the straight line of love that gives and saves, the love that brings light to our lives and peace to our hearts. That night, the shepherds understood this. They were among the marginalised of those times. Yet no one is marginalised in the sight of God, and that Christmas, they themselves were the guests. People who felt sure of themselves, self-sufficient, were at home with their possessions. It was the shepherds who "set out with haste". Tonight, may we too be challenged and called by Jesus. Let us approach him with trust, starting from all those things that make us feel marginalised, from our limitations and our sins. Let us be touched by the tenderness that saves. Let us draw close to God who draws close to us.

(Pope Francis)

Entrance Antiphon Cf. Is 9:1,5; Lk 1:33

TODAY a light will shine upon us,
for the Lord is born for us;
and he will be called Wondrous God,
Prince of peace, Father of future ages:
and his reign will be without end.

Ant. ad introitum

LUX fulgebit hodie super nos,
quia natus est nobis Dominus;
et vocabitur admirabilis, Deus,
    Princeps pacis,
Pater futuri sæculi:
    cuius regni non erit finis.

The Gloria in excelsis (Glory to God in the highest) is said.

Collect

Grant, we pray, almighty God,
that, as we are bathed in the new
    radiance of your incarnate Word,
the light of faith, which illumines
    our minds,
may also shine through in our deeds.
Through our Lord Jesus Christ,
    your Son,
who lives and reigns with you
    in the unity of the Holy Spirit,
one God, for ever and ever.

Collecta

Da, quæsumus, omnipotens Deus,
ut dum nova incarnati Verbi
    tui luce perfundimur,
hoc in nostro resplendeat opere,
quod per fidem fulget in mente.
Per Dominum nostrum Iesum
    Christum Filium tuum,
qui tecum vivit et regnat
    in unitate Spiritus Sancti,
Deus, per omnia sæcula sæculorum.

FIRST READING

A reading from the prophet Isaiah   62:11-12

Look, your saviour comes.

This the Lord proclaims
to the ends of the earth:

> Say to the daughter of Zion, 'Look,
> your saviour comes,
> the prize of his victory with him,
> his trophies before him.'
> They shall be called 'The Holy People',
> 'The Lord's Redeemed'.
> And you shall be called 'The-sought-after',
> 'City-not-forsaken'.

The word of the Lord.

Responsorial Psalm   Ps 96:1,6,11-12

R. **This day new light will shine upon the earth:
the Lord is born for us.**

> The Lord is king, let earth rejoice,
> the many coastlands be glad.
> The skies proclaim his justice;
> all peoples see his glory. R.

> Light shines forth for the just
> and joy for the upright of heart.
> Rejoice, you just, in the Lord;
> give glory to his holy name. R.

SECOND READING

A reading from the letter of St Paul to Titus   3:4-7

It was for no reason except his own compassion that he saved us.

When the kindness and love of God our saviour for mankind were revealed,
it was not because he was concerned with any righteous actions we might
have done ourselves; it was for no reason except his own compassion that
he saved us, by means of the cleansing water of rebirth and by renewing
us with the Holy Spirit which he has so generously poured over us through
Jesus Christ our saviour. He did this so that we should be justified by his
grace, to become heirs looking forward to inheriting eternal life.

The word of the Lord.

Gospel Acclamation   Lk 2:14

R. **Alleluia, alleluia!**
Glory to God in the highest heaven,
and peace to men who enjoy his favour.

R. **Alleluia!**

GOSPEL

A reading from the holy Gospel according to Luke   2:15-20
The shepherds found Mary and Joseph and the baby.

Now when the angels had gone from them into heaven, the shepherds
said to one another, 'Let us go to Bethlehem and see this thing that has
happened which the Lord has made known to us.' So they hurried away
and found Mary and Joseph, and the baby lying in the manger. When
they saw the child they repeated what they had been told about him, and
everyone who heard it was astonished at what the shepherds had to say. As
for Mary, she treasured all these things and pondered them in her heart.
And the shepherds went back glorifying and praising God for all they had
heard and seen; it was exactly as they had been told.

The Gospel of the Lord.

The Creed is said. All kneel at the words **and by the Holy Spirit was incarnate**.

Prayer over the Offerings	Super oblata
May our offerings be worthy, we pray, O Lord, of the mysteries of the Nativity this day, that, just as Christ was born a man and also shone forth as God, so these earthly gifts may confer on us what is divine. Through Christ our Lord.	Munera nostra, quæsumus, Domine, nativitatis hodiernæ mysteriis apta proveniant, ut sicut homo genitus idem præfulsit et Deus, sic nobis hæc terrena substantia conferat quod divinum est. Per Christum Dominum nostrum.

Preface I, II or III of the Nativity of the Lord, pp.44-47.

Communion Antiphon Cf. Zc 9:9	Ant. ad communionem
Rejoice, O Daughter Sion; lift up praise, Daughter Jerusalem: Behold, your King will come, the Holy One and Saviour of the world.	Exsulta, filia Sion, lauda, filia Ierusalem: ecce Rex tuus veniet sanctus et salvator mundi.

Prayer after Communion	Post communionem

Grant us, Lord, as we honour
    with joyful devotion
the Nativity of your Son,
that we may come to know
    with fullness of faith
the hidden depths of this mystery
and to love them
    ever more and more.
Through Christ our Lord.
	Da nobis, Domine,
	    Filii tui nativitatem
	læta devotione colentibus,
	huius arcana mysterii
	    et plena fide cognoscere,
	et pleniore caritatis ardore diligere.
	Per Christum Dominum nostrum.

A formula of Solemn Blessing, pp.132-135 may be used.

At the Mass during the Day

Inevitably the question arises, what would happen if Mary and Joseph were to knock at my door. Would there be room for them? And then it occurs to us that St John takes up this seemingly chance comment about the lack of room at the inn, which drove the Holy Family into the stable; he explores it more deeply and arrives at the heart of the matter when he writes: "he came to his own home, and his own people received him not". The great moral question of our attitude towards the homeless, towards refugees and migrants, takes on a deeper dimension: do we really have room for God when he seeks to enter under our roof? Do we have time and space for him? Do we not actually turn away God himself? We begin to do so when we have no time for God. The faster we can move, the more efficient our time-saving appliances become, the less time we have. And God? The question of God never seems urgent. Our time is already completely full. But matters go deeper still. Does God actually have a place in our thinking? Our process of thinking is structured in such a way that he simply ought not to exist. Even if he seems to knock at the door of our thinking, he has to be explained away. If thinking is to be taken seriously, it must be structured in such a way that the "God hypothesis" becomes superfluous. There is no room for him. Not even in our feelings and desires is there any room for him. We want ourselves. We want what we can seize hold of, we want happiness that is within our reach, we want our plans and purposes to succeed. We are so "full" of ourselves that there is no room left for God. And that means there is no room for others either, for children, for the poor, for the stranger.

(Pope Benedict XVI)

Entrance Antiphon Cf. Is 9:5	Ant. ad introitum

A CHILD is born for us,
  and a son is given to us;
his sceptre of power rests
    upon his shoulder,
and his name will be called
    Messenger of great counsel.

PUER natus est nobis,
  et filius datus est nobis,
cuius imperium super
    humerum eius,
et vocabitur nomen eius magni
    consilii Angelus.

The Gloria in excelsis (Glory to God in the highest) is said.

Collect	Collecta

O God, who wonderfully created
    the dignity of human nature
and still more wonderfully
    restored it,
grant, we pray,
that we may share in the divinity
    of Christ,
who humbled himself to share
    in our humanity.
Who lives and reigns with you
    in the unity of the Holy Spirit,
one God, for ever and ever.

Deus, qui humanæ
    substantiæ dignitatem
et mirabiliter condidisti,
    et mirabilius reformasti,
da, quæsumus, nobis eius
    divinitatis esse consortes,
qui humanitatis nostræ fieri
    dignatus est particeps.
Qui tecum vivit et regnat
    in unitate Spiritus Sancti,
Deus, per omnia sæcula sæculorum.

FIRST READING

A reading from the prophet Isaiah   52:7-10
All the ends of the earth shall see the salvation of our God.

How beautiful on the mountains,
are the feet of one who brings good news,
who heralds peace, brings happiness,
proclaims salvation,
and tells Zion,
'Your God is king!'
Listen! Your watchmen raise their voices,
they shout for joy together,
for they see the Lord face to face,
as he returns to Zion.
Break into shouts of joy together,
you ruins of Jerusalem;

for the Lord is consoling his people,
redeeming Jerusalem.
The Lord bares his holy arm
in the sight of all the nations,
and all the ends of the earth shall see
the salvation of our God.

The word of the Lord.

Responsorial Psalm   Ps 97:1-6. R. v.3

R. **All the ends of the earth have seen
the salvation of our God.**

Sing a new song to the Lord
for he has worked wonders.
His right hand and his holy arm
have brought salvation. R.

The Lord has made known his salvation;
has shown his justice to the nations.
He has remembered his truth and love
for the house of Israel. R.

All the ends of the earth have seen
the salvation of our God.
Shout to the Lord all the earth,
ring out your joy. R.

Sing psalms to the Lord with the harp,
with the sound of music.
With trumpets and the sound of the horn
acclaim the King, the Lord. R.

SECOND READING

A reading from the letter to the Hebrews   1:1-6
God has spoken to us through his Son.

At various times in the past and in various different ways, God spoke to
our ancestors through the prophets; but in our own time, the last days, he
has spoken to us through his Son, the Son that he has appointed to inherit
everything and through whom he made everything there is. He is the
radiant light of God's glory and the perfect copy of his nature, sustaining

the universe by his powerful command; and now that he has destroyed the
defilement of sin, he has gone to take his place in heaven at the right hand
of divine Majesty. So he is now as far above the angels as the title which he
has inherited is higher than their own name.

God has never said to any angel: You are my Son, today I have become
your father; or: I will be a father to him and he a son to me. Again, when
he brings the First-born into the world, he says: Let all the angels of God
worship him.

The word of the Lord.

Gospel Acclamation.

R. **Alleluia, alleluia!**
A hallowed day has dawned upon us.
Come, you nations, worship the Lord,
for today a great light has shone down upon the earth.

R. **Alleluia!**

GOSPEL

A reading from the holy Gospel according to John   1:1-18
The Word was made flesh, and lived among us.

[In the beginning was the Word:
the Word was with God
and the Word was God.
He was with God in the beginning.
Through him all things came to be,
not one thing had its being but through him.
All that came to be had life in him
and that life was the light of men,
a light that shines in the dark,
a light that darkness could not overpower.]

A man came, sent by God.
His name was John.
He came as a witness,
as a witness to speak for the light,
so that everyone might believe through him.
He was not the light,
only a witness to speak for the light.

[The Word was the true light
that enlightens all men;
and he was coming into the world.
He was in the world
that had its being through him,
and the world did not know him.
He came to his own domain
and his own people did not accept him.
But to all who did accept him
he gave power to become children of God,
to all who believe in the name of him
who was born not out of human stock
or urge of the flesh
or will of man
but of God himself.
The Word was made flesh,
he lived among us,
and we saw his glory,
the glory that is his as the only Son of the Father,
full of grace and truth.]

John appears as his witness. He proclaims:
'This is the one of whom I said:
He who comes after me
ranks before me
because he existed before me.'
Indeed, from his fullness we have, all of us, received –
yes, grace in return for grace,
since, though the Law was given through Moses,
grace and truth have come through Jesus Christ.
No one has ever seen God,
it is the only Son, who is nearest to the Father's heart,
who has made him known.

[The Gospel of the Lord.]

Shorter Form, verses 1-5,9-14. Read between [ ]

The Creed is said. All kneel at the words **and by the Holy Spirit was incarnate**.

Prayer over the Offerings	Super oblata

Make acceptable, O Lord,
  our oblation on this solemn day,
when you manifested
  the reconciliation
that makes us wholly pleasing
  in your sight
and inaugurated for us the fullness
  of divine worship.
Through Christ our Lord.

Oblatio tibi sit, Domine,
  hodiernæ sollemnitatis accepta,
qua et nostræ reconciliationis
  processit perfecta placatio,

et divini cultus nobis
  est indita plenitudo.
Per Christum Dominum nostrum.

Preface I, II or III of the Nativity of the Lord, pp.44-47.

Communion Antiphon Cf. Ps 97:3	Ant. ad communionem

All the ends of the earth have seen
  the salvation of our God.

Viderunt omnes fines terræ
  salutare Dei nostri.

Prayer after Communion	Post communionem

Grant, O merciful God,
that, just as the Saviour of the
  world, born this day,
is the author of divine generation
  for us,
so he may be the giver even
  of immortality.
Who lives and reigns
  for ever and ever.

Præsta, misericors Deus,
  ut natus hodie Salvator mundi,
sicut divinæ nobis generationis
  est auctor,
ita et immortalitatis sit ipse largitor.
Qui vivit et regnat
  in sæcula sæculorum.

A formula of Solemn Blessing, pp.132-135, may be used.

31 December

THE HOLY FAMILY OF JESUS, MARY AND JOSEPH

We can imagine this tiny family, in the midst of so many people, in the Temple's grand courtyards. They do not stand out, they are not distinguishable.... Yet they do not pass unnoticed! Two elderly people, Simeon and Anna, moved by the Holy Spirit, approach and praise God for that Child, in whom they recognise the Messiah, the light of the people and the salvation of Israel. It is a simple moment but rich with prophecy: the encounter between two young spouses full of joy and faith due to the grace of the Lord; and two elderly people also filled with joy and faith through the action of the Spirit. Who causes them to meet? Jesus. Jesus makes them meet: young and old. Jesus is he who brings generations closer. He is the font of that love which unites families and people, conquering all diffidence, all isolation, all distance.

(Pope Francis)

Feast

Entrance Antiphon   Lk 2:16

THE shepherds went in haste,
and found Mary and Joseph
and the Infant lying in a manger.

Ant. ad introitum

VENERUNT pastores festinantes,
et invenerunt Mariam
et Ioseph et Infantem positum
in præsepio.

The Gloria in excelsis (Glory to God in the highest) is said.

Collect

O God, who were pleased to give us
the shining example
   of the Holy Family,
graciously grant that we may
   imitate them
in practising the virtues of family life
   and in the bonds of charity,
and so, in the joy of your house,
delight one day in eternal rewards.

Collecta

Deus, qui præclara nobis
   sanctæ Familiæ
dignatus es exempla præbere,
concede propitius,
ut, domesticis virtutibus caritatisque
   vinculis illam sectantes,
in lætitia domus tuæ præmiis
   fruamur æternis.

Through our Lord Jesus Christ, your Son, who lives and reigns with you in the unity of the Holy Spirit, one God, for ever and ever.	Per Dominum nostrum Iesum Christum Filium tuum, qui tecum vivit et regnat in unitate Spiritus Sancti, Deus, per omnia sæcula sæculorum.

The readings for Year B are included in full below. The readings for Year A may also be used on this feast: Si 3:2-6,12-14; Ps 127:1-5; Col 3:12-21; Col 3:15,16.

FIRST READING

A reading from the book of Genesis   15:1-6,21:1-3

Your heir shall be your own flesh and blood.

The word of the Lord was spoken to Abram in a vision, 'Have no fear, Abram, I am your shield; your reward will be very great.'

'My Lord,' Abram replied 'what do you intend to give me? I go childless...' Then Abram said, 'See, you have given me no descendants; some man of my household will be my heir.' And then this word of the Lord was spoken to him, 'He shall not be your heir; your heir shall be of your own flesh and blood.' Then taking him outside he said, 'Look up to heaven and count the stars if you can. Such will be your descendants' he told him. Abram put his faith in the Lord, who counted this as making him justified.

The Lord dealt kindly with Sarah as he had said, and did what he had promised her. So Sarah conceived and bore a son to Abraham in his old age, at the time God had promised. Abraham named the son born to him Isaac, the son to whom Sarah had given birth.

The word of the Lord.

Responsorial Psalm   Ps 104:1-6,8-9. R. vv.7-8

R. **He, the Lord, is our God.**
  He remembers his covenant for ever.

  Give thanks to the Lord, tell his name,
  make known his deeds among the peoples.
  O sing to him, sing his praise;
  tell all his wonderful works! R.

  Be proud of his holy name,
  let the hearts that seek the Lord rejoice.
  Consider the Lord and his strength;
  constantly seek his face. R.

Remember the wonders he has done,
his miracles, the judgements he spoke.
O children of Abraham, his servant,
O sons of the Jacob he chose. R.

He remembers his covenant for ever,
his promise for a thousand generations,
the covenant he made with Abraham,
the oath he swore to Isaac. R.

SECOND READING

A reading from the letter to the Hebrews   11:8,11-12,17-19
The faith of Abraham, Sarah and Isaac.

It was by faith that Abraham obeyed the call to set out for a country that
was the inheritance given to him and his descendants, and that he set out
without knowing where he was going.

It was equally by faith that Sarah, in spite of being past the age, was made
able to conceive, because she believed that he who had made the promise
would be faithful to it. Because of this, there came from one man, and one
who was already as good as dead himself, more descendants than could be
counted, as many as the stars of heaven or the grains of sand on the seashore.

It was by faith that Abraham, when put to the test, offered up Isaac.
He offered to sacrifice his only son even though the promises had been
made to him and he had been told: It is through Isaac that your name will
be carried on. He was confident that God had the power even to raise the
dead; and so, figuratively speaking, he was given back Isaac from the dead.

The word of the Lord.

Gospel Acclamation   Heb 1:1-2
R. **Alleluia, alleluia!**
At various times in the past
and in various different ways,
God spoke to our ancestors through the prophets;
but in our own time, the last days,
he has spoken to us through his Son.
R. **Alleluia!**

GOSPEL

A reading from the holy Gospel according to Luke   2:22-40
The child grew, filled with wisdom.

[When the day came for them to be purified as laid down by the Law of

Moses, the parents of Jesus took him up to Jerusalem to present him to the Lord] – observing what stands written in the law of the Lord: Every first-born male must be consecrated to the Lord – and also to offer in sacrifice, in accordance with what is said in the Law of the Lord, a pair of turtledoves or two young pigeons. Now in Jerusalem there was a man named Simeon. He was an upright and devout man; he looked forward to Israel's comforting and the Holy Spirit rested on him. It had been revealed to him by the Holy Spirit that he would not see death until he had set eyes on the Christ of the Lord. Prompted by the Spirit he came to the Temple, and when the parents brought in the child Jesus to do for him what the Law required, he took him into his arms and blessed God; and he said:

'Now, Master, you can let your servant go in peace,
just as you promised;
because my eyes have seen the salvation
which you have prepared for all the nations to see,
a light to enlighten the pagans
and the glory of your people Israel.'

As the child's father and mother stood there wondering at the things that were being said about him, Simeon blessed them and said to Mary his mother, 'You see this child: he is destined for the fall and for the rising of many in Israel, destined to be a sign that is rejected – and a sword will pierce your own soul too – so that the secret thoughts of many may be laid bare.'

There was a prophetess also, Anna the daughter of Phanuel, of the tribe of Asher. She was well on in years. Her days of girlhood over, she had been married for seven years before becoming a widow. She was now eighty-four years old and never left the Temple, serving God night and day with fasting and prayer. She came by just at that moment and began to praise God; and she spoke of the child to all who looked forward to the deliverance of Jerusalem.

[When they had done everything the Law of the Lord required, they went back to Galilee, to their own town of Nazareth. Meanwhile the child grew to maturity, and he was filled with wisdom; and God's favour was with him.

The Gospel of the Lord.]

Shorter Form, verses 22,39-40. Read between [ ]
The Creed is said.

Prayer over the Offerings

We offer you, Lord,
   the sacrifice of conciliation,
humbly asking that,
through the intercession of the Virgin
   Mother of God and Saint Joseph,
you may establish our families firmly
   in your grace and your peace.
Through Christ our Lord.

Super oblata

Hostiam tibi placationis offerimus,
   Domine,
suppliciter deprecantes,
ut, Deiparæ Virginis beatique
   Ioseph interveniente suffragio,
familias nostras in tua gratia
   firmiter et pace constituas.
Per Christum Dominum nostrum.

Preface I, II or III of the Nativity of the Lord, pp.44-47.

Communion Antiphon   Ba 3:38

Our God has appeared on the earth,
   and lived among us.

Ant. ad communionem

Deus noster in terris visus est,
et cum hominibus conversatus est.

Prayer after Communion

Bring those you refresh
   with this heavenly Sacrament,
most merciful Father,
to imitate constantly the example
   of the Holy Family,
so that, after the trials of this world,
we may share their company for ever.
Through Christ our Lord.

Post communionem

Quos cælestibus reficis sacramentis,
fac, clementissime Pater,
sanctæ Familiæ exempla
   iugiter imitari,
ut, post ærumnas sæculi,
eius consortium
   consequamur æternum.
Per Christum Dominum nostrum.

1 January

SOLEMNITY OF MARY, THE HOLY MOTHER OF GOD

At the beginning of a new year, the Church invites us to contemplate Mary's divine maternity as an icon of peace. The ancient promise finds fulfilment in her person. She believed in the words of the angel, conceived her Son and thus became the Mother of the Lord. Through her, through her "yes", the fulness of time came about. The Gospel we have just heard tells us that the Virgin Mary "treasured all these words and pondered them in her heart". She appears to us as a vessel filled to the brim with the memory of Jesus, as the Seat of Wisdom to whom we can have recourse to understand his teaching aright. Today Mary makes it possible for us to grasp the meaning of events which affect us personally, events which also affect our families, our countries and the entire world.

(Pope Francis)

Solemnity

Entrance Antiphon

HAIL, Holy Mother,
who gave birth to the King
who rules heaven and earth for ever.

Ant. ad introitum

SALVE, sancta Parens,
enixa puerpera Regem,
qui cælum terramque regit
in sæcula sæculorum.

Or: Cf. Is 9:1,5; Lk 1:33

Today a light will shine upon us,
    for the Lord is born for us;
and he will be called Wondrous God,
Prince of peace, Father of future ages:
and his reign will be without end.

Vel:

Lux fulgebit hodie super nos,
quia natus est nobis Dominus;
et vocabitur admirabilis, Deus,
    Princeps pacis,
Pater futuri sæculi:
    cuius regni non erit finis.

The Gloria in excelsis (Glory to God in the highest) is said.

Collect	Collecta
O God, who through the fruitful virginity of Blessed Mary bestowed on the human race the grace of eternal salvation, grant, we pray, that we may experience the intercession of her, through whom we were found worthy to receive the author of life, our Lord Jesus Christ, your Son. Who lives and reigns with you in the unity of the Holy Spirit, one God, for ever and ever.	Deus, qui salutis æternæ, beatæ Mariæ virginitate fecunda, humano generi præmia præstitisti, tribue, quæsumus, ut ipsam pro nobis intercedere sentiamus, per quam meruimus auctorem vitæ suscipere, Dominum nostrum Iesum Christum, Filium tuum. Qui tecum vivit et regnat in unitate Spiritus Sancti, Deus, per omnia sæcula sæculorum.

FIRST READING

A reading from the book of Numbers   6:22-27

They are to call down my name on the sons of Israel, and I will bless them.

The Lord spoke to Moses and said, 'Say this to Aaron and his sons: "This is how you are to bless the sons of Israel. You shall say to them:

May the Lord bless you and keep you.
May the Lord let his face shine on you and be gracious to you.
May the Lord uncover his face to you and bring you peace."

This is how they are to call down my name on the sons of Israel, and I will bless them.'

The word of the Lord.

Responsorial Psalm   Ps 66:2-3,5,6,8. R. v.2

R. **O God, be gracious and bless us.**

God, be gracious and bless us
and let your face shed its light upon us.
So will your ways be known upon earth
and all nations learn your saving help. R.

Let the nations be glad and exult
for you rule the world with justice.
With fairness you rule the peoples,
you guide the nations on earth. R.

Let the peoples praise you, O God;
let all the peoples praise you.
May God still give us his blessing
till the ends of the earth revere him. R.

R. **O God, be gracious and bless us.**

SECOND READING

A reading from the letter of St Paul to the Galatians   4:4-7
God sent his Son, born of a woman.

When the appointed time came, God sent his Son, born of a woman, born
a subject of the Law, to redeem the subjects of the Law and to enable us to
be adopted as sons. The proof that you are sons is that God has sent the
Spirit of his Son into our hearts: the Spirit that cries, 'Abba, Father', and it
is this that makes you a son, you are not a slave any more; and if God has
made you son, then he has made you heir.

    The word of the Lord.

Gospel Acclamation   Heb 1:1-2

R. **Alleluia, alleluia!**

At various times in the past
and in various different ways,
God spoke to our ancestors through the prophets;
but in our own time, the last days,
he has spoken to us through his Son.

R. **Alleluia!**

GOSPEL

A reading from the holy Gospel according to Luke   2:16-21
*They found Mary and Joseph and the baby ... When the eighth day came, they gave
him the name Jesus.*

The shepherds hurried away to Bethlehem and found Mary and Joseph,
and the baby lying in the manger. When they saw the child they repeated
what they had been told about him, and everyone who heard it was
astonished at what the shepherds had to say. As for Mary, she treasured
all these things and pondered them in her heart. And the shepherds went
back glorifying and praising God for all they had heard and seen; it was
exactly as they had been told.

When the eighth day came and the child was to be circumcised, they gave him the name Jesus, the name the angel had given him before his conception.

The Gospel of the Lord.

The Creed is said.

Prayer over the Offerings	Super oblata
O God, who in your kindness begin all good things and bring them to fulfilment, grant to us, who find joy in the Solemnity of the holy Mother of God, that, just as we glory in the beginnings of your grace, so one day we may rejoice in its completion. Through Christ our Lord.	Deus, qui bona cuncta inchoas benignus et perficis, da nobis, de sollemnitate sanctæ Dei Genetricis lætantibus, sicut de initiis tuæ gratiæ gloriamur, ita de perfectione gaudere. Per Christum Dominum nostrum.

Preface: The Motherhood of the Blessed Virgin Mary.	Præfatio: De Maternitate beatæ Mariæ Virginis.
It is truly right and just, our duty and our salvation, always and everywhere to give you thanks, Lord, holy Father, almighty and eternal God, and to praise, bless, and glorify your name on the Solemnity of the Motherhood of the Blessed ever-Virgin Mary.	Vere dignum et iustum est, æquum et salutare, nos tibi semper et ubique gratias agere: Domine, sancte Pater, omnipotens æterne Deus:
For by the overshadowing of the Holy Spirit she conceived your Only Begotten Son, and without losing the glory of virginity, brought forth into the world the eternal Light, Jesus Christ our Lord.	Et te in maternitate beatæ Mariæ semper Virginis collaudare, benedicere et prædicare. Quæ et Unigenitum tuum Sancti Spiritus obumbratione concepit, et, virginitatis gloria permanente, lumen æternum mundo effudit, Iesum Christum Dominum nostrum.

Through him the Angels praise
   your majesty,
Dominions adore and Powers
   tremble before you.
Heaven and the Virtues of heaven
   and the blessed Seraphim
worship together with exultation.
May our voices, we pray,
   join with theirs
in humble praise, as we acclaim:

Holy, Holy, Holy Lord God of hosts...

Per quem maiestatem
   laudant Angeli,
adorant Dominationes,
   tremunt Potestates.
Cæli cælorumque Virtutes,
   ac beata Seraphim,
socia exsultatione concelebrant.
Cum quibis et nostras voces ut
   admitti iubeas, deprecamur,
supplici confessione dicentes:

Sanctus, Sanctus, Sanctus. . .

Communion Antiphon   Heb 13:8

Jesus Christ is the same yesterday,
   today, and for ever.

Ant. ad communionem

Iesus Christus heri et hodie,
   ipse et in sæcula.

Prayer after Communion

We have received this heavenly
   Sacrament with joy, O Lord:
grant, we pray,
that it may lead us to eternal life,
for we rejoice to proclaim
   the blessed ever-Virgin Mary
Mother of your Son
   and Mother of the Church.
Through Christ our Lord.

Post communionem

Sumpsimus, Domine,
   læti sacramenta cælestia:
præsta, quæsumus,
ut ad vitam nobis
   proficiant sempiternam,
qui beatam semper Virginem Mariam
Filii tui Genetricem
   et Ecclesiæ Matrem
profiteri gloriamur.
Per Christum Dominum nostrum.

A formula of Solemn Blessing, pp.134-135, may be used.

In Ireland
6 January

In England, Wales & Scotland
7 January

THE EPIPHANY OF THE LORD

The Magi thus personify all those who believe, those who long for God, who yearn for their home, their heavenly homeland. They reflect the image of all those who in their lives have not let their hearts be anesthetised. A holy longing for God wells up in the heart of believers because they know that the Gospel is not an event of the past but of the present. A holy longing for God helps us keep alert in the face of every attempt to reduce and impoverish our life. A holy longing for God is the memory of faith, which rebels before all prophets of doom. That longing keeps hope alive in the community of believers, which from week to week continues to plead: "Come, Lord Jesus".

(Pope Francis)

Solemnity

At the Vigil Mass

This Mass is used on the evening of the day before the Solemnity, either before or after First Vespers (Evening Prayer I) of the Epiphany.

Entrance Antiphon Cf. Ba 5:5	Ant. ad introitum
ARISE, Jerusalem, and look to the East and see your children gathered from the rising to the setting of the sun.	SURGE, Ierusalem, et circumspice ad orientem et vide congregatos filios tuos a solis ortu usque ad occasum.

The Gloria in excelsis (Glory to God in the highest) is said.

Collect	Collecta

May the splendour of your majesty,
  O Lord, we pray,
shed its light upon our hearts,
that we may pass through
   the shadows of this world
and reach the brightness
   of our eternal home.
	Corda nostra, quæsumus, Domine,
	tuæ maiestatis splendor illustret,
	quo per mundi huius tenebras
	   transire valeamus,
	et perveniamus ad patriam
	   claritatis æternæ.

| Through our Lord Jesus Christ, your Son, who lives and reigns with you in the unity of the Holy Spirit, one God, for ever and ever. | Per Dominum nostrum Iesum Christum Filium tuum, qui tecum vivit et regnat in unitate Spiritus Sancti, Deus, per omnia sæcula sæculorum. |

FIRST READING

A reading from the prophet Isaiah   60:1-6
Above you the glory of the Lord appears.

Arise, shine out Jerusalem, for your light has come,
the glory of the Lord is rising on you,
though night still covers the earth
and darkness the peoples.

Above you the Lord now rises
and above you his glory appears.
The nations come to your light
and kings to your dawning brightness.

Lift up your eyes and look around:
all are assembling and coming towards you,
your sons from far away
and daughters being tenderly carried.

At this sight you will glow radiant,
your heart throbbing and full;
since the riches of the sea will flow to you;
the wealth of the nations come to you;

camels in throngs will cover you,
and dromedaries of Midian and Ephah;
everyone in Sheba will come,
bringing gold and incense
and singing the praise of the Lord.

The word of the Lord.

Responsorial Psalm   Ps 71:1-2,7-8,10-13. R. Cf. v.11

R. **All nations shall fall prostrate before you, O Lord.**

> O God, give your judgement to the king,
> to a king's son your justice,
> that he may judge your people in justice
> and your poor in right judgement. R.

> In his days justice shall flourish
> and peace till the moon fails.
> He shall rule from sea to sea,
> from the Great River to earth's bounds. R.

> The Kings of Tarshish and the sea coasts
> shall pay him tribute.
> The kings of Sheba and Seba
> shall bring him gifts.
> Before him all kings shall fall prostrate,
> all nations shall serve him. R.

> For he shall save the poor when they cry
> and the needy who are helpless.
> He will have pity on the weak
> and save the lives of the poor. R.

SECOND READING

A reading from the letter of St Paul to the Ephesians   3:2-3,5-6
It has now been revealed that pagans share the same inheritance.

You have probably heard how I have been entrusted by God with the
grace he meant for you, and that it was by a revelation that I was given
the knowledge of the mystery. This mystery that has now been revealed
through the Spirit to his holy apostles and prophets was unknown to
any men in past generations; it means that pagans now share the same
inheritance, that they are parts of the same body, and that the same
promise has been made to them, in Christ Jesus, through the gospel.

The word of the Lord.

Gospel Acclamation   Mt 2:2

R. **Alleluia, alleluia!**
We saw his star as it rose
and have come to do the Lord homage.
R. **Alleluia!**

GOSPEL

A reading from the holy Gospel according to Matthew　　　　2:1-12

We saw his star and have come to do the king homage.

After Jesus had been born at Bethlehem in Judaea during the reign of King Herod, some wise men came to Jerusalem from the east. 'Where is the infant king of the Jews?' they asked. 'We saw his star as it rose and have come to do him homage.' When King Herod heard this he was perturbed, and so was the whole of Jerusalem. He called together all the chief priests and the scribes of the people, and enquired of them where the Christ was to be born. 'At Bethlehem in Judaea,' they told him 'for this is what the prophet wrote:

> And you, Bethlehem, in the land of Judah
> you are by no means least among the leaders of Judah,
> for out of you will come a leader
> who will shepherd my people Israel.'

Then Herod summoned the wise men to see him privately. He asked them the exact date on which the star had appeared, and sent them on to Bethlehem. 'Go and find out all about the child,' he said 'and when you have found him, let me know, so that I too may go and do him homage.' Having listened to what the king had to say, they set out. And there in front of them was the star they had seen rising; it went forward and halted over the place where the child was. The sight of the star filled them with delight, and going into the house they saw the child with his mother Mary, and falling to their knees they did him homage. Then, opening their treasures, they offered him gifts of gold and frankincense and myrrh. But they were warned in a dream not to go back to Herod, and returned to their own country by a different way.

The Gospel of the Lord.

The Creed is said.

Prayer over the Offerings	Super oblata
Accept we pray, O Lord, our offerings, in honour of the appearing of your Only Begotten Son and the first fruits of the nations, that to you praise may be rendered and eternal salvation be ours. Through Christ our Lord.	Suscipe, quæsumus, Domine, munera nostra pro apparitione Unigeniti Filii tui et primitiis gentium dicata, ut et tibi celebretur laudatio et nobis fiat æterna salvatio. Per Christum Dominum nostrum.

Preface of the Epiphany of the Lord, pp.48-49.

Communion Antiphon Cf. Rv 21:23	Ant. ad communionem

The brightness of God illumined
the holy city Jerusalem,
and the nations will walk by its light.

Claritas Dei illuminavit civitatem
sanctam Ierusalem
et ambulabant gentes in lumine eius.

Prayer after Communion	Post communionem

Renewed by sacred nourishment,
we implore your mercy, O Lord,
that the star of your justice
may shine always bright in our minds
and that our true treasure may ever
consist in our confession of you.
Through Christ our Lord.

Sacra alimonia renovati,
tuam, Domine,
misericordiam deprecamur,
ut semper in mentibus nostris
tuæ appareat stella iustitiæ
et noster in tua sit
confessione thesaurus.
Per Christum Dominum nostrum.

A formula of Solemn Blessing, pp.134-137, may be used.

At the Mass during the Day

Entrance Antiphon Cf.Ml 3:1;1Ch 29:12	Ant. ad introitum

BEHOLD, the Lord,
the Mighty One, has come;
and kingship is in his grasp,
and power and dominion.

ECCE advenit
Dominator Dominus;
et regnum in manu eius
et potestas et imperium.

The Gloria in excelsis (Glory to God in the highest) is said.

Collect	Collecta

O God, who on this day
revealed your Only Begotten Son
to the nations
by the guidance of a star,
grant in your mercy
that we, who know you already
by faith,
may be brought to behold
the beauty of your sublime glory.
Through our Lord Jesus Christ,
your Son,
who lives and reigns with you
in the unity of the Holy Spirit,
one God, for ever and ever.

Deus, qui hodierna die
Unigenitum tuum
gentibus stella duce revelasti,
concede propitius, ut qui iam
te ex fide cognovimus,
usque ad contemplandam speciem
tuæ celsitudinis perducamur.
Per Dominum nostrum Iesum
Christum Filium tuum,
qui tecum vivit et regnat
in unitate Spiritus Sancti,
Deus, per omnia sæcula sæculorum.

FIRST READING

A reading from the prophet Isaiah   60:1-6
Above you the glory of the Lord appears.

Arise, shine out Jerusalem, for your light has come,
the glory of the Lord is rising on you,
though night still covers the earth
and darkness the peoples.
Above you the Lord now rises
and above you his glory appears.
The nations come to your light
and kings to your dawning brightness.

Lift up your eyes and look around:
all are assembling and coming towards you,
your sons from far away
and daughters being tenderly carried.

At this sight you will glow radiant,
your heart throbbing and full;
since the riches of the sea will flow to you;
the wealth of the nations come to you;

camels in throngs will cover you,
and dromedaries of Midian and Ephah;
everyone in Sheba will come,
bringing gold and incense
and singing the praise of the Lord.

   The word of the Lord.

Responsorial Psalm   Ps 71:1-2,7-8,10-13. R. Cf. v.11

R. **All nations shall fall prostrate before you, O Lord.**

   O God, give your judgement to the king,
   to a king's son your justice,
   that he may judge your people in justice
   and your poor in right judgement. R.

   In his days justice shall flourish
   and peace till the moon fails.
   He shall rule from sea to sea,
   from the Great River to earth's bounds. R.

The Kings of Tarshish and the sea coasts
shall pay him tribute.
The kings of Sheba and Seba
shall bring him gifts.
Before him all kings shall fall prostrate,
all nations shall serve him. R.

For he shall save the poor when they cry
and the needy who are helpless.
He will have pity on the weak
and save the lives of the poor. R.

SECOND READING

A reading from the letter of St Paul to the Ephesians   3:2-3,5-6
It has now been revealed that pagans share the same inheritance.

You have probably heard how I have been entrusted by God with the grace he meant for you, and that it was by a revelation that I was given the knowledge of the mystery. This mystery that has now been revealed through the Spirit to his holy apostles and prophets was unknown to any men in past generations; it means that pagans now share the same inheritance, that they are parts of the same body, and that the same promise has been made to them, in Christ Jesus, through the gospel.

The word of the Lord.

Gospel Acclamation   Mt 2:2

R. **Alleluia, alleluia!**
We saw his star as it rose
and have come to do the Lord homage.
R. **Alleluia!**

GOSPEL

A reading from the holy Gospel according to Matthew   2:1-12
We saw his star and have come to do the king homage.

After Jesus had been born at Bethlehem in Judaea during the reign of King Herod, some wise men came to Jerusalem from the east. 'Where is the infant king of the Jews?' they asked. 'We saw his star as it rose and have come to do him homage.' When King Herod heard this he was perturbed, and so was the whole of Jerusalem. He called together all the chief priests and the scribes of the people, and enquired of them where the Christ was to be born. 'At Bethlehem in Judaea,' they told him 'for this is what the prophet wrote:

> And you, Bethlehem, in the land of Judah
> you are by no means least among the leaders of Judah,
> for out of you will come a leader
> who will shepherd my people Israel.'

Then Herod summoned the wise men to see him privately. He asked them the exact date on which the star had appeared, and sent them on to Bethlehem. 'Go and find out all about the child,' he said 'and when you have found him, let me know, so that I too may go and do him homage.' Having listened to what the king had to say, they set out. And there in front of them was the star they had seen rising; it went forward and halted over the place where the child was. The sight of the star filled them with delight, and going into the house they saw the child with his mother Mary, and falling to their knees they did him homage. Then, opening their treasures, they offered him gifts of gold and frankincense and myrrh. But they were warned in a dream not to go back to Herod, and returned to their own country by a different way.

The Gospel of the Lord.

The Creed is said.

Prayer over the Offerings	Super oblata
Look with favour, Lord, we pray, on these gifts of your Church, in which are offered now not gold or frankincense or myrrh, but he who by them is proclaimed, sacrificed and received, Jesus Christ. Who lives and reigns for ever and ever.	Ecclesiæ tuæ, quæsumus, Domine, dona propitius intuere, quibus non iam aurum, thus et myrrha profertur, sed quod eisdem muneribus declaratur, immolatur et sumitur, Iesus Christus. Qui vivit et regnat in sæcula sæculorum.

Preface of the Epiphany of the Lord, pp.48-49.

Communion Antiphon Cf. Mt 2:2	Ant. ad communionem
We have seen his star in the East, and have come with gifts to adore the Lord.	Vidimus stellam eius in Oriente, et venimus cum muneribus adorare Dominum.

Prayer after Communion	Post communionem
Go before us with heavenly light, O Lord,	Cælesti lumine, quæsumus, Domine,
always and everywhere,	semper et ubique nos præveni,
that we may perceive with clear sight	ut mysterium, cuius nos participes
and revere with true affection	esse voluisti,
the mystery in which you have willed us to participate.	et puro cernamus intuitu, et digno percipiamus affectu.
Through Christ our Lord.	Per Christum Dominum nostrum.

A formula of Solemn Blessing, pp.134-137, may be used.

In Ireland

7 January

In England, Wales & Scotland

8 January

THE BAPTISM OF THE LORD

In the First Reading we heard that the Lord takes care of his children like a parent: he takes care to provide his children with nourishing food... And what is this nourishing food that God gives us? It is his Word: his Word makes us grow, it enables us to bear good fruit in life, just as the rain and snow imbue the earth, making it fruitful. Likewise you, parents, and you too, godmothers and godfathers, grandparents, aunts and uncles, will help these children grow if you give them the Word of God, the Gospel of Jesus. And give it also by your example! Every day, make it a habit to read a passage of the Gospel, a small one, and always carry a little Gospel with you in your pocket, in your purse, so you can read it.

(Pope Francis)

Feast

Entrance Antiphon Cf. Mt 3:16-17	Ant. ad introitum

AFTER the Lord was baptised,
the heavens were opened,
and the Spirit descended upon him
   like a dove,
and the voice of the
   Father thundered:
This is my beloved Son,
   with whom I am well pleased.

BAPTIZATO Domino,
aperti sunt cæli,
et sicut columba super eum
   Spiritus mansit,
et vox Patris intonuit:
Hic est Filius meus dilectus,
in quo mihi bene complacui.

The Gloria in excelsis (Glory to God in the highest) is said.

Collect	Collecta

Almighty ever-living God,
who, when Christ had been
   baptised in the River Jordan
and as the Holy Spirit descended
   upon him,
solemnly declared him
   your beloved Son,
grant that your children
   by adoption,
reborn of water and the Holy Spirit,
may always be well pleasing to you.
Through our Lord Jesus Christ,
   your Son,
who lives and reigns with you in
   the unity of the Holy Spirit,
one God, for ever and ever.

Omnipotens sempiterne Deus,
qui Christum,
   in Iordane flumine baptizatum,
Spiritu Sancto super
   eum descendente,
dilectum Filium tuum sollemniter
   declarasti,
concede filiis adoptionis tuæ,
ex aqua et Spiritu Sancto renatis,
ut in beneplacito tuo
   iugiter perseverent.
Per Dominum nostrum
Iesum Christum Filium tuum,
   qui tecum vivit et regnat
   in unitate Spiritus Sancti,
Deus, per omnia sæcula sæculorum.

Or:	Vel:
O God, whose Only Begotten Son has appeared in our very flesh, grant, we pray, that we may be inwardly transformed through him whom we recognise as outwardly like ourselves. Who lives and reigns with you in the unity of the Holy Spirit, one God, for ever and ever.	Deus, cuius Unigenitus in substantia nostræ carnis apparuit, præsta, quæsumus, ut per eum, quem similem nobis foris agnovimus, intus reformari mereamur. Qui tecum vivit et regnat in unitate Spiritus Sancti, Deus, per omnia sæcula sæculorum.

The readings for Year B are included in full below. The readings for Year A may also be used on this feast: Is 42:1-4,6-7; Ps 28:1-4,9-10; Ac 10:34-38; Cf. Mk 9:8.

In England, Wales and Scotland only one of the readings may be used before the Gospel.

FIRST READING

A reading from the prophet Isaiah   55:1-11

Come to the water. Listen and your soul will live.

Oh, come to the water all you who are thirsty;
though you have no money, come!
Buy corn without money, and eat,
and, at no cost, wine and milk.
Why spend money on what is not bread,
your wages on what fails to satisfy?
Listen, listen to me, and you will have good things to eat
and rich food to enjoy.
Pay attention, come to me;
listen, and your soul will live.

With you I will make an everlasting covenant
out of the favours promised to David.
See, I have made of you a witness to the peoples,
a leader and a master of the nations.
See, you will summon a nation you never knew,
those unknown will come hurrying to you,
for the sake of the Lord your God,
of the Holy One of Israel who will glorify you.

Seek the Lord while he is still to be found,
call to him while he is still near.
Let the wicked man abandon his way,
the evil man his thoughts.
Let him turn back to the Lord who will take pity on him,
to our God who is rich in forgiving;
for my thoughts are not your thoughts,
my ways not your ways – it is the Lord who speaks.
Yes, the heavens are as high above earth
as my ways are above your ways,
my thoughts above your thoughts.

Yes, as the rain and the snow come down from the heavens and do not
return without watering the earth, making it yield and giving growth to
provide seed for the sower and bread for the eating, so the word that goes
from my mouth does not return to me empty, without carrying out my
will and succeeding in what it was sent to do.

   The word of the Lord.

Responsorial Psalm   Is 12:2-6 R. v.3

R. **With joy you will draw water
    from the wells of salvation.**

   Truly, God is my salvation,
   I trust, I shall not fear.
   For the Lord is my strength, my song,
   he became my saviour.
   With joy you will draw water
   from the wells of salvation. R.

   Give thanks to the Lord, give praise to his name!
   Make his mighty deeds known to the peoples!
   Declare the greatness of his name. R.

   Sing a psalm to the Lord
   for he has done glorious deeds,
   make them known to all the earth!
   People of Zion, sing and shout for joy
   for great in your midst is the Holy One of Israel. R.

SECOND READING

A reading from the first letter of St John   5:1-9
The Spirit and water and blood.

Whoever believes that Jesus is the Christ
has been begotten by God;
and whoever loves the Father that begot him
loves the child whom he begets.
We can be sure that we love God's children
if we love God himself and do what he has commanded us;
this is what loving God is –
keeping his commandments;
and his commandments are not difficult,
because anyone who has been begotten by God
has already overcome the world;
this is the victory over the world –
our faith.
Who can overcome the world?
Only the man who believes that Jesus is the Son of God:
Jesus Christ who came by water and blood,
not with water only,
but with water and blood;
with the Spirit as another witness –
since the Spirit is the truth –
so that there are three witnesses,
the Spirit, the water and the blood,
and all three of them agree.
We accept the testimony of human witnesses,
but God's testimony is much greater,
and this is God's testimony,
given as evidence for his Son.

   The word of the Lord.

Gospel Acclamation   cf. Jn 1:29

R. **Alleluia, alleluia!**
John saw Jesus coming towards him, and said:
This is the Lamb of God who takes away the sin of the world.
R. **Alleluia!**

GOSPEL

A reading from the holy Gospel according to Mark   1:7-11

You are my Son, the Beloved; my favour rests on you.

In the course of his preaching John the Baptist said, 'Someone is following me, someone who is more powerful than I am, and I am not fit to kneel down and undo the strap of his sandals. I have baptised you with water, but he will baptise you with the Holy Spirit.'

It was at this time that Jesus came from Nazareth in Galilee and was baptised in the Jordan by John. No sooner had he come up out of the water than he saw the heavens torn apart and the Spirit, like a dove, descending on him. And a voice came from heaven, 'You are my Son, the Beloved; my favour rests on you.'

The Gospel of the Lord.

The Creed is only said in Ireland.

Prayer over the Offerings

Accept, O Lord, the offerings
we have brought to honour
   the revealing of your
   beloved Son,
so that the oblation of your faithful
may be transformed into
   the sacrifice of him
who willed in his compassion
to wash away the sins of the world.
Who lives and reigns
   for ever and ever.

Super oblata

Suscipe munera, Domine,
in dilecti Filii tui revelatione delata,
ut fidelium tuorum oblatio
   in eius sacrificium transeat,
qui mundi voluit peccata
   miseratus abluere.
Qui vivit et regnat
   in sæcula sæculorum.

Preface: The Baptism of the lord.

Præfatio: de Baptismate domini.

It is truly right and just, our duty
     and our salvation,
always and everywhere
     to give you thanks,
Lord, holy Father,
     almighty and eternal God.

Vere dignum et iustum est,
     æquum et salutare,
nos tibi semper et ubique
     gratias agere:
 Domine, sancte Pater,
     omnipotens æterne deus:

For in the waters of the Jordan
     you revealed with signs
     and wonders a new Baptism,
so that through the voice
     that came down from heaven
we might come to believe in your
     Word dwelling among us,
and by the Spirit's descending
     in the likeness of a dove
we might know that Christ
     your Servant
has been anointed with the oil
     of gladness
and sent to bring the good news
     to the poor.

Qui miris signasti mysteriis novum
     in Iordane lavacrum,
ut, per vocem de cælo delapsam,
habitare Verbum tuum inter
     homines crederetur;

et, per Spiritum in columbæ
     specie descendentem,
Christus Servus tuus oleo
     perungi lætitiæ
ac mitti ad evangelizandum
     pauperibus nosceretur.

And so, with the Powers of heaven,
we worship you constantly on earth,
and before your majesty
without end we acclaim:
Holy, Holy, Holy Lord God of hosts...

Et ideo cum cælorum virtutibus
in terris te iugiter celebramus,
maiestati tuæ sine fine clamantes:
Sanctus, Sanctus, Sanctus. . .

Communion Antiphon Jn 1:32,34

Behold the One of whom
    John said:
I have seen and testified that
    this is the Son of God.

Prayer after Communion

Nourished with these sacred gifts,
we humbly entreat your mercy,
    O Lord,
that, faithfully listening to your
    Only Begotten Son,
we may be your children in
    name and in truth.
Through Christ our Lord.

Ant. ad communionem

Ecce de quo dicebat Ioannes:
Ego vidi et testimonium perhibui,
    quia hic est Filius Dei.

Post communionem

Sacro munere satiati,
clementiam tuam, Domine,
    suppliciter exoramus,
ut, Unigenitum tuum
    fideliter audientes,
filii tui vere nominemur et simus.
Per Christum Dominum nostrum.

14 January

SECOND SUNDAY IN ORDINARY TIME

Entrance Antiphon Ps 65:4	Ant. ad introitum

A LL the earth shall bow down
  before you, O God,
and shall sing to you,
shall sing to your name,
    O Most High!

O MNIS terra adoret te, Deus,
   et psallat tibi;
psalmum dicat nomini tuo,
    Altissime.

Collect	Collecta

Almighty ever-living God,
who govern all things,
both in heaven and on earth,
mercifully hear the pleading
    of your people
and bestow your peace on our times.
Through our Lord Jesus Christ,
    your Son,
who lives and reigns with you
    in the unity of the Holy Spirit,
one God, for ever and ever.

Omnipotens sempiterne Deus,
qui cælestia simul
    et terrena moderaris,
supplicationes populi tui
    clementer exaudi,
et pacem tuam nostris
    concede temporibus.
Per Dominum nostrum Iesum
    Christum Filium tuum,
qui tecum vivit et regnat
    in unitate Spiritus Sancti,
Deus, per omnia sæcula sæculorum.

FIRST READING

A reading from the first book of Samuel   3:3-10,19

Speak, Lord, your servant is listening.

Samuel was lying in the sanctuary of the Lord where the ark of God was,
when the Lord called, 'Samuel! Samuel!' He answered, 'Here I am.' Then
he ran to Eli and said, 'Here I am, since you called me.' Eli said, 'I did not
call. Go back and lie down.' So he went and lay down. Once again the Lord
called, 'Samuel! Samuel!' Samuel got up and went to Eli and said, 'Here I
am, since you called me.' He replied, 'I did not call you, my son; go back and
lie down.' Samuel had as yet no knowledge of the Lord and the word of the
Lord had not yet been revealed to him. Once again the Lord called, the third
time. He got up and went to Eli and said, 'Here I am, since you called me.'
Eli then understood that it was the Lord who was calling the boy, and he said
to Samuel, 'Go and lie down, and if someone calls say, "Speak, Lord, your
servant is listening."' So Samuel went and lay down in his place.

The Lord then came and stood by, calling as he had done before, 'Samuel! Samuel!' Samuel answered, 'Speak, Lord, your servant is listening.'

Samuel grew up and the Lord was with him and let no word of his fall to the ground.

The word of the Lord.

Responsorial Psalm   Ps 39:2,4,7-10 R. vv.8,9

R. **Here I am, Lord!**
I come to do your will.

I waited, I waited for the Lord
and he stooped down to me.
He heard my cry
He put a new song into my mouth,
praise of our God. R.

You do not ask for sacrifice and offerings,
but an open ear.
You do not ask for holocaust and victim.
Instead, here am I. R.

In the scroll of the book it stands written
that I should do your will.
My God, I delight in your law
in the depth of my heart. R.

Your justice I have proclaimed
in the great assembly.
My lips I have not sealed;
you know it, O Lord. R.

SECOND READING

A reading from the first letter of St Paul to the Corinthians   6:13-15,17-20
Your bodies are members making up the body of Christ.

The body is not meant for fornication; it is for the Lord, and the Lord for the body. God who raised the Lord from the dead, will by his power raise us up too.

You know, surely, that your bodies are members making up the body of Christ; anyone who is joined to the Lord is one spirit with him.

Keep away from fornication. All the other sins are committed outside the body; but to fornicate is to sin against your own body. Your body, you know, is the temple of the Holy Spirit, who is in you since you received him from God. You are not your own property; you have been bought and paid for. That is why you should use your body for the glory of God.

The word of the Lord.

Gospel Acclamation   1 S 3:9; Jn 6:68

R. **Alleluia, alleluia!**
Speak, Lord, your servant is listening:
you have the message of eternal life.
R. **Alleluia!**

Or: Jn 1:14,17

R. **Alleluia, alleluia!**
We have found the Messiah - which means the Christ -
grace and truth have come through him.
R. **Alleluia!**

GOSPEL

A reading from holy Gospel according to John   Jn 1:35-42
They saw where he lived, and stayed with him.

As John stood with two of his disciples, Jesus passed, and John stared hard at
him and said, 'Look, there is the lamb of God.' Hearing this, the two disciples
followed Jesus. Jesus turned round, saw them following and said, 'What do
you want?' They answered, 'Rabbi,' – which means Teacher – 'where do you
live?' 'Come and see' he replied; so they went and saw where he lived and
stayed with him the rest of that day. It was about the tenth hour.

One of these two who became followers of Jesus after hearing what John
had said was Andrew, the brother of Simon Peter. Early next morning, Andrew
met his brother and said to him 'We have found the Messiah' – which means
the Christ – and he took Simon to Jesus. Jesus looked hard at him and said,
'You are Simon son of John; you are to be called Cephas' – meaning Rock.

The Gospel of the Lord.

Prayer over the Offerings	Super oblata
Grant us, O Lord, we pray, that we may participate worthily in these mysteries, for whenever the memorial of this sacrifice is celebrated the work of our redemption is accomplished. Through Christ our Lord.	Concede nobis, quæsumus, Domine, hæc digne frequentare mysteria, quia, quoties huius hostiæ commemoratio celebratur, opus nostræ redemptionis exercetur. Per Christum Dominum nostrum.

Preface of Sundays in Ordinary Time I-VIII, pp.61-67.

Communion Antiphon Cf. Ps 22:5 | Ant. ad communionem

You have prepared a table before me, and how precious is the chalice
that quenches my thirst.

Parasti in conspectu meo mensam, et calix meus inebrians quam
præclarus est!

Or: 1 Jn 4:16

Vel:

We have come to know
and to believe
in the love that God has for us.

Nos cognovimus
et credidimus caritati,
quam Deus habet in nobis.

Prayer after Communion | Post communionem

Pour on us, O Lord,
the Spirit of your love,
and in your kindness
make those you have nourished
by this one heavenly Bread
one in mind and heart.
Through Christ our Lord.

Spiritum nobis, Domine,
tuæ caritatis infunde,
ut, quos uno cælesti pane satiasti,
una facias pietate concordes.
Per Christum Dominum nostrum.

21 January

THIRD SUNDAY IN ORDINARY TIME

Entrance Antiphon   Cf. Ps 95:1,6 | Ant. ad introitum

O SING a new song to the Lord;
sing to the Lord, all the earth.
In his presence are majesty
and splendour,
strength and honour
in his holy place.

CANTATE Domino
canticum novum,
cantate Domino, omnis terra.
Confessio et pulchritudo
in conspectu eius,
sanctitas et magnificentia
in sanctificatione eius.

Collect | Collecta

Almighty ever-living God,
direct our actions according
to your good pleasure,
that in the name of your beloved Son
we may abound in good works.
Through our Lord Jesus Christ,
your Son,
who lives and reigns with you
in the unity of the Holy Spirit,
one God, for ever and ever.

Omnipotens sempiterne Deus,
dirige actus nostros
in beneplacito tuo,
ut in nomine dilecti Filii tui
mereamur bonis operibus abundare.
Per Dominum nostrum Iesum
Christum Filium tuum,
qui tecum vivit et regnat
in unitate Spiritus Sancti,
Deus, per omnia sæcula sæculorum.

FIRST READING

A reading from the prophet Jonah   3:1-5,10

The people of Nineveh renounce their evil behaviour.

The word of the Lord was addressed to Jonah: 'Up!' he said 'Go to Nineveh, the great city, and preach to them as I told you to.' Jonah set out and went to Nineveh in obedience to the word of the Lord. Now Nineveh was a city great beyond compare: it took three days to cross it. Jonah went on into the city, making a day's journey. He preached in these words, 'Only forty days more and Nineveh is going to be destroyed.' And the people of Nineveh believed in God; they proclaimed a fast and put on sackcloth, from the greatest to the least.

God saw their efforts to renounce their evil behaviour. And God relented: he did not inflict on them the disaster which he had threatened.

The word of the Lord.

Responsorial Psalm   Ps 24:4-9. R. v.4

R. **Lord, make me know your ways.**

Lord, make me know your ways.
Lord, teach me your paths.
Make me walk in your truth, and teach me:
for you are God my saviour. R.

Remember your mercy, Lord,
and the love you have shown from of old.
In your love remember me,
because of your goodness, O Lord. R.

The Lord is good and upright.
He shows the path to those who stray,
he guides the humble in the right path;
he teaches his way to the poor. R.

SECOND READING

A reading from the first letter of St Paul to the Corinthians   7:29-31

The world as we know it is passing away.

Brothers: our time is growing short. Those who have wives should live as though they had none, and those who mourn should live as though they had nothing to mourn for; those who are enjoying life should live as though there were nothing to laugh about; those whose life is buying things should live as though they had nothing of their own; and those who have to deal with the world should not become engrossed in it. I say this because the world as we know it is passing away.

The word of the Lord.

Gospel Acclamation   Mk 1:15
R. **Alleluia, alleluia!**
The kingdom of God is close at hand;
believe the Good News.
R. **Alleluia!**

GOSPEL

A reading from the holy Gospel according to Mark   1:14-20
Repent, and believe the Good News.

After John had been arrested, Jesus went into Galilee. There he proclaimed the Good News from God. 'The time has come' he said 'and the kingdom of God is close at hand. Repent, and believe the Good News.'

As he was walking along by the Sea of Galilee he saw Simon and his brother Andrew casting a net in the lake – for they were fishermen. And Jesus said to them, 'Follow me and I will make you into fishers of men.' And at once they left their nets and followed him.

Going on a little further, he saw James son of Zebedee and his brother John; they too were in their boat, mending their nets. He called them at once and, leaving their father Zebedee in the boat with the men he employed, they went after him.

The Gospel of the Lord.

Prayer over the Offerings | Super oblata

Accept our offerings, O Lord, | Munera nostra, Domine,
  we pray, | suscipe placatus,
and in sanctifying them | quæ sanctificando
grant that they may profit us | nobis, quæsumus,
  for salvation. | salutaria fore concede.
Through Christ our Lord. | Per Christum Dominum nostrum.

Preface of Sundays in Ordinary Time I-VIII, pp.61-67.

Communion Antiphon Cf. Ps 33:6 | Ant. ad communionem

Look toward the Lord | Accedite ad Dominum
  and be radiant; | et illuminamini,
let your faces not be abashed. | et facies vestræ non confundentur.

Or: Jn 8:12

I am the light of the world,
   says the Lord;
whoever follows me will not walk
   in darkness,
but will have the light of life.

Vel:

Ego sum lux mundi, dicit Dominus:
qui sequitur me non ambulat
   in tenebris,
sed habebit lumen vitæ.

Prayer after Communion

Grant, we pray, almighty God,
that, receiving the grace
by which you bring us to new life,
we may always glory in your gift.
Through Christ our Lord.

Post communionem

Præsta nobis, quæsumus,
   omnipotens Deus,
ut, vivificationis tuæ
   gratiam consequentes,
in tuo semper munere gloriemur.
Per Christum Dominum nostrum.

28 January

FOURTH SUNDAY IN ORDINARY TIME

Entrance Antiphon   Ps 105:47

SAVE us, O Lord our God!
  And gather us from the nations,
to give thanks to your holy name,
and make it our glory to praise you.

Ant. ad introitum

SALVOS nos fac,
  Domine Deus noster,
et congrega nos de nationibus,
ut confiteamur nomini sancto tuo,
et gloriemur in laude tua.

Collect

Grant us, Lord our God,
that we may honour you
   with all our mind,
and love everyone in truth of heart.
Through our Lord Jesus Christ,
   your Son,
who lives and reigns with you
   in the unity of the Holy Spirit,
one God, for ever and ever.

Collecta

Concede nobis,
   Domine Deus noster,
ut te tota mente veneremur,
et omnes homines rationabili
   diligamus affectu.
Per Dominum nostrum Iesum
   Christum Filium tuum,
qui tecum vivit et regnat
   in unitate Spiritus Sancti,
Deus, per omnia sæcula sæculorum.

FIRST READING

A reading from the book of Deuteronomy   18:15-20

I will raise up a prophet and I will put my words into his mouth.

Moses said to the people: 'Your God will raise up for you a prophet like myself, from among yourselves, from your own brothers; to him you must listen. This is what you yourselves asked of the Lord your God at Horeb on the day of the Assembly. "Do not let me hear again" you said, "the voice of the Lord my God, nor look any longer on this great fire, or I shall die"; and the Lord said to me, "All they have spoken is well said. I will raise up a prophet like yourself for them from their own brothers; I will put my words into his mouth and he shall tell them all I command him. The man who does not listen to my words that he speaks in my name, shall be held answerable to me for it. But the prophet who presumes to say in my name a thing I have not commanded him to say, or who speaks in the name of other gods, that prophet shall die."'

The word of the Lord.

Responsorial Psalm   Ps 94:1-2,6-9. R. v.9

R. **O that today you would listen to his voice!**
Harden not your hearts.

Come, ring out our joy to the Lord,
hail the rock who saves us.
Let us come before him, giving thanks,
with songs let us hail the Lord. R.

Come in; let us kneel and bend low;
let us kneel before the God who made us
for he is our God and we
the people who belong to his pasture,
the flock that is led by his hand. R.

O that today you would listen to his voice!
'Harden not your hearts as at Meribah,
as on that day at Massah in the desert
when your fathers put me to the test;
when they tried me, though they saw my work.' R.

SECOND READING

A reading from the first letter of St Paul to the Corinthians   7:32-35

An unmarried woman can devote herself to the Lord's affairs; all she need worry about is being holy.

I would like to see you free from all worry. An unmarried man can devote himself to the Lord's affairs, all he need worry about is pleasing the Lord; but a married man has to bother about the world's affairs and devote himself to pleasing his wife: he is torn two ways. In the same way an unmarried woman, like a young girl, can devote herself to the Lord's affairs; all she need worry about is being holy in body and spirit. The married woman, on the other hand, has to worry about the world's affairs and devote herself to pleasing her husband. I say this only to help you, not to put a halter round your necks, but simply to make sure that everything is as it should be, and that you give you undivided attention to the Lord.

The word of the Lord.

Gospel Acclamation   Mt 11:25

R. **Alleluia, alleluia!**
Blessed are you, Father,
Lord of heaven and earth,
for revealing the mysteries of the kingdom
to mere children.
R. **Alleluia!**
Or: Mt 4:16
R. **Alleluia, alleluia!**
The people that lived in darkness
has seen a great light;
on those who dwell in the land and shadow of death
a light has dawned.
R. **Alleluia!**

GOSPEL

A reading from the holy Gospel according to Mark   1:21-28
He taught them with authority.

Jesus and his followers went as far as Capernaum, and as soon as the Sabbath came Jesus went to the synagogue and began to teach. And his teaching made a deep impression on them because, unlike the scribes, he taught them with authority.

In their synagogue just then there was a man possessed by an unclean spirit, and it shouted, 'What do you want with us, Jesus of Nazareth? Have you come to destroy us? I know who you are: the Holy One of God.' But Jesus said sharply, 'Be quiet! Come out of him!' And the unclean spirit threw the man into convulsions and with a loud cry went out of him. The people were so astonished that they started asking each other what it all meant. 'Here is a teaching that is new' they said 'and with authority behind it: he gives orders even to unclean spirits and they obey him.' And his reputation rapidly spread everywhere, through all the surrounding Galilean countryside.

The Gospel of the Lord.

Prayer over the Offerings	Super oblata
O Lord, we bring to your altar these offerings of our service: be pleased to receive them, we pray, and transform them into the Sacrament of our redemption. Through Christ our Lord.	Altaribus tuis, Domine, munera nostræ servitutis inferimus, quæ, placatus assumens, sacramentum nostræ redemptionis efficias. Per Christum Dominum nostrum.

Preface of Sundays in Ordinary Time I-VIII, pp.61-67.

Communion Antiphon Cf. Ps 30:17-18	Ant. ad communionem
Let your face shine on your servant. Save me in your merciful love. O Lord, let me never be put to shame, for I call on you.	Illumina faciem tuam super servum tuum, et salvum me fac in tua misericordia. Domine, non confundar, quoniam invocavi te.

Or: Mt 5:3-4	Vel:
Blessed are the poor in spirit, for theirs is the Kingdom of Heaven. Blessed are the meek, for they shall possess the land.	Beati pauperes spiritu, quoniam ipsorum est regnum cælorum. Beati mites, quoniam ipsi possidebunt terram.

Prayer after Communion	Post communionem
Nourished by these redeeming gifts, we pray, O Lord, that through this help to eternal salvation true faith may ever increase. Through Christ our Lord.	Redemptionis nostræ munere vegetati, quæsumus, Domine, ut hoc perpetuæ salutis auxilio fides semper vera proficiat. Per Christum Dominum nostrum.

4 February

FIFTH SUNDAY IN ORDINARY TIME

Entrance Antiphon   Ps 94:6-7

O COME, let us worship God
and bow low before the God
who made us,
for he is the Lord our God.

Ant. ad introitum

V ENITE, adoremus Deum,
et procidamus ante Dominum,
qui fecit nos;
quia ipse est Dominus Deus noster.

Collect

Keep your family safe, O Lord,
with unfailing care,
that, relying solely on the hope
of heavenly grace,
they may be defended always
by your protection.
Through our Lord Jesus Christ,
your Son,
who lives and reigns with you
in the unity of the Holy Spirit,
one God, for ever and ever.

Collecta

Familiam tuam,
quæsumus, Domine,
continua pietate custodi,
ut, quæ in sola spe gratiæ
cælestis innititur,
tua semper protectione muniatur.
Per Dominum nostrum Iesum
Christum Filium tuum,
qui tecum vivit et regnat
in unitate Spiritus Sancti,
Deus, per omnia sæcula sæculorum.

FIRST READING

A reading from the book of Job   7:1-4,6-7

Restlessly I fret till twilight falls.

Job began to speak:

Is not man's life on earth nothing more than pressed service,
his time no better than hired drudgery?
Like the slave, sighing for the shade,
or the workman with no thought but his wages,
months of delusion I have assigned to me,
nothing for my own but nights of grief.
Lying in bed I wonder, 'When will it be day?'
Risen I think, 'How slowly evening comes!'
Restlessly I fret till twilight falls.
Swifter than a weaver's shuttle my days have passed,
and vanished, leaving no hope behind.
Remember that my life is but a breath,
and that my eyes will never again see joy.

The word of the Lord.

Responsorial Psalm   Ps 146:1-6. R. v.3

R. **Praise the Lord who heals the broken-hearted.**
   Or: **Alleluia!**
   Praise the Lord for he is good;
   sing to our God for he is loving:
   to him our praise is due. R.

   The Lord builds up Jerusalem
   and brings back Israel's exiles,
   He heals the broken-hearted,
   he binds up all their wounds.
   He fixes the number of the stars;
   he calls each one by its name. R.

   Our Lord is great and almighty;
   his wisdom can never be measured.
   The Lord raises the lowly;
   he humbles the wicked to the dust. R.

SECOND READING

A reading from the first letter of St Paul to the Corinthians   9:16-19,22-23
I should be punished if I did not preach the Gospel.

I do not boast of preaching the gospel, since it is a duty which has been
laid on me; I should be punished if I did not preach it! If I had chosen
this work myself, I might have been paid for it, but as I have not, it is a
responsibility which has been put into my hands. Do you know what my
reward is? It is this: in my preaching, to be able to offer the Good News
free, and not insist on the rights which the gospel gives me.

So though I am not a slave of any man I have made myself the slave of
everyone so as to win as many as I could. For the weak I made myself weak.
I made myself all things to all men in order to save some at any cost; and I
still do this, for the sake of the gospel, to have a share in its blessing.

The word of the Lord.

Gospel Acclamation   Jn 8:12

R. **Alleluia, alleluia!**
I am the light of the world, says the Lord,
anyone who follows me
will have the light of life.
R. **Alleluia!**

Or: Mt 8:17
R. **Alleluia, alleluia!**
He took our sicknesses away,
and carried our diseases for us.
R. **Alleluia!**

GOSPEL

A reading from the holy Gospel according to Mark   1:29-39
He cured many who were suffering from diseases of one kind or another.

On leaving the synagogue, Jesus went with James and John straight to the
house of Simon and Andrew. Now Simon's mother-in-law had gone to bed
with fever, and they told him about her straightaway. He went to her, took
her by the hand and helped her up. And the fever left her and she began
to wait on them.

That evening, after sunset, they brought to him all who were sick and
those who were possessed by devils. The whole town came crowding round
the door, and he cured many who were suffering from diseases of one kind
or another; he also cast out many devils, but he would not allow them to
speak, because they knew who he was.

In the morning, long before dawn, he got up and left the house, and
went off to a lonely place and prayed there. Simon and his companions set
out in search of him; and when they found him they said, 'Everybody is
looking for you.' He answered, 'Let us go elsewhere, to the neighbouring
country towns, so that I can preach there too, because that is why I came.'
And he went all through Galilee, preaching in their synagogues and casting
out devils.

The Gospel of the Lord.

Prayer over the Offerings	Super oblata
O Lord our God,	Domine Deus noster,
who once established these	qui has potius creaturas
created things	ad fragilitatis nostræ
to sustain us in our frailty,	subsidium condidisti,
grant, we pray,	tribue, quæsumus,
that they may become for us now	ut etiam æternitatis nobis
the Sacrament of eternal life.	fiant sacramentum.
Through Christ our Lord.	Per Christum Dominum nostrum.

Preface of Sundays in Ordinary Time I-VIII, pp.61-67.

Communion Antiphon Cf. Ps 106:8-9 | Ant. ad communionem

Let them thank the Lord
  for his mercy,
his wonders for the children of men
for he satisfies the thirsty soul,
and the hungry he fills
  with good things.

Confiteantur Domino
  misericordiæ eius,
et mirabilia eius filiis hominum,
quia satiavit animam inanem,
et animam esurientem
  satiavit bonis.

Or: Mt 5:5-6 | Vel:

Blessed are those who mourn,
  for they shall be consoled.
Blessed are those who hunger
  and thirst for righteousness,
for they shall have their fill.

Beati qui lugent,
  quoniam ipsi consolabuntur.
Beati qui esuriunt
  et sitiunt iustitiam,
quoniam ipsi saturabuntur.

Prayer after Communion | Post communionem

O God, who have willed
  that we be partakers
in the one Bread and the one Chalice,
grant us, we pray, so to live that,
  made one in Christ,
we may joyfully bear fruit
for the salvation of the world.
Through Christ our Lord.

Deus, qui nos de uno pane
  et de uno calice
participes esse voluisti,
da nobis, quæsumus, ita vivere, ut,
  unum in Christo effecti,
fructum afferamus pro mundi
  salute gaudentes.
Per Christum Dominum nostrum.

11 February

SIXTH SUNDAY IN ORDINARY TIME

Entrance Antiphon   Cf. Ps 30:3-4 | Ant. ad introitum

BE my protector, O God,
  a mighty stronghold to save me.
For you are my rock, my stronghold!
Lead me, guide me,
  for the sake of your name.

ESTO mihi
  in Deum protectorem,
et in locum refugii,
  ut salvum me facias.
Quoniam firmamentum meum
  et refugium meum es tu,
et propter nomen tuum dux
  mihi eris, et enutries me.

Collect	Collecta
O God, who teach us that you abide in hearts that are just and true, grant that we may be so fashioned by your grace as to become a dwelling pleasing to you. Through our Lord Jesus Christ, your Son, who lives and reigns with you in the unity of the Holy Spirit, one God, for ever and ever.	Deus, qui te in rectis et sinceris manere pectoribus asseris, da nobis tua gratia tales exsistere, in quibus habitare digneris. Per Dominum nostrum Iesum Christum Filium tuum, qui tecum vivit et regnat in unitate Spiritus Sancti, Deus, per omnia sæcula sæculorum.

FIRST READING

A reading from the book of Leviticus   13:1-2,44-46
The leper must live apart: he must live outside the camp.

The Lord said to Moses and Aaron, 'If a swelling or scab or shiny spot appears on a man's skin, a case of leprosy of the skin is to be suspected. The man must be taken to Aaron, the priest, or to one of the priests who are his sons.

'The man is leprous: he is unclean. The priest must declare him unclean; he is suffering from leprosy of the head. A man infected with leprosy must wear his clothing torn and his hair disordered; he must shield his upper lip and cry, "Unclean, unclean." As long as the disease lasts he must be unclean; and therefore he must live apart; he must live outside the camp.'

The word of the Lord.

Responsorial Psalm   Ps 31:1-2,5,11. R. v.7

R. **You are my refuge, O Lord;**
   you fill me with the joy of salvation.

   Happy the man whose offence is forgiven,
   whose sin is remitted.
   O happy the man to whom the Lord
   imputes no guilt,
   in whose spirit is no guile. R.

   But now I have acknowledged my sins;
   my guilt I did not hide.
   I said: 'I will confess
   my offence to the Lord.'

And you, Lord, have forgiven
the guilt of my sin. R.

Rejoice, rejoice in the Lord,
exult, you just!
O come, ring out your joy,
all you upright of heart. R.

R. **You are my refuge, O Lord;
you fill me with the joy of salvation.**

SECOND READING

A reading from the first letter of St Paul to the Corinthians   10:31-11:1
Take me for your model, as I take Christ.

Whatever you eat, whatever you drink, whatever you do at all, do it for the glory of God. Never do anything offensive to anyone – to Jews or Greeks or to the Church of God; just as I try to be helpful to everyone at all times, not anxious for my own advantage but for the advantage of everybody else, so that they may be saved.

Take me for your model, as I take Christ.

The word of the Lord.

Gospel Acclamation   Cf. Ep 1:17,18
R. **Alleluia, alleluia!**
May the Father of our Lord Jesus Christ
enlighten the eyes of our mind,
so that we can see what hope his call holds for us.
R. **Alleluia!**
Or: Lk 7:16
R. **Alleluia, alleluia!**
A great prophet has appeared among us;
God has visited his people.
R. **Alleluia!**

GOSPEL

A reading from the holy Gospel according to Mark   1:40-45
The leprosy left him at once and he was cured.

A leper came to Jesus and pleaded on his knees: 'If you want to' he said 'you can cure me.' Feeling sorry for him, Jesus stretched out his hand and touched him. 'Of course I want to!' he said. 'Be cured!' And the leprosy

left him at once and he was cured. Jesus immediately sent him away and
sternly ordered him, 'Mind you say nothing to anyone, but go and show
yourself to the priest, and make the offering for your healing prescribed by
Moses as evidence of your recovery.' The man went away, but then started
talking about it freely and telling the story everywhere, so that Jesus could
no longer go openly into any town, but had to stay outside in places where
nobody lived. Even so, people from all around would come to him.

The Gospel of the Lord.

Prayer over the Offerings	Super oblata
May this oblation, O Lord, we pray, cleanse and renew us and may it become for those who do your will the source of eternal reward. Through Christ our Lord.	Hæc nos oblatio, quæsumus, Domine, mundet et renovet, atque tuam exsequentibus voluntatem fiat causa remunerationis æternæ. Per Christum Dominum nostrum.

Preface of Sundays in Ordinary Time I-VIII, pp.61-67.

Communion Antiphon Cf. Ps 77:29-30	Ant. ad communionem
They ate and had their fill, and what they craved the Lord gave them; they were not disappointed in what they craved.	Manducaverunt, et saturati sunt nimis, et desiderium eorum attulit eis Dominus; non sunt fraudati a desiderio suo.

Or: Jn 3:16	Vel:
God so loved the world that he gave his Only Begotten Son, so that all who believe in him may not perish, but may have eternal life.	Sic Deus dilexit mundum, ut Filium suum Unigenitum daret, ut omnis qui credit in eum non pereat, sed habeat vitam æternam.

Prayer after Communion	Post communionem
Having fed upon these heavenly delights, we pray, O Lord, that we may always long for that food by which we truly live. Through Christ our Lord.	Cælestibus, Domine, pasti deliciis, quæsumus, ut semper eadem, per quæ veraciter vivimus, appetamus. Per Christum Dominum nostrum.

14 February

ASH WEDNESDAY

*Lent is a time for remembering. It is the time to reflect and ask ourselves what
we would be if God had closed his doors to us. What would we be without
his mercy that never tires of forgiving us and always gives us the chance to
begin anew? Lent is the time to ask ourselves where we would be without the
help of so many people who in a thousand quiet ways have stretched out their
hands and in very concrete ways given us hope and enabled us to make a new
beginning? Lent is the time to start breathing again. It is the time to open our
hearts to the breath of the One capable of turning our dust into humanity. It
is not the time to rend our garments before the evil all around us, but instead
to make room in our life for all the good we are able to do.*

(Pope Francis)

In the course of today's Mass, ashes are blessed and distributed. These are made from
the olive branches or branches of other trees that were blessed the previous year.

Entrance Antiphon Ws 11:24,25,27

YOU are merciful to all, O Lord,
and despise nothing that you
have made.
You overlook people's sins,
to bring them to repentance,
and you spare them,
for you are the Lord our God.

Ant. ad introitum

MISERERIS omnium, Domine,
et nihil odisti eorum
quæ fecisti,
dissimulans peccata hominum
propter pænitentiam
et parcens illis,
quia tu es Dominus Deus noster.

The Penitential Act is omitted, and the Distribution of Ashes takes its place.

Collect

Grant, O Lord, that we may begin
with holy fasting
this campaign of Christian service,
so that, as we take up battle
against spiritual evils,
we may be armed with weapons
of self-restraint.
Through our Lord Jesus Christ,
your Son,

Collecta

Concede nobis, Domine,
præsidia militiæ christianæ sanctis
inchoare ieiuniis,
ut, contra spiritales
nequitias pugnaturi,
continentiæ muniamur auxiliis.
Per Dominum nostrum
Iesum Christum Filium tuum,

who lives and reigns with you	qui tecum vivit et regnat
in the unity of the Holy Spirit,	in unitate Spiritus Sancti,
one God, for ever and ever.	Deus, per omnia sæcula sæculorum.

FIRST READING

A reading from the prophet Joel   2:12-18

Let your hearts be broken, not your garments torn.

'Now, now – it is the Lord who speaks –
come back to me with all your heart,
fasting, weeping, mourning.'
Let your hearts be broken not your garments torn,
turn to the Lord your God again,
for he is all tenderness and compassion,
slow to anger, rich in graciousness,
and ready to relent.
Who knows if he will not turn again, will not relent,
will not leave a blessing as he passes,
oblation and libation
for the Lord your God?
Sound the trumpet in Zion!
Order a fast,
proclaim a solemn assembly,
call the people together,
summon the community,
assemble the elders,
gather the children,
even the infants at the breast.
Let the bridegroom leave his bedroom
and the bride her alcove.
Between vestibule and altar let the priests,
the ministers of the Lord, lament.
Let them say,
'Spare your people, Lord!
Do not make your heritage a thing of shame,
a byword for the nations.
Why should it be said among the nations,
"Where is their God?"'
Then the Lord, jealous on behalf of his land,
took pity on his people.

The word of the Lord.

Responsorial Psalm   Ps 50:3-6,12-14,17. R. v.3

R. **Have mercy on us, O Lord, for we have sinned.**

Have mercy on me, God, in your kindness.
In your compassion blot out my offence.
O wash me more and more from my guilt
and cleanse me from my sin. R.

My offences truly I know them;
my sin is always before me.
Against you, you alone, have I sinned:
what is evil in your sight I have done. R.

A pure heart create for me, O God,
put a steadfast spirit within me.
Do not cast me away from your presence,
nor deprive me of your holy spirit. R.

Give me again the joy of your help;
with a spirit of fervour sustain me.
O Lord, open my lips
and my mouth shall declare your praise. R.

SECOND READING

A reading from the second letter of St Paul to the Corinthians   5:20-6:2
Be reconciled to God ... now is the favourable time.

We are ambassadors for Christ; it is as though God were appealing through
us, and the appeal that we make in Christ's name is: be reconciled to God.
For our sake God made the sinless one into sin, so that in him we might
become the goodness of God. As his fellow workers, we beg you once again
not to neglect the grace of God that you have received. For he says: At the
favourable time, I have listened to you, on the day of salvation I came to
your help. Well, now is the favourable time; this is the day of salvation.

The word of the Lord.

Gospel Acclamation   Ps 50:12,14

R. **Praise to you, O Christ, king of eternal glory!**
A pure heart create for me, O God,
and give me again the joy of your help.
R. **Praise to you, O Christ, king of eternal glory!**

Or: Cf. Ps 94:8

R. **Praise to you, O Christ, king of eternal glory!**
Harden not your hearts today,
but listen to the voice of the Lord.
R. **Praise to you, O Christ, king of eternal glory!**

GOSPEL

A reading from holy Gospel according to Matthew   6:1-6,16-18
Your Father, who sees all that is done in secret, will reward you.

Jesus said to his disciples:

'Be careful not to parade your good deeds before men to attract their
notice; by doing this you will lose all reward from your Father in heaven.
So when you give alms, do not have it trumpeted before you; this is what
the hypocrites do in the synagogues and in the streets to win men's
admiration. I tell you solemnly, they have had their reward. But when you
give alms, your left hand must not know what your right is doing; your
almsgiving must be secret, and your Father who sees all that is done in
secret will reward you.

'And when you pray, do not imitate the hypocrites: they love to say
their prayers standing up in the synagogues and at the street corners for
people to see them. I tell you solemnly, they have had their reward. But
when you pray go to your private room and, when you have shut your
door, pray to your Father who is in that secret place, and your Father who
sees all that is done in secret will reward you.

'When you fast do not put on a gloomy look as the hypocrites do: they
pull long faces to let men know they are fasting. I tell you solemnly, they
have had their reward. But when you fast, put oil on your head and wash
your face, so that no one will know you are fasting except your Father who
sees all that is done in secret; and your Father who sees all that is done in
secret will reward you.'

The Gospel of the Lord.

Blessing and Distribution of Ashes

After the Homily, the Priest, standing with hands joined, says:

Dear brethren (brothers and sisters),
   let us humbly ask God our Father
that he be pleased to bless
   with the abundance of his grace
these ashes, which we will put
   on our heads in penitence.

Deum Patrem, fratres carissimi,
   suppliciter deprecemur,
ut hos cineres, quos pænitentiæ causa
capitibus nostris imponimus,
ubertate gratiæ suæ
   benedicere dignetur.

After a brief prayer in silence, and, with hands extended, he continues:

O God, who are moved
   by acts of humility
and respond with forgiveness
   to works of penance,
lend your merciful ear to our prayers
and in your kindness pour out
   the grace of your ✠ blessing
on your servants who are marked
   with these ashes,
that, as they follow
   the Lenten observances,
they may be worthy to come
   with minds made pure
to celebrate the Paschal Mystery
   of your Son.
Who lives and reigns
   for ever and ever.
R. Amen.

Deus, qui humiliatione flecteris
   et satisfactione placaris,
aurem tuæ pietatis precibus
   nostris inclina,
et super famulos tuos,
horum cinerum aspersione contactos,
gratiam tuæ benedictionis ✠
   effunde propitius,
ut, quadragesimalem
   observantiam prosequentes,
ad Filii tui paschale
   mysterium celebrandum
purificatis mentibus
   pervenire mereantur.
Per Christum Dominum nostrum.
R. Amen.

Or:

Vel:

O God, who desire not
   the death of sinners,
but their conversion,
mercifully hear our prayers
and in your kindness be pleased
   to bless ✠ these ashes,
which we intend to receive
   upon our heads,
that we, who acknowledge
   we are but ashes

Deus, qui non mortem
   sed conversionem
desideras peccatorum,
preces nostras clementer exaudi,
et hos cineres,
quos capitibus nostris
   imponi decernimus,
benedicere ✠ pro tua pietate dignare,
ut qui nos cinerem esse
et in pulverem
   reversuros cognoscimus,

and shall return to dust,
may, through a steadfast
   observance of Lent,
gain pardon for sins
   and newness of life
after the likeness of your Risen Son.
Who lives and reigns
   for ever and ever.

R. Amen.

quadragesimalis exercitationis studio,
peccatorum veniam
et novitatem vitæ,
ad imaginem Filii tui resurgentis,
   consequi valeamus.
Qui vivit et regnat
   in sæcula sæculorum.

R. Amen.

He sprinkles the ashes with holy water, without saying anything.

Then the Priest places ashes on the head of all those present who come to him, and says to each one:

Repent, and believe in the Gospel.

Pænitemini, et credite Evangelio.

Or:

Vel:

Remember that you are dust,
   and to dust you shall return.

Memento, homo, quia pulvis es,
   et in pulverem reverteris.

Meanwhile, the following are sung:

Antiphon 1

Let us change our garments
   to sackcloth and ashes,
let us fast and weep before the Lord,
that our God, rich in mercy,
   might forgive us our sins.

Antiphona 1

Immutemur habitu,
   in cinere et cilicio,
ieiunemus,
   et ploremus ante Dominum,
quia multum misericors est
dimittere peccata nostra Deus noster.

Antiphon 2   Cf. Jl 2:17; Est 4:17

Let the priests,
   the ministers of the Lord,
stand between the porch and
   the altar and weep and cry out:
Spare, O Lord, spare your people;
do not close the mouths of those
   who sing your praise, O Lord.

Antiphona 2

Inter vestibulum et altare
plorabunt sacerdotes
   ministri Domini,
et dicent: Parce, Domine,
   parce populo tuo,
et ne claudas ora canentium te,
   Domine.

Antiphon 3   Ps 50:3

Blot out my transgressions, O Lord.

Antiphona 3

Dele, Domine, iniquitatem meam.

This may be repeated after each verse of Psalm 50

(Have mercy on me, O God).

Miserere mei, Deus.

Responsory Cf. Ba 3:2; Ps 78:9	Responsorium
R. Let us correct our faults which we have committed in ignorance, let us not be taken unawares by the day of our death, looking in vain for leisure to repent. * Hear us, O Lord, and show us your mercy, for we have sinned against you.	R. Emendemus in melius, quæ ignoranter peccavimus, ne subito præoccupati die mortis quæramus spatium pænitentiæ, et invenire non possimus. *Attende, Domine, et miserere, quia peccavimus tibi.
V. Help us, O God our Saviour; for the sake of your name, O Lord, set us free. * Hear us, O Lord. . .	V. Adiuva nos, Deus salutaris noster, et propter honorem nominis tui, Domine, libera nos. *Attende, Domine. . .

Another appropriate chant may also be sung.

After the distribution of ashes, the Priest washes his hands and proceeds to the Universal Prayer, and continues the Mass in the usual way.

The Creed is not said.

The Liturgy of the Eucharist

Prayer over the Offerings	Super oblata

As we solemnly offer
the annual sacrifice for
    the beginning of Lent,
we entreat you, O Lord,
that, through works of penance
    and charity,
we may turn away from
    harmful pleasures
and, cleansed from our sins,
    may become worthy
to celebrate devoutly the Passion
    of your Son.
Who lives and reigns
    for ever and ever.
	Sacrificium quadragesimalis initii
	    sollemniter immolamus,
	te, Domine, deprecantes,
	ut per pænitentiæ
	    caritatisque labores
	a noxiis voluptatibus temperemus,
	et, a peccatis mundati,
	ad celebrandam Filii tui passionem
	mereamur esse devoti.
	Qui vivit et regnet
	    in sæcula sæculorum.

Preface III or IV of Lent, pp.50-53.

Communion Antiphon Cf. Ps 1:2-3

He who ponders the law
    of the Lord day and night
will yield fruit in due season.

Prayer after Communion

May the Sacrament we have
    received sustain us, O Lord,
that our Lenten fast may
    be pleasing to you
and be for us a healing remedy.
Through Christ our Lord.

Ant. ad communionem

Qui meditabitur in lege
    Domini die ac nocte,
dabit fructum suum in tempore suo.

Post communionem

Percepta nobis, Domine,
præbeant sacramenta subsidium,
ut tibi grata sint nostra ieiunia,
et nobis proficiant ad medelam.
Per Christum Dominum nostrum.

For the dismissal, the Priest stands facing the people and, extending his hands over them, says this prayer:

Prayer over the People

Pour out a spirit of compunction,
    O God,
on those who bow before
    your majesty,
and by your mercy may they
    merit the rewards you promise
to those who do penance.
Through Christ our Lord.

Oratio super populum

Super inclinantes se tuæ maiestati,
    Deus,
spiritum compunctionis
    propitius effunde,
et præmia pænitentibus repromissa
misericorditer consequi mereantur.
Per Christum Dominum nostrum.

The blessing and distribution of ashes may also take place outside Mass. In this case, the rite is preceded by a Liturgy of the Word, with the Entrance Antiphon, the Collect, and the readings with their chants as at Mass. Then there follow the Homily and the blessing and distribution of ashes. The rite is concluded with the Universal Prayer, the Blessing, and the Dismissal of the Faithful.

18 February

FIRST SUNDAY OF LENT

This is the meaning of this First Sunday of Lent: to place ourselves decisively on the path of Jesus, the road that leads to life. To look at Jesus. Look at what Jesus has done and go with him. This path of Jesus passes through the desert. The desert is the place where the voice of God and the voice of the tempter can be heard. In the noise, in the confusion, this cannot be done; only superficial voices can be heard. Instead we can go deeper in the desert, where our destiny is truly played out, life or death. And how do we hear the voice of God? We hear it in his Word. For this reason, it is important to know Scripture, because otherwise we do not know how to react to the snares of the Evil One.

(Pope Francis)

Entrance Antiphon Cf. Ps 90:15-16

WHEN he calls on me,
I will answer him;
I will deliver him and give him glory,
I will grant him length of days.

Ant. ad introitum

INVOCABIT me,
et ego exaudiam eum;
eripiam eum, et glorificabo eum,
longitudine dierum adimplebo eum.

The Gloria in excelsis (Glory to God in the highest) is not said.

Collect

Grant, almighty God,
through the yearly observances
  of holy Lent,
that we may grow in understanding
of the riches hidden in Christ
and by worthy conduct pursue
  their effects.
Through our Lord Jesus Christ,
  your Son,
who lives and reigns with you
  in the unity of the Holy Spirit,
one God, for ever and ever.

Collecta

Concede nobis, omnipotens Deus,
ut, per annua quadragesimalis
  exercitia sacramenti,
et ad intellegendum Christi
  proficiamus arcanum,
et effectus eius digna
  conversatione sectemur.
Per Dominum nostrum Iesum
  Christum Filium tuum,
qui tecum vivit et regnat
  in unitate Spiritus Sancti,
Deus, per omnia sæcula sæculorum.

FIRST READING

A reading from the book of Genesis   9:8-15

God's covenant with Noah after he had saved him from the waters of the flood.

God spoke to Noah and his sons, 'See, I establish my Covenant with you, and with your descendants after you; also with every living creature to be found with you, birds, cattle and every wild beast with you: everything that came out of the ark, everything that lives on the earth. I establish my Covenant with you: no thing of flesh shall be swept away again by the waters of the flood. There shall be no flood to destroy the earth again.'

God said, 'Here is the sign of the Covenant I make between myself and you and every living creature with you for all generations: I set my bow in the clouds and it shall be a sign of the Covenant between me and the earth. When I gather the clouds over the earth and the bow appears in the clouds, I will recall the Covenant between myself and you and every living creature of every kind. And so the waters shall never again become a flood to destroy all things of flesh.'

The word of the Lord.

Responsorial Psalm   Ps 24:4-9. R. Cf. v.10

R. **Your ways, Lord, are faithfulness and love**
   for those who keep your covenant.

   Lord, make me know your ways.
   Lord, teach me your paths.
   Make me walk in your truth, and teach me:
   for you are God my saviour. R.

   Remember your mercy, Lord
   and the love you have shown from of old.
   In your love remember me,
   because of your goodness, O Lord. R.

   The Lord is good and upright.
   He shows the path to those who stray,
   he guides the humble in the right path;
   he teaches his way to the poor. R.

SECOND READING

A reading from the first letter of St Peter   3:18-22

That water is a type of the baptism which saves you now.

Christ himself, innocent though he was, died once for sins, died for the guilty, to lead us to God. In the body he was put to death, in the spirit he was raised to life, and, in the spirit, he went to preach to the spirits in prison. Now it was long ago, when Noah was still building that ark which saved only a small group of eight people 'by water', and when God was still waiting patiently, that these spirits refused to believe. That water is a type of the baptism which saves you now, and which is not the washing off of physical dirt but a pledge made to God from a good conscience, through the resurrection of Jesus Christ, who has entered heaven and is at God's right hand, now that he has made the angels and Dominations and Powers his subjects.

The word of the Lord.

Gospel Acclamation   Mt 4:4

R. **Praise to you, O Christ, king of eternal glory!**
Man does not live on bread alone,
but on every word that comes from the mouth of God.
R. **Praise to you, O Christ, king of eternal glory!**

GOSPEL

A reading from the holy Gospel according to Mark   1:12-15
Jesus was tempted by Satan, and the angels looked after him.

The Spirit drove Jesus out into the wilderness and he remained there for forty days, and was tempted by Satan. He was with the wild beasts, and the angels looked after him.

After John had been arrested, Jesus went into Galilee. There he proclaimed the Good News from God. 'The time has come' he said 'and the kingdom of God is close at hand. Repent, and believe the Good News.'

The Gospel of the Lord.

The Creed is said.

Prayer over the Offerings

Give us the right dispositions,
    O Lord, we pray,
to make these offerings,
for with them we celebrate
    the beginning
of this venerable and sacred time.
Through Christ our Lord.

Super oblata

Fac nos, quæsumus, Domine,
his muneribus offerendis
    convenienter aptari,
quibus ipsius venerabilis sacramenti
    celebramus exordium.
Per Christum Dominum nostrum.

Preface: The Temptation of the Lord.

It is truly right and just,
  our duty and our salvation,
always and everywhere
  to give you thanks,
Lord, holy Father,
  almighty and eternal God,
through Christ our Lord.

By abstaining forty long days
  from earthly food,
he consecrated through his fast
the pattern of our Lenten observance
and, by overturning all the snares
  of the ancient serpent,
taught us to cast out the leaven
  of malice,
so that, celebrating worthily
  the Paschal Mystery,
we might pass over at last
  to the eternal paschal feast.

And so, with the company
  of Angels and Saints,
we sing the hymn of your praise,
as without end we acclaim:

Holy, Holy, Holy Lord God of hosts...

Praefatio: De tentatione Domini.

Vere dignum et iustum est,
  aequum et salutare,
nos tibi semper et ubique
  gratias agere:
Domine, sancte Pater, omnipotens
  aeterne Deus:
per Christum Dominum nostrum:

Qui quadraginta diebus,
  terrenis abstinens alimentis,
formam huius observantiae
  ieiunio dedicavit,
et, omnes evertens antiqui
  serpentis insidias,
fermentum malitiae nos
  docuit superare,
ut, paschale mysterium dignis
  mentibus celebrantes,
ad pascha demum
  perpetuum transeamus.

Et ideo, cum Angelorum
  atque Sanctorum turba,
hymnum laudis tibi canimus,
  sine fine dicentes:

Sanctus, Sanctus, Sanctus. . .

Communion Antiphon   Mt 4:4

One does not live by bread alone,
but by every word that comes forth
  from the mouth of God.

Ant. ad communionem

Non in solo pane vivit homo,
sed in omni verbo quod procedit
  de ore Dei.

Or: Cf. Ps 90:4

The Lord will conceal you
  with his pinions,
and under his wings you will trust.

Vel:

Scapulis suis obumbrabit
  tibi Dominus,
et sub pennis eius sperabis.

Prayer after Communion

Renewed now with heavenly bread,
by which faith is nourished,
    hope increased,
and charity strengthened,
we pray, O Lord,
that we may learn to hunger
    for Christ,
the true and living Bread,
and strive to live by every word
which proceeds from your mouth.
Through Christ our Lord.

Post communionem

Cælesti pane refecti,
quo fides alitur, spes provehitur
    et caritas roboratur,
quæsumus, Domine,
ut ipsum, qui est panis vivus
    et verus, esurire discamus,
et in omni verbo,
    quod procedit de ore tuo,
vivere valeamus.
Per Christum Dominum nostrum.

Prayer over the People

May bountiful blessing,
    O Lord, we pray,
come down upon your people,
that hope may grow in tribulation,
virtue be strengthened in temptation,
and eternal redemption be assured.
Through Christ our Lord.

Oratio super populum

Super populum tuum,
    Domine, quæsumus,
benedictio copiosa descendat,
ut spes in tribulatione succrescat,
virtus in tentatione firmetur,
æterna redemptio tribuatur.
Per Christum Dominum nostrum.

25 February

SECOND SUNDAY OF LENT

The path to Jesus always leads us to happiness, don't forget it! There will always be a cross, trials in the middle, but at the end we are always led to happiness. Jesus does not deceive us; he promised us happiness and will give it to us if we follow his ways. With Peter, James and John we too climb the Mount of the Transfiguration today and stop in contemplation of the face of Jesus to retrieve the message and translate it into our lives; for we too can be transfigured by love. In reality, love is capable of transfiguring everything.

(Pope Francis)

Entrance Antiphon Cf. Ps 26:8-9	Ant. ad introitum
OF you my heart has spoken: Seek his face. It is your face, O Lord, that I seek; hide not your face from me.	TIBI dixit cor meum quæsivi vultum tuum, vultum tuum, Domine, requiram. Ne avertas faciem tuam a me.
Or: Cf. Ps 24:6,2,22	Vel:
Remember your compassion, O Lord, and your merciful love, for they are from of old. Let not our enemies exult over us. Redeem us, O God of Israel, from all our distress.	Reminiscere miserationum tuarum, Domine, et misericordiæ tuæ, quæ a sæculo sunt. Ne umquam dominentur nobis inimici nostri; libera nos, Deus Israel, ex omnibus angustiis nostris.

The Gloria in excelsis (Glory to God in the highest) is not said.

Collect

O God, who have commanded us
  to listen to your beloved Son,
be pleased, we pray,
to nourish us inwardly by your word,
that, with spiritual sight made pure,
we may rejoice to behold your glory.
Through our Lord Jesus Christ,
  your Son,
who lives and reigns with you
  in the unity of the Holy Spirit,
one God, for ever and ever.

Collecta

Deus, qui nobis dilectum Filium
  tuum audire præcepisti,
verbo tuo interius
  nos pascere digneris,
ut, spiritali purificato intuitu,
gloriæ tuæ lætemur aspectu.
Per Dominum nostrum Iesum
  Christum Filium tuum,
qui tecum vivit et regnat
  in unitate Spiritus Sancti,
Deus, per omnia sæcula sæculorum.

FIRST READING

A reading from the book of Genesis   22:1-2,9-13,15-18
The sacrifice of Abraham, our father in faith.

God put Abraham to the test. 'Abraham, Abraham' he called. 'Here I am' he replied. 'Take your son,' God said 'your only child Isaac, whom you love, and go to the land of Moriah. There you shall offer him as a burnt offering, on a mountain I will point out to you.'

When they arrived at the place God had pointed out to him, Abraham built an altar there, and arranged the wood. Then he stretched out his hand and seized the knife to kill his son.

But the angel of the Lord called to him from heaven. 'Abraham, Abraham' he said. 'I am here' he replied. 'Do not raise your hand against the boy' the angel said. 'Do not harm him, for now I know you fear God. You have not refused me your son, your only son.' Then looking up, Abraham saw a ram caught by its horns in a bush. Abraham took the ram and offered it as a burnt-offering in place of his son.

The angel of the Lord called Abraham a second time from heaven. 'I swear by my own self – it is the Lord who speaks – because you have done this, because you have not refused me your son, your only son, I will shower blessings on you, I will make your descendants as many as the stars of heaven and the grains of sand on the seashore. Your descendants shall gain possession of the gates of their enemies. All the nations of the earth shall bless themselves by your descendants, as a reward for your obedience.'

The word of the Lord.

Responsorial Psalm   Ps 115:10,15-19. R. Ps 114:9

R. **I will walk in the presence of the Lord**
   in the land of the living.

I trusted, even when I said:
'I am sorely afflicted.'
O precious in the eyes of the Lord
is the death of his faithful. R.

Your servant, Lord, your servant am I;
you have loosened my bonds.
A thanksgiving sacrifice I make:
I will call on the Lord's name. R.

My vows to the Lord I will fulfil
before all his people,
in the courts of the house of the Lord,
in your midst, O Jerusalem. R.

SECOND READING

A reading from the letter of St Paul to the Romans   8:31-34
God did not spare his own Son.

With God on our side who can be against us? Since God did not spare his
own Son, but gave him up to benefit us all, we may be certain, after such
a gift, that he will not refuse anything he can give. Could anyone accuse
those that God has chosen? When God acquits, could anyone condemn?
Could Christ Jesus? No! He not only died for us – he rose from the dead,
and there at God's right hand he stands and pleads for us.

The word of the Lord.

Gospel Acclamation   Mt 17:5

R. **Glory and praise to you, O Christ!**
From the bright cloud the Father's voice was heard:
'This is my Son, the Beloved. Listen to him.'
R. **Glory and praise to you, O Christ!**

GOSPEL

A reading from the holy Gospel according to Mark   9:2-10
This is my Son, the Beloved.

Jesus took with him Peter and James and John and led them up a high
mountain where they could be alone by themselves. There in their
presence he was transfigured: his clothes became dazzlingly white, whiter

than any earthly bleacher could make them. Elijah appeared to them with
Moses; and they were talking with Jesus. Then Peter spoke to Jesus: 'Rabbi,'
he said 'it is wonderful for us to be here; so let us make three tents, one for
you, one for Moses and one for Elijah.' He did not know what to say; they
were so frightened. And a cloud came, covering them in shadow; and there
came a voice from the cloud, 'This is my Son, the Beloved. Listen to him.'
Then suddenly, when they looked round, they saw no one with them any
more but only Jesus.

As they came down the mountain he warned them to tell no one what
they had seen, until after the Son of Man had risen from the dead. They
observed the warning faithfully, though among themselves they discussed
what 'rising from the dead' could mean.

The Gospel of the Lord.

The Creed is said.

Prayer over the Offerings

May this sacrifice, O Lord, we pray,
cleanse us of our faults
and sanctify your faithful
     in body and mind
for the celebration
     of the paschal festivities.
Through Christ our Lord.

Super oblata

Hæc hostia, Domine, quæsumus,
     emundet nostra delicta,
et ad celebranda festa paschalia
fidelium tuorum corpora
     mentesque sanctificet.
Per Christum Dominum nostrum.

Preface: The Transfiguration of the Lord.

It is truly right and just,
     our duty and our salvation,
always and everywhere
     to give you thanks,
Lord, holy Father,
     almighty and eternal God,
through Christ our Lord.

For after he had told the disciples
     of his coming Death,
on the holy mountain
     he manifested to them his glory,

Praefatio: De transfiguratione Domini.

Vere dignum et iustum est,
     aequum et salutare,
nos tibi semper et ubique
     gratias agere:
Domine, sancte Pater,
     omnipotens aeterne Deus:
per Christum Dominum nostrum:

Qui, propria morte
     praenuntiata discipulis,
in monte sancto suam eis
     aperuit claritatem,

to show, even by the testimony
of the law and the prophets,
that the Passion leads to the glory
of the Resurrection.

And so, with the Powers of heaven,
we worship you constantly on earth,
and before your majesty
without end we acclaim:

Holy, Holy, Holy Lord God of hosts...

ut per passionem, etiam lege
prophetisque testantibus,
ad gloriam resurrectionis
perveniri constaret.

Et ideo, cum caelorum Virtutibus,
in terris te iugiter celebramus,
maiestati tuae sine fine clamantes:

Sanctus, Sanctus, Sanctus. . .

Communion Antiphon   Mt 17:5

This is my beloved Son,
with whom I am well pleased;
listen to him.

Ant. ad communionem

Hic est Filius meus dilectus,
in quo mihi bene complacui;
ipsum audite.

Prayer after Communion

As we receive these glorious mysteries,
we make thanksgiving to you,
O Lord,
for allowing us while still on earth
to be partakers even now
of the things of heaven.
Through Christ our Lord.

Post communionem

Percipientes, Domine,
gloriosa mysteria,
gratias tibi referre satagimus,
quod, in terra positos,
iam cælestium præstas
esse participes.
Per Christum Dominum nostrum.

Prayer over the People

Bless your faithful, we pray, O Lord,
with a blessing that endures for ever,
and keep them faithful
to the Gospel of your
Only Begotten Son,
so that they may always desire
and at last attain
that glory whose beauty he showed
in his own Body,
to the amazement of his Apostles.
Through Christ our Lord.

Oratio super populum

Benedic, Domine, fideles tuos
benedictione perpetua,
et fac eos Unigeniti tui Evangelio
sic adhærere,
ut ad illam gloriam, cuius in se
speciem Apostolis ostendit,
et suspirare iugiter et feliciter
valeant pervenire.
Per Christum Dominum nostrum.

In Wales

1 March

SAINT DAVID, BISHOP, PATRON OF WALES

Saint David was one of the great saints of the sixth century, that golden age of saints and missionaries in these isles, and he was thus a founder of the Christian culture which lies at the root of modern Europe. David's preaching was simple yet profound: his dying words to his monks were, "Be joyful, keep the faith, and do the little things". It is the little things that reveal our love for the one who loved us first (Cf. 1 Jn 4:19) and that bind people into a community of faith, love and service. May Saint David's message, in all its simplicity and richness, continue to resound today, drawing the hearts of people to renewed love for Christ and his Church.

(*Pope Benedict XVI*)

Solemnity

Entrance Antiphon   Is 52:7

How beautiful upon the mountains are the feet of him
who brings glad tidings of peace,
bearing good news, announcing salvation!

The Gloria in excelsis (Glory to God in the highest) is said.

Collect

O God, who graciously bestowed on your Bishop Saint David of Wales
the virtue of wisdom and the gift of eloquence
and made him an example of prayer and pastoral zeal,
grant that, through his intercession
your Church may ever prosper and render you joyful praise.
Through our Lord Jesus Christ, your Son,
who lives and reigns with you in the unity of the Holy Spirit,
one God, for ever and ever.

Readings such as the following may be chosen from the Common of Pastors, or from the Common of Holy Men and Women. First readings outside Easter are always from the Old Testament.

FIRST READING

A reading from the book of Genesis   12:1-4

The call of Abraham, the father the People of God.

The Lord said to Abram, 'Leave your country, your family and your father's house, for the land I will show you. I will make you a great nation; I will bless you and make your name so famous that it will be used as a blessing.

'I will bless those who bless you:
I will curse those who slight you.

All the tribes of the earth
  shall bless themselves by you.'
So Abram went as the Lord told him.
  The word of the Lord.

Responsorial Psalm   Ps 1. R. Ps 39:5

R. **Happy the man who has placed
   his trust in the Lord.**

  Happy indeed is the man
  who follows not the counsel of the wicked;
  nor lingers in the way of sinners
  nor sits in the company of scorners,
  but whose delight is the law of the Lord
  and who ponders his law day and night. R.

  He is like a tree that is planted
  beside the flowing waters,
  that yields its fruit in due season
  and whose leaves shall never fade;
  and all that he does shall prosper. R.

  Not so are the wicked, not so!
  For they like winnowed chaff
  shall be driven away by the wind;
  for the Lord guards the way of the just
  but the way of the wicked leads to doom. R.

SECOND READING

A reading from the letter of St Paul to the Philippians   3:8-14

*I am racing for the finish, for the prize to which God calls us upwards to receive in
Christ Jesus.*

I believe nothing can happen that will outweigh the supreme advantage
of knowing Christ Jesus my Lord. For him I have accepted the loss of
everything, and I look on everything as so much rubbish if only I can have
Christ and be given a place in him. I am no longer trying for perfection by
my own efforts, the perfection that comes from the Law, but I want only the
perfection that comes through faith in Christ, and is from God and based
on faith. All I want is to know Christ and the power of his resurrection and
to share his sufferings by reproducing the pattern of his death. That is the
way I can hope to take my place in the resurrection of the dead. Not that I
have become perfect yet: I have not yet won, but I am still running, trying
to capture the prize for which Christ Jesus captured me. I can assure you my
brothers, I am far from thinking that I have already won. All I can say is that I

forget the past and I strain ahead for what is still to come; I am racing for the finish, for the prize to which God calls us upwards to receive in Christ Jesus.

The word of the Lord.

Gospel Acclamation   Jn 8:31-32

R. **Praise to you, O Christ, king of eternal glory!**
If you make my word your home
you will indeed be my disciples,
and you will learn the truth, says the Lord.
R. **Praise to you, O Christ, king of eternal glory!**

GOSPEL

A reading from the holy Gospel according to Matthew   5:13-16
You are the light of the world.

Jesus said to his disciples: 'You are the salt of the earth. But if salt becomes tasteless, what can make it salty again? It is good for nothing, and can only be thrown out to be trampled underfoot by men.

'You are the light of the world. A city built on a hill-top cannot be hidden. No one lights a lamp to put it under a tub; they put it on the lamp-stand where it shines for everyone in the house. In the same way your light must shine in the sight of men, so that, seeing your good works, they may give the praise to your Father in heaven.'

The Gospel of the Lord.

The Creed is said.

Prayer over the Offerings

Look with favour, O Lord, we pray,
on the offerings we set upon this sacred altar
on the feast day of the Bishop Saint David,
that, bestowing on us your pardon,
our oblations may give honour to your name.
Through Christ our Lord.

Communion Antiphon   Cf. 1 Co 1:23-24

We proclaim Christ crucified,
Christ, the power of God, and the wisdom of God.

Prayer after Communion

We pray, almighty God,
that we, who are fortified by the power of this Sacrament,
may learn through the example of your Bishop Saint David
to seek you always above all things
and to bear in this world the likeness of the New Man.
Who lives and reigns for ever and ever.

4 March

THIRD SUNDAY OF LENT

On the occasion of Jewish Passover, Jesus goes to Jerusalem. When he arrives at the Temple, he does not find people seeking God, but people conducting business. This provokes a forceful response from Jesus. He overturns the tables and throws the money to the ground, and sends the merchants away, telling them: "you shall not make my Father's house a house of trade"! This expression does not merely refer to the dealings in the temple courtyards. It instead refers to a type of religiosity. This act is a reference to authentic worship, to a correspondence between liturgy and life. The liturgy is not something unusual, over there, far away, and while celebrating I think about many things, or I pray the Rosary. No, no. There is a correspondence, between the liturgical celebration which we then carry in our life; and we must always persevere in this.

(Pope Francis)

Entrance Antiphon Cf. Ps 24:15-16

MY eyes are always on the Lord,
for he rescues my feet
from the snare.
Turn to me and have mercy on me,
for I am alone and poor.

Or: Cf. Ezk 36:23-26

When I prove my holiness
among you,
I will gather you from all
the foreign lands;
and I will pour clean water upon you
and cleanse you from
all your impurities,
and I will give you a new spirit,
says the Lord.

Ant. ad introitum

OCULI mei semper
ad Dominum,
quia ipse evellet de laqueo
pedes meos.
Respice in me et miserere mei,
quoniam unicus et pauper sum ego.

Vel:

Cum sanctificatus fuero in vobis,
congregabo vos
de universis terris;
et effundam super vos
aquam mundam,
et mundabimini ab omnibus
inquinamentis vestris,
et dabo vobis spiritum novum,
dicit Dominus.

The Gloria in excelsis (Glory to God in the highest) is not said.

Collect

O God, author of every mercy
    and of all goodness,
who in fasting, prayer and almsgiving
have shown us a remedy for sin,
look graciously on this confession
    of our lowliness,
that we, who are bowed down
    by our conscience,
may always be lifted up
    by your mercy.
Through our Lord Jesus Christ,
    your Son,
who lives and reigns with you
    in the unity of the Holy Spirit,
one God, for ever and ever.

Collecta

Deus, omnium misericordiarum
    et totius bonitatis auctor,
qui peccatorum remedia in ieiuniis,
orationibus et eleemosynis
    demonstrasti,
hanc humilitatis nostræ
    confessionem propitius intuere,
ut, qui inclinamur
    conscientia nostra,
tua semper misericordia sublevemur.
Per Dominum nostrum Iesum
    Christum Filium tuum,
qui tecum vivit et regnat
    in unitate Spiritus Sancti,
Deus, per omnia sæcula sæculorum.

The readings for Year B are included in full below. The readings for Year A may also be used on this Sunday: Ex 17:3-7; Ps 94:1-2,6-9. R. v.8; Rom 5:1-2,5-8; Jn 4:5-42 or Jn 4:5-15,19-26,39-42; Cf. Jn 4:42,15. If this is done, the Preface: The Samaritan Woman (pp.275-276) and Communion Antiphon: Jn 4:13-14 as in Year A are also used.

FIRST READING

A reading from the book of Exodus   20:1-17
The Law was given through Moses.

[God spoke all these words. He said, 'I am the Lord your God who brought you out of the land of Egypt, out of the house of slavery.

'You shall have no gods except me.]

'You shall not make yourself a carved image or any likeness of anything in heaven or on earth beneath or in the waters under the earth; you shall not bow down to them or serve them. For I, the Lord your God, am a jealous God and I punish the father's fault in the sons, the grandsons, and the great-grandsons of those who hate me; but I show kindness to thousands of those who love me and keep my commandments.

['You shall not utter the name of the Lord your God to misuse it, for the Lord will not leave unpunished the man who utters his name to misuse it.]

'Remember the sabbath day and keep it holy. For six days you shall labour and do all your work, but the seventh day is a sabbath for the

Lord your God. You shall do no work that day, neither you nor your son nor your daughter nor your servants, men or women, nor your animals nor the stranger who lives with you. For in six days the Lord made the heavens and the earth and the sea and all that these hold, but on the seventh day he rested; that is why the Lord has blessed the sabbath day and made it sacred.

[‘Honour your father and your mother so that you may have a long life in the land that the Lord your God has given to you.

‘You shall not kill.

‘You shall not commit adultery.

‘You shall not steal.

‘You shall not bear false witness against your neighbour.

‘You shall not covet your neighbour’s house. You shall not covet your neighbour’s wife, or his servant, man or woman, or his ox, or his donkey, or anything that is his.’

The word of the Lord.]

Shorter Form, verses 1-3,7-8,12-17. Read between [ ]

Responsial Psalm   Ps 18:8-11. R. Jn 6:68

R. **You, Lord, have the message of eternal life.**

The law of the Lord is perfect,
it revives the soul.
The rule of the Lord is to be trusted,
it gives wisdom to the simple. R.

The precepts of the Lord are right,
they gladden the heart.
The command of the Lord is clear,
it gives light to the eyes. R.

The fear of the Lord is holy,
abiding for ever.
The decrees of the Lord are truth
and all of them just. R.

They are more to be desired than gold,
than the purest of gold
and sweeter are they than honey,
than honey from the comb. R.

SECOND READING

A reading from the first letter of St Paul to the Corinthians   1:22-25
Here we are preaching a crucified Christ, an obstacle to men, but to those who are
called, the wisdom of God.

While the Jews demand miracles and the Greeks look for wisdom, here are
we preaching a crucified Christ; to the Jews an obstacle that they cannot get
over, to the pagans madness, but to those who have been called, whether
they are Jews or Greeks, a Christ who is the power and the wisdom of God.
For God's foolishness is wiser than human wisdom, and God's weakness is
stronger than human strength.

   The word of the Lord.

Gospel Acclamation   Jn 11:25,26

R. **Praise to you, O Christ, king of eternal glory!**
I am the resurrection and the life, says the Lord,
whoever believes in me will never die.
R. **Praise to you, O Christ, king of eternal glory!**
Or: Jn 3:16

R. **Praise to you, O Christ, king of eternal glory!**
God loved the world so much that he gave his only Son;
everyone who believes in him has eternal life.
R. **Praise to you, O Christ, king of eternal glory!**

GOSPEL

A reading from the holy Gospel according to John   2:13-25
Destroy this sanctuary, and in three days I will raise it up.

Just before the Jewish Passover Jesus went up to Jerusalem, and in the Temple
he found people selling cattle and sheep and pigeons, and the money
changers sitting at their counters there. Making a whip out of some cord,
he drove them all out of the Temple, cattle and sheep as well, scattered the
money changers' coins, knocked their tables over and said to the pigeon-
sellers, 'Take all this out of here and stop turning my Father's house into
a market.' Then his disciples remembered the words of scripture: Zeal for
your house will devour me. The Jews intervened and said, 'What sign can
you show us to justify what you have done?' Jesus answered, 'Destroy this
sanctuary, and in three days I will raise it up.' The Jews replied, 'It has
taken forty-six years to build this sanctuary: are you going to raise it up in
three days?' But he was speaking of the sanctuary that was his body, and

when Jesus rose from the dead, his disciples remembered that he had said this, and they believed the scripture and the words he had said.

During his stay in Jerusalem for the Passover many believed in his name when they saw the signs that he gave, but Jesus knew them all and did not trust himself to them; he never needed evidence about any man; he could tell what a man had in him.

The Gospel of the Lord.

The Creed is said.

Prayer over the Offerings

Be pleased, O Lord,
    with these sacrificial offerings,
and grant that we who beseech
    pardon for our own sins,
may take care to forgive
    our neighbour.
Through Christ our Lord.

Preface I or II of Lent, pp.48-51.

Super oblata

His sacrificiis, Domine,
    concede placatus,
ut, qui propriis oramus
    absolvi delictis,
fraterna dimittere studeamus.
Per Christum Dominum nostrum.

ALTERNATIVE PREFACE

If the alternative readings from Year A are used the following Preface is also used.

Preface: The Samaritan Woman.

It is truly right and just,
    our duty and our salvation,
always and everywhere
    to give you thanks,
Lord, holy Father,
    almighty and eternal God,
through Christ our Lord.

For when he asked the Samaritan
    woman for water to drink,
he had already created
    the gift of faith within her
and so ardently did he thirst
    for her faith,
that he kindled in her the fire
    of divine love.

Praefatio: De Samaritana.

Vere dignum et iustum est,
    aequum et salutare,
nos tibi semper et ubique
    gratias agere:
Domine, sancte Pater,
    omnipotens aeterne Deus:
per Christum Dominum nostrum:

Qui, dum aquae sibi petiit potum
    a Samaritana praeberi,
iam in ea fidei donum ipse creaverat,
et ita eius fidem sitire dignatus est,
ut ignem in illa divini
    amoris accenderet.

And so we, too, give you thanks
and with the Angels
praise your mighty deeds,
    as we acclaim:

Holy, Holy, Holy Lord God of hosts...

Unde et nos tibi gratias agimus,
et tuas virtutes cum Angelis
    praedicamus, dicentes:

Sanctus, Sanctus, Sanctus. . .

Communion Antiphon Cf. Ps 83:4-5

The sparrow finds a home,
and the swallow a nest for her young:
by your altars, O Lord of hosts,
    my King and my God.
Blessed are they who dwell
    in your house,
for ever singing your praise.

Ant. ad communionem

Passer invenit sibi domum,
et turtur nidum,
    ubi reponat pullos suos:
altaria tua, Domine virtutum,
    Rex meus, et Deus meus!
Beati qui habitant in domo tua,
in sæculum sæculi laudabunt te.

Prayer after Communion

As we receive the pledge
of things yet hidden in heaven
and are nourished while still on earth
with the Bread that comes
    from on high,
we humbly entreat you, O Lord,
that what is being brought about
    in us in mystery
may come to true completion.
Through Christ our Lord.

Post communionem

Sumentes pignus cælestis arcani,
et in terra positi iam superno
    pane satiati,
te, Domine, supplices deprecamur,
ut, quod in nobis mysterio geritur,
    opere impleatur.
Per Christum Dominum nostrum.

Prayer over the People

Direct, O Lord, we pray,
    the hearts of your faithful,
and in your kindness grant
    your servants this grace:
that, abiding in the love of you
    and their neighbour,
they may fulfil the whole
    of your commands.
Through Christ our Lord.

Oratio super populum

Rege, Domine, quæsumus,
    tuorum corda fidelium,
et servis tuis hanc gratiam
    largire propitius,
ut in tui et proximi
    dilectione manentes
plenitudinem mandatorum
    tuorum adimpleant.
Per Christum Dominum nostrum.

11 March

FOURTH SUNDAY OF LENT

Today's Gospel again offers us the words that Jesus addressed to Nicodemus: "For God so loved the world that he gave his only Son". In hearing these words, we turn our heart's gaze to Jesus Crucified and we feel within us that God loves us, truly loves us, and he loves us so much! This is the simplest expression that epitomises all of the Gospel, all of the faith, all of theology: God loves us with a free and boundless love. The Cross of Christ is the supreme proof of the mercy and love that God has for us: Jesus loved us "to the end", meaning not only to the last instant of his earthly life, but to the farthest limit of love.

(Pope Francis)

Entrance Antiphon   Cf. Is 66:10-11

REJOICE, Jerusalem,
and all who love her.
Be joyful, all who were in mourning;
exult and be satisfied at her
    consoling breast.

Ant. ad introitum

LÆTARE, Ierusalem,
et conventum facite,
    omnes qui diligitis eam;
gaudete cum lætitia,
    qui in tristitia fuistis,
ut exsultetis, et satiemini ab
    uberibus consolationis vestræ.

The Gloria in excelsis (Glory to God in the highest) is not said.

Collect

O God, who through your Word
reconcile the human race
    to yourself in a wonderful way,
grant, we pray,
that with prompt devotion
    and eager faith
the Christian people may hasten
toward the solemn celebrations
    to come.
Through our Lord Jesus Christ,
    your Son,
who lives and reigns with you
    in the unity of the Holy Spirit,
one God, for ever and ever.

Collecta

Deus, qui per Verbum tuum
humani generis reconciliationem
    mirabiliter operaris,
præsta, quæsumus,
    ut populus christianus
prompta devotione et alacri fide
ad ventura sollemnia
    valeat festinare.
Per Dominum nostrum Iesum
    Christum Filium tuum,
qui tecum vivit et regnat
    in unitate Spiritus Sancti,
Deus, per omnia sæcula sæculorum.

The readings for Year B are included in full below. The readings for Year A may also be used on this Sunday: Sam 16:1,6-7,10-13; Ps 22. R. v.1; Eph 5:8-14; Jn 8:12; Jn 9:1-41 or Jn 9:1,6-9,13-17,34-38. If this is done, the Preface: The Man Born Blind (p. 285) and Communion Antiphon: Cf. Jn 9:11,38 as in Year A are also used.

FIRST READING

A reading from the second book of Chronicles   36:14-16,19-23

The wrath and mercy of God are revealed in the exile and in the release of his people.

All the heads of the priesthood, and the people too, added infidelity to infidelity, copying all the shameful practices of the nations and defiling the Temple that the Lord had consecrated for himself in Jerusalem. The Lord, the God of their ancestors, tirelessly sent them messenger after messenger, since he wished to spare his people and his house. But they ridiculed the messengers of God, they despised his words, they laughed at his prophets, until at last the wrath of the Lord rose so high against his people that there was no further remedy.

Their enemies burned down the Temple of God, demolished the walls of Jerusalem, set fire to all its palaces, and destroyed everything of value in it. The survivors were deported by Nebuchadnezzar to Babylon; they were to serve him and his sons until the kingdom of Persia came to power. This is how the word of the Lord was fulfilled that he spoke through Jeremiah, 'Until this land has enjoyed its sabbath rest, until seventy years have gone by, it will keep sabbath throughout the days of its desolation.'

And in the first year of Cyrus king of Persia, to fulfil the word of the Lord that was spoken through Jeremiah, the Lord roused the spirit of Cyrus king of Persia to issue a proclamation and to have it publicly displayed throughout his kingdom: 'Thus speaks Cyrus king of Persia, "The Lord, the God of heaven, has given me all the kingdoms of the earth; he has ordered me to build him a Temple in Jerusalem, in Judah. Whoever there is among you of all his people, may his God be with him! Let him go up."'

The word of the Lord.

Responsorial Psalm   Ps 136:1-6. R. v.6

R. **O let my tongue**
     cleave to my mouth
     if I remember you not!

By the rivers of Babylon
there we sat and wept,
remembering Zion;
on the poplars that grew there
we hung up our harps. R.

For it was there that they asked us,
our captors, for songs,
our oppressors, for joy.
'Sing to us,' they said,
'one of Zion's songs.' R.

O how could we sing
the song of the Lord
on alien soil?
If I forget you, Jerusalem,
let my right hand wither! R.

O let my tongue
cleave to my mouth
if I remember you not,
if I prize not Jerusalem
above all my joys! R.

SECOND READING

A reading from the letter of St Paul to the Ephesians   2:4-10
You who were dead through your sins have been saved through grace.

God loved us with so much love that he was generous with his mercy:
when we were dead through our sins, he brought us to life with Christ – it
is through grace that you have been saved – and raised us up with him and
gave us a place with him in heaven, in Christ Jesus.

   This was to show for all ages to come, through his goodness towards us
in Christ Jesus, how infinitely rich he is in grace. Because it is by grace that
you have been saved, through faith; not by anything of your own, but by
a gift from God; not by anything that you have done, so that nobody can
claim the credit. We are God's work of art, created in Christ Jesus to live the
good life as from the beginning he had meant us to live it.

   The word of the Lord.

Gospel Acclamation   Jn 3:16
R. **Glory and praise to you, O Christ!**
God loved the world so much that he gave his only Son;
everyone who believes in him has eternal life.
R. **Glory and praise to you, O Christ!**

GOSPEL

A reading from the holy Gospel according to John   3:14-21

God sent his Son so that through him the world might be saved.

Jesus said to Nicodemus:

'The Son of Man must be lifted up
as Moses lifted up the serpent in the desert,
so that everyone who believes may have eternal life in him.
Yes, God loved the world so much
that he gave his only Son,
so that everyone who believes in him may not be lost
but may have eternal life.
For God sent his Son into the world
not to condemn the world,
but so that through him the world might be saved.
No one who believes in him will be condemned;
but whoever refuses to believe is condemned already,
because he has refused to believe
in the name of God's only Son.
On these grounds is sentence pronounced:
that though the light has come into the world
men have shown they prefer
darkness to the light
because their deeds were evil.
And indeed, everybody who does wrong
hates the light and avoids it,
for fear his actions should be exposed;
but the man who lives by the truth
comes out into the light,
so that it may be plainly seen that what he does is done in God.'

The Gospel of the Lord.

The Creed is said.

Prayer over the Offerings	Super oblata

We place before you with joy
    these offerings,
which bring eternal remedy, O Lord,
praying that we may both faithfully
    revere them
and present them to you, as is fitting,
for the salvation of all the world.
Through Christ our Lord.
	Remedii sempiterni munera,
	    Domine,
	lætantes offerimus,
	    suppliciter exorantes,
	ut eadem nos et fideliter venerari,
	et pro salute mundi congruenter
	    exhibere perficias.
	Per Christum Dominum nostrum.

Preface I or II of Lent, pp.48-51.

ALTERNATIVE PREFACE

If the alternative readings from Year A are used the following Preface is also used.

Preface: The Man Born Blind.	Praefatio: De caeco nato.

It is truly right and just,
    our duty and our salvation,
always and everywhere
    to give you thanks,
Lord, holy Father,
    almighty and eternal God,
through Christ our Lord.
	Vere dignum et iustum est,
	    aequum et salutare,
	nos tibi semper et ubique
	    gratias agere:
	Domine, sancte Pater,
	    omnipotens aeterne Deus:
	per Christum Dominum nostrum:

By the mystery of the Incarnation,
he has led the human race
    that walked in darkness
into the radiance of the faith
and has brought those born
    in slavery to ancient sin
through the waters of regeneration
to make them your adopted children.
	Qui genus humanum,
	    in tenebris ambulans,
	ad fidei claritatem
	per mysterium incarnationis adduxit,
	et, qui servi peccati
	    veteris nascebantur,
	per lavacrum regenerationis
	in filios adoptionis assumpsit.

Therefore, all creatures
    of heaven and earth
sing a new song in adoration,
and we, with all the host of Angels,
cry out, and without end acclaim:
	Propter quod caelestia tibi
	    atque terrestria
	canticum novum
	    concinunt adorando,
	et nos cum omni exercitu Angelorum
	proclamamus, sine fine dicentes:

Holy, Holy, Holy Lord God of hosts...	**Sanctus, Sanctus, Sanctus. . .**

Communion Antiphon Cf. Ps 121:3-4

Jerusalem is built as a city bonded
    as one together.
It is there that the tribes go up,
    the tribes of the Lord,
to praise the name of the Lord.

Prayer after Communion

O God, who enlighten everyone
    who comes into this world,
illuminate our hearts, we pray,
with the splendour of your grace,
that we may always ponder
what is worthy and pleasing
    to your majesty
and love you in all sincerity.
Through Christ our Lord.

Prayer over the People

Look upon those who call to you,
    O Lord,
and sustain the weak;
give life by your unfailing light
to those who walk in the shadow
    of death,
and bring those rescued by your
    mercy from every evil
to reach the highest good.
Through Christ our Lord.

Ant. ad communionem

Ierusalem, quæ ædificatur ut civitas,
cuius participatio eius in idipsum.
Illuc enim ascenderunt tribus,
    tribus Domini,
ad confitendum nomini tuo,
    Domine.

Post communionem

Deus, qui illuminas
    omnem hominem
venientem in hunc mundum,
illumina, quæsumus, corda nostra
    gratiæ tuæ splendore,
ut digna ac placita maiestati tuæ
    cogitare semper,
et te sincere diligere valeamus.
Per Christum Dominum nostrum.

Oratio super populum

Tuere, Domine, supplices tuos,
    sustenta fragiles,
et inter tenebras mortalium
    ambulantes
tua semper luce vivifica,
atque a malis omnibus
    clementer ereptos,
ad summa bona pervenire concede.
Per Christum Dominum nostrum.

In Ireland

17 March

SAINT PATRICK, BISHOP, PATRON OF IRELAND

From his days as a shepherd boy at Slemish right up to his death at Saul, Patrick was a witness to Jesus Christ. Not far from this spot, on the Hill of Slane, it is said that he lit, for the first time in Ireland, the Paschal Fire, so that the light of Christ might shine forth on all of Ireland and unite all of its people in the love of the one Jesus Christ. He is the Lord of history, the Light of the world, the Hope of the future of all humanity. In the words of the Easter Liturgy, celebrated for the first time in Ireland by Saint Patrick on the Hill of Slane, we greet Christ today: he is the Alpha and the Omega, the beginning of all things and their end. All time is his and all the ages. To him be glory for ever and ever. Lumen Christi: Deo gratias. *That he might be faithful to the end of his life to the light of Christ was Saint Patrick's prayer for himself. That the people of Ireland might remain faithful always to the light of Christ was his constant prayer for the Irish.*

(St John Paul II)

Solemnity

Entrance Antiphon   Gn 12:1-2

GO from your country and your kindred and your father's house to the land that I will show you.
I will make of you a great nation, and I will bless you,
and make your name great, so that you will be a blessing.

The Gloria in excelsis (Glory to God in the highest) is said.

Collect

Lord, through the work of Saint Patrick in Ireland
we have come to acknowledge the mystery of the one true God
and give thanks for our salvation in Christ;
grant by his prayers
that we who celebrate this festival
may keep alive the fire of faith he kindled.
Through our Lord Jesus Christ, your Son,
who lives and reigns with you in the unity of the Holy Spirit,
one God, for ever and ever.

FIRST READING

A reading from the prophet Jeremiah   1:4-9

Go now to those to whom I send you.

The word of the Lord was addressed to me, saying,
    'Before I formed you in the womb I knew you;
    before you came to birth I consecrated you;
    I have appointed you as prophet to the nations.'
    I said, 'Ah, Lord; look, I do not know how to speak: I am a child!'

But the Lord replied,
    'Do not say, "I am a child."
    Go now to those to whom I send you
    and say whatever I command you.
    Do not be afraid of them,
    for I am with you to protect you –
    it is the Lord who speaks!'

    Then the Lord put out his hand and touched my mouth and said to me:

    'There! I am putting my words into your mouth.'

    The word of the Lord.

Responsorial Psalm   Ps 116. R. Mk 16:15

R. **Go out to all the world,**
    and tell the Good News.
    O praise the Lord, all you nations,
    acclaim him all you peoples! R.

    Strong is his love for us;
    he is faithful for ever. R.

SECOND READING

A reading from the letter of St Paul to the Romans   10:9-18

Faith comes from what is preached, and what is preached comes from the word of Christ.

If your lips confess that Jesus is Lord and if you believe in your heart that God raised him from the dead, then you will be saved. By believing from the heart you are made righteous; by confessing with your lips you are saved. When scripture says: those who believe in him will have no cause for shame, it makes no distinction between Jew and Greek: all belong to the same Lord who is rich enough, however many ask his help, for everyone who calls on the name of the Lord will be saved.

But they will not ask his help unless they believe in him, and they will not believe in him unless they have heard him, and they will not hear him unless they get a preacher, and they will never have a preacher unless one is sent, but as scripture says: The footsteps of those who bring good news are a welcome sound. Not everyone, of course, listens to the Good News. As Isaiah says: Lord, how many believe what we proclaimed? So faith comes from what is preached, and what is preached comes from the word of Christ.

Let me put the question: is it possible that they did not hear? Indeed they did; in the words of the psalm, their voice has gone out through all the earth, and their message to the ends of the world.

The word of the Lord.

Gospel Acclamation   Mt 28:19-20

R. **Glory to you, O Christ, you are the Word of God.**
Go, make disciples of all the nations, says the Lord;
I am with you always, yes, to the end of time.
R. **Glory to you, O Christ, you are the Word of God.**

GOSPEL

A reading from the holy Gospel according to Mark   16:15-20
He was taken up into heaven: there at the right hand of God he took his place.

Jesus showed himself to the Eleven, and said to them, 'Go out to the whole world; proclaim the Good News to all creation. He who believes and is baptised will be saved; he who does not believe will be condemned. These are the signs that will be associated with believers: in my name they will cast out devils; they will have the gift of tongues; they will pick up snakes in their hands, and be unharmed should they drink deadly poison; they will lay their hands on the sick, who will recover.'

And so the Lord Jesus, after he had spoken to them, was taken up into heaven: there at the right hand of God he took his place, while they, going out, preached everywhere, the Lord working with them and confirming the word by the signs that accompanied it.

The Gospel of the Lord.

The Creed is said.

This second set of proper readings, from Year A, may also be read in Year B and Year C.

FIRST READING

A reading from the book of Ecclesiasticus   39:6-10

His memory will not disappear, generation after generation his name will live.

If it is the will of the great Lord,
the scholar will be filled with the spirit of understanding,
he will shower forth words of wisdom,
and in prayer give thanks to the Lord.
He will grow upright in purpose and learning,
he will ponder the Lord's hidden mysteries.
He will display the instruction he has received,
taking his pride in the Law of the Lord's covenant.
Many will praise his understanding,
and it will never be forgotten.
His memory will not disappear,
generation after generation his name will live.
Nations will proclaim his wisdom,
the assembly will celebrate his praises.

   The word of the Lord.

Responsorial Psalm   Ps 115:12-19. R. 12

R. **How can I repay the Lord for his goodness to me?**
   How can I repay the Lord
   for his goodness to me?
   The cup of salvation I will raise;
   I will call on the Lord's name. R.

   My vows to the Lord I will fulfil
   before all his people.
   O precious in the eyes of the Lord
   is the death of his faithful. R.

   Your servant, O Lord, your servant am I;
   you have loosened my bonds.
   A thanksgiving sacrifice I make;
   I will call on the Lord's name. R.

   My vows to the Lord I will fulfil
   before all his people,
   in the courts of the house of the Lord,
   in your midst, O Jerusalem. R.

SECOND READING

A reading from the second letter of St Paul to Timothy   4:1-8

Refute falsehood, correct error, call to obedience - but do all with patience and with the intention of teaching.

Before God and before Christ Jesus who is to be judge of the living and the dead, I put this duty to you, in the name of his Appearing and of his kingdom: proclaim the message and, welcome or unwelcome, insist on it. Refute falsehood, correct error, call to obedience – but do all with patience and with the intention of teaching. The time is sure to come when, far from being content with sound teaching, people will be avid for the latest novelty and collect themselves a whole series of teachers according to their own tastes; and then, instead of listening to the truth, they will turn to myths. Be careful always to choose the right course; be brave under trials; make the preaching of the Good News your life's work, in thoroughgoing service.

As for me, my life is already being poured away as a libation, and the time has come for me to be gone. I have fought the good fight to the end; I have run the race to the finish; I have kept the faith; all there is to come now is the crown of righteousness reserved for me, which the Lord, the righteous judge, will give me on that Day; and not only to me but to all those who have longed for his Appearing.

The word of the Lord.

Gospel Acclamation   Jm 1:21

R. **Glory to you, O Christ, you are the Word of God!**
Accept and submit to the word which has been planted in you
and can save your souls.
R. **Glory to you, O Christ, you are the Word of God!**

GOSPEL

A reading from the holy Gospel according to Matthew   13:24-32

It is the smallest of all seeds, but when it has grown it is the greatest of shrubs.

Jesus put a parable before the crowds, 'The kingdom of heaven may be compared to a man who sowed good seed in his field. While everybody was asleep his enemy came, sowed darnel all among the wheat, and made off. When the new wheat sprouted and ripened, the darnel appeared as well. The owner's servants went to him and said, "Sir, was it not good seed that you sowed in your field? If so, where does the darnel come from?" "Some enemy has done this" he answered. And the servants said, "Do you want us to go and weed it out?" But he said, "No, because when you weed out the darnel you might pull up the wheat with it. Let them both grow till the harvest; and at harvest time I shall say to the reapers: First collect the darnel and tie it in bundles to be burnt, then gather the wheat into my barn.'''

He put another parable before them, 'The kingdom of heaven is like a mustard seed which a man took and sowed in his field. It is the smallest of all the seeds, but when it has grown it is the biggest shrub of all and becomes a tree so that the birds of the air come and shelter in its branches.'

The Gospel of the Lord.

The Creed is said.

Prayer over the Offerings

Lord, accept this pure sacrifice
which, through the labours of Saint Patrick,
your grateful people make
to the glory of your name.
Through Christ our Lord.

Preface

It is truly right and just, our duty and our salvation,
always and everywhere to give you thanks,
Lord, holy Father, almighty and eternal God,
and proclaim your greatness with due praise
as we honour Saint Patrick.

For you drew him through daily prayer
in captivity and hardship
to know you as a loving Father.

You chose him out of all the world
to return to the land of his captors,
that they might acknowledge Jesus Christ, their Redeemer.

In the power of your Spirit you directed his paths
to win the sons and daughters of the Irish
to the service of the Triune God.

And so, with the Angels and Archangels,
and with the great multitude of the Saints,
we sing the hymn of your praise, as without end we acclaim:

Holy, Holy, Holy Lord God of hosts ...

Communion Antiphon

Cf. Mt 8:11

Many will come from east and west
and sit down with Abraham, Isaac and Jacob
at the feast in the Kingdom of Heaven, says the Lord.

Prayer after Communion

Strengthen us, O Lord, by this sacrament
so that we may profess the faith taught by Saint Patrick
and to proclaim it in our way of living.
Through Christ our Lord.

Solemn Blessing

May God the Father, who called us together
to celebrate this feast of Saint Patrick,
bless you, protect you and keep you faithful.

R. **Amen.**

May Christ the Lord, the High King of Heaven,
be near you at all times and shield you from evil.

R. **Amen.**

May the Holy Spirit, who is the source of all holiness,
make you rich in the love of God's people.

R. **Amen.**

And may the blessing of almighty God,
the Father, and the Son, ✠ and the Holy Spirit,
come down on you and remain with you for ever.

R. **Amen.**

---

18 March

FIFTH SUNDAY OF LENT

*On this Fifth Sunday of Lent, John the Evangelist draws our attention with
a curious detail: some "Greeks", of the Jewish religion, who have come to
Jerusalem for the feast of Passover, turn to Philip and say to him: "We wish
to see Jesus". These words, like so many others in the Gospels, go beyond this
particular episode and express something universal; they reveal a desire that
passes through the ages and cultures, a desire present in the heart of so many
people who have heard of Christ, but have not yet encountered him. To all
these people we can offer three things: the Gospel, the Crucifix and the witness
of our faith, poor but sincere. The Gospel: there we can encounter Jesus, listen
to him, know him. The Crucifix: the sign of the love of Jesus who gave himself
for us. And then a faith that is expressed in simple gestures of fraternal charity.
But mainly in the coherence of life, between what we say and what we do.*

(Pope Francis)

290 FIFTH SUNDAY OF LENT

Entrance Antiphon Cf. Ps 42:1-2	Ant. ad introitum
GIVE me justice, O God, and plead my cause against a nation that is faithless. From the deceitful and cunning rescue me, for you, O God, are my strength.	IUDICA me, Deus, et discerne causam meam de gente non sancta; ab homine iniquo et doloso eripe me, quia tu es Deus meus et fortitudo mea.

The Gloria in excelsis (Glory to God in the highest) is not said.

Collect	Collecta
By your help, we beseech you, Lord our God, may we walk eagerly in that same charity with which, out of love for the world, your Son handed himself over to death. Through our Lord Jesus Christ, your Son, who lives and reigns with you in the unity of the Holy Spirit, one God, for ever and ever.	Quæsumus, Domine Deus noster, ut in illa caritate qua Filius tuus diligens mundum morti se tradidit, inveniamur ipsi, te opitulante, alacriter ambulantes. Per Dominum nostrum Iesum Christum Filium tuum, qui tecum vivit et regnat in unitate Spiritus Sancti, Deus, per omnia sæcula sæculorum.

The readings for Year B are included in full below. The readings for Year A may also be used on this Sunday: Ezk 37:12-14; Ps 129. R. v.7; Rom 8:8-11; Jn 11:25-26; Jn 11:1-45 or Jn 11:3-7,17,20-27,33-45. If this is done, the Preface: Lazarus (p.293) and Communion Antiphon: Cf. Jn 11:26 as in Year A are also used.

FIRST READING

A reading from the prophet Jeremiah   31:31-34

I will make a new covenant and never call their sin to mind.

See, the days are coming – it is the Lord who speaks – when I will make a new covenant with the House of Israel and the House of Judah, but not a covenant like the one I made with their ancestors on the day I took them by the hand to bring them out of the land of Egypt. They broke that covenant of mine, so I had to show them who was master. It is the Lord who speaks. No, this is the covenant I will make with the House of Israel when those days arrive – it is the Lord who speaks. Deep within them I will plant my Law, writing it on their hearts. Then I will be their God and they shall be my people. There will be no further need for neighbour to try to teach neighbour, or brother to say to brother, 'Learn to know the Lord!' No, they

will all know me, the least no less than the greatest – it is the Lord who
speaks – since I will forgive their iniquity and never call their sin to mind.

The word of the Lord.

Responsorial Psalm   Ps 50:3-4,12-15. R. v.12

R. **A pure heart create for me, O God.**

Have mercy on me, God, in your kindness.
In your compassion blot out my offence.
O wash me more and more from my guilt
and cleanse me from my sin. R.

A pure heart create for me, O God,
put a steadfast spirit within me.
Do not cast me away from your presence,
nor deprive me of your holy spirit. R.

Give me again the joy of your help;
with a spirit of fervour sustain me,
that I may teach transgressors your ways
and sinners may return to you. R.

SECOND READING

A reading from the letter to the Hebrews   5:7-9
He learnt to obey and became for all the source of eternal salvation.

During his life on earth, Christ offered up prayer and entreaty, aloud and
in silent tears, to the one who had the power to save him out of death, and
he submitted so humbly that his prayer was heard. Although he was Son,
he learnt to obey through suffering; but having been made perfect, he
became for all who obey him the source of eternal salvation.

The word of the Lord.

Gospel Acclamation   Jn 12:26

R. **Glory to you, O Christ, you are the Word of God!**
If a man serves me, says the Lord, he must follow me;
wherever I am, my servant will be there too.
R. **Glory to you, O Christ, you are the Word of God!**

GOSPEL

A reading from the holy Gospel according to John   12:20-30

If a grain of wheat falls on the ground and dies, it yields a rich harvest.

Among those who went up to worship at the festival were some Greeks.
These approached Philip, who came from Bethsaida in Galilee, and put this
request to him, 'Sir, we should like to see Jesus.' Philip went to tell Andrew,
and Andrew and Philip together went to tell Jesus. Jesus replied to them:

'Now the hour has come
for the Son of Man to be glorified.
I tell you, most solemnly,
unless a wheat grain falls on the ground and dies,
it remains only a single grain;
but if it dies,
it yields a rich harvest.
Anyone who loves his life loses it;
anyone who hates his life in this world
will keep it for the eternal life.
If a man serves me, he must follow me,
wherever I am, my servant will be there too.
If anyone serves me, my Father will honour him.
Now my soul is troubled.
What shall I say:
Father, save me from this hour?
But it was for this very reason that I have come to this hour.
Father, glorify your name!'

A voice came from heaven, 'I have glorified it, and I will glorify it again.'
People standing by, who heard this, said it was a clap of thunder; others
said, 'It was an angel speaking to him.' Jesus answered, 'It was not for my
sake that this voice came, but for yours.

'Now sentence is being passed on this world;
now the prince of this world is to be overthrown.
And when I am lifted up from the earth,
I shall draw all men to myself.'

By these words he indicated the kind of death he would die.

The Gospel of the Lord.

The Creed is said.

Prayer over the Offerings

Hear us, almighty God,
and, having instilled in your servants
the teachings of the Christian faith,
graciously purify them
by the working of this sacrifice.
Through Christ our Lord.

Preface I or II of Lent, pp.48-51.

Super oblata

Exaudi nos, omnipotens Deus,
et famulos tuos, quos fidei
    christianæ eruditionibus imbuisti,
huius sacrificii tribuas
    operatione mundari.
Per Christum Dominum nostrum.

ALTERNATIVE PREFACE

If the alternative readings from Year A are used the following Preface is also used.

Preface: Lazarus.

It is truly right and just,
    our duty and our salvation,
always and everywhere
    to give you thanks,
Lord, holy Father,
    almighty and eternal God,
through Christ our Lord.

For as true man he wept
    for Lazarus his friend
and as eternal God raised him
    from the tomb,
just as, taking pity on
    the human race,
he leads us by sacred mysteries
    to new life.

Through him the host
    of Angels adores your majesty
and rejoices in your presence
    for ever.
May our voices, we pray,
    join with theirs
in one chorus of exultant praise,
    as we acclaim:

Holy, Holy, Holy Lord God of hosts...

Praefatio: De Lazaro.

Vere dignum et iustum est,
    aequum et salutare,
nos tibi semper
    et ubique gratias agere:
Domine, sancte Pater,
    omnipotens aeterne Deus:
per Christum Dominum nostrum:

Ipse enim verus homo Lazarum
    flevit amicum,
et Deus aeternus
    e tumulo suscitavit,
qui, humani generis miseratus,
ad novam vitam sacris
    mysteriis nos adducit.

Per quem maiestatem tuam adorat
    exercitus Angelorum,
ante conspectum tuum
    in aeternitate laetantium.
Cum quibus et nostras voces
    ut admitti iubeas, deprecamur,
socia exsultatione dicentes:

Sanctus, Sanctus, Sanctus. . .

Communion Antiphon   Jn 12:24

Amen, Amen I say to you:
   Unless a grain of wheat
falls to the ground and dies,
   it remains a single grain.
But if it dies, it bears much fruit.

Prayer after Communion

We pray, almighty God,
that we may always be counted
   among the members of Christ,
in whose Body and Blood
   we have communion.
Who lives and reigns
   for ever and ever.

Prayer over the People

Bless, O Lord, your people,
who long for the gift of your mercy,
and grant that what,
   at your prompting, they desire
they may receive
   by your generous gift.
Through Christ our Lord.

Ant. ad communionem

Amen, amen dico vobis:
   Nisi granum frumenti
cadens in terram mortuum fuerit,
   ipsum solum manet;
si autem mortuum fuerit,
   multum fructum affert.

Post communionem

Quæsumus, omnipotens Deus,
ut inter eius membra
   semper numeremur,
cuius Corpori communicamus
   et Sanguini.
Qui vivit et regnat
   in sæcula sæculorum.

Oratio super populum

Benedic, Domine, plebem tuam,
quæ munus tuæ
   miserationis exspectat,
et concede, ut, quod,
   te inspirante, desiderat,
te largiente percipiat.
Per Christum Dominum nostrum.

19 March

SAINT JOSEPH,
SPOUSE OF THE BLESSED VIRGIN MARY

Joseph was for Jesus the example and the teacher of the wisdom that is nourished by the Word of God. We could ponder how Joseph formed the little Jesus to listen to the Sacred Scriptures, above all by accompanying him on Saturday to the Synagogue in Nazareth. Joseph accompanied Jesus so that he would listen to the Word of God in the Synagogue. And lastly, the dimension of "grace". St Luke always says of Jesus: "the favour of God was upon him" (2:40). Here, of course, the role reserved to St Joseph is more limited than it was in the area of age and wisdom. But it would be a grave error to think that a father and mother can do nothing to form their child to grow in the grace of God. Dear brothers and sisters, Joseph's mission is certainly unique and unrepeatable, because Jesus is absolutely unique. And yet, in his guardianship of Jesus, forming him to grow in age, wisdom and grace, he is a model for every educator, especially every father. St Joseph is the model of the educator and the dad, the father. I, therefore, entrust to his protection, all parents, priests — who are fathers — and those who have an educational role in the Church and in society.

(Pope Francis)

Solemnity

Entrance Antiphon	Cf. Lk 12:42	Ant. ad introitum

BEHOLD, a faithful and prudent steward, whom the Lord set over his household.

ECCE fidelis servus et prudens, quem constituit Dominus super familiam suam.

The Gloria in excelsis (Glory to God in the highest) is said.

Collect	Collecta

Grant, we pray, almighty God, that by Saint Joseph's intercession your Church may constantly watch over
the unfolding of the mysteries of human salvation,
whose beginnings you entrusted to his faithful care.
Through our Lord Jesus Christ, your Son,

Præsta, quæsumus,
    omnipotens Deus,
ut humanæ salutis mysteria,
cuius primordia beati Ioseph fideli
    custodiæ commisisti,
Ecclesia tua, ipso intercedente,
    iugiter servet implenda.

Per Dominum nostrum Iesum
    Christum Filium tuum,

who lives and reigns with you
    in the unity of the Holy Spirit,
one God, for ever and ever.
	qui tecum vivit et regnat
	    in unitate Spiritus Sancti,
	Deus, per omnia sæcula sæculorum.

FIRST READING

A reading from the second book of Samuel   7:4-5,12-14,16

The Lord will give him the throne of his ancestor David.

The word of the Lord came to Nathan:

'Go and tell my servant David, "Thus the Lord speaks: When your days are ended and you are laid to rest with your ancestors, I will preserve the offspring of your body after you and make his sovereignty secure. (It is he who shall build a house for my name and I will make his royal throne secure for ever.) I will be a father to him and he a son to me. Your House and your sovereignty will always stand secure before me and your throne be established for ever.'''

The word of the Lord.

Responsorial Psalm   Ps 88:2-5,27,29. R. v.37

R. **His dynasty shall last for ever.**

I will sing for ever of your love, O Lord;
through all ages my mouth will proclaim your truth.
Of this I am sure, that your love lasts for ever,
that your truth is firmly established as the heavens. R.

'I have made a covenant with my chosen one;
I have sworn to David my servant:
I will establish your dynasty for ever
and set up your throne through all ages.' R.

He will say to me: 'You are my father,
my God, the rock who saves me.'
I will keep my love for him always;
for him my covenant shall endure. R.

SECOND READING

A reading from the letter of St Paul to the Romans   4:13,16-18,22

Though it seemed Abraham's hope could not be fulfilled, he hoped and he believed.

The promise of inheriting the world was not made to Abraham and his descendants on account of any law but on account of the righteousness which consists in faith. That is why what fulfils the promise depends on faith, so that it may be a free gift and be available to all of Abraham's descendants, not only those who belong to the Law but also to those who belong to the faith of Abraham who is the father of all of us. As scripture says: I have made you the ancestor of many nations – Abraham is our father in the eyes of God, in whom he put his faith, and who brings the dead to life and calls into being what does not exist.

Though it seemed Abraham's hope could not be fulfilled, he hoped and he believed, and through doing so he did become the father of many nations exactly as he had been promised: Your descendants will be as many as the stars. This is the faith that was 'considered as justifying him'.

The word of the Lord.

Gospel Acclamation   Ps 83:5
R. **Glory and praise to you, O Christ.**
They are happy who dwell in your house, O Lord,
for ever singing your praise.
R. **Glory and praise to you, O Christ.**

GOSPEL

A reading from the holy Gospel according to Matthew   1:16,18-21,24
Joseph did what the angel of the Lord had told him to do.

Jacob was the father of Joseph the husband of Mary; of her was born Jesus who is called Christ.

This is how Jesus Christ came to be born. His mother Mary was betrothed to Joseph; but before they came to live together she was found to be with child through the Holy Spirit. Her husband Joseph, being a man of honour and wanting to spare her publicity, decided to divorce her informally. He had made up his mind to do this when the angel of the Lord appeared to him in a dream and said, 'Joseph son of David, do not be afraid to take Mary home as your wife, because she has conceived what is in her by the Holy Spirit. She will give birth to a son and you must name him Jesus, because he is the one who is to save his people from their sins.' When Joseph woke up he did what the angel of the Lord had told him to do.

The Gospel of the Lord

ALTERNATIVE GOSPEL

A reading from the holy Gospel according to Luke   2:41-51
See how worried your father and I have been, looking for you.

Every year the parents of Jesus used to go to Jerusalem for the feast of the Passover. When he was twelve years old, they went up for the feast as usual. When they were on their way home after the feast, the boy Jesus stayed behind in Jerusalem without his parents knowing it. They assumed he was with the caravan, and it was only after a day's journey that they went to look for him among their relations and acquaintances. When they failed to find him they went back to Jerusalem looking for him everywhere.

Three days later, they found him in the Temple, sitting among the doctors, listening to them, and asking them questions; and all those who heard him were astounded at his intelligence and his replies. They were overcome when they saw him and his mother said to him, 'My child, why have you done this to us? See how worried your father and I have been, looking for you.' 'Why were you looking for me?' he replied. 'Did you not know that I must be busy with my Father's affairs?' But they did not understand what he meant.

He then went down with them and came to Nazareth and lived under their authority.

The Gospel of the Lord.

The Creed is said.

Prayer over the Offerings	Super oblata

We pray, O Lord,
that, just as Saint Joseph
    served with loving care
your Only Begotten Son,
    born of the Virgin Mary,
so we may be worthy to minister
with a pure heart at your altar.
Through Christ our Lord.
	Quæsumus, Domine, ut,
	    sicut beatus Ioseph
	Unigenito tuo,
	    nato de Maria Virgine,
	pia devotione deserviit,
	ita et nos mundo corde
	tuis altaribus mereamur ministrare.
	Per Christum Dominum nostrum.

Preface: The mission of Saint Joseph.	Præfatio: De missione sancti Ioseph.

It is truly right and just,
    our duty and our salvation,
always and everywhere
    to give you thanks,
Lord, holy Father,
    almighty and eternal God,
and on the Solemnity of Saint Joseph
to give you fitting praise,
to glorify you and bless you.
	Vere dignum et iustum est,
	    æquum et salutare,
	nos tibi semper et ubique
	    gratias agere:
	Domine, sancte Pater,
	    omnipotens æterne Deus:
	Et te in sollemnitate beati Ioseph
	debitis magnificare præconiis,
	    benedicere et prædicare.

For this just man was given by you
as spouse to the Virgin Mother of God
and set as a wise and faithful servant
in charge of your household
to watch like a father over your
   Only Begotten Son,
who was conceived by the
   overshadowing of the Holy Spirit,
our Lord Jesus Christ.

Through him the Angels praise
   your majesty,
Dominions adore and Powers
   tremble before you.
Heaven and the Virtues of heaven
   and the blessed Seraphim
worship together with exultation.

May our voices, we pray,
   join with theirs
in humble praise, as we acclaim:

Holy, Holy, Holy Lord God of hosts...

Qui et vir iustus, a te Deiparæ
   Virgini Sponsus est datus,
et fidelis servus ac prudens,
super Familiam tuam est constitutus,
ut Unigenitum tuum,
Sancti Spiritus obumbratione
   conceptum,
paterna vice custodiret,
Iesum Christum Dominum nostrum.

Per quem maiestatem tuam
   laudant Angeli,
adorant Dominationes,
   tremunt Potestates.
Cæli cælorumque Virtutes,
   ac beata Seraphim,
socia exsultatione concelebrant.

Cum quibus et nostras voces ut
   admitti iubeas, deprecamur,
supplici confessione dicentes:

Sanctus, Sanctus, Sanctus. . .

Communion Antiphon Mt 25:21

Ant. ad communionem

Well done, good and faithful servant.
Come, share your master's joy.

Euge, serve bone et fidelis:
   intra in gaudium Domini tui.

Prayer after Communion

Post communionem

Defend with unfailing protection,
O Lord, we pray,
the family you have nourished
with food from this altar,
as they rejoice at the Solemnity
   of Saint Joseph,
and graciously keep safe your gifts
   among them.
Through Christ our Lord.

Familiam tuam, quæsumus,
   Domine,
quam de beati Ioseph
   sollemnitate lætantem
ex huius altaris alimonia satiasti,
perpetua protectione defende,
et tua in ea propitiatus
   dona custodi.
Per Christum Dominum nostru.

25 March

PALM SUNDAY OF THE PASSION OF THE LORD

At the heart of this celebration, which seems so festive, are the words we heard in the Letter to the Philippians: "He humbled himself" . These words show us God's way and, consequently, that which must be the way of Christians: it is humility. A way which constantly amazes and disturbs us: we will never get used to a humble God! God humbles himself to walk with his people, to put up with their infidelity. This is clear when we read the story of the Exodus. This week, Holy Week, which leads us to Easter, we will take this path of Jesus's own humiliation. Only in this way will this week be "holy" for us too! This is God's way, the way of humility...In the end, humility also means service. It means making room for God by stripping oneself, "emptying oneself", as Scripture says. This – the pouring out of oneself - is the greatest humiliation of all.

(Pope Francis)

On this day the Church recalls the entrance of Christ the Lord into Jerusalem to accomplish his Paschal Mystery. Accordingly, the memorial of this entrance of the Lord takes place at all Masses, by means of the Procession or the Solemn Entrance before the principal Mass or the Simple Entrance before other Masses. The Solemn Entrance, but not the Procession, may be repeated before other Masses that are usually celebrated with a large gathering of people.

It is desirable that, where neither the Procession nor the Solemn Entrance can take place, there be a sacred celebration of the Word of God on the messianic entrance and on the Passion of the Lord, either on Saturday evening or on Sunday at a convenient time.

The Commemoration of the Lord's Entrance into Jerusalem

First Form: The Procession

At an appropriate hour, a gathering takes place at a smaller church or other suitable place other than inside the church to which the procession will go. The faithful hold branches in their hands.

Wearing the red sacred vestments as for Mass, the Priest and the Deacon, accompanied by other ministers, approach the place where the people are gathered. Instead of the chasuble, the Priest may wear a cope, which he leaves aside when the procession is over, and puts on a chasuble.

Meanwhile, the following antiphon or another appropriate chant is sung.

Ant. Mt 21:9	Ant.
Hosanna to the Son of David;	Hosanna filio David:
blessed is he who comes	benedictus qui venit
in the name of the Lord,	in nomine Domini.
the King of Israel.	Rex Israel:
Hosanna in the highest.	Hosanna in excelsis.

After this, the Priest and people sign themselves, while the Priest says: In the name of the Father, and of the Son, and of the Holy Spirit. Then he greets the people in the usual way. A brief address is given, in which the faithful are invited to participate actively and consciously in the celebration of this day, in these or similar words:

Dear brethren (brothers and sisters),	Fratres carissimi,
since the beginning of Lent until now	postquam iam ab initio
we have prepared our hearts	Quadragesimæ corda nostra
by penance and charitable works.	pænitentia et operibus
Today we gather together to herald	caritatis præparavimus,
with the whole Church	hodierna die congregamur,
the beginning of the celebration	ut cum tota Ecclesia præludamus
of our Lord's Paschal Mystery,	paschale Domini nostri mysterium,
that is to say, of his Passion	eius nempe passionem
and Resurrection.	atque resurrectionem,
For it was to accomplish this mystery	ad quod implendum
that he entered his own city	ipse ingressus est civitatem
of Jerusalem.	suam Ierusalem.
Therefore, with all faith	Quare cum omni fide et devotione
and devotion,	memoriam agentes
let us commemorate	huius salutiferi ingressus,
the Lord's entry into the city	sequamur Dominum,
for our salvation,	ut, per gratiam consortes
following in his footsteps,	effecti crucis,
so that, being made by his grace	partem habeamus resurrectionis
partakers of the Cross,	et vitæ.
we may have a share also in his	
Resurrection and in his life.	

After the address, the Priest says one of the following prayers with hands extended.

Let us pray.

Almighty ever-living God,
sanctify ✠ these branches
   with your blessing,
that we, who follow Christ the King
   in exultation,
may reach the eternal Jerusalem
   through him.
Who lives and reigns
   for ever and ever.
R. Amen.

Or:

Increase the faith of those who
   place their hope in you, O God,
and graciously hear the prayers
   of those who call on you,
that we, who today hold high
   these branches
to hail Christ in his triumph,
may bear fruit for you by good
   works accomplished in him.
Who lives and reigns
   for ever and ever.
R. Amen.

Oremus.

Omnipotens sempiterne Deus,
hos palmites tua
   benedictione ✠ sanctifica,
ut nos, qui Christum Regem
   exsultando prosequimur,
per ipsum valeamus ad æternam
   Ierusalem pervenire.
Qui vivit et regnat
   in sæcula sæculorum.
R. Amen.

Vel:

Auge fidem in te sperantium, Deus,
et supplicum preces
   clementer exaudi,
ut, qui hodie Christo triumphanti
   palmites exhibemus,
in ipso fructus tibi bonorum
   operum afferamus.
Qui vivit et regnat
   in sæcula sæculorum.
R. Amen.

He sprinkles the branches with holy water without saying anything.

Then a Deacon or, if there is no Deacon, a Priest, proclaims in the usual way the Gospel concerning the Lord's entrance according to one of the four Gospels. If appropriate, incense may be used.

A reading from the holy Gospel according to Mark   11:1-10

Blessings on him who comes in the name of the Lord.

When they drew near to Jerusalem,
to Bethphage and Bethany, at the Mount of Olives,
Jesus sent two of his disciples, and said to them,
'Go into the village opposite you,
and immediately as you enter it
you will find a colt tied, on which no one has ever sat;
untie it and bring it.

If any one says to you,
"Why are you doing this?" say,
"The Lord has need of it
and will send it back here immediately."'
And they went away,
and found a colt tied at the door out in the open street;
and they untied it.
And those who stood there said to them,
'What are you doing, untying the colt?'
And they told them what Jesus had said;
and they let them go.
And they brought the colt to Jesus,
and threw their garments on it;
and he sat upon it.
And many spread their garments on the road,
and others spread leafy branches
which they had cut from the fields.
And those who went before
and those who followed cried out,
'Hosanna!
Blessed is he who comes in the name of the Lord!
Blessed is the kingdom of our father David that is coming!
Hosanna in the highest!'

    The Gospel of the Lord.

ALTERNATIVE GOSPEL

A reading from the holy Gospel according to John   12:12-16
Blessings on him who comes in the name of the Lord.

A great crowd who had come to the feast
heard that Jesus was coming to Jerusalem.
So they took branches of palm trees
and went out to meet him, crying,
'Hosanna!
Blessed is he who comes in the name of the Lord,
even the king of Israel!'
And Jesus found a young ass and sat upon it; as is written,

'Fear not, daughter of Sion;
behold, your king is coming,
sitting on an ass's colt!'
His disciples did not understand this at first;
but when Jesus was glorified,
then they remembered that this had been written of him
and had been done to him.

The Gospel of the Lord.

After the Gospel, a brief homily may be given. Then, to begin the Procession, an invitation may be given by a Priest or a Deacon or a lay minister, in these or similar words:

Dear brethren (brothers and sisters), like the crowds who acclaimed Jesus in Jerusalem, let us go forth in peace.	Imitemur, fratres carissimi, turbas acclamantes Iesum, et procedamus in pace.
Or:	Vel:
Let us go forth in peace.	Procedamus in pace.
In this latter case, all respond:	
In the name of Christ. Amen.	In nomine Christi. Amen.

The Procession to the church where Mass will be celebrated then sets off in the usual way. If incense is used, the thurifer goes first, carrying a thurible with burning incense, then an acolyte or another minister, carrying a cross decorated with palm branches according to local custom, between two ministers with lighted candles. Then follow the Deacon carrying the Book of the Gospels, the Priest with the ministers, and, after them, all the faithful carrying branches.

As the Procession moves forward, the following or other suitable chants in honour of Christ the King are sung by the choir and people.

Antiphon 1	Antiphona 1
The children of the Hebrews, carrying olive branches, went to meet the Lord, crying out and saying: Hosanna in the highest.	Pueri Hebræorum, portantes ramos olivarum, obviaverunt Domino, clamantes et dicentes: Hosanna in excelsis.

If appropriate, this antiphon is repeated between the strophes of the following Psalm.

PSALM 23

The Lord's is the earth
  and its fullness,*
the world, and those who dwell in it.
It is he who set it on the seas;*
on the rivers he made it firm. Ant.

Who shall climb the mountain
  of the Lord?*
The clean of hands and pure of heart,
whose soul is not set on vain things,†
who has not sworn
  deceitful words.* Ant.

Blessings from the Lord
  shall he receive,*
and right reward from the God
  who saves him.
Such are the people who seek him,*
who seek the face of the God
  of Jacob. Ant.

O gates, lift high your heads,†
grow higher, ancient doors.*
Let him enter, the king of glory!
Who is this king of glory?*
The Lord, the mighty, the valiant;
the Lord, the valiant in war. Ant.

O gates, lift high your heads;†
grow higher, ancient doors.*
Let him enter, the king of glory!
Who is this king of glory?*
He, the Lord of hosts,
he is the king of glory. Ant.

Antiphon 2

The children of the Hebrews spread
  their garments on the road,
crying out and saying:
  Hosanna to the Son of David;
blessed is he who comes
  in the name of the Lord.

Domini est terra et plenitudo eius,*
orbis terrarum et qui habitant in eo.
Quia ipse super maria fundavit eum*
et super flumina firmavit eum. Ant.

Quis ascendet in montem Domini,*
aut quis stabit in loco sancto eius?
Innocens manibus et mundo corde,†
qui non levavit ad vana
  animam suam,*
nec iuravit in dolum. Ant.

Hic accipiet benedictionem
  a Domino*
et iustificationem a Deo salutari suo.
Hæc est generatio
  quærentium eum,*
quærentium faciem Dei Iacob. Ant.

Attollite, portæ, capita vestra,†
et elevamini, portæ æternales,*
et introibit rex gloriæ.
Quis est iste rex gloriæ?*
Dominus fortis et potens,
Dominus potens in prœlio. Ant.

Attollite, portæ, capita vestra, †
et elevamini, portæ æternales,*
et introibit rex gloriæ.
Quis est iste rex gloriæ?*
Dominus virtutum ipse est
  rex gloriæ. Ant.

Antiphona 2

Pueri Hebræorum vestimenta
  prosternebant in via,
et clamabant dicentes:
  Hosanna filio David;
benedictus, qui venit
  in nomine Domini.

If appropriate, this antiphon is repeated between the strophes of the following Psalm.

PSALM 46

All peoples, clap your hands.*
Cry to God with shouts of joy!
For the Lord, the Most high,
    is awesome,*
the great king over all the earth. Ant.

He humbles peoples under us*
and nations under our feet.
Our heritage he chose for us,*
the pride of Jacob whom he loves.
God goes up with shouts of joy.*
The Lord goes up
    with trumpet blast. Ant.

Sing praise for God; sing praise!*
Sing praise to our king; sing praise!
God is king of all earth.*
Sing praise with all your skill. Ant.

God reigns over the nations.*
God sits upon his holy throne.
The princes of the peoples
    are assembled
with the people of the God
    of Abraham. †
The rulers of the earth belong
    to God,*
who is greatly exalted. Ant.

Omnes gentes, plaudite manibus,*
iubilate Deo in voce exsultationis,
quoniam Dominus Altissimus,
    terribilis,*
rex magnus super omnem terram. Ant.

Subiecit populos nobis,*
et gentes sub pedibus nostris.
Elegit nobis hereditatem nostram,*
gloriam Iacob, quem dilexit.
Ascendit Deus in iubilo,*
et Dominus in voce tubæ. Ant.

Psallite Deo, psallite;*
psallite regi nostro, psallite.
Quoniam rex omnis terræ Deus,*
psallite sapienter. Ant.

Regnavit Deus super gentes,*
Deus sedet super sedem
    sanctam suam.
Principes populorum congregati sunt
cum populo Dei Abraham,†
quoniam Dei sunt scuta terræ:*
vehementer elevatus est. Ant.

Hymn to Christ the King
Chorus:

Glory and honour and praise be to
    you, Christ, King and Redeemer,
to whom young children cried out
    loving Hosannas with joy.
All repeat: Glory and honour. . .
Chorus:

Israel's King are you, King David's
    magnificent offspring;
you are the ruler who come blest
    in the name of the Lord.
All repeat: Glory and honour. . .

Hymnus ad Christum Regem

Gloria, laus et honor tibi sit,
    rex Christe redemptor,
cui puerile decus prompsit
    Hosanna pium.
Omnes repetunt: Gloria, laus. . .

Israel es tu rex, Davidis
    et inclita proles,
nomine qui in Domini,
    rex benedicte, venis.
Omnes repetunt: Gloria, laus. . .

Chorus:

Heavenly hosts on high unite
    in singing your praises;
men and women on earth
    and all creation join in.
All repeat: Glory and honour. . .

Chorus:

Bearing branches of palm, Hebrews
    came crowding to greet you;
see how with prayers and hymns
    we come to pay you our vows.
All repeat: Glory and honour. . .

Chorus:

They offered gifts of praise to you,
    so near to your Passion;
see how we sing this song now
    to you reigning on high.
All repeat: Glory and honour. . .

Chorus:

Those you were pleased to accept;
    now accept our gifts of devotion,
good and merciful King,
    lover of all that is good.
All repeat: Glory and honour. . .

Cœtus in excelsis te laudat
    cælicus omnis,
et mortalis homo,
    et cuncta creata simul.
Omnes repetunt: Gloria, laus. . .

Plebs Hebræa tibi cum palmis
    obvia venit;
cum prece, voto,
    hymnis adsumus ecce tibi.
Omnes repetunt: Gloria, laus. . .

Hi tibi passuro solvebant
    munia laudis;
nos tibi regnanti
    pangimus ecce melos.
Omnes repetunt: Gloria, laus. . .

Hi placuere tibi,
    placeat devotio nostra:
rex bone, rex clemens,
    cui bona cuncta placent.
Omnes repetunt: Gloria, laus. . .

As the procession enters the church, there is sung the following responsory or
another chant, which should speak of the Lord's entrance.

R. As the Lord entered the holy city,
the children of the Hebrews
proclaimed the resurrection of life.
*Waving their branches of palm,
    they cried:
Hosanna in the Highest.

V. When the people heard that
    Jesus was coming to Jerusalem,
    they went out to meet him.

*Waving their branches. . .

R. Ingrediente Domino
    in sanctam civitatem,
Hebræorum pueri, resurrectionem
    vitæ pronuntiantes,
*Cum ramis palmarum:
Hosanna, clamabant, in excelsis.

V. Cum audisset populus, quod
    Iesus veniret Hierosolymam,
    exierunt obviam ei.

*Cum ramis. . .

When the Priest arrives at the altar, he venerates it and, if appropriate, incenses it. Then he goes to the chair, where he puts aside the cope, if he has worn one, and puts on the chasuble. Omitting the other Introductory Rites of the Mass and, if appropriate, the Kyrie (Lord, have mercy), he says the Collect of the Mass, and then continues the Mass in the usual way.

Second Form: The Solemn Entrance

When a procession outside the church cannot take place, the entrance of the Lord is celebrated inside the church by means of a Solemn Entrance before the principal Mass.

Holding branches in their hands, the faithful gather either outside, in front of the church door, or inside the church itself. The Priest and ministers and a representative group of the faithful go to a suitable place in the church outside the sanctuary, where at least the greater part of the faithful can see the rite.

While the Priest approaches the appointed place, the antiphon Hosanna or another appropriate chant is sung. Then the blessing of branches and the proclamation of the Gospel of the Lord's entrance into Jerusalem take place. After the Gospel, the Priest processes solemnly with the ministers and the representative group of the faithful through the church to the sanctuary, while the responsory As the Lord entered or another appropriate chant is sung.

Arriving at the altar, the Priest venerates it. He then goes to the chair and, omitting the Introductory Rites of the Mass and, if appropriate, the Kyrie (Lord, have mercy), he says the Collect of the Mass, and then continues the Mass in the usual way.

Third Form: The Simple Entrance

At all other Masses of this Sunday at which the Solemn Entrance is not held, the memorial of the Lord's entrance into Jerusalem takes place by means of a Simple Entrance.

While the Priest proceeds to the altar, the Entrance Antiphon with its Psalm or another chant on the same theme is sung. Arriving at the altar, the Priest venerates it and goes to the chair. After the Sign of the Cross, he greets the people and continues the Mass in the usual way.

At other Masses, in which singing at the entrance cannot take place, the Priest, as soon as he has arrived at the altar and venerated it, greets the people, reads the Entrance Antiphon, and continues the Mass in the usual way.

Entrance Antiphon Cf. Jn 12:1,12-13; Ps 23:9-10	Ant. ad introitum

SIX days before the Passover,
when the Lord came into
the city of Jerusalem,
the children ran to meet him;
in their hands they carried
palm branches
and with a loud voice cried out:

*Hosanna in the highest!
Blessed are you, who have come
in your abundant mercy!

O gates, lift high your heads;
grow higher, ancient doors.
Let him enter, the king of glory!
Who is this king of glory?
He, the Lord of hosts,
he is the king of glory.

*Hosanna in the highest!
Blessed are you, who have come
in your abundant mercy!

ANTE sex dies sollemnis Paschæ,
quando venit Dominus
in civitatem Ierusalem,
occurrerunt ei pueri:
et in manibus portabant
ramos palmarum
et clamabant voce magna, dicentes:

*Hosanna in excelsis:
Benedictus, qui venisti
in multitudine misericordiæ tuæ.

Attollite, portæ, capita vestra,
et elevamini, portæ æternales,
et introibit rex gloriæ.
Quis est iste rex gloriæ?
Dominus virtutum ipse est
rex gloriæ.

*Hosanna in excelsis:
Benedictus, qui venisti
in multitudine misericordiæ tuæ.

At the Mass

After the Procession or Solemn Entrance the Priest begins the Mass with the Collect.

Collect | Collecta

Almighty ever-living God,
who as an example of humility
for the human race to follow
caused our Saviour to take flesh
and submit to the Cross,
graciously grant that we may heed
his lesson of patient suffering
and so merit a share
in his Resurrection.
Who lives and reigns with you
in the unity of the Holy Spirit,
one God, for ever and ever.

Omnipotens sempiterne Deus,
qui humano generi, ad imitandum
humilitatis exemplum,
Salvatorem nostrum carnem sumere,
et crucem subire fecisti,
concede propitius,
ut et patientiæ ipsius
habere documenta
et resurrectionis consortia mereamur.
Qui tecum vivit et regnat
in unitate Spiritus Sancti,
Deus, per omnia sæcula sæculorum.

FIRST READING

A reading from the prophet Isaiah   50:4-7

I did not cover my face against insult - I know I shall not be shamed.

The Lord has given me
a disciple's tongue.
So that I may know how to reply to the wearied
he provides me with speech.
Each morning he wakes me to hear,
to listen like a disciple.
The Lord has opened my ear.
For my part, I made no resistance,
neither did I turn away.
I offered my back to those who struck me,
my cheeks to those who tore at my beard;
I did not cover my face
against insult and spittle.
The Lord comes to my help,
so that I am untouched by the insults.
So, too, I set my face like flint,
I know I shall not be shamed.

   The word of the Lord.

Responsorial Psalm   Ps 21:8-9,17-20,23-24. R. v.2

R. **My God, my God, why have you forsaken me?**

   All who see me deride me.
   They curl their lips, they toss their heads.
   'He trusted in the Lord, let him save him;
   let him release him if this is his friend.' R.

   Many dogs have surrounded me,
   a band of the wicked beset me.
   They tear holes in my hands and my feet.
   I can count every one of my bones. R.

   They divide my clothing among them.
   They cast lots for my robe.
   O Lord, do not leave me alone,
   my strength, make haste to help me! R.

   I will tell of your name to my brethren
   and praise you where they are assembled.
   'You who fear the Lord give him praise;
   all sons of Jacob, give him glory.
   Revere him, Israel's sons.' R.

SECOND READING

A reading from the letter of St Paul to the Philippians   2:6-11

He humbled himself, but God raised him high.

His state was divine,
yet Christ Jesus did not cling
to his equality with God
but emptied himself
to assume the condition of a slave,
and became as men are;
and being as all men are,
he was humbler yet,
even to accepting death,
death on a cross.
But God raised him high
and gave him the name
which is above all other names
so that all beings
in the heavens, on earth and in the underworld,
should bend the knee at the name of Jesus
and that every tongue should acclaim
Jesus Christ as Lord,
to the glory of God the Father.

The word of the Lord.

Gospel Acclamation   Ph 2:8-9

R. **Praise to you, O Christ, king of eternal glory.**
Christ was humbler yet,
even to accepting death, death on a cross.
But God raised him high
and gave him the name which is above all names.
R. **Praise to you, O Christ, king of eternal glory.**

The narrative of the Lord's Passion is read without candles and without incense, with no greeting or signing of the book. It is read by a Deacon or, if there is no Deacon, by a Priest. It may also be read by readers, with the part of Christ, if possible, reserved to a Priest.

Deacons, but not others, ask for the blessing of the Priest before singing the Passion, as at other times before the Gospel.

GOSPEL

The symbols in the following passion narrative represent:

N Narrator J Jesus O Other single speaker
C Crowd, or more than one speaker

The passion of our Lord Jesus Christ according to Mark   14:1-15:47

N It was two days before the Passover and the feast of Unleavened Bread, and the chief priests and scribes were looking for a way to arrest Jesus by some trick and have him put to death. For they said,

C It must not be during the festivities, or there will be a disturbance among the people.

N Jesus was at Bethany in the house of Simon the leper; he was at dinner when a woman came in with an alabaster jar of very costly ointment, pure nard. She broke the jar and poured the ointment on his head. Some who were there said to one another indignantly,

C Why this waste of ointment? Ointment like this could have been sold for over three hundred denarii and the money given to the poor;

N and they were angry with her. But Jesus said,

J Leave her alone. Why are you upsetting her? What she has done for me is one of the good works. You have the poor with you always and you can be kind to them whenever you wish but you will not always have me. She has done what was in her power to do; she has anointed my body beforehand for its burial. I tell you solemnly, wherever throughout all the world the Good News is proclaimed, what she has done will be told also, in remembrance of her.

N Judas Iscariot, one of the Twelve, approached the chief priests with an offer to hand Jesus over to them. They were delighted to hear it, and promised to give him money; and he looked for a way of betraying him when the opportunity should occur.

      On the first day of Unleavened Bread, when the Passover lamb was sacrificed, his disciples said to him,

C Where do you want us to go and make the preparations for you to eat the Passover?

N So he sent two of his disciples, saying to them,

J Go into the city and you will meet a man carrying a pitcher of water. Follow him, and say to the owner of the house which he enters, 'The Master says: Where is my dining room in which I can eat the Passover with my disciples?' He will show you a large upper room furnished with couches, all prepared. Make the preparations for us there.

N   The disciples set out and went to the city and found everything as he had told them, and prepared the Passover.

      When evening came he arrived with the Twelve. And while they were at table eating, Jesus said,

J   I tell you solemnly, one of you is about to betray me, one of you eating with me.

N   They were distressed and asked him, one after another,

O   Not I, surely?

N   He said to them,

J   It is one of the Twelve, one who is dipping into the same dish with me. Yes, the Son of Man is going to his fate, as the scriptures say he will, but alas for that man by whom the Son of Man is betrayed! Better for that man if he had never been born!

N   And as they were eating he took some bread, and when he had said the blessing he broke it and gave it to them, saying,

J   Take it; this is my body.

N   Then he took a cup, and when he had returned thanks he gave it to them, and all drank from it, and he said to them,

J   This is my blood, the blood of the covenant, which is to be poured out for many. I tell you solemnly, I shall not drink any more wine until the day I drink the new wine in the kingdom of God.

N   After psalms had been sung they left for the Mount of Olives. And Jesus said to them,

J   You will all lose faith, for the scripture says, 'I shall strike the shepherd and the sheep will be scattered.' However after my resurrection I shall go before you to Galilee.

N   Peter said,

O   Even if all lose faith, I will not.

N   And Jesus said to him,

J   I tell you solemnly, this day, this very night, before the cock crows twice, you will have disowned me three times.

N   But he repeated still more earnestly,

O   If I have to die with you, I will never disown you.

N   And they all said the same.

      They came to a small estate called Gethsemane, and Jesus said to his disciples,

J   Stay here while I pray.

N   Then he took Peter and James and John with him. And a sudden fear came over him, and great distress. And he said to them,

J   My soul is sorrowful to the point of death. Wait here, and keep awake.

N   And going on a little further he threw himself on the ground and prayed that, if it were possible, this hour might pass him by. He said,

J   Abba (Father)! Everything is possible for you. Take this cup away from me. But let it be as you, not I, would have it.

N   He came back and found them sleeping, and he said to Peter,

J   Simon, are you asleep? Had you not the strength to keep awake one hour? You should be awake, and praying not to be put to the test. The spirit is willing but the flesh is weak.

N   Again he went away and prayed, saying the same words. And once more he came back and found them sleeping, their eyes were so heavy; and they could find no answer for him. He came back a third time and said to them,

J   You can sleep on now and take your rest. It is all over. The hour has come. Now the Son of Man is to be betrayed into the hands of sinners. Get up! Let us go! My betrayer is close at hand already.

N   Even while he was still speaking, Judas, one of the Twelve, came up with a number of men armed with swords and clubs, sent by the chief priests and the scribes and the elders. Now the traitor had arranged a signal with them. He had said,

O   The one I kiss, he is the man. Take him in charge, and see he is well guarded when you lead him away.'

N   So when the traitor came, he went straight up to Jesus and said,

O   Rabbi!

N   and kissed him. The others seized him and took him in charge. Then one of the bystanders drew his sword and struck out at the high priest's servant, and cut off his ear.

Then Jesus spoke,

J   Am I a brigand that you had to set out to capture me with swords and clubs? I was among you teaching in the Temple day after day and you never laid hands on me. But this is to fulfil the scriptures.

N   And they all deserted him and ran away. A young man who followed him had nothing on but a linen cloth. They caught hold of him, but he left the cloth in their hands and ran away naked.

They led Jesus off to the high priest; and all the chief priests and the elders and the scribes assembled there. Peter had followed him at a distance, right into the high priest's palace, and was sitting with the attendants warming himself at the fire.

The chief priests and the whole Sanhedrin were looking for evidence against Jesus on which they might pass the death-sentence.

But they could not find any. Several, indeed, brought false evidence against him, but their evidence was conflicting. Some stood up and submitted this false evidence against him,

C We heard him say, 'I am going to destroy this Temple made by human hands, and in three days build another, not made by human hands.'

N But even on this point their evidence was conflicting. The high priest then stood up before the whole assembly and put this question to Jesus,

O Have you no answer to that? What is this evidence these men are bringing against you?

N But he was silent and made no answer at all. The high priest put a second question to him,

O Are you the Christ the Son of the Blessed One?

N Jesus said,

J I am, and you will see the Son of Man seated at the right hand of the Power and coming with the clouds of heaven.

N The high priest tore his robes, and said,

O What need of witnesses have we now? You heard the blasphemy. What is your finding?

N And they all gave their verdict: he deserved to die.
   Some of them started spitting at him and, blindfolding him, began hitting him with their fists and shouting,

C Play the prophet!

N And the attendants rained blows on him.
   While Peter was down below in the courtyard, one of the high-priest's servant-girls came up. She saw Peter warming himself there, stared at him and said,

O You too were with Jesus, the man from Nazareth.

N But he denied it, saying,

O I do not know, I do not understand what you are talking about.

N And he went out into the forecourt. The servant-girl saw him and again started telling the bystanders,

O This fellow is one of them.

N But he again denied it. A little later the bystanders themselves said to Peter,

C You are one of them for sure! Why, you are a Galilean.

N But he started calling down curses on himself and swearing,

O I do not know the man you speak of.

N At that moment the cock crew for the second time, and Peter recalled how Jesus had said to him, 'Before the cock crows twice, you will have disowned me three times.' And he burst into tears.

[First thing in the morning, the chief priest together with the elders and scribes, in short the whole Sanhedrin, had their plan ready. They had Jesus bound and took him away and handed him over to Pilate.

Pilate questioned him,

O Are you the king of the Jews?

N He answered,

J It is you who say it.

N And the chief priests brought many accusations against him. Pilate questioned him again,

O Have you no reply at all? See how many accusations they are bringing against you!

N But to Pilate's amazement, Jesus made no further reply.

At festival time Pilate used to release a prisoner for them, anyone they asked for. Now a man called Barabbas was then in prison with the rioters who had committed murder during the uprising. When the crowd went up and began to ask Pilate the customary favour, Pilate answered them,

O Do you want me to release for you the king of the Jews?

N For he realised it was out of jealousy that the chief priests had handed Jesus over. The chief priests, however, had incited the crowd to demand that he should release Barabbas for them instead. Then Pilate spoke again.

O But in that case, what am I to do with the man you call king of the Jews?

N They shouted back.

C Crucify him!

N Pilate asked them,

O Why? What harm has he done?

N But they shouted all the louder,

C Crucify him!

N So Pilate, anxious to placate the crowd, released Barabbas for them and, having ordered Jesus to be scourged, handed him over to be crucified.

The soldiers led him away to the inner part of the palace, that is, the Praetorium, and called the whole cohort together. They dressed him up in purple, twisted some thorns into a crown and put it on him. And they began saluting him,

C Hail, king of the Jews!

N They struck his head with a reed and spat on him; and they went down on their knees to do him homage. And when they had finished making fun of him, they took off the purple and dressed him in his own clothes.

They led him out to crucify him. They enlisted a passer-by, Simon of Cyrene, father of Alexander and Rufus, who was coming in from the country, to carry his cross. They brought Jesus to the place called Golgotha, which means the place of the skull.

They offered him wine mixed with myrrh, but he refused it. Then they crucified him, and shared out his clothing, casting lots to decide what each should get. It was the third hour when they crucified him. The inscription giving the charge against him read: 'The King of the Jews.' And they crucified two robbers with him, one on his right and one on his left.

The passers-by jeered at him; they shook their heads and said,

C Aha! So you would destroy the Temple and rebuild it in three days! Then save yourself: come down from the cross!

N The chief priests and the scribes mocked him among themselves in the same way. They said,

C He saved others, he cannot save himself. Let the Christ, the king of Israel, come down from the cross now, for us to see it and believe.

N Even those who were crucified with him taunted him.

When the sixth hour came there was darkness over the whole land until the ninth hour. And at the ninth hour Jesus cried out in a loud voice,

J Eloi, Eloi, lama sabachthani?

N This means 'My God, my God, why have you deserted me?' When some of those who stood by heard this, they said,

C Listen, he is calling on Elijah.

N Someone ran and soaked a sponge in vinegar and, putting it on a reed, gave it him to drink, saying,

O Wait and see if Elijah will come to take him down.

N But Jesus gave a loud cry and breathed his last.

All kneel and pause a moment.

N And the veil of the Temple was torn in two from top to bottom. The centurion, who was standing in front of him, had seen how he had died, and he said,

O In truth this man was a son of God.]

N There were some women watching from a distance. Among them were Mary of Magdala, Mary who was the mother of James the younger, and Joset, and Salome. These used to follow him and look after him when he was in Galilee. And there were many other women there who had come up to Jerusalem with him.

It was now evening, and since it was Preparation Day (that is the vigil of the sabbath), there came Joseph of Arimathaea, a prominent member of the Council, who himself lived in the hope of seeing the kingdom of God, and he boldly went to Pilate and asked for the body of Jesus. Pilate, astonished that he should have died so soon, summoned the centurion and enquired if he was already dead. Having been assured of this by the centurion, he granted the corpse to Joseph who brought a shroud, took Jesus down from the cross, wrapped him in the shroud and laid him in a tomb which had been hewn out of the rock. He then rolled a stone against the entrance to the tomb. Mary of Magdala and Mary the mother of Joset were watching and took note of where he was laid.

[The Gospel of the Lord.]

Shorter Form, verses 15:1-39. Read between [ ]

After the narrative of the Passion, a brief homily should take place, if appropriate. A period of silence may also be observed.

The Creed is said, and the Universal Prayer takes place.

Prayer over the Offerings | ## Super oblata

Through the Passion of your Only
   Begotten Son, O Lord,
may our reconciliation with you
   be near at hand,
so that, though we do not merit it
   by our own deeds,
yet by this sacrifice made once
   for all,
we may feel already the effects
   of your mercy.
Through Christ our Lord.

Per Unigeniti tui passionem
placatio tua nobis, Domine,
   sit propinqua,
quam, etsi nostris operibus
   non meremur,
interveniente sacrificio singulari,
tua percipiamus
   miseratione præventi.
Per Christum Dominum nostrum.

Preface: The Passion of the Lord. | ## Præfatio: De dominica Passione.

It is truly right and just,
   our duty and our salvation,
always and everywhere to give
   you thanks,
Lord, holy Father, almighty
   and eternal God,
through Christ our Lord.

Vere dignum et iustum est,
   æquum et salutare,
nos tibi semper et ubique
   gratias agere:
Domine, sancte Pater, omnipotens
   æterne Deus:
per Christum Dominum nostrum.

For, though innocent, he suffered
willingly for sinners
and accepted unjust condemnation
to save the guilty.
His Death has washed away our sins,
and his Resurrection has purchased
our justification.

And so, with all the Angels,
we praise you, as in joyful
celebration we acclaim:

Holy, Holy, Holy Lord God of hosts...

Qui pati pro impiis dignatus
est innocens,
et pro sceleratis
indebite condemnari.
Cuius mors delicta nostra detersit,
et iustificationem nobis
resurrectio comparavit.

Unde et nos cum omnibus Angelis
te laudamus,
iucunda celebratione clamantes:

Sanctus, Sanctus, Sanctus. . .

Communion Antiphon   Mt 26:42

Father, if this chalice cannot pass
without my drinking it,
your will be done.

Ant. ad communionem

Pater, si non potest
hic calix transire,
nisi bibam illum, fiat voluntas tua.

Prayer after Communion

Nourished with these sacred gifts,
we humbly beseech you, O Lord,
that, just as through the death
of your Son
you have brought us to hope
for what we believe,
so by his Resurrection
you may lead us to where you call.
Through Christ our Lord.

Post communionem

Sacro munere satiati,
supplices te, Domine, deprecamur,
ut, qui fecisti nos
morte Filii tui sperare
quod credimus,
facias nos, eodem resurgente,
pervenire quo tendimus.
Per Christum Dominum nostrum.

Prayer over the People

Look, we pray, O Lord,
on this your family,
for whom our Lord Jesus Christ
did not hesitate to be delivered
into the hands of the wicked
and submit to the agony
of the Cross.
Who lives and reigns
for ever and ever.

Oratio super populum

Respice, quæsumus, Domine,
super hanc familiam tuam,
pro qua Dominus noster
Iesus Christus
non dubitavit manibus
tradi nocentium,
et crucis subire tormentum.
Qui vivit et regnat
in sæcula sæculorum.

THE SACRED PASCHAL TRIDUUM

In the Sacred Triduum, the Church solemnly celebrates the greatest mysteries of our redemption, keeping by means of special celebrations the memorial of her Lord, crucified, buried, and risen.

The Paschal Fast should also be kept sacred. It is to be celebrated everywhere on the Friday of the Lord's Passion and, where appropriate, prolonged also through Holy Saturday as a way of coming, with spirit uplifted, to the joys of the Lord's Resurrection.

For a fitting celebration of the Sacred Triduum, a sufficient number of lay ministers is required, who must be carefully instructed as to what they are to do.

The singing of the people, the ministers, and the Priest Celebrant has a special importance in the celebrations of these days, for when texts are sung, they have their proper impact.

Pastors should, therefore, not fail to explain to the Christian faithful, as best they can, the meaning and order of the celebrations and to prepare them for active and fruitful participation.

The celebrations of the Sacred Triduum are to be carried out in cathedral and parochial churches and only in those churches in which they can be performed with dignity, that is, with a good attendance of the faithful, an appropriate number of ministers, and the means to sing at least some of the parts.

Consequently, it is desirable that small communities, associations, and special groups of various kinds join together in these churches to carry out the sacred celebrations in a more noble manner.

29 March

THURSDAY OF THE LORD'S SUPPER

(MAUNDY THURSDAY)

This is moving. Jesus, washing the feet of his disciples. Peter didn't understood it at all, he refused. But Jesus explained it for him. Jesus - God - did this! He himself explains to his disciples: "Do you know what I have done to you? You call me Teacher and Lord - and you are right, for that is what I am. So if I, your Lord and Teacher, have washed your feet, you also ought to wash one another's feet. For I have set you an example, that you also should do as I have done to you" (Jn 13:12-15). It is the Lord's example: he is the most important, and he washes feet, because with us what is highest must be at the service of others. This is a symbol, it is a sign, right? Washing feet means: "I am at your service". And with us too, don't we have to wash each other's feet day after day? But what does this mean? That all of us must help one another. Sometimes I am angry with someone or other ... but... let it go, let it go, and if he or she asks you a favour, do it. Help one another: this is what Jesus teaches us and this what I am doing, and doing with all my heart, because it is my duty. As a priest and a bishop, I must be at your service. But it is a duty which comes from my heart: I love it. I love this and I love to do it because that is what the Lord has taught me to do. But you too, help one another: help one another always. One another. In this way, by helping one another, we will do some good. Now we will perform this ceremony of washing feet, and let us think, let each one of us think: "Am I really willing, willing to serve, to help others?". Let us think about this, just this. And let us think that this sign is a caress of Jesus, which Jesus gives, because this is the real reason why Jesus came: to serve, to help us.

(Pope Francis)

In accordance with a most ancient tradition of the Church, on this day all Masses without the people are forbidden.

At the Evening Mass

The Mass of the Lord's Supper is celebrated in the evening, at a convenient time, with the full participation of the whole local community and with all the Priests and ministers exercising their office.

All Priests may concelebrate even if they have already concelebrated the Chrism Mass on this day, or if they have to celebrate another Mass for the good of the Christian faithful.

Where a pastoral reason requires it, the local Ordinary may permit another Mass to be celebrated in churches and oratories in the evening and, in case of genuine necessity, even in the morning, but only for the faithful who are in no way able to participate in the evening Mass. Care should, nevertheless, be taken that celebrations of this sort do not take place for the advantage of private persons or special small groups, and do not prejudice the evening Mass.

Holy Communion may only be distributed to the faithful during Mass; but it may be brought to the sick at any hour of the day.

The altar may be decorated with flowers with a moderation that accords with the character of this day. The tabernacle should be entirely empty; but a sufficient amount of bread should be consecrated in this Mass for the Communion of the clergy and the people on this and the following day.

Entrance Antiphon   Cf. Ga 6:14

WE should glory in the Cross
of our Lord Jesus Christ,
in whom is our salvation,
    life and resurrection,
through whom we are saved
    and delivered.

Ant. ad introitum

NOS autem gloriari oportet
in cruce Domini nostri
    Iesu Christi,
in quo est salus,
    vita et resurrectio nostra,
per quem salvati et liberati sumus.

The Gloria in excelsis (Glory to God in the highest) is said. While the hymn is being sung, bells are rung, and when it is finished, they remain silent until the Gloria in excelsis of the Easter Vigil, unless, if appropriate, the Diocesan Bishop has decided otherwise. Likewise, during this same period, the organ and other musical instruments may be used only so as to support the singing.

Collect

O God, who have called us
    to participate
in this most sacred Supper,
in which your Only Begotten Son,
when about to hand himself over
    to death,
entrusted to the Church a sacrifice
    new for all eternity,
the banquet of his love,
grant, we pray,
that we may draw from so great
    a mystery,
the fullness of charity and of life.
Through our Lord Jesus Christ,
    your Son,
who lives and reigns with you
    in the unity of the Holy Spirit,
one God, for ever and ever.

Collecta

Sacratissimam, Deus,
    frequentantibus Cenam,
in qua Unigenitus tuus,
    morti se traditurus,
novum in sæcula sacrificium
dilectionisque suæ convivium
    Ecclesiæ commendavit,
da nobis, quæsumus,
    ut ex tanto mysterio
plenitudinem caritatis hauriamus
    et vitæ.
Per Dominum nostrum Iesum
    Christum Filium tuum,
qui tecum vivit et regnat
    in unitate Spiritus Sancti,
Deus, per omnia sæcula sæculorum.

FIRST READING

A reading from the book of Exodus   12:1-8,11-14
Instructions concerning the Passover meal.

The Lord said to Moses and Aaron in the land of Egypt, 'This month is to be the first of all the others for you, the first month of your year. Speak to the whole community of Israel and say, "On the tenth day of this month each man must take an animal from the flock, one for each family: one animal for each household. If the household is too small to eat the animal, a man must join with his neighbour, the nearest to his house, as the number of persons requires. You must take into account what each can eat in deciding the number for the animal. It must be an animal without blemish, a male one year old; you may take it from either sheep or goats. You must keep it till the fourteenth day of the month when the whole assembly of the community of Israel shall slaughter it between the two evenings. Some of the blood must then be taken and put on the two doorposts and the lintel of the houses where it is eaten. That night, the flesh is to be eaten, roasted over the fire; it must be eaten with unleavened bread and bitter herbs. You shall eat it like this: with a girdle round your waist, sandals on your feet, a staff in your hand. You shall eat it hastily; it is a passover in honour of the Lord. That night, I will go through the land of Egypt and strike down all the first-born in the land of Egypt, man and beast alike, and I shall deal out punishment to all the gods of Egypt, I am the Lord. The blood shall serve to mark the houses that you live in. When I see the blood I will pass over you and you shall escape the destroying plague when I strike the land of Egypt. This day is to be a day of remembrance for you, and you must celebrate it as a feast in the Lord's honour. For all generations you are to declare it a day of festival, for ever.'"

The word of the Lord.

Responsorial Psalm   Ps 115:12-13,15-18. R. Cf. 1 Co 10:16

R. **The blessing-cup that we bless**
   is a communion with the blood of Christ.

How can I repay the Lord
for his goodness to me?
The cup of salvation I will raise;
I will call on the Lord's name. R.

O precious in the eyes of the Lord
is the death of his faithful.
Your servant, Lord, your servant am I;
you have loosened my bonds. R.

A thanksgiving sacrifice I make:
I will call on the Lord's name.
My vows to the Lord I will fulfil
before all his people. R.

SECOND READING

A reading from the first letter of St Paul to the Corinthians   11:23-26

Every time you eat this bread and drink this cup, you are proclaiming the death of the Lord.

This is what I received from the Lord, and in turn passed on to you: that on the same night that he was betrayed, the Lord Jesus took some bread, and thanked God for it and broke it, and he said, 'This is my body, which is for you; do this as a memorial of me.' In the same way he took the cup after supper, and said, 'This cup is the new covenant in my blood. Whenever you drink it, do this as a memorial of me.' Until the Lord comes, therefore, every time you eat this bread and drink this cup, you are proclaiming his death.

The word of the Lord.

Gospel Acclamation   Jn 13:34

R. **Praise and honour to you, Lord Jesus!**
I give you a new commandment:
love one another just as I have loved you, says the Lord.
R. **Praise and honour to you, Lord Jesus!**

GOSPEL

A reading from the holy Gospel according to John   13:1-15

Now he showed how perfect his love was.

It was before the festival of the Passover, and Jesus knew that the hour had come for him to pass from this world to the Father. He had always loved those who were his in the world, but now he showed how perfect his love was.

They were at supper, and the devil had already put it into the mind of Judas Iscariot son of Simon, to betray him. Jesus knew that the Father had put everything into his hands, and that he had come from God and was returning to God, and he got up from table, removed his outer garment and, taking a towel, wrapped it round his waist; he then poured water into a basin and began to wash the disciples' feet and to wipe them with the towel he was wearing.

He came to Simon Peter, who said to him, 'Lord, are you going to wash my feet?' Jesus answered, 'At the moment you do not know what I am doing, but later you will understand.' 'Never!' said Peter 'You shall never wash my feet.' Jesus replied, 'If I do not wash you, you can have nothing in common with me.' 'Then, Lord,' said Simon Peter 'not only my feet, but my hands and my head as well!' Jesus said, 'No one who has taken a bath needs washing, he is clean all over. You too are clean, though not all of you are.' He knew who was going to betray him, that was why he said, 'though not all of you are.'

When he had washed their feet and put on his clothes again he went back to the table. 'Do you understand' he said 'what I have done to you? You call me Master and Lord, and rightly; so I am. If I, then, the Lord and Master, have washed your feet, you should wash each other's feet. I have given you an example so that you may copy what I have done to you.'

The Gospel of the Lord.

After the proclamation of the Gospel, the Priest gives a homily in which light is shed on the principal mysteries that are commemorated in this Mass, namely, the institution of the Holy Eucharist and of the priestly Order, and the commandment of the Lord concerning fraternal charity.

The Washing of Feet

After the Homily, where a pastoral reason suggests it, the Washing of Feet follows.

Those who have been chosen are led by the ministers to seats prepared in a suitable place. Then the Priest (removing his chasuble if necessary) goes to each one, and, with the help of the ministers, pours water over each one's feet and then dries them. Meanwhile some of the following antiphons or other appropriate chants are sung.

Antiphon 1 Cf. Jn 13:4,5,15	Antiphona 1
After the Lord had risen from supper, he poured water into a basin and began to wash the feet of his disciples: he left them this example.	Postquam surrexit Dominus a cena, misit aquam in pelvim, et cœpit lavare pedes discipulorum: hoc exemplum reliquit eis.
Antiphon 2 Cf. Jn 13:12,13,15	Antiphona 2
The Lord Jesus, after eating supper with his disciples, washed their feet and said to them: Do you know what I, your Lord and Master, have done for you? I have given you an example, that you should do likewise.	Dominus Iesus, postquam cenavit cum discipulis suis, lavit pedes eorum, et ait illis: 'Scitis quid fecerim vobis ego, Dominus et Magister? Exemplum dedi vobis, ut et vos ita faciatis.'

Antiphon 3   Jn 13:6,7,8

Lord, are you to wash my feet?
    Jesus said to him in answer:
If I do not wash your feet,
    you will have no share with me.

V. So he came to Simon Peter
    and Peter said to him:
– Lord, are you to wash my feet?. . .

V. What I am doing,
    you do not know for now,
    but later you will come to know.
– Lord, are you to wash my feet?. . .

Antiphon 4   Cf. Jn 13:14

If I, your Lord and Master,
    have washed your feet,
how much more should you wash
    each other's feet?

Antiphon 5   Jn 13:35

This is how all will know that you
    are my disciples:
if you have love for one another.

V. Jesus said to his disciples:
– This is how all will know. . .

Antiphon 6   Jn 13:34

I give you a new commandment,
that you love one another
as I have loved you, says the Lord.

Antiphon 7   1 Co 13:13

Let faith, hope and charity,
    these three, remain among you,
but the greatest of these is charity.

V. Now faith, hope and charity,
    these three, remain;
but the greatest of these is charity.
– Let faith, hope and charity. . .

Antiphona 3

Domine, tu mihi lavas pedes?
    Respondit Iesus et dixit ei:
Se non lavero tibi pedes,
    non habebis partem mecum.

V. Venit ergo ad Simonem Petrum,
    et dixit ei Petrus:
– Domine, tu mihi lavas pedes?. . .

V. Quod ego facio,
    tu nescis modo:
    scies autem postea.
– Domine, tu mihi lavas pedes?. . .

Antiphona 4

Si ego, Dominus et Magister vester,
    lavi vobis pedes:
quanto magis debetis alter alterius
    lavare pedes?

Antiphona 5

In hoc cognoscent omnes,
    quia discipuli mei estis,
si dilectionem habueritis
    ad invicem.

V. Dixit Iesus discipulis suis.
– In hoc cognoscent omnes. . .

Antiphona 6

Mandatum novum do vobis,
    ut diligatis invicem,
sicut dilexi vos, dicit Dominus.

Antiphona 7

Maneant in vobis fides, spes,
    caritas, tria hæc:
maior autem horum est caritas.

V. Nunc autem manent fides, spes,
    caritas, tria hæc:
maior horum est caritas.
– Maneant in vobis fides. . .

The Liturgy of the Eucharist

At the beginning of the Liturgy of the Eucharist, there may be a procession of the faithful in which gifts for the poor may be presented with the bread and wine.

Meanwhile the following, or another appropriate chant, is sung.

Ant. Where true charity is dwelling, God is present there.

V. By the love of Christ we have been brought together:

V. let us find in him our gladness and our pleasure;

V. may we love him and revere him, God the living,

V. and in love respect each other with sincere hearts.

Ant. Where true charity is dwelling, God is present there.

V. So when we as one are gathered all together,

V. let us strive to keep our minds free of division;

V. may there be an end to malice, strife and quarrels,

V. and let Christ our God be dwelling here among us.

Ant. Where true charity is dwelling, God is present there.

V. May your face thus be our vision, bright in glory,

V. Christ our God, with all the blessed Saints in heaven:

V. such delight is pure and faultless, joy unbounded,

V. which endures through countless ages world without end. Amen.

Ant. Ubi caritas est vera, Deus ibi est.

V. Exsultemus et in ipso iucundemur.

V. Congregavit nos in unum Christi amor.

V. Timeamus et amemus Deum vivum.

V. Et ex corde diligamus nos sincero

Ant. Ubi caritas est vera, Deus ibi est.

V. Simul ergo cum in unum congregamur:

V. Ne nos mente dividamur, caveamus.

V. Cessent iurgia maligna, cessent lites.

V. Et in medio nostri sit Christus Deus.

Ant. Ubi caritas est vera, Deus ibi est.

V. Simul quoque cum beatis videamus

V. Glorianter vultum tuum, Christe Deus:

V. Gaudium, quod est immensum atque probum,

V. Sæcula per infinita sæculorum. Amen.

Prayer over the Offerings	Super oblata
Grant us, O Lord, we pray,	Concede nobis,
that we may participate worthily	quæsumus, Domine,
in these mysteries,	hæc digne frequentare mysteria,
for whenever the memorial	quia, quoties huius hostiæ
of this sacrifice is celebrated	commemoratio celebratur,
the work of our redemption	opus nostræ redemptionis exercetur.
is accomplished.	Per Christum Dominum nostrum.
Through Christ our Lord.	

Preface I of the Most Holy Eucharist, pp.68-69.

If the Roman Canon is said, the following special forms are used.

Celebrating the most sacred day	Communicantes, et diem
on which our Lord Jesus Christ	sacratissimum celebrantes,
was handed over for our sake,	quo Dominus noster Iesus Christus
and in communion with those	pro nobis est traditus,
whose memory we venerate,	sed et memoriam venerantes,
especially the glorious	in primis gloriosæ semper
ever-Virgin Mary,	Virginis Mariæ,
Mother of our God and Lord,	Genetricis eiusdem Dei et Domini
Jesus Christ,	nostri Iesu Christi:
and blessed Joseph, her Spouse,	sed et beati Ioseph,
your blessed Apostles and Martyrs,	eiusdem Virginis Sponsi,
Peter and Paul, Andrew,	et beatorum Apostolorum ac
(James, John,	Martyrum tuorum,
Thomas, James, Philip,	Petri et Pauli, Andreæ,
Bartholomew, Matthew,	(Iacobi, Ioannis,
Simon and Jude;	Thomæ, Iacobi, Philippi,
Linus, Cletus, Clement, Sixtus,	Bartholomæi, Matthæi,
Cornelius, Cyprian,	Simonis et Thaddæi:
Lawrence, Chrysogonus,	Lini, Cleti, Clementis, Xysti,
John and Paul,	Cornelii, Cypriani,
Cosmas and Damian)	Laurentii, Chrysogoni,
and all your Saints;	Ioannis et Pauli,
we ask that through their merits	Cosmæ et Damiani)
and prayers,	et omnium Sanctorum tuorum;
in all things we may be defended	quorum meritis precibusque concedas,
by your protecting help.	ut in omnibus protectionis tuæ
(Through Christ our Lord. Amen.)	muniamur auxilio.
	(Per Christum Dominum nostrum.
	Amen.)

Therefore, Lord, we pray:
graciously accept this oblation of
    our service,
that of your whole family,
which we make to you
as we observe the day
on which our Lord Jesus Christ
handed on the mysteries
    of his Body and Blood
for his disciples to celebrate;
order our days in your peace,
and command that we be delivered
    from eternal damnation
and counted among the flock of
    those you have chosen.
(Through Christ our Lord. Amen.)

Be pleased, O God, we pray,
to bless, acknowledge,
and approve this offering
    in every respect;
make it spiritual and acceptable,
so that it may become for us
the Body and Blood of your most
    beloved Son,
our Lord Jesus Christ.

On the day before he was to suffer
for our salvation and the salvation
    of all,
that is today,
he took bread in his holy
    and venerable hands,
and with eyes raised to heaven
to you, O God, his almighty Father,
giving you thanks,
    he said the blessing,
broke the bread
and gave it to his disciples, saying:

TAKE THIS, ALL OF YOU,
    AND EAT OF IT,
FOR THIS IS MY BODY,
WHICH WILL BE GIVEN UP FOR YOU.

Hanc igitur oblationem
    servitutis nostræ,
sed et cunctæ familiæ tuæ,
quam tibi offerimus ob diem,
in qua Dominus noster Iesus Christus
tradidit discipulis suis
Corporis et Sanguinis
    sui mysteria celebranda,
quæsumus, Domine,
    ut placatus accipias:
diesque nostros in tua pace
    disponas,
atque ab æterna damnatione
    nos eripi
et in electorum tuorum iubeas
    grege numerari.
(Per Christum Dominum nostrum.
    Amen.)

Quam oblationem tu, Deus,
    in omnibus, quæsumus,
benedictam, adscriptam, ratam,
rationabilem, acceptabilemque
    facere digneris:
ut nobis Corpus et Sanguis fiat
    dilectissimi Filii tui,
Domini nostri Iesu Christi.

Qui, pridie quam pro nostra
omniumque salute pateretur,
hoc est hodie,
accepit panem in sanctus ac
    venerabiles manus suas,
et elevatis oculis in cælum
ad te Deum Patrem
    suum omnipotentem,
tibi gratias agens benedixit,
fregit, deditque discipulis suis, dicens:

ACCIPITE ET MANDUCATE
    EX HOC OMNES:
HOC EST ENIM CORPUS MEUM,
QUOD PRO VOBIS TRADETUR.

Then follows the remainder of the Roman Canon as usual (see pp.86-93) and the Communion Rite, pp.120-129.

At an appropriate moment during Communion, the Priest entrusts the Eucharist from the table of the altar to Deacons or acolytes or other extraordinary ministers, so that afterwards it may be brought to the sick who are to receive Holy Communion at home.

Communion Antiphon 1 Co 11:24-25

This is the Body that will be given
    up for you;
this is the Chalice of the new
    covenant in my Blood,
    says the Lord;
do this, whenever you receive it,
    in memory of me.

Ant. ad communionem

Hoc Corpus, quod pro
    vobis tradetur:
hic calix novi testamenti
    est in meo Sanguine,
dicit Dominus;
hoc facite, quotiescumque sumitis,
in meam commemorationem.

After the distribution of Communion, the ciborium with hosts for Communion on the following day is left on the altar. The Priest, standing at the chair, says the Prayer after Communion.

Prayer after Communion

Grant, almighty God,
that, just as we are renewed
by the Supper of your Son
    in this present age,
so we may enjoy his banquet
    for all eternity.
Who lives and reigns
    for ever and ever.

Post communionem

Concede nobis, omnipotens Deus,
ut, sicut Cena Filii tui
    reficimur temporali,
ita satiari mereamur æterna.
Per Christum Dominum nostrum.

The Transfer of the Most Blessed Sacrament

After the Prayer after Communion, the Priest puts incense in the thurible while standing, blesses it and then, kneeling, incenses the Blessed Sacrament three times. Then, having put on a white humeral veil, he rises, takes the ciborium, and covers it with the ends of the veil.

A procession is formed in which the Blessed Sacrament, accompanied by torches and incense, is carried through the church to a place of repose prepared in a part of the church or in a chapel suitably decorated. A lay minister with a cross, standing between two other ministers with lighted candles leads off. Others carrying lighted candles follow. Before the Priest carrying the Blessed Sacrament comes the thurifer with a smoking thurible. Meanwhile, the hymn Pange, lingua (exclusive of the last two stanzas) or another eucharistic chant is sung.

When the procession reaches the place of repose, the Priest, with the help of the Deacon if necessary, places the ciborium in the tabernacle, the door of which remains open. Then he puts incense in the thurible and, kneeling, incenses the Blessed Sacrament, while Tantum ergo Sacramentum or another eucharistic chant is sung. Then the Deacon or the Priest himself places the Sacrament in the tabernacle and closes the door.

After a period of adoration in silence, the Priest and ministers genuflect and return to the sacristy.

At an appropriate time, the altar is stripped and, if possible, the crosses are removed from the church. It is expedient that any crosses which remain in the church be veiled.

Vespers (Evening Prayer) is not celebrated by those who have attended the Mass of the Lord's Supper.

The faithful are invited to continue adoration before the Blessed Sacrament for a suitable length of time during the night, according to local circumstances, but after midnight the adoration should take place without solemnity.

If the celebration of the Passion of the Lord on the following Friday does not take place in the same church, the Mass is concluded in the usual way and the Blessed Sacrament is placed in the tabernacle.

30 March

FRIDAY OF THE PASSION OF THE LORD
(GOOD FRIDAY)

O Cross of Christ, today too we see you in those who dream, those with the heart of a child, who work to make the world a better place, ever more human and just. O Cross of Christ, teach us that the rising of the sun is more powerful than the darkness of night. O Cross of Christ, teach us that the apparent victory of evil vanishes before the empty tomb and before the certainty of the Resurrection and the love of God which nothing can defeat, obscure or weaken.

(Pope Francis)

On this and the following day, by a most ancient tradition, the Church does not celebrate the Sacraments at all, except for Penance and the Anointing of the Sick.

On this day, Holy Communion is distributed to the faithful only within the celebration of the Lord's Passion; but it may be brought at any hour of the day to the sick who cannot participate in this celebration.

The altar should be completely bare: without a cross, without candles and without cloths.

The Celebration of the Passion of the Lord

On the afternoon of this day, about three o'clock (unless a later hour is chosen for a pastoral reason), there takes place the celebration of the Lord's Passion consisting of three parts, namely, the Liturgy of the Word, the Adoration of the Cross, and Holy Communion.

The Priest and the Deacon, if a Deacon is present, wearing red vestments as for Mass, go to the altar in silence and, after making a reverence to the altar, prostrate themselves or, if appropriate, kneel and pray in silence for a while. All others kneel.

Then the Priest, with the ministers, goes to the chair where, facing the people, who are standing, he says, with hands extended, one of the following prayers, omitting the invitation Let us pray.

Prayer

Remember your mercies, O Lord,
and with your eternal protection
    sanctify your servants,
for whom Christ your Son,
by the shedding of his Blood,
established the Paschal Mystery.
Who lives and reigns
    for ever and ever.
R. Amen.

Or:

O God, who by the Passion
    of Christ your Son, our Lord,
abolished the death inherited
    from ancient sin
by every succeeding generation,
grant that just as,
    being conformed to him,
we have borne by the law of nature
the image of the man of earth,
so by the sanctification of grace
we may bear the image of the Man
    of heaven.
Through Christ our Lord.
R. Amen.

Oratio

Reminiscere miserationum
    tuarum, Domine,
et famulos tuos æterna
    protectione sanctifica,
pro quibus Christus, Filius tuus,
per suum cruorem instituit
    paschale mysterium.
Qui vivit et regnat
    in sæcula sæculorum.
R. Amen.

Vel:

Deus, qui peccati veteris
    hereditariam mortem,
in qua posteritatis genus
    omne successerat,
Christi Filii tui, Domini nostri,
    passione solvisti,
da, ut conformes eidem facti,
sicut imaginem terreni hominis
naturæ necessitate portavimus,
ita imaginem cælestis
gratiæ sanctificatione portemus.
Per Christum Dominum nostrum.

R. Amen.

FIRST PART:

The Liturgy of the Word

FIRST READING

A reading from the prophet Isaiah   52:13-53:12

He was pierced through our faults.

See, my servant will prosper,
he shall be lifted up, exalted, rise to great heights.

As the crowds were appalled on seeing him
 – so disfigured did he look
that he seemed no longer human –
so will the crowds be astonished at him,
and kings stand speechless before him;
for they shall see something never told
and witness something never heard before:
'Who could believe what we have heard,
and to whom has the power of the Lord been revealed?'

Like a sapling he grew up in front of us,
like a root in arid ground.
Without beauty, without majesty (we saw him),
no looks to attract our eyes;
a thing despised and rejected by men,
a man of sorrows and familiar with suffering,
a man to make people screen their faces;
he was despised and we took no account of him.

And yet ours were the sufferings he bore,
ours the sorrows he carried.
But we, we thought of him as someone punished,
struck by God, and brought low.
Yet he was pierced through for our faults,
crushed for our sins.
On him lies a punishment that brings us peace,
and through his wounds we are healed.

We had all gone astray like sheep,
each taking his own way,
and the Lord burdened him
with the sins of all of us.

Harshly dealt with, he bore it humbly,
he never opened his mouth,
like a lamb that is led to the slaughter-house,
like a sheep that is dumb before its shearers
never opening its mouth.

By force and by law he was taken;
would anyone plead his cause?
Yes, he was torn away from the land of the living;
for our faults struck down in death.
They gave him a grave with the wicked,
a tomb with the rich,
though he had done no wrong
and there had been no perjury in his mouth.
The Lord has been pleased to crush him with suffering.
If he offers his life in atonement,
he shall see his heirs, he shall have a long life
and through him what the Lord wishes will be done.
His soul's anguish over
he shall see the light and be content.
By his sufferings shall my servant justify many,
taking their faults on himself.

Hence I will grant whole hordes for his tribute,
he shall divide the spoil with the mighty,
for surrendering himself to death
and letting himself be taken for a sinner,
while he was bearing the faults of many
and praying all the time for sinners.

    The word of the Lord.

Responsorial Psalm   Ps 30:2,6,12-13,15-17,25. R. Lk 23:46

R. **Father, into your hands I commend my spirit.**

    In you, O Lord, I take refuge.
    Let me never be put to shame.
    In your justice, set me free.
    Into your hands I commend my spirit.
    It is you who will redeem me, Lord. R.

In the face of all my foes
I am a reproach,
an object of scorn to my neighbours
and of fear to my friends. R.

Those who see me in the street
run far away from me.
I am like a dead man, forgotten in men's hearts,
like a thing thrown away. R.

But as for me, I trust in you, Lord,
I say: 'You are my God.'
My life is in your hands, deliver me
from the hands of those who hate me. R.

Let your face shine on your servant.
Save me in your love.
Be strong, let your heart take courage,
all who hope in the Lord. R.

SECOND READING

A reading from the letter to the Hebrews   4:14-16; 5:7-9

He learnt to obey through suffering and became for all who obey him the source of eternal salvation.

Since in Jesus, the Son of God, we have the supreme high priest who has gone through to the highest heaven, we must never let go of the faith that we have professed. For it is not as if we had a high priest who was incapable of feeling our weaknesses with us; but we have one who has been tempted in every way that we are, though he is without sin. Let us be confident, then, in approaching the throne of grace, that we shall have mercy from him and find grace when we are in need of help.

During his life on earth, he offered up prayer and entreaty, aloud and in silent tears, to the one who had the power to save him out of death, and he submitted so humbly that his prayer was heard. Although he was Son, he learnt to obey through suffering; but having been made perfect, he became for all who obey him the source of eternal salvation.

The word of the Lord.

Gospel Acclamation   Ph 2:8-9

R. **Glory and praise to you, O Christ!**
Christ was humbler yet,
even accepting death, death on a cross.
But God raised him high
and gave him the name which is above all names.
R. **Glory and praise to you, O Christ!**

GOSPEL

The symbols in the following passion narrative represent:

N Narrator   J Jesus   O Other single speaker

C Crowd, or more than one speaker

The passion of our Lord Jesus Christ according to John   18:1-19:42

N   Jesus left with his disciples and crossed the Kedron valley. There was a
    garden there, and he went into it with his disciples. Judas the traitor
    knew the place well, since Jesus had often met his disciples there, and
    he brought the cohort to this place together with a detachment of
    guards sent by the chief priests and the Pharisees, all with lanterns and
    torches and weapons. Knowing everything that was going to happen to
    him, Jesus then came forward and said,

J   Who are you looking for?

N   They answered,

C   Jesus the Nazarene.

N   He said,

J   I am he.

N   Now Judas the traitor was standing among them. When Jesus said,
    'I am he', they moved back and fell to the ground. He asked them a
    second time,

J   Who are you looking for?

N   They said,

C   Jesus the Nazarene.

N   Jesus replied,

J   I have told you that I am he. If I am the one you are looking for, let
    these others go.

N   This was to fulfil the words he has spoken: 'Not one of those you gave
    me have I lost.'
        Simon Peter, who carried a sword, drew it and wounded the high
    priest's servant, cutting off his right ear. The servant's name was
    Malchus. Jesus said to Peter,

J   Put your sword back in its scabbard; am I not to drink the cup that the Father has given me?

N   The cohort and its captain and the Jewish guards seized Jesus and bound him. They took him first to Annas, because Annas was the father-in-law of Caiaphas, who was high priest that year. It was Caiaphas who had suggested to the Jews, 'It is better for one man to die for the people.'

Simon Peter, with another disciple, followed Jesus. This disciple, who was known to the high priest, went with Jesus into the high priest's palace, but Peter stayed outside the door. So the other disciple, the one known to the high priest, went out, spoke to the woman who was keeping the door and brought Peter in. The maid on duty at the door said to Peter,

O   Aren't you another of that man's disciples?

N   He answered,

O   I am not.

N   Now it was cold, and the servants and guards had lit a charcoal fire and were standing there warming themselves; so Peter stood there too, warming himself with the others.

The high priest questioned Jesus about his disciples and his teaching. Jesus answered,

J   I have spoken openly for all the world to hear; I have always taught in the synagogue and in the Temple where all the Jews meet together: I have said nothing in secret. But why ask me? Ask my hearers what I taught: they know what I said.

N   At these words, one of the guards standing by gave Jesus a slap in the face, saying,

O   Is that the way to answer the high priest?

N   Jesus replied,

J   If there is something wrong in what I said, point it out; but if there is no offence in it, why do you strike me?

N   Then Annas sent him, still bound, to Caiaphas, the high priest. As Simon Peter stood there warming himself, someone said to him,

O   Aren't you another of his disciples?

N   He denied it saying,

O   I am not.

N   One of the high priest's servants, a relation of the man whose ear Peter had cut off, said,

O   Didn't I see you in the garden with him?

N   Again Peter denied it, and at once a cock crew.

They then led Jesus from the house of Caiaphas to the Praetorium. It was now morning. They did not go into the Praetorium themselves or they would be defiled and unable to eat the passover. So Pilate came outside to them and said,

O What charge do you bring against this man?

N They replied,

C If he were not a criminal, we should not be handing him over to you.

N Pilate said,

O Take him yourselves, and try him by your own Law.

N The Jews answered,

C We are not allowed to put a man to death.

N This was to fulfil the words Jesus had spoken indicating the way he was going to die.

So Pilate went back into the Praetorium and called Jesus to him, and asked,

O Are you the king of Jews?

N Jesus replied,

J Do you ask this of your own accord, or have others spoken to you about me?

N Pilate answered,

O Am I a Jew? It is your own people and the chief priests who have handed you over to me: what have you done?

N Jesus replied,

J Mine is not a kingdom of this world; if my kingdom were of this world, my men would have fought to prevent me being surrendered to the Jews. But my kingdom is not of this kind.

N Pilate said,

O So you are the king then?

N Jesus answered,

J It is you who say it. Yes, I am a king. I was born for this; I came into the world for this; to bear witness to the truth, and all who are on the side of truth listen to my voice.

N Pilate said,

O Truth? What is that?

N And with that he went out again to the Jews and said,

O I find no case against him. But according to a custom of yours I should release one prisoner at the Passover; would you like me, then, to release the king of Jews?

N At this they shouted:

C   Not this man, but Barabbas.

N   Barabbas was a brigand.

> Pilate then had Jesus taken away and scourged; and after this, the soldiers twisted some thorns into a crown and put it on his head, and dressed him in a purple robe. They kept coming up to him and saying,

C   Hail, king of the Jews!

N   and they slapped him in the face.

> Pilate came outside again and said to them,

O   Look, I am going to bring him out to you to let you see that I find no case.

N   Jesus then came out wearing the crown of thorns and the purple robe. Pilate said,

O   Here is the man.

N   When they saw him the chief priests and the guards shouted,

C   Crucify him! Crucify him!

N   Pilate said,

O   Take him yourselves and crucify him: I can find no case against him

N   The Jews replied,

C   We have a Law, and according to the Law he ought to die, because he has claimed to be the son of God.

N   When Pilate heard them say this his fears increased. Re-entering the Praetorium, he said to Jesus,

O   Where do you come from?

N   But Jesus made no answer. Pilate then said to him,

O   Are you refusing to speak to me? Surely you know I have power to release you and I have power to crucify you?

N   Jesus replied,

J   You would have no power over me if it had not been given you from above; that is why the one who handed me over to you has the greater guilt.

N   From that moment Pilate was anxious to set him free, but the Jews shouted,

C   If you set him free you are no friend of Caesar's; anyone who makes himself king is defying Caesar.

N   Hearing these words, Pilate had Jesus brought out, and seated himself on the chair of judgement at a place called the Pavement, in Hebrew Gabbatha. It was Passover Preparation Day, about the sixth hour. Pilate said to the Jews,

O   Here is your king.

N   They said,

C   Take him away, take him away. Crucify him!

N Pilate said,

O Do you want me to crucify your king?

N The chief priests answered,

C We have no king except Caesar.

N So in the end Pilate handed him over to them to be crucified.

They then took charge of Jesus, and carrying his own cross he went out of the city to the place of the skull, or, as it was called in Hebrew, Golgotha, where they crucified him with two others, one on either side with Jesus in the middle. Pilate wrote out a notice and had it fixed to the cross; it ran: 'Jesus the Nazarene, King of the Jews.' This notice was read by many of the Jews, because the place where Jesus was crucified was not far from the city, and the writing was in Hebrew, Latin and Greek. So the Jewish chief priests said to Pilate,

C You should not write 'King of the Jews', but 'This man said: I am King of the Jews'.

N Pilate answered,

O What I have written, I have written.

N When the soldiers had finished crucifying Jesus they took his clothing and divided it into four shares, one for each soldier. His undergarment was seamless, woven in one piece from neck to hem; so they said to one another,

C Instead of tearing it, let's throw dice to decide who is to have it.

N In this way the words of scripture were fulfilled:

They shared out my clothing among them.

They cast lots for my clothes.

This is exactly what the soldiers did.

Near the cross of Jesus stood his mother and his mother's sister, Mary the wife of Clopas, and Mary of Magdala. Seeing his mother and the disciple he loved standing near her, Jesus said to his mother,

J Woman, this is your son.

N Then to the disciple he said,

J This is your mother.

N And from that moment the disciple made a place for her in his home.

After this, Jesus knew that everything had now been completed, and to fulfil the scripture perfectly he said:

J I am thirsty.

N A jar full of vinegar stood there, so putting a sponge soaked in vinegar on a hyssop stick they held it up to his mouth. After Jesus had taken the vinegar he said,

J   It is accomplished;

N   and bowing his head he gave up the spirit.

All kneel and pause a moment.

N   It was Preparation Day, and to prevent the bodies remaining on the cross during the sabbath – since that sabbath was a day of special solemnity – the Jews asked Pilate to have the legs broken and the bodies taken away. Consequently the soldiers came and broke the legs of the first man who had been crucified with him and then of the other. When they came to Jesus, they found that he was already dead, and so instead of breaking his legs one of the soldiers pierced his side with a lance; and immediately there came out blood and water. This is the evidence of one who saw it – trustworthy evidence, and he knows he speaks the truth – and he gives it so that you may believe as well. Because all this happened to fulfil the words of scripture:

> Not one bone of his will be broken,

and again, in another place scripture says:

> They will look on the one whom they have pierced.

After this, Joseph of Arimathaea, who was a disciple of Jesus – though a secret one because he was afraid of the Jews – asked Pilate to let him remove the body of Jesus. Pilate gave permission, so they came and took it away. Nicodemus came as well – the same one who had first come to Jesus at night – time – and he brought a mixture of myrrh and aloes, weighing about a hundred pounds. They took the body of Jesus and wrapped it with the spices in linen cloths, following the Jewish burial custom. At the place where he had been crucified there was a garden, and in the garden a new tomb in which no one had yet been buried. Since it was the Jewish Day of Preparation and the tomb was near at hand, they laid Jesus there.

   The Gospel of the Lord.

After the reading of the Lord's Passion, the Priest gives a brief homily and, at its end, the faithful may be invited to spend a short time in prayer.

The Solemn Intercessions

The Liturgy of the Word concludes with the Solemn Intercessions, which take place in this way: the Deacon, if a Deacon is present, or if he is not, a lay minister, stands at the ambo, and sings or says the invitation in which the intention is expressed. Then all pray in silence for a while, and afterwards the Priest, standing at the chair or, if appropriate, at the altar, with hands extended, sings or says the prayer.

The faithful may remain either kneeling or standing throughout the entire period of the prayers.

Before the Priest's prayer, in accord with tradition, it is permissible to use the Deacon's invitations Let us kneel – Let us stand, (Flectamus genua – Levate), with all kneeling for silent prayer.

The Conferences of Bishops may provide other invitations to introduce the prayer of the Priest.

In a situation of grave public need, the Diocesan Bishop may permit or order the addition of a special intention.

The prayer is sung in the simple tone or, if the invitations Let us kneel – Let us stand (Flectamus genua – Levate) are used, in the solemn tone.

I. For Holy Church

Let us pray, dearly beloved,
  for the holy Church of God,
that our God and Lord be pleased
  to give her peace,
to guard her and to unite her
  throughout the whole world
and grant that, leading our life
  in tranquillity and quiet,
we may glorify God
  the Father almighty.

Prayer in silence. Then the Priest says:

Almighty ever-living God,
who in Christ revealed your glory
  to all the nations,
watch over the works of your mercy,
that your Church, spread
  throughout all the world,
may persevere with steadfast faith
  in confessing your name.
Through Christ our Lord.
R. Amen.

II. For the Pope

Let us pray also for our most
  Holy Father Pope N.,
that our God and Lord,
who chose him for the
  Order of Bishops,

I. Pro sancta Ecclesia

Oremus, dilectissimi nobis,
  pro Ecclesia sancta Dei,
ut eam Deus et Dominus noster
pacificare, adunare
  et custodire dignetur
toto orbe terrarum,
detque nobis, quietam et tranquillam
  vitam degentibus,
glorificare Deum
  Patrem omnipotentem.

Omnipotens sempiterne Deus,
qui gloriam tuam omnibus
  in Christo gentibus revelasti:
custodi opera misericordiæ tuæ,
ut Ecclesia tua, toto orbe diffusa,
stabili fide in confessione
  tui nominis perseveret.
Per Christum Dominum nostrum.
R. Amen.

II. Pro Papa

Oremus et pro beatissimo
  Papa nostro N.,
ut Deus et Dominus noster,
qui elegit eum
  in ordine episcopatus,

may keep him safe and unharmed
   for the Lord's holy Church,
to govern the holy People of God.

salvum atque incolumem custodiat
   Ecclesiæ suæ sanctæ,
ad regendum populum
   sanctum Dei.

Prayer in silence. Then the Priest says:

Almighty ever-living God,
by whose decree all things
   are founded,
look with favour on our prayers
and in your kindness protect
   the Pope chosen for us,
that, under him,
   the Christian people,
governed by you their maker,
may grow in merit by reason
   of their faith.
Through Christ our Lord.
R. Amen.

Omnipotens sempiterne Deus,
cuius iudicio universa fundantur,
respice propitius ad preces nostras,
et electum nobis Antistitem
   tua pietate conserva,
ut christiana plebs,
   quæ te gubernatur auctore,
sub ipso Pontifice,
   fidei suæ meritis augeatur.
Per Christum Dominum nostrum.
R. Amen.

III. For all orders and degrees of the faithful

III. Pro omnibus ordinibus gradibusque fidelium

Let us pray also for our Bishop N.,
for all Bishops, Priests,
   and Deacons of the Church
and for the whole
   of the faithful people.

Oremus et pro Episcopo nostro N.,
pro omnibus Episcopis, presbyteris,
   diaconis Ecclesiæ,
et universa plebe fidelium.

Prayer in silence. Then the Priest says:

Almighty ever-living God,
by whose Spirit the whole body
   of the Church
is sanctified and governed,
hear our humble prayer
   for your ministers,
that, by the gift of your grace,
all may serve you faithfully.
Through Christ our Lord.
R. Amen.

Omnipotens sempiterne Deus,
cuius Spiritu totum corpus Ecclesiæ
sanctificatur et regitur,
exaudi nos pro ministris
   tuis supplicantes,
ut, gratiæ tuæ munere, ab omnibus
   tibi fideliter serviatur.
Per Christum Dominum nostrum.
R. Amen.

IV. For catechumens

Let us pray also
    for (our) catechumens,
that our God and Lord
may open wide the ears
    of their inmost hearts
and unlock the gates of his mercy,
that, having received forgiveness
    of all their sins
through the waters of rebirth,
they, too, may be one with Christ
    Jesus our Lord.

Prayer in silence. Then the Priest says:

Almighty ever-living God,
who make your Church ever
    fruitful with new offspring,
increase the faith and understanding
    of (our) catechumens,
that, reborn in the font of Baptism,
they may be added to the number
    of your adopted children.
Through Christ our Lord.
R. Amen.

V. For the unity of Christians

Let us pray also for all our brothers
    and sisters who believe in Christ,
that our God and Lord may
    be pleased,
as they live the truth,
to gather them together and keep
    them in his one Church.

Prayer in silence. Then the Priest says:

Almighty ever-living God,
who gather what is scattered
and keep together what you
    have gathered,
look kindly on the flock of your Son,

IV. Pro catechumenis

Oremus et pro
    catechumenis (nostris),
ut Deus et Dominus noster
adaperiat aures
    præcordiorum ipsorum
ianuamque misericordiæ,
ut, per lavacrum regenerationis
accepta remissione
    omnium peccatorum,
et ipsi inveniantur in Christo Iesu
    Domino nostro.

Omnipotens sempiterne Deus,
qui Ecclesiam tuam nova semper
    prole fecundas,
auge fidem et intellectum
    catechumenis (nostris),
ut, renati fonte baptismatis,
tadoptionis tuæ filiis aggregentur.
Per Christum Dominum nostrum.
R. Amen.

V. Pro unitate Christianorum

Oremus et pro universis fratribus
    in Christum credentibus,
ut Deus et Dominus noster eos,
    veritatem facientes,
in una Ecclesia sua congregare
    et custodire dignetur.

Omnipotens sempiterne Deus,
qui dispersa congregas
    et congregata conservas,
ad gregem Filii tui placatus intende,
ut, quos unum baptisma sacravit,

that those whom one Baptism
  has consecrated
may be joined together by integrity
  of faith
and united in the bond of charity.
Through Christ our Lord.
R. Amen.

eos et fidei iungat integritas
et vinculum societ caritatis.
Per Christum Dominum nostrum.
R. Amen.

VI. For the Jewish people

Let us pray also for the Jewish people,
to whom the Lord our God
  spoke first,
that he may grant them to advance
  in love of his name
and in faithfulness to his covenant.

Prayer in silence. Then the Priest says:

Almighty ever-living God,
who bestowed your promises on
  Abraham and his descendants,
graciously hear the prayers
  of your Church,
that the people you first made
  your own
may attain the fullness
  of redemption.
Through Christ our Lord.
R. Amen.

VI. Pro Iudæis

Oremus et pro Iudæis,
ut, ad quos prius locutus est
  Dominus Deus noster,
eis tribuat in sui nominis amore
et in sui fœderis fidelitate proficere.

Omnipotens sempiterne Deus,
qui promissiones tuas Abrahæ
  eiusque semini contulisti,
Ecclesiæ tuæ preces
  clementer exaudi,
ut populus acquisitionis prioris
ad redemptionis mereatur
  plenitudinem pervenire.
Per Christum Dominum nostrum.
R. Amen.

VII. For those who do not believe in Christ

Let us pray also for those who
  do not believe in Christ,
that, enlightened by the Holy Spirit,
they, too, may enter on the way
  of salvation.

Prayer in silence. Then the Priest says:

Almighty ever-living God,
grant to those who do not
  confess Christ
that, by walking before you
  with a sincere heart,

VII. Pro iis qui Christum non credunt

Oremus et pro iis qui in Christum
  non credunt,
ut, luce Sancti Spiritus illustrati,
viam salutis et ipsi valeant introire.

Omnipotens sempiterne Deus,
fac ut qui Christum
  non confitentur,
coram te sincero corde ambulantes,
  inveniant veritatem,

they may find the truth,
and that we ourselves, being
   constant in mutual love
and striving to understand more
   fully the mystery of your life,
may be made more perfect witnesses
   to your love in the world.
Through Christ our Lord. R. Amen.

nosque, mutuo proficientes
   semper amore
et ad tuæ vitæ mysterium plenius
   percipiendum sollicitos,
perfectiores effice tuæ testes
   caritatis in mundo.
Per Christum Dominum nostrum.
R. Amen.

VIII. For those who do not believe in God

Let us pray also for those who
   do not acknowledge God,
that, following what is right
   in sincerity of heart,
they may find the way
   to God himself.

VIII. Pro iis qui in Deum non credunt

Oremus et pro iis qui Deum
   non agnoscunt,
ut, quæ recta sunt sincero
   corde sectantes,
ad ipsum Deum
   pervenire mereantur.

Prayer in silence. Then the Priest says:

Almighty ever-living God,
who created all people
to seek you always by desiring you
and, by finding you, come to rest,
grant, we pray,
that, despite every harmful obstacle,
all may recognise the signs
   of your fatherly love
and the witness of the good works
done by those who believe in you,
and so in gladness confess you,
the one true God and Father
   of our human race.
Through Christ our Lord. R. Amen.

Omnipotens sempiterne Deus,
qui cunctos homines condidisti,
ut te semper desiderando quærerent
et inveniendo quiescerent,
præsta, quæsumus,
ut inter noxia quæque obstacula
omnes, tuæ signa pietatis
et in te credentium testimonium
bonorum operum percipientes,
te solum verum Deum nostrique
   generis Patrem
gaudeant confiteri.
Per Christum Dominum nostrum.
R. Amen.

IX. For those in public office

Let us pray also for those
   in public office,
that our God and Lord
may direct their minds and hearts
   according to his will
for the true peace and freedom of all.

IX. Pro rempublicam moderantibus

Oremus et pro omnibus
   rempublicam moderantibus,
ut Deus et Dominus noster
mentes et corda eorum secundum
   voluntatem suam dirigat
ad veram omnium pacem
   et libertatem.

Prayer in silence. Then the Priest says:

Almighty ever-living God,
in whose hand lies every
   human heart
and the rights of peoples,
look with favour, we pray,
on those who govern
   with authority over us,
that throughout the whole world,
the prosperity of peoples,
the assurance of peace,
and freedom of religion
may through your gift
   be made secure.
Through Christ our Lord. R. Amen.

Omnipotens sempiterne Deus,
in cuius manu sunt hominum
   corda et iura populorum,
respice benignus ad eos,
   qui nos in potestate moderantur,
ut ubique terrarum populorum
   prosperitas,
pacis securitas et religionis libertas,
te largiente, consistant.
Per Christum Dominum nostrum.
R. Amen.

X. For those in tribulation

Let us pray, dearly beloved,
to God the Father almighty,
that he may cleanse the world
   of all errors,
banish disease, drive out hunger,
unlock prisons, loosen fetters,
granting to travellers safety,
   to pilgrims return,
health to the sick,
   and salvation to the dying.

X. Pro tribulatis

Oremus, dilectissimi nobis,
   Deum Patrem omnipotentem,
ut cunctis mundum
   purget erroribus,
morbos auferat, famem depellat,
aperiat carceres, vincula solvat,
viatoribus securitatem,
   peregrinantibus reditum,
infirmantibus sanitatem
atque morientibus
   salutem indulgeat.

Prayer in silence. Then the Priest says:

Almighty ever-living God,
comfort of mourners,
   strength of all who toil,
may the prayers of those who cry out
   in any tribulation
come before you,
that all may rejoice,
because in their hour of need
your mercy was at hand.
Through Christ our Lord.
R. Amen.

Omnipotens sempiterne Deus,
mæstorum consolatio,
   laborantium fortitudo,
perveniant ad te preces
de quacumque
   tribulatione clamantium,
ut omnes sibi in necessitatibus suis
misericordiam tuam
   gaudeant affuisse.
Per Christum Dominum nostrum.
R. Amen.

SECOND PART:

THE ADORATION OF THE HOLY CROSS

After the Solemn Intercessions, the solemn Adoration of the Holy Cross takes place. Of the two forms of the showing of the Cross presented here, the more appropriate one, according to pastoral needs, should be chosen.

The Showing of the Holy Cross

First Form

The Deacon accompanied by ministers, or another suitable minister, goes to the sacristy, from which, in procession, accompanied by two ministers with lighted candles, he carries the Cross, covered with a violet veil, through the church to the middle of the sanctuary.

The Priest, standing before the altar and facing the people, receives the Cross, uncovers a little of its upper part and elevates it while beginning the **Ecce lignum Crucis** (**Behold the wood of the Cross**). He is assisted in singing by the Deacon or, if need be, by the choir. All respond, **Come, let us adore**. At the end of the singing, all kneel and for a brief moment adore in silence, while the Priest stands and holds the Cross raised.

Behold the wood of the Cross, **on which hung the salvation** **of the world.** R. Come, let us adore.	Ecce lignum Crucis, in quo salus mundi pependit. R. Venite, adoremus.

Then the Priest uncovers the right arm of the Cross and again, raising up the Cross, begins, **Behold the wood of the Cross** and everything takes place as above.

Finally, he uncovers the Cross entirely and, raising it up, he begins the invitation **Behold the wood of the Cross** a third time and everything takes place like the first time.

Second Form

The Priest or the Deacon accompanied by ministers, or another suitable minister, goes to the door of the church, where he receives the unveiled Cross, and the ministers take lighted candles; then the procession sets off through the church to the sanctuary. Near the door, in the middle of the church, and before the entrance of the sanctuary, the one who carries the Cross elevates it, singing, **Behold the wood of the Cross**, to which all respond, **Come, let us adore**. After each response all kneel and for a brief moment adore in silence, as above.

The Adoration of the Holy Cross

Then, accompanied by two ministers with lighted candles, the Priest or the Deacon carries the Cross to the entrance of the sanctuary or to another suitable place and there puts it down or hands it over to the ministers to hold. Candles are placed on the right and left sides of the Cross.

For the Adoration of the Cross, first the Priest Celebrant alone approaches, with the chasuble and his shoes removed, if appropriate. Then the clergy, the lay ministers, and the faithful approach, moving as if in procession, and showing reverence to the Cross by a simple genuflection or by some other sign appropriate to the usage of the region, for example, by kissing the Cross.

Only one Cross should be offered for adoration. If, because of the large number of people, it is not possible for all to approach individually, the Priest, after some of the clergy and faithful have adored, takes the Cross and, standing in the middle before the altar, invites the people in a few words to adore the Holy Cross and afterwards holds the Cross elevated higher for a brief time, for the faithful to adore it in silence.

While the adoration of the Holy Cross is taking place, the antiphon **Crucem tuam adoramus** (**We adore your Cross, O Lord**), the Reproaches, the hymn **Crux fidelis** (**Faithful Cross**) or other suitable chants are sung, during which all who have already adored the Cross remain seated.

Chants to be Sung
during the Adoration of the Holy Cross

Ant. We adore your Cross, O Lord,
we praise and glorify your
   holy Resurrection,
for behold, because of the wood
   of a tree
joy has come to the whole world.

Ant. Crucem tuam
   adoramus, Domine,
et sanctam resurrectionem tuam
   laudamus et glorificamus:
ecce enim propter lignum
venit gaudium in universo mundo.

Cf. Ps 66:2

May God have mercy on us
   and bless us;
may he let his face shed its light
   upon us
and have mercy on us.

Deus misereatur nostri,
   et benedicat nobis:
illuminet vultum suum super nos,
et misereatur nostri.

And the antiphon is repeated:

We adore. . .

| Crucem tuam. . .

THE REPROACHES

Parts assigned to one of the two choirs separately are indicated by the numbers 1 (first choir) and 2 (second choir); parts sung by both choirs together are marked: 1 and 2. Some of the verses may also be sung by two cantors.

1 and 2 My people,
   what have I done to you?
Or how have I grieved you?
   Answer me!

1 et 2 Popule meus,
   quid feci tibi?
Aut in quo contristavi te?
   Responde mihi!

1 Because I led you out of the land
   of Egypt,
you have prepared a Cross
   for your Saviour.

1 Quia eduxi te de terra Ægypti:
parasti Crucem Salvatori tuo.

1 Hagios o Theos,
2 Holy is God,
1 Hagios Ischyros,
2 Holy and Mighty,
1 Hagios Athanatos,
   eleison himas.
2 Holy and Immortal One,
   have mercy on us.

1 Hagios o Theos.
2 Sanctus Deus.
1 Hagios Ischyros.
2 Sanctus Fortis.
1 Hagios Athanatos,
   eleison himas.
2 Sanctus Immortalis,
   miserere nobis.

1 and 2 Because I led you out
   through the desert forty years
and fed you with manna and
   brought you into a land of plenty,
you have prepared a Cross
   for your Saviour.

1 et 2 Quia eduxi te per desertum
   quadraginta annis,
et manna cibavi te,
et introduxi te in terram
   satis bonam:
parasti Crucem Salvatori tuo.

1 Hagios o Theos,
2 Holy is God,
1 Hagios Ischyros,
2 Holy and Mighty,
1 Hagios Athanatos, eleison himas.
2 Holy and Immortal One,
   have mercy on us.

1 Hagios o Theos.
2 Sanctus Deus.
1 Hagios Ischyros.
2 Sanctus Fortis.
1 Hagios Athanatos, eleison himas.
2 Sanctus Immortalis,
   miserere nobis.

1 and 2 What more should I have
   done for you and have not done?
Indeed, I planted you as my most
   beautiful chosen vine
and you have turned very bitter
   for me,
for in my thirst you gave me
   vinegar to drink
and with a lance you pierced your
   Saviour's side.

1 et 2 Quid ultra debui facere tibi,
   et non feci?
Ego quidem plantavi te
vineam electam
   meam speciosissimam:
et tu facta es mihi nimis amara:
aceto namque sitim meam potasti,
et lancea perforasti latus
   Salvatori tuo.

1 Hagios o Theos,
2 Holy is God,

1 Hagios o Theos.
2 Sanctus Deus.

1 Hagios Ischyros,
2 Holy and Mighty,
1 Hagios Athanatos,
   eleison himas.
2 Holy and Immortal One, have
   mercy on us.

1 Hagios Ischyros.
2 Sanctus Fortis.
1 Hagios Athanatos,
   eleison himas.
2 Sanctus Immortalis,
   miserere nobis.

II

Cantors:

I scourged Egypt for your sake
   with its firstborn sons,
and you scourged me and handed
   me over.

1 and 2 repeat:

My people, what have I done to you?
Or how have I grieved you?
Answer me!

Cantors:

I led you out from Egypt as Pharaoh
   lay sunk in the Red Sea,
and you handed me over
   to the chief priests.

1 and 2 repeat:

My people. . .

Cantors:

I opened up the sea before you,
and you opened my side with a lance.

1 and 2 repeat:

My people. . .

Cantors:

I went before you in a pillar of cloud,
and you led me into Pilate's palace.

1 and 2 repeat:

My people. . .

Cantores:

Ego propter te flagellavi Ægyptum
cum primogenitis suis:
et tu me flagellatum tradidisti.

1 et 2 repetunt:

Popule meus, quid feci tibi?
Aut in quo contristavi te?
Responde mihi!

Cantores:

Ego eduxi te de Ægypto,
demerso Pharaone in Mare Rubrum:
et tu me tradidisti
   principibus sacerdotum.

1 et 2 repetunt:

Popule meus. . .

Cantores:

Ego ante te aperui mare:
et tu aperuisti lancea latus meum.

1 et 2 repetunt:

Popule meus. . .

Cantores:

Ego ante te præivi in columna nubis:
et tu me duxisti ad prætorium Pilati.

1 et 2 repetunt:

Popule meus. . .

Cantors:

I fed you with manna in the desert,
and on me you rained blows
      and lashes.

1 and 2 repeat:
My people. . .

Cantors:

I gave you saving water
      from the rock to drink,
and for drink you gave me gall
      and vinegar.

1 and 2 repeat:
My people. . .

Cantors:

I struck down for you the kings
      of the Canaanites,
and you struck my head with a reed.

1 and 2 repeat:
My people. . .

Cantors:

I put in your hand a royal sceptre,
and you put on my head
      a crown of thorns.

1 and 2 repeat:
My people. . .

Cantors:

I exalted you with great power,
and you hung me on the scaffold
      of the Cross.

1 and 2 repeat:
My people. . .

Cantores:

Ego te pavi manna per desertum:
et tu me cecidisti alapis et flagellis.

1 et 2 repetunt:
Popule meus. . .

Cantores:

Ego te potavi aqua salutis de petra:
et tu me potasti felle et aceto.

1 et 2 repetunt:
Popule meus. . .

Cantores:

Ego propter te Chananæorum
      reges percussi:
et tu percussisti arundine
      caput meum.

1 et 2 repetunt:
Popule meus. . .

Cantores:

Ego dedi tibi sceptrum regale:
et tu dedisti capiti meo spineam
      coronam.

1 et 2 repetunt:
Popule meus. . .

Cantores:

Ego te exaltavi magna virtute:
et tu me suspendisti
      in patibulo Crucis.

1 et 2 repetunt:
Popule meus. . .

HYMN

All:

Faithful Cross the Saints rely on,
Noble tree beyond compare!
Never was there such a scion,
Never leaf or flower so rare.
Sweet the timber, sweet the iron,
Sweet the burden that they bear!

Cantors:

Sing, my tongue, in exultation
Of our banner and device!
Make a solemn proclamation
Of a triumph and its price:
How the Saviour of creation
Conquered by his sacrifice!

All:

Faithful Cross the Saints rely on,
Noble tree beyond compare!
Never was there such a scion,
Never leaf or flower so rare.

Cantors:

For, when Adam first offended,
Eating that forbidden fruit,
Not all hopes of glory ended
With the serpent at the root:
Broken nature would be mended
By a second tree and shoot.

All:

Sweet the timber, sweet the iron,
Sweet the burden that they bear!

Cantors:

Thus the tempter was outwitted
By a wisdom deeper still:
Remedy and ailment fitted,
Means to cure and means to kill;
That the world might be acquitted,
Christ would do his Father's will.

Omnes:

Crux fidelis, inter omnes
    arbor una nobilis,
Nulla talem silva profert,
    flore, fronde, germine!
Dulce lignum dulci clavo
    dulce pondus sustinens!

Cantores:

Pange, lingua, gloriosi
    prœlium certaminis,
Et super crucis tropæo
    dic triumphum nobilem,
Qualiter Redemptor orbis
    immolatus vicerit.

Omnes:

Crux fidelis, inter omnes
    arbor una nobilis,
Nulla talem silva profert,
    flore, fronde, germine!

Cantores:

De parentis protoplasti
    fraude factor condolens,
Quando pomi noxialis
    morte morsu corruit,
Ipse lignum tunc notavit,
    damna ligni ut solveret.

Omnes:

Dulce lignum dulci clavo
    dulce pondus sustinens!

Cantores:

Hoc opus nostræ salutis
    ordo depoposcerat,
Multiformis perditoris
    arte ut artem falleret,
Et medelam ferret inde,
    hostis unde læserat.

All:

Faithful Cross the Saints rely on,
Noble tree beyond compare!
Never was there such a scion,
Never leaf or flower so rare.

Cantors:

So the Father, out of pity
For our self-inflicted doom,
Sent him from the heavenly city
When the holy time had come:
He, the Son and the Almighty,
Took our flesh in Mary's womb.

All:

Sweet the timber, sweet the iron,
Sweet the burden that they bear!

Cantors:

Hear a tiny baby crying,
Founder of the seas and strands;
See his virgin Mother tying
Cloth around his feet and hands;
Find him in a manger lying
Tightly wrapped in swaddling-bands!

All:

Faithful Cross the Saints rely on,
Noble tree beyond compare!
Never was there such a scion,
Never leaf or flower so rare.

Cantors:

So he came, the long-expected,
Not in glory, not to reign;
Only born to be rejected,
Choosing hunger, toil and pain,
Till the scaffold was erected
And the Paschal Lamb was slain.

All:

Sweet the timber, sweet the iron,
Sweet the burden that they bear!

Cantors:

No disgrace was too abhorrent:
Nailed and mocked and

Omnes:

Crux fidelis, inter omnes
    arbor una nobilis,
Nulla talem silva profert,
    flore, fronde, germine!

Cantores:

Quando venit ergo sacri
    plenitudo temporis,
Missus est ab arce Patris
Natus, orbis conditor,
Atque ventre virginali
    carne factus prodiit.

Omnes:

Dulce lignum dulci clavo
    dulce pondus sustinens!

Cantores:

Vagit infans inter arta
    conditus præsepia,
Membra pannis involuta
    Virgo Mater alligat,
Et manus pedesque et crura
    stricta cingit fascia.

Omnes:

Crux fidelis, inter omnes
    arbor una nobilis,
Nulla talem silva profert,
    flore, fronde, germine!

Cantores:

Lustra sex qui iam peracta,
    tempus implens corporis,
se volente, natus ad hoc,
    passioni deditus,
agnus in crucis levatur
    immolandus stipite.

Omnes:

Dulce lignum dulci clavo
    dulce pondus sustinens!

Cantores:

En acetum, fel, arundo,
Mite corpus perforatur,

parched he died;
Blood and water, double warrant,
Issue from his wounded side,
Washing in a mighty torrent
Earth and stars and oceantide.

All:

Faithful Cross the Saints rely on,
Noble tree beyond compare!
Never was there such a scion,
Never leaf or flower so rare.

Cantors:

Lofty timber,
    smooth your roughness,
Flex your boughs for blossoming;
Let your fibres lose their toughness,
Gently let your tendrils cling;
Lay aside your native gruffness,
Clasp the body of your King!

All:

Sweet the timber, sweet the iron,
Sweet the burden that they bear!

Cantors:

Noblest tree of all created,
Richly jewelled and embossed:
Post by Lamb's blood consecrated;
Spar that saves the tempest-tossed;
Scaffold-beam which, elevated,
Carries what the world has cost!

All:

Faithful Cross the Saints rely on,
Noble tree beyond compare!
Never was there such a scion,
Never leaf or flower so rare.

The following conclusion is never to be omitted:

All:

Wisdom, power, and adoration
To the blessed Trinity

---

sputa, clavi, lancea;
sanguis unde profluit;
Terra, pontus, astra, mundus
    quo lavantur flumine!

Omnes:

Crux fidelis, inter omnes
    arbor una nobilis,
Nulla talem silva profert,
    flore, fronde, germine!

Cantores:

Flecte ramos, arbor alta,
    tensa laxa viscera,
Et rigor lentescat ille,
    quem dedit nativitas,
Ut superni membra Regis
    miti tendas stipite.

Omnes:

Dulce lignum dulci clavo
    dulce pondus sustinens!

Cantores:

Sola digna tu fuisti
    ferre sæcli pretium
Atque portum præparare
    nauta mundo naufrago,
Quem sacer cruor perunxit
    fusus Agni corpore.

Omnes:

Crux fidelis, inter omnes
    arbor una nobilis,
Nulla talem silva profert,
    flore, fronde, germine!

Omnes:

Æqua Patri Filioque,
    inclito Paraclito,

For redemption and salvation	Sempiterna sit beatæ
Through the Paschal Mystery,	Trinitati gloria;
Now, in every generation,	cuius alma nos redemit
And for all eternity. Amen.	atque servat gratia. Amen.

In accordance with local circumstances or popular traditions and if it is pastorally appropriate, the Stabat Mater may be sung, as found in the Graduale Romanum, or another suitable chant in memory of the compassion of the Blessed Virgin Mary.

When the adoration has been concluded, the Cross is carried by the Deacon or a minister to its place at the altar. Lighted candles are placed around or on the altar or near the Cross.

THIRD PART:
Holy Communion

A cloth is spread on the altar, and a corporal and the Missal put in place. Meanwhile the Deacon or, if there is no Deacon, the Priest himself, putting on a humeral veil, brings the Blessed Sacrament back from the place of repose to the altar by a shorter route, while all stand in silence. Two ministers with lighted candles accompany the Blessed Sacrament and place their candlesticks around or upon the altar.

When the Deacon, if a Deacon is present, has placed the Blessed Sacrament upon the altar and uncovered the ciborium, the Priest goes to the altar and genuflects.

Then the Priest, with hands joined, says aloud:

At the Saviour's command	Præceptis salutaribus moniti,
and formed by divine teaching,	et divina institutione formati,
we dare to say:	audemus dicere:

The Priest, with hands extended says, and all present continue:

Our Father, who art in heaven,	Pater noster, qui es in cælis:
hallowed be thy name;	sanctificetur nomen tuum;
thy kingdom come,	adveniat regnum tuum;
thy will be done	fiat voluntas tua, sicut in cælo,
on earth as it is in heaven.	et in terra.
Give us this day our daily bread,	Panem nostrum cotidianum
and forgive us our trespasses,	da nobis hodie;
as we forgive those who trespass	et dimitte nobis debita nostra,
against us;	sicut et nos dimittimus
and lead us not into temptation,	debitoribus nostris;
but deliver us from evil.	et ne nos inducas in tentationem;
	sed libera nos a malo.

With hands extended, the Priest continues alone:

Deliver us, Lord, we pray,	Libera nos, quæsumus, Domine,
from every evil,	ab omnibus malis,

graciously grant peace in our days,
that, by the help of your mercy,
and safe from all distress,
as we await the blessed hope
and the coming of our Saviour,
    Jesus Christ.

da propitius pacem in diebus nostris,
ut, ope misericordiæ tuæ adiuti,
we may be always free from sin
et a peccato simus semper liberi
et ab omni perturbatione securi:
exspectantes beatam spem
et adventum Salvatoris nostri
    Iesu Christi.

He joins his hands.

The people conclude the prayer, acclaiming:

For the kingdom,
the power and the glory are yours
now and for ever.

Quia tuum est regnum,
et potestas,
et gloria in sæcula.

Then the Priest, with hands joined, says quietly:

May the receiving of your Body
    and Blood,
Lord Jesus Christ,
not bring me to judgement
    and condemnation,
but through your loving mercy
be for me protection in mind
    and body
and a healing remedy.

Perceptio Corporis tui,
    Domine Iesu Christe,
non mihi proveniat in iudicium
    et condemnationem:
sed pro tua pietate prosit mihi
ad tutamentum mentis et corporis,
et ad medelam percipiendam.

The Priest then genuflects, takes a particle, and, holding it slightly raised over the ciborium, while facing the people, says aloud:

Behold the Lamb of God,
behold him who takes away
    the sins of the world.
Blessed are those called
    to the supper of the Lamb.

Ecce Agnus Dei, ecce qui tollit
    peccata mundi.
Beati qui ad cenam
    Agni vocati sunt.

And together with the people he adds once:

Lord, I am not worthy
that you should enter under my roof,
but only say the word
and my soul shall be healed.

Domine, non sum dignus,
    ut intres sub tectum meum,
sed tantum dic verbo,
    et sanabitur anima mea.

And facing the altar, he reverently consumes the Body of Christ, saying quietly:

May the Body of Christ keep me
    safe for eternal life.

Corpus Christi custodiat me
    in vitam æternam.

He then proceeds to distribute Communion to the faithful. During Communion, Psalm 21 or another appropriate chant may be sung.

When the distribution of Communion has been completed, the ciborium is taken by the Deacon or another suitable minister to a place prepared outside the church or, if circumstances so require, it is placed in the tabernacle.

Then the Priest says: Let us pray, and, after a period of sacred silence, if circumstances so suggest, has been observed, he says the Prayer after Communion.

Almighty ever-living God,
who have restored us to life
by the blessed Death
    and Resurrection of your Christ,
preserve in us the work
    of your mercy,
that, by partaking of this mystery,
we may have a life unceasingly
    devoted to you.
Through Christ our Lord. R. Amen.
	Omnipotens sempiterne Deus,
	qui nos Christi tui beata morte
	    et resurrectione reparasti,
	conserva in nobis opus
	    misericordiæ tuæ,
	ut huius mysterii participatione
	perpetua devotione vivamus.
	Per Christum Dominum nostrum.
	R. Amen.

For the Dismissal the Deacon or, if there is no Deacon, the Priest himself, may say the invitation Bow down for the blessing.

Then the Priest, standing facing the people and extending his hands over them, says this Prayer over the People:

May abundant blessing, O Lord,
    we pray,
descend upon your people,
who have honoured the Death
    of your Son
in the hope of their resurrection:
may pardon come,
comfort be given,
holy faith increase,
and everlasting redemption
    be made secure.
Through Christ our Lord. R. Amen.
	Super populum tuum,
	    quæsumus, Domine,
	qui mortem Filii tui in spe suæ
	    resurrectionis recoluit,
	benedictio copiosa descendat,
	indulgentia veniat,
	    consolatio tribuatur,
	fides sancta succrescat,
	    redemptio sempiterna firmetur.
	Per Christum Dominum nostrum.
	R. Amen.

And all, after genuflecting to the Cross, depart in silence.

After the celebration, the altar is stripped, but the Cross remains on the altar with two or four candlesticks.

Vespers (Evening Prayer) is not celebrated by those who have been present at the solemn afternoon liturgical celebration.

EASTER SUNDAY OF THE RESURRECTION OF THE LORD

31 March

THE EASTER VIGIL IN THE HOLY NIGHT

How can we strengthen our hope? The liturgy of this night offers some guidance. It teaches us to remember the works of God. The readings describe God's faithfulness, the history of his love towards us. The living word of God is able to involve us in this history of love, nourishing our hope and renewing our joy. Remember the words of Jesus, remember all that he has done in our lives. Let us not forget his words and his works, otherwise we will lose hope and become "hopeless" Christians. Let us instead remember the Lord, his goodness and his life-giving words which have touched us. Let us remember them and make them ours, to be sentinels of the morning who know how to help others see the signs of the Risen Lord.

(Pope Francis)

By most ancient tradition, this is the night of keeping vigil for the Lord (Ex 12:42), in which, following the Gospel admonition (Lk 12:35-37), the faithful, carrying lighted lamps in their hands, should be like those looking for the Lord when he returns, so that at his coming he may find them awake and have them sit at his table.

Of this night's Vigil, which is the greatest and most noble of all solemnities, there is to be only one celebration in each church. It is arranged, moreover, in such a way that after the Lucernarium and Easter Proclamation (which constitutes the first part of this Vigil), Holy Church meditates on the wonders the Lord God has done for his people from the beginning, trusting in his word and promise (the second part, that is, the Liturgy of the Word) until, as day approaches, with new members reborn in Baptism (the third part), the Church is called to the table the Lord has prepared for his people, the memorial of his Death and Resurrection until he comes again (the fourth part).

The entire celebration of the Easter Vigil must take place during the night, so that it begins after nightfall and ends before daybreak on the Sunday.

The Mass of the Vigil, even if it is celebrated before midnight, is a paschal Mass of the Sunday of the Resurrection.

Anyone who participates in the Mass of the night may receive Communion again at Mass during the day. A Priest who celebrates or concelebrates the Mass of the night may again celebrate or concelebrate Mass during the day.

The Easter Vigil takes the place of the Office of Readings.

The Priest is usually assisted by a Deacon. If, however, there is no Deacon, the duties of his Order, except those indicated below, are assumed by the Priest Celebrant or by a concelebrant.

The Priest and Deacon vest as at Mass, in white vestments.

Candles should be prepared for all who participate in the Vigil. The lights of the church are extinguished.

FIRST PART:

THE SOLEMN BEGINNING OF THE VIGIL OR LUCERNARIUM

The Blessing of the Fire and Preparation of the Candle

A blazing fire is prepared in a suitable place outside the church. When the people are gathered there, the Priest approaches with the ministers, one of whom carries the paschal candle. The processional cross and candles are not carried.

Where, however, a fire cannot be lit outside the church, the rite is carried out as below.

The Priest and faithful sign themselves while the Priest says: In the name of the Father, and of the Son, and of the Holy Spirit, and then he greets the assembled people in the usual way and briefly instructs them about the night vigil in these or similar words:

Dear brethren (brothers and sisters),	Fratres carissimi,
on this most sacred night,	hac sacratissima nocte,
in which our Lord Jesus Christ	in qua Dominus noster
passed over from death to life,	Iesus Christus
the Church calls upon her sons and daughters,	de morte transivit ad vitam,
scattered throughout the world,	Ecclesia invitat filios dispersos per orbem terrarum,
to come together to watch and pray.	ut ad vigilandum et orandum conveniant.
If we keep the memorial of the Lord's paschal solemnity in this way,	Si ita memoriam egerimus Paschatis Domini,
listening to his word and celebrating his mysteries,	audientes verbum et celebrantes mysteria eius,
then we shall have the sure hope of sharing his triumph over death and living with him in God.	spem habebimus participandi triumphum eius de morte et vivendi cum ipso in Deo.

Then the Priest blesses the fire, saying with hands extended:

Let us pray.	Oremus.

O God, who through your Son bestowed upon the faithful the fire of your glory, sanctify ✠ this new fire, we pray, and grant that, by these paschal celebrations, we may be so inflamed with heavenly desires, that with minds made pure we may attain festivities of unending splendour. Through Christ our Lord. R. Amen.	Deus, qui per Filium tuum claritatis tuæ ignem fidelibus contulisti, novum hunc ignem ✠ sanctifica, et concede nobis, ita per hæc festa paschalia cælestibus desideriis inflammari, ut ad perpetuæ claritatis puris mentibus valeamus festa pertingere. Per Christum Dominum nostrum. R. Amen.

After the blessing of the new fire, one of the ministers brings the paschal candle to the Priest, who cuts a cross into the candle with a stylus. Then he makes the Greek letter Alpha above the cross, the letter Omega below, and the four numerals of the current year between the arms of the cross, saying meanwhile:

1. Christ yesterday and today	1. Christus heri et hodie
2. the Beginning and the End	2. Principium et Finis
3. the Alpha	3. Alpha
4. and the Omega	4. et Omega
5. All time belongs to him	5. Ipsius sunt tempora
6. and all the ages	6. et sæcula
7. To him be glory and power	7. Ipsi gloria et imperium
8. through every age and for ever. Amen	8. per universa æternitatis sæcula. Amen

When the cutting of the cross and of the other signs has been completed, the Priest may insert five grains of incense into the candle in the form of a cross, meanwhile saying:

1. By his holy	1. Per sua sancta vulnera
2. and glorious wounds,	2. gloriosa
3. may Christ the Lord	3. custodiat
4. guard us	4. et conservet nos
5. and protect us. Amen.	5. Christus Dominus. Amen.

Where, because of difficulties that may occur, a fire is not lit, the blessing of fire is adapted to the circumstances. When the people are gathered in the church as on other occasions, the Priest comes to the door of the church, along with the ministers carrying the paschal candle. The people, insofar as is possible, turn to face the Priest.

The greeting and address take place as above; then the fire is blessed and the candle is prepared, as above.

The Priest lights the paschal candle from the new fire, saying:

| May the light of Christ rising in glory dispel the darkness of our hearts and minds. | Lumen Christi gloriose resurgentis dissipet tenebras cordis et mentis. |

As regards the preceding elements, Conferences of Bishops may also establish other forms more adapted to the culture of the different peoples.

Procession

When the candle has been lit, one of the ministers takes burning coals from the fire and places them in the thurible, and the Priest puts incense into it in the usual way. The Deacon or, if there is no Deacon, another suitable minister, takes the paschal candle and a procession forms. The thurifer with the smoking thurible precedes the Deacon or other minister who carries the paschal candle. After them follows the Priest with the ministers and the people, all holding in their hands unlit candles.

At the door of the church the Deacon, standing and raising up the candle, sings:

| The Light of Christ. | Lumen Christi. |

And all reply:

| Thanks be to God. | Deo gratias. |

The Priest lights his candle from the flame of the paschal candle.

Then the Deacon moves forward to the middle of the church and, standing and raising up the candle, sings a second time:

| The Light of Christ. | Lumen Christi. |

And all reply:

| Thanks be to God. | Deo gratias. |

All light their candles from the flame of the paschal candle and continue in procession.

When the Deacon arrives before the altar, he stands facing the people, raises up the candle and sings a third time:

| The Light of Christ. | Lumen Christi. |

And all reply:

| Thanks be to God. | Deo gratias. |

Then the Deacon places the paschal candle on a large candlestand prepared next to the ambo or in the middle of the sanctuary.

And lights are lit throughout the church, except for the altar candles.

The Easter Proclamation (Exsultet)

Arriving at the altar, the Priest goes to his chair, gives his candle to a minister, puts incense into the thurible and blesses the incense as at the Gospel at Mass. The Deacon goes to the Priest and saying, **Your blessing, Father**, asks for and receives a blessing from the Priest, who says in a low voice:

May the Lord be in your heart
    and on your lips,
that you may proclaim his paschal
    praise worthily and well,
in the name of the Father and of
    the Son, ✠ and of the Holy Spirit.
The Deacon replies: Amen.
	Dominus sit in corde tuo
	    et in labiis tuis,
	ut digne et competenter annunties
	suum paschale præconium:
	in nomine Patris, et Filii,
	    ✠ et Spiritus Sancti.
	Amen.

This blessing is omitted if the Proclamation is made by someone who is not a Deacon.

The Deacon, after incensing the book and the candle, proclaims the Easter Proclamation (Exsultet) at the ambo or at a lectern, with all standing and holding lighted candles in their hands.

The Easter Proclamation may be made, in the absence of a Deacon, by the Priest himself or by another concelebrating Priest. If, however, because of necessity, a lay cantor sings the Proclamation, the words Therefore, dearest friends up to the end of the invitation are omitted, along with the greeting The Lord be with you.

The Proclamation may also be sung in the shorter form p.367.

Longer Form of the Easter Proclamation

Exult, let them exult,
    the hosts of heaven,
exult, let Angel ministers
    of God exult,
let the trumpet of salvation
sound aloud our mighty
    King's triumph!
Be glad, let earth be glad,
    as glory floods her,
ablaze with light from her
    eternal King,
let all corners of the earth be glad,
knowing an end to gloom
    and darkness.
	Exsultet iam angelica
	    turba cælorum:
	exsultent divina mysteria:
	et pro tanti Regis victoria tuba
	    insonet salutaris.
	
	Gaudeat et tellus tantis
	    irradiata fulgoribus:
	et, æterni Regis splendore illustrata,
	totius orbis se sentiat
	    amisisse caliginem.

Rejoice, let Mother Church
   also rejoice,
arrayed with the lightning
   of his glory,
let this holy building shake with joy,
filled with the mighty voices
   of the peoples.

(Therefore, dearest friends,
standing in the awesome glory
   of this holy light,
invoke with me, I ask you,
the mercy of God almighty,
that he, who has been pleased
   to number me,
though unworthy, among the Levites,
may pour into me his light
   unshadowed,
that I may sing this candle's
   perfect praises.)

(V. The Lord be with you.
R. And with your spirit.)
V. Lift up your hearts.
R. We lift them up to the Lord.
V. Let us give thanks to the Lord
   our God.
R. It is right and just.
It is truly right and just,
with ardent love of mind and heart
and with devoted service of our voice,
to acclaim our God invisible,
   the almighty Father,
and Jesus Christ, our Lord, his Son,
   his Only Begotten.

Who for our sake paid Adam's debt
   to the eternal Father,
and, pouring out his own dear Blood,
wiped clean the record of our
   ancient sinfulness.

Lætetur et mater Ecclesia,
tanti luminis adornata fulgoribus:
et magnis populorum vocibus hæc
   aula resultet.

(Quapropter astantes vos,
   fratres carissimi,
ad tam miram huius sancti
   luminis claritatem,
una mecum, quæso,
Dei omnipotentis
   misericordiam invocate.
Ut, qui me non meis meritis
intra Levitarum numerum dignatus
   est aggregare,
luminis sui claritatem infundens,
cerei huius laudem
   implere perficiat.)

(V. Dominus vobiscum.
R. Et cum spiritu tuo.)
V. Sursum corda.
R. Habemus ad Dominum.
V. Gratias agamus Domino
   Deo nostro.
R. Dignum et iustum est.
Vere dignum et iustum est,
invisibilem Deum
   Patrem omnipotentem
Filiumque eius Unigenitum,
Dominum nostrum
   Iesum Christum,
toto cordis ac mentis affectu
   et vocis ministerio personare.

Qui pro nobis æterno Patri Adæ
   debitum solvit,
et veteris piaculi cautionem
   pio cruore detersit.

These then are the feasts of Passover,
in which is slain the Lamb,
 the one true Lamb,
whose Blood anoints the doorposts
 of believers.

Hæc sunt enim festa paschalia,
in quibus verus ille Agnus occiditur,
cuius sanguine postes
 fidelium consecrantur.

This is the night,
when once you led our forebears,
 Israel's children,
from slavery in Egypt
and made them pass dry-shod
 through the Red Sea.

Hæc nox est,
in qua primum patres nostros,
filios Israel eductos de Ægypto,
Mare Rubrum sicco vestigio
 transire fecisti.

This is the night
that with a pillar of fire
banished the darkness of sin.

Hæc igitur nox est,
quæ peccatorum tenebras columnæ
 illuminatione purgavit.

This is the night
that even now, throughout the world,
sets Christian believers apart
 from worldly vices
and from the gloom of sin,
leading them to grace
and joining them to his holy ones.

Hæc nox est,
quæ hodie per universum mundum
 in Christo credentes,
a vitiis sæculi et caligine
 peccatorum segregatos,
reddit gratiæ, sociat sanctitati.

This is the night,
when Christ broke the prison-bars
 of death
and rose victorious
 from the underworld.

Hæc nox est,
in qua, destructis vinculis mortis,
Christus ab inferis victor ascendit.

Our birth would have been no gain,
had we not been redeemed.
O wonder of your humble care for us!
O love, O charity beyond all telling,
to ransom a slave you gave away
 your Son!

Nihil enim nobis nasci profuit,
 nisi redimi profuisset.
O mira circa nos tuæ pietatis
 dignatio!
O inæstimablilis dilectio caritatis:
ut servum redimeres,
 Filium tradidisti!

O truly necessary sin of Adam,
destroyed completely by the Death
 of Christ!

O certe necessarium
 Adæ peccatum,
quod Christi morte deletum est!

O happy fault
that earned so great,
   so glorious a Redeemer!

O truly blessed night,
worthy alone to know the time
   and hour
when Christ rose
   from the underworld!

This is the night
of which it is written:
The night shall be as bright as day,
dazzling is the night for me,
and full of gladness.

The sanctifying power of this night
dispels wickedness,
   washes faults away,
restores innocence to the fallen,
   and joy to mourners,
drives out hatred, fosters concord,
   and brings down the mighty.

On this, your night of grace,
   O holy Father,
accept this candle, a solemn offering,
the work of bees and of your
   servants' hands,
an evening sacrifice of praise,
this gift from your most holy Church.

But now we know the praises
   of this pillar,
which glowing fire ignites
   for God's honour,
a fire into many flames divided,
yet never dimmed by sharing
   of its light,
for it is fed by melting wax,
drawn out by mother bees
to build a torch so precious.

O felix culpa,
quæ talem ac tantum meruit
   habere Redemptorem!

O vere beata nox,
quæ sola meruit scire tempus
   et horam,
in qua Christus ab inferis resurrexit!

Hæc nox est, de qua scriptum est:
Et nox sicut dies illuminabitur:
et nox illuminatio mea
   in deliciis meis.

Huius igitur sanctificatio noctis
   fugat scelera, culpas lavat:
et reddit innocentiam lapsis
   et mæstis lætitiam.
Fugat odia, concordiam parat
   et curvat imperia.

In huius igitur noctis gratia,
suscipe, sancte Pater, laudis huius
   sacrificium vespertinum,
quod tibi in hac cerei
   oblatione sollemni,
per ministrorum manus
de operibus apum,
   sacrosancta reddit Ecclesia.

Sed iam columnæ huius
   præconia novimus,
quam in honorem Dei rutilans
   ignis accendit.
Qui, licet sit divisus in partes,
mutuati tamen luminis detrimenta
   non novit.
Alitur enim liquantibus ceris,
quas in substantiam pretiosæ
   huius lampadis
apis mater eduxit.

O truly blessed night,
when things of heaven are wed
   to those of earth,
and divine to the human.

Therefore, O Lord,
we pray you that this candle,
hallowed to the honour of
   your name,
may persevere undimmed,
to overcome the darkness
   of this night.
Receive it as a pleasing fragrance,
and let it mingle with
   the lights of heaven.
May this flame be found still burning
by the Morning Star:
the one Morning Star who never sets,
Christ your Son,
who, coming back
   from death's domain,
has shed his peaceful light
   on humanity,
and lives and reigns
   for ever and ever.
R. Amen.

O vere beata nox,
in qua terrenis cælestia,
   humanis divina iunguntur!

Oramus ergo te, Domine,
ut cereus iste in honorem tui
   nominis consecratus,
ad noctis huius
   caliginem destruendam,
indeficiens perseveret.

Et in odorem suavitatis acceptus,
supernis luminaribus misceatur.
Flammas eius lucifer
   matutinus inveniat:

Ille, inquam, lucifer,
   qui nescit occasum:
Christus Filius tuus,
qui, regressus ab inferis, humano
   generi serenus illuxit,
et vivit et regnat
   in sæcula sæculorum.

R. Amen.

Shorter Form of the Easter Proclamation

Exult, let them exult,
   the hosts of heaven,
exult, let Angel ministers
   of God exult,
let the trumpet of salvation
sound aloud our mighty
   King's triumph!
Be glad, let earth be glad, as glory
   floods her,
ablaze with light from her
   eternal King,
let all corners of the earth be glad,
knowing an end to gloom
   and darkness.

Exsultet iam angelica
   turba cælorum:
exsultent divina mysteria:
et pro tanti Regis victoria tuba
   insonet salutaris.

Gaudeat et tellus tantis
   irradiata fulgoribus:
et, æterni Regis splendore illustrata,
totius orbis se sentiat
   amisisse caliginem.

Rejoice, let Mother Church
    also rejoice,
arrayed with the lightning
    of his glory,
let this holy building shake with joy,
filled with the mighty voices
    of the peoples.

(V. The Lord be with you.
R. And with your spirit.)
V. Lift up your hearts.
R. We lift them up to the Lord.
V. Let us give thanks to the Lord
    our God.
R. It is right and just.

It is truly right and just,
with ardent love of mind and heart
and with devoted service of our voice,
to acclaim our God invisible,
    the almighty Father,
and Jesus Christ, our Lord, his Son,
    his Only Begotten.

Who for our sake paid Adam's debt
    to the eternal Father,
and, pouring out his own dear Blood,
wiped clean the record
    of our ancient sinfulness.

These then are the feasts of Passover,
in which is slain the Lamb,
    the one true Lamb,
whose Blood anoints the doorposts
    of believers.

This is the night,
when once you led our forebears,
    Israel's children,
from slavery in Egypt
and made them pass dry-shod
    through the Red Sea.

Lætetur et mater Ecclesia,
tanti luminis adornata fulgoribus:
et magnis populorum vocibus hæc
    aula resultet.

(V. Dominus vobiscum.
R. Et cum spiritu tuo.)
V. Sursum corda.
R. Habemus ad Dominum.
V. Gratias agamus Domino
    Deo nostro.
R. Dignum et iustum est.

Vere dignum et iustum est,
invisibilem Deum
    Patrem omnipotentem
Filiumque eius Unigenitum,
Dominum nostrum
    Iesum Christum,
toto cordis ac mentis affectu
    et vocis ministerio personare.

Qui pro nobis æterno Patri Adæ
    debitum solvit,
et veteris piaculi cautionem pio
    cruore detersit.

Hæc sunt enim festa paschalia,
in quibus verus ille
    Agnus occiditur,
cuius sanguine postes
    fidelium consecrantur.

Hæc nox est,
in qua primum patres nostros,
    filios Israel
eductos de Ægypto,
Mare Rubrum sicco vestigio
    transire fecisti.

This is the night
that with a pillar of fire
banished the darkness of sin.

Hæc igitur nox est,
quæ peccatorum tenebras columnæ
    illuminatione purgavit.

This is the night
that even now, throughout the world,
sets Christian believers apart
    from worldly vices
and from the gloom of sin,
leading them to grace
and joining them to his holy ones.

Hæc nox est,
quæ hodie per universum mundum
    in Christo credentes,
a vitiis sæculi et caligine
peccatorum segregatos,
reddit gratiæ, sociat sanctitati.

This is the night,
when Christ broke the prison-bars
    of death
and rose victorious
    from the underworld.

Hæc nox est,
in qua, destructis vinculis mortis,
Christus ab inferis victor ascendit.

O wonder of your humble care for us!
O love, O charity beyond all telling,
to ransom a slave you gave away
    your Son!

O mira circa nos tuæ
    pietatis dignatio!
O inæstimablilis dilectio caritatis:
ut servum redimeres,
    Filium tradidisti!

O truly necessary sin of Adam,
destroyed completely by the Death
    of Christ!

O certe necessarium Adæ peccatum,
quod Christi morte deletum est!

O happy fault
that earned so great,
    so glorious a Redeemer!

O felix culpa,
quæ talem ac tantum meruit
    habere Redemptorem!

The sanctifying power of this night
dispels wickedness,
    washes faults away,
restores innocence to the fallen,
    and joy to mourners.

Huius igitur sanctificatio noctis
    fugat scelera, culpas lavat:
et reddit innocentiam lapsis
    et mæstis lætitiam.

O truly blessed night,
when things of heaven are wed
    to those of earth,
and divine to the human.

O vere beata nox,
in qua terrenis cælestia,
    humanis divina iunguntur!

On this, your night of grace,
    O holy Father,
accept this candle, a solemn offering,
the work of bees and of your

In huius igitur noctis gratia,
suscipe, sancte Pater, laudis huius
    sacrificium vespertinum,
quod tibi in hac cerei

servants' hands,
an evening sacrifice of praise,
this gift from your most
    holy Church.

Therefore, O Lord,
we pray you that this candle,
hallowed to the honour
    of your name,
may persevere undimmed,
to overcome the darkness
    of this night.
Receive it as a pleasing fragrance,
and let it mingle with the lights
    of heaven.
May this flame be found
    still burning
by the Morning Star:
the one Morning Star who never sets,
Christ your Son,
who, coming back from
    death's domain,
has shed his peaceful light
    on humanity,
and lives and reigns
    for ever and ever.
R. Amen.

oblatione sollemni,
per ministrorum manus
de operibus apum,
    sacrosancta reddit Ecclesia.

Oramus ergo te, Domine,
ut cereus iste in honorem tui
    nominis consecratus,
ad noctis huius
    caliginem destruendam,
indeficiens perseveret.
Et in odorem suavitatis acceptus,
supernis luminaribus misceatur.
Flammas eius lucifer
    matutinus inveniat:
Ille, inquam, lucifer,
    qui nescit occasum:
Christus Filius tuus,
qui, regressus ab inferis,
    humano generi serenus illuxit,
et vivit et regnat
    in sæcula sæculorum.
R. Amen.

SECOND PART:
The Liturgy of the Word

In this Vigil, the mother of all Vigils, nine readings are provided, namely seven from the Old Testament and two from the New (the Epistle and Gospel), all of which should be read whenever this can be done, so that the character of the Vigil, which demands an extended period of time, may be preserved.

Nevertheless, where more serious pastoral circumstances demand it, the number of readings from the Old Testament may be reduced, always bearing in mind that the reading of the Word of God is a fundamental part of this Easter Vigil. At least three readings should be read from the Old Testament, both from the Law and from the Prophets, and their respective Responsorial Psalms should be sung. Never, moreover, should the reading of chapter 14 of Exodus with its canticle be omitted.

After setting aside their candles, all sit. Before the readings begin, the Priest instructs the people in these or similar words:

Dear brethren (brothers and sisters), now that we have begun
  our solemn Vigil,
let us listen with quiet hearts
  to the Word of God.
Let us meditate on how God in
  times past saved his people
and in these, the last days, has sent
  us his Son as our Redeemer.
Let us pray that our God may
  complete this paschal work
  of salvation
by the fullness of redemption.

Vigiliam sollemniter ingressi,
  fratres carissimi,
quieto corde nunc verbum
  Dei audiamus.
Meditemur, quomodo Deus
  populum suum
elapsis temporibus salvum fecerit,
et novissime nobis Filium suum
  miserit Redemptorem.
Oremus, ut Deus noster hoc
  paschale salvationis opus
ad plenam redemptionem perficiat.

Then the readings follow. A reader goes to the ambo and proclaims the reading. Afterwards a psalmist or a cantor sings or says the Psalm with the people making the response. Then all rise, the Priest says, Let us pray and, after all have prayed for a while in silence, he says the prayer corresponding to the reading. In place of the Responsorial Psalm a period of sacred silence may be observed, in which case the pause after Let us pray is omitted.

FIRST READING

A reading from the book of Genesis   1:1-2:2

God saw all he made, and indeed it was very good.

[In the beginning God created the heavens and the earth.] Now the earth was a formless void, there was darkness over the deep, and God's spirit hovered over the water.

God said, 'Let there be light,' and there was light. God saw that light was good, and God divided light from darkness. God called light 'day', and darkness he called 'night'. Evening came and morning came: the first day.

God said, 'Let there be a vault in the waters to divide the waters in two.' And so it was. God made the vault, and it divided the waters above the vault from the waters under the vault. God called the vault 'heaven'. Evening came and morning came: the second day.

God said, 'Let the waters under heaven come together into a single mass, and let dry land appear.' And so it was. God called the dry land 'earth' and the mass of waters 'seas', and God saw that it was good.

God said, 'Let the earth produce vegetation: seed-bearing plants, and fruit trees bearing fruit with their seed inside, on the earth.' And so it was.

The earth produced vegetation: plants bearing seed in their several kinds, and trees bearing fruit with their seed inside in their several kinds. God saw that it was good. Evening came and morning came: the third day.

God said, 'Let there be lights in the vault of heaven to divide day from night, and let them indicate festivals, days and years. Let them be lights in the vault of heaven to shine on the earth.' And so it was. God made the two great lights: the greater light to govern the day, the smaller light to govern the night, and the stars. God set them in the vault of heaven to shine on the earth, to govern the day and the night and to divide light from darkness. God saw that it was good. Evening came and morning came: the fourth day.

God said, 'Let the waters teem with living creatures, and let birds fly above the earth within the vault of heaven.' And so it was. God created great sea-serpents and every kind of living creature with which the waters teem, and every kind of winged creature. God saw that it was good. God blessed them, saying, 'Be fruitful, multiply, and fill the waters of the seas, and let the birds multiply upon the earth.' Evening came and morning came: the fifth day.

God said, 'Let the earth produce every kind of living creature: cattle, reptiles, and every kind of wild beast.' And so it was. God made every kind of wild beast, every kind of cattle, and every kind of land reptile. God saw that it was good.

[God said, 'Let us make man in our own image, in the likeness of ourselves, and let them be masters of the fish of the sea, the birds of heaven, the cattle, all the wild beasts and all the reptiles that crawl upon the earth.'

God created man in the image of himself,
in the image of God he created him,
male and female he created them.

God blessed them, saying to them, 'Be fruitful, multiply, fill the earth and conquer it. Be masters of the fish of the sea, the birds of heaven and all living animals on the earth.' God said, 'See, I give you all the seed-bearing plants that are upon the whole earth, and all the trees with seed-bearing fruit; this shall be your food. To all wild beasts, all birds of heaven and all living reptiles on the earth I give all the foliage of plants for food.' And so it was. God saw all he had made, and indeed it was very good. Evening came and morning came: the sixth day.

Thus heaven and earth were completed with all their array. On the seventh day God completed the work he had been doing. He rested on the seventh day after all the work he had been doing.

The word of the Lord.]

Shorter Form, verses 1, 26-31. Read between [ ]

Responsorial Psalm   Ps 103:1-2,5-6,10,12-14,24,35. R. Cf. v.30

R. **Send forth your spirit, O Lord,**
  and renew the face of the earth.

  Bless the Lord, my soul!
  Lord God, how great you are,
  clothed in majesty and glory,
  wrapped in light as in a robe! R.

  You founded the earth on its base,
  to stand firm from age to age.
  You wrapped it with the ocean like a cloak:
  the waters stood higher than the mountains. R.

  You make springs gush forth in the valleys:
  they flow in between the hills.
  On their banks dwell the birds of heaven;
  from the branches they sing their song. R.

  From your dwelling you water the hills;
  earth drinks its fill of your gift.
  You make the grass grow for the cattle
  and the plants to serve man's needs. R.

  How many are your works, O Lord!
  In wisdom you have made them all.
  The earth is full of your riches.
  Bless the Lord, my soul! R.

Alternative Psalm   Ps 32:4-7,12-13,20,22. R. v.5

R. **The Lord fills the earth with his love.**

  The word of the Lord is faithful
  and all his works to be trusted.
  The Lord loves justice and right
  and fills the earth with his love. R.

  By his word the heavens were made,
  by the breath of his mouth all the stars.
  He collects the waves of the ocean;
  he stores up the depths of the sea. R.

  They are happy, whose God is the Lord,
  the people he has chosen as his own.
  From the heavens the Lord looks forth,
  he sees all the children of men. R.

Our soul is waiting for the Lord.
The Lord is our help and our shield.
May your love be upon us, O Lord,
as we place all our hope in you. R.

R. **The Lord fills the earth with his love.**

Prayer

Let us pray.

Almighty ever-living God,
who are wonderful in the ordering
 of all your works,
may those you have
 redeemed understand
that there exists nothing
 more marvellous
than the world's creation
 in the beginning
except that, at the end of the ages,
Christ our Passover
 has been sacrificed.
Who lives and reigns
 for ever and ever.
R. Amen.

Oremus.

Omnipotens sempiterne Deus,
qui es in omnium operum tuorum
 dispensatione mirabilis,
intellegant redempti tui,
 non fuisse excellentius,
quod initio factus est mundus,
quam quod in fine sæculorum
Pascha nostrum immolatus
 est Christus.
Qui vivit et regnat
 in sæcula sæculorum.
R. Amen.

Or, On the creation of man:

O God, who wonderfully created
 human nature
and still more wonderfully
 redeemed it,
grant us, we pray,
to set our minds against
 the enticements of sin,
that we may merit to attain
 eternal joys.
Through Christ our Lord.
R. Amen.

Deus, qui mirabiliter creasti hominem
et mirabilius redemisti,
da nobis, quæsumus,
contra oblectamenta peccati mentis
 ratione persistere,
ut mereamur ad æterna
 gaudia pervenire.
Per Christum Dominum nostrum.
R. Amen.

SECOND READING

A reading from the book of Genesis   22:1-18

The sacrifice of Abraham, our father in faith.

[God put Abraham to the test. 'Abraham, Abraham,' he called. 'Here I am'
he replied. 'Take your son,' God said 'your only child Isaac, whom you

love, and go to the land of Moriah. There you shall offer him as a burnt offering, on a mountain I will point out to you.']

Rising early next morning Abraham saddled his ass and took with him two of his servants and his son Isaac. He chopped wood for the burnt offering and started on his journey to the place God had pointed out to him. On the third day Abraham looked up and saw the place in the distance. Then Abraham said to his servants, 'Stay here with the donkey. The boy and I will go over there; we will worship and come back to you.'

Abraham took the wood for the burnt offering, loaded it on Isaac, and carried in his own hands the fire and the knife. Then the two of them set out together. Isaac spoke to his father Abraham, 'Father' he said. 'Yes, my son' he replied. 'Look,' he said 'here are the fire and the wood, but where is the lamb for the burnt offering?' Abraham answered, 'My son, God himself will provide the lamb for the burnt offering.' Then the two of them went on together.

[When they arrived at the place God had pointed out to him, Abraham built an altar there, and arranged the wood. Then he bound his son Isaac and put him on the altar on top of the wood. Abraham stretched out his hand and seized the knife to kill his son.

But the angel of the Lord called to him from heaven. 'Abraham, Abraham' he said. 'I am here' he replied. 'Do not raise your hand against the boy' the angel said. 'Do not harm him, for now I know you fear God. You have not refused me your son, your only son.' Then looking up, Abraham saw a ram caught by its horns in a bush. Abraham took the ram and offered it as a burnt-offering in place of his son.] Abraham called this place 'The Lord provides', and hence the saying today: On the mountain the Lord provides.

[The angel of the Lord called Abraham a second time from heaven. 'I swear by my own self – it is the Lord who speaks – because you have done this, because you have not refused me your son, your only son, I will shower blessings on you, I will make your descendants as many as the stars of heaven and the grains of sand on the seashore. Your descendants shall gain possession of the gates of their enemies. All the nations of the earth shall bless themselves by your descendants, as a reward for your obedience.

The word of the Lord.]

Shorter Form, verses 1-2,9-13,15-18. Read between [ ]

Responsial Psalm   Ps 15:5,8-11, R. v.1

R. **Preserve me, God, I take refuge in you.**

O Lord, it is you who are my portion and cup;
it is you yourself who are my prize.
I keep the Lord ever in my sight:
since he is at my right hand, I shall stand firm. R.

And so my heart rejoices, my soul is glad;
even my body shall rest in safety.
For you will not leave my soul among the dead,
nor let your beloved know decay. R.

You will show me the path of life,
the fullness of joy in your presence,
at your right hand happiness for ever. R.

Prayer

Let us pray.

O God, supreme Father of the faithful, who increase the children of your promise by pouring out the grace of adoption throughout the whole world and who through the Paschal Mystery make your servant Abraham father of nations, as once you swore, grant, we pray, that your peoples may enter worthily into the grace to which you call them. Through Christ our Lord. R. Amen.	Oremus. Deus, Pater summe fidelium, qui promissionis tuæ filios diffusa adoptionis gratia in toto terrarum orbe multiplicas, et per paschale sacramentum Abraham puerum tuum universarum, sicut iurasti, gentium efficis patrem, da populis tuis digne ad gratiam tuæ vocationis intrare. Per Christum Dominum nostrum. R. Amen.

The following reading must always be read.

THIRD READING

A reading from the book of Exodus   14:15-15:1

The sons of Israel went on dry ground right into the sea.

The Lord said to Moses, 'Why do you cry to me so? Tell the sons of Israel to
march on. For yourself, raise your staff and stretch out your hand over the

sea and part it for the sons of Israel to walk through the sea on dry ground. I for my part will make the heart of the Egyptians so stubborn that they will follow them. So shall I win myself glory at the expense of Pharaoh, of all his army, his chariots, his horsemen. And when I have won glory for myself, at the expense of Pharaoh and his chariots and his army, the Egyptians will learn that I am the Lord.'

Then the angel of the Lord, who marched at the front of the army of Israel, changed station and moved to their rear. The pillar of cloud changed station from the front to the rear of them, and remained there. It came between the camp of the Egyptians and the camp of Israel. The cloud was dark, and the night passed without the armies drawing any closer the whole night long. Moses stretched out his hand over the sea. The Lord drove back the sea with a strong easterly wind all night, and he made dry land of the sea. The waters parted and the sons of Israel went on dry ground right into the sea, walls of water to right and to left of them. The Egyptians gave chase: after them they went, right into the sea, all Pharaoh's horses, his chariots, and his horsemen. In the morning watch, the Lord looked down on the army of the Egyptians from the pillar of fire and of cloud, and threw the army into confusion. He so clogged their chariot wheels that they could scarcely make headway. 'Let us flee from the Israelites,' the Egyptians cried 'the Lord is fighting for them against the Egyptians!' 'Stretch out your hand over the sea,' the Lord said to Moses 'that the waters may flow back on the Egyptians and their chariots and their horsemen.' Moses stretched out his hand over the sea and, as day broke, the sea returned to its bed. The fleeing Egyptians marched right into it, and the Lord overthrew the Egyptians in the very middle of the sea. The returning waters overwhelmed the chariots and the horsemen of Pharaoh's whole army, which had followed the Israelites into the sea; not a single one of them was left. But the sons of Israel had marched through the sea on dry ground, walls of water to right and to left of them. That day, the Lord rescued Israel from the Egyptians, and Israel saw the Egyptians lying dead on the shore. Israel witnessed the great act that the Lord had performed against the Egyptians, and the people venerated the Lord; they put their faith in the Lord and in Moses, his servant.

It was then that Moses and the sons of Israel sang this song in honour of the Lord:

The choir takes up the Responsorial Psalm immediately.

Responsorial Psalm   Ex 15:1-6,17-18. R. v.1

R. **I will sing to the Lord, glorious his triumph!**

I will sing to the Lord, glorious his triumph!
Horse and rider he has thrown into the sea!
The Lord is my strength, my song, my salvation.
This is my God and I extol him,
my father's God and I give him praise. R.

The Lord is a warrior! The Lord is his name.
The chariots of Pharaoh he hurled into the sea,
the flower of his army is drowned in the sea.
The deeps hide them; they sank like a stone. R.

Your right hand, Lord, glorious in its power,
your right hand, Lord, has shattered the enemy.
In the greatness of your glory you crushed the foe. R.

You will lead your people and plant them on your mountain,
the place, O Lord, where you have made your home,
the sanctuary, Lord, which your hands have made.
The Lord will reign for ever and ever. R.

Prayer

Let us pray.

O God, whose ancient wonders
remain undimmed in splendour
    even in our day,
for what you once bestowed
    on a single people,
freeing them from
    Pharaoh's persecution
by the power of your right hand,
now you bring about as the salvation
    of the nations
through the waters of rebirth,
grant, we pray,
    that the whole world
may become children of Abraham
and inherit the dignity
    of Israel's birthright.
Through Christ our Lord.
R. Amen.

Oremus.

Deus, cuius antiqua miracula
etiam nostris temporibus
    coruscare sentimus,
dum, quod uni populo
a persecutione Pharaonis liberando
dexteræ tuæ potentia contulisti,
id in salutem gentium
per aquam regenerationis operaris,
præsta, ut in Abrahæ filios
et in Israeliticam dignitatem
totius mundi transeat plenitudo.
Per Christum Dominum nostrum.
R. Amen.

Or:	Vel:
O God, who by the light of the New Testament have unlocked the meaning of wonders worked in former times, so that the Red Sea prefigures the sacred font and the nation delivered from slavery foreshadows the Christian people, grant, we pray, that all nations, obtaining the privilege of Israel by merit of faith, may be reborn by partaking of your Spirit. Through Christ our Lord. R. Amen.	Deus, qui primis temporibus impleta miracula novi testamenti luce reserasti, ut et Mare Rubrum forma sacri fontis exsisteret, et plebs a servitute liberata christiani populi sacramenta præferret, da, ut omnes gentes, Israelis privilegium merito fidei consecutæ, Spiritus tui participatione regenerentur. Per Christum Dominum nostrum. R. Amen.

FOURTH READING

A reading from the prophet Isaiah   54:5-14

With everlasting love the Lord your redeemer has taken pity on you.

Now your creator will be your husband,
his name, the Lord of hosts;
your redeemer will be the Holy One of Israel,
he is called the God of the whole earth.
Yes, like a forsaken wife, distressed in spirit,
the Lord calls you back.
Does a man cast off the wife of his youth?
says your God.

I did forsake you for a brief moment,
but with great love will I take you back.
In excess of anger, for a moment
I hid my face from you.
But with everlasting love I have taken pity on you,
says the Lord, your redeemer.

I am now as I was in the days of Noah
when I swore that Noah's waters
should never flood the world again.
So now I swear concerning my anger with you
and the threats I made against you;

for the mountains may depart,
the hills be shaken,
but my love for you will never leave you;
and my covenant of peace with you will never be shaken,
says the Lord who takes pity on you.

Unhappy creature, storm-tossed, disconsolate,
see, I will set your stones on carbuncles
and your foundations on sapphires.
I will make rubies your battlements,
your gates crystal,
and your entire wall precious stones.
Your sons will all be taught by the Lord.
The prosperity of your sons will be great.
You will be founded on integrity;
remote from oppression, you will have nothing to fear;
remote from terror, it will not approach you.

   The word of the Lord.

Responsorial Psalm   Ps 29:2,4-6,11-13. R. v.2

R. **I will praise you, Lord, you have rescued me.**

   I will praise you, Lord, you have rescued me
   and have not let my enemies rejoice over me.
   O Lord, you have raised my soul from the dead,
   restored me to life from those who sink into the grave. R.

   Sing psalms to the Lord, you who love him,
   give thanks to his holy name.
   His anger lasts but a moment; his favour through life.
   At night there are tears, but joy comes with dawn. R.

   The Lord listened and had pity.
   The Lord came to my help.
   For me you have changed my mourning into dancing,
   O Lord my God, I will thank you for ever. R.

Prayer

Let us pray.   Oremus.
Almighty ever-living God,   Omnipotens sempiterne Deus,
surpass, for the honour of your name, multiplica in honorem nominis tui
what you pledged to the Patriarchs   quod patrum fidei spopondisti,
   by reason of their faith,   et promissionis filios sacra
and through sacred adoption increase   adoptione dilata,
   the children of your promise,   ut, quod priores sancti non

so that what the Saints of old never
    doubted would come to pass
your Church may now see in great
    part fulfilled.
Through Christ our Lord. R. Amen.

dubitaverunt futurum,
Ecclesia tua magna ex parte iam
    cognoscat impletum.
Per Christum Dominum nostrum.
R. Amen.

Alternatively, other prayers may be used from among those which follow the
readings that have been omitted.

FIFTH READING

A reading from the prophet Isaiah   55:1-11

Come to me and your soul will live, and I will make an everlasting covenant with you.

Thus says the Lord:
    Oh, come to the water all you who are thirsty;
    though you have no money, come!
    Buy corn without money, and eat,
    and, at no cost, wine and milk.
    Why spend money on what is not bread,
    your wages on what fails to satisfy?
    Listen, listen to me, and you will have good things to eat
    and rich food to enjoy.
    Pay attention, come to me;
    and your soul will live.

With you I will make an everlasting covenant
    out of the favours promised to David.
    See, I have made of you a witness to the peoples,
    a leader and a master of the nations.
    See, you will summon a nation you never knew,
    those unknown will come hurrying to you,
    for the sake of the Lord your God,
    of the Holy One of Israel who will glorify you.

Seek the Lord while he is still to be found,
    call to him while he is still near.
    Let the wicked man abandon his way,
    the evil man his thoughts.
    Let him turn back to the Lord who will take pity on him,
    to our God who is rich in forgiving;
    for my thoughts are not your thoughts,
    my ways not your ways – it is the Lord who speaks.
    Yes, the heavens are as high above earth
    as my ways are above your ways,
    my thoughts above your thoughts.

Yes, as the rain and the snow come down from the heavens and do not return without watering the earth, making it yield and giving growth to provide seed for the sower and bread for the eating, so the word that goes from my mouth does not return to me empty, without carrying out my will and succeeding in what it was sent to do.

The word of the Lord.

Responsorial Psalm   Is 12:2-6. R. v.3

R. **With joy you will draw water from the wells of salvation.**

Truly God is my salvation,
I trust, I shall not fear.
For the Lord is my strength, my song,
he became my saviour.
With joy you will draw water
from the wells of salvation. R.

Give thanks to the Lord, give praise to his name!
Make his mighty deeds known to the peoples,
declare the greatness of his name. R.

Sing a psalm to the Lord
for he has done glorious deeds,
make them known to all the earth!
People of Zion, sing and shout for joy
for great in your midst is the Holy One of Israel. R.

Prayer

Let us pray.

Almighty ever-living God, sole hope of the world, who by the preaching of your Prophets unveiled the mysteries of this present age, graciously increase the longing of your people, for only at the prompting of your grace do the faithful progress in any kind of virtue. Through Christ our Lord. R. Amen.	Oremus. Omnipotens sempiterne Deus, spes unica mundi, qui prophetarum tuorum præconio præsentium temporum declarasti mysteria, auge populi tui vota placatus, quia in nullo fidelium nisi ex tua inspiratione proveniunt quarumlibet incrementa virtutum. Per Christum Dominum nostrum. R. Amen.

SIXTH READING

A reading from the prophet Baruch   3:9-15,32–4:4

In the radiance of the Lord make your way to light.

Listen, Israel, to commands that bring life;
hear, and learn what knowledge means.
Why, Israel, why are you in the country of your enemies,
growing older and older in an alien land,
sharing defilement with the dead,
reckoned with those who go to Sheol?
Because you have forsaken the fountain of wisdom.
Had you walked in the way of God,
you would have lived in peace for ever.
Learn where knowledge is, where strength,
where understanding, and so learn
where length of days is, where life,
where the light of the eyes and where peace.
But who has found out where she lives,
who has entered her treasure house?

But the One who knows all knows her,
he has grasped her with his own intellect,
he has set the earth firm for ever
and filled it with four-footed beasts,
he sends the light – and it goes,
he recalls it – and trembling it obeys;
the stars shine joyfully at their set times:
when he calls them, they answer, 'Here we are';
they gladly shine for their creator.
It is he who is our God,
no other can compare with him.
He has grasped the whole way of knowledge,
and confided it to his servant Jacob,
to Israel his well-beloved;
so causing her to appear on earth
and move among men.

This is the book of the commandments of God,
the Law that stands for ever;
those who keep her live,
those who desert her die.
Turn back, Jacob, seize her,
in her radiance make your way to light:

do not yield your glory to another,
your privilege to a people not your own.
Israel, blessed are we:
what pleases God has been revealed to us.

   The word of the Lord.

Responsorial Psalm   Ps 18:8-11. R. Jn 6:69

R. **You have the message of eternal life, O Lord.**

The law of the Lord is perfect,
it revives the soul.
The rule of the Lord is to be trusted,
it gives wisdom to the simple. R.

The precepts of the Lord are right,
they gladden the heart.
The command of the Lord is clear,
it gives light to the eyes. R.

The fear of the Lord is holy,
abiding for ever.
The decrees of the Lord are truth
and all of them just. R.

They are more to be desired than gold,
than the purest of gold
and sweeter are they than honey,
than honey from the comb. R.

Prayer

Let us pray.

O God, who constantly increase
   your Church
by your call to the nations,
graciously grant
to those you wash clean
   in the waters of Baptism
the assurance of your
   unfailing protection.
Through Christ our Lord.
R. Amen.

Oremus.

Deus, qui Ecclesiam tuam
semper gentium
   vocatione multiplicas,
concede propitius,
ut, quos aqua baptismatis abluis,
continua protectione tuearis.
Per Christum Dominum nostrum.
R. Amen.

SEVENTH READING

A reading from the prophet Ezekiel   36:16-28

I shall pour clean water over you, and I shall give you a new heart.

The word of the Lord was addressed to me as follows: 'Son of man, the members of the House of Israel used to live in their own land, but they defiled it by their conduct and actions. I then discharged my fury at them because of the blood they shed in their land and the idols with which they defiled it. I scattered them among the nations and dispersed them in foreign countries. I sentenced them as their conduct and actions deserved. And now they have profaned my holy name among the nations where they have gone, so that people say of them, "These are the people of the Lord; they have been exiled from his land." But I have been concerned about my holy name, which the House of Israel has profaned among the nations where they have gone. And so, say to the House of Israel, "The Lord says this: I am not doing this for my sake, House of Israel, but for the sake of my holy name, which you have profaned among the nations where you have gone. I mean to display the holiness of my great name, which has been profaned among the nations, which you have profaned among them. And the nations will learn that I am the Lord – it is the Lord who speaks – when I display my holiness for your sake before their eyes. Then I am going to take you from among the nations and gather you together from all the foreign countries, and bring you home to your own land. I shall pour clean water over you and you will be cleansed; I shall cleanse you of all your defilement and all your idols. I shall give you a new heart, and put a new spirit in you; I shall remove the heart of stone from your bodies and give you a heart of flesh instead. I shall put my spirit in you, and make you keep my laws and sincerely respect my observances. You will live in the land which I gave your ancestors. You shall be my people and I will be your God."'

The word of the Lord.

Responsorial Psalm   Pss 41:3,5; 42:3,4. R. Ps 41:1

R. **Like the deer that yearns for running streams,
so my soul is yearning for you, my God.**

My soul is thirsting for God.
the God of my life;
when can I enter and see
the face of God? R.

These things I will remember
as I pour out my soul:
how I would lead the rejoicing crowd
into the house of God,
amid cries of gladness and thanksgiving,
the throng wild with joy. R.

O send forth your light and your truth;
let these be my guide.
Let them bring me to your holy mountain
to the place where you dwell. R.

And I will come to the altar of God,
the God of my joy.
My redeemer, I will thank you on the harp,
O God, my God. R.

R. **Like the deer that yearns for running streams,
so my soul is yearning for you, my God.**

If a Baptism takes place the Responsorial Psalm which follows the Fifth Reading, see
p.382 is used, or Psalm 50 as follows.

Responsorial Psalm   Ps 50:12-15,18,19. R. v.12

R. **A pure heart create for me, O God.**
A pure heart create for me, O God,
put a steadfast spirit within me.
Do not cast me away from your presence,
nor deprive me of your holy spirit. R.

Give me again the joy of your help;
with a spirit of fervour sustain me,
that I may teach transgressors your ways
and sinners may return to you. R.

For in sacrifice you take no delight,
burnt offering from me you would refuse,
my sacrifice, a contrite spirit.
A humbled, contrite heart you will not spurn. R.

Prayer

Let us pray.	Oremus.
O God of unchanging power and eternal light, look with favour on the wondrous mystery of the whole Church	Deus, incommutabilis virtus et lumen æternum, respice propitius ad totius Ecclesiæ mirabile sacramentum,

and serenely accomplish the work
of human salvation,
which you planned from all eternity;
may the whole world know and see
that what was cast down is raised up,
what had become old is made new,
and all things are restored
    to integrity through Christ,
just as by him they came into being.
Who lives and reigns
    for ever and ever.
R. Amen.

Or:

O God, who by the pages
    of both Testaments
instruct and prepare us to celebrate
    the Paschal Mystery,
grant that we may comprehend
    your mercy,
so that the gifts we receive
    from you this night
may confirm our hope of the gifts
    to come.
Through Christ our Lord.
R. Amen.

et opus salutis humanæ
perpetuæ dispositionis effectu
tranquillius operare;
totusque mundus experiatur
    et videat
deiecta erigi, inveterata renovari
et per ipsum Christum redire
    omnia in integrum,
a quo sumpsere principium.
Qui vivit et regnat
    in sæcula sæculorum.
R. Amen.

Vel:

Deus, qui nos ad celebrandum
    paschale sacramentum
utriusque Testamenti
    paginis instruis,
da nobis intellegere
    misericordiam tuam,
ut ex perceptione
    præsentium munerum
firma sit exspectatio futurorum.
Per Christum Dominum nostrum.
R. Amen.

After the last reading from the Old Testament with its Responsorial Psalm and its prayer, the altar candles are lit, and the Priest intones the hymn **Gloria in excelsis Deo** (Glory to God in the highest), which is taken up by all, while bells are rung, according to local custom.

The complete musical setting of the Latin text is found in the Graduale Romanum. When the hymn is concluded, the Priest says the Collect in the usual way.

Collect	Collecta

Let us pray.

O God, who make this most sacred
    night radiant
with the glory
    of the Lord's Resurrection,
stir up in your Church a spirit
    of adoption,

Oremus.

Deus, qui hanc
    sacratissimam noctem
gloria dominicæ
    resurrectionis illustras,
excita in Ecclesia tua
    adoptionis spiritum,

so that, renewed in body and mind,	ut, corpore et mente renovati,
we may render you undivided service.	puram tibi exhibeamus servitutem.
Through our Lord Jesus Christ,	Per Dominum nostrum Iesum
your Son,	Christum Filium tuum,
who lives and reigns with you	qui tecum vivit et regnat
in the unity of the Holy Spirit,	in unitate Spiritus Sancti,
one God, for ever and ever.	Deus, per omnia sǽcula sæculorum.

FIRST READING

A reading from the letter of St Paul to the Romans   6:3-11

Christ, having been raised from the dead, will never die again.

When we were baptised in Christ Jesus we were baptised in his death; in other words, when we were baptised we went into the tomb with him and joined him in death, so that as Christ was raised from the dead by the Father's glory, we too might live a new life.

If in union with Christ we have imitated his death, we shall also imitate him in his resurrection. We must realise that our former selves have been crucified with him to destroy this sinful body and to free us from the slavery of sin. When a man dies, of course, he has finished with sin.

But we believe that having died with Christ we shall return to life with him: Christ, as we know, having been raised from the dead will never die again. Death has no power over him any more. When he died, he died, once for all, to sin, so his life now is life with God; and in that way, you too must consider yourselves to be dead to sin but alive for God in Christ Jesus.

The word of the Lord.

After the Epistle has been read, all rise, then the Priest solemnly intones the Alleluia three times, raising his voice by a step each time, with all repeating it. If necessary, the psalmist intones the Alleluia.

Responsorial Psalm   Ps 117:1-2,16-17,22-23

R. **Alleluia, alleluia, alleluia!**
   Give thanks to the Lord for he is good,
   for his love has no end.
   Let the sons of Israel say:
   'His love has no end.' R.

   The Lord's right hand has triumphed;
   his right hand raised me.
   I shall not die, I shall live
   and recount his deeds. R.

The stone which the builders rejected
has become the corner stone.
This is the work of the Lord,
a marvel in our eyes. R.

The Priest, in the usual way, puts incense in the thurible and blesses the Deacon. At the Gospel lights are not carried, but only incense.

GOSPEL

A reading from the holy Gospel according to Mark   16:1-7
Jesus of Nazareth, who was crucified, has risen.

When the sabbath was over, Mary of Magdala, Mary the mother of James, and Salome, bought spices with which to go and anoint him. And very early in the morning on the first day of the week they went to the tomb, just as the sun was rising.

They had been saying to one another, 'Who will roll away the stone for us from the entrance to the tomb?' But when they looked they could see that the stone – which was very big – had already been rolled back. On entering the tomb they saw a young man in a white robe seated on the right-hand side, and they were struck with amazement. But he said to them, 'There is no need for alarm. You are looking for Jesus of Nazareth, who was crucified: he has risen, he is not here. See, here is the place where they laid him. But you must go and tell his disciples and Peter, "He is going before you to Galilee; it is there you will see him, just as he told you."'

The Gospel of the Lord.

After the Gospel, the Homily, even if brief, is not to be omitted.

THIRD PART:

Baptismal Liturgy

After the Homily the Baptismal Liturgy begins. The Priest goes with the ministers to the baptismal font, if this can be seen by the faithful. Otherwise a vessel with water is placed in the sanctuary.

Catechumens, if there are any, are called forward and presented by their godparents in front of the assembled Church or, if they are small children, are carried by their parents and godparents.

Then, if there is to be a procession to the baptistery or to the font, it forms immediately. A minister with the paschal candle leads off, and those to be baptised follow him with their godparents, then the ministers, the Deacon, and the Priest. During the procession, the Litany is sung. When the Litany is completed, the Priest gives the address.

If, however, the Baptismal Liturgy takes place in the sanctuary, the Priest immediately makes an introductory statement in these or similar words.

If there are candidates to be baptised:

Dearly beloved,	Precibus nostris, carissimi,
with one heart and one soul,	fratrum nostrorum beatam spem
let us by our prayers	unanimes adiuvemus,
come to the aid of these our brothers	ut Pater omnipotens ad fontem
and sisters in their blessed hope,	regenerationis euntes
so that, as they approach the font	omni misericordiæ suæ
of rebirth,	auxilio prosequatur.
the almighty Father may bestow	
on them	
all his merciful help.	

If the font is to be blessed, but no one is to be baptised:

Dearly beloved,	Dei Patris omnipotentis gratiam,
let us humbly invoke upon	carissimi,
this font	super hunc fontem
the grace of God the almighty Father,	supplices invocemus,
that those who from it are born anew	ut qui ex eo renascentur
may be numbered among the	adoptionis filiis in
children of adoption in Christ.	Christo aggregentur.

The Litany

The Litany is sung by two cantors, with all standing (because it is Easter Time) and responding.

If, however, there is to be a procession of some length to the baptistery, the Litany is sung during the procession; in this case, those to be baptised are called forward before the procession begins, and the procession takes place led by the paschal candle, followed by the catechumens with their godparents, then the ministers, the Deacon, and the Priest. The address should occur before the Blessing of Water.

If no one is to be baptised and the font is not to be blessed, the Litany is omitted, and the Blessing of Water takes place at once.

In the Litany the names of some Saints may be added, especially the Titular Saint of the church and the Patron Saints of the place and of those to be baptised.

Lord, have mercy.		Kyrie, eleison.	
	Lord, have mercy.		Kyrie, eleison.
Christ, have mercy.		Christe, eleison.	
	Christ, have mercy.		Christe, eleison.
Lord, have mercy.		Kyrie, eleison.	
	Lord have mercy.		Kyrie, eleison.
Holy Mary, Mother of God,	pray for us.	Sancta Maria, Mater Dei,	ora pro nobis.
Saint Michael,	pray for us.	Sancte Michael,	ora pro nobis.
Holy Angels of God,	pray for us.	Sancti Angeli Dei,	orate pro nobis.
Saint John the Baptist,	pray for us.	Sancte Ioannes Baptista,	ora pro nobis.
Saint Joseph,	pray for us.	Sancte Ioseph,	ora pro nobis.
Saint Peter and Saint Paul,	pray for us.	Sancti Petre et Paule,	orate pro nobis.
Saint Andrew,	pray for us.	Sancte Andrea,	ora pro nobis.
Saint John,	pray for us.	Sancte Ioannes,	ora pro nobis.
Saint Mary Magdalene,	pray for us.	Sancta Maria Magdalena,	ora pro nobis.
Saint Stephen,	pray for us.	Sancte Stephane,	ora pro nobis.
Saint Ignatius of Antioch,	pray for us.	Sancte Ignati Antiochene,	ora pro nobis.
Saint Lawrence,	pray for us.	Sancte Laurenti,	ora pro nobis.
Saint Perpetua and Saint Felicity,	pray for us.	Sanctæ Perpetua et Felicitas,	orate pro nobis.
Saint Agnes,	pray for us.	Sancta Agnes,	ora pro nobis.
Saint Gregory,	pray for us.	Sancte Gregori,	ora pro nobis.
Saint Augustine,	pray for us.	Sancte Augustine,	ora pro nobis.

Saint Athanasius,	pray for us.	Sancte Athanasi,	ora pro nobis.
Saint Basil,	pray for us.	Sancte Basili,	ora pro nobis.
Saint Martin,	pray for us.	Sancte Martine,	ora pro nobis.
Saint Benedict,	pray for us.	Sancte Benedicte,	ora pro nobis.
Saint Francis and Saint Dominic,	pray for us.	Sancti Francisce et Dominice,	orate pro nobis.
Saint Francis Xavier,	pray for us.	Sancte Francisce (Xavier),	ora pro nobis.
Saint John Vianney,	pray for us.	Sancte Ioannes Maria (Vianney),	ora pro nobis.
Saint Catherine of Siena,	pray for us.	Sancta Catharina (Senensis),	ora pro nobis.
Saint Teresa of Jesus,	pray for us.	Sancta Teresia a Iesu,	ora pro nobis.
All holy men and women, Saints of God,	pray for us.	Omnes Sancti et Sanctæ Dei,	orate pro nobis.
Lord, be merciful	Lord, deliver us, we pray.	Propitius esto,	libera nos, Domine.
From all evil,	Lord, deliver us, we pray.	Ab omni malo,	libera nos, Domine.
From every sin,	Lord, deliver us, we pray.	Ab omni peccato,	libera nos, Domine.
From everlasting death,	Lord, deliver us, we pray.	A morte perpetua,	libera nos, Domine.
By your Incarnation,	Lord, deliver us, we pray.	Per incarnationem tuam,	libera nos, Domine.
By your Death and Resurrection,	Lord, deliver us, we pray.	Per mortem et resurrectionem tuam,	libera nos, Domine.
By the out-pouring of the Holy Spirit,	Lord, deliver us, we pray.	Per effusionem Spiritus Sancti,	libera nos, Domine.
Be merciful to us sinners,	Lord we ask you to hear our prayer.	Peccatores,	te rogamus, audi nos.

If there are candidates to be baptised

Bring these chosen ones to new birth through the grace of Baptism, Lord, we ask you, hear our prayer.	Ut hos electos per gratiam Baptismi regenerare digneris te rogamus, audi nos.

If there is no one to be baptised:

Make this font holy by your grace
    for the new birth of your children,
Lord, we ask you, hear our prayer.

Jesus, Son of the Living God,
    Lord, we ask you, hear our prayer.

Christ, hear us.   Christ, hear us.
Christ, graciously hear us.
       Christ graciously hear us.

Ut hunc fontem,
    regenerandis tibi filiis,
      gratia tua sanctificare digneris
           te rogamus, audi nos.

Iesu, Fili Dei vivi,
           te rogamus, audi nos.

Christe, audi nos. Christe, audi nos.
Christe, exaudi nos.
           Christe, exaudi nos.

If there are candidates to be baptised, the Priest, with hands extended, says the following prayer:

Almighty ever-living God,
be present by the mysteries of your
    great love
and send forth the spirit of adoption
to create the new peoples
brought to birth for you in the font
    of Baptism,
so that what is to be carried out
    by our humble service
may be brought to fulfilment
    by your mighty power.
Through Christ our Lord.
R. Amen.

Omnipotens sempiterne Deus,
adesto magnæ pietatis
    tuæ sacramentis,
et ad recreandos novos populos,
quos tibi fons baptismatis parturit,
spiritum adoptionis emitte,
ut, quod nostræ humilitatis
    gerendum est ministerio,
virtutis tuæ impleatur effectu.
Per Christum Dominum nostrum.
R. Amen.

Blessing of Baptismal Water

The Priest then blesses the baptismal water, saying the following prayer with hands extended:

O God, who by invisible power
accomplish a wondrous effect
through sacramental signs
and who in many ways have
    prepared water, your creation,
to show forth the grace of Baptism;

Deus, qui invisibili potentia
per sacramentorum signa
    mirabilem operaris effectum,
et creaturam aquæ multis
    modis præparasti,
ut baptismi gratiam demonstraret;

O God, whose Spirit
in the first moments
   of the world's creation
hovered over the waters,
so that the very substance of water
would even then take to itself
   the power to sanctify;

O God, who by the outpouring
   of the flood
foreshadowed regeneration,
so that from the mystery of one
   and the same element of water
would come an end to vice
   and a beginning of virtue;

O God, who caused the children
   of Abraham
to pass dry-shod through the Red Sea,
so that the chosen people,
set free from slavery to Pharaoh,
would prefigure the people
   of the baptised;

O God, whose Son,
baptised by John in the waters
   of the Jordan,
was anointed with the Holy Spirit,
and, as he hung upon the Cross,
gave forth water from his side
   along with blood,
and after his Resurrection,
   commanded his disciples:
'Go forth, teach all nations,
   baptising them
in the name of the Father and of the
   Son and of the Holy Spirit',
look now, we pray, upon the face
   of your Church
and graciously unseal for her
   the fountain of Baptism.

Deus, cuius Spiritus
super aquas inter ipsa mundi
   primordia ferebatur,
ut iam tunc virtutem sanctificandi
aquarum natura conciperet;

Deus, qui regenerationis speciem
in ipsa diluvii effusione signasti,
ut unius eiusdemque
   elementi mysterio
et finis esset vitiis et origo virtutum;

Deus, qui Abrahæ filios
per Mare Rubrum sicco vestigio
   transire fecisti,
ut plebs, a Pharaonis
   servitute liberata,
populum baptizatorum
   præfiguraret;

Deus, cuius Filius, in aqua Iordanis
   a Ioanne baptizatus,
Sancto Spiritu est inunctus,
et, in cruce pendens,
una cum sanguine aquam de latere
   suo produxit,
ac, post resurrectionem suam,
   discipulis iussit:

'Ite, docete omnes gentes,
   baptizantes eos
in nomine Patris et Filii
   et Spiritus Sancti':
respice in faciem Ecclesiæ tuæ,
eique dignare fontem
   baptismatis aperire.

May this water receive
  by the Holy Spirit
the grace of your Only Begotten Son,
so that human nature,
  created in your image,
and washed clean through
  the Sacrament of Baptism
from all the squalor of the life of old,
may be found worthy to rise
  to the life of newborn children
through water and the Holy Spirit.

Sumat hæc aqua Unigeniti tui
  gratiam de Spiritu Sancto,
ut homo, ad imaginem
  tuam conditus,
sacramento baptismatis
a cunctis squaloribus
  vetustatis ablutus,
in novam infantiam
ex aqua et Spiritu Sancto
  resurgere mereatur.

And, if appropriate, lowering the paschal candle into the water either once or three times, he continues:

May the power of the Holy Spirit,
O Lord, we pray,
come down through your Son
into the fullness of this font,

Descendat, quæsumus, Domine,
in hanc plenitudinem fontis
per Filium tuum virtus
  Spiritus Sancti,

and, holding the candle in the water, he continues:

so that all who have been buried
  with Christ
by Baptism into death
may rise again to life with him.
Who lives and reigns with you
  in the unity of the Holy Spirit,
one God, for ever and ever.
R. **Amen.**

ut omnes, cum Christo consepulti
per baptismum in mortem,
ad vitam cum ipso resurgant.
Qui tecum vivit et regnat
  in unitate Spiritus Sancti,
Deus, per omnia sæcula sæculorum.
R. **Amen.**

Then the candle is lifted out of the water, as the people acclaim:

Springs of water, bless the Lord;
praise and exalt him above all
  for ever.

Benedicite, fontes, Domino,
laudate et superexaltate eum
  in sæcula.

After the blessing of baptismal water and the acclamation of the people, the Priest, standing, puts the prescribed questions to the adults and the parents or godparents of the children, as is set out in the respective Rites of the Roman Ritual, in order for them to make the required renunciation.

If the anointing of the adults with the Oil of Catechumens has not taken place beforehand, as part of the immediately preparatory rites, it occurs at this moment.

Then the Priest questions the adults individually about the faith and, if there are children to be baptised, he requests the triple profession of faith from all the parents and godparents together, as is indicated in the respective Rites.

Where many are to be baptised on this night, it is possible to arrange the rite so that, immediately after the response of those to be baptised and of the godparents and the parents, the Celebrant asks for and receives the renewal of baptismal promises of all present.

When the interrogation is concluded, the Priest baptises the adult elect and the children.

After the Baptism, the Priest anoints the infants with chrism. A white garment is given to each, whether adults or children. Then the Priest or Deacon receives the paschal candle from the hand of the minister, and the candles of the newly baptised are lighted. For infants the rite of Ephphetha is omitted.

Afterwards, unless the baptismal washing and the other explanatory rites have occurred in the sanctuary, a procession returns to the sanctuary, formed as before, with the newly baptised or the godparents or parents carrying lighted candles. During this procession, the baptismal canticle Vidi aquam (I saw water) or another appropriate chant is sung.

If adults have been baptised, the Bishop or, in his absence, the Priest who has conferred Baptism, should at once administer the Sacrament of Confirmation to them in the sanctuary, as is indicated in the Roman Pontifical or Roman Ritual.

The Blessing of Water

If no one present is to be baptised and the font is not to be blessed, the Priest introduces the faithful to the blessing of water, saying:

Dear brothers and sisters, let us humbly beseech the Lord our God to bless this water he has created, which will be sprinkled upon us as a memorial of our Baptism. May he graciously renew us, that we may remain faithful to the Spirit whom we have received.	Dominum Deum nostrum, fratres carissimi, suppliciter exoremus, ut hanc creaturam aquæ benedicere dignetur, super nos aspergendam in nostri memoriam baptismi. Ipse autem nos adiuvare dignetur, ut Spiritui, quem accepimus, fideles maneamus.

And after a brief pause in silence, he proclaims the following prayer, with hands extended:

Lord our God,
in your mercy be present
    to your people
who keep vigil on this most
    sacred night,
and, for us who recall the wondrous
    work of our creation
and the still greater work
    of our redemption,
graciously bless this water.
For you created water to make
    the fields fruitful
and to refresh and cleanse our bodies.
You also made water the instrument
    of your mercy:
for through water you freed
    your people from slavery
and quenched their thirst
    in the desert;
through water the Prophets
    proclaimed the new covenant
you were to enter upon
    with the human race;
and last of all,
through water, which Christ made
    holy in the Jordan,
you have renewed our
    corrupted nature
in the bath of regeneration.
Therefore, may this water be for us
a memorial of the Baptism
    we have received,
and grant that we may share
in the gladness of our brothers
    and sisters,
who at Easter have received
    their Baptism.
Through Christ our Lord.
℟. Amen.

Domine Deus noster,
populo tuo hac nocte
    sacratissima vigilanti
adesto propitius;
et nobis, mirabile nostræ
    creationis opus,
sed et redemptionis nostræ
    mirabilius, memorantibus,
hanc aquam benedicere tu dignare.

Ipsam enim tu fecisti,
ut et arva fecunditate donaret,
et levamen corporibus nostris
    munditiamque præberet.

Aquam etiam tuæ ministram
    misericordiæ condidisti;
nam per ipsam solvisti tui
    populi servitutem
illiusque sitim in deserto sedasti;
per ipsam novum fœdus
    nuntiaverunt prophetæ,
quod eras cum hominibus initurus;
per ipsam denique, quam Christus
    in Iordane sacravit,
corruptam naturæ
    nostræ substantiam
in regenerationis lavacro renovasti.

Sit igitur hæc aqua nobis suscepti
    baptismatis memoria,
et cum fratribus nostris,
    qui sunt in Paschate baptizati,
gaudia nos tribuas sociare.
Per Christum Dominum nostrum.
℟. Amen.

The Renewal of Baptismal Promises

When the Rite of Baptism (and Confirmation) has been completed or, if this has not taken place, after the blessing of water, all stand, holding lighted candles in their hands, and renew the promise of baptismal faith, unless this has already been done together with those to be baptised.

The Priest addresses the faithful in these or similar words:

Dear brethren (brothers and sisters),
  through the Paschal Mystery
we have been buried with Christ
  in Baptism,
so that we may walk with him
  in newness of life.
And so, now that our Lenten
  observance is concluded,
let us renew the promises
  of Holy Baptism,
by which we once renounced Satan
  and his works
and promised to serve God
  in the holy Catholic Church.
And so I ask you:

Priest: Do you renounce Satan?
All: **I do.**

Priest: And all his works?
All: **I do.**

Priest: And all his empty show?
All: **I do.**

Or:

Priest: Do you renounce sin,
so as to live in the freedom
  of the children of God?
All: **I do.**

Priest: Do you renounce the lure
  of evil,
so that sin may have no mastery
  over you?
All: **I do.**

Per paschale mysterium,
  fratres carissimi,
in baptismo consepulti sumus
  cum Christo,
ut cum eo in novitate
  vitæ ambulemus.
Quapropter, quadragesimali
  observatione absoluta,
sancti baptismatis
  promissiones renovemus,
quibus olim Satanæ et operibus
  eius abrenuntiavimus,
et Deo in sancta Ecclesia catholica
  servire promisimus.
Quapropter:

Sacerdos: Abrenutiatis Satanæ?
Omnes: **Abrenuntio.**

Sacerdos: Et omnibus operibus eius?
Omnes: **Abrenuntio.**

Sacerdos: Et omnibus pompis eius?
Omnes: **Abrenuntio.**

Vel:

Sacerdos: Abrenuntiatis peccato,
ut in libertate filiorum Dei vivatis?
Omnes: **Abrenuntio.**

Sacerdos: Abrenuntiatis
  seductionibus iniquitatis,
ne pecccatum vobis dominetur?
Omnes: **Abrenuntio.**

Priest: **Do you renounce Satan,**
the author and prince of sin?
All: **I do.**

Sacerdos: **Abrenuntiatis Satanæ,**
qui est auctor et princeps peccati?
Omnes: **Abrenuntio.**

If the situation warrants, this second formula may be adapted by Conferences of Bishops according to local needs.

Then the Priest continues:

Priest: **Do you believe in God,**
the Father almighty,
Creator of heaven and earth?
All: **I do.**

Sacerdos: **Creditis in Deum Patrem**
omnipotentem,
creatorem cæli et terræ?
Omnes: **Credo.**

Priest: **Do you believe in Jesus**
Christ, his only Son, our Lord,
who was born of the Virgin Mary,
suffered death and was buried,
rose again from the dead
and is seated at the right hand
of the Father?
All: **I do.**

Sacerdos: **Creditis in Iesum**
Christum, Filium eius unicum,
Dominum nostrum,
natum ex Maria Virgine,
passum et sepultum,
qui a mortuis resurrexit
et sedet ad dexteram Patris?
Omnes: **Credo.**

Priest: **Do you believe**
in the Holy Spirit,
the holy Catholic Church,
the communion of saints,
the forgiveness of sins,
the resurrection of the body,
and life everlasting?
All: **I do.**

Sacerdos: **Creditis in Spiritum**
Sanctum,
sanctam Ecclesiam catholicam,
sanctorum communionem,
remissionem peccatorum,
carnis resurrectionem et
vitam æternam?
Omnes: **Credo.**

And the Priest concludes:

And may almighty God, the Father
of our Lord Jesus Christ,
who has given us new birth by water
and the Holy Spirit
and bestowed on us forgiveness
of our sins,
keep us by his grace,
in Christ Jesus our Lord,
for eternal life.
All: **Amen.**

Et Deus omnipotens, Pater Domini
nostri Iesu Christi,
qui nos regeneravit ex aqua
et Spiritu Sancto,
quique nobis dedit
remissionem peccatorum,
ipse nos custodiat gratia sua,
in Christo Iesu Domino nostro,
in vitam æternam.
Omnes: **Amen.**

The Priest sprinkles the people with the blessed water, while all sing:

Antiphon

I saw water flowing
    from the Temple,
from its right-hand side, alleluia;
and all to whom this water
    came were saved
and shall say: Alleluia, alleluia.
	Vidi aquam egredientem
	    de templo,
	a latere dextro, alleluia;
	et omnes, ad quos pervenit aqua
	    ista, salvi facti sunt
	et dicent: Alleluia, alleluia.

Another chant that is baptismal in character may also be sung.

Meanwhile the newly baptised are led to their place among the faithful.

If the blessing of baptismal water has not taken place in the baptistery, the Deacon and the ministers reverently carry the vessel of water to the font.

If the blessing of the font has not occurred, the blessed water is put aside in an appropriate place.

After the sprinkling, the Priest returns to the chair where, omitting the Creed, he directs the Universal Prayer, in which the newly baptised participate for the first time.

FOURTH PART:
The Liturgy of the Eucharist

The Priest goes to the altar and begins the Liturgy of the Eucharist in the usual way.

It is desirable that the bread and wine be brought forward by the newly baptised or, if they are children, by their parents or godparents.

Prayer over the Offerings	Super oblata

Accept, we ask, O Lord,
the prayers of your people
with the sacrificial offerings,
that what has begun
    in the paschal mysteries
may, by the working of your power,
bring us to the healing of eternity.
Through Christ our Lord.
	Suscipe, quæsumus, Domine,
	    preces populi tui
	cum oblationibus hostiarum,
	ut, paschalibus initiata mysteriis,
	ad æternitatis nobis medelam,
	    te operante, proficiant.
	Per Christum Dominum nostrum.

Preface I of Easter: The Paschal Mystery (. . .on this night above all. . .), pp.52-55.

In the Eucharistic Prayer, a commemoration is made of the baptised and their godparents in accord with the formulas which are found in the Roman Missal and Roman Ritual for each of the Eucharistic Prayers.

Before the Ecce Agnus Dei (Behold the Lamb of God), the Priest may briefly address the newly baptised about receiving their first Communion and about the excellence of this great mystery, which is the climax of Initiation and the centre of the whole of Christian life.

It is desirable that the newly baptised receive Holy Communion under both kinds, together with their godfathers, godmothers, and Catholic parents and spouses, as well as their lay catechists. It is even appropriate that, with the consent of the Diocesan Bishop, where the occasion suggests this, all the faithful be admitted to Holy Communion under both kinds.

Communion Antiphon 1 Co 5:7-8	Ant. ad communionem
Christ our Passover	Pascha nostrum immolatus
has been sacrificed;	est Christus;
therefore let us keep the feast	itaque epulemur in azymis
with the unleavened bread	sinceritatis et veritatis, alleluia.
of purity and truth, alleluia.	

Psalm 117 may appropriately be sung.

Prayer after Communion — Post communionem

Pour out on us, O Lord,	Spiritum nobis, Domine,
the Spirit of your love,	tuæ caritatis infunde,
and in your kindness make those	ut, quos sacramentis
you have nourished	paschalibus satiasti,
by this paschal Sacrament	tua facias pietate concordes.
one in mind and heart.	Per Christum Dominum nostrum.
Through Christ our Lord.	

Solemn Blessing — Benedictio sollemnis

May almighty God bless you	Benedicat vos omnipotens Deus,
through today's Easter Solemnity	hodierna interveniente
and, in his compassion,	sollemnitate paschali,
defend you from every assault of sin.	et ab omni miseratus defendat
R. Amen.	incursione peccati.
	R. Amen.

And may he, who restores you	Et qui ad æternam vitam
to eternal life	in Unigeniti sui resurrectione
in the Resurrection	vos reparat,
of his Only Begotten,	vos præmiis
endow you with the prize	immortalitatis adimpleat.
of immortality.	R. Amen.
R. Amen.	

Now that the days of the Lord's	Et qui, expletis passionis
Passion have drawn to a close,	dominicæ diebus,
may you who celebrate	paschalis festi gaudia celebratis,
the gladness of the Paschal Feast	ad ea festa, quæ lætitiis
come with Christ's help,	peraguntur æternis,
and exulting in spirit,	ipso opitulante, exsultantibus
to those feasts that are celebrated	animis veniatis.
in eternal joy.	R. Amen.
R. Amen.	

| And may the blessing of almighty God, the Father, and the Son, ✠ and the Holy Spirit, come down on you and remain with you for ever.
R. Amen. | Et benedictio Dei omnipotentis, Patris, et Filii, ✠ et Spiritus Sancti, descendat super vos et maneat semper.
R. Amen. |

The final blessing formula from the Rite of Baptism of Adults or of Children may also be used, according to circumstances.

To dismiss the people the Deacon or, if there is no Deacon, the Priest himself sings or says:

| Go forth, the Mass is ended, alleluia, alleluia. | Ite, missa est, alleluia, alleluia. |

Or:

Vel:

| Go in peace, alleluia, alleluia. | Ite in pace, alleluia, alleluia |

All reply:

Omnes respondent:

| Thanks be to God, alleluia, alleluia. | Deo gratias, alleluia, alleluia. |

This practice is observed throughout the Octave of Easter.

The paschal candle is lit in all the more solemn liturgical celebrations of this period.

1 April

At the Mass during the Day

Life has conquered death. Mercy and Love have conquered sin! We need faith and hope in order to open ourselves to this new and marvellous horizon. And we know that faith and hope are gifts from God, and we need to ask for them: "Lord, grant me faith, grant me hope! I need them so much!". Let us be permeated by the emotions that resound in the Easter sequence: "Yes, we are sure of it: Christ indeed from death is risen". The Lord has risen among us! This truth indelibly marked the lives of the Apostles who, after the Resurrection, again sensed the need to follow their Teacher and, having received the Holy Spirit, set out fearlessly to proclaim to all what they had seen with their own eyes and personally experienced.

(Pope Francis)

Entrance Antiphon Cf. Ps 138:18,5-6

I HAVE risen, and I am with you still, alleluia.
You have laid your hand upon me, alleluia.
Too wonderful for me,
  this knowledge, alleluia, alleluia.

Or: Lk 24:34; Cf. Rv 1:6

The Lord is truly risen, alleluia.
To him be glory and power
for all the ages of eternity, alleluia,
  alleluia.

Ant. ad introitum

RESURREXI, et adhuc tecum sum, alleluia:
posuisti super me manum tuam,
  alleluia:
mirabilis facta est scientia tua,
  alleluia, alleluia.

Vel:

Surrexit Dominus vere, alleluia.
Ipsi gloria et imperium
per universa æternitatis sæcula,
  alleluia, alleluia.

The Gloria in excelsis (Glory to God in the highest) is said.

Collect

O God, who on this day,
through your Only Begotten Son,
have conquered death
and unlocked for us the path
  to eternity,
grant, we pray, that we who keep

Collecta

Deus, qui hodierna die,
  per Unigenitum tuum,
æternitatis nobis aditum,
  devicta morte, reserasti,
da nobis, quæsumus,
ut, qui resurrectionis dominicæ

the solemnity of
   the Lord's Resurrection
may, through the renewal brought
   by your Spirit,
rise up in the light of life.
Through our Lord Jesus Christ,
   your Son,
who lives and reigns with you
   in the unity of the Holy Spirit,
one God, for ever and ever.

sollemnia colimus,
per innovationem tui Spiritus
in lumine vitæ resurgamus.
Per Dominum nostrum Iesum
   Christum Filium tuum,
qui tecum vivit et regnat
   in unitate Spiritus Sancti,
Deus, per omnia sæcula sæculorum.

FIRST READING

A reading from the Acts of the Apostles   10:34,37-43

We have eaten and drunk with him after his resurrection.

Peter addressed Cornelius and his household: 'You must have heard about the recent happenings in Judaea; about Jesus of Nazareth and how he began in Galilee, after John had been preaching baptism. God had anointed him with the Holy Spirit and with power, and because God was with him, Jesus went about doing good and curing all who had fallen into the power of the devil. Now I, and those with me, can witness to everything he did throughout the countryside of Judaea and in Jerusalem itself: and also to the fact that they killed him by hanging him on a tree, yet three days afterwards God raised him to life and allowed him to be seen, not by the whole people but only by certain witnesses God had chosen beforehand. Now we are those witnesses – we have eaten and drunk with him after his resurrection from the dead – and he has ordered us to proclaim this to his people and to tell them that God has appointed him to judge everyone, alive or dead. It is to him that all the prophets bear this witness: that all who believe in Jesus will have their sins forgiven through his name.'

   The word of the Lord.

Responsorial Psalm   Ps 117:1-2,16-17,22-23. R. v. 24

R. **This day was made by the Lord;**
   we rejoice and are glad.
   Or: **Alleluia, alleluia, alleluia!**

   Give thanks to the Lord for he is good,
   for his love has no end.
   Let the sons of Israel say:
   'His love has no end.' R.

   The Lord's right hand has triumphed;
   his right hand raised me.

I shall not die, I shall live
and recount his deeds. R.
The stone which the builders rejected
has become the corner stone.
This is the work of the Lord,
a marvel in our eyes. R.

SECOND READING

A reading from the letter of St Paul to the Colossians 3:1-4
You must look for the things that are in heaven, where Christ is.

Since you have been brought back to true life with Christ, you must look
for the things that are in heaven, where Christ is, sitting at God's right
hand. Let your thoughts be on heavenly things, not on the things that are
on the earth, because you have died, and now the life you have is hidden
with Christ in God. But when Christ is revealed – and he is your life – you
too will be revealed in all your glory with him.

The word of the Lord.

ALTERNATIVE SECOND READING

A reading from the first letter of St Paul to the Corinthians 5:6-8
Get rid of the old yeast, and make yourselves into a completely new batch of bread.

You must know how even a small amount of yeast is enough to leaven all the
dough, so get rid of all the old yeast, and make yourselves into a completely
new batch of bread, unleavened as you are meant to be. Christ, our Passover,
has been sacrificed; let us celebrate the feast, by getting rid of all the old yeast of
evil and wickedness, having only the unleavened bread of sincerity and truth.

The word of the Lord.

The sequence is said or sung on this day. On the weekdays of the Octave of Easter,
its use is optional.

SEQUENCE

Christians, to the Paschal Victim
    offer sacrifice and praise.
The sheep are ransomed
    by the Lamb;
and Christ, the undefiled,
hath sinners to his Father reconciled.
Death with life contended:
    combat strangely ended!
Life's own Champion, slain,
    yet lives to reign.
	Victimæ paschali laudes
	    immolent Christiani.
	Agnus redemit oves:
	    Christus innocens Patri
	reconciliavit peccatores.
	
	Mors et vita duello
	    conflixere mirando:
	    dux vitæ mortuus regnat vivus.

Tell us, Mary:
    say what thou didst see
    upon the way.
	Dic nobis, Maria,
	    quid vidisti in via?

The tomb the Living did enclose; I saw Christ's glory as he rose!	Sepulcrum Christi viventis, gloriam vidi resurgentis.
The angels there attesting; shroud with grave-clothes resting.	Angelicos testes, sudarium et vestes.
Christ, my hope, has risen: he goes before you into Galilee.	Surrexit Christus spes mea: præcedet vos in Galilæam.

That Christ is truly risen
    from the dead we know.
	Scimus Christum surrexisse
	    a mortuis vere:

Victorious king, thy mercy show!	tu nobis, victor Rex, miserere.

Gospel Acclamation   1 Co 5:7-8

R. **Alleluia, alleluia!**
Christ, our passover, has been sacrificed;
let us celebrate the feast then, in the Lord.
R. **Alleluia!**

GOSPEL

A reading from the holy Gospel according to John   20:1-9
He must rise from the dead.

It was very early on the first day of the week and still dark, when Mary of Magdala came to the tomb. She saw that the stone had been moved away from the tomb and came running to Simon Peter and the other disciple, the one Jesus loved. 'They have taken the Lord out of the tomb' she said 'and we don't know where they have put him.'

So Peter set out with the other disciple to go to the tomb. They ran together, but the other disciple, running faster than Peter, reached the tomb first; he bent down and saw the linen cloths lying on the ground, but did not go in. Simon Peter who was following now came up, went right into the tomb, saw the linen cloths on the ground, and also the cloth that had been over his head; this was not with the linen cloths but rolled up in a place by itself. Then the other disciple who had reached the tomb first also went in; he saw and he believed. Till this moment they had failed to understand the teaching of scripture, that he must rise from the dead.

The Gospel of the Lord.

The Creed is said. However, in Easter Sunday Masses which are celebrated with a congregation, the rite of the renewal of baptismal promises may take place after the homily, according to the text used at the Easter Vigil (pp.398-400). In that case the Creed is omitted.

Prayer over the Offerings | Super oblata

Exultant with paschal gladness,
   O Lord,
we offer the sacrifice
by which your Church
is wondrously reborn and nourished.
Through Christ our Lord.

Sacrificia, Domine,
   paschalibus gaudiis
exsultantes offerimus,
quibus Ecclesia tua
mirabiliter renascitur et nutritur.
Per Christum Dominum nostrum.

Preface I of Easter, The Paschal Mystery, pp.52-55.

When the Roman Canon is used, the proper forms of the **Communicantes** (In communion with those) and **Hanc igitur** (Therefore, Lord, we pray) are said.

Communion Antiphon 1 Co 5:7-8 | Ant. ad communionem

Christ our Passover has been
   sacrificed, alleluia;
therefore let us keep the feast
   with the unleavened bread
of purity and truth, alleluia, alleluia.

Pascha nostrum immolatus
   est Christus, alleluia;
itaque epulemur
   in azymis sinceritatis
et veritatis, alleluia, alleluia.

Prayer after Communion | Post communionem

Look upon your Church, O God,
with unfailing love and favour,
so that, renewed by the paschal
   mysteries,
she may come to the glory
   of the resurrection.
Through Christ our Lord.

Perpetuo, Deus, Ecclesiam tuam
   pio favore tuere,
ut, paschalibus renovata mysteriis,
ad resurrectionis perveniat claritatem.
Per Christum Dominum nostrum.

To impart the blessing at the end of Mass, the Priest may appropriately use the formula of Solemn Blessing for the Mass of the Easter Vigil, p.401-402.

For the dismissal of the people, the following is sung or said:

Go forth, the Mass is ended,
   alleluia, alleluia.

Ite, missa est, alleluia, alleluia.

Or:

Go in peace, alleluia, alleluia.
R. Thanks be to God, alleluia, alleluia.

Vel:

Ite in pace, alleluia, alleluia
R. Deo gratias, alleluia, alleluia.

8 April

SECOND SUNDAY OF EASTER

(or of Divine Mercy)

"Peace be with you!" is the greeting of Jesus to his disciples; this same peace awaits men and women of our own day. It is not a negotiated peace, it is not the absence of conflict: it is his peace, the peace that comes from the heart of the Risen Lord, the peace that has defeated sin, fear and death. It is a peace that does not divide but unites; it is a peace that does not abandon us but makes us feel listened to and loved; it is a peace that persists even in pain and enables hope to blossom. This peace, as on the day of Easter, is born ever anew by the forgiveness of God which calms our anxious hearts. To be bearers of his peace: this is the mission entrusted to the Church on Easter day. In Christ, we are born to be instruments of reconciliation, to bring the Father's forgiveness to everyone, to reveal his loving face through concrete gestures of mercy.

(Pope Francis)

Entrance Antiphon   1 P 2:2

L IKE newborn infants,
you must long for the pure,
spiritual milk,
that in him you may grow
    to salvation, alleluia.

Or: 4 Esdr 2:36-37

Receive the joy of your glory,
    giving thanks to God,
who has called you into the heavenly
    kingdom, alleluia.

The Gloria in excelsis (Glory to God in the highest) is said.

Collect

God of everlasting mercy,
who, in the very recurrence
    of the paschal feast
kindle the faith of the people you
    have made your own,
increase, we pray, the grace you
    have bestowed,
that all may grasp
and rightly understand

Ant. ad introitum

Q UASI modo geniti infantes,
    rationabile, sine dolo
    lac concupiscite,
ut in eo crescatis in salutem,
    alleluia.

Vel:

Accipite iucunditatem gloriæ vestræ,
gratias agentes Deo,
qui vos ad cælestia regna vocavit,
    alleluia.

Collecta

Deus misericordiæ sempiternæ,
qui in ipso paschalis festi recursu
fidem sacratæ tibi plebis accendis,
auge gratiam quam dedisti,
ut digna omnes intellegentia
    comprehendant,
quo lavacro abluti,
    quo Spiritu regenerati,
quo sanguine sunt redempti.

in what font they have been washed,
by whose Spirit they have
been reborn,
by whose Blood they have
been redeemed.
Through our Lord Jesus Christ,
your Son,
who lives and reigns with you
in the unity of the Holy Spirit,
one God, for ever and ever.

Per Dominum nostrum Iesum
Christum Filium tuum,
qui tecum vivit et regnat
in unitate Spiritus Sancti,
Deus, per omnia sæcula sæculorum.

FIRST READING

A reading from the Acts of the Apostles   4:32-35

United, heart and soul.

The whole group of believers was united, heart and soul; no one claimed
for his own use anything that he had, as everything they owned was held
in common.

The apostles continued to testify to the resurrection of the Lord Jesus
with great power, and they were all given great respect.

None of their members was ever in want, as all those who owned land
or houses would sell them, and bring the money from them, to present it to
the apostles; it was then distributed to any members who might be in need.

The word of the Lord.

Responsorial Psalm   Ps 117:2-4,15-18,22-24. R. v.1

R. **Give thanks to the Lord for he is good,**
for his love has no end.
Or: **Alleluia, alleluia, alleluia!**

Let the sons of Israel say:
'His love has no end.'
Let the sons of Aaron say:
'His love has no end.'
Let those who fear the Lord say:
'His love has no end.' R.

The Lord's right hand has triumphed;
his right hand raised me up.
I shall not die, I shall live
and recount his deeds.
I was punished, I was punished by the Lord,
but not doomed to die. R.

The stone which the builders rejected
has become the corner stone.
This is the work of the Lord
a marvel in our eyes.
This day was made by the Lord;
we rejoice and are glad. R.

R. **Give thanks to the Lord for he is good,**
for his love has no end.
Or: **Alleluia, alleluia, alleluia!**

SECOND READING

A reading from the first letter of St John   5:1-6

Anyone who has been begotten by God has already overcome the world.

Whoever believes that Jesus is the Christ
has been begotten by God;
and whoever loves the Father that begot him
loves the child whom he begets.
We can be sure that we love God's children
if we love God himself and do what he has commanded us;
this is what loving God is –
keeping his commandments;
and his commandments are not difficult,
because anyone who has been begotten by God
has already overcome the world;
this is the victory over the world –
our faith.
Who can overcome the world?
Only the man who believes that Jesus is the Son of God:
Jesus Christ who came by water and blood,
not with water only,
but with water and blood;
with the Spirit as another witness –
since the Spirit is the truth.

The word of the Lord.

Easter Sequence can be sung here, see pp.405-406.

Gospel Acclamation   Jn 20:29

R. **Alleluia, alleluia!**
Jesus said: 'You believe because you can see me.
Happy are those who have not seen and yet believe.'
R. **Alleluia!**

GOSPEL

A reading from the holy Gospel according to John   20:19-31

Eight days later, Jesus came.

In the evening of that same day, the first day of the week, the doors were closed in the room where the disciples were, for fear of the Jews. Jesus came and stood among them. He said to them 'Peace be with you,' and showed them his hands and his side. The disciples were filled with joy when they saw the Lord, and he said to them again, 'Peace be with you.

'As the Father sent me,
so am I sending you.'

After saying this he breathed on them and said:

'Receive the Holy Spirit.
For those whose sins you forgive,
they are forgiven;
for those whose sins you retain,
they are retained.'

Thomas, called the Twin, who was one of the Twelve, was not with them when Jesus came. When the disciples said, 'We have seen the Lord,' he answered, 'Unless I see the holes that the nails made in his hands and can put my finger into the holes they made, and unless I can put my hand into his side, I refuse to believe.' Eight days later the disciples were in the house again and Thomas was with them. The doors were closed, but Jesus came in and stood among them. 'Peace be with you,' he said. Then he spoke to Thomas, 'Put your finger here; look, here are my hands. Give me your hand; put it into my side. Doubt no longer but believe.' Thomas replied, 'My Lord and my God!' Jesus said to him:

'You believe because you can see me.
Happy are those who have not seen and yet believe.'

There were many other signs that Jesus worked and the disciples saw, but they are not recorded in this book. These are recorded so that you may believe that Jesus is the Christ, the Son of God, and that believing this you may have life through his name.

The Gospel of the Lord.

The Creed is said.

Prayer over the Offerings	Super oblata
Accept, O Lord, we pray,	Suscipe, quæsumus, Domine,
the oblations of your people	plebis tuæ
(and of those you have brought	(et tuorum renatorum) oblationes,
to new birth),	ut, confessione tui nominis et
that, renewed by confession of your	baptismate renovati,
name and by Baptism,	sempiternam beatitudinem
they may attain unending happiness.	consequantur.
Through Christ our Lord.	Per Christum Dominum nostrum.

Preface I of Easter (. . .on this day above all. . .), pp.52-55.

When the Roman Canon is used, the proper forms of Communicantes (In communion with those) and Hanc igitur (Therefore, Lord, we pray) are said.

Communion Antiphon Cf. Jn 20:27	Ant. ad communionem
Bring your hand and feel the place	Mitte manum tuam, et cognosce
of the nails,	loca clavorum,
and do not be unbelieving	et noli esse incredulus, sed fidelis,
but believing, alleluia.	alleluia.

Prayer after Communion	Post communionem
Grant, we pray, almighty God,	Concede, quæsumus,
that our reception of this paschal	omnipotens Deus,
Sacrament	ut paschalis perceptio sacramenti
may have a continuing effect	continua in nostris
in our minds and hearts.	mentibus perseveret.
Through Christ our Lord.	Per Christum Dominum nostrum.

A formula of Solemn Blessing, pp.136-139, may be used.

For the dismissal of the people, there is sung or said: **Go forth, the Mass is ended, alleluia, alleluia.** Or: **Go in peace, alleluia, alleluia.** The people respond: **Thanks be to God, alleluia, alleluia.**

9 April

THE ANNUNCIATION OF THE LORD

Mary's journey to heaven began with the "yes" spoken in Nazareth in response to the heavenly messenger's announcement of God's will to her. And in reality it is just like this: every "yes" to God is a step toward heaven, toward eternal life. Because this is what the Lord wants: that all his children may have life in abundance! God wants us all with him, in his house!

(Pope Francis)

Solemnity

Entrance Antiphon Heb 10:5,7	Ant. ad introitum

THE Lord said,
as he entered the world:
Behold, I come to do your will,
O God.

DOMINUS ingrediens
mundum dixit:
Ecce venio ut faciam, Deus,
voluntatem tuam.

The Gloria in excelsis (Glory to God in the highest) is said.

Collect — Collecta

O God, who willed that your Word
should take on the reality
    of human flesh
in the womb of the Virgin Mary,
grant, we pray,
that we, who confess our Redeemer
to be God and man,
may merit to become partakers
    even in his divine nature.
Who lives and reigns with you
    in the unity of the Holy Spirit,
one God, for ever and ever.

Deus, qui Verbum tuum in utero
    Virginis Mariæ
veritatem carnis humanæ
    suscipere voluisti,
concede, quæsumus,
ut, qui Redemptorem nostrum
Deum et hominem confitemur,
ipsius etiam divinæ naturæ
    mereamur esse consortes.
Per Dominum nostrum Iesum
    Christum Filium tuum,
qui tecum vivit et regnat
    in unitate Spiritus Sancti,
Deus, per omnia sæcula sæculorum.

FIRST READING

A reading from the prophet Isaiah   7:10-14,8:10

The maiden is with child.

The Lord spoke to Ahaz and said, 'Ask the Lord your God for a sign for yourself coming either from the depths of Sheol or from the heights above.' 'No,' Ahaz answered, 'I will not put the Lord to the test.'

Then Isaiah said:

Listen now, House of David:
are you not satisfied with trying the patience of men
without trying the patience of my God, too?
The Lord himself, therefore,
will give you a sign.
It is this: the maiden is with child
and will soon give birth to a son
whom she will call Emmanuel,
a name which means 'God-is-with-us'.

The word of the Lord.

Responsorial Psalm   Ps 39:7-11. R. vv.8,9

R. **Here I am, Lord!**
I come to do your will.

You do not ask for sacrifice and offerings,
but an open ear.
You do not ask for holocaust and victim.
Instead, here am I. R.

In the scroll of the book it stands written
that I should do your will.
My God, I delight in your law
in the depth of my heart. R.

Your justice I have proclaimed
in the great assembly.
My lips I have not sealed;
you know it, O Lord. R.

I have not hidden your justice in my heart
but declared your faithful help.
I have not hidden your love and your truth
from the great assembly. R.

SECOND READING

A reading from the letter to the Hebrews   10:4-10

I was commanded in the scroll of the book, 'God, here I am! I am coming to obey your will.'

Bulls' blood and goats' blood are useless for taking away sins, and this is what Christ said, on coming into the world:

> You who wanted no sacrifice or oblation,
> prepared a body for me.
> you took no pleasure in holocausts or sacrifices for sin;
> then I said,
> just as I was commanded in the scroll of the book,
>   'God, here I am! I am coming to obey your will.'

Notice that he says first: You did not want what the Law lays down as the things to be offered, that is: the sacrifices, the oblations, the holocausts and the sacrifices for sin, and you took no pleasure in them; and then he says: Here I am! I am coming to obey your will. He is abolishing the first sort to replace it with the second. And this will was for us to be made holy by the offering of his body made once and for all by Jesus Christ.

The word of the Lord.

Gospel Acclamation   Jn 1:14

R. **Alleluia, alleluia!**
The Word was made flesh,
he lived among us,
and we saw his glory.
R. **Alleluia!**

GOSPEL

A reading from the Gospel according to Luke   1:26-38

Listen! You are to conceive and bear a son.

The angel Gabriel was sent by God to a town in Galilee called Nazareth, to a virgin betrothed to a man named Joseph, of the house of David; and the virgin's name was Mary. He went in and said to her, "Rejoice, so highly favoured! The Lord is with you.' She was deeply disturbed by these words and asked herself what this greeting could mean, but the angel said to her, 'Mary, do not be afraid; you have won God's favour. Listen! You are to conceive and bear a son, and you must name him Jesus. He will be great and will be called Son of the Most High. The Lord God will give him the throne of his ancestor David; he will rule over the House of Jacob for ever and his reign will have no end.' Mary said to the angel, 'But how can this come about, since I am a virgin?' 'The Holy Spirit will come upon you, the angel answered, 'and the power of the Most High will cover you with its shadow. And so the child will be holy and will be called Son of God. Know this too: your kinswoman Elizabeth also, in her old age, herself conceived a son, and she whom people called barren is now in her sixth month, for nothing is impossible to God.' 'I am the handmaid of the Lord,' said Mary, 'let what you have said be done to me.' And the angel left her.

The Gospel of the Lord.

The Creed is said. At the words **and was incarnate** all genuflect.

Prayer over the Offerings

Be pleased, almighty God,
to accept your Church's offering,
so that she,
    who is aware that her beginnings
lie in the Incarnation of your Only
    Begotten Son,
may rejoice to celebrate his mysteries
    on this Solemnity.
Who lives and reigns
    for ever and ever.

Super oblata

Ecclesiæ tuæ munus, omnipotens
    Deus, dignare suscipere,
ut, quæ in Unigeniti
    tui incarnatione
primordia sua constare cognoscit,
ipsius gaudeat hac sollemnitate
    celebrare mysteria.
Per Christum Dominum nostrum.

Preface: The Mystery of the Incarnation.

It is truly right and just,
    our duty and our salvation,
always and everywhere
    to give you thanks,
Lord, holy Father,
    almighty and eternal God,
through Christ our Lord.

For the Virgin Mary heard with faith
that the Christ was to be born
    among men and for men's sake
by the overshadowing power
    of the Holy Spirit.
Lovingly she bore him in her

Præfatio: De mysterio Incarnationis.

Vere dignum et iustum est,
    æquum et salutare,
nos tibi semper et ubique
    gratias agere:
Domine, sancte Pater,
    omnipotens æterne Deus:
per Christum Dominum nostrum.

Quem inter homines et propter
    homines nasciturum,
Spiritus Sancti obumbrante virtute,
a cælesti nuntio Virgo
    fidenter audivit
et immaculatis visceribus

immaculate womb,
that the promises to the children
  of Israel might come about
and the hope of nations be
  accomplished beyond all telling.

Through him the host of Angels
  adores your majesty
and rejoices in your presence for ever.

May our voices, we pray,
  join with theirs
in one chorus of exultant praise,
  as we acclaim:

Holy, Holy, Holy Lord God of hosts...

amanter portavit,
ut et promissiones filiis Israel
  perficeret veritas,
et gentium exspectatio pateret
  ineffabiliter adimplenda.

Per quem maiestatem tuam adorat
  exercitus Angelorum,
ante conspectum tuum
  in æternitate lætantium.

Cum quibus et nostras voces
  ut admitti iubeas, deprecamur,
socia exsultatione dicentes:

Sanctus, Sanctus, Sanctus. . .

Communion Antiphon   Is 7:14

Behold, a Virgin shall conceive
  and bear a son;
and his name will be
  called Emmanuel.

Ant. ad communionem

Ecce Virgo concipiet,
  et pariet Filium;
et vocabitur nomen
  eius Emmanuel.

Prayer after Communion

Confirm in our minds
  the mysteries of the true faith,
we pray, O Lord,
so that, confessing that he who was
  conceived of the Virgin Mary
is true God and true man,
we may, through the saving power
  of his Resurrection,
merit to attain eternal joy.
Through Christ our Lord.

Post communionem

In mentibus nostris, quæsumus,
  Domine,
veræ fidei sacramenta confirma,
ut, qui conceptum de Virgine
Deum verum
  et hominem confitemur,
per eius salutiferæ
  resurrectionis potentiam,
ad æternam mereamur
  pervenire lætitiam.
Per Christum Dominum nostrum.

15 April

THIRD SUNDAY OF EASTER

This history of the first Christian community tells us something very important which applies to the Church in all times and also to us. When a person truly knows Jesus Christ and believes in him, that person experiences his presence in life as well as the power of his Resurrection and cannot but communicate this experience. And if this person meets with misunderstanding or adversity, he behaves like Jesus in his Passion: he answers with love and with the power of the truth.

(Pope Francis)

Entrance Antiphon Cf. Ps 65:1-2	Ant. ad introitum
CRY out with joy to God, all the earth; O sing to the glory of his name. O render him glorious praise, alleluia.	IUBILATE Deo, omnis terra, psalmum dicite nomini eius, date gloriam laudi eius, alleluia.

The Gloria in excelsis (Glory to God in the highest) is said.

Collect	Collecta
May your people exult for ever, O God, in renewed youthfulness of spirit, so that, rejoicing now in the restored glory of our adoption, we may look forward in confident hope to the rejoicing of the day of resurrection. Through our Lord Jesus Christ, your Son, who lives and reigns with you in the unity of the Holy Spirit, one God, for ever and ever.	Semper exsultet populus tuus, Deus, renovata animæ iuventute, ut, qui nunc lætatur in adoptionis se gloriam restitutum, resurrectionis diem spe certæ gratulationis exspectet. Per Dominum nostrum Iesum Christum Filium tuum, qui tecum vivit et regnat in unitate Spiritus Sancti, Deus, per omnia sæcula sæculorum.

FIRST READING

A reading from the Acts of the Apostles   3:13-15,17-19

You killed the prince of life. God, however, raised him from the dead.

Peter said to the people: 'You are Israelites, and it is the God of Abraham, Isaac and Jacob, the God of our ancestors, who has glorified his servant Jesus, the same Jesus you handed over and then disowned in the presence of Pilate, after Pilate had decided to release him. It was you who accused the Holy One, the Just One, you who demanded the reprieve of a murderer while you killed the prince of life. God, however, raised him from the dead, and to that fact we are the witnesses.

'Now I know, brothers, that neither you nor your leaders had any idea what you were really doing; this was the way God carried out what he had foretold, when he said through all his prophets that his Christ would suffer. Now you must repent and turn to God, so that your sins may be wiped out.'

The word of the Lord.

Responsorial Psalm   Ps 4:2,4,7,9. R. v.7

R. **Lift up the light of your face on us, O Lord.**
   Or: **Alleluia!**

When I call, answer me, O God of justice;
from anguish you released me, have mercy and hear me! R.

It is the Lord who grants favours to those whom he loves;
the Lord hears me whenever I call him. R.

'What can bring us happiness?' many say.
Lift up the light of your face on us, O Lord. R.

I will lie down in peace and sleep comes at once,
for you alone, Lord, make me dwell in safety. R.

SECOND READING

A reading from the first letter of St John   2:1-5

He is the sacrifice that takes our sins away, and not only ours, but the whole world's.

I am writing this, my children,
to stop you sinning;
but if anyone should sin,
we have our advocate with the Father,
Jesus Christ, who is just;
he is the sacrifice that takes our sins away,
and not only ours,
but the whole world's.

We can be sure that we know God
only by keeping his commandments.
Anyone who says, 'I know him',
and does not keep his commandments,
is a liar,
refusing to admit the truth.
But when anyone does obey what he has said,
God's love comes to perfection in him.

The word of the Lord.

Gospel Acclamation   Cf. Lk 24:32

R. **Alleluia, alleluia!**
Lord Jesus, explain the scriptures to us.
Make our hearts burn within us as you talk to us.
R. **Alleluia!**

GOSPEL

A reading from the holy Gospel according to Luke   24:35-48

So you see how it is written that the Christ would suffer and on the third day rise from the dead.

The disciples told their story of what had happened on the road and how they had recognised Jesus at the breaking of bread.

They were still talking about this when Jesus himself stood among them and said to them, 'Peace be with you!' In a state of alarm and fright, they thought they were seeing a ghost. But he said, 'Why are you so agitated, and why are these doubts rising in your hearts? Look at my hands and feet; yes, it is I indeed. Touch me and see for yourselves; a ghost has no flesh and bones as you can see I have.' And as he said this he showed them his hands and feet. Their joy was so great that they could not believe it, and they stood there dumbfounded; so he said to them, 'Have you anything here to eat?' And they offered him a piece of grilled fish, which he took and ate before their eyes.

Then he told them, 'This is what I meant when I said, while I was still with you, that everything written about me in the Law of Moses, in the Prophets and in the Psalms, has to be fulfilled.' He then opened their minds to understand the scriptures, and he said to them, 'So you see how it is written that the Christ would suffer and on the third day rise from the dead, and that, in his name, repentance for the forgiveness of sins would be preached to all the nations, beginning from Jerusalem. You are witnesses to this.'

The Gospel of the Lord.

The Creed is said.

Prayer over the Offerings

Receive, O Lord, we pray,
these offerings of your
    exultant Church,
and, as you have given her cause
    for such great gladness,
grant also that the gifts we bring
may bear fruit
    in perpetual happiness.
Through Christ our Lord.

Preface of Easter, pp.52-57.

Super oblata

Suscipe munera, Domine,
    quæsumus, exsultantis Ecclesiæ,
et cui causam tanti
    gaudii præstitisti,
perpetuæ fructum concede lætitiæ.
Per Christum Dominum nostrum.

Communion Antiphon   Lk 24:35

The disciples recognised
    the Lord Jesus
in the breaking of the bread,
    alleluia.

Ant. ad communionem

Cognoverunt discipuli
    Dominum Iesum
in fractione panis, alleluia.

Optional for Year B: Lk 24:46-47

The Christ had to suffer and on
    the third day rise from the dead;
in his name repentance
    and remission of sins
must be preached to all the nations,
    alleluia.

Ad libitum pro anno B

Oportebat Christum pati,
    et resurgere a mortuis tertia die,
et prædicari in nomine
    eius pænitentiam,
et remissionem peccatorum
    in omnes gentes, alleluia.

Prayer after Communion

Look with kindness upon your
    people, O Lord,
and grant, we pray,
that those you were pleased
    to renew by eternal mysteries
may attain in their flesh
the incorruptible glory
    of the resurrection.
Through Christ our Lord.

Post communionem

Populum tuum, quæsumus,
    Domine, intuere benignus,
et, quem æternis dignatus
    es renovare mysteriis,
ad incorruptibilem glorificandæ
    carnis resurrectionem
pervenire concede.
Per Christum Dominum nostrum.

A formula of Solemn Blessing, pp.136-139, may be used.

22 April

FOURTH SUNDAY OF EASTER

In the figure of Jesus, the Good Shepherd, we contemplate the Providence of God, his paternal solicitude for each one of us. He does not leave us on our own! The result of this contemplation of Jesus the true and good Shepherd, is the exclamation of poignant astonishment that we find in the Second Reading of the day's Liturgy: "See what love the Father has given us...". Before this love of God, we feel immense joy and we open ourselves to recognising how much we have freely received. But it is not enough to contemplate and give thanks. It is also necessary to follow the Good Shepherd. In particular, those whose mission is to be a guide in the Church — priests, bishops, popes — are called to take on not the mentality of manager but that of servant, in imitation of Jesus who, in emptying himself, saved us with his mercy.

(Pope Francis)

Entrance Antiphon   Cf. Ps 32:5-6

THE merciful love of the Lord
  fills the earth;
by the word of the Lord the heavens
  were made, alleluia.

Ant. ad introitum

MISERICORDIA Domini plena
  est terra;
verbo Domini cæli firmati sunt,
  alleluia

The Gloria in excelsis (Glory to God in the highest) is said.

Collect

Almighty ever-living God,
lead us to a share in the joys
  of heaven,
so that the humble flock may reach
where the brave Shepherd
  has gone before.
Who lives and reigns with you
  in the unity of the Holy Spirit,
one God, for ever and ever.

Collecta

Omnipotens sempiterne Deus,
deduc nos ad societatem
  cælestium gaudiorum,
ut eo perveniat humilitas gregis,
quo processit fortitudo pastoris.
Per Dominum nostrum
  Iesum Christum Filium tuum,
qui tecum vivit et regnat
  in unitate Spiritus Sancti,
Deus, per omnia sæcula sæculorum.

FIRST READING

A reading from the Acts of the Apostles   4:8-12

This is the only name by which we can be saved.

Filled with the Holy Spirit, Peter said: 'Rulers of the people, and elders! If you are questioning us today about an act of kindness to a cripple, and asking us how he was healed, then I am glad to tell you all, and would indeed be glad to tell the whole people of Israel, that it was by the name of Jesus Christ the Nazarene, the one you crucified, whom God raised from the dead, by this name and by no other that this man is able to stand up perfectly healthy, here in your presence, today. This is the stone rejected by you the builders, but which has proved to be the keystone. For of all the names in the world given to men, this is the only one by which we can be saved.'

The word of the Lord.

Responsorial Psalm   Ps 117:1,8-9,21-23,26,28-29. R. v.22

R. **The stone which the builders rejected
has become the corner stone.**
Or: **Alleluia!**

Give thanks to the Lord for he is good,
for his love has no end.
It is better to take refuge in the Lord
than to trust in men:
it is better to take refuge in the Lord
than to trust in princes. R.

I will thank you for you have given answer
and you are my saviour.
The stone which the builders rejected
has become the corner stone.
This is the work of the Lord,
a marvel in our eyes. R.

Blessed in the name of the Lord
is he who comes.
We bless you from the house of the Lord;
I will thank you for you have given answer
and you are my saviour.
Give thanks to the Lord for he is good;
for his love has no end. R.

SECOND READING

A reading from the first letter of St John   3:1-2
We shall see God as he really is.

Think of the love that the Father has lavished on us,
by letting us be called God's children;
and that is what we are.
Because the world refused to acknowledge him,
therefore it does not acknowledge us.
My dear people, we are already the children of God
but what we are to be in the future has not yet been revealed;
all we know is, that when it is revealed
we shall be like him
because we shall see him as he really is.

   The word of the Lord.

Gospel Acclamation   Jn 10:14

R. **Alleluia, alleluia!**
I am the good shepherd, says the Lord;
I know my own sheep and my own know me.
R. **Alleluia!**

GOSPEL

A reading from the holy Gospel according to John   10:11-18
The good shepherd is one who lays down his life for his sheep.

Jesus said:
   'I am the good shepherd:
   the good shepherd is one who lays down his life for his sheep.
   The hired man, since he is not the shepherd
   and the sheep do not belong to him,
   abandons the sheep and runs away
   as soon as he sees a wolf coming,
   and then the wolf attacks and scatters the sheep;
   this is because he is only a hired man
   and has no concern for the sheep.
   I am the good shepherd;
   I know my own
   and my own know me,
   just as the Father knows me
   and I know the Father;

and I lay down my life for my sheep.
And there are other sheep I have
that are not of this fold,
and these I have to lead as well.
They too will listen to my voice,
and there will be only one flock,
and one shepherd.
The Father loves me,
because I lay down my life
in order to take it up again.
No one takes it from me;
I lay it down of my own free will,
and as it is in my power to lay it down,
so it is in my power to take it up again;
and this is the command I have been given by my Father.'

The Gospel of the Lord.

The Creed is said.

Prayer over the Offerings

Grant, we pray, O Lord,
that we may always find delight
   in these paschal mysteries,
so that the renewal constantly
   at work within us
may be the cause of our
   unending joy.
Through Christ our Lord.

Preface of Easter, pp.52-57.

Super oblata

Concede, quæsumus, Domine,
semper nos per hæc mysteria
   paschalia gratulari,
ut continua nostræ
   reparationis operatio
perpetuæ nobis fiat causa lætitiæ.
Per Christum Dominum nostrum.

Communion Antiphon

The Good Shepherd has risen,
who laid down his life for his sheep
and willingly died for his flock,
   alleluia.

Ant. ad communionem

Surrexit Pastor bonus,
qui animam suam posuit pro
   ovibus suis,
et pro grege suo mori dignatus est,
   alleluia.

Prayer after Communion	Post communionem
Look upon your flock, kind Shepherd, and be pleased to settle in eternal pastures the sheep you have redeemed by the Precious Blood of your Son. Who lives and reigns for ever and ever.	Gregem tuum, Pastor bone, placatus intende, et oves, quas pretioso Filii tui sanguine redemisti, in æternis pascuis collocare digneris. Per Christum Dominum nostrum.

A formula of Solemn Blessing, pp.136-139, may be used.

In England

23 April

SAINT GEORGE, MARTYR, PATRON OF ENGLAND

The Church's action is credible and effective only to the extent to which those who belong to her are prepared to pay in person for their fidelity to Christ in every circumstance. When this readiness is lacking, the crucial argument of truth on which the Church herself depends is also absent. Dear brothers and sisters, as in early times, today too Christ needs apostles ready to sacrifice themselves. He needs witnesses and martyrs.

(Pope Benedict XVI)

Solemnity

Entrance Antiphon   Cf. Mt 25:34

REJOICE, you Saints, in the presence of the Lamb;
a kingdom has been prepared for you
from the foundation of the world, alleluia.

Or: Ps 90:13

On the asp and the viper you will tread,
and trample the young lion and the dragon, alleluia.

The Gloria in excelsis (Glory to God in the highest) is said.

Collect

God of hosts,
who so kindled the fire of charity
in the heart of Saint George your martyr
that he bore witness to the risen Lord
both by his life and by his death,
grant us through his intercession, we pray,
the same faith and power of love,
that we who rejoice in his triumph
may be led to share with him
in the fullness of the resurrection.
Through our Lord Jesus Christ, your Son,
who lives and reigns with you in the unity of the Holy Spirit,
one God, for ever and ever.

FIRST READING

A reading from the book of the Apocalypse   12:10-12

In the face of death they would not cling to life.

I, John, heard a voice shout from heaven, 'Victory and power and empire
for ever have been won by our God, and all authority for his Christ, now
that the persecutor, who accused our brothers day and night before our
God, has been brought down. They have triumphed over him by the blood
of the Lamb and by the witness of their martyrdom, because even in the
face of death they would not cling to life. Let the heavens rejoice and all
who live there.'

The word of the Lord.

Responsorial Psalm   Ps 125. R v.5

R. **Those who are sowing in tears**
will sing when they reap.

When the Lord delivered Zion from bondage,
it seemed like a dream.
Then was our mouth filled with laughter,
on our lips there were songs. R.

The heathens themselves said: 'What marvels
the Lord worked for them!'
What marvels the Lord worked for us!
Indeed we were glad. R.

Deliver us, O Lord, from our bondage
as streams in dry land.
Those who are sowing in tears
will sing when they reap. R.

They go out, they go out, full of tears,
carrying seed for the sowing;
they come back, they come back, full of song,
carrying their sheaves. R.

A second reading is chosen from the Common of Martyrs.

Gospel Acclamation   Mt 23:9-10

R. **Alleluia, alleluia!**
Happy the man who stands firm,
for he has proved himself,
and will win the crown of life.
R. **Alleluia!**

GOSPEL

A reading from the holy Gospel according to John   15:18-21

If they persecuted me, they will persecute you.

Jesus said to his disciples:
    'If the world hates you,
      remember that it hated me before you.
    If you belonged to the world,
      the world would love you as its own;
    but because you do not belong to the world,
    because my choice withdrew you from the world,
      therefore the world hates you.

Remember the words I said to you:
A servant is not greater than his master.
If they persecuted me,
they will persecute you too;
if they kept my word,
they will keep yours as well.
But it will be on my account that they will do all this,
because they do not know the one who sent me.'

The Gospel of the Lord.

ALTERNATIVE GOSPEL

A reading from the holy Gospel according to John   15:1-8
Whoever remains in me, with me in him, bears fruit in plenty.

Jesus said to his disciples:
'I am the true vine,
and my Father is the vinedresser.
Every branch in me that bears no fruit
he cuts away,
and every branch that does bear fruit he prunes
to make it bear even more.
You are pruned already,
by means of the word that I have spoken to you.
Make your home in me, as I make mine in you.
As a branch cannot bear fruit all by itself,
but must remain part of the vine,
neither can you unless you remain in me.
I am the vine,
you are the branches.
Whoever remains in me, with me in him,
bears fruit in plenty;
for cut off from me you can do nothing.
Anyone who does not remain in me
is like a branch that has been thrown away
– he withers;
these branches are collected and thrown on the fire,
and they are burnt.

If you remain in me
and my words remain in you,
you may ask what you will
and you shall get it.
It is to the glory of my Father that you should bear much fruit,
and then you will be my disciples.'

The Gospel of the Lord.

The Creed is said.

Prayer over the Offerings

Receive, we pray, O Lord,
the sacrifice of conciliation and praise,
which we offer to your majesty
in commemoration of the blessed Martyr Saint George,
that it may lead us to forgiveness
and confirm us in constant thanksgiving.
Through Christ our Lord.

Preface I or II of Holy Martyrs, pp.72-73.

Communion Antiphon
Cf. 2 Tm 2:11-12

If we have died with Christ, we shall also live with him;
if we persevere, we shall also reign with him, alleluia.

Prayer after Communion

Rejoicing on this festival day, O Lord,
we have received your heavenly gifts;
grant, we pray,
that we who in this divine banquet
proclaim the death of your Son
may merit with Saint George to be partakers
in his resurrection and glory.
Through Christ our Lord.

29 April

FIFTH SUNDAY OF EASTER

This is Christian life: to abide in Jesus. And Jesus, in order to explain to us what he means by this, uses this beautiful figure of the vine: "I am the true vine, you the branches". And every branch that is not joined to the vine ends up dying, it bears no fruit; and then is thrown away to feed the fire. Many are used for this, to feed the fire — they are very, very useful — but not in bearing fruit. Rather, the branches that are united to the vine receive the lifeblood and thus develop, grow and bear fruit. It's a simple, simple image...if we detach from him, if we do not abide in the Lord, we are Christians in name only, but not in life; we are Christians, but dead ones, because we bear no fruit, like branches broken away from the vine.

(Pope Francis)

Entrance Antiphon   Cf. Ps 97:1-2

O SING a new song to the Lord,
  for he has worked wonders;
in the sight of the nations
he has shown his deliverance,
  alleluia.

Ant. ad introitum

C ANTATE Domino
  canticum novum,
quia mirabilia fecit Dominus;
ante conspectum gentium revelavit
  iustitiam suam, alleluia.

The Gloria in excelsis (Glory to God in the highest) is said.

Collect

Almighty ever-living God,
constantly accomplish the Paschal
  Mystery within us,
that those you were pleased
  to make new in Holy Baptism
may, under your protective care,
  bear much fruit
and come to the joys of life eternal.
Through our Lord Jesus Christ,
  your Son,
who lives and reigns with you
  in the unity of the Holy Spirit,
one God, for ever and ever.

Collecta

Omnipotens sempiterne Deus,
semper in nobis paschale
perfice sacramentum,
ut, quos sacro baptismate dignatus
  es renovare,
sub tuæ protectionis auxilio multos
  fructus afferant,
et ad æternæ vitæ gaudia
pervenire concedas.
Per Dominum nostrum Iesum
  Christum Filium tuum,
qui tecum vivit et regnat
  in unitate Spiritus Sancti,
Deus, per omnia sæcula sæculorum.

FIRST READING

A reading from the Acts of the Apostles   9:26-31
Barnabas explained how the Lord had appeared to Saul on his journey.

When Saul got to Jerusalem he tried to join the disciples, but they were all afraid of him: they could not believe he was really a disciple. Barnabas, however, took charge of him, introduced him to the apostles, and explained how the Lord had appeared to Saul and spoken to him on his journey, and how he had preached boldly at Damascus in the name of Jesus. Saul now started to go round with them in Jerusalem, preaching fearlessly in the name of the Lord. But after he had spoken to the Hellenists, and argued with them, they became determined to kill him. When the brothers knew, they took him to Caesarea, and sent him off from there to Tarsus.

The churches throughout Judaea, Galilee and Samaria were now left in peace, building themselves up, living in the fear of the Lord, and filled with the consolation of the Holy Spirit.

The word of the Lord.

Responsorial Pslam   Ps 21:26-28,30-32. R. v.26

R. **You, Lord, are my praise in the great assembly.**
   Or: **Alleluia!**

My vows I will pay before those who fear him.
The poor shall eat and shall have their fill.
They shall praise the Lord, those who seek him.
May their hearts live for ever and ever! R.

All the earth shall remember and return to the Lord,
all families of the nations worship before him.
They shall worship him, all the mighty of the earth;
before him shall bow all who go down to the dust. R.

And my soul shall live for him, my children serve him.
They shall tell of the Lord to generations yet to come,
declare his faithfulness to peoples yet unborn:
'These things the Lord has done.' R.

SECOND READING

A reading from the first letter of St John 3:18-24

His commandments are these: that we believe in his Son and that we love one another.

My children,
our love is not to be just words or mere talk,
but something real and active;
only by this can we be certain
that we are the children of the truth
and be able to quieten our conscience in his presence,
whatever accusations it may raise against us,
because God is greater than our conscience and he knows everything.
My dear people,
if we cannot be condemned by our own conscience,
we need not be afraid in God's presence,
and whatever we ask him,
we shall receive,
because we keep his commandments
and live the kind of life that he wants.
His commandments are these:
that we believe in the name of his Son Jesus Christ
and that we love one another
as he told us to.
Whoever keeps his commandments
lives in God and God lives in him.
We know that he lives in us
by the Spirit that he has given us.

   The word of the Lord.

Gospel Acclamation   Jn 15:4,5

R. **Alleluia, alleluia!**
Make your home in me, as I make mine in you.
Whoever remains in me bears fruit in plenty.
R. **Alleluia!**

GOSPEL

A reading from the holy Gospel according to John 15:1-8

Whoever remains in me, with me in him, bears fruit in plenty.

Jesus said to his disciples:
   'I am the true vine,
   and my Father is the vinedresser.

Every branch in me that bears no fruit
he cuts away,
and every branch that does bear fruit he prunes
to make it bear even more.
You are pruned already,
by means of the word that I have spoken to you.
Make your home in me, as I make mine in you.
As a branch cannot bear fruit all by itself,
but must remain part of the vine,
neither can you unless you remain in me.
I am the vine,
you are the branches.
Whoever remains in me, with me in him,
bears fruit in plenty;
for cut off from me you can do nothing.
Anyone who does not remain in me
is like a branch that has been thrown away
 – he withers;
these branches are collected and thrown on the fire,
and they are burnt.
If you remain in me
and my words remain in you,
you may ask what you will
and you shall get it.
It is to the glory of my Father that you should bear much fruit,
and then you will be my disciples.'

The Gospel of the Lord.

The Creed is said.

Prayer over the Offerings

O God, who by the wonderful
   exchange effected in this sacrifice
have made us partakers of the one
   supreme Godhead,
grant, we pray,
that, as we have come to know
   your truth,
we may make it ours by a worthy
   way of life.
Through Christ our Lord.

Super oblata

Deus, qui nos, per huius sacrificii
   veneranda commercia,
unius summæque divinitatis
   participes effecisti,
præsta, quæsumus,
ut, sicut tuam
   cognovimus veritatem,
sic eam dignis
   moribus assequamur.
Per Christum Dominum nostrum.

Preface of Easter, pp.52-57.

Communion Antiphon Cf. Jn 15:1,5	Ant. ad communionem
I am the true vine and you are the branches, says the Lord. Whoever remains in me, and I in him, bears fruit in plenty, alleluia.	Ego sum vitis vera et vos palmites, dicit Dominus; qui manet in me et ego in eo, hic fert fructum multum, alleluia.

Prayer after Communion	Post communionem
Graciously be present to your people, we pray, O Lord, and lead those you have imbued with heavenly mysteries to pass from former ways to newness of life. Through Christ our Lord.	Populo tuo, quæsumus, Domine, adesto propitius, et, quem mysteriis cælestibus imbuisti, fac ad novitatem vitæ de vetustate transire. Per Christum Dominum nostrum.

A formula of Solemn Blessing, pp.136-139, may be used.

6 May

SIXTH SUNDAY OF EASTER

Today's Gospel brings us back to the Last Supper, when we hear Jesus's new commandment. These words summarise Jesus's full message. Actually they summarise all that he did: Jesus gave his life for his friends. Friends who did not understand him, in fact they abandoned, betrayed and denied him at the crucial moment. This tells us that he loves us, even though we don't deserve his love. Thus Jesus shows us the path to follow him: the path of love. It is a real path, a path that leads us to come out of ourselves and go towards others. Jesus showed us that the love of God is realised in love for our neighbour.

(Pope Francis)

Entrance Antiphon Cf. Is 48:20	Ant. ad introitum
PROCLAIM a joyful sound and let it be heard; proclaim to the ends of the earth: The Lord has freed his people, alleluia.	VOCEM iucunditatis annuntiate, et audiatur, annuntiate usque ad extremum terræ: liberavit Dominus populum suum, alleluia.

The Gloria in excelsis (Glory to God in the highest) is said.

Collect

Grant, almighty God,
that we may celebrate with heartfelt
    devotion these days of joy,
which we keep in honour
    of the risen Lord,
and that what we relive
    in remembrance
we may always hold to in what we do.
Through our Lord Jesus Christ,
    your Son,
who lives and reigns with you
    in the unity of the Holy Spirit,
one God, for ever and ever.

Collecta

Fac nos, omnipotens Deus,
    hos lætitiæ dies,
quos in honorem Domini
    resurgentis exsequimur,
affectu sedulo celebrare,
ut quod recordatione percurrimus
semper in opere teneamus.
Per Dominum nostrum Iesum
    Christum Filium tuum,
qui tecum vivit et regnat
    in unitate Spiritus Sancti,
Deus, per omnia sæcula sæculorum.

FIRST READING

A reading from the Acts of the Apostles   10:25-26,34-35,44-48
The Holy Spirit has been poured out on the pagans too.

As Peter reached the house Cornelius went out to meet him, knelt at his feet and prostrated himself. But Peter helped him up. 'Stand up,' he said 'I am only a man after all!'

Then Peter addressed them: 'The truth I have now come to realise' he said 'is that God does not have favourites, but that anybody of any nationality who fears God and does what is right is acceptable to him.'

While Peter was still speaking the Holy Spirit came down on all the listeners. Jewish believers who had accompanied Peter were all astonished that the gift of the Holy Spirit should be poured out on the pagans too, since they could hear them speaking strange languages and proclaiming the greatness of God. Peter himself then said, 'Could anyone refuse the water of baptism to these people, now they have received the Holy Spirit just as much as we have?' He then gave orders for them to be baptised in the name of Jesus Christ. Afterwards they begged him to stay on for some days.

The word of the Lord.

Responsial Psalm   Ps 97:1-4. R. Cf. v.2

R. **The Lord has shown his salvation to the nations.**
    Or: **Alleluia!**

Sing a new song to the Lord
for he has worked wonders.
His right hand and his holy arm
have brought salvation. R.

The Lord has made known his salvation;
has shown his justice to the nations.
He has remembered his truth and love
for the house of Israel. R.

All the ends of the earth have seen
the salvation of our God.
Shout to the Lord all the earth,
ring out your joy. R.

When the Ascension is celebrated on the Seventh Sunday of Easter, the Second
Reading and Gospel assigned to the Seventh Sunday, may be read on the Sixth Sunday
(pp.451-453).

SECOND READING

A reading from the first letter of St John   4:7-10
God is love.

My dear people,
let us love one another
since love comes from God
and everyone who loves is begotten by God and knows God.
Anyone who fails to love can never have known God,
because God is love.
God's love for us was revealed
when God sent into the world his only Son
so that we could have life through him;
this is the love I mean:
not our love for God,
but God's love for us when he sent his Son
to be the sacrifice that takes our sins away.

    The word of the Lord.

Gospel Acclamation   Jn 14:23
R. **Alleluia, alleluia!**
Jesus said: 'If anyone loves me he will keep my word,
and my Father will love him, and we shall come to him.'
R. **Alleluia!**

GOSPEL

A reading from the holy Gospel according to John   15:9-17
A man can have no greater love than to lay down his life for his friends.

Jesus said to his disciples:

'As the Father has loved me,
so I have loved you.
Remain in my love.
If you keep my commandments
you will remain in my love,
just as I have kept my Father's commandments
and remain in his love.
I have told you this
so that my own joy may be in you
and your joy be complete.
This is my commandment:
love one another,
as I have loved you.
A man can have no greater love
than to lay down his life for his friends.
You are my friends,
if you do what I command you.
I shall not call you servants any more,
because a servant does not know
his master's business;
I call you friends,
because I have made known to you
everything I have learnt from my Father.
You did not choose me,
no, I chose you;
and I commissioned you
to go out and to bear fruit,
fruit that will last;
and then the Father will give you
anything you ask him in my name.

What I command you
is to love one another.'

The Gospel of the Lord.

The Creed is said.

Prayer over the Offerings | Super oblata

May our prayers rise up to you,
   O Lord,
together with the sacrificial offerings,
so that, purified by your graciousness,
we may be conformed to
   the mysteries of your mighty love.
Through Christ our Lord.

Ascendant ad te, Domine,
   preces nostræ
cum oblationibus hostiarum,
ut, tua dignatione mundati,
sacramentis magnæ
   pietatis aptemur.
Per Christum Dominum nostrum.

Preface of Easter, pp.52-57.

Communion Antiphon Jn 14:15-16 | Ant. ad communionem

If you love me, keep my
   commandments, says the Lord,
and I will ask the Father and he will
   send you another Paraclete,
to abide with you for ever, alleluia.

Si diligitis me, mandata mea
   servate, dicit Dominus.
Et ego rogabo Patrem, et alium
   Paraclitum dabit vobis,
ut maneat vobiscum in æternum,
   alleluia.

Prayer after Communion | Post communionem

Almighty ever-living God,
who restore us to eternal life
   in the Resurrection of Christ,
increase in us, we pray, the fruits
   of this paschal Sacrament
and pour into our hearts
   the strength of this saving food.
Through Christ our Lord.

Omnipotens sempiterne Deus,
qui ad æternam vitam in Christi
   resurrectione nos reparas,
fructus in nobis paschalis
   multiplica sacramenti,
et fortitudinem cibi salutaris nostris
   infunde pectoribus.
Per Christum Dominum nostrum.

A formula of Solemn Blessing, pp.136-139, may be used.

In Scotland

10 May

In England, Wales & Ireland

13 May

THE ASCENSION OF THE LORD

Jesus departs, he ascends to heaven, that is, he returns to the Father from whom he had been sent to the world. But this does not mean a separation, for he remains forever with us, in a new way. By his ascension, the Risen Lord draws the gaze of the Apostles — and our gaze — to the heights of heaven to show us that the end of our journey is the Father. He himself said that he would go to prepare a place for us in heaven. Yet, Jesus remains present and active in the affairs of human history through the power and the gifts of his Spirit; he is beside each of us: even if we do not see him with our eyes, he is there! He accompanies us, he guides us, he takes us by the hand and he lifts us up when we fall down. The risen Jesus is close to persecuted and discriminated Christians; he is close to every man and woman who suffers. He is close to us all.

(*Pope Francis*)

Solemnity

At the Vigil Mass

This Mass is used on the evening of the day before the Solemnity, either before or after First Vespers (Evening Prayer I) of the Ascension.

Entrance Antiphon   Ps 67:33,35 | Ant. ad introitum

YOU kingdoms of the earth,
    sing to God;
praise the Lord, who ascends above
    the highest heavens;
his majesty and might
    are in the skies, alleluia.

REGNA terræ cantate Deo,
    psallite Domino,
qui ascendit super cælum cæli;
magnificentia et virtus eius
    in nubibus, alleluia.

The Gloria in excelsis (Glory to God in the highest) is said.

Collect

O God, whose Son today ascended
    to the heavens
as the Apostles looked on,
grant, we pray, that, in accordance
    with his promise,
we may be worthy for him to live
    with us always on earth,
and we with him in heaven.
Who lives and reigns with you
    in the unity of the Holy Spirit,
one God, for ever and ever.

Collecta

Deus, cuius Filius hodie in cælos,
Apostolis astantibus, ascendit,
concede nobis, quæsumus,
ut secundum eius promissionem
et ille nobiscum semper in terris
et nos cum eo in cælo
    vivere mereamur.
Qui tecum vivit et regnat
    in unitate Spiritus Sanci, Deus,
per omnia sæcula sæculorum.

FIRST READING

A reading from the Acts of the Apostles   1:1-11
He was lifted up while they looked on.

In my earlier work, Theophilus, I dealt with everything Jesus had done and taught from the beginning until the day he gave his instructions to the apostles he had chosen through the Holy Spirit, and was taken up to heaven. He had shown himself alive to them after his Passion by many demonstrations: for forty days he had continued to appear to them and tell them about the kingdom of God. When he had been at table with them, he had told them not to leave Jerusalem, but to wait there for what the Father had promised. 'It is', he had said, 'what you have heard me speak about: John baptised with water but you, not many days from now, will be baptised with the Holy Spirit.'

Now having met together, they asked him, 'Lord, has the time come? Are you going to restore the kingdom to Israel?' He replied, 'It is not for you to know times or dates that the Father has decided by his own authority, but you will receive power when the Holy Spirit comes on you, and then you will be my witnesses not only in Jerusalem but throughout Judaea and Samaria, and indeed to the ends of the earth.'

As he said this he was lifted up while they looked on, and a cloud took him from their sight. They were still staring into the sky when suddenly two men in white were standing near them and they said, 'Why are you men from Galilee standing here looking into the sky? Jesus who has been taken up from you into heaven, this same Jesus will come back in the same way as you have seen him go there.'

The word of the Lord.

Responsorial Psalm   Ps 46:2-3,6-9. R. v.6

R. **God goes up with shouts of joy;**
   the Lord goes up with trumpet blast.
   Or: **Alleluia!**

All peoples, clap your hands,
cry to God with shouts of joy!
For the Lord, the Most High, we must fear,
great king over all the earth. R.

God goes up with shouts of joy;
the Lord goes up with trumpet blast.
Sing praise for God, sing praise,
sing praise to our king, sing praise. R.

God is king of all the earth.
Sing praise with all your skill.
God is king over the nations;
God reigns on his holy throne. R.

SECOND READING

The reading of Year A, Ep 1:17-23, may be used in place of the following.

A reading from the letter of St Paul to the Ephesians   4:1-13
Fully mature with the fullness of Christ.

[I, the prisoner in the Lord, implore you therefore to lead a life worthy of
your vocation. Bear with one another charitably, in complete selflessness,
gentleness and patience. Do all you can to preserve the unity of the Spirit
by the peace that binds you together. There is one Body, one Spirit, just
as you were all called into one and the same hope when you were called.
There is one Lord, one faith, one baptism, and one God who is Father of
all, over all, through all and within all.

Each one of us, however, has been given his own share of grace, given
as Christ allotted it.] It was said that he would:

When he ascended to the height, he captured prisoners,
he gave gifts to men.

When it says, 'he ascended', what can it mean if not that he descended
right down to the lower regions of the earth? [The one who rose higher
than all the heavens to fill all things is none other than the one who
descended. And to some, his gift was that they should be apostles; to some,
prophets; to some, evangelists; to some, pastors and teachers; so that the
saints together make a unity in the work of service, building up the body
of Christ. In this way we are all to come to unity in our faith and in our

knowledge of the Son of God, until we become the perfect Man, fully mature with the fullness of Christ himself.

The word of the Lord.]

Shorter Form, verses 1-7,11-13. Read between [ ]

Gospel Acclamation   Mt 28:19,20

R. **Alleluia, alleluia!**
Go, make disciples of all nations;
I am with you always; yes, to the end of time.
R. **Alleluia!**

GOSPEL

A reading from the holy Gospel according to Mark   16:15-20

He was taken up into heaven: there at the right hand of God he took his place.

Jesus showed himself to the Eleven, and said to them, 'Go out to the whole world; proclaim the Good News to all creation. He who believes and is baptised will be saved; he who does not believe will be condemned. These are the signs that will be associated with believers: in my name they will cast out devils; they will have the gift of tongues; they will pick up snakes in their hands, and be unharmed should they drink deadly poison; they will lay their hands on the sick, who will recover.'

And so the Lord Jesus, after he had spoken to them, was taken up into heaven: there at the right hand of God he took his place, while they, going out, preached everywhere, the Lord working with them and confirming the word by the signs that accompanied it.

The Gospel of the Lord.

The Creed is said.

Prayer over the Offerings

O God, whose Only Begotten Son,
    our High Priest,
is seated ever-living at your right
    hand to intercede for us,
grant that we may approach with
    confidence the throne of grace
and there obtain your mercy.
Through Christ our Lord.

Super oblata

Deus, cuius Unigenitus,
    Pontifex noster,
semper vivens sedet
    ad dexteram tuam
ad interpellandum pro nobis,
concede nos adire cum fiducia
    ad thronum gratiæ,
ut misericordiam tuam consequamur.
Per Christum Dominum nostrum.

Preface I or II of the Ascension of the Lord, pp.58-59.
When the Roman Canon is used, the proper form of the Communicantes (In communion with those) is said.

Communion Antiphon Cf. Heb 10:12

Christ, offering a single sacrifice
    for sins,
is seated for ever at God's right hand,
    alleluia.

Prayer after Communion

May the gifts we have received
    from your altar, Lord,
kindle in our hearts a longing
    for the heavenly homeland
and cause us to press forward,
    following in
    the Saviour's footsteps,
to the place where for our sake
    he entered before us.
Who lives and reigns
    for ever and ever.

Ant. ad communionem

Christus, unam pro peccatis
    offerens hostiam,
in sempiternum sedet in dextera Dei,
    alleluia.

Post communionem

Quæ ex altari tuo, Domine,
    dona percepimus,
accendant in cordibus nostris
    cælestis patriæ desiderium,
et quo præcursor pro nobis
    introivit Salvator,
faciant nos, eius vestigia sectantes,
    contendere.
Qui vivit et regnat
    in sæcula sæculorum.

A formula of Solemn Blessing, pp.138-139, may be used.

At the Mass during the Day

Entrance Antiphon   Ac 1:11

MEN of Galilee, why gaze
in wonder at the heavens?
This Jesus whom you saw
    ascending into heaven
will return as you saw him go,
    alleluia.

Ant. ad introitum

VIRI Galilæi, quid admiramini
aspicientes in cælum?
Quemadmodum vidistis eum
    ascendentem in cælum,
ita veniet, alleluia.

The Gloria in excelsis (Glory to God in the highest) is said.

Collect

Gladden us with holy joys,
    almighty God,
and make us rejoice with devout
    thanksgiving,
for the Ascension of Christ your Son
is our exaltation,
and, where the Head has gone
    before in glory,
the Body is called to follow in hope.

Collecta

Fac nos, omnipotens Deus,
    sanctis exsultare gaudiis,
et pia gratiarum actione lætari,
quia Christi Filii tui ascensio
    est nostra provectio,
et quo processit gloria capitis,
    eo spes vocatur et corporis.

Through our Lord Jesus Christ,
    your Son,
who lives and reigns with you
    in the unity of the Holy Spirit,
one God, for ever and ever.

Per Dominum nostrum Iesum
    Christum Filium tuum,
qui tecum vivit et regnat
    in unitate Spiritus Sancti,
Deus, per omnia sæcula sæculorum.

Or:

Vel:

Grant, we pray, almighty God,
that we, who believe that your Only
    Begotten Son, our Redeemer,
ascended this day to the heavens,
may in spirit dwell already
    in heavenly realms.
Who lives and reigns with you
    in the unity of the Holy Spirit,
one God, for ever and ever.

Concede, quæsumus,
    omnipotens Deus,
ut, qui hodierna die
Unigenitum tuum
    Redemptorem nostrum
ad cælos ascendisse credimus,
ipsi quoque mente
    in cælestibus habitemus.
Qui tecum vivit et regnat
    in unitate Spiritus Sancti,
Deus, per omnia sæcula sæculorum.

FIRST READING

A reading from the Acts of the Apostles   1:1-11

He was lifted up while they looked on.

In my earlier work, Theophilus, I dealt with everything Jesus had done and taught from the beginning until the day he gave his instructions to the apostles he had chosen through the Holy Spirit, and was taken up to heaven. He had shown himself alive to them after his Passion by many demonstrations: for forty days he had continued to appear to them and tell them about the kingdom of God. When he had been at table with them, he had told them not to leave Jerusalem, but to wait there for what the Father had promised. 'It is' he had said 'what you have heard me speak about: John baptised with water but you, not many days from now, will be baptised with the Holy Spirit.'

Now having met together, they asked him, 'Lord, has the time come? Are you going to restore the kingdom to Israel?' He replied, 'It is not for you to know times or dates that the Father has decided by his own authority, but you will receive power when the Holy Spirit comes on you, and then you will be my witnesses not only in Jerusalem but throughout Judaea and Samaria, and indeed to the ends of the earth.'

As he said this he was lifted up while they looked on, and a cloud took him from their sight. They were still staring into the sky when suddenly two men in white were standing near them and they said, 'Why are you men from Galilee standing here looking into the sky? Jesus who has been taken up from you into heaven, this same Jesus will come back in the same way as you have seen him go there.'

The word of the Lord.

Responsorial Psalm   Ps 46:2-3,6-9. R. v.6

R. **God goes up with shouts of joy**
   the Lord goes up with trumpet blast.
   Or: **Alleluia!**

All peoples, clap your hands,
cry to God with shouts of joy!
For the Lord, the Most High, we must fear,
great king over all the earth. R.

God goes up with shouts of joy;
the Lord goes up with trumpet blast.
Sing praise for God, sing praise,
sing praise to our king, sing praise. R.

God is king of all the earth.
Sing praise with all your skill.
God is king over the nations;
God reigns on his holy throne. R.

SECOND READING

The reading of Year A, Ep 1:17-23, may be used in place of the following.

A reading from the letter of St Paul to the Ephesians   4:1-13
Fully mature with the fullness of Christ.

[I, the prisoner in the Lord, implore you therefore to lead a life worthy of your vocation. Bear with one another charitably, in complete selflessness, gentleness and patience. Do all you can to preserve the unity of the Spirit by the peace that binds you together. There is one Body, one Spirit, just as you were all called into one and the same hope when you were called. There is one Lord, one faith, one baptism, and one God who is Father of all, over all, through all and within all.

Each one of us, however, has been given his own share of grace, given as Christ allotted it.] It was said that he would:

When he ascended to the height, he captured prisoners,
he gave gifts to men.

When it says, 'he ascended', what can it mean if not that he descended right down to the lower regions of the earth? [The one who rose higher than all the heavens to fill all things is none other than the one who descended. And to some, his gift was that they should be apostles; to some, prophets; to some, evangelists; to some, pastors and teachers; so that the saints together make a unity in the work of service, building up the body of Christ. In this way we are all to come to unity in our faith and in our knowledge of the Son of God, until we become the perfect Man, fully mature with the fullness of Christ himself.

The word of the Lord.]

Shorter Form, verses 1-7,11-13. Read between [ ]

Gospel Acclamation   Mt 28:19,20

R. **Alleluia, alleluia!**
Go, make disciples of all nations;
I am with you always; yes, to the end of time.
R. **Alleluia!**

GOSPEL

A reading from the holy Gospel according to Mark   16:15-20
He was taken up into heaven: there at the right hand of God he took his place.

Jesus showed himself to the Eleven, and said to them, 'Go out to the whole world; proclaim the Good News to all creation. He who believes and is baptised will be saved; he who does not believe will be condemned. These are the signs that will be associated with believers: in my name they will cast out devils; they will have the gift of tongues; they will pick up snakes in their hands, and be unharmed should they drink deadly poison; they will lay their hands on the sick, who will recover.'

And so the Lord Jesus, after he had spoken to them, was taken up into heaven: there at the right hand of God he took his place, while they, going out, preached everywhere, the Lord working with them and confirming the word by the signs that accompanied it.

The Gospel of the Lord.

The Creed is said.

Prayer over the Offerings	Super oblata

We offer sacrifice now
    in supplication, O Lord,
to honour the wondrous Ascension
    of your Son:
grant, we pray,
that through this most holy exchange
we, too, may rise up
    to the heavenly realms.
Through Christ our Lord.
	Sacrificium, Domine,
	    pro Filii tui supplices
	venerabili nunc
	    ascensione deferimus:
	præsta, quæsumus, ut his
	    commerciis sacrosanctis
	ad cælestia consurgamus.
	Per Christum Dominum nostrum.

Preface I or II of the Ascension of the Lord, pp.58-59.

When the Roman Canon is used, the proper form of the Communicantes (In communion with those) is said.

Communion Antiphon Mt 28:20	Ant. ad communionem

Behold, I am with you always,
even to the end of the age, alleluia.
	Ecce ego vobiscum sum
	    omnibus diebus,
	usque ad consummationem sæculi,
	    alleluia.

Prayer after Communion	Post communionem

Almighty ever-living God,
who allow those on earth
    to celebrate divine mysteries,
grant, we pray,
that Christian hope may draw
    us onward
to where our nature is united
    with you.
Through Christ our Lord.
	Omnipotens sempiterne Deus,
	qui in terra constitutos divina
	    tractare concedis,
	præsta, quæsumus,
	ut illuc tendat christianæ
	    devotionis affectus,
	quo tecum est nostra substantia.
	Per Christum Dominum nostrum.

A formula of Solemn Blessing, pp.138-139, may be used.

In Scotland

13 May

SEVENTH SUNDAY OF EASTER

The Apostles had a direct and overwhelming experience of the resurrection; they were eyewitnesses to that event. Thanks to their authoritative testimony, many people came to believe; from faith in the risen Lord, Christian communities were born and are born continually. We too, today, base our faith in the risen Lord on the witness of the Apostles, which has come down to us through the mission of the Church. Our faith is firmly linked to their testimony, as to an unbroken chain which spans the centuries, made up not only by the successors of the Apostles, but also by succeeding generations of Christians. Like the Apostles, each one of Christ's followers is called to become a witness to his resurrection, above all in those human settings where forgetfulness of God and human disorientation are most evident.

(Pope Francis)

Entrance Antiphon Cf. Ps 26:7-9	Ant. ad introitum
O LORD, hear my voice, for I have called to you; of you my heart has spoken: Seek his face; hide not your face from me, alleluia.	E XAUDI, Domine, vocem meam, qua clamavi ad te. Tibi dixit cor meum, quæsivi vultum tuum, vultum tuum requiram; ne avertas faciem tuam a me, alleluia.

The Gloria in excelsis (Glory to God in the highest) is said.

Collect

Graciously hear our supplications,
   O Lord,
so that we, who believe that
   the Saviour of the human race
is with you in your glory,
may experience, as he promised,
until the end of the world,
his abiding presence among us.
Who lives and reigns with you
   in the unity of the Holy Spirit,
one God, for ever and ever.

Collecta

Supplicationibus nostris, Domine,
   adesto propitius,
ut, sicut humani generis Salvatorem
tecum in tua credimus maiestate,
ita eum usque ad
   consummationem sæculi
manere nobiscum,
sicut ipse promisit, sentiamus.
Qui tecum vivit et regnat
   in unitate Spiritus Sancti,
Deus, per omnia sæcula sæculorum.

FIRST READING

A reading from the Acts of the Apostles   1:15-17,20-26
We must choose one of these to be a witness to his resurrection with us.

One day Peter stood up to speak to the brothers – there were about a hundred and twenty persons in the congregation: 'Brothers, the passage of scripture had to be fulfilled in which the Holy Spirit, speaking through David, foretells the fate of Judas, who offered himself as a guide to the men who arrested Jesus – after having been one of our number and actually sharing this ministry of ours.

   'In the Book of Psalms it says:

   Let someone else take his office.

'We must therefore choose someone who has been with us the whole time that the Lord Jesus was travelling around with us, someone who was with us right from the time when John was baptising until the day when he was taken up from us – and he can act with us as a witness to his resurrection.'

   Having nominated two candidates, Joseph known as Barsabbas, whose surname was Justus, and Matthias, they prayed, 'Lord, you can read everyone's heart; show us therefore which of these two you have chosen to take over this ministry and apostolate, which Judas abandoned to go to his proper place.' They then drew lots for them, and as the lot fell to Matthias, he was listed as one of the twelve apostles.

   The word of the Lord.

Responsorial Psalm   Ps 102:1-2,11-12,19-20. R. v.19

R. **The Lord has set his sway in heaven.**
   Or: **Alleluia!**

My soul, give thanks to the Lord;
all my being, bless his holy name.
My soul, give thanks to the Lord
and never forget all his blessings. R.

For as the heavens are high above the earth
so strong is his love for those who fear him.
As far as the east is from the west
so far does he remove our sins. R.

The Lord has set his sway in heaven
and his kingdom is ruling over all.
Give thanks to the Lord, all his angels,
mighty in power, fulfilling his word. R.

SECOND READING

A reading from the first letter of St John   4:11-16

Anyone who lives in love lives in God, and God lives in him.

My dear people,
since God has loved us so much,
we too should love one another.
No one has ever seen God;
but as long as we love one another
God will live in us
and his love will be complete in us.
We can know that we are living in him
and he is living in us
because he lets us share his Spirit.
We ourselves saw and we testify
that the Father sent his Son
as saviour of the world.
If anyone acknowledges that Jesus is the Son of God,
God lives in him, and he in God.
We ourselves have known and put our faith in
God's love towards ourselves.

God is love
and anyone who lives in love lives in God,
and God lives in him.

   The word of the Lord.

Gospel Acclamation   Cf. Jn 14:18

R. **Alleluia, alleluia!**
I will not leave you orphans, says the Lord;
I will come back to you, and your hearts will be full of joy.
R. **Alleluia!**

GOSPEL

A reading from the holy Gospel according to John   17:11-19
That they may be one like us!

Jesus raised his eyes to heaven and said:

   'Holy Father,
   keep those you have given me true to your name,
   so that they may be one like us.
   While I was with them,
   I kept those you had given me true to your name.
   I have watched over them and not one is lost
   except the one who chose to be lost,
   and this was to fulfil the scriptures.
   But now I am coming to you
   and while still in the world I say these things
   to share my joy with them to the full.
   I passed your word on to them,
   and the world hated them,
   because they belong to the world
   no more than I belong to the world.
   I am not asking you to remove them from the world,
   but to protect them from the evil one.
   They do not belong to the world
   any more than I belong to the world.
   Consecrate them in the truth,
   your word is truth.
   As you sent me into the world,
   I have sent them into the world,

and for their sake I consecrate myself
   so that they too may be consecrated in truth.'

   The Gospel of the Lord.

The Creed is said.

Prayer over the Offerings | Super oblata

Accept, O Lord, the prayers
   of your faithful
with the sacrificial offerings,
that through these acts
   of devotedness
we may pass over to the glory
   of heaven.
Through Christ our Lord.

Suscipe, Domine, fidelium preces
cum oblationibus hostiarum,
ut, per hæc piæ devotionis officia,
ad cælestem gloriam transeamus.
Per Christum Dominum nostrum.

Preface of Easter, or of the Ascension, pp.52-59.

Communion Antiphon   Jn 17:22 | Ant. ad communionem

Father, I pray that they may be one
as we also are one, alleluia.

Rogo, Pater, ut sint unum,
sicut et nos unum sumus, alleluia.

Prayer after Communion | Post communionem

Hear us, O God our Saviour,
and grant us confidence,
that through these sacred mysteries
there will be accomplished
   in the body of the whole Church
what has already come to pass
   in Christ her Head.
Who lives and reigns
   for ever and ever.

Exaudi nos, Deus, salutaris noster,
ut per hæc sacrosancta mysteria
in totius Ecclesiæ confidamus
   corpore faciendum,
quod eius præcessit in capite.
Per Christum Dominum nostrum.

A formula of Solemn Blessing, pp.136-139, may be used.

20 May

PENTECOST SUNDAY

The world needs men and women who are not closed in on themselves, but filled with the Holy Spirit. Closing oneself off from the Holy Spirit means not only a lack of freedom; it is a sin. There are many ways one can close oneself off to the Holy Spirit: by selfishness for one's own gain; by rigid legalism – seen in the attitude of the doctors of the law to whom Jesus referred as "hypocrites"; by neglect of what Jesus taught; by living the Christian life not as service to others but in the pursuit of personal interests; and in so many other ways. The gift of the Holy Spirit has been bestowed upon the Church and upon each one of us, so that we may live lives of genuine faith and active charity, that we may sow the seeds of reconciliation and peace.

(Pope Francis)

Solemnity

At the Vigil Mass

EXTENDED FORM

This Vigil Mass may be celebrated on the Saturday evening, either before or after First Vespers (Evening Prayer I) of Pentecost Sunday.

In churches where the Vigil Mass is celebrated in an extended form, this may be done as follows.

a) If First Vespers (Evening Prayer I) celebrated in choir or in common immediately precede Mass, the celebration may begin either from the introductory verse and the hymn (**Veni, creator Spiritus**) or else from the singing of the Entrance Antiphon with the procession and greeting of the Priest; in either case the Penitential Act is omitted (Cf. General Instruction of the Liturgy of the Hours, nos. 94 and 96).

Then the Psalmody prescribed for Vespers follows, up to but not including the Short Reading.

After the Psalmody, omitting the Penitential Act, and if appropriate, the Kyrie (Lord, have mercy), the Priest says the prayer **Grant, we pray, almighty God, that the splendour**, as at the Vigil Mass.

b) If Mass is begun in the usual way, after the Kyrie (Lord, have mercy), the Priest says the prayer **Grant, we pray, almighty God, that the splendour,** as at the Vigil Mass.

Then the Priest may address the people in these or similar words:

Dear brethren (brothers and sisters), we have now begun our Pentecost Vigil, after the example of the Apostles and disciples who with Mary, the Mother of Jesus, persevered in prayer, awaiting the Spirit promised by the Lord; like them, let us, too, listen with quiet hearts to the Word of God. Let us meditate on how many great deeds God in times past did for his people and let us pray that the Holy Spirit, whom the Father sent as the first fruits for those who believe, may bring to perfection his work in the world.	Vigiliam Pentecostes ingressi, fratres carissimi, ad exemplum Apostolorum et discipulorum qui, cum Maria, Matre Iesu, instabant in oratione, exspectantes Spiritum a Domino promissum, quieto corde nunc verbum Dei audiamus. Meditemur quanta fecit Deus populo suo et oremus, ut Spiritus Sanctus quem Pater misit primitias credentibus, opus suum in mundo perficiat.

Then follow the readings proposed as options in the Lectionary. A reader goes to the ambo and proclaims the reading. Afterwards a psalmist or a cantor sings or says the Psalm with the people making the response. Then all rise, the Priest says, **Let us pray** and, after all have prayed for a while in silence, he says the prayer corresponding to the reading. In place of the Responsorial Psalm a period of sacred silence may be observed, in which case the pause after **Let us pray** is omitted.

FIRST READING

A reading from the book of Genesis   11:1-9

It was named Babel because there the language of the whole earth was confused.

Throughout the earth men spoke the same language, with the same vocabulary. Now as they moved eastwards they found a plain in the land of Shinar where they settled. They said to one another, 'Come, let us make bricks and bake them in the fire.' – For stone they used bricks, and for mortar they used bitumen. – 'Come,' they said 'let us build ourselves a town and a tower with its top reaching heaven. Let us make a name for ourselves, so that we may not be scattered about the whole earth.'

Now the Lord came down to see the town and the tower that the sons of man had built. 'So they are all a single people with a single language!'

said the Lord. 'This is but the start of their undertakings! There will be nothing too hard for them to do. Come, let us go down and confuse their language on the spot so that they can no longer understand one another.' The Lord scattered them thence over the whole face of the earth, and they stopped building the town. It was named Babel therefore, because there the Lord confused the language of the whole earth. It was from there that the Lord scattered them over the whole face of the earth.

The word of the Lord.

Responsorial Psalm   Ps 32:10-11,12-13,14-15 R. v.12b

R. **Happy the people the Lord has chosen as his own.**

He frustrates the designs of the nations,
he defeats the plans of the peoples.
His own designs shall stand for ever,
the plans of his heart from age to age. R.

They are happy, whose God is the Lord,
the people he has chosen as his own.
From the heavens the Lord looks forth,
he sees all the children of men. R.

From the place where he dwells he gazes
on all the dwellers on the earth,
he who shapes the hearts of them all
and considers all their deeds. R.

Prayer

Let us pray.	Oremus.
Grant, we pray, almighty God, that your Church may always remain that holy people, formed as one by the unity of Father, Son and Holy Spirit, which manifests to the world the Sacrament of your holiness and unity and leads it to the perfection of your charity. Through Christ our Lord.	Concede, quæsumus, omnipotens Deus, ut Ecclesia tua semper ea plebs sancta permaneat de unitate Patris et Filii et Spiritus Sancti adunata, quce tuce sanctitatis et unitatis sacramentum mundo manifestet et ipsum ad perfectionem tuce conducat caritatis. Per Christum Dominum nostrum.
R. Amen.	R. Amen.

SECOND READING

A reading from the book of Exodus   19:3-8,16-20

The Lord came down on the mountain of Sinai before all the people.

Moses went up to God, and the Lord called to him from the mountain, saying, 'Say this to the House of Jacob, declare this to the sons of Israel, "You yourselves have seen what I did with the Egyptians, how I carried you on eagle's wings and brought you to myself. From this you know that now, if you obey my voice and hold fast to my covenant, you of all the nations shall be my very own, for all the earth is mine. I will count you a kingdom of priests, a consecrated nation." Those are the words you are to speak to the sons of Israel.' So Moses went and summoned the elders of the people, putting before them all that the Lord had bidden him. Then all the people answered as one, 'All that the Lord has said, we will do.'

Now at daybreak on the third day there were peals of thunder on the mountain and lightning flashes, a dense cloud, and a loud trumpet blast, and inside the camp all the people trembled. Then Moses led the people out of the camp to meet God; and they stood at the bottom of the mountain. The mountain of Sinai was entirely wrapped in smoke, because the Lord had descended on it in the form of fire. Like smoke from a furnace the smoke went up, and the whole mountain shook violently. Louder and louder grew the sound of the trumpet. Moses spoke, and God answered him with peals of thunder. The Lord came down on the mountain of Sinai, on the mountain top, and the Lord called Moses to the top of the mountain.

The word of the Lord.

Responsorial Psalm   Dn 3:52,53,54,55,56. R. v.52b

R. **To you glory and praise for evermore.**

You are blest, Lord God of our fathers. R.
Blest your glorious holy name. R.
You are blest in the temple of your glory. R.
You are blest on the throne of your kingdom. R.
You are blest who gaze into the depths. R.
You are blest in the firmament of heaven. R.

Or   Ps 18:8,9,10,11. R. Jn v.6:68c

R. **You have the message of eternal life, O Lord.**

The law of the Lord is perfect,
it revives the soul.
The rule of the Lord is to be trusted,
it gives wisdom to the simple. R.

The precepts of the Lord are right,
they gladden the heart.
The command of the Lord is clear,
it gives light to the eyes. R.

The fear of the Lord is holy,
abiding for ever.
The decrees of the Lord are truth
and all of them just. R.

They are more to be desired than gold,
than the purest of gold
and sweeter are they than honey,
than honey from the comb. R.

R. **You have the message of eternal life, O Lord.**

Prayer

Let us pray.

O God, who in fire and lightning
gave the ancient Law to Moses
   on Mount Sinai
and on this day manifested
   the new covenant
in the fire of the Spirit,
grant, we pray,
that we may always be aflame
   with that same Spirit
whom you wondrously poured out
   on your Apostles,
and that the new Israel,
gathered from every people,
may receive with rejoicing
the eternal commandment
   of your love.
Through Christ our Lord.
R. Amen.

Oremus.

Deus, qui in fulgure ignis
   in monte Sinai
legem antiquam Moysi dedisti
et fœdus novum in igne Spiritus
hoc die manifestasti,
presta, quæsumus,
ut illo iugiter Spiritu ferveamus,
quem Apostolis tuis
   ineffabiliter infudisti,

et novus Israel,
ex omni populo congregatus,
mandatum æternum tui amoris
   lætanter accipiat.
Per Christum Dominum nostrum.
R. Amen.

THIRD READING

A reading from the prophet Ezekiel   37:1-14
Dry bones, I am going to make the breath enter you, and you will live.

The hand of the Lord was laid on me, and he carried me away by the
spirit of the Lord and set me down in the middle of a valley, a valley full

of bones. He made me walk up and down among them. There were vast quantities of these bones on the ground the whole length of the valley; and they were quite dried up. He said to me, 'Son of man, can these bones live?' I said, 'You know, Lord.' He said, 'Prophesy over these bones. Say, "Dry bones, hear the word of the Lord. The Lord says this to these bones: I am now going to make the breath enter you, and you will live. I shall put sinews on you, I shall make flesh grow on you, I shall cover you with skin and give you breath, and you will live, and you will learn that I am the Lord."' I prophesied as I had been ordered. While I was prophesying, there was a noise, a sound of clattering; and the bones joined together. I looked, and saw that they were covered with sinews; flesh was growing on them and skin was covering them, but there was no breath in them. He said to me, 'Prophesy to the breath; prophesy, son of man. Say to the breath, "The Lord says this: Come from the four winds, breath; breathe on these dead; let them live!"' I prophesied as he had ordered me, and the breath entered them; they came to life again and stood up on their feet, a great, an immense army.

Then he said, 'Son of man, these bones are the whole House of Israel. They keep saying, "Our bones are dried up, our hope has gone; we are as good as dead." So prophesy. Say to them, "The Lord says this: I am now going to open your graves; I mean to raise you from your graves, my people, and lead you back to the soil of Israel. And you will know that I am the Lord, when I open your graves and raise you from your graves, my people. And I shall put my spirit in you, and you will live, and I shall resettle you on your own soil; and you will know that I, the Lord have said and done this – it is the Lord who speaks."'

The word of the Lord.

Responsorial Psalm   Ps 106:2-3,4-5,6–7,8–9. R. v.1

R. **O give thanks to the Lord, for he is good;**
   for his love has no end.
   Or: **Alleluia!**

Let them say this, the Lord's redeemed,
whom he redeemed from the hand of the foe
and gathered from far-off lands,
from east and west, north and south. R.

Some wandered in the desert, in the wilderness,
finding no way to a city they could dwell in.
Hungry they were and thirsty;
their soul was fainting within them. R.

Then they cried to the Lord in their need
and he rescued them from their distress
and he led them along the right way,
to reach a city they could dwell in. R.

Let them thank the Lord for his love,
for the wonders he does for men.
For he satisfies the thirsty soul;
he fills the hungry with good things. R.

R. **O give thanks to the Lord, for he is good;
for his love has no end.**
Or: **Alleluia!**

Prayer

Let us pray.
Lord, God of power,
who restore what has fallen
and preserve what you have restored,
increase, we pray, the peoples
to be renewed by the sanctification
    of your name,
that all who are washed clean
    by holy Baptism
may always be directed
    by your prompting.
Through Christ our Lord.
R. Amen.

Oremus.
Domine, Deus virtutum,
qui coliapsa reparas
    et reparata conservas,
auge populos in tui nominis
    sanctificatione renovandos,
ut omnes, qui sacro
    Baptismate diluuntur,
tua semper inspiratione dirigantur.
Per Christum Dominum nostrum.
R. Amen.

Or:
O God, who have brought us
    to rebirth by the word of life,
pour out upon us your Holy Spirit,
that, walking in oneness of faith,
we may attain in our flesh
the incorruptible glory
    of the resurrection.
Through Christ our Lord.
R. Amen.

Vel:
Deus, qui nos verbo vitæ regenerasti,
effunde super nos
    Spiritum Sanctum tuum,
ut, in unitate fidei ambulantes,
ad incorruptibilem glorificandæ
    carnis resurrectionem
pervenire mereamur.
Per Christum Dominum nostrum.
R. Amen.

Or:
May your people exult for ever,
    O God,
in renewed youthfulness of spirit,

Vel:
Semper exsultet populus
    tuus, Deus,
Spiritu Sancto tuo renovata

so that, rejoicing now in the restored
   glory of our adoption,
we may look forward
in confident hope
to the rejoicing of the day
   of resurrection.
Through Christ our Lord.
R. Amen.

animce iuventute,
ut, qui nunc lætatur in adoptionis
   se gloriam restitutum,
resurrectionis diem spe certæ
gratulationis exspectet.
Per Christum Dominum nostrum.
R. Amen.

FOURTH READING

A reading from the prophet Joel   3:1-5

I will pour out my spirit on all people.

Thus says the Lord:

   'I will pour out my spirit on all mankind.
   Your sons and daughters shall prophesy,
   your old men shall dream dreams,
   and your young men see visions.
   Even on the slaves, men and women,
   will I pour out my spirit in those days.
   I will display portents in heaven and on earth,
   blood and fire and columns of smoke.'

The sun will be turned into darkness,
and the moon into blood,
before the day of the Lord dawns,
that great and terrible day.
All who call on the name of the Lord will be saved,
for on Mount Zion there will be some who have escaped,
as the Lord has said,
and in Jerusalem some survivors whom the Lord will call.

   The word of the Lord.

Responsorial Psalm   Ps103:1-2a,24,35c,27–28,29bc-30. R. v.30

R. **Send forth your Spirit, O Lord,**
   and renew the face of the earth.

   Or: **Alleluia!**

   Bless the Lord, my soul!
   Lord God, how great you are,
   clothed in majesty and glory,
   wrapped in light as in a robe! R.

How many are your works, O Lord!
In wisdom you have made them all.
The earth is full of your riches.
Bless the Lord, my soul. R.

All of these look to you
to give them their food in due season.
You give it, they gather it up:
you open your hand, they have their fill. R.

You take back your spirit, they die,
returning to the dust from which they came.
You send forth your spirit, they are created;
and you renew the face of the earth. R.

R. **Send forth your Spirit, O Lord,
and renew the face of the earth.**
Or: **Alleluia!**

Prayer

Let us pray.	Oremus.
Fulfil for us your gracious promise, O Lord, we pray, so that by his coming the Holy Spirit may make us witnesses before the world to the Gospel of our Lord Jesus Christ. Who lives and reigns for ever and ever.	Promissionem tuam, quæsumus, Domine, super nos propitiatus adimple, ut Spiritus Sanctus adveniens nos coram mundo testes efficiat Evangelii Domini nostri Iesu Christi. Qui tecum vivit et regnat in sæcula sæculorum.
R. Amen.	R. Amen.

Then the Priest intones the hymn Gloria in excelsis Deo (Glory to God in the highest).

When the hymn is concluded, the Priest says the Collect in the usual way: **Almighty ever-living God, who willed**, as here below (p.463).

Then the reader proclaims the reading from the Apostle (Rm 8:22-27) pp.464-465, and Mass continues in the usual way.

If Vespers (Evening Prayer) are joined to Mass, after Communion with the Communion Antiphon (**On the last day**), the Magnificat is sung, with its Vespers antiphon (**Veni, Sancte Spiritus**); then the Prayer after Communion is said and the rest follows as usual.

At the Vigil Mass

SIMPLE FORM

This Mass is used on the Saturday evening, either before or after First Vespers (Evening Prayer I) of Pentecost Sunday.

Entrance Antiphon Rm 5:5; Cf. 8:11 | Ant. ad introitum

THE love of God has been poured into our hearts through the Spirit of God dwelling within us, alleluia.

CARITAS Dei diffusa est in cordibus nostris per inhabitantem Spiritum eius in nobis, alleluia.

The Gloria in excelsis (Glory to God in the highest) is said.

Collect

Almighty ever-living God,
who willed the Paschal Mystery
to be encompassed as a sign
    in fifty days,
grant that from out
    of the scattered nations
the confusion of many tongues
may be gathered by heavenly grace
into one great confession
    of your name.
Through our Lord Jesus Christ,
    your Son,
who lives and reigns with you
    in the unity of the Holy Spirit,
one God, for ever and ever.

Collecta

Omnipotens sempiterne Deus,
qui paschale sacramentum
quinquaginta dierum voluisti
    mysterio contineri,
præsta, ut, gentium
    facta dispersione,
divisiones linguarum ad unam
    confessionem tui nominis
cælesti munere congregentur.
Per Dominum nostrum Iesum
    Christum Filium tuum,
qui tecum vivit et regnat
    in unitate Spiritus Sancti,
Deus, per omnia sæcula sæculorum.

Or:

Grant, we pray, almighty God,
that the splendour of your glory
may shine forth upon us
and that, by the bright rays
    of the Holy Spirit,
the light of your light may confirm
    the hearts
of those born again by your grace.

Vel:

Præsta, quæsumus,
    omnipotens Deus,
ut claritatis tuæ super nos
    splendor effulgeat,
et lux tuæ lucis corda eorum,
qui per tuam gratiam sunt renati,
Sancti Spiritus
    illustratione confirmet.

| Through our Lord Jesus Christ, your Son, who lives and reigns with you in the unity of the Holy Spirit, one God, for ever and ever. | Per Dominum nostrum Iesum Christum Filium tuum, qui tecum vivit et regnat in unitate Spiritus Sancti, Deus, per omnia sæcula sæculorum. |

FIRST READING

There is a choice of four texts for the First Reading: Either Genesis 11:1-9 (On Babel), p.455; or Exodus 19:3-8,16-20 (On God's descent on Mount Sinai), p.457; or Ezekiel 37:1-14 (On the dry bones and God's spirit), p.458; or Joel 3:1-5 (On the outpouring of the Spirit), p.461.

Responsorial Psalm   Ps 103:1-2,24,27-30,35. R. Cf. v.30

R. **Send forth your spirit, O Lord,**
   and renew the face of the earth.
   Or: **Alleluia!**

Bless the Lord, my soul!
Lord God, how great you are,
clothed in majesty and glory,
wrapped in light as in a robe! R.

How many are your works, O Lord!
In wisdom you have made them all.
The earth is full of your riches.
Bless the Lord, my soul. R.

All of these look to you
to give them their food in due season.
You give it, they gather it up:
you open your hand, they have their fill. R.

You take back your spirit, they die,
returning to the dust from which they came.
You send forth your spirit, they are created;
and you renew the face of the earth. R.

SECOND READING

A reading from the letter of St Paul to the Romans   8:22-27

The Spirit himself expresses our plea in a way that could never be put into words.

From the beginning till now the entire creation, as we know, has been groaning in one great act of giving birth; and not only creation, but all of us who possess the first-fruits of the Spirit, we too groan inwardly as we wait for our bodies to be set free. For we must be content to hope that we shall be saved – our salvation is not in sight, we should not have to be hoping for it if it were – but, as I say, we must hope to be saved since we are not saved yet – it is something we must wait for with patience.

The Spirit too comes to help us in our weakness. For when we cannot choose words in order to pray properly, the Spirit himself expresses our plea in a way that could never be put into words, and God who knows everything in our hearts knows perfectly well what he means, and that the pleas of the saints expressed by the Spirit are according to the mind of God.

The word of the Lord.

Gospel Acclamation

R. **Alleluia, alleluia!**
Come, Holy Spirit, fill the hearts of your faithful
and kindle in them the fire of your love.
R. **Alleluia!**

GOSPEL

A reading from the holy Gospel according to John   7:37-39
From his breast shall flow fountains of living water.

On the last day and greatest day of the festival, Jesus stood there and cried out:

'If any man is thirsty, let him come to me!
Let the man come and drink who believes in me!'

As scripture says: From his breast shall flow fountains of living water.

He was speaking of the Spirit which those who believed in him were to receive; for there was no Spirit as yet because Jesus had not yet been glorified.

The Gospel of the Lord.

The Creed is said.

Prayer over the Offerings

Pour out upon these gifts
    the blessing of your Spirit,
we pray, O Lord,
so that through them your Church
    may be imbued with such love
that the truth of your saving mystery
may shine forth for the whole world.
Through Christ our Lord.

Super oblata

Præsentia munera,
    quæsumus, Domine,
Spiritus tui benedictione perfunde,
ut per ipsa Ecclesiæ tuæ
    ea dilectio tribuatur,
per quam salutaris mysterii toto
    mundo veritas enitescat.
Per Christum Dominum nostrum.

Preface: The Mystery of Pentecost.

It is truly right and just,
    our duty and our salvation,
always and everywhere
    to give you thanks,
Lord, holy Father,
    almighty and eternal God.

For, bringing your Paschal Mystery
    to completion,
you bestowed the Holy Spirit today
on those you made
    your adopted children
by uniting them to your Only
    Begotten Son.

This same Spirit,
    as the Church came to birth,
opened to all peoples
    the knowledge of God
and brought together the many
    languages of the earth
in profession of the one faith.

Therefore, overcome with paschal joy,
every land, every people exults
    in your praise
and even the heavenly Powers,
    with the angelic hosts,
sing together the unending hymn
    of your glory,
as they acclaim:

Holy, Holy, Holy Lord God of hosts...

Præfatio: De mysterio Pentecostes.

Vere dignum et iustum est,
    æquum et salutare,
nos tibi semper et ubique
    gratias agere:
Domine, sancte Pater,
    omnipotens æterne Deus.

Tu enim, sacramentum
    paschale consummans,
quibus, per Unigeniti tui consortium,
filios adoptionis esse tribuisti,
hodie Spiritum Sanctum es largitus;
qui, principio nascentis Ecclesiæ,
et cunctis gentibus scientiam
    indidit deitatis,
et linguarum diversitatem in unius
    fidei confessione sociavit.

Quapropter, profusis
    paschalibus gaudiis,
totus in orbe terrarum
    mundus exsultat.
Sed et supernæ virtutes atque
    angelicæ potestates
hymnum gloriæ tuæ concinunt,
    sine fine dicentes:

Sanctus, Sanctus, Sanctus. . .

When the Roman Canon is used, the proper form of the **Communicantes** (In communion with those) is said.

Communion Antiphon   Jn 7:37

On the last day of the festival,
    Jesus stood and cried out:
If anyone is thirsty, let him come
    to me and drink, alleluia.

Ant. ad communionem

Ultimo festivitatis die, stabat Iesus
    et clamabat dicens:
Si quis sitit, veniat ad me et bibat,
    alleluia.

Prayer after Communion

May these gifts we have consumed
benefit us, O Lord,
that we may always be aflame
    with the same Spirit,
whom you wondrously poured out
    on your Apostles.
Through Christ our Lord.

Post communionem

Hæc nobis, Domine,
    munera sumpta proficiant,
ut illo iugiter Spiritu ferveamus,
quem Apostolis tuis
    ineffabiliter infudisti.
Per Christum Dominum nostrum.

A formula of Solemn Blessing, pp.138-141, may be used.

To dismiss the people the Deacon or, if there is no Deacon, the Priest himself sings or says:

Go forth, the Mass is ended,
    alleluia, alleluia.

Ite, missa est, alleluia, alleluia.

Or:

Vel:

Go in peace, alleluia, alleluia.

Ite in pace, alleluia, alleluia.

And the people reply:

Omnes respondent:

Thanks be to God, alleluia, alleluia.

℟. Deo gratias, alleluia, alleluia.

At the Mass during the Day

Entrance Antiphon   Ws 1:7

Ant. ad introitum

THE Spirit of the Lord has filled
the whole world
and that which contains all things
understands what is said, alleluia.

SPIRITUS Domini replevit
orbem terrarum,
et hoc quod continet omnia
scientiam habet vocis, alleluia.

Or: Rm 5:5; Cf. 8:11

Vel:

The love of God has been poured
    into our hearts
through the Spirit of God dwelling
    within us, alleluia.

Caritas Dei diffusa est in
    cordibus nostris
per inhabitantem Spiritum eius in
    nobis, alleluia.

The Gloria in excelsis (Glory to God in the highest) is said.

Collect

O God, who by the mystery
    of today's great feast
sanctify your whole Church
    in every people and nation,
pour out, we pray, the gifts
    of the Holy Spirit

Collecta

Deus, qui sacramento
    festivitatis hodiernæ
universam Ecclesiam tuam
in omni gente et
    natione sanctificas,
in totam mundi latitudinem

across the face of the earth
and, with the divine grace that
   was at work
when the Gospel was first proclaimed,
fill now once more the hearts
   of believers.
Through our Lord Jesus Christ,
   your Son,
who lives and reigns with you
   in the unity of the Holy Spirit,
one God, for ever and ever.

Spiritus Sancti dona defunde,
et, quod inter ipsa evangelicæ
   prædicationis exordia
operata est divina dignatio,
nunc quoque per credentium corda
   perfunde.
Per Dominum nostrum Iesum
   Christum Filium tuum,
qui tecum vivit et regnat
   in unitate Spiritus Sancti,
Deus, per omnia sæcula sæculorum.

FIRST READING

A reading from the Acts of the Apostles   2:1-11

They were all filled with the Holy Spirit and began to speak.

When Pentecost day came round, the apostles had all met in one room, when suddenly they heard what sounded like a powerful wind from heaven, the noise of which filled the entire house in which they were sitting; and something appeared to them that seemed like tongues of fire; these separated and came to rest on the head of each of them. They were all filled with the Holy Spirit, and began to speak foreign languages as the Spirit gave them the gift of speech.

Now there were devout men living in Jerusalem from every nation under heaven, and at this sound they all assembled, each one bewildered to hear these men speaking his own language. They were amazed and astonished. 'Surely' they said 'all these men speaking are Galileans? How does it happen that each of us hears them in his own native language? Parthians, Medes and Elamites; people from Mesopotamia, Judaea and Cappadocia, Pontus and Asia, Phrygia and Pamphylia, Egypt and the parts of Libya round Cyrene; as well as visitors from Rome – Jews and proselytes alike – Cretans and Arabs; we hear them preaching in our own language about the marvels of God.'

The word of the Lord.

Responsorial Psalm   Ps 103:1,24,29-31,34. R. Cf. v.30

R. **Send forth your Spirit, O Lord,**
   and renew the face of the earth.
   Or: **Alleluia!**

   Bless the Lord, my soul!
   Lord God, how great you are.
   How many are your works, O Lord!
   The earth is full of your riches. R.

   You take back your spirit, they die,
   returning to the dust from which they came.
   You send forth your spirit, they are created;
   and you renew the face of the earth. R.

   May the glory of the Lord last for ever!
   May the Lord rejoice in his works!
   May my thoughts be pleasing to him.
   I find my joy in the Lord. R.

The Second Reading and the Gospel may be taken from Year A: Co 12:3-7,12-13; Jn
20:19-23. Alternatively, the Second Reading and the Gospel given below may be used.

SECOND READING

A reading from the letter of St Paul to the Galatians   5:16-25
The fruit of the Spirit.

If you are guided by the Spirit you will be in no danger of yielding to self-
indulgence, since self-indulgence is the opposite of the Spirit, the Spirit
is totally against such a thing, and it is precisely because the two are so
opposed that you do not always carry out your good intentions. If you
are led by the Spirit, no law can touch you. When self-indulgence is at
work the results are obvious: fornication, gross indecency and sexual
irresponsibility; idolatry and sorcery; feuds and wrangling, jealousy, bad
temper and quarrels; disagreements, factions, envy; drunkenness, orgies
and similar things. I warn you now, as I warned you before: those who
behave like this will not inherit the kingdom of God. What the Spirit
brings is very different: love, joy, peace, patience, kindness, goodness,
trustfulness, gentleness and self-control. There can be no law against
things like that, of course. You cannot belong to Christ Jesus unless you
crucify all self-indulgent passions and desire.

   Since the Spirit is our life, let us be directed by the Spirit.

   The word of the Lord.

SEQUENCE

The sequence may be said or sung.

Holy Spirit, Lord of light,
From the clear celestial height
Thy pure beaming radiance give.

Come, thou Father of the poor,
Come with treasures which endure;
Come, thou light of all that live!

Thou, of all consolers best,
Thou, the soul's delightful guest,
Dost refreshing peace bestow.

Thou in toil art comfort sweet;
Pleasant coolness in the heat;
Solace in the midst of woe.

Light immortal, light divine,
Visit thou these hearts of thine,
And our inmost being fill:

If thou take thy grace away,
Nothing pure in man will stay;
All his good is turned to ill.

Heal our wounds,
    our strength renew;
On our dryness pour thy dew;
Wash the stains of guilt away.

Bend the stubborn heart and will;
Melt the frozen, warm the chill;
Guide the steps that go astray.

Thou, on us who evermore
Thee confess and thee adore,
thy sevenfold gifts descend:

Give us comfort when we die,
Give us life with thee on high;
Give us joys that never end.

Veni, Sancte Spiritus,
    et emitte cælitus
lucis tuæ radium.

Veni, pater pauperum,
    veni, dator munerum,
veni, lumen cordium.

Consolator optime,
    dulcis hospes animæ,
dulce refrigerium.

In labore requies,
    in æstu temperies,
in fletu solacium.

O lux beatissima,
    reple cordis intima
tuorum fidelium.

Sine tuo numine,
nihil est in homine,
nihi est innoxium.

Lava quod est sordidum,
riga quod est aridum,
sana quod est saucium.

Flecte quod est rigidum,
fove quod est frigidum,
rege quod est devium.

Da tuis fidelibus,
    in te confidentibus,
sacrum septenarium.

Da virtutis meritum
    da salutis exitum,
da perenne gaudium.

Gospel Acclamation
R. **Alleluia, alleluia!**
Come, Holy Spirit, fill the hearts of your faithful
and kindle in them the fire of your love.
R. **Alleluia!**

GOSPEL
A reading from the holy Gospel according to John   15:26-27; 16:12-15
The Spirit of truth will lead you to the complete truth.

Jesus said to his disciples:
'When the Advocate comes,
whom I shall send to you from the Father,
the Spirit of truth who issues from the Father,
he will be my witness.
And you too will be witnesses,
because you have been with me from the outset.

I still have many things to say to you
but they would be too much for you now.
But when the Spirit of truth comes
he will lead you to the complete truth,
since he will not be speaking as from himself
but will say only what he has learnt,
and he will tell you of the things to come.
He will glorify me,
since all he tells you
will be taken from what is mine.
Everything the Father has is mine;
that is why I said:
All he tells you
will be taken from what is mine.'

The Gospel of the Lord.

The Creed is said.

Prayer over the Offerings	Super oblata
Grant, we pray, O Lord,	Præsta, quæsumus, Domine,
that, as promised by your Son,	ut, secundum promissionem Filii tui,
the Holy Spirit may reveal to us	Spiritus Sanctus huius
more abundantly	nobis sacrificii
the hidden mystery of this sacrifice	copiosius revelet arcanum,
and graciously lead us into all truth.	et omnem propitius reseret veritatem.
Through Christ our Lord.	Per Christum Dominum nostrum.

Preface: The Mystery of Pentecost, p.466.

Communion Antiphon   Ac 2:4,11

They were all filled with
   the Holy Spirit
and spoke of the marvels of God,
   alleluia.

Ant. ad communionem

Repleti sunt omnes Spiritu Sancto,
loquentes magnalia Dei, alleluia.

Prayer after Communion

O God, who bestow heavenly gifts
   upon your Church,
safeguard, we pray, the grace you
   have given,
that the gift of the Holy Spirit
   poured out upon her
may retain all its force
and that this spiritual food
may gain her abundance
   of eternal redemption.
Through Christ our Lord.

Post communionem

Deus, qui Ecclesiæ tuæ cælestia
   dona largiris,
custodi gratiam quam dedisti,
ut Spiritus Sancti vigeat semper
   munus infusum,
et ad æternæ
   redemptionis augmentum
spiritalis esca proficiat.
Per Christum Dominum nostrum.

A formula of Solemn Blessing, pp.138-141 may be used.

To dismiss the people the Deacon or, if there is no Deacon, the Priest himself sings
or says:

Go forth, the Mass is ended,
   alleluia, alleluia.

Ite, missa est,
   alleluia, alleluia.

Or:

Go in peace, alleluia, aleluia.

Vel:

Ite in pace, alleluia, alleluia.

And the people reply:

Thanks be to God, alleluia, alleluia.

Omnes respondent:

Deo gratias, alleluia, alleluia.

With Easter Time now concluded, the paschal candle is extinguished. It is desirable
to keep the paschal candle in the baptistery with due honour so that it is lit at the
celebration of Baptism and the candles of those baptised are lit from it.

27 May

THE MOST HOLY TRINITY

Today's liturgical solemnity, while making us contemplate the amazing mystery from which we come and toward which we are going, renews for us the mission of living in communion with God and living in communion among ourselves on the model of the divine communion. We are called to live not as one without the others, above or against the others, but one with the others, for the others, and in the others. This means to accept and witness in harmony the beauty of the Gospel; experiencing love for one another and for all, sharing joy and suffering, learning to ask and grant forgiveness, appreciating various charisms under the guidance of Pastors.

(Pope Francis)

Solemnity

Entrance Antiphon

BLEST be God the Father,
and the Only Begotten Son
of God,
and also the Holy Spirit,
for he has shown us his
merciful love.

Ant. ad introitum

BENEDICTUS sit Deus Pater,
Unigenitusque Dei Filius,
Sanctus quoque Spiritus,
quia fecit nobiscum
misericordiam suam.

The Gloria in excelsis (Glory to God in the highest) is said.

Collect

God our Father, who by sending
into the world
the Word of truth and the Spirit
of sanctification
made known to the human race
your wondrous mystery,
grant us, we pray, that in professing
the true faith,

Collecta

Deus Pater, qui Verbum veritatis
et Spiritum sanctificationis
mittens in mundum,
admirabile mysterium tuum
hominibus declarasti,
da nobis, in confessione veræ fidei,
æternæ gloriam

we may acknowledge the Trinity
   of eternal glory
and adore your Unity,
   powerful in majesty.
Through our Lord Jesus Christ,
   your Son,
who lives and reigns with you
   in the unity of the Holy Spirit,
one God, for ever and ever.

Trinitatis agnoscere,
et Unitatem adorare
   in potentia maiestatis.
Per Dominum nostrum Iesum
   Christum Filium tuum,
qui tecum vivit et regnat
   in unitate Spiritus Sancti,
Deus, per omnia sæcula sæculorum.

FIRST READING

A reading from the book of Deuteronomy   4:32-34,39-40

The Lord is God indeed, in heaven above as on earth beneath, he and no other.

Moses said to the people: 'Put this question to the ages that are past, that went before you, from the time God created man on earth: Was there ever a word so majestic, from one end of heaven to the other? Was anything ever heard? Did ever a people hear the voice of the living God speaking from the heart of the fire, as you heard it, and remain alive? Has any god ventured to take to himself one nation from the midst of another by ordeals, signs, wonders, war with mighty hand and outstretched arm, by fearsome terrors – all this that the Lord your God did for you before your eyes in Egypt?

'Understand this today, therefore, and take it to heart: the Lord is God indeed, in heaven above as on earth beneath, he and no other. Keep his laws and commandments as I give them to you today, so that you and your children may prosper and live long in the land that the Lord your God gives you for ever.'

The word of the Lord.

Responsorial Psalm   Ps 32:4-6,9,18-20. R. v.12

R. **Happy the people the Lord has chosen as his own.**

The word of the Lord is faithful
and all his works to be trusted.
The Lord loves justice and right
and fills the earth with his love. R.

By his word the heavens were made,
by the breath of his mouth all the stars.
He spoke; and they came to be.
He commanded; they sprang into being. R.

The Lord looks on those who revere him,
on those who hope in his love,
to rescue their souls from death,
to keep them alive in famine. R.

Our soul is waiting for the Lord.
The Lord is our help and our shield.
May your love be upon us, O Lord,
as we place all our hope in you. R.

SECOND READING

A reading from the letter of St Paul to the Romans   8:14-17
You received the spirit of sons, and it makes us cry out, 'Abba, Father!'

Everyone moved by the Spirit is a son of God. The spirit you received is
not the spirit of slaves bringing fear into your lives again; it is the spirit
of sons, and it makes us cry out, 'Abba Father!' The Spirit himself and
our spirit bear united witness that we are children of God. And if we are
children we are heirs as well: heirs of God and coheirs with Christ, sharing
his sufferings so as to share his glory.

The word of the Lord.

Gospel Acclamation   Cf. Rv 1:8

R. **Alleluia, alleluia!**
Glory be to the Father, and to the Son, and to the Holy Spirit,
the God who is, who was, and who is to come.
R. **Alleluia!**

GOSPEL

A reading from the holy Gospel according to Matthew   28:16-20
Baptise them in the name of the Father and of the Son and of the Holy Spirit.

The eleven disciples set out for Galilee, to the mountain where Jesus had
arranged to meet them. When they saw him they fell down before him,
though some hesitated. Jesus came up and spoke to them. He said, 'All
authority in heaven and on earth has been given to me. Go, therefore,
make disciples of all the nations; baptise them in the name of the Father

and of the Son and of the Holy Spirit, and teach them to observe all the commands I gave you. And know that I am with you always; yes, to the end of time.'

The Gospel of the Lord.

The Creed is said.

Prayer over the Offerings	Super oblata
Sanctify by the invocation of your name, we pray, O Lord our God, this oblation of our service, and by it make of us an eternal offering to you. Through Christ our Lord.	Sanctifica, quæsumus, Domine Deus noster, per tui nominis invocationem, hæc munera nostræ servitutis, et per ea nosmetipsos tibi perfice munus æternum. Per Christum Dominum nostrum.
Preface: The Mystery of the Most Holy Trinity.	**Præfatio:** De mysterio Sanctissimæ Trinitatis.
It is truly right and just, our duty and our salvation, always and everywhere to give you thanks, Lord, holy Father, almighty and eternal God.	Vere dignum et iustum est, æquum et salutare, nos tibi semper et ubique gratias agere: Domine, sancte Pater, omnipotens æterne Deus:
For with your Only Begotten Son and the Holy Spirit you are one God, one Lord: not in the unity of a single person, but in a Trinity of one substance.	Qui cum Unigenito Filio tuo et Spiritu Sancto unus es Deus, unus es Dominus: non in unius singularitate personæ, sed in unius Trinitate substantiæ.
For what you have revealed to us of your glory we believe equally of your Son and of the Holy Spirit, so that, in the confessing of the true and eternal Godhead, you might be adored in what is proper to each Person, their unity in substance, and their equality in majesty.	Quod enim de tua gloria, revelante te, credimus, hoc de Filio tuo, hoc de Spiritu Sancto, sine discretione sentimus. Ut in confessione veræ sempiternæque Deitatis, et in personis proprietas, et in essentia unitas, et in maiestate adoretur æqualitas.

For this is praised by Angels
   and Archangels,
Cherubim, too, and Seraphim,
who never cease to cry out each day,
as with one voice they acclaim:

Holy, Holy, Holy Lord God of hosts...

Quem laudant Angeli
   atque Archangeli,
Cherubim quoque ac Seraphim,
qui non cessant clamare cotidie,
   una voce dicentes:

Sanctus, Sanctus, Sanctus . . .

Communion Antiphon   Ga 4:6

Since you are children of God,
God has sent into your hearts
   the Spirit of his Son,
the Spirit who cries out:
   Abba, Father.

Ant. ad communionem

Quoniam autem estis filii,
misit Deus Spiritum Filii sui
   in corda vestra
clamantem: Abba, Pater.

Prayer after Communion

May receiving this Sacrament,
   O Lord our God,
bring us health of body and soul,
as we confess your eternal holy
   Trinity and undivided Unity.
Through Christ our Lord.

Post communionem

Proficiat nobis ad salutem
   corporis et animæ,
Domine Deus noster,
   huius sacramenti susceptio,
et sempiternæ sanctæ Trinitatis
eiusdemque individuæ
   Unitatis confessio.
Per Christum Dominum nostrum.

3 June

THE MOST HOLY BODY AND BLOOD OF CHRIST (CORPUS CHRISTI)

The Last Supper represents the culmination of Christ's entire life... a life offered for the salvation of the whole of humanity. Therefore, it is not enough to state that Jesus is present in the Eucharist, but one must see in it the presence of a life given and partake in it. When we take and eat that Bread, we are associated into the life of Jesus, we enter into communion with him, we commit to achieve communion among ourselves, to transform our life into a gift, especially to the poorest. Today's feast urges us to become, with our life, imitators of that which we celebrate in the Liturgy. The Christ, who nourishes us under the consecrated species of bread and wine, is the same One who comes to us in the everyday happenings; he is in the poor person who holds out his hand, in the suffering one who begs for help, in the brother or sister who asks for our availability and awaits our welcome. He is in the child who knows nothing about Jesus or salvation, who does not have faith. He is in every human being, even the smallest and the defenceless.

(Pope Francis)

Solemnity

Entrance Antiphon   Cf. Ps 80:17

HE fed them with the finest wheat and satisfied them with honey from the rock.

Ant. ad introitum

CIBAVIT eos ex adipe frumenti, et de petra melle saturavit eos.

The Gloria in excelsis (Glory to God in the highest) is said.

Collect

O God, who in this
   wonderful Sacrament
have left us a memorial
   of your Passion,
grant us, we pray,
so to revere the sacred mysteries
   of your Body and Blood
that we may always experience
   in ourselves
the fruits of your redemption.
Who live and reign with God
   the Father
in the unity of the Holy Spirit,
   one God, for ever and ever.

Collecta

Deus, qui nobis sub
   sacramento mirabili
passionis tuæ memoriam reliquisti,
tribue, quæsumus,
ita nos Corporis et Sanguinis tui
   sacra mysteria venerari,
ut redemptionis tuæ fructum
   in nobis iugiter sentiamus.
Qui vivis et regnas cum Deo Patre
in unitate Spiritus Sancti,
   Deus, per omnia sæcula
   sæculorum.

FIRST READING

A reading from the book of Exodus   24:3-8

This is the blood of the Covenant that the Lord has made with you.

Moses went and told the people all the commands of the Lord and all the
ordinances. In answer, all the people said with one voice, 'We will observe
all the commands that the Lord has decreed.' Moses put all the commands
of the Lord into writing, and early next morning he built an altar at the
foot of the mountain, with twelve standing-stones for the twelve tribes of
Israel. Then he directed certain young Israelites to offer holocausts and to
immolate bullocks to the Lord as communion sacrifices. Half of the blood
Moses took up and put into basins, the other half he cast on the altar. And
taking the Book of the Covenant he read it to the listening people, and
they said, 'We will observe all that the Lord has decreed; we will obey.'
Then Moses took the blood and cast it towards the people. 'This' he said
'is the blood of the Covenant that the Lord has made with you, containing
all these rules.'

   The word of the Lord.

Responsorial Psalm   Ps 115:12-13,15-18. R. v.13

R. **The cup of salvation I will raise;**
   I will call on the Lord's name.
   Or: **Alleluia!**

How can I repay the Lord
for his goodness to me?
The cup of salvation I will raise;
I will call on the Lord's name. R.

O precious in the eyes of the Lord
is the death of his faithful.
Your servant, Lord, your servant am I;
you have loosened my bonds. R.

A thanksgiving sacrifice I make:
I will call on the Lord's name.
My vows to the Lord I will fulfil
before all his people. R.

SECOND READING

A reading from the letter to the Hebrews   9:11-15
The blood of Christ can purify our inner self from dead actions.

Now Christ has come, as the high priest of all the blessings which were
to come. He has passed through the greater, the more perfect tent, which
is better than one made by men's hands because it is not of this created
order; and he has entered the sanctuary once and for all, taking with him
not the blood of goats and bull calves, but his own blood, having won an
eternal redemption for us. The blood of goats and bulls and the ashes of
a heifer are sprinkled on those who have incurred defilement and they
restore the holiness of their outward lives; how much more effectively
the blood of Christ, who offered himself as the perfect sacrifice to God
through the eternal Spirit, can purify our inner self from dead actions so
that we do our service to the living God.

He brings a new covenant, as the mediator, only so that the people
who were called to an eternal inheritance may actually receive what
was promised: his death took place to cancel the sins that infringed the
earlier covenant.

The word of the Lord.

SEQUENCE

The Sequence may be said or sung in full, or using the shorter form indicated by the asterisked verses.

Sing forth, O Zion, sweetly sing
The praises of thy Shepherd-King,
   In hymns and canticles divine;
Dare all thou canst, thou hast no song
Worthy his praises to prolong,
   So far surpassing powers like thine.

Today no theme of common praise
Forms the sweet burden of thy lays –
   The living, life-dispensing food –
That food which at the sacred board
Unto the brethren twelve our Lord
   His parting legacy bestowed.

Then be the anthem clear and strong,
Thy fullest note, thy sweetest song,
   The very music of thy breast:
For now shines forth the day sublime
That brings remembrance of the time
   When Jesus first his table blessed.

Within our new King's banquet-hall
They meet to keep the festival
   That closed the ancient paschal rite:
The old is by the new replaced;
The substance hath
   the shadows chased;
   And rising day dispels the night.
Christ willed what He Himself
   had done
Should be renewed while time
   should run,
   in memory of His parting hour:
Thus, tutored in His school divine,
We consecrate the bread and wine;
   And lo – a Host of saving power.

Lauda Sion Salvatorem
Lauda ducem et pastorem
   In hymnis et canticis.
Quantum potes, tantum aude:
Quia major omni laude,
   Nec laudare sufficis.

Laudis thema specialis,
Panis vivus et vitalis,
   Hodie proponitur.
Quem in sacræ mensa cenæ,
Turbæ fratrum duodenæ
   Datum non ambigitur.

Sit laus plena, sit sonora,
Sit iucunda, sit decora
   Mentis iubilatio.
Dies enim solemnis agitur,
In qua mensæ prima recolitur
   Huius institutio.

In hac mensa novi Regis,
Novum Pascha novæ legis,
   Phase vetus terminat.
Vetustatem novitas,
Umbram fugat veritas,
   Noctem lux eliminat.
Quod in cœna Christus gessit,
Faciendum hoc expressit
   In sui memoriam.
Docti sacris institutis,
Panem, vinum, in salutis
   Consecramus hostiam.

This faith to Christian men is given –
Bread is made flesh by words
    from heaven:
      Into his Blood the wine is turned:
What though it baffles
    nature's powers
Of sense and sight? This faith of ours
    Proves more than nature
    e'er discerned.

Dogma datur Christianis,
Quod in carnem transit panis,
    Et vinum in sanguinem.
Quod non capis, quod non vides,
Animosa firmat fides,
    Præter rerum ordinem.

Concealed beneath the two-fold sign
Meet symbols of the gifts divine,
    There lie the mysteries adored:
The living body is our food;
Our drink the ever precious blood;
    In each, one undivided Lord.

Sub diversis speciebus,
Signis tantum, et non rebus,
    Latent res eximiæ.
Caro cibus, sanguis potus:
Manet tamen Christus totus,
    Sub utraque specie.

Not he that eateth it divides
The sacred food, which whole abides
    Unbroken still, nor knows decay;
Be one, or be a thousand fed,
They eat alike the Living Bread
    Which, still received,
    ne'er wastes away.

A sumente non concisus,
Non confractus, non divisus:
    Integer accipitur.
Sumit unus, sumunt mille:
Quantum isti, tantum ille:
    Nec sumptus consumitur.

The good, the guilty share therein,
With sure increase of grace or sin,
    The ghostly life, or ghostly death:
Death to the guilty; to the good
Immortal life. See how one food
    Man's joy or woe accomplisheth.

Sumunt boni, sumunt mali:
Sorte tamen inæquali,
    Vitæ vel interitus.
Mors est malis, vita bonis:
Vide paris sumptionis
    Quam sit dispar exitus.

We break the Sacrament; but bold
And firm thy faith shall keep its hold;
Deem not the whole doth
    more enfold
    Than in the fractured part resides:
Deem not that Christ doth broken lie;
'Tis but the sign that meets the eye;
The hidden deep reality
    In all its fulness still abides.

Fracto demum Sacramento,
Ne vacilles, sed memento,
Tantum esse sub fragmento,
    Quantum toto tegitur.
Nulla rei fit scissura:
Signi tantum fit fractura:
Qua nec status nec statura
    Signati minuitur.

*Behold the bread of angels, sent
For pilgrims in their banishment,
The bread for God's true
  children meant,
  That may not unto dogs be given:
Oft in the olden types foreshadowed;
In Isaac on the altar bowed,
And in the ancient paschal food,
  And in the manna sent
  from heaven.

*Come then, good shepherd,
  bread divine,
Still show to us Thy mercy sign;
Oh, feed us still, still keep us Thine;
So may we see Thy glories shine
  In fields of immortality;

*O Thou, the wisest, mightiest, best,
Our present food, our future rest,
Come, make us each Thy
  chosen guest,
Coheirs of Thine, and comrades blest
  With saints whose dwelling
  is with Thee.

*Ecce panis Angelorum,
Factus cibus viatorum:
Vere panis filiorum,
  Non mittendus canibus.
In figuris præsignatur,
Cum Isaac immolatur:
Agnus paschæ deputatur
  Datur manna patribus.

*Bone pastor, panis vere,
Iesu, nostri miserere:
Tu nos pasce, nos tuere:
Tu nos bona fac videre
  In terra viventium.

*Tu, qui cuncta scis et vales:
Qui nos pascis hic mortales:
Tuos ibi commensales,
Cohæredes et sodales,
  Fac sanctorum civium.

Gospel Acclamation   Jn 6:51

R. **Alleluia, alleluia!**
I am the living bread which has come down from heaven,
says the Lord;
Anyone who eats this bread will live for ever.
R. **Alleluia!**

GOSPEL

A reading from the holy Gospel according to Mark   14:12-16,22-26
This is my body. This is my blood.

On the first day of Unleavened Bread, when the Passover lamb was
sacrificed, his disciples said to Jesus, 'Where do you want us to go and
make the preparations for you to eat the Passover?' So he sent two of
his disciples, saying to them, 'Go into the city and you will meet a man

carrying a pitcher of water. Follow him, and say to the owner of the house which he enters, "The Master says: Where is my dining room in which I can eat the Passover with my disciples?" He will show you a large upper room furnished with couches, all prepared. Make the preparations for us there.' The disciples set out and went to the city and found everything as he had told them, and prepared the Passover.

And as they were eating he took some bread, and when he had said the blessing he broke it and gave it to them. 'Take it,' he said 'this is my body.' Then he took a cup, and when he had returned thanks he gave it to them, and all drank from it, and he said to them, 'This is my blood, the blood of the covenant, which is to be poured out for many. I tell you solemnly, I shall not drink any more wine until the day I drink the new wine in the kingdom of God.'

After psalms had been sung they left for the Mount of Olives.

The Gospel of the Lord.

The Creed is said.

Prayer over the Offerings	Super oblata

Grant your Church, O Lord,
    we pray,
the gifts of unity and peace,
whose signs are to be seen in mystery
in the offerings we here present.
Through Christ our Lord.
	Ecclesiæ tuæ, quæsumus, Domine,
	unitatis et pacis propitius
	    dona concede,
	quæ sub oblatis muneribus
	    mystice designantur.
	Per Christum Dominum nostrum.

Preface of the Most Holy Eucharist I or II, pp.68-69.

Communion Antiphon Jn 6:57	Ant. ad communionem

Whoever eats my flesh
    and drinks my blood
remains in me and I in him,
    says the Lord.
	Qui manducat meam carnem
	    et bibit meum sanguinem,
	in me manet et ego in eo,
	    dicit Dominus.

Prayer after Communion

Grant, O Lord, we pray,
that we may delight for all eternity
in that share in your divine life,
which is foreshadowed
    in the present age
by our reception of your precious
    Body and Blood.
Who live and reign
    for ever and ever.

Post communionem

Fac nos, quæsumus, Domine,
divinitatis tuæ sempiterna
    fruitione repleri,
quam pretiosi Corporis
    et Sanguinis tui
temporalis perceptio præfigurat.
Qui vivis et regnas
    in sæcula sæculorum.

It is desirable that a procession take place after the Mass in which the Host to be carried in the procession is consecrated. However, nothing prohibits a procession from taking place even after a public and lengthy period of adoration following the Mass. If a procession takes place after Mass, when the Communion of the faithful is over, the monstrance in which the consecrated host has been placed is set on the altar. When the Prayer after Communion has been said, the Concluding Rites are omitted and the procession forms.

8 June

THE MOST SACRED HEART OF JESUS

In the First Reading we enter into the tenderness of God: God tells his people how much he loves them, how much he cares for them. What God says to his people in this Reading, he says to each one of us. And it would be good to take this text, in a moment of solitude, and set ourselves in the presence of God and listen: "I saved you from slavery", from the slavery of sin, from the slavery of self-destruction and from every kind of slavery that each of us knows, has had and has within. "I saved you. I taught you how to walk". The Almighty abases himself and teaches me how to walk. Without him I wouldn't know how to walk in the Spirit. This is our history, at least it is my history. Each of us can read his own history here. In the moments when we are afraid, at the times that we are uncertain, he says to us: "If I did this for you, how can you think I would leave you alone, that I could abandon you?"

(Pope Francis)

Solemnity

Entrance Antiphon   Ps 32:11,19

THE designs of his Heart
   are from age to age,
to rescue their souls from death,
and to keep them alive in famine.

Ant. ad introitum

COGITATIONES Cordis eius
   in generatione et generationem,
ut eruat a morte animas eorum
   et alat eos in fame.

The Gloria in excelsis (Glory to God in the highest) is said.

Collect

Grant, we pray, almighty God,
that we, who glory in the Heart
   of your beloved Son
and recall the wonders of his love
   for us,
may be made worthy to receive
an overflowing measure of grace
from that fount of heavenly gifts.
Through our Lord Jesus Christ,
   your Son,
who lives and reigns with you
   in the unity of the Holy Spirit,
one God, for ever and ever.

Collecta

Concede, quæsumus,
   omnipotens Deus,
ut qui, dilecti Filii tui
   Corde gloriantes,
eius præcipua in nos beneficia
   recolimus caritatis,
de illo donorum fonte cælesti
supereffluentem gratiam
   mereamur accipere.
Per Dominum nostrum Iesum
   Christum Filium tuum,
qui tecum vivit et regnat
   in unitate Spiritus Sancti,
Deus, per omnia sæcula sæculorum.

Or:

O God, who in the Heart of your Son,
wounded by our sins,
bestow on us in mercy
the boundless treasures of your love,
grant, we pray,
that, in paying him the homage
    of our devotion
we may also offer
    worthy reparation.
Through our Lord Jesus Christ,
    your Son,
who lives and reigns with you
    in the unity of the Holy Spirit,
one God, for ever and ever.

Vel:

Deus, qui nobis in Corde Filii tui,
nostris vulnerato peccatis,
infinitos dilectionis thesauros
misericorditer largiri dignaris,
concede, quæsumus,
ut, illi devotum pietatis nostræ
    præstantes obsequium,
dignæ quoque satisfactionis
    exhibeamus officium.
Per Dominum nostrum Iesum
    Christum Filium tuum,
qui tecum vivit et regnat
    in unitate Spiritus Sancti,
Deus, per omnia sæcula sæculorum.

FIRST READING

A reading from the prophet Hosea   11:1,3-4,8-9

My heart recoils from it.

Listen to the word of the Lord:

> When Israel was a child I loved him,
> and I called my son out of Egypt.
> I myself taught Ephraim to walk,
> I took them in my arms;
> yet they have not understood that I was the one looking after them.
> I led them with reins of kindness,
> with leading-strings of love.
> I was like someone who lifts an infant close against his cheek;
> stooping down to him I gave him his food.
> How could I treat you like Admah,
> or deal with you like Zeboiim?
> My heart recoils from it,
> my whole being
> trembles at the thought.
> I will not give rein to my fierce anger,
> I will not destroy Ephraim again,
> for I am God, not man:
> I am the Holy One in your midst
> and have no wish to destroy.

The word of the Lord.

Responsorial Psalm   Is 12:2-6. R. v.3

R. **With joy you will draw water**
   from the wells of the Saviour.

Truly God is my salvation,
I trust, I shall not fear.
For the Lord is my strength, my song,
he became my saviour.
With joy you will draw water
from the wells of Salvation. R.

Give thanks to the Lord, give praise to his name!
Make his mighty deeds known to the peoples!
Declare the greatness of his name. R.

Sing a psalm to the Lord
for he has done glorious deeds;
make them known to all the earth!
People of Zion, sing and shout for joy
for great in your midst is the Holy One of Israel. R.

SECOND READING

A reading from the letter of St Paul to the Ephesians   3:8-12,14-19
The love of Christ is beyond all knowledge.

I, Paul, who am less than the least of all the saints, have been entrusted
with this special grace, not only of proclaiming to the pagans the
infinite treasure of Christ but also of explaining how the mystery is to be
dispensed. Through all the ages, this has been kept hidden in God, the
creator of everything. Why? So that the Sovereignties and Powers should
learn only now, through the Church, how comprehensive God's wisdom
really is, exactly according to the plan which he had had from all eternity
in Christ Jesus our Lord. This is why we are bold enough to approach God
in complete confidence, through our faith in him.

   This, then, is what I pray, kneeling before the Father, from whom every
family, whether spiritual or natural, takes its name.

   Out of his infinite glory, may he give you the power through his
Spirit for your hidden self to grow strong, so that Christ may live in your
hearts through faith, and then, planted in love and built on love, you
will with all the saints have strength to grasp the breadth and the length,
the height and the depth; until, knowing the love of Christ, which is
beyond all knowledge, you are filled with the utter fullness of God.

   The word of the Lord.

Gospel Acclamation   Mt 11:29

R. **Alleluia, alleluia!**
Shoulder my yoke and learn from me,
for I am gentle and humble in heart.
R. **Alleluia!**

Or: 1 Jn 4:10

R. **Alleluia, alleluia!**
This is the love I mean:
God's love for us when he sent his Son
to be the sacrifice that takes our sins away.
R. **Alleluia!**

GOSPEL

A reading from the holy Gospel according to John   19:31-37

One of the soldiers pierced his side and there came out blood and water.

It was Preparation Day, and to prevent the bodies remaining on the cross during the sabbath – since that sabbath was a day of special solemnity – the Jews asked Pilate to have the legs broken and the bodies taken away. Consequently the soldiers came and broke the legs of the first man who had been crucified with him and then of the other. When they came to Jesus, they found he was already dead, and so instead of breaking his legs one of the soldiers pierced his side with a lance; and immediately there came out blood and water. This is the evidence of one who saw it – trustworthy evidence, and he knows he speaks the truth – and he gives it so that you may believe as well. Because all this happened to fulfil the words of scripture:

Not one bone of his will be broken;
and again, in another place scripture says:

They will look on the one whom they have pierced.

The Gospel of the Lord.

The Creed is said.

Prayer over the Offerings	Super oblata
Look, O Lord, we pray, on the surpassing charity in the Heart of your beloved Son, that what we offer may be a gift acceptable to you and an expiation of our offences. Through Christ our Lord.	Respice, quæsumus, Domine, ad ineffabilem Cordis dilecti Filii tui caritatem, ut quod offerimus sit tibi munus acceptum et nostrorum expiatio delictorum. Per Christum Dominum nostrum.

It is truly right and just,
  our duty and our salvation,
always and everywhere
  to give you thanks,
Lord, holy Father,
  almighty and eternal God,
through Christ our Lord.

For raised up high on the Cross,
he gave himself up for us
  with a wonderful love
and poured out blood and water
  from his pierced side,
the wellspring of the
  Church's Sacraments,
so that, won over to the open heart
  of the Saviour,
all might draw water joyfully
  from the springs of salvation.

And so, with all the Angels
  and Saints,
we praise you, as without end
  we acclaim:

Holy, Holy, Holy Lord God of hosts...

Vere dignum et iustum est,
  æquum et salutare,
nos tibi semper et ubique
  gratias agere:
Domine, sancte Pater,
  omnipotens æterne Deus:
per Christum Dominum nostrum:

Qui, mira caritate, exaltatus in cruce,
pro nobis tradidit semetipsum,
atque de transfixo latere sanguinem
  fudit et aquam,
ex quo manarent
  Ecclesiæ sacramenta,
ut omnes, ad Cor apertum
  Salvatoris attracti,
iugiter haurirent e fontibus salutis
  in gaudio.

Et ideo, cum Sanctis
  et Angelis universis,
te collaudamus, sine fine dicentes:
Sanctus, Sanctus, Sanctus . . .

Thus says the Lord:
Let whoever is thirsty come to me
  and drink.
Streams of living water will flow
from within the one who believes
  in me.

Dicit Dominus:
Si quis sitit, veniat ad me et bibat.
Qui credit in me, flumina de ventre
  eius fluent aquæ vivæ.

Or: Jn 19:34 | Vel:

One of the soldiers opened his side
   with a lance,
and at once there came forth blood
   and water.

Unus militum lancea
   latus eius aperuit,
et continuo exivit sanguis et aqua.

Prayer after Communion

Post communionem

May this sacrament of charity,
   O Lord,
make us fervent with the fire
   of holy love,
so that, drawn always to your Son,
we may learn to see him
   in our neighbour.
Through Christ our Lord.

Sacramentum caritatis, Domine,
sancta nos faciat dilectione fervere,
qua, ad Filium tuum
   semper attracti,
ipsum in fratribus
   agnoscere discamus.
Qui vivit et regnat
   in sæcula sæculorum.

10 June

TENTH SUNDAY IN ORDINARY TIME

Entrance Antiphon   Cf. Ps 26:1-2

THE Lord is my light and my
salvation; whom shall I fear?
The Lord is the stronghold
    of my life; whom should I dread?
When those who do evil draw near,
    they stumble and fall.

Ant. ad introitum

DOMINUS illuminatio mea,
et salus mea, quem timebo?
Dominus defensor vitæ meæ,
    a quo trepidabo?
Qui tribulant me inimici mei,
    ipsi infirmati sunt.

Collect

O God, from whom all good
    things come,
grant that we, who call on you
    in our need,
may at your prompting discern
    what is right,
and by your guidance do it.
Through our Lord Jesus Christ,
    your Son,
who lives and reigns with you
    in the unity of the Holy Spirit,
one God, for ever and ever.

Collecta

Deus, a quo bona
    cuncta procedunt,
tuis largire supplicibus,
ut cogitemus, te inspirante,
    quæ recta sunt,
et, te gubernante, eadem faciamus.
Per Dominum nostrum Iesum
    Christum Filium tuum,
qui tecum vivit et regnat
    in unitate Spiritus Sancti,
Deus, per omnia sæcula sæculorum.

FIRST READING

A reading from the book of Genesis   3:9-15

I will make you enemies of each other: you and the woman, your offspring and her offspring.

The Lord God called to the man. 'Where are you?' he asked. 'I heard the sound of you in the garden,' he replied 'I was afraid because I was naked, so I hid.' 'Who told you that you were naked?' he asked. 'Have you been eating of the tree I forbade you to eat?' The man replied, 'It was the woman you put with me; she gave me the fruit, and I ate it.' Then the Lord God asked the woman, 'What is this you have done?' The woman replied, 'The serpent tempted me and I ate.'

Then the Lord God said to the serpent, 'Because you have done this,

'Be accursed beyond all cattle,
all wild beasts.

You shall crawl on your belly and eat dust
every day of your life.
I will make you enemies of each other:
you and the woman,
your offspring and her offspring.
It will crush your head
and you will strike its heel.'

The word of the Lord.

R. **With the Lord there is mercy
and fullness of redemption.**

Out of the depths I cry to you, O Lord,
Lord, hear my voice!
O let your ears be attentive
to the voice of my pleading. R.

If you, O Lord, should mark our guilt,
Lord, who would survive?
But with you is found forgiveness:
for this we revere you. R.

My soul is waiting for the Lord,
I count on his word.
My soul is longing for the Lord
more than watchman for daybreak. R.

Because with the Lord there is mercy
and fullness of redemption,
Israel indeed he will redeem
from all its iniquity. R.

SECOND READING

A reading from the second letter of St Paul to the Corinthians   4:13-5:1
We believe and therefore we also speak.

As we have the same spirit of faith that is mentioned in scripture – I
believed, and therefore I spoke – we too believe and therefore we too
speak, knowing that he who raised the Lord Jesus to life will raise us with
Jesus in our turn, and put us by his side and you with us. You see, all this
is for your benefit, so that the more grace is multiplied among people, the
more thanksgiving there will be, to the glory of God.

That is why there is no weakening on our part, and instead, though
this outer man of ours may be falling into decay, the inner man is renewed

day by day. Yes, the troubles which are soon over, though they weigh little, train us for the carrying of a weight of eternal glory which is out of all proportion to them. And so we have no eyes for things that are visible, but only for things that are invisible; for visible things last only for a time, and the invisible things are eternal.

For we know that when the tent that we live in on earth is folded up, there is a house built by God for us, an everlasting home not made by human hands, in the heavens.

The word of the Lord.

Gospel Acclamation

Jn 14:23

R. **Alleluia, alleluia!**
If anyone loves me he will keep my word,
and my Father will love him,
and we shall come to him.
R. **Alleluia!**

Or:

Jn 12:31-32

R. **Alleluia, alleluia!**
Now the prince of this world is to be overthrown,
says the Lord.
And when I am lifted up from the earth,
I shall draw all men to myself.
R. **Alleluia!**

GOSPEL

A reading from the holy Gospel according to Mark   3:20-35

It is the end of Satan.

Jesus went home with his disciples, and such a crowd collected that they could not even have a meal. When his relatives heard of this, they set out to take charge of him, convinced he was out of his mind.

The scribes who had come down from Jerusalem were saying, 'Beelzebul is in him,' and, 'It is through the prince of devils that he casts devils out.' So he called them to him and spoke to them in parables, 'How can Satan cast out Satan? If a kingdom is divided against itself, that kingdom cannot last. And if a household is divided against itself, that household can never stand. Now if Satan has rebelled against himself and is divided, he cannot stand either – it is the end of him. But no one can make his way into a strong man's house and burgle his property unless he has tied up the strong man first. Only then can he burgle his house.

'I tell you solemnly, all men's sins will be forgiven, and all their blasphemies; but let anyone blaspheme against the Holy Spirit and he will never have forgiveness: he is guilty of an eternal sin.' This was because they were saying, 'An unclean spirit is in him.'

His mother and brothers now arrived and, standing outside, sent in a message asking for him. A crowd was sitting round him at the time the message was passed to him, 'Your mother and brothers and sisters are outside asking for you.' He replied, 'Who are my mother and my brothers? And looking round at those sitting in a circle about him, he said, 'Here are my mother and my brothers. Anyone who does the will of God, that person is my brother and sister and mother.'

The Gospel of the Lord.

Prayer over the Offerings

Look kindly upon our service,
    O Lord, we pray,
that what we offer
may be an acceptable oblation to you
and lead us to grow in charity.
Through Christ our Lord.

Super oblata

Respice, Domine, quæsumus,
    nostram propitius servitutem,
ut quod offerimus sit tibi
    munus acceptum,
et nostræ caritatis augmentum.
Per Christum Dominum nostrum.

Preface of Sundays in Ordinary Time I-VIII, pp.60-67.

Communion Antiphon   Ps 17:3

The Lord is my rock, my fortress,
    and my deliverer;
my God is my saving strength.

Or: 1 Jn 4:16

God is love, and whoever abides
    in love
abides in God, and God in him.

Ant. ad communionem

Dominus firmamentum meum,
et refugium meum, et liberator meus.
Deus meus adiutor meus.

Vel:

Deus caritas est,
    et qui manet in caritate
in Deo manet et Deus in eo.

Prayer after Communion

May your healing work, O Lord,
free us, we pray, from doing evil
and lead us to what is right.
Through Christ our Lord.

Post communionem

Tua nos, Domine,
    medicinalis operatio,
et a nostris perversitatibus
    clementer expediat,
et ad ea quæ sunt recta perducat.
Per Christum Dominum nostrum.

17 June

ELEVENTH SUNDAY IN ORDINARY TIME

Entrance Antiphon   Cf. Ps 26:7,9

O LORD, hear my voice,
   for I have called to you;
   be my help.
Do not abandon or forsake me,
   O God, my Saviour!

Ant. ad introitum

EXAUDI, Domine, vocem meam,
   qua clamavi ad te.
Adiutor meus esto,
   ne derelinquas me,
neque despicias me,
   Deus salutaris meus.

Collect

O God, strength of those
   who hope in you,
graciously hear our pleas,
and, since without you mortal
   frailty can do nothing,
grant us always the help of your grace,
that in following your commands
we may please you by our resolve
   and our deeds.
Through our Lord Jesus Christ,
   your Son,
who lives and reigns with you
   in the unity of the Holy Spirit,
one God, for ever and ever.

Collecta

Deus, in te sperantium fortitudo,
invocationibus nostris
   adesto propitius,
et, quia sine te nihil potest
   mortalis infirmitas,
gratiæ tuæ præsta semper auxilium,
ut, in exsequendis mandatis tuis,
et voluntate tibi
   et actione placeamus.
Per Dominum nostrum Iesum
   Christum Filium tuum,
qui tecum vivit et regnat
   in unitate Spiritus Sancti,
Deus, per omnia sæcula sæculorum.

FIRST READING

A reading from the prophet Ezekiel   17:22-24
I make low trees grow.

The Lord says this:

   'From the top of the cedar,
   from the highest branch I will take a shoot
   and plant it myself on a very high mountain.
   I will plant it on the high mountain of Israel.
   It will sprout branches and bear fruit,
   and become a noble cedar.
   Every kind of bird will live beneath it,
   every winged creature rest in the shade of its branches.

And every tree of the field will learn that I, the Lord, am the one
who stunts tall trees and makes the low ones grow,
who withers green trees and makes the withered green.
I, the Lord, have spoken, and I will do it.'

The word of the Lord.

Responsorial Psalm   Ps 91:2-3,13-16. R. Cf.v.2

R. **It is good to give you thanks, O Lord.**

It is good to give thanks to the Lord
to make music to your name, O Most High,
to proclaim your love in the morning
and your truth in the watches of the night. R.

The just will flourish like the palm-tree
and grow like a Lebanon cedar. R.

Planted in the house of the Lord
they will flourish in the courts of our God,
still bearing fruit when they are old,
still full of sap, still green,
to proclaim that the Lord is just.
In him, my rock, there is no wrong. R.

SECOND READING

A reading from the second letter of St Paul to the Corinthians   5:6-10
Whether we are living in the body or exiled from it, we are intent on pleasing the Lord.

We are always full of confidence when we remember that to live in the
body means to be exiled from the Lord, going as we do by faith and not
by sight – we are full of confidence, I say, and actually want to be exiled
from the body and make our home with the Lord. Whether we are living
in the body or exiled from it, we are intent on pleasing him. For all the
truth about us will be brought out in the law court of Christ, and each of
us will get what he deserves for the things he did in the body, good or bad.

The word of the Lord.

Gospel Acclamation   Jn 15:15

R. **Alleluia, alleluia!**
I call you friends, says the Lord,
because I have made known to you
everything I have learnt from my Father.
R. **Alleluia!**

Or:

R. **Alleluia, alleluia!**
The seed is the word of God, Christ the sower;
whoever finds the seed will remain for ever.
R. **Alleluia!**

GOSPEL

A reading from the holy Gospel according to Mark   4:26-34

It is the smallest of all the seeds; yet it grows into the biggest shrub of them all.

Jesus said to the crowds: 'This is what the kingdom of God is like. A man throws seed on the land. Night and day, while he sleeps, when he is awake, the seed is sprouting and growing; how, he does not know. Of its own accord the land produces first the shoot, then the ear, then the full grain in the ear. And when the crop is ready, he loses no time: he starts to reap because the harvest has come.'

He also said, 'What can we say the kingdom of God is like? What parable can we find for it? It is like a mustard seed which the time of its sowing in the soil is the smallest of all the seeds on earth; yet once it is sown it grows into the biggest shrub of them all and puts out big branches so that the birds of the air can shelter in its shade.'

Using many parables like these, he spoke the word to them, so far as they were capable of understanding it. He would not speak to them except in parables, but he explained everything to his disciples when they were alone.

The Gospel of the Lord.

Prayer over the Offerings	Super oblata
O God, who in the offerings presented here provide for the twofold needs of human nature, nourishing us with food and renewing us with your Sacrament, grant, we pray, that the sustenance they provide may not fail us in body or in spirit. Through Christ our Lord.	Deus, qui humani generis utramque substantiam præsentium munerum et alimento vegetas et renovas sacramento, tribue, quæsumus, ut eorum et corporibus nostris subsidium non desit et mentibus. Per Christum Dominum nostrum.

Preface of Sundays in Ordinary Time I-VIII, pp.61-67.

Communion Antiphon Ps 26:4	Ant. ad communionem

There is one thing I ask of the Lord,
   only this do I seek:
to live in the house of the Lord
   all the days of my life.

Unum petii a Domino,
   hoc requiram,
ut inhabitem in domo Domini
omnibus diebus vitæ meæ.

Or: Jn 17:11

Holy Father, keep in your name
   those you have given me,
that they may be one as we are one,
   says the Lord.

Vel:

Pater sancte,
   serva eos in nomine tuo,
quos dedisti mihi, ut sint unum
   sicut et nos, dicit Dominus.

Prayer after Communion

As this reception of your
   Holy Communion, O Lord,
foreshadows the union
   of the faithful in you,
so may it bring about unity
   in your Church.
Through Christ our Lord.

Post communionem

Hæc tua, Domine,
   sumpta sacra communio,
sicut fidelium in te
   unionem præsignat,
sic in Ecclesia tua unitatis
   operetur effectum.
Per Christum Dominum nostrum.

24 June

THE NATIVITY OF SAINT JOHN THE BAPTIST

One of those who gave his life for the truth is John the Baptist. John was chosen by God to prepare the way for Jesus, and he revealed him to the people of Israel as the Messiah, the Lamb of God who takes away the sin of the world (cf. Jn 1:29). John consecrated himself entirely to God and to his envoy, Jesus. But, in the end, what happened? He died for the sake of the truth, when he denounced the adultery of King Herod and Herodias. How many people pay dearly for their commitment to truth! Upright people who are not afraid to go against the current! How many just men prefer to go against the current, so as not to deny the voice of conscience, the voice of truth! And we, we must not be afraid. Among you are many young people. To you young people I say: do not be afraid to go against the current, when they want to rob us of hope, when they propose rotten values, values like food gone bad — and when food has gone bad, it harms us; these values harm us. We must go against the current! Forward, be brave and go against the tide! And be proud of doing so.

(Pope Francis)

Solemnity

At the Vigil Mass

This Mass is used on the evening of 23 June, either before or after First Vespers (Evening Prayer I) of the Solemnity.

Entrance Antiphon Lk 1:15-14	Ant. ad introitum
HE will be great in the sight of the Lord	HIC erit magnus coram Domino,
and will be filled with the Holy Spirit,	et Spiritu Sancto replebitur adhuc
even from his mother's womb;	ex utero matris suæ,
and many will rejoice at his birth.	et multi in nativitate eius gaudebunt.

The Gloria in excelsis (Glory to God in the highest) is said.

Collect	Collecta
Grant, we pray, almighty God,	Præsta, quæsumus,
that your family may walk in the	omnipotens Deus,
way of salvation	ut familia tua per viam

and, attentive to what Saint John the Precursor urged,	salutis incedat, et, beati Ioannis Præcursoris hortamenta sectando,
may come safely to the One he foretold,	ad eum quem prædixit, secura perveniat,
our Lord Jesus Christ.	Dominum nostrum Iesum Christum.
Who lives and reigns with you in the unity of the Holy Spirit,	Qui tecum vivit et regnat in unitate Spiritus Sancti,
one God, for ever and ever.	Deus, per omnia sæcula sæculorum.

FIRST READING

A reading from the prophet Jeremiah   1:4-10

Before I formed you in the womb, I knew you.

In the days of Josiah, the word of the Lord was addressed to me, saying,

'Before I formed you in the womb I knew you;
before you came to birth I consecrated you;
I have appointed you as prophet to the nations.'

I said, 'Ah, Lord, look, I do not know how to speak: I am a child!'

But the Lord replied,

'Do not say, "I am a child."
Go now to those to whom I send you
and say whatever I command you.
Do not be afraid of them,
for I am with you to protect you –
it is the Lord who speaks!'

Then the Lord put out his hand and touched my mouth and said to me:

'There! I am putting my words into your mouth.
Look, today I am setting you
over nations and over kingdoms,
to tear up and to knock down,
to destroy and to overthrow,
to build and to plant.'

The word of the Lord.

Responsional Psalm   Ps 70:1-6,15,17. R. v.6

R. **From my mother's womb you have been my help.**
In you, O Lord, I take refuge;
let me never be put to shame.

In your justice rescue me, free me:
pay heed to me and save me. R.

Be a rock where I can take refuge,
a mighty stronghold to save me;
for you are my rock, my stronghold.
Free me from the hand of the wicked. R.

It is you, O Lord, who are my hope,
my trust, O Lord, since my youth.
On you I have leaned from my birth,
from my mother's womb you have been my help. R.

My lips will tell of your justice
and day by day of your help.
O God, you have taught me from my youth
and I proclaim your wonders still. R.

R. **From my mother's womb you have been my help.**

SECOND READING

A reading from the first letter of St Peter   1:8-12

It was this salvation that the prophets were looking and searching so hard for.

You did not see Jesus Christ, yet you love him; and still without seeing
him, you are already filled with joy so glorious that it cannot be described,
because you believe; and you are sure of the end to which your faith looks
forward, that is, the salvation of your souls.

   It was this salvation that the prophets were looking and searching so
hard for; their prophecies were about the grace which was to come to you.
The Spirit of Christ which was in them foretold the sufferings of Christ and
the glories that would come after them, and they tried to find out at what
time and in what circumstances all this was to be expected. It was revealed
to them that the news they brought of all the things which have now been
announced to you, by those who preached to you the Good News through
the Holy Spirit sent from heaven, was for you and not for themselves. Even
the angels long to catch a glimpse of these things.

   The word of the Lord.

Gospel Acclamation   Cf. Jn 1:7; Lk 1:17

R. **Alleluia, alleluia!**
He came as a witness,
as a witness to speak for the light,
preparing for the Lord a people fit for him.
R. **Alleluia!**

GOSPEL

A reading from the holy Gospel according to Luke   1:5-17

She is to bear you a son and you must name him John.

In the days of King Herod of Judaea there lived a priest called Zechariah who belonged to the Abijah section of the priesthood, and he had a wife, Elizabeth by name, who was a descendant of Aaron. Both were worthy in the sight of God, and scrupulously observed all the commandments and observances of the Lord. But they were childless: Elizabeth was barren and they were both getting on in years.

Now it was the turn of Zechariah's section to serve, and he was exercising his priestly office before God when it fell to him by lot, as the ritual custom was, to enter the Lord's sanctuary and burn incense there. And at the hour of incense the whole congregation was outside, praying.

Then there appeared to him the angel of the Lord, standing on the right of the altar of incense. The sight disturbed Zechariah and he was overcome with fear. But the angel said to him, 'Zechariah, do not be afraid, your prayer has been heard. Your wife Elizabeth is to bear you a son and you must name him John. He will be your joy and delight and many will rejoice at his birth, for he will be great in the sight of the Lord; he must drink no wine, no strong drink. Even from his mother's womb he will be filled with the Holy Spirit, and he will bring back many of the sons of Israel to the Lord their God. With the spirit and power of Elijah, he will go before him to turn the hearts of fathers towards their children and the disobedient back to the wisdom that the virtuous have, preparing for the Lord a people fit for him.'

The Gospel of the Lord.

The Creed is said.

Prayer over the Offerings

Look with favour, O Lord,
upon the offerings made
   by your people
on the Solemnity of
   Saint John the Baptist,
and grant that what we celebrate
   in mystery
we may follow with deeds
   of devoted service.
Through Christ our Lord.

Super oblata

Munera populi tui, Domine,
   propitius intende,
in beati Ioannis Baptistæ
   sollemnitate delata,
et præsta, ut,
   quæ mysterio gerimus,
debitæ servitutis actione sectemur.
Per Christum Dominum nostrum.

Proper Preface, as in the following Mass, pp.507-508.

Communion Antiphon   Lk 1:68

Blessed be the Lord,
the God of Israel!
He has visited his people
and redeemed them.

Ant. ad communionem

Benedictus Dominus Deus Israel,
quia visitavit et fecit redemptionem
plebi suæ.

Prayer after Communion

May the marvellous prayer of Saint
John the Baptist
accompany us who have
eaten our fill
at this sacrificial feast, O Lord,
and, since Saint John
proclaimed your Son
to be the Lamb who would
take away our sins,
may he implore now for us
your favour.
Through Christ our Lord.

Post communionem

Sacris dapibus satiatos,
beati Ioannis Baptistæ nos,
Domine,
præclara comitetur oratio,
et, quem Agnum nostra ablaturum
crimina nuntiavit,
ipsum Filium tuum poscat nobis
fore placatum.
Qui vivit et regnat
in sæcula sæculorum.

At the Mass during the Day

Entrance Antiphon   Jn 1:6-7; Lk 1:17

A MAN was sent from God,
whose name was John.
He came to testify to the light,
to prepare a people fit for the Lord.

Ant. ad introitum

FUIT homo missus a Deo,
cui nomen erat Ioannes.
Hic venit, ut testimonium
perhiberet de lumine,
parare Domino plebem perfectam.

The Gloria in excelsis (Glory to God in the highest) is said.

Collect

O God, who raised up
Saint John the Baptist
to make ready a nation fit for
Christ the Lord,
give your people, we pray,
the grace of spiritual joys
and direct the hearts
of all the faithful
into the way of salvation and peace.
Through our Lord Jesus Christ,
your Son,

Collecta

Deus, qui beatum Ioannem
Baptistam suscitasti,
ut perfectam plebem
Christo Domino præpararet,
da populis tuis spiritalium
gratiam gaudiorum,
et omnium fidelium mentes
dirige in viam salutis et pacis.
Per Dominum nostrum
Iesum Christum Filium tuum,
qui tecum vivit et regnat

who lives and reigns with you | in unitate Spiritus Sancti,
   in the unity of the Holy Spirit, | Deus, per omnia sæcula sæculorum.
one God, for ever and ever.

FIRST READING

A reading from the prophet Isaiah   49:1-6

I will make you the light of the nations.

Islands, listen to me,
pay attention, remotest peoples.
The Lord called me before I was born,
from my mother's womb he pronounced my name.

He made my mouth a sharp sword,
and hid me in the shadow of his hand.
He made me into a sharpened arrow,
and concealed me in his quiver.

He said to me, 'You are my servant (Israel)
in whom I shall be glorified';
while I was thinking, 'I have toiled in vain,
I have exhausted myself for nothing';
and all the while my cause was with the Lord,
my reward with my God.
I was honoured in the eyes of the Lord,
my God was my strength.

And now the Lord has spoken,
he who formed me in the womb to be his servant,
to bring Jacob back to him,
to gather Israel to him:
'It is not enough for you to be my servant,
to restore the tribes of Jacob and bring back the survivors of Israel;
I will make you the light of the nations
so that my salvation may reach to the ends of the earth.'

   The word of the Lord.

Responsorial Psalm   Ps 138:1-3,13-15. R. v.14

R. **I thank you for the wonder of my being.**
   O Lord, you search me and you know me,
   you know my resting and my rising,
   you discern my purpose from afar.
   You mark when I walk or lie down,
   all my ways lie open to you. R.

For it was you who created my being,
knit me together in my mother's womb.
I thank you for the wonder of my being,
for the wonders of all your creation. R.

Already you knew my soul,
my body held no secret from you
when I was being fashioned in secret
and moulded in the depths of the earth. R.

R. **I thank you for the wonder of my being.**

SECOND READING

A reading from the Acts of the Apostles   13:22-26

Jesus, whose coming was heralded by John.

Paul said: 'God made David the king of our ancestors, of whom he approved in these words, "I have elected David son of Jesse, a man after my own heart, who will carry out my whole purpose." To keep his promise, God has raised up for Israel one of David's descendants, Jesus, as Saviour, whose coming was heralded by John when he proclaimed a baptism of repentance for the whole people of Israel. Before John ended his career he said, "I am not the one you imagine me to be; that one is coming after me and I am not fit to undo his sandal."

'My brothers, sons of Abraham's race, and all you who fear God, this message of salvation is meant for you.'

The word of the Lord.

Gospel Acclamation   Cf. Lk 1:76

R. **Alleluia, alleluia!**
As for you, little child, you shall be called
a prophet of God, the Most High.
You shall go ahead of the Lord
to prepare his ways before him.
R. **Alleluia!**

GOSPEL

A reading from the holy Gospel according to Luke   1:57-66,80

His name is John.

The time came for Elizabeth to have her child, and she gave birth to a son; and when her neighbours and relations heard that the Lord had shown her so great a kindness, they shared her joy.

Now on the eighth day they came to circumcise the child; they were going to call him Zechariah after his father, but his mother spoke up. 'No,' she said 'he is to be called John.' They said to her, 'But no one in your family has that name', and made signs to his father to find out what he wanted him called. The father asked for a writing-tablet and wrote, 'His name is John.' And they were all astonished. At that instant his power of speech returned and he spoke and praised God. All their neighbours were filled with awe and the whole affair was talked about throughout the hill country of Judaea. All those who heard of it treasured it in their hearts. 'What will this child turn out to be?' they wondered. And indeed the hand of the Lord was with him. Meanwhile, the child grew up and his spirit matured. And he lived out in the wilderness until the day he appeared openly to Israel.

The Gospel of the Lord.

The Creed is said.

Prayer over the Offerings

We place these offerings on your
    altar, O Lord,
to celebrate with fitting honour
    the nativity of him
who both foretold the coming
    of the world's Saviour
and pointed him out
    when he came.
Who lives and reigns
    for ever and ever.

Super oblata

Tua, Domine, muneribus
    altaria cumulamus,
illius nativitatem honore
    debito celebrantes,
qui Salvatorem mundi
    et cecinit affuturum,
et adesse monstravit.
Qui vivit et regnat
    in sæcula sæculorum.

Preface: The mission of the Precursor

It is truly right and just,
    our duty and our salvation,
always and everywhere
    to give you thanks,
Lord, holy Father,
    almighty and eternal God,
through Christ our Lord.

In his Precursor, Saint John
    the Baptist,
we praise your great glory,
for you consecrated him

Præfatio: De missione Præcursoris

Vere dignum et iustum est,
    æquum et salutare,
nos tibi semper et ubique
    gratias agere:
Domine, sancte Pater,
    omnipotens æterne Deus:
per Christum Dominum nostrum.

In cuius Præcursore beato Ioanne
tuam magnificentiam collaudamus,
quem inter natos mulierum honore
    præcipuo consecrasti.

for a singular honour
among those born of women.

His birth brought great rejoicing;
even in the womb he leapt for joy
at the coming of human salvation.
He alone of all the prophets
pointed out the Lamb of redemption.

And to make holy the flowing waters,
he baptised the very author
      of Baptism
and was privileged to bear him
      supreme witness
by the shedding of his blood.

And so, with the Powers of heaven,
we worship you constantly on earth,
and before your majesty
without end we acclaim:

Holy, Holy, Holy Lord God of hosts...

Qui cum nascendo multa gaudia
      præstitisset,
et nondum editus exsultasset
      ad humanæ salutis adventum,
ipse solus omnium prophetarum
Agnum redemptionis ostendit.

Sed et sanctificandis etiam
      aquæ fluentis
ipsum baptismatis lavit auctorem,
et meruit fuso sanguine supremum
illi testimonium exhibere.

Et ideo, cum cælorum virtutibus,
in terris te iugiter prædicamus,
maiestati tuæ sine fine clamantes:

Sanctus, Sanctus, Sanctus. . .

Communion Antiphon Cf. Lk 1:78

Through the tender mercy
      of our God,
the Dawn from on high will visit us.

Ant. ad communionem

Per viscera misericordiæ Dei nostri,
visitavit nos Oriens ex alto.

Prayer after Communion

Having feasted at the banquet
      of the heavenly Lamb,
we pray, O Lord,
that, finding joy in the nativity
      of Saint John the Baptist,
your Church may know as
      the author of her rebirth
the Christ whose coming
      John foretold.
Who lives and reigns
      for ever and ever.

Post communionem

Cælestis Agni convivio refecti,
quæsumus, Domine,
      ut Ecclesia tua,
sumens de beati Ioannis Baptistæ
      generatione lætitiam,
quem ille prænuntiavit venturum,
suæ regenerationis
      cognoscat auctorem.
Qui vivit et regnat
      in sæcula sæculorum.

29 June

SAINTS PETER AND PAUL, APOSTLES

St Peter and St Paul, so different from each other on a human level, were personally chosen by the Lord Jesus and they answered the call by offering their entire life. In both of them the grace of Christ accomplished great things, it transformed them. It transformed them, and how! Simon denied Jesus in a dramatic moment of the Passion; Saul harshly persecuted the Christians. But they both welcomed God's love and allowed themselves to be transformed by his mercy; they thus became friends and apostles of Christ. This is why they continue to speak to the Church and still today they show us the way to salvation. And should we perchance fall into the most serious sins and the darkest of nights, God is always capable of transforming us too, the way he transformed Peter and Paul; transforming the heart and forgiving us for everything, thus transforming the darkness of our sin into a dawn of light. God is like this: he transforms us, he always forgives us, as he did with Peter and as he did with Paul.

(Pope Francis)

Solemnity

At the Vigil Mass

This Mass is used on the evening before the Solemnity, either before or after First Vespers (Evening Prayer I) of the Solemnity.

Entrance Antiphon	Ant. ad introitum
PETER the Apostle, and Paul the teacher of the Gentiles, these have taught us your law, O Lord.	PETRUS apostolus et Paulus doctor gentium, ipsi nos docuerunt legem tuam, Domine.

The Gloria in excelsis (Glory to God in the highest) is said.

Collect	Collecta
Grant, we pray, O Lord our God, that we may be sustained by the intercession of the blessed Apostles Peter and Paul, that, as through them you gave your Church the foundations of her heavenly office, so through them you may help her to eternal salvation. Through our Lord Jesus Christ, your Son, who lives and reigns with you in the unity of the Holy Spirit, one God, for ever and ever.	Da nobis, quæsumus, Domine Deus noster, beatorum apostolorum Petri et Pauli intercessionibus sublevari, ut, per quos Ecclesiæ tuæ superni muneris rudimenta donasti, per eos subsidia perpetuæ salutis impendas. Per Dominum nostrum Iesum Christum Filium tuum, qui tecum vivit et regnat in unitate Spiritus Sancti, Deus, per omnia sæcula sæculorum.

FIRST READING

A reading from the Acts of the Apostles   3:1-10
I will give you what I have: in the name of Jesus, walk!

Once, when Peter and John were going up to the Temple for the prayers at the ninth hour, it happened that there was a man being carried past. He was a cripple from birth; and they used to put him down every day near the Temple entrance called the Beautiful Gate so that he could beg from the people going in. When this man saw Peter and John on their way into the Temple he begged from them. Both Peter and John looked straight at him and said, 'Look at us.' He turned to them expectantly, hoping to get something from them, but Peter said, 'I have neither silver nor gold, but I will give you what I have: in the name of Jesus Christ the Nazarene, walk!' Peter then took him by the hand and helped him to stand up. Instantly his feet and ankles became firm, he jumped up, stood, and began to walk, and he went with them into the Temple, walking and jumping and praising God. Everyone could see him walking and praising God, and they recognised him as the man who used to sit begging at the Beautiful Gate of the Temple. They were all astonished and unable to explain what had happened to him.

The word of the Lord.

Responsorial Psalm   Ps 18:2-5. R. v.5

R. **Their word goes forth through all the earth.**

The heavens proclaim the glory of God
and the firmament shows forth the work of his hands.
Day unto day takes up the story
and night unto night makes known the message. R.

No speech, no word, no voice is heard
yet their span extends through all the earth,
their words to the utmost bounds of the world. R.

SECOND READING

A reading from the letter of St Paul to the Galatians   1:11-20
God specially chose me while I was still in my mother's womb.

The Good News I preached is not a human message that I was given by
men, it is something I learnt only through a revelation of Jesus Christ. You
must have heard of my career as a practising Jew, how merciless I was in
persecuting the Church of God, how much damage I did to it, how I stood
out among other Jews of my generation, and how enthusiastic I was for the
traditions of my ancestors.

Then God, who had specially chosen me while I was still in my mother's
womb, called me through his grace and chose to reveal his Son in me, so
that I might preach the Good News about him to the pagans. I did not
stop to discuss this with any human being, nor did I go up to Jerusalem to
see those who were already apostles before me, but I went off to Arabia at
once and later went straight back from there to Damascus. Even when after
three years I went up to Jerusalem to visit Cephas and stayed with him for
fifteen days, I did not see any of the other apostles; I only saw James, the
brother of the Lord, and I swear before God that what I have just written is
the literal truth.

The word of the Lord.

Gospel Acclamation   Jn 21:17

R. **Alleluia, alleluia!**
Lord, you know everything;
you know I love you.
R. **Alleluia!**

GOSPEL

A reading from the holy Gospel according to John   21:15-19
Feed my lambs, feed my sheep.

After Jesus had shown himself to his disciples and eaten with them, he said to Simon Peter, 'Simon son of John, do you love me more than these others do?' He answered, 'Yes Lord, you know I love you.' Jesus said to him, 'Feed my lambs.' A second time he said to him, 'Simon son of John, do you love me?' He replied, 'Yes, Lord, you know I love you.' Jesus said to him, 'Look after my sheep.' Then he said to him a third time, 'Simon son of John, do you love me?' Peter was upset that he asked him the third time, 'Do you love me?' and said, 'Lord, you know everything; you know I love you.' Jesus said to him, 'Feed my sheep.

> 'I tell you most solemnly,
> when you were young
> you put on your own belt
> and walked where you liked;
> but when you grow old
> you will stretch out your hands,
> and somebody else will put a belt round you
> and take you where you would rather not go.'

In these words he indicated the kind of death by which Peter would give glory to God. After this he said, 'Follow me.'

The Gospel of the Lord.

The Creed is said.

Prayer over the Offerings	Super oblata
We bring offerings to your altar, O Lord, as we glory in the solemn feast of the blessed Apostles Peter and Paul, so that the more we doubt our own merits, the more we may rejoice that we are to be saved by your loving kindness. Through Christ our Lord.	Munera, Domine, tuis altaribus adhibemus, de beatorum apostolorum Petri et Pauli sollemnitatibus gloriantes, ut quantum sumus de nostro merito formidantes, tantum de tua benignitate gloriemur salvandi. Per Christum Dominum nostrum.

Proper Preface, as in the following Mass, p.517.

Communion Antiphon Cf. Jn 21:15,17 | Ant. ad communionem

Simon, Son of John,
  do you love me more than these?
Lord, you know everything;
  you know that I love you.

Simon Ioannis, diligis me plus his?
Domine, tu omnia nosti;
tu scis, Domine, quia amo te.

Prayer after Communion | Post communionem

By this heavenly Sacrament,
  O Lord, we pray,
strengthen your faithful,
whom you have enlightened
  with the teaching of the Apostles.
Through Christ our Lord.

Cælestibus sacramentis,
  quæsumus, Domine,
fideles tuos corrobora,
quos Apostolorum
  doctrina illuminasti.
Per Christum Dominum nostrum.

A formula of Solemn Blessing, pp.144-147, may be used.

At the Mass during the Day

Entrance Antiphon | Ant. ad introitum

THESE are the ones who,
  living in the flesh,
planted the Church with their blood;
they drank the chalice of the Lord
and became the friends of God.

ISTI sunt qui, viventes in carne,
  plantaverunt Ecclesiam
  sanguine suo:
calicem Domini biberunt,
  et amici Dei facti sunt.

The Gloria in excelsis (Glory to God in the highest) is said.

Collect | Collecta

O God, who on the Solemnity
  of the Apostles Peter and Paul
give us the noble and holy joy
  of this day,
grant, we pray, that your Church
may in all things follow the teaching
of those through whom she received
the beginnings of right religion.
Through our Lord Jesus Christ,
  your Son,
who lives and reigns with you
  in the unity of the Holy Spirit,
one God, for ever and ever.

Deus, qui huius diei venerandam
  sanctamque lætitiam
in apostolorum Petri et Pauli
  sollemnitate tribuisti,
da Ecclesiæ tuæ eorum in omnibus
  sequi præceptum,
per quos religionis sumpsit exordium.

Per Dominum nostrum Iesum
  Christum Filium tuum,
qui tecum vivit et regnat
  in unitate Spiritus Sancti,
Deus, per omnia sæcula sæculorum.

FIRST READING

A reading from the Acts of the Apostles   12:1-11
Now I know the Lord really did save me from Herod.

King Herod started persecuting certain members of the Church. He
beheaded James the brother of John, and when he saw that this pleased
the Jews he decided to arrest Peter as well. This was during the days of
Unleavened Bread, and he put Peter in prison, assigning four squads of
four soldiers each to guard him in turns. Herod meant to try Peter in public
after the end of Passover week. All the time Peter was under guard the
Church prayed to God for him unremittingly.

   On the night before Herod was to try him, Peter was sleeping between
two soldiers, fastened with double chains, while guards kept watch at the
main entrance to the prison. Then suddenly the angel of the Lord stood
there, and the cell was filled with light. He tapped Peter on the side and
woke him. 'Get up!' he said 'Hurry!' – and the chains fell from his hands.
The angel then said, 'Put on your belt and sandals.' After he had done this,
the angel next said, 'Wrap your cloak round you and follow me.' Peter
followed him, but had no idea that what the angel did was all happening
in reality; he thought he was seeing a vision. They passed through two
guard posts one after the other, and reached the iron gate leading to the
city. This opened of its own accord; they went through it and had walked
the whole length of one street when suddenly the angel left him. It was
only then that Peter came to himself. 'Now I know it is all true,' he said.
'The Lord really did send his angel and has saved me from Herod and from
all that the Jewish people were so certain would happen to me.'

   The word of the Lord.

Responsional Psalm   Ps 33:2-9. R̊. v.5. Alt. R̊. v.8

R̊. **From all my terrors the Lord set me free.**
   Or: **The angel of the Lord rescues those who revere him.**

   I will bless the Lord at all times
   his praise always on my lips;
   in the Lord my soul shall make its boast.
   The humble shall hear and be glad. R̊.

   Glorify the Lord with me.
   Together let us praise his name.
   I sought the Lord and he answered me;
   from all my terrors he set me free. R̊.

Look towards him and be radiant;
let your faces not be abashed.
This poor man called; the Lord heard him
and rescued him from all his distress. R.

The angel of the Lord is encamped
around those who revere him, to rescue them.
Taste and see that the Lord is good.
He is happy who seeks refuge in him. R.

SECOND READING

A reading from the second letter of St Paul to Timothy   4:6-8,17-18
All there is to come now is the crown of righteousness reserved for me.

My life is already being poured away as a libation, and the time has come for me to be gone. I have fought the good fight to the end; I have run the race to the finish; I have kept the faith; all there is to come now is the crown of righteousness reserved for me, which the Lord, the righteous judge, will give to me on that Day; and not only to me but to all those who have longed for his Appearing.

The Lord stood by me and gave me power, so that through me the whole message might be proclaimed for all the pagans to hear; and so I was rescued from the lion's mouth. The Lord will rescue me from all evil attempts on me, and bring me safely to his heavenly kingdom. To him be glory for ever and ever. Amen.

The word of the Lord.

Gospel Acclamation   Mt 16:18
R. **Alleluia, alleluia!**
You are Peter and on this rock I will build my Church.
And the gates of the underworld can never hold out against it.
R. **Alleluia!**

GOSPEL

A reading from the holy Gospel according to Matthew   16:13-19

You are Peter, and I will give you the keys of the kingdom of heaven.

When Jesus came to the region of Caesarea Philippi he put this question
to his disciples, 'Who do people say the Son of Man is?' And they said,
'Some say he is John the Baptist, some Elijah, and others Jeremiah or one
of the prophets.' 'But you,' he said 'who do you say I am?' Then Simon
Peter spoke up, 'You are the Christ,' he said 'the Son of the living God.'
Jesus replied, 'Simon son of Jonah, you are a happy man! Because it was
not flesh and blood that revealed this to you but my Father in heaven. So
I now say to you: You are Peter and on this rock I will build my Church.
And the gates of the underworld can never hold out against it. I will give
you the keys of the kingdom of heaven: whatever you bind on earth shall
be considered bound in heaven; whatever you loose on earth shall be
considered loosed in heaven.'

The Gospel of the Lord.

The Creed is said.

Prayer over the Offerings | Super oblata

May the prayer of the Apostles,
    O Lord,
accompany the sacrificial gift
that we present to your name
    for consecration,
and may their intercession make
    us devoted to you
in celebration of the sacrifice.
Through Christ our Lord.

Hostiam, Domine, quam nomini
    tuo exhibemus sacrandam,
apostolica prosequatur oratio,
nosque tibi reddat in sacrificio
    celebrando devotos.
Per Christum Dominum nostrum.

Preface: The twofold mission of Peter and Paul in the Church.

Præfatio: De duplici missione Petri et Pauli in Ecclesia.

It is truly right and just,
  our duty and our salvation,
always and everywhere to give
  you thanks,
Lord, holy Father,
  almighty and eternal God.

Vere dignum et iustum est,
  æquum et salutare,
nos tibi semper et ubique
  gratias agere:
Domine, sancte Pater,
  omnipotens æterne Deus.

For by your providence
the blessed Apostles Peter and Paul
  bring us joy:
Peter, foremost in confessing
  the faith,
Paul, its outstanding preacher,
Peter, who established the early
  Church from the remnant
  of Israel,
Paul, master and teacher
  of the Gentiles that you call.

Quia nos beati apostoli
  Petrus et Paulus
tua dispositione lætificant:
hic princeps fidei confitendæ,
ille intellegendæ clarus assertor;
hic reliquiis Israel instituens
  Ecclesiam primitivam,
ille magister et doctor
  gentium vocandarum.

And so, each in a different way
gathered together the one family
  of Christ;
and revered together throughout
  the world,
they share one Martyr's crown.

Sic diverso consilio unam Christi
  familiam congregantes,
par mundo venerabile,
  una corona sociavit.

And therefore, with all the Angels
  and Saints,
we praise you, as without end
  we acclaim:

Et ideo, cum Sanctis
  et Angelis universis
te collaudamus, sine fine dicentes:

Holy, Holy, Holy Lord God of hosts...

Sanctus, Sanctus, Sanctus. . .

Communion Antiphon Cf. Mt 16:16,18

Ant. ad communionem

Peter said to Jesus:
  You are the Christ,
  the Son of the living God.
And Jesus replied: You are Peter,
and upon this rock I will build
  my Church.

Dixit Petrus ad Iesum:
  Tu es Christus, Filius Dei vivi.
Respondit Iesus: Tu es Petrus,
et super hanc petram ædificabo
  Ecclesiam meam.

Prayer after Communion
Grant us, O Lord,
who have been renewed
    by this Sacrament,
so to live in the Church,
that, persevering in the breaking
    of the Bread
and in the teaching of the Apostles,
we may be one heart and one soul,
made steadfast in your love.
Through Christ our Lord.

Post communionem
Da nobis, Domine,
    hoc sacramento refectis,
ita in Ecclesia conversari,
ut, perseverantes in fractione panis
Apostolorumque doctrina,
cor unum simus et anima una,
    tua caritate firmati.
Per Christum Dominum nostrum.

A formula of Solemn Blessing, pp.144-147, may be used.

1 July

THIRTEENTH SUNDAY IN ORDINARY TIME

Entrance Antiphon   Ps 46:2
ALL peoples, clap your hands.
    Cry to God with shouts of joy!

Ant. ad introitum
OMNES gentes,
    plaudite manibus,
iubilate Deo in voce exsultationis.

Collect
O God, who through the grace
    of adoption
chose us to be children of light,
grant, we pray,
that we may not be wrapped
    in the darkness of error
but always be seen to stand
    in the bright light of truth.
Through our Lord Jesus Christ,
    your Son,
who lives and reigns with you
    in the unity of the Holy Spirit,
one God, for ever and ever.

Collecta
Deus, qui, per adoptionem gratiæ,
lucis nos esse filios voluisti,
præsta, quæsumus, ut errorum
    non involvamur tenebris,
sed in splendore veritatis semper
    maneamus conspicui.
Per Dominum nostrum Iesum
    Christum Filium tuum,
qui tecum vivit et regnat
    in unitate Spiritus Sancti,
Deus, per omnia sæcula sæculorum.

FIRST READING

A reading from the book of Wisdom   1:13-15; 2:23-24

It was the devil's envy that brought death into the world.

Death was not God's doing,
he takes no pleasure in the extinction of the living.
To be – for this he created all;
the world's created things have health in them,
in them no fatal poison can be found,
and Hades holds no power on earth;
for virtue is undying.
Yet God did make man imperishable,
he made him in the image of his own nature;
it was the devil's envy that brought death into the world,
as those who are his partners will discover.

   The word of the Lord.

Responsional Psalm   Ps 29:2,4-6,11-13. R. v.2

R. **I will praise you, Lord, you have rescued me.**

   I will praise you, Lord, you have rescued me
   and have not let my enemies rejoice over me.
   O Lord, you have raised my soul from the dead,
   restored me to life from those who sink into the grave. R.

   Sing psalms to the Lord, you who love him,
   give thanks to his holy name.
   His anger lasts but a moment; his favour through life.
   At night there are tears, but joy comes with dawn. R.

   The Lord listened and had pity.
   The Lord came to my help.
   For me you have changed my mourning into dancing,
   O Lord my God, I will thank you for ever. R.

SECOND READING

A reading from the second letter of St Paul to the Corinthians   8:7,9,13-15

In giving relief to others, balance what happens to be your surplus now against their present need.

You always have the most of everything – of faith, of eloquence, of understanding, of keenness for any cause, and the biggest share of our affection – so we expect you to put the most into this work of mercy too. Remember how generous the Lord Jesus was: he was rich, but he became poor for your sake, to make you rich out of his poverty. This does not mean that to give relief to others you ought to make things difficult for yourselves: it is a question of balancing what happens to be your surplus now against their present need, and one day they may have something to spare that will supply your own need. That is how we strike a balance: as scripture says: The man who gathered much had none too much, the man who gathered little did not go short.

The word of the Lord.

Gospel Acclamation   Cf. Jn 6:63,68
R. **Alleluia, alleluia!**
Your words are spirit, Lord,
and they are life:
you have the message of eternal life.
R. **Alleluia!**

Or: Cf. 2 Tm 1:10

R. **Alleluia, alleluia!**
Our Saviour Christ Jesus abolished death,
and he has proclaimed life through the Good News.
R. **Alleluia!**

GOSPEL

A reading from the holy Gospel according to Mark   5:21-43
Little girl, I tell you to get up.

[When Jesus had crossed in the boat to the other side, a large crowd gathered round him and he stayed by the lakeside. Then one of the synagogue officials came up, Jairus by name, and seeing him, fell at his feet and pleaded with him earnestly, saying, 'My little daughter is desperately sick. Do come and lay your hands on her to make her better and save her life.' Jesus went with him and a large crowd followed him; they were pressing all round him.]

Now there was a woman who had suffered from a haemorrhage for twelve years; after long and painful treatment under various doctors, she had spent all she had without being any the better for it, in fact, she was getting worse. She had heard about Jesus, and she came up behind him through the crowd and touched his cloak. 'If I can touch even his clothes,' she had told herself 'I shall be well again.' And the source of the bleeding dried up instantly, and she felt in herself that she was cured of her complaint. Immediately aware that power had gone out from him Jesus turned round in the crowd and said, 'Who touched my clothes?'

His disciples said to him, 'You see how the crowd is pressing round you and yet you say, "Who touched me?"' But he continued to look all round to see who had done it. Then the woman came forward, frightened and trembling because she knew what had happened to her, and she fell at his feet and told him the whole truth. 'My daughter,' he said 'your faith has restored you to health; go in peace and be free from your complaint.'

[While he was still speaking some people arrived from the house of the synagogue official to say, 'Your daughter is dead: why put the Master to any further trouble?' But Jesus had overheard this remark of theirs and he said to the official, 'Do not be afraid; only have faith.' And he allowed no one to go with him except Peter and James and John the brother of James. So they came to the official's house and Jesus noticed all the commotion, with people weeping and wailing unrestrainedly. He went in and said to them, 'Why all this commotion and crying? The child is not dead, but asleep.' But they laughed at him. So he turned them all out and, taking with him the child's father and mother and his own companions, he went into the place where the child lay. And taking the child by the hand he said to her, 'Talitha, kum!' which means, 'Little girl, I tell you to get up.' The little girl got up at once and began to walk about, for she was twelve years old. At this they were overcome with astonishment, and he ordered them strictly not to let anyone know about it, and told them to give her something to eat.

The Gospel of the Lord.]

Shorter Form, verses 21-24, 35-43. Read between [ ]

Prayer over the Offerings	Super oblata
O God, who graciously accomplish the effects of your mysteries, grant, we pray, that the deeds by which we serve you may be worthy of these sacred gifts. Through Christ our Lord.	Deus, qui mysteriorum tuorum dignanter operaris effectus, præsta, quæsumus, ut sacris apta muneribus fiant nostra servitia. Per Christum Dominum nostrum.

Preface of Sundays in Ordinary Time I-VIII, pp.60-67.

Communion Antiphon Cf. Ps 102:1	Ant. ad communionem
Bless the Lord, O my soul, and all within me, his holy name.	Benedic, anima mea, Domino, et ea quæ intra me sunt nomini sancto eius.

Or: Jn 17:20-21

O Father, I pray for them,
    that they may be one in us,
that the world may believe that you
    have sent me, says the Lord.

Vel:

Pater, pro eis rogo,
    ut ipsi in nobis unum sint,
ut credat mundus quia tu me
    misisti, dicit Dominus.

Prayer after Communion

May this divine sacrifice
    we have offered and received
fill us with life, O Lord, we pray,
so that, bound to you
    in lasting charity,
we may bear fruit that lasts for ever.
Through Christ our Lord.

Post communionem

Vivificet nos, quæsumus, Domine,
divina quam obtulimus
    et sumpsimus hostia,
ut, perpetua tibi caritate coniuncti,
fructum qui semper
    maneat afferamus.
Per Christum Dominum nostrum.

8 July

FOURTEENTH SUNDAY IN ORDINARY TIME

Entrance Antiphon Cf. Ps 47:10-11

YOUR merciful love, O God,
    we have received in the midst
    of your temple.
Your praise, O God, like your name,
reaches the ends of the earth;
your right hand is filled
    with saving justice.

Ant. ad introitum

SUSCEPIMUS, Deus,
    misericordiam tuam
in medio templi tui.
Secundum nomen tuum, Deus,
ita et laus tua in fines terræ;
iustitia plena est dextera tua.

Collect

O God, who in the abasement
    of your Son
have raised up a fallen world,
fill your faithful with holy joy,
for on those you have rescued
    from slavery to sin
you bestow eternal gladness.
Through our Lord Jesus Christ,
    your Son,
who lives and reigns with you
    in the unity of the Holy Spirit,
one God, for ever and ever.

Collecta

Deus, qui in Filii tui humilitate
iacentem mundum erexisti,
fidelibus tuis sanctam
    concede lætitiam,
ut, quos eripuisti
    a servitute peccati,
gaudiis facias perfrui sempiternis.
Per Dominum nostrum Iesum
    Christum Filium tuum,
qui tecum vivit et regnat
    in unitate Spiritus Sancti,
Deus, per omnia sæcula sæculorum.

FIRST READING

A reading from the prophet Ezekiel   2:2-5

The sons are defiant and obstinate and they shall know that there is a prophet among them.

The spirit came into me and made me stand up, and I heard the Lord speaking to me. He said, 'Son of man, I am sending you to the Israelites, to the rebels who have turned against me. Till now they and their ancestors have been in revolt against me. The sons are defiant and obstinate; I am sending you to them, to say, "The Lord says this." Whether they listen or not, this set of rebels shall know there is a prophet among them.'

The word of the Lord.

Responsorial Psalm   Ps 122: R. v.2

R. **Our eyes are on the Lord**
   till he shows us his mercy.

To you have I lifted up my eyes,
you who dwell in the heavens:
my eyes, like the eyes of slaves
on the hand of their lords. R.

Like the eyes of a servant
on the hand of her mistress,
so our eyes are on the Lord our God
till he show us his mercy. R.

Have mercy on us, Lord, have mercy.
We are filled with contempt.
Indeed all too full is our soul
with the scorn of the rich,
with the proud man's disdain. R.

SECOND READING

A reading from the second letter of St Paul to the Corinthians   12:7-10

I shall be very happy to make my weaknesses my special boast so that the power of Christ may stay over me.

In view of the extraordinary nature of these revelations, to stop me from getting too proud I was given a thorn in the flesh, an angel of Satan to beat me and stop me from getting too proud! About this thing, I have pleaded with the Lord three times for it to leave me, but he has said, 'My grace is enough for you: my power is at its best in weakness.' So I shall be very happy to make my weaknesses my special boast so that the power of Christ may stay over me, and that is why I am quite content with my weaknesses, and with insults, hardships, persecutions, and the agonies I go through for Christ's sake. For it is when I am weak that I am strong.

The word of the Lord.

Jn 1:14,12

R. **Alleluia, alleluia!**
The Word was made flesh and lived among us;
to all who did accept him
he gave power to become children of God.
R. **Alleluia!**
Or: Cf. Lk 4:18
R. **Alleluia, alleluia!**
The Lord has sent me to bring the good news to
    the poor,
to proclaim liberty to captives.
R. **Alleluia!**

GOSPEL

A reading from the holy Gospel according to Mark   6:1-6
A prophet is despised only in his own country.

Jesus went to his home town and his disciples accompanied him. With the coming of the sabbath he began teaching in the synagogue and most of them were astonished when they heard him. They said, 'Where did the man get all this? What is this wisdom that has been granted him, and these miracles that are worked through him? This is the carpenter, surely, the son of Mary, the brother of James and Joset and Jude and Simon? His sisters, too are they not here with us?' And they would not accept him. And Jesus said to them, 'A prophet is only despised in his own country among his own relations and in his own house'; and he could work no miracle there, though he cured a few sick people by laying his hands on them. He was amazed at their lack of faith.

The Gospel of the Lord.

Prayer over the Offerings

May this oblation dedicated
    to your name
purify us, O Lord,
and day by day bring our conduct
closer to the life of heaven.
Through Christ our Lord.

Super oblata

Oblatio nos, Domine,
    tuo nomini dicata purificet,
et de die in diem ad cælestis vitæ
    transferat actionem.
Per Christum Dominum nostrum.

Preface of Sundays in Ordinary Time I-VIII, pp.61-67.

Communion Antiphon   Ps 33:9

Taste and see that the Lord is good;
blessed the man who seeks refuge
    in him.

Or: Mt 11:28

Come to me, all who labour
    and are burdened,
and I will refresh you, says the Lord.

Prayer after Communion

Grant, we pray, O Lord,
that, having been replenished
    by such great gifts,
we may gain the prize of salvation
and never cease to praise you.
Through Christ our Lord.

Ant. ad communionem

Gustate et videte, quoniam suavis
    est Dominus;
beatus vir, qui sperat in eo.

Vel:

Venite ad me, omnes qui laboratis
    et onerati estis,
et ego reficiam vos, dicit Dominus.

Post communionem

Tantis, Domine, repleti muneribus,
præsta, quæsumus, ut et salutaria
    dona capiamus,
et a tua numquam laude cessemus.
Per Christum Dominum nostrum.

15 July

FIFTEENTH SUNDAY IN ORDINARY TIME

Entrance Antiphon   Cf. Ps 16:15

AS for me, in justice I shall
   behold your face;
I shall be filled with the vision
    of your glory.

Collect

O God, who show the light
    of your truth
to those who go astray,
so that they may return
    to the right path,
give all who for the faith they profess
are accounted Christians
the grace to reject whatever
    is contrary to the name of Christ
and to strive after all that does
    it honour.
Through our Lord Jesus Christ,
    your Son,

Ant. ad introitum

EGO autem cum iustitia
   apparebo in conspectu tuo;
satiabor dum manifestabitur
    gloria tua.

Collecta

Deus, qui errantibus,
    ut in viam possint redire,
veritatis tuæ lumen ostendis,
da cunctis qui christiana
    professione censentur,
et illa respuere, quæ huic inimica
    sunt nomini,
et ea quæ sunt apta sectari.
Per Dominum nostrum Iesum
    Christum Filium tuum,
qui tecum vivit et regnat
    in unitate Spiritus Sancti,
Deus, per omnia sæcula sæculorum.

who lives and reigns with you
   in the unity of the Holy Spirit,
one God, for ever and ever.

FIRST READING

A reading from the prophet Amos   7:12-15

Go, prophesy to my people.

Amaziah, the priest of Bethel, said to Amos, 'Go away, seer; get back to the
land of Judah; earn your bread there, do your prophesying there. We want
no more prophesying in Bethel; this is the royal sanctuary, the national
temple.' 'I was no prophet, neither did I belong to any of the brotherhoods
of prophets,' Amos replied to Amaziah. 'I was a shepherd, and looked after
sycamores: but it was the Lord who took me from herding the flock, and
the Lord who said, "Go, prophesy to my people Israel."'

   The word of the Lord.

Responsorial Psalm   Ps 84:9-14. R. v.8

R. **Let us see, O Lord, your mercy**
   and give us your saving help.

   I will hear what the Lord God has to say,
   a voice that speaks of peace,
   peace for his people.
   His help is near for those who fear him
   and his glory will dwell in our land. R.

   Mercy and faithfulness have met;
   justice and peace have embraced.
   Faithfulness shall spring from the earth
   and justice look down from heaven. R.

   The Lord will make us prosper
   and our earth shall yield its fruit.
   Justice shall march before him
   and peace shall follow his steps. R.

SECOND READING

A reading from the letter of St Paul to the Ephesians   1:3-14

Before the world was made, God chose us.

[Blessed be God the Father of our Lord Jesus Christ,
who has blessed us with all the spiritual blessings of heaven in Christ.
Before the world was made, he chose us, chose us in Christ,
to be holy and spotless, and to live through love in his presence,
determining that we should become his adopted sons, through Jesus Christ
for his own kind purposes,

to make us praise the glory of his grace,
his free gift to us in the Beloved
in whom, through his blood, we gain our freedom, the forgiveness of our sins.
Such is the richness of the grace
which he has showered on us
in all wisdom and insight.
He has let us know the mystery of his purpose,
the hidden plan he so kindly made in Christ from the beginning
to act upon when the times had run their course to the end:
that he would bring everything together under Christ, as head
everything in the heavens and everything on earth.]

And it is in him that we were claimed as God's own,
chosen from the beginning,
under the predetermined plan of the one who guides all things
as he decides by his own will;
chosen to be,
for his greater glory,
the people who would put their hopes in Christ before he came.
Now you too, in him,
have heard the message of the truth and the good news of your salvation,
and have believed it:
and you too have been stamped with the seal of the Holy Spirit of the Promise,
the pledge of our inheritance
which brings freedom for those whom God has taken for his own,
to make his glory praised.

| [The word of the Lord.]

Shorter Form, verses 3-10. Read between [ ]

Gospel Acclamation   Cf. Jn 6:63,68

R. **Alleluia, alleluia!**
Your words are spirit, Lord,
and they are life:
you have the message of eternal life.
R. **Alleluia!**

Or: Cf. Ep 1:17,18

R. **Alleluia, alleluia!**
May the Father of our Lord Jesus Christ
enlighten the eyes of our mind
so that we can see what hope his call holds for us.
R. **Alleluia!**

GOSPEL

A reading from the holy Gospel according to Mark   6:7-13
He began to send them out.

Jesus summoned the Twelve and began to send them out in pairs giving
them authority over the unclean spirits. And he instructed them to take
nothing for the journey except a staff – no bread, no haversack, no coppers
for their purses. They were to wear sandals but, he added, 'Do not take a spare
tunic.' And he said to them, 'If you enter a house anywhere, stay there until
you leave the district. And if any place does not welcome you and people
refuse to listen to you, as you walk away shake off the dust from under your
feet as a sign to them.' So they set off to preach repentance; and they cast
out many devils, and anointed many sick people with oil and cured them.

The Gospel of the Lord.

Prayer over the Offerings	Super oblata

Look upon the offerings
   of the Church, O Lord,
as she makes her prayer to you,
and grant that, when consumed
   by those who believe,
they may bring ever greater holiness.
Through Christ our Lord.
	Respice, Domine, munera
	   supplicantis Ecclesiæ,
	et pro credentium
	   sanctificationis incremento
	sumenda concede.
	Per Christum Dominum nostrum.

Preface of Sundays in Ordinary Time I-VIII, pp.61-67.

Communion Antiphon Cf. Ps 83:4-5	Ant. ad communionem

The sparrow finds a home,
and the swallow a nest for her young:
by your altars, O Lord of hosts,
   my King and my God.
Blessed are they who dwell
   in your house,
for ever singing your praise.
	Passer invenit sibi domum,
	et turtur nidum,
	   ubi reponat pullos suos.
	Altaria tua, Domine virtutum,
	   Rex meus, et Deus meus!
	Beati qui habitant in domo tua,
	in sæculum sæculi laudabunt te.

Or: Jn 6:57	Vel:

Whoever eats my flesh and drinks
   my blood
remains in me and I in him,
   says the Lord.
	Qui manducat meam carnem
	   et bibit meum sanguinem,
	in me manet et ego in eo,
	   dicit Dominus.

Prayer after Communion	Post communionem
Having consumed these gifts, we pray, O Lord, that, by our participation in this mystery, its saving effects upon us may grow. Through Christ our Lord.	Sumptis muneribus, quæsumus, Domine, ut, cum frequentatione mysterii, crescat nostræ salutis effectus. Per Christum Dominum nostrum.

22 July

SIXTEENTH SUNDAY IN ORDINARY TIME

Entrance Antiphon Ps 53:6,8	Ant. ad introitum
SEE, I have God for my help. The Lord sustains my soul. I will sacrifice to you with willing heart, and praise your name, O Lord, for it is good.	ECCE Deus adiuvat me, et Dominus susceptor est animæ meæ. Voluntarie sacrificabo tibi, et confitebor nomini tuo, Domine, quoniam bonum est.

Collect	Collecta
Show favour, O Lord, to your servants and mercifully increase the gifts of your grace, that, made fervent in hope, faith and charity, they may be ever watchful in keeping your commands. Through our Lord Jesus Christ, your Son, who lives and reigns with you in the unity of the Holy Spirit, one God, for ever and ever.	Propitiare, Domine, famulis tuis, et clementer gratiæ tuæ super eos dona multiplica, ut, spe, fide et caritate ferventes, semper in mandatis tuis vigili custodia perseverent. Per Dominum nostrum Iesum Christum Filium tuum, qui tecum vivit et regnat in unitate Spiritus Sancti, Deus, per omnia sæcula sæculorum.

FIRST READING

A reading from the prophet Jeremiah   23:1-6

The remnant of my flock I will gather and I will raise up shepherds to look after them.

'Doom for the shepherds who allow the flock of my pasture to be destroyed and scattered – it is the Lord who speaks! This, therefore, is what the Lord,

the God of Israel, says about the shepherds in charge of my people: You
have let my flock be scattered and go wandering and have not taken care
of them. Right, I will take care of you for your misdeeds – it is the Lord
who speaks! But the remnant of my flock I myself will gather from all
the countries where I have dispersed them, and will bring them back to
their pastures: they shall be fruitful and increase in numbers. I will raise up
shepherds to look after them and pasture them; no fear, no terror for them
anymore; not one shall be lost – it is the Lord who speaks!

'See, the days are coming – it is the Lord who speaks –
when I will raise a virtuous Branch for David,
who will reign as true king and be wise,
practising honesty and integrity in the land.
In his days Judah will be saved
and Israel dwell in confidence.
And this is the name he will be called:
The Lord-our-integrity.'

The word of the Lord.

Responsial Psalm   Ps 22. R. v.1

R. **The Lord is my shepherd;**
   there is nothing I shall want.

The Lord is my shepherd;
there is nothing I shall want.
Fresh and green are the pastures
where he gives me repose.
Near restful waters he leads me,
to revive my drooping spirit. R.

He guides me along the right path;
he is true to his name.
If I should walk in the valley of darkness
no evil would I fear.
You are there with your crook and your staff;
with these you give me comfort. R.

You have prepared a banquet for me
in the sight of my foes.
My head you have anointed with oil;
my cup is overflowing. R.

Surely goodness and kindness shall follow me
all the days of my life.
In the Lord's own house shall I dwell
for ever and ever. R.

SECOND READING

A reading from the letter of St Paul to the Ephesians 2:13-18

Christ Jesus is the peace between us, and has made the two into one.

In Christ Jesus, you that used to be so far apart from us have been brought very close, by the blood of Christ. For he is the peace between us, and has made the two into one and broken down the barrier which used to keep them apart, actually destroying in his own person the hostility caused by the rules and decrees of the Law. This was to create one single New Man in himself out of the two of them and by restoring peace through the cross, to unite them both in a single Body and reconcile them with God. In his own person he killed the hostility. Later he came to bring the good news of peace, peace to you who were far away and peace to those who were near at hand. Through him, both of us have in the one Spirit our way to come to the Father.

The word of the Lord.

Gospel Acclamation Jn 10:27

R. **Alleluia, alleluia!**
The sheep that belong to me listen to my voice,
says the Lord,
I know them and they follow me.
R. **Alleluia!**

GOSPEL

A reading from the holy Gospel according to Mark 6:30-34

They were like sheep without a shepherd.

The apostles rejoined Jesus and told him all they had done and taught. Then he said to them, 'You must come away to some lonely place all by yourselves and rest for a while'; for there were so many coming and going that the apostles had no time even to eat. So they went off in a boat to a lonely place where they could be by themselves. But people saw them going, and many could guess where; and from every town they all hurried to the place on foot and reached it before them. So as he stepped ashore he saw a large crowd; and he took pity on them because they were like sheep without a shepherd, and he set himself to teach them at some length.

The Gospel of the Lord.

Prayer over the Offerings

O God, who in the one
   perfect sacrifice
brought to completion varied
   offerings of the law,
accept, we pray, this sacrifice
   from your faithful servants
and make it holy, as you blessed
   the gifts of Abel,
so that what each has offered
   to the honour of your majesty
may benefit the salvation of all.
Through Christ our Lord.

Super oblata

Deus, qui legalium
   differentiam hostiarum
unius sacrificii perfectione sanxisti,
accipe sacrificium a devotis
   tibi famulis,
et pari benedictione,
   sicut munera Abel, sanctifica,
ut, quod singuli obtulerunt
   ad maiestatis tuæ honorem,
cunctis proficiat ad salutem.
Per Christum Dominum nostrum.

Preface of Sundays in Ordinary Time I-VIII, pp.61-67.

Communion Antiphon Ps 110:4-5

The Lord, the gracious, the merciful,
has made a memorial of his wonders;
he gives food to those who fear him.

Ant. ad communionem

Memoriam fecit mirabilium suorum
misericors et miserator Dominus;
escam dedit timentibus se.

Or: Rv 3:20

Behold, I stand at the door
   and knock, says the Lord.
If anyone hears my voice
   and opens the door to me,
I will enter his house and dine
   with him, and he with me.

Vel:

Ecce sto ad ostium et pulso,
   dicit Dominus:
si quis audierit vocem meam,
   et aperuerit mihi ianuam,
intrabo ad illum, et cenabo
   cum illo, et ipse mecum.

Prayer after Communion

Graciously be present to your people,
   we pray, O Lord,
and lead those you have imbued
   with heavenly mysteries
to pass from former ways
   to newness of life.
Through Christ our Lord.

Post communionem

Populo tuo, quæsumus, Domine,
   adesto propitius,
et, quem mysteriis
   cælestibus imbuisti,
fac ad novitatem vitæ
   de vetustate transire.
Per Christum Dominum nostrum.

29 July

SEVENTEENTH SUNDAY IN ORDINARY TIME

Entrance Antiphon Cf. Ps 67:6-7,36

GOD is in his holy place,
God who unites those
    who dwell in his house;
he himself gives might and strength
    to his people.

Ant. ad introitum

DEUS in loco sancto suo;
Deus qui inhabitare facit
    unanimes in domo,
ipse dabit virtutem et fortitudinem
    plebi suæ.

Collect

O God, protector of those
    who hope in you,
without whom nothing has firm
    foundation, nothing is holy,
bestow in abundance your mercy
    upon us
and grant that, with you as our ruler
    and guide,
we may use the good things that pass
in such a way as to hold fast even now
to those that ever endure.
Through our Lord Jesus Christ,
    your Son,
who lives and reigns with you
    in the unity of the Holy Spirit,
one God, for ever and ever.

Collecta

Protector in te sperantium, Deus,
sine quo nihil est validum,
    nihil sanctum,
multiplica super nos
    misericordiam tuam
ut, te rectore, te duce, sic bonis
    transeuntibus nunc utamur,
ut iam possimus
    inhærere mansuris.
Per Dominum nostrum Iesum
    Christum Filium tuum,
qui tecum vivit et regnat
    in unitate Spiritus Sancti,
Deus, per omnia sæcula sæculorum.

FIRST READING

A reading from the second book of the Kings   4:42-44

They will eat and have some left over.

A man came from Baal-shalishah, bringing Elisha, the man of God, bread from the first-fruits, twenty barley loaves and fresh grain in the ear. 'Give it to the people to eat,' Elisha said. But his servant replied, 'How can l serve this to a hundred men?' 'Give it to the people to eat' he insisted 'for the Lord says this, "They will eat and have some left over."' He served them; they ate and had some over, as the Lord had said.

The word of the Lord.

Responsorial Psalm   Ps 144:10-11,15-18. R. v.16

R. **You open wide your hand, O Lord,**
   you grant our desires.

All your creatures shall thank you, O Lord
and your friends shall repeat their blessing.
They shall speak of the glory of your reign
and declare your might, O God. R.

The eyes of all creatures look to you
and you give them their food in due time.
You open wide your hand,
grant the desires of all who live. R.

The Lord is just in all his ways
and loving in all his deeds.
He is close to all who call him,
who call on him from their hearts. R.

SECOND READING

A reading from the letter of St Paul to the Ephesians   4:1-6
One Body, one Lord, one faith, one baptism.

I, the prisoner in the Lord, implore you to lead a life worthy of your
vocation. Bear with one another charitably, in complete selflessness,
gentleness and patience. Do all you can to preserve the unity of the Spirit
by the peace that binds you together. There is one Body, one Spirit, just
as you were all called into one and the same hope when you were called.
There is one Lord, one faith, one baptism, and one God who is Father of
all, through all and within all.

   The word of the Lord.

Gospel Acclamation   Cf. Jn 6:63,68

R. **Alleluia, alleluia!**
Your words are spirit, Lord,
and they are life:
you have the message of eternal life.
R. **Alleluia!**

Or: Lk 7:16

R. **Alleluia, alleluia!**
A great prophet has appeared among us;
God has visited his people.
R. **Alleluia!**

GOSPEL

A reading from the holy Gospel according to John   6:1-15

Jesus gave out as much as was wanted to all who were sitting ready.

Jesus went off to the other side of the Sea of Galilee – or of Tiberias – and a large crowd followed him, impressed by the signs he gave by curing the sick. Jesus climbed the hillside, and sat down there with his disciples. It was shortly before the Jewish feast of Passover.

Looking up, Jesus saw the crowds approaching and said to Philip, 'Where can we buy some bread for these people to eat?' He only said this to test Philip; he himself knew exactly what he was going to do. Philip answered, 'Two hundred denarii would only buy enough to give them a small piece each.' One of his disciples, Andrew, Simon Peter's brother, said, 'There is a small boy here with five barley loaves and two fish; but what is that between so many?' Jesus said to them, 'Make the people sit down.' There was plenty of grass there, and as many as five thousand men sat down. Then Jesus took the loaves, gave thanks, and gave them out to all who were sitting ready; he then did the same with the fish, giving out as much as was wanted. When they had eaten enough he said to the disciples, 'Pick up the pieces left over, so that nothing gets wasted.' So they picked them up, and filled twelve hampers with scraps left over from the meal of five barley loaves. The people, seeing this sign that he had given, said, 'This really is the prophet who is to come into the world.' Jesus, who could see they were about to come and take him by force and make him king, escaped back to the hills by himself.

The Gospel of the Lord.

Prayer over the Offerings	Super oblata
Accept, O Lord, we pray, the offerings which we bring from the abundance of your gifts, that through the powerful working of your grace these most sacred mysteries may sanctify our present way of life and lead us to eternal gladness. Through Christ our Lord.	Suscipe, quæsumus, Domine, munera, quæ tibi de tua largitate deferimus, ut hæc sacrosancta mysteria, gratiæ tuæ operante virtute, et præsentis vitæ nos conversatione sanctificent, et ad gaudia sempiterna perducant. Per Christum Dominum nostrum.

Preface of Sundays in Ordinary Time I-VIII, pp.61-67.

Communion Antiphon Ps 102:2	Ant. ad communionem
Bless the Lord, O my soul, and never forget all his benefits.	Benedic, anima mea, Domino, et noli oblivisci omnes retributiones eius.
Or: Mt 5:7-8	Vel:

Blessed are the merciful,
    for they shall receive mercy.
Blessed are the clean of heart,
    for they shall see God.
	Beati misericordes,
	quoniam ipsi
	    misericordiam consequentur.
	Beati mundo corde,
	quoniam ipsi Deum videbunt.

Prayer after Communion	Post communionem

We have consumed, O Lord,
    this divine Sacrament,
the perpetual memorial
    of the Passion of your Son;
grant, we pray, that this gift,
which he himself gave us with love
    beyond all telling,
may profit us for salvation.
Through Christ our Lord.
	Sumpsimus, Domine,
	    divinum sacramentum,
	passionis Filii tui
	    memoriale perpetuum;
	tribue, quæsumus,
	ut ad nostram salutem hoc
	    munus proficiat,
	quod ineffabili nobis caritate
	    ipse donavit.
	Qui vivit et regnat
	    in sæcula sæculorum.

5 August

EIGHTEENTH SUNDAY IN ORDINARY TIME

Entrance Antiphon Ps 69:2,6	Ant. ad introitum
O GOD, come to my assistance; O Lord, make haste to help me! You are my rescuer, my help; O Lord, do not delay.	DEUS, in adiutorium meum intende; Domine, ad adiuvandum me festina. Adiutor meus et liberator meus es tu; Domine, ne moreris.

Collect

Draw near to your servants, O Lord,
and answer their prayers
    with unceasing kindness,
that, for those who glory in you
    as their Creator and guide,
you may restore what you
    have created
and keep safe what you have restored.
Through our Lord Jesus Christ,
    your Son,
who lives and reigns with you
    in the unity of the Holy Spirit,
one God, for ever and ever.

Collecta

Adesto, Domine, famulis tuis,
et perpetuam benignitatem
    largire poscentibus,
ut his, qui te auctorem et
    gubernatorem gloriantur habere,
et creata restaures,
    et restaurata conserves.
Per Dominum nostrum Iesum
    Christum Filium tuum,
qui tecum vivit et regnat
    in unitate Spiritus Sancti,
Deus, per omnia sæcula sæculorum.

FIRST READING

A reading from the book of Exodus   16:2-4,12-15

I will rain down bread for you from the heavens.

The whole community of the sons of Israel began to complain against Moses and Aaron in the wilderness and said to them, 'Why did we not die at the Lord's hand in the land of Egypt, when we were able to sit down to pans of meat and could eat bread to our heart's content! As it is, you have brought us to this wilderness to starve this whole company to death!'

Then the Lord said to Moses, 'Now I will rain down bread for you from the heavens. Each day the people are to go out and gather the day's portion; I proposed to test them in this way to see whether they will follow my law or not.'

'I have heard the complaints of the sons of Israel. Say this to them, "Between the two evenings you shall eat meat, and in the morning you shall have bread to your heart's content. Then you will learn that I, the Lord, am your God."' And so it came about: quails flew up in the evening, and they covered the camp; in the morning there was a coating of dew all round the camp. When the coating of dew lifted, there on the surface of the desert was a thing delicate, powdery, as fine as hoarfrost on the ground. When they saw this, the sons of Israel said to one another, 'What is that?' not knowing what it was. 'That' said Moses to them 'is the bread the Lord gives you to eat.'

The word of the Lord.

Responsorial Psalm   Ps 77:3-4,23-25,54. R. v.24

R. **The Lord gave them bread from heaven.**

The things we have heard and understood,
the things our fathers have told us,
we will tell to the next generation:
the glories of the Lord and his might. R.

He commanded the clouds above
and opened the gates of heaven.
He rained down manna for their food,
and gave them bread from heaven. R.

Mere men ate the bread of angels.
He sent them abundance of food.
He brought them to his holy land,
to the mountain which his right hand had won. R.

SECOND READING

A reading from the letter of St Paul to the Ephesians   4:17,20-24
Put on the new self that has been created in God's way.

I want to urge you in the name of the Lord, not to go on living the aimless
kind of life that pagans live. Now that is hardly the way you have learnt
from Christ, unless you failed to hear him properly when you were taught
what the truth is in Jesus. You must give up your old way of life; you must
put aside your old self, which gets corrupted by following illusory desires.
Your mind must be renewed by a spiritual revolution so that you can put
on the new self that has been created in God's way, in the goodness and
holiness of the truth.

The word of the Lord.

Gospel Acclamation   Jn 14:5

R. **Alleluia, alleluia!**
I am the Way, the Truth and the Life, says the Lord;
no one can come to the Father except through me.
R. **Alleluia!**

Or: Mt 4:4

R. **Alleluia, alleluia!**
Man does not live on bread alone,
but on every word that comes from the mouth of God.
R. **Alleluia!**

GOSPEL

A reading from the holy Gospel according to John 6:24-35

He who comes to me will never be hungry; he who believes in me will never thirst.

When the people saw that neither Jesus nor his disciples were there, they got into boats and crossed to Capernaum to look for Jesus. When they found him on the other side, they said to him, 'Rabbi, when did you come here?' Jesus answered:

'I tell you most solemnly,
you are not looking for me
because you have seen the signs
but because you had all the bread you wanted to eat.
Do not work for food that cannot last,
but work for food that endures to eternal life,
the kind of food the Son of Man is offering you,
for on him the Father, God himself, has set his seal.'

Then they said to him, 'What must we do if we are to do the works that God wants?' Jesus gave them this answer, 'This is working for God: you must believe in the one he has sent.' So they said, 'What sign will you give to show us that we should believe in you? What work will you do? Our fathers had manna to eat in the desert; as scripture says: He gave them bread from heaven to eat.'

Jesus answered:
'I tell you most solemnly,
it was not Moses who gave you bread from heaven,
it is my Father who gives you the bread from heaven,
the true bread;
for the bread of God
is that which comes down from heaven
and gives life to the world.'

'Sir,' they said 'give us that bread always.' Jesus answered:
'I am the bread of life.
He who comes to me will never be hungry;
he who believes in me will never thirst.'

The Gospel of the Lord.

Prayer over the Offerings

Graciously sanctify these gifts,
    O Lord, we pray,
and, accepting the oblation
    of this spiritual sacrifice,
make of us an eternal offering to you.
Through Christ our Lord.

Super oblata

Propitius, Domine, quæsumus,
    hæc dona sanctifica,
et, hostiæ spiritalis
    oblatione suscepta,
nosmetipsos tibi perfice
    munus æternum.
Per Christum Dominum nostrum.

Preface of Sundays in Ordinary Time I-VIII, pp.61-67.

Communion Antiphon   Wis 16:20

You have given us, O Lord,
    bread from heaven,
endowed with all delights
    and sweetness in every taste.

Ant. ad communionem

Panem de cælo dedisti
    nobis, Domine,
habentem omne delectamentum,
et omnem saporem suavitatis.

Or: Jn 6:35

I am the bread of life, says the Lord;
whoever comes to me will not hunger
and whoever believes in me
    will not thirst.

Vel:

Ego sum panis vitæ, dicit Dominus.
Qui venit ad me non esuriet,
    et qui credit in me non sitiet.

Prayer after Communion

Accompany with constant
    protection, O Lord,
those you renew with these
    heavenly gifts
and, in your never-failing care
    for them,
make them worthy
    of eternal redemption.
Through Christ our Lord.

Post communionem

Quos cælesti recreas munere,
perpetuo, Domine,
    comitare præsidio,
et, quos fovere non desinis,
dignos fieri sempiterna
    redemptione concede.
Per Christum Dominum nostrum.

12 August

NINETEENTH SUNDAY IN ORDINARY TIME

Entrance Antiphon Cf. Ps 73:20,19,22,23 | Ant. ad introitum

LOOK to your covenant, O Lord,
and forget not the life of your
  poor ones for ever.
Arise, O God, and defend your cause,
and forget not the cries of those
  who seek you.

RESPICE, Domine,
in testamentum tuum,
et animas pauperum tuorum
  ne derelinquas in finem.
Exsurge, Domine,
  et iudica causam tuam,
et ne obliviscaris voces
  quærentium te.

Collect | Collecta

Almighty ever-living God,
whom, taught by the Holy Spirit,
we dare to call our Father,
bring, we pray, to perfection
  in our hearts
the spirit of adoption as your sons
  and daughters,
that we may merit to enter
  into the inheritance
which you have promised.
Through our Lord Jesus Christ,
  your Son,
who lives and reigns with you
  in the unity of the Holy Spirit,
one God, for ever and ever.

Omnipotens sempiterne Deus,
quem, docente Spiritu Sancto,
paterno nomine
  invocare præsumimus,
perfice in cordibus nostris spiritum
  adoptionis filiorum,
ut promissam hereditatem
  ingredi mereamur.
Per Dominum nostrum Iesum
  Christum Filium tuum,
qui tecum vivit et regnat
  in unitate Spiritus Sancti,
Deus, per omnia sæcula sæculorum.

FIRST READING

A reading from the first book of Kings   19:4-8

Strengthened by the food he walked until he reached the mountain of God.

Elijah went into the wilderness, a day's journey, and sitting under a furze
bush wished he were dead. 'Lord,' he said 'I have had enough. Take my life;
I am no better than my ancestors.' Then he lay down and went to sleep.
But an angel touched him and said, 'Get up and eat.' He looked round, and
there at his head was a scone baked on hot stones, and a jar of water. He ate

and drank and then lay down again. But the angel of the Lord came back a second time and touched him and said, 'Get up and eat, or the journey will be too long for you.' So he got up and ate and drank, and strengthened by that food he walked for forty days and forty nights until he reached Horeb, the mountain of God.

The word of the Lord.

Responsorial Psalm   Ps 33:2-9. R. v.9

R. **Taste and see that the Lord is good.**

I will bless the Lord at all times,
his praise always on my lips;
in the Lord my soul shall make its boast.
The humble shall hear and be glad. R.

Glorify the Lord with me.
Together let us praise his name.
I sought the Lord and he answered me;
from all my terrors he set me free. R.

Look towards him and be radiant;
let your faces not be abashed.
This poor man called; the Lord heard him
and rescued him from all his distress. R.

The angel of the Lord is encamped
around those who revere him, to rescue them.
Taste and see that the Lord is good.
He is happy who seeks refuge in him. R.

SECOND READING

A reading from the letter of St Paul to the Ephesians   4:30-5:2
Follow Christ by loving as he loved you.

Do not grieve the Holy Spirit of God who has marked you with his seal for you to be set free when the day comes. Never have grudges against others, or lose your temper, or raise your voice to anybody, or call each other names, or allow any sort of spitefulness. Be friends with one another, and kind, forgiving each other as readily as God forgave you in Christ.

Try, then, to imitate God, as children of his that he loves, and follow Christ by loving as he loved you, giving himself up in our place as a fragrant offering and a sacrifice to God.

The word of the Lord.

Gospel Acclamation   Jn 14:23

R. **Alleluia, alleluia!**
If anyone loves me he will keep my word,
and my Father will love him,
and we shall come to him.
R. **Alleluia!**

Or: Jn 6:51

R. **Alleluia, alleluia!**
I am the living bread which has come down from heaven,
says the Lord.
Anyone who eats this bread will live for ever.
R. **Alleluia!**

GOSPEL

A reading from the holy Gospel according to John   6:41-51

I am the living bread which has come down from heaven.

The Jews were complaining to each other about Jesus, because he had said,
'I am the bread that came down from heaven.' 'Surely this is Jesus son of
Joseph' they said. 'We know his father and mother. How can he now say,
"I have come down from heaven"?' Jesus said in reply, 'Stop complaining
to each other.

'No one can come to me
unless he is drawn by the Father who sent me,
and I will raise him up at the last day.
It is written in the prophets:
They will all be taught by God,
and to hear the teaching of the Father,
and learn from it,
is to come to me.
Not that anybody has seen the Father,
except the one who comes from God:
he has seen the Father.
I tell you most solemnly,
everybody who believes has eternal life.
I am the bread of life.
Your fathers ate the manna in the desert
and they are dead;
but this is the bread that comes down from heaven,
so that a man may eat it and not die.
I am the living bread which has come down from heaven.

Anyone who eats this bread will live for ever;
and the bread that I shall give
is my flesh, for the life of the world.'
The Gospel of the Lord.

Prayer over the Offerings

Be pleased, O Lord, to accept
    the offerings of your Church,
for in your mercy you have given
    them to be offered
and by your power
    you transform them
into the mystery of our salvation.
Through Christ our Lord.

Super oblata

Ecclesiæ tuæ, Domine,
    munera placatus assume,
quæ et misericors
    offerenda tribuisti,
et in nostræ salutis potenter efficis
    transire mysterium.
Per Christum Dominum nostrum.

Preface of Sundays in Ordinary Time I-VIII, pp.61-67.

Communion Antiphon Ps 147:12,14

O Jerusalem, glorify the Lord,
who gives you your fill
    of finest wheat.

Ant. ad communionem

Lauda, Ierusalem, Dominum,
qui adipe frumenti satiat te.

Or: Cf. Jn 6:51

The bread that I will give,
    says the Lord,
is my flesh for the life of the world.

Vel:

Panis, quem ego dedero,
caro mea est pro sæculi vita,
dicit Dominus.

Prayer after Communion

May the communion
    in your Sacrament
that we have consumed, save us,
    O Lord,
and confirm us in the light
    of your truth.
Through Christ our Lord.

Post communionem

Sacramentorum tuorum, Domine,
communio sumpta nos salvet,
et in tuæ veritatis luce confirmet.
Per Christum Dominum nostrum.

15 August

THE ASSUMPTION
OF THE BLESSED VIRGIN MARY

The Assumption of Mary is a great mystery which regards each one of us, it regards our future. Mary, in fact, precedes us on the path walked upon by those who, through their Baptism, have bound their life to Jesus, as Mary bound her own life to him. Today's feast makes us look to heaven, foretells the "new heaven and new earth", with the Risen Christ's victory over death and the definitive defeat of evil. Therefore, the exultation of the humble maiden of Galilee, expressed in the Canticle of the Magnificat, *becomes the song of all humanity, which sees with satisfaction the Lord stoop over all men and all women, humble creatures, and assume them with him into heaven.*

(Pope Francis)

Solemnity

At the Vigil Mass

This Mass is used on the evening before the Solemnity, either before or after First Vespers (Evening Prayer I) of the Solemnity.

Entrance Antiphon	Ant. ad introitum
GLORIOUS things are spoken of you, O Mary, who today were exalted above the choirs of Angels into eternal triumph with Christ.	GLORIOSA dicta sunt de te, Maria, quæ hodie exaltata es super choros Angelorum, et in æternum cum Christo triumphas.

The Gloria in excelsis (Glory to God in the highest) is said.

Collect	Collecta
O God, who, looking on the lowliness of the Blessed Virgin Mary, raised her to this grace, that your Only Begotten Son was born of her according to the flesh	Deus, qui beatam Virginem Mariam, eius humilitatem respiciens, ad hanc gratiam evexisti, ut Unigenitus tuus ex ipsa secundum carnem nasceretur,

and that she was crowned this day with surpassing glory,	et hodierna die superexcellenti gloria coronasti,
grant through her prayers,	eius nobis precibus concede,
that, saved by the mystery of your redemption,	ut, redemptionis tuæ mysterio salvati,
we may merit to be exalted by you on high.	a te exaltari mereamur.
Through our Lord Jesus Christ, your Son,	Per Dominum nostrum Iesum Christum Filium tuum,
who lives and reigns with you in the unity of the Holy Spirit,	qui tecum vivit et regnat in unitate Spiritus Sancti,
one God, for ever and ever.	Deus, per omnia sæcula sæculorum.

FIRST READING

A reading from the first book of Chronicles   15:3-4,15-16; 16:1-2

They brought in the ark of God and set it inside the tent which David had pitched for it.

David gathered all Israel together in Jerusalem to bring the ark of God up to the place he had prepared for it. David called together the sons of Aaron and the sons of Levi. And the Levites carried the ark of God with the shafts on their shoulders, as Moses had ordered in accordance with the word of the Lord.

David then told the heads of the Levites to assign duties for their kinsmen as cantors, with their various instruments of music, harps and lyres and cymbals, to play joyful tunes. They brought the ark of God in and put it inside the tent that David had pitched for it; and they offered holocausts before God, and communion sacrifices. And when David had finished offering holocausts and communion sacrifices, he blessed the people in the name of the Lord.

The word of the Lord.

Responsorial Psalm   Ps 131:6-7,9-10,13-14. R. v.8

R. **Go up, Lord, to the place of your rest,**
   you and the ark of your strength.

   At Ephrata we heard of the ark;
   we found it in the plains of Yearim.
   'Let us go to the place of his dwelling;
   let us go to kneel at his footstool.' R.

Your priests shall be clothed with holiness:
your faithful shall ring out their joy.
For the sake of David your servant
do not reject your anointed. R.

For the Lord has chosen Zion;
he has desired it for his dwelling:
'This is my resting-place for ever,
here have I chosen to live.' R.

SECOND READING

A reading from the first letter of St Paul to the Corinthians   15:54-57
He gave us victory through our Lord Jesus Christ.

When this perishable nature has put on imperishability, and when this
mortal nature has put on immortality, then the words of scripture will
come true: Death is swallowed up in victory. Death, where is your victory?
Death, where is your sting? Now the sting of death is sin, and sin gets its
power from the Law. So let us thank God for giving us the victory through
our Lord Jesus Christ.

   The word of the Lord.

Gospel Acclamation   Lk 11:28

R. **Alleluia, alleluia!**
Happy are those
who hear the word of God,
and keep it.
R. **Alleluia!**

GOSPEL

A reading from the holy Gospel according to Luke   11:27-28
Happy the womb that bore you!

As Jesus was speaking, a woman in the crowd raised her voice and said,
'Happy the womb that bore you and the breasts you sucked!' But he
replied, 'Still happier those who hear the word of God and keep it!'

   The Gospel of the Lord.

The Creed is said.

Prayer over the Offerings

Receive, we pray, O Lord,
the sacrifice of conciliation
    and praise,
which we celebrate on
    the Assumption of the holy
    Mother of God,
that it may lead us to your pardon
and confirm us in perpetual
    thanksgiving.
Through Christ our Lord.

Proper Preface, as in the following Mass, p.552.

Communion Antiphon Cf. Lk 11:27

Blessed is the womb
    of the Virgin Mary,
which bore the Son
    of the eternal Father.

Prayer after Communion

Having partaken of this
    heavenly table,
we beseech your mercy,
    Lord our God,
that we, who honour
    the Assumption of the Mother
    of God,
may be freed from every threat
    of harm.
Through Christ our Lord.

A formula of Solemn Blessing, pp.144-145, may be used.

Super oblata

Suscipe, quæsumus, Domine,
sacrificium placationis et laudis,
quod in sanctæ Dei Genetricis
    Assumptione celebramus,
ut ad veniam nos
    obtinendam perducat,
et in perpetua gratiarum
    constituat actione.
Per Christum Dominum nostrum.

Ant. ad communionem

Beata viscera Mariæ Virginis,
quæ portaverunt æterni
    Patris Filium.

Post communionem

Mensæ cælestis participes effecti,
imploramus clementiam tuam,
    Domine Deus noster,
ut, qui Assumptionem Dei
    Genetricis colimus,
a cunctis malis
    imminentibus liberemur.
Per Christum Dominum nostrum.

At the Mass during the Day

Entrance Antiphon   Cf. Rv 12:1

A GREAT sign appeared
in heaven:
a woman clothed with the sun,
    and the moon beneath her feet,
and on her head a crown
    of twelve stars.

Ant. ad introitum

S IGNUM magnum apparuit
in cælo:
mulier amicta sole, et luna sub
    pedibus eius,
et in capite eius corona
    stellarum duodecim.

Or: | Vel:

Let us all rejoice in the Lord,
as we celebrate the feast day
   in honour of the Virgin Mary,
at whose Assumption
   the Angels rejoice
and praise the Son of God.

Gaudeamus omnes in Domino,
diem festum celebrantes sub
   honore Mariæ Virginis,
de cuius Assumptione
   gaudent Angeli,
et collaudant Filium Dei.

The Gloria in excelsis (Glory to God in the highest) is said.

Collect | Collecta

Almighty ever-living God,
who assumed the Immaculate Virgin
   Mary, the Mother of your Son,
body and soul into heavenly glory,
grant, we pray,
that, always attentive to the things
   that are above,
we may merit to be sharers
   of her glory.
Through our Lord Jesus Christ,
   your Son,
who lives and reigns with you
   in the unity of the Holy Spirit,
one God, for ever and ever.

Omnipotens sempiterne Deus,
qui immaculatam Virginem
   Mariam, Filii tui Genetricem,
corpore et anima ad cælestem
   gloriam assumpsisti,
concede, quæsumus, ut,
   ad superna semper intenti,
ipsius gloriæ mereamur
   esse consortes.
Per Dominum nostrum Iesum
   Christum Filium tuum,
qui tecum vivit et regnat
in unitate Spiritus Sancti,
Deus, per omnia sæcula sæculorum.

FIRST READING

A reading from the book of the Apocalypse   11:19; 12:1-6,10

A woman adorned with the sun standing on the moon.

The sanctuary of God in heaven opened, and the ark of the covenant could be seen inside it.

Now a great sign appeared in heaven: a woman, adorned with the sun, standing on the moon, and with the twelve stars on her head for a crown. She was pregnant, and in labour, crying aloud in the pangs of childbirth. Then a second sign appeared in the sky, a huge red dragon which had seven heads and ten horns, and each of the seven heads crowned with a coronet. Its tail dragged a third of the stars from the sky and dropped them to the earth, and the dragon stopped in front of the woman as she was having the child, so that he could eat it as soon as it was born from its mother. The woman brought a male child into the world, the son who was to rule all nations with an iron sceptre, and the child was taken straight up to God and to his throne, while the woman escaped into the desert, where God had made a place of safety ready. Then I heard a voice shout from heaven, 'Victory and power and empire for ever have been won by our God, and all authority for his Christ.'

The word of the Lord.

Responsorial Psalm   Ps 44:10-12,16. R. v.10

R. **On your right stands the queen,
    in garments of gold.**

The daughters of kings are among your loved ones.
On your right stands the queen in gold of Ophir.
Listen, O daughter, give ear to my words:
forget your own people and your father's house. R.

So will the king desire your beauty:
He is your lord, pay homage to him.
They are escorted amid gladness and joy;
they pass within the palace of the king. R.

SECOND READING

A reading from the first letter of St Paul to the Corinthians   15:20-26
Christ as the first-fruits and then, those who belong to him.

Christ has been raised from the dead, the first-fruits of all who have fallen asleep. Death came through one man and in the same way the resurrection of the dead has come through one man. Just as all men die in Adam, so all men will be brought to life in Christ; but all of them in their proper order: Christ as the first-fruits and then, after the coming of Christ, those who belong to him. After that will come the end, when he hands over the kingdom to God the Father, having done away with every sovereignty, authority and power. For he must be king until he has put all his enemies under his feet and the last of the enemies to be destroyed is death, for everything is to be put under his feet.

The word of the Lord.

Gospel Acclamation

R. **Alleluia, alleluia!**
Mary has been taken up into heaven;
all the choirs of angels are rejoicing.
R. **Alleluia!**

GOSPEL

A reading from the holy Gospel according to Luke   1:39-56
The Almighty has done great things for me, he has exalted up the lowly.

Mary set out and went as quickly as she could to a town in the hill country
of Judah. She went into Zechariah's house and greeted Elizabeth. Now as
soon as Elizabeth heard Mary's greeting, the child leapt in her womb and
Elizabeth was filled with the Holy Spirit. She gave a loud cry and said, 'Of
all women you are the most blessed, and blessed is the fruit of your womb.
Why should I be honoured with a visit from the mother of my Lord? For
the moment your greeting reached my ears, the child in my womb leapt
for joy. Yes, blessed is she who believed that the promise made her by the
Lord would be fulfilled.'

And Mary said:

'My soul proclaims the greatness of the Lord
and my spirit exults in God my saviour;
because he has looked upon his lowly handmaid.
Yes, from this day forward all generations will call me blessed,
for the Almighty has done great things for me.
Holy is his name,
and his mercy reaches from age to age for those who fear him.
He has shown the power of his arm,
he has routed the proud of heart.
He has pulled down princes from their thrones and exalted the lowly.
The hungry he has filled with good things, the rich sent empty away.
He has come to the help of Israel his servant, mindful of his mercy
– according to the promise he made to our ancestors –
of his mercy to Abraham and to his descendants for ever.'

Mary stayed with Elizabeth about three months and then went back home.

The Gospel of the Lord.

The Creed is said.

Prayer over the Offerings

May this oblation, our tribute
  of homage,
rise up to you, O Lord,
and, through the intercession
  of the most Blessed Virgin Mary,
whom you assumed into heaven,
may our hearts,
  aflame with the fire of love,
constantly long for you.
Through Christ our Lord.

Preface: The Glory of Mary assumed into heaven.

It is truly right and just, our duty
  and our salvation,
always and everywhere to give
  you thanks,
Lord, holy Father, almighty
  and eternal God,
through Christ our Lord.

For today the Virgin Mother of God
was assumed into heaven
as the beginning and image
of your Church's coming
  to perfection
and a sign of sure hope and comfort
  to your pilgrim people;
rightly you would not allow her
to see the corruption of the tomb,
since from her own body she
  marvellously brought forth
your incarnate Son,
  the Author of all life.

And so, in company with the choirs
  of Angels,
we praise you, and with joy
  we proclaim:

Holy, Holy, Holy Lord God of hosts...

Super oblata

Ascendat ad te, Domine, nostræ
  devotionis oblatio,
et, beatissima Virgine Maria
in cælum assumpta intercedente,
corda nostra, caritatis igne succensa,
ad te iugiter aspirent.
Per Christum Dominum nostrum.

Præfatio: De Gloria Mariæ Assumptæ.

Vere dignum et iustum est,
  æquum et salutare,
nos tibi semper et ubique
  gratias agere:
Domine, sancte Pater,
  omnipotens æterne Deus:
per Christum Dominum nostrum.

Quoniam hodie Virgo Deipara
  in cælos assumpta est,
Ecclesiæ tuæ consummandæ
  initium et imago,
ac populo peregrinanti certæ spei
  et solacii documentum;
corruptionem enim sepulcri
eam videre merito noluisti,
quæ Filium tuum,
  vitæ omnis auctorem,
ineffabiliter de se
  genuit incarnatum.

Et ideo, choris angelicis sociati,
te laudamus, in gaudio confitentes:

Sanctus, Sanctus, Sanctus. . .

Communion Antiphon Lk 1:48-49

All generations will call me blessed,
for he who is mighty has done
     great things for me.

Prayer after Communion

Having received the Sacrament
     of salvation,
we ask you to grant, O Lord,
that, through the intercession
     of the Blessed Virgin Mary,
whom you assumed into heaven,
we may be brought to the glory
     of the resurrection.
Through Christ our Lord.

Ant. ad communionem

Beatam me dicent
     omnes generationes,
quia fecit mihi magna
     qui potens est.

Post communionem

Sumptis, Domine,
     salutaribus sacramentis,
da, quæsumus,
ut, intercessione beatæ Mariæ
     Virginis in cælum assumptæ,
ad resurrectionis
     gloriam perducamur.
Per Christum Dominum nostrum.

A formula of Solemn Blessing, p.144-145, may be used.

19 August

TWENTIETH SUNDAY IN ORDINARY TIME

Entrance Antiphon   Ps 83:10-11

TURN your eyes, O God,
    our shield;
and look on the face
    of your anointed one;
one day within your courts
is better than a thousand elsewhere.

Ant. ad introitum

PROTECTOR noster,
    aspice, Deus,
et respice in faciem Christi tui,
quia melior est dies una in atriis
    tuis super millia.

Collect

O God, who have prepared
    for those who love you
good things which no eye can see,
fill our hearts, we pray,
    with the warmth of your love,
so that, loving you in all things
    and above all things,
we may attain your promises,
which surpass every human desire.
Through our Lord Jesus Christ,
    your Son,
who lives and reigns with you
    in the unity of the Holy Spirit,
one God, for ever and ever.

Collecta

Deus, qui diligentibus te bona
    invisibilia præparasti,
infunde cordibus nostris
    tui amoris affectum,
ut, te in omnibus et super
    omnia diligentes,
promissiones tuas, quæ omne
    desiderium superant,
consequamur.
Per Dominum nostrum Iesum
    Christum Filium tuum,
qui tecum vivit et regnat
    in unitate Spiritus Sancti,
Deus, per omnia sæcula sæculorum.

FIRST READING

A reading from the book of Proverbs   9:1-6

Eat my bread, drink the wine I have prepared for you.

Wisdom has built herself a house,
she has erected her seven pillars,
she has slaughtered her beasts, prepared her wine,
she has laid her table.
She has despatched her maidservants
and proclaimed from the city's heights:
'Who is ignorant? Let him step this way.'

To the fool she says,
'Come and eat my bread,
drink the wine I have prepared!
Leave your folly and you will live,
walk in the ways of perception.'

    The word of the Lord.

Responsorial Psalm   Ps 33:2-3,10-15. R. v.9

R. **Taste and see the Lord is good.**

    I will bless the Lord at all times,
    his praise always on my lips;
    in the Lord my soul shall make its boast.
    The humble shall hear and be glad. R.

    Revere the Lord, you his saints.
    They lack nothing, those who revere him.
    Strong lions suffer want and go hungry
    but those who seek the Lord lack no blessing. R.

    Come, children, and hear me
    that I may teach you the fear of the Lord.
    Who is he who longs for life
    and many days, to enjoy his prosperity? R.

    Then keep your tongue from evil
    and your lips from speaking deceit.
    Turn aside from evil and do good;
    seek and strive after peace. R.

SECOND READING

A reading from the letter of St Paul to the Ephesians   5:15-20
Recognise what is the will of God.

Be very careful about the sort of lives you lead, like intelligent and not like
senseless people. This may be a wicked age, but your lives should redeem
it. And do not be thoughtless but recognise what is the will of the Lord.
Do not drug yourselves with wine, this is simply dissipation; be filled with
the Spirit. Sing the words and tunes of the psalms and hymns when you
are together, and go on singing and chanting to the Lord in your hearts, so
that always and everywhere you are giving thanks to God who is our Father
in the name of our Lord Jesus Christ.

    The word of the Lord.

Gospel Acclamation   Jn 1:14,12

R. **Alleluia, alleluia!**
The Word was made flesh and lived among us;
to all who did accept him
he gave power to become children of God.
R. **Alleluia!**

Or: Jn 6:56

R. **Alleluia, alleluia!**
He who eats my flesh and drinks my blood
lives in me, and I live in him,
says the Lord.
R. **Alleluia!**

GOSPEL

A reading from the holy Gospel according to John   6:51-58
My flesh is real food and my blood is real drink.

Jesus said to the crowd:

'I am the living bread which has come down from heaven.
Anyone who eats this bread will live for ever;
and the bread that I shall give
is my flesh, for the life of the world.'

Then the Jews started arguing with one another: 'How can this man give
us his flesh to eat?' they said. Jesus replied:

'I tell you most solemnly,
if you do not eat the flesh of the Son of Man
and drink his blood,
you will not have life in you.
Anyone who does eat my flesh and drink my blood
has eternal life,
and I shall raise him up on the last day.
For my flesh is real food
and my blood is real drink.
He who eats my flesh and drinks my blood
lives in me
and I live in him.
As I, who am sent by the living Father,
myself draw life from the Father,
so whoever eats me will draw life from me.

> This the bread come down from heaven;
> not like the bread our ancestors ate:
> they are dead,
> but anyone who eats this bread will live for ever.'

The Gospel of the Lord.

Prayer over the Offerings	Super oblata

Receive our oblation, O Lord,
by which is brought about
  a glorious exchange,
that, by offering what you have given,
we may merit to receive
  your very self.
Through Christ our Lord.
	Suscipe, Domine, munera nostra,
	quibus exercentur
	  commercia gloriosa,
	ut, offerentes quæ dedisti,
	teipsum mereamur accipere.
	Per Christum Dominum nostrum.

Preface of Sundays in Ordinary Time I-VIII, pp.61-67.

Communion Antiphon Ps 129:7	Ant. ad communionem
With the Lord there is mercy; in him is plentiful redemption.	Apud Dominum misericordia, et copiosa apud eum redemptio.

Or: Jn 6:51	Vel:

I am the living bread that came
  down from heaven, says the Lord.
Whoever eats of this bread
  will live for ever.
	Ego sum panis vivus, qui de cælo
	  descendi, dicit Dominus:
	si quis manducaverit ex hoc pane,
	  vivet in æternum.

Prayer after Communion	Post communionem

Made partakers of Christ through
  these Sacraments,
we humbly implore your
  mercy, Lord,
that, conformed to his image
  on earth,
we may merit also to be his coheirs
  in heaven.
Who lives and reigns
  for ever and ever.
	Per hæc sacramenta, Domine,
	  Christi participes effecti,
	clementiam tuam
	  humiliter imploramus,
	ut, eius imaginis conformes
	  in terris,
	et eius consortes in cælis
	  fieri mereamur.
	Qui vivit et regnat
	  in sæcula sæculorum.

26 August

TWENTY-FIRST SUNDAY IN ORDINARY TIME

Entrance Antiphon   Cf. Ps 85:1-3 | Ant. ad introitum

TURN your ear, O Lord,
and answer me;
save the servant who trusts in you,
  my God.
Have mercy on me, O Lord,
  for I cry to you all the day long.

INCLINA, Domine, aurem tuam
ad me, et exaudi me.
Salvum fac servum tuum,
  Deus meus, sperantem in te.
Miserere mihi, Domine,
  quoniam ad te clamavi tota die.

Collect | Collecta

O God, who cause the minds
  of the faithful
to unite in a single purpose,
grant your people to love
  what you command
and to desire what you promise,
that, amid the uncertainties
  of this world,
our hearts may be fixed on that place
where true gladness is found.
Through our Lord Jesus Christ,
  your Son,
who lives and reigns with you
  in the unity of the Holy Spirit,
one God, for ever and ever.

Deus, qui fidelium mentes unius
  efficis voluntatis,
da populis tuis id amare
  quod præcipis,
id desiderare quod promittis,
ut, inter mundanas varietates,
ibi nostra fixa sint corda,
  ubi vera sunt gaudia.
Per Dominum nostrum Iesum
  Christum Filium tuum,
qui tecum vivit et regnat
  in unitate Spiritus Sancti,
Deus, per omnia sæcula sæculorum.

FIRST READING

A reading from the book of Joshua   24:1-2,15-17,18
We will serve the Lord, for he is our God.

Joshua gathered all the tribes of Israel together at Shechem; then he called
the elders, leaders, judges and scribes of Israel, and they presented themselves
before God. Then Joshua said to all the people: 'If you will not serve the Lord,
choose today whom you wish to serve, whether the gods that your ancestors
served beyond the River, or the gods of the Amorites in whose land you are
now living. As for me and my House, we will serve the Lord.'

The people answered, 'We have no intention of deserting the Lord our
God and serving other gods! Was it not the Lord our God who brought

us and our ancestors out of the land of Egypt, the house of slavery, who worked those great wonders before our eyes and preserved us all along the way we travelled and among all the peoples through whom we journeyed? We too will serve the Lord, for he is our God.'

The word of the Lord.

Responsorial Psalm   Ps 33:2-3,16-23. R. v.9

R. **Taste and see that the Lord is good.**

I will bless the Lord at all times,
his praise always on my lips;
in the Lord my soul shall make its boast.
The humble shall hear and be glad. R.

The Lord turns his face against the wicked
to destroy their remembrance from the earth.
The Lord turns his eyes to the just
and his ears to their appeal. R.

They call and the Lord hears
and rescues them in all their distress.
The Lord is close to the broken-hearted;
those whose spirit is crushed he will save. R.

Many are the trials of the just man
but from them all the Lord will rescue him.
He will keep guard over all his bones,
not one of his bones shall be broken. R.

Evil brings death to the wicked;
those who hate the good are doomed.
The Lord ransoms the souls of his servants.
Those who hide in him shall not be condemned. R.

SECOND READING

A reading from the letter of St Paul to the Ephesians   5:21-32
This mystery has many implications for Christ and his Church.

Give way to one another in obedience to Christ. Wives should regard their husbands as they regard the Lord, since as Christ is head of the Church and saves the whole body, so is a husband the head of his wife; and as the Church submits to Christ, so should wives to their husbands, in everything. Husbands should love their wives just as Christ loved the Church and sacrificed himself for her to make her holy. He made her clean by washing her in water with a form of words, so that when he took her to himself she would be glorious, with no speck or wrinkle or anything like that, but holy and faultless. In the same way, husbands must love their wives as they love their own bodies; for a man to love his wife is for him to love himself. A man never hates his own body, but he feeds it and looks after it; and that is the way Christ treats the Church, because it is his body – and we are its living parts. For this reason, a man must leave his father and mother and be joined to his wife, and the two will become one body. This mystery has many implications; but I am saying it applies to Christ and the Church.

The word of the Lord.

Gospel Acclamation   Cf. Jn 6:63,68

R. **Alleluia, alleluia!**
Your words are spirit, Lord,
and they are life:
you have the message of eternal life.
R. **Alleluia!**

GOSPEL

A reading from the holy Gospel according to John   6:60-69
Who shall we go to? You have the message of eternal life.

After hearing his doctrine many of the followers of Jesus said, 'This is intolerable language. How could anyone accept it?' Jesus was aware that his followers were complaining about it and said, 'Does this upset you? What if you should see the Son of Man ascend to where he was before?

'It is the spirit that gives life,
the flesh has nothing to offer.
The words I have spoken to you are spirit
and they are life.

'But there are some of you who do not believe.' For Jesus knew from the outset those who did not believe, and who it was that would betray him. He went on, 'This is why I told you that no one could come to me unless the Father allows him.' After this, many of his disciples left him and stopped going with him.

Then Jesus said to the Twelve, 'What about you, do you want to go away too?' Simon Peter answered, 'Lord, who shall we go to? You have the message of eternal life, and we believe; we know that you are the Holy One of God.'

The Gospel of the Lord.

Prayer over the Offerings

O Lord, who gained for yourself
    a people by adoption
through the one sacrifice offered
    once for all,
bestow graciously on us, we pray,
the gifts of unity and peace
    in your Church.
Through Christ our Lord.

Super oblata

Qui una semel hostia, Domine,
adoptionis tibi populum acquisisti,
unitatis et pacis in Ecclesia tua
propitius nobis dona concedas.
Per Christum Dominum nostrum.

Preface of Sundays in Ordinary Time I-VIII, pp.61-67.

Communion Antiphon Cf. Ps 103:13-15

The earth is replete with the fruits
    of your work, O Lord;
you bring forth bread from the earth
and wine to cheer the heart.

Ant. ad communionem

De fructu operum tuorum,
    Domine, satiabitur terra,
ut educas panem de terra,
    et vinum lætificet cor hominis.

Or: Cf. Jn 6:54

Whoever eats my flesh
    and drinks my blood
has eternal life, says the Lord,
and I will raise him up
    on the last day.

Vel:

Qui manducat meam carnem
    et bibit meum sanguinem,
habet vitam æternam,
    dicit Dominus;
et ego resuscitabo eum
    in novissimo die.

Prayer after Communion

Complete within us, O Lord,
    we pray,
the healing work of your mercy
and graciously perfect
    and sustain us,
so that in all things we may
    please you.
Through Christ our Lord.

Post communionem

Plenum, quæsumus, Domine,
in nobis remedium tuæ
    miserationis operare
ac tales nos esse perfice propitius
    et sic foveri,
ut tibi in omnibus
    placere valeamus.
Per Christum Dominum nostrum.

2 September

TWENTY-SECOND SUNDAY IN ORDINARY TIME

Entrance Antiphon   Cf. Ps 85:3,5

HAVE mercy on me, O Lord,
     for I cry to you all the day long.
O Lord, you are good and forgiving,
full of mercy to all who call to you.

Ant. ad introitum

MISERERE mihi, Domine,
     quoniam ad te clamavi
     tota die:
quia tu, Domine, suavis ac mitis es,
et copiosus in misericordia
     omnibus invocantibus te.

Collect

God of might, giver of every
     good gift,
put into our hearts the love
     of your name,
so that, by deepening our sense
     of reverence,
you may nurture in us what is good
and, by your watchful care,
keep safe what you have nurtured.
Through our Lord Jesus Christ,
     your Son,
who lives and reigns with you
     in the unity of the Holy Spirit,
one God, for ever and ever.

Collecta

Deus virtutum, cuius est totum
     quod est optimum,
insere pectoribus nostris
     tui nominis amorem,
et præsta, ut in nobis,
religionis augmento,
     quæ sunt bona nutrias,
ac, vigilanti studio,
     quæ sunt nutrita custodias.
Per Dominum nostrum Iesum
     Christum Filium tuum,
qui tecum vivit et regnat
     in unitate Spiritus Sancti,
Deus, per omnia sæcula sæculorum.

FIRST READING

A reading from the book of Deuteronomy   4:1-2,6-8
Add nothing to what I command you, keep the commandments of the Lord.

Moses said to the people: 'Now, Israel, take notice of the laws and customs
that I teach you today, and observe them, that you may have life and may
enter and take possession of the land that the Lord the God of your fathers
is giving you. You must add nothing to what I command you, and take
nothing from it, but keep the commandments of the Lord your God just as
I lay them down for you. Keep them, observe them, and they will demon-
strate to the peoples your wisdom and understanding. When they come to

know of all these laws they will exclaim, "No other people is as wise and prudent as this great nation." And indeed, what great nation is there that has its gods so near as the Lord our God is to us whenever we call to him? And what great nation is there that has laws and customs to match this whole Law that I put before you today?'

The word of the Lord.

Responsorial Psalm   Ps 14:2-5. R. v.1

R. **The just will live in the presence of the Lord.**

Lord, who shall dwell on your holy mountain?
He who walks without fault,
he who acts with justice
and speaks the truth from his heart. R.

He who does no wrong to his brother,
who casts no slur on his neighbour,
who holds the godless in disdain,
but honours those who fear the Lord. R.

He who keeps his pledge, come what may;
who takes no interest on a loan
and accepts no bribes against the innocent.
Such a man will stand firm for ever. R.

SECOND READING

A reading from the letter of St James   1:17-18,21-22,27

You must do what the word tells you.

It is all that is good, everything that is perfect, which is given us from above; it comes down from the Father of all light; with him there is no such thing as alteration, no shadow of a change. By his own choice he made us his children by the message of the truth so that we should be a sort of first-fruits of all that he had created.

Accept and submit to the word which has been planted in you and can save your souls. But you must do what the word tells you, and not just listen to it and deceive yourselves.

Pure unspoilt religion, in the eyes of God our Father is this: coming to the help of orphans and widows when they need it, and keeping oneself uncontaminated by the world.

The word of the Lord.

Gospel Acclamation   Cf. Jn 6:63,68
R. **Alleluia, alleluia!**
Your words are spirit, Lord,
and they are life:
you have the message of eternal life.
R. **Alleluia!**

Or: Jm 1:18

R. **Alleluia, alleluia!**
By his own choice the Father made us his children
by the message of the truth,
so that we should be a sort of first-fruits
of all that he created.
R. **Alleluia!**

GOSPEL

A reading from the holy Gospel according to Mark   7:1-8,14-15,21-23
You put aside the commandment of God to cling to human traditions.

The Pharisees and some of the scribes who had come from Jerusalem
gathered round Jesus, and they noticed that some of his disciples were eating
with unclean hands, that is, without washing them. For the Pharisees, and
the Jews in general, follow the tradition of the elders and never eat without
washing their arms as far as the elbow; and on returning from the market
place they never eat without first sprinkling themselves. There are also many
other observances which have been handed down to them concerning the
washing of cups and pots and bronze dishes. So these Pharisees and scribes
asked him, 'Why do your disciples not respect the tradition of the elders but
eat their food with unclean hands?' He answered, 'It was of you hypocrites
that Isaiah so rightly prophesied in this passage of scripture:

This people honours me only with lip-service,
    while their hearts are far from me.
The worship they offer me is worthless,
    the doctrines they teach are only human regulations.

You put aside the commandment of God to cling to human traditions.'

He called the people to him again and said, 'Listen to me, all of you,
and understand. Nothing that goes into a man from outside can make him
unclean; it is the things that come out of a man that make him unclean. For
it is from within, from men's hearts, that evil intentions emerge: fornication,
theft, murder, adultery, avarice, malice, deceit, indecency, envy, slander,
pride, folly. All these evil things come from within and make a man unclean.'

The Gospel of the Lord.

Prayer over the Offerings	**Super oblata**
May this sacred offering, O Lord, confer on us always the blessing of salvation, that what it celebrates in mystery it may accomplish in power. Through Christ our Lord.	Benedictionem nobis, Domine, conferat salutarem sacra semper oblatio, ut, quod agit mysterio, virtute perficiat. Per Christum Dominum nostrum.

Preface of Sundays in Ordinary Time I-VIII, pp.61-67.

Communion Antiphon Ps 30:20	**Ant. ad communionem**
How great is the goodness, Lord, that you keep for those who fear you.	Quam magna multitudo dulcedinis tuæ, Domine, quam abscondisti timentibus te.
Or: Mt 5:9-10	Vel:
Blessed are the peacemakers, for they shall be called children of God. Blessed are they who are persecuted for the sake of righteousness, for theirs is the Kingdom of Heaven.	Beati pacifici, quoniam filii Dei vocabuntur. Beati qui persecutionem patiuntur propter iustitiam, quoniam ipsorum est regnum cælorum.
Prayer after Communion	**Post communionem**
Renewed by this bread from the heavenly table, we beseech you, Lord, that, being the food of charity, it may confirm our hearts and stir us to serve you in our neighbour. Through Christ our Lord.	Pane mensæ cælestis refecti, te, Domine, deprecamur, ut hoc nutrimentum caritatis corda nostra confirmet, quatenus ad tibi ministrandum in fratribus excitemur. Per Christum Dominum nostrum.

9 September

TWENTY-THIRD SUNDAY IN ORDINARY TIME

Entrance Antiphon Ps 118:137,124	Ant. ad introitum
YOU are just, O Lord, and your judgement is right; treat your servant in accord with your merciful love.	IUSTUS es, Domine, et rectum iudicium tuum; fac cum servo tuo secundum misericordiam tuam.

Collect

O God, by whom we are redeemed
and receive adoption,
look graciously upon your beloved
sons and daughters,
that those who believe in Christ
may receive true freedom
and an everlasting inheritance.
Through our Lord Jesus Christ,
your Son,
who lives and reigns with you
in the unity of the Holy Spirit,
one God, for ever and ever.

Collecta

Deus, per quem nobis
et redemptio venit
et præstatur adoptio,
filios dilectionis tuæ
benignus intende,
ut in Christo credentibus
et vera tribuatur libertas,
et hereditas æterna.
Per Dominum nostrum Iesum
Christum Filium tuum,
qui tecum vivit et regnat
in unitate Spiritus Sancti,
Deus, per omnia sæcula sæculorum.

FIRST READING

A reading from the prophet Isaiah   35:4-7

The ears of the deaf shall be unsealed and the tongues of the dumb shall be loosed.

Say to all faint hearts,
'Courage! Do not be afraid.

'Look, your God is coming,
vengeance is coming,
the retribution of God;
he is coming to save you.'

Then the eyes of the blind shall be opened,
the ears of the deaf unsealed,
then the lame shall leap like a deer
and the tongues of the dumb sing for joy;

for water gushes in the desert,
streams in the wasteland,
the scorched earth becomes a lake,
the parched land springs of water.

This word of the Lord.

Responsorial Psalm   Ps 145:7-10. R. v.1

R. **My soul, give praise to the Lord.**
Or: **Alleluia!**

It is the Lord who keeps faith for ever,
who is just to those who are oppressed.
It is he who gives bread to the hungry,
the Lord, who sets prisoners free. R.

It is the Lord who gives sight to the blind,
who raises up those who are bowed down,
the Lord who loves the just,
the Lord, who protects the stranger. R.

The Lord upholds the widow and orphan,
but thwarts the path of the wicked.
The Lord will reign for ever,
Zion's God, from age to age. R.

SECOND READING

A reading from the letter of St James   2:1-5

God chose the poor to be the heirs to the kingdom.

My brothers, do not try to combine faith in Jesus Christ, our glorified Lord,
with the making of distinctions between classes of people. Now suppose a
man comes into your synagogue, beautifully dressed and with a gold ring
on, and at the same time a poor man comes in, in shabby clothes, and you
take notice of the well-dressed man, and say, 'Come this way to the best
seats'; then you tell the poor man, 'Stand over there' or 'You can sit on
the floor by my foot-rest.' Can't you see that you have used two different
standards in your mind, and turned yourselves into judges, and corrupt
judges at that?

Listen, my dear brothers: it was those who are poor according to the
world that God chose, to be rich in faith and to be the heirs to the kingdom
which he promised to those who love him.

The word of the Lord.

Gospel Acclamation   1 S 3:9; Jn 6:68

R. **Alleluia, alleluia!**
Speak, Lord, your servant is listening:
you have the message of eternal life.
R. **Alleluia!**

Or: Cf. Mt 4:23

R. **Alleluia, alleluia!**
Jesus proclaimed the Good News of the kingdom,
and cured all kinds of sickness among the people.
R. **Alleluia!**

GOSPEL

A reading from the holy Gospel according to Mark　　　　7:31-37

He makes the deaf hear and the dumb speak.

Returning from the district of Tyre, Jesus went by way of Sidon towards the Sea of Galilee, right through the Decapolis region. And they brought him a deaf man who had an impediment in his speech; and they asked him to lay his hand on him. He took him aside in private, away from the crowd, put his fingers into the man's ears and touched his tongue with spittle. Then looking up to heaven he sighed; and he said to him, 'Ephphatha,' that is, 'Be opened.' And his ears were opened, and the ligament of his tongue was loosened and he spoke clearly. And Jesus ordered them to tell no one about it, but the more he insisted, the more widely they published it. Their admiration was unbounded. 'He has done all things well,' they said 'he makes the deaf hear and the dumb speak.'

The Gospel of the Lord.

Prayer over the Offerings	Super oblata
O God, who give us the gift of true prayer and of peace, graciously grant that, through this offering, we may do fitting homage to your divine majesty and, by partaking of the sacred mystery, we may be faithfully united in mind and heart. Through Christ our Lord.	Deus, auctor sinceræ devotionis et pacis, da, quæsumus, ut et maiestatem tuam convenienter hoc munere veneremur, et sacri participatione mysterii fideliter sensibus uniamur. Per Christum Dominum nostrum.

Preface of Sundays in Ordinary Time I-VIII, pp.61-67.

Communion Antiphon Cf. Ps 41:2-3	Ant. ad communionem
Like the deer that yearns for running streams, so my soul is yearning for you, my God; my soul is thirsting for God, the living God.	Quemadmodum desiderat cervus ad fontes aquarum, ita desiderat anima mea ad te, Deus: sitivit anima mea ad Deum fortem vivum.

Or: Jn 8:12

I am the light of the world,
  says the Lord;
whoever follows me will not walk
  in darkness,
but will have the light of life.

Prayer after Communion

Grant that your faithful, O Lord,
whom you nourish and endow
  with life
through the food of your Word
  and heavenly Sacrament,
may so benefit from your beloved
  Son's great gifts
that we may merit an eternal share
  in his life.
Who lives and reigns
  for ever and ever.

Vel:

Ego sum lux mundi,
  dicit Dominus:
qui sequitur me non ambulat
  in tenebris,
sed habebit lumen vitæ.

Post communionem

Da fidelibus tuis, Domine,
quos et verbi tui et cælestis
  sacramenti pabulo
nutris et vivificas,
ita dilecti Filii tui tantis
  muneribus proficere,
ut eius vitæ semper consortes
  effici mereamur.
Qui vivit et regnat
  in sæcula sæculorum.

16 September

TWENTY-FOURTH SUNDAY IN ORDINARY TIME

Entrance Antiphon Cf. Si 36:18

GIVE peace, O Lord,
  to those who wait for you,
that your prophets be found true.
Hear the prayers of your servant,
and of your people Israel.

Collect

Look upon us, O God,
Creator and ruler of all things,
and, that we may feel the working
  of your mercy,
grant that we may serve you
  with all our heart.
Through our Lord Jesus Christ,
  your Son,
who lives and reigns with you
  in the unity of the Holy Spirit,
one God, for ever and ever.

Ant. ad introitum

DA pacem, Domine,
  sustinentibus te,
ut prophetæ tui fideles inveniantur;
exaudi preces servi tui,
  et plebis tuæ Israel.

Collecta

Respice nos, rerum omnium Deus
  creator et rector,
et, ut tuæ propitiationis
  sentiamus effectum,
toto nos tribue tibi corde servire.
Per Dominum nostrum Iesum
  Christum Filium tuum,
qui tecum vivit et regnat
  in unitate Spiritus Sancti,
Deus, per omnia sæcula sæculorum.

FIRST READING

A reading from the prophet Isaiah   50:5-9
I offered my back to those who struck me.

The Lord has opened my ear.

For my part, I made no resistance,
neither did I turn away.
I offered my back to those who struck me,
my cheeks to those who tore at my beard;
I did not cover my face
against insult and spittle.

The Lord comes to my help,
so that I am untouched by the insults.
So, too, I set my face like flint;
I know I shall not be shamed.

My vindicator is here at hand. Does anyone start proceedings against me?
Then let us go to court together.
Who thinks he has a case against me?
Let him approach me.
The Lord is coming to my help,
who dare condemn me?

    The word of the Lord.

Responsorial Psalm   Ps 114:1-6,8-9. R. v.9

R. **I will walk in the presence of the Lord,**
    in the land of the living.
    Or: **Alleluia!**

I love the Lord for he has heard
the cry of my appeal;
for he turned his ear to me
in the day when I called him. R.

They surrounded me, the snares of death,
with the anguish of the tomb;
they caught me, sorrow and distress.
I called on the Lord's name.
O Lord my God, deliver me! R.

How gracious is the Lord, and just;
our God has compassion.
The Lord protects the simple hearts;
I was helpless so he saved me. R.

He has kept my soul from death,
my eyes from tears
and my feet from stumbling.
I will walk in the presence of the Lord
in the land of the living. R.

SECOND READING

A reading from the letter of St James   2:14-18

If good works do not go with faith, it is quite dead.

Take the case, my brothers, of someone who has never done a single good act but claims that he has faith. Will that faith save him? If one of the brothers or one of the sisters is in need of clothes and has not enough food to live on, and one of you says to them, 'I wish you well; keep yourself warm and eat plenty,' without giving them these bare necessities of life, then what good is that? Faith is like that: if good works do not go with it, it is quite dead.

This is the way to talk to people of that kind: 'You say you have faith and I have good deeds; I will prove to you that I have faith by showing my good deeds – now you prove to me that you have faith without any good deeds to show.'

The word of the Lord.

Gospel Acclamation   Jn 14:5

R. **Alleluia, alleluia!**
I am the Way, the Truth and the Life, says the Lord;
no one can come to the Father except through me.
R. **Alleluia!**

Or: Ga 6:14

R. **Alleluia, alleluia!**
The only thing I can boast about is the cross
    of our Lord,
through whom the world is crucified to me, and I to the world.
R. **Alleluia!**

GOSPEL

A reading from the holy Gospel according to Mark   8:27-35

You are the Christ. The Son of Man is destined to suffer grievously.

Jesus and his disciples left for the villages round Caesarea Philippi. On the way he put this question to his disciples, 'Who do people say I am?' And they told him. 'John the Baptist,' they said 'others Elijah; others again, one of the prophets.' 'But you,' he asked 'who do you say I am?' Peter spoke up and said to him, 'You are the Christ.' And he gave them strict orders not to tell anyone about him.

And he began to teach them that the Son of Man was destined to suffer grievously, to be rejected by the elders and the chief priests and the scribes, and to be put to death, and after three days to rise again; and he said all this quite openly. Then, taking him aside, Peter started to remonstrate with him. But, turning and seeing his disciples, he rebuked Peter and said to him, 'Get behind me, Satan! Because the way you think is not God's way but man's.'

He called the people and his disciples to him and said, 'If anyone wants to be a follower of mine, let him renounce himself and take up his cross and follow me. For anyone who wants to save his life will lose it; but anyone who loses his life for my sake, and for the sake of the gospel, will save it.'

The Gospel of the Lord.

Prayer over the Offerings

Look with favour on our
   supplications, O Lord,
and in your kindness accept these,
   your servants' offerings,
that what each has offered
   to the honour of your name
may serve the salvation of all.
Through Christ our Lord.

Super oblata

Propitiare, Domine,
   supplicationibus nostris,
et has oblationes famulorum
   tuorum benignus assume,
ut, quod singuli ad honorem
   tui nominis obtulerunt,
cunctis proficiat ad salutem.
Per Christum Dominum nostrum.

Preface of Sundays in Ordinary Time I-VIII, pp.61-67.

Communion Antiphon Cf. Ps 35:8

How precious is your mercy, O God!
The children of men seek shelter
   in the shadow of your wings.

Ant. ad communionem

Quam pretiosa
   est misericordia tua, Deus!
Filii hominum sub umbra alarum
   tuarum confugient.

Or: Cf. 1 Co 10:16

The chalice of blessing that we bless
is a communion in the Blood
   of Christ;
and the bread that we break
is a sharing in the Body of the Lord.

Vel:

Calix benedictionis,
   cui benedicimus,
communicatio Sanguinis Christi est;
et panis, quem frangimus,
participatio Corporis Domini est.

Prayer after Communion

May the working of this heavenly
    gift, O Lord, we pray,
take possession of our minds
    and bodies,
so that its effects,
    and not our own desires,
may always prevail in us.
Through Christ our Lord.

Post communionem

Mentes nostras et corpora possideat,
quæsumus, Domine,
    doni cælestis operatio,
ut non noster sensus in nobis,
sed eius præveniat semper effectus.
Per Christum Dominum nostrum.

23 September

TWENTY-FIFTH SUNDAY IN ORDINARY TIME

Entrance Antiphon

I AM the salvation of the people,
  says the Lord.
Should they cry to me in any distress,
I will hear them, and I will be
    their Lord for ever.

Ant. ad introitum

S ALUS populi ego sum,
  dicit Dominus.
De quacumque tribulatione
    clamaverint ad me,
exaudiam eos, et ero illorum
    Dominus in perpetuum.

Collect

O God, who founded all the
    commands of your sacred Law
upon love of you
    and of our neighbour,
grant that, by keeping your precepts,
we may merit to attain eternal life.
Through our Lord Jesus Christ,
    your Son,
who lives and reigns with you
    in the unity of the Holy Spirit,
one God, for ever and ever.

Collecta

Deus, qui sacræ legis
    omnia constituta
in tua et proximi dilectione posuisti,
da nobis, ut, tua præcepta servantes,
ad vitam mereamur
    pervenire perpetuam.
Per Dominum nostrum Iesum
    Christum Filium tuum,
qui tecum vivit et regnat
    in unitate Spiritus Sancti,
Deus, per omnia sæcula sæculorum.

FIRST READING

A reading from the book of Wisdom   2:12,17-20

Let us condemn him to a shameful death.

The godless say to themselves,
'Let us lie in wait for the virtuous man, since he annoys us
and opposes our way of life,
reproaches us for our breaches of the law
and accuses us of playing false to our upbringing.
Let us see if what he says is true,
let us observe what kind of end he himself will have.
If the virtuous man is God's son, God will take his part
and rescue him from the clutches of his enemies.
Let us test him with cruelty and with torture,
and thus explore this gentleness of his
and put his endurance to the proof.
Let us condemn him to a shameful death
since he will be looked after – we have his word for it.'

   The word of the Lord.

Responsorial Psalm   Ps 53:3-6,8. R. v.6

R. **The Lord upholds my life.**

   O God, save me by your name;
   by your power, uphold my cause.
   O God, hear my prayer;
   listen to the words of my mouth. R.

   For proud men have risen against me,
   ruthless men seek my life.
   They have no regard for God. R.

   But I have God for my help.
   The Lord upholds my life.
   I will sacrifice to you with willing heart
   and praise your name for it is good. R.

SECOND READING

A reading from the letter of St James   3:16-4:3

Peacemakers, when they work for peace, sow the seeds which will bear fruit in holiness.

Wherever you find jealousy and ambition, you find disharmony, and
wicked things of every kind being done; whereas the wisdom that comes
down from above is essentially something pure; it also makes for peace, and

is kindly and considerate, it is full of compassion and shows itself by doing good; nor is there any trace of partiality or hypocrisy in it. Peacemakers, when they work for peace, sow the seeds which will bear fruit in holiness.

Where do these wars and battles between yourselves first start? Isn't it precisely in the desires fighting inside your own selves? You want something and you haven't got it; so you are prepared to kill. You have an ambition that you cannot satisfy; so you fight to get your way by force. Why you don't have what you want is because you don't pray for it; when you do pray and don't get it, it is because you have not prayed properly, you have prayed for something to indulge your own desires.

The word of the Lord.

Gospel Acclamation													Jn 8:12

R. **Alleluia, alleluia!**
I am the light of the world, says the Lord,
anyone who follows me
will have the light of life.
R. **Alleluia!**

Or:													Cf. 2 Th 2:14

R. **Alleluia, alleluia!**
Through the Good News God called us
to share the glory of our Lord Jesus Christ.
R. **Alleluia!**

GOSPEL

A reading from the holy Gospel according to Mark					9:30-37

The Son of Man will be delivered. If anyone wants to be first, he must make himself servant of all.

After leaving the mountain Jesus and his disciples made their way through Galilee; and he did not want anyone to know because he was instructing his disciples; he was telling them, 'The Son of Man will be delivered into the hands of men; they will put him to death; and three days after he has been put to death he will rise again.' But they did not understand what he said and were afraid to ask him.

They came to Capernaum, and when he was in the house he asked them, 'What were you arguing about on the road?' They said nothing because they had been arguing which of them was the greatest. So he sat down, called the Twelve to him and said, 'If anyone wants to be first, he must make himself last of all and servant of all.' He then took a little child, set him in front of them put his arms round him, and said to them, 'Anyone who welcomes one of these little children in my name, welcomes me; and anyone who welcomes me welcomes not me but the one who sent me.'

The Gospel of the Lord.

Prayer over the Offerings	Super oblata
Receive with favour, O Lord, we pray, the offerings of your people, that what they profess with devotion and faith may be theirs through these heavenly mysteries. Through Christ our Lord.	Munera, quæsumus, Domine, tuæ plebis propitiatus assume, ut, quæ fidei pietate profitentur, sacramentis cælestibus apprehendant. Per Christum Dominum nostrum.

Preface of Sundays in Ordinary Time I-VIII, pp.61-67.

Communion Antiphon Ps 118:4-5	Ant. ad communionem
You have laid down your precepts to be carefully kept; may my ways be firm in keeping your statutes.	Tu mandasti mandata tua custodiri nimis; utinam dirigantur viæ meæ ad custodiendas iustificationes tuas.

Or: Jn 10:14	Vel:
I am the Good Shepherd, says the Lord; I know my sheep, and mine know me.	Ego sum pastor bonus, dicit Dominus; et cognosco oves meas, et cognoscunt me meæ.

Prayer after Communion	Post communionem
Graciously raise up, O Lord, those you renew with this Sacrament, that we may come to possess your redemption both in mystery and in the manner of our life. Through Christ our Lord.	Quos tuis, Domine, reficis sacramentis, continuis attolle benignus auxiliis, ut redemptionis effectum et mysteriis capiamus et moribus. Per Christum Dominum nostrum.

30 September

TWENTY-SIXTH SUNDAY IN ORDINARY TIME

Entrance Antiphon Dn 3:31,29,30,43,42

ALL that you have done to us,
O Lord,
you have done with true judgement,
for we have sinned against you
and not obeyed
    your commandments.
But give glory to your name
and deal with us according
    to the bounty of your mercy.

Ant. ad introitum

OMNIA, quæ fecisti nobis,
Domine,
in vero iudicio fecisti,
    quia peccavimus tibi,
et mandatis tuis non obœdivimus;
sed da gloriam nomini tuo,
et fac nobiscum secundum
    multitudinem misericordiæ tuæ.

Collect

O God, who manifest
    your almighty power
above all by pardoning
    and showing mercy,
bestow, we pray, your grace
    abundantly upon us
and make those hastening to attain
    your promises
heirs to the treasures of heaven.
Through our Lord Jesus Christ,
    your Son,
who lives and reigns with you
    in the unity of the Holy Spirit,
one God, for ever and ever.

Collecta

Deus, qui omnipotentiam tuam
parcendo maxime
    et miserando manifestas,
multiplica super nos gratiam tuam,
ut, ad tua promissa currentes,
cælestium bonorum facias
    esse consortes.
Per Dominum nostrum Iesum
    Christum Filium tuum,
qui tecum vivit et regnat
    in unitate Spiritus Sancti,
Deus, per omnia sæcula sæculorum.

FIRST READING

A reading from the book of Numbers   11:25-29

Are you jealous on my account? If only the whole people of the Lord were prophets!

The Lord came down in the Cloud. He spoke with Moses, but took some of
the spirit that was on him and put it on the seventy elders. When the spirit
came on them they prophesied, but not again.

Two men had stayed back in the camp; one was called Eldad and the
other Medad. The spirit came down on them; though they had not gone to
the Tent, their names were enrolled among the rest. These began to prophesy

in the camp. The young man ran to tell this to Moses, 'Look,' he said 'Eldad and Medad are prophesying in the camp.' Then said Joshua the son of Nun, who had served Moses from his youth, 'My Lord Moses, stop them!' Moses answered him, 'Are you jealous on my account? If only the whole people of the Lord were prophets, and the Lord gave his Spirit to them all!'

The word of the Lord.

Responsorial Psalm   Ps 18:8,10,12-14. R. v.9

R. **The precepts of the Lord gladden the heart.**

The law of the Lord is perfect,
it revives the soul.
The rule of the Lord is to be trusted,
it gives wisdom to the simple. R.

The fear of the Lord is holy,
abiding for ever.
The decrees of the Lord are truth
and all of them just. R.

So in them your servant finds instruction;
great reward is in their keeping.
But who can detect all his errors?
From hidden faults acquit me. R.

From presumption restrain your servant
and let it not rule me.
Then shall I be blameless,
clean from grave sin. R.

SECOND READING

A reading from the letter of St James   5:1-6
Your wealth is rotting.

An answer for the rich. Start crying, weep for the miseries that are coming to you. Your wealth is all rotting, your clothes are all eaten up by moths. All your gold and your silver are corroding away, and the same corrosion will be your own sentence, and eat into your body. It was a burning fire that you stored up as your treasure for the last days. Labourers mowed your fields, and you cheated them – listen to the wages that you kept back, calling out; realise that the cries of the reapers have reached the ears of the Lord of hosts. On earth you have had a life of comfort and luxury; in the time of slaughter you went on eating to your heart's

content. It was you who condemned the innocent and killed them; they
offered you no resistance.

The word of the Lord.

Gospel Acclamation   Cf. Jn 17:17

R. **Alleluia, alleluia!**
Your word is truth, O Lord,
consecrate us in the truth.
R. **Alleluia!**

GOSPEL

A reading from the holy Gospel according to Mark   9:38-43,45,47-48
Anyone who is not against us is for us. If your hand should cause you to sin, cut it off.

John said to Jesus, 'Master, we saw a man who is not one of us casting out
devils in your name; and because he was not one of us we tried to stop him.'
But Jesus said, 'You must not stop him: no one who works a miracle in my
name is likely to speak evil of me. Anyone who is not against us is for us.

'If anyone gives you a cup of water to drink just because you belong to
Christ, then I tell you solemnly, he will most certainly not lose his reward.

'But anyone who is an obstacle to bring down one of these little ones
who have faith, would be better thrown into the sea with a great millstone
round his neck. And if your hand should cause you to sin, cut it off; it is
better for you to enter into life crippled, than to have two hands and go to
hell, into the fire that cannot be put out. And if your foot should cause you
to sin, cut it off; it is better for you to enter into life lame, than to have two
feet and be thrown into hell. And if your eye should cause you to sin, tear
it out; it is better for you to enter into the kingdom of God with one eye,
than to have two eyes and be thrown into hell where their worm does not
die nor their fire go out.'

The Gospel of the Lord.

Prayer over the Offerings	Super oblata
Grant us, O merciful God,	Concede nobis, misericors Deus,
that this our offering may find acceptance with you	ut hæc nostra oblatio tibi sit accepta,
and that through it the wellspring of all blessing	et per eam nobis fons omnis benedictionis aperiatur.
may be laid open before us.	Per Christum Dominum nostrum.
Through Christ our Lord.	

Preface of Sundays in Ordinary Time I-VIII, pp.61-67.

Communion Antiphon Cf.Ps118:49-50 | Ant. ad communionem

Remember your word to your servant,
    O Lord,
by which you have given me hope.
This is my comfort when I am
    brought low.

Memento verbi tui
    servo tuo, Domine,
in quo mihi spem dedisti;
hæc me consolata
    est in humilitate mea.

Or: 1 Jn 3:16 | Vel:

By this we came to know
    the love of God:
that Christ laid down his life for us;
so we ought to lay down our lives
    for one another.

In hoc cognovimus caritatem Dei:
quoniam ille animam suam
    pro nobis posuit;
et nos debemus pro fratribus
    animas ponere.

Prayer after Communion | Post communionem

May this heavenly mystery, O Lord,
restore us in mind and body,
that we may be coheirs in glory
    with Christ,
to whose suffering we are united
whenever we proclaim his Death.
Who lives and reigns
    for ever and ever.

Sit nobis, Domine,
    reparatio mentis et corporis
cæleste mysterium, ut simus eius
    in gloria coheredes,
cui, mortem ipsius
    annuntiando, compatimur.
Qui vivit et regnat
    in sæcula sæculorum.

7 October

TWENTY-SEVENTH SUNDAY IN ORDINARY TIME

Entrance Antiphon   Cf. Est 4:17 | Ant. ad introitum

WITHIN your will, O Lord,
    all things are established,
and there is none that can resist
    your will.
For you have made all things,
    the heaven and the earth,
and all that is held within the circle
    of heaven;
you are the Lord of all.

IN voluntate tua, Domine,
    universa sunt posita,
et non est qui possit resistere
    voluntati tuæ.
Tu enim fecisti omnia,
    cælum et terram,
et universa quæ cæli
    ambitu continentur;
Dominus universorum tu es.

Collect

Almighty ever-living God,
who in the abundance
of your kindness
surpass the merits and the desires
of those who entreat you,
pour out your mercy upon us
to pardon what conscience dreads
and to give what prayer does
not dare to ask.
Through our Lord Jesus Christ,
your Son,
who lives and reigns with you
in the unity of the Holy Spirit,
one God, for ever and ever.

Collecta

Omnipotens sempiterne Deus,
qui abundantia pietatis tuæ
et merita supplicum excedis et vota,
effunde super nos
misericordiam tuam,
ut dimittas quæ conscientia metuit,
et adicias quod oratio non præsumit.
Per Dominum nostrum
Iesum Christum Filium tuum,
qui tecum vivit et regnat
in unitate Spiritus Sancti,
Deus, per omnia sæcula sæculorum.

FIRST READING

A reading from the book of Genesis   2:18-24

They become one body.

The Lord God said, 'It is not good that the man should be alone. I will make him a helpmate.' So from the soil the Lord God fashioned all the wild beasts and all the birds of heaven. These he brought to the man to see what he would call them; each one was to bear the name the man would give it. The man gave names to all the cattle, all the birds of heaven and all the wild beasts. But no helpmate suitable for man was found for him. So the Lord God made the man fall into a deep sleep. And while he slept, he took one of his ribs and enclosed it in flesh. The Lord God built the rib he had taken from the man into a woman, and brought her to the man. The man exclaimed:

'This at last is bone from my bones
and flesh from my flesh!
This is to be called woman,
for this was taken from man.'

This is why a man leaves his father and mother and joins himself to his wife, and they become one body.

The word of the Lord.

Responsorial Psalm   Ps 127. R. v.5

R. **May the Lord bless us
all the days of our lives.**

O blessed are those who fear the Lord
and walk in his ways!

By the labour of your hands you shall eat.
You will be happy and prosper. R.

Your wife will be like a fruitful vine
in the heart of your house;
your children like shoots of the olive,
around your table. R.

Indeed thus shall be blessed
the man who fears the Lord.
May the Lord bless you from Zion
in a happy Jerusalem
all the days of your life!
May you see your children's children.
On Israel, peace! R.

R. **May the Lord bless us
all the days of our lives.**

SECOND READING

A reading from the letter to the Hebrews   2:9-11

The one who sanctifies, and the ones who are sanctified, are of the same stock.

We see in Jesus one who was for a short while made lower than the angels and is now crowned with glory and splendour because he submitted to death; by God's grace he had to experience death for all mankind.

As it was his purpose to bring a great many of his sons into glory, it was appropriate that God, for whom everything exists and through whom everything exists, should make perfect, through suffering, the leader who would take them to their salvation. For the one who sanctifies, and the ones who are sanctified, are of the same stock; that is why he openly calls them brothers.

The word of the Lord.

Gospel Acclamation   Cf. Jn 17:17

R. **Alleluia, alleluia!**
Your word is truth, O Lord,
consecrate us in the truth.
R. **Alleluia!**
Or: 1 Jn 4:12
R. **Alleluia, alleluia!**
As long as we love one another
God will live in us
and his love will be complete in us.
R. **Alleluia!**

GOSPEL

A reading from the holy Gospel according to Mark   10:2-16

What God has united, man must not divide.

[Some Pharisees approached Jesus and asked, 'Is it against the law for a man to divorce his wife?' They were testing him. He answered them, 'What did Moses command you?' 'Moses allowed us' they said 'to draw up a writ of dismissal and so to divorce.' Then Jesus said to them, 'It was because you were so unteachable that he wrote this commandment for you. But from the beginning of creation God made them male and female. This is why a man must leave father and mother, and the two become one body. They are no longer two, therefore, but one body. So then, what God has united, man must not divide.' Back in the house the disciples questioned him again about this, and he said to them, 'The man who divorces his wife and marries another is guilty of adultery against her. And if a woman divorces her husband and marries another she is guilty of adultery too.']

People were bringing little children to him, for him to touch them. The disciples turned them away, but when Jesus saw this he was indignant and said to them, 'Let the little children come to me; do not stop them; for it is to such as these that the kingdom of God belongs. I tell you solemnly, anyone who does not welcome the kingdom of God like a little child will never enter it.' Then he put his arms round them, laid his hands on them and gave them his blessing.

[The Gospel of the Lord.]

Shorter Form, verses 2-12. Read between [ ]

Prayer over the Offerings	Super oblata
Accept, O Lord, we pray, the sacrifices instituted by your commands and, through the sacred mysteries, which we celebrate with dutiful service, graciously complete the sanctifying work by which you are pleased to redeem us. Through Christ our Lord.	Suscipe, quæsumus, Domine, sacrificia tuis instituta præceptis, et sacris mysteriis, quæ debitæ servitutis celebramus officio, sanctificationem tuæ nobis redemptionis dignanter adimple. Per Christum Dominum nostrum.

Preface of Sundays in Ordinary Time I-VIII, pp.61-67.

Communion Antiphon Lm 3:25

The Lord is good to those
  who hope in him,
to the soul that seeks him.

Or: Cf. 1 Co 10:17

Though many, we are one bread,
  one body,
for we all partake of the one Bread
  and one Chalice.

Prayer after Communion

Grant us, almighty God,
that we may be refreshed
  and nourished
by the Sacrament which
  we have received,
so as to be transformed
  into what we consume.
Through Christ our Lord.

Ant. ad communionem

Bonus est Dominus
  sperantibus in eum,
animæ quærenti illum.

Vel:

Unus panis et unum corpus
  multi sumus,
omnes qui de uno pane et de uno
  calice participamus.

Post communionem

Concede nobis, omnipotens Deus,
ut de perceptis sacramentis
  inebriemur atque pascamur,
quatenus in id quod
  sumimus transeamus.
Per Christum Dominum nostrum.

14 October

TWENTY-EIGHTH SUNDAY IN ORDINARY TIME

Entrance Antiphon Ps 129:3-4

IF you, O Lord,
  should mark iniquities,
Lord, who could stand?
But with you is found forgiveness,
O God of Israel.

Collect

May your grace, O Lord, we pray,
at all times go before us
  and follow after
and make us always determined
to carry out good works.
Through our Lord Jesus Christ,
  your Son,
who lives and reigns with you
  in the unity of the Holy Spirit,
one God, for ever and ever.

Ant. ad introitum

SI iniquitates observaveris,
  Domine,
Domine, quis sustinebit?
Quia apud te propitiatio est,
  Deus Israel.

Collecta

Tua nos, quæsumus,
  Domine, gratia
semper et præveniat et sequatur,
ac bonis operibus iugiter præstet
  esse intentos.
Per Dominum nostrum Iesum
  Christum Filium tuum,
qui tecum vivit et regnat
  in unitate Spiritus Sancti,
Deus, per omnia sæcula sæculorum.

FIRST READING

A reading from the book of Wisdom 7:7-11

Compared with wisdom, I held riches as nothing.

I prayed, and understanding was given me;
I entreated, and the spirit of Wisdom came to me.
I esteemed her more than sceptres and thrones;
compared with her, I held riches as nothing.
I reckoned no priceless stone to be her peer,
for compared with her, all gold is a pinch of sand,
and beside her silver ranks as mud.
I loved her more than health or beauty,
preferred her to the light,
since her radiance never sleeps.
In her company all good things came to me,
at her hands riches not to be numbered.

The word of the Lord.

Responsorial Psalm Ps 89:12-17. R. v.14

R. **Fill us with your love that we may rejoice.**

Make us know the shortness of our life
that we may gain wisdom of heart.
Lord, relent! Is your anger for ever?
Show pity to your servants. R.

In the morning, fill us with your love;
we shall exult and rejoice all our days.
Give us joy to balance our affliction
for the years when we knew misfortune. R.

Show forth your work to your servants;
let your glory shine on their children.
Let the favour of the Lord be upon us:
give success to the work of our hands. R.

SECOND READING

A reading from the letter to the Hebrews 4:12-13

The word of God can judge secret emotions and thoughts.

The word of God is something alive and active: it cuts like any double-edged sword but more finely: it can slip through the place where the soul is divided from the spirit, or joints from the marrow; it can judge the secret emotions and thoughts. No created thing can hide from him; everything is uncovered and open to the eyes of the one to whom we must give account of ourselves.

The word of the Lord.

Gospel Acclamation   Cf. Mt 11:25

R. **Alleluia, alleluia!**
Blessed are you, Father,
Lord of heaven and earth,
for revealing the mysteries of the kingdom
to mere children.
R. **Alleluia!**

Or: Mt 5:3

R. **Alleluia, alleluia!**
How happy the poor in spirit;
theirs is the kingdom of heaven.
R. **Alleluia!**

GOSPEL

A reading from the holy Gospel according to Mark   10:17-30
Go and sell everything you own and follow me.

[Jesus was setting out on a journey when a man ran up, knelt before him and put this question to him, 'Good master, what must I do to inherit eternal life?' Jesus said to him, 'Why do you call me good? No one is good but God alone. You know the commandments: You must not kill; You must not commit adultery, You must not steal; You must not bring false witness; You must not defraud; Honour your father and mother.' And he said to him, 'Master, I have kept all these from my earliest days.' Jesus looked steadily at him and loved him, and he said, 'There is one thing you lack. Go and sell everything you own and give the money to the poor, and you will have treasure in heaven; then come, follow me.' But his face fell at these words and he went away sad, for he was a man of great wealth.

Jesus looked round and said to his disciples, 'How hard it is for those who have riches to enter the kingdom of God!' The disciples were astounded by these words, but Jesus insisted, 'My children,' he said to them, 'how hard it is to enter the kingdom of God! It is easier for a camel to pass through the eye of a needle than for a rich man to enter the kingdom of God.' They were more astonished than ever. 'In that case' they said to one another 'who can be saved?' Jesus gazed at them. 'For men' he said 'it is impossible, but not for God: because everything is possible for God.']

Peter took this up. 'What about us?' he asked him. 'We have left everything and followed you.' Jesus said, 'I tell you solemnly, there is no one who has left house, brothers, sisters, father, children or land for my sake and for the sake of the gospel who will not be repaid a hundred times over, houses, brothers, sisters, mothers, children and land – not without persecutions – now in this present time and, in the world to come, eternal life.'

[The Gospel of the Lord.]

Shorter Form, verses 17-27. Read between [ ]

Prayer over the Offerings

Accept, O Lord, the prayers
  of your faithful
with the sacrificial offerings,
that, through these acts
  of devotedness,
we may pass over to the glory
  of heaven.
Through Christ our Lord.

Super oblata

Suscipe, Domine,
fidelium preces cum
    oblationibus hostiarum,
ut, per hæc piæ devotionis officia,
ad cælestem gloriam transeamus.
Per Christum Dominum nostrum.

Preface of Sundays in Ordinary Time I-VIII, pp.61-67.

Communion Antiphon Cf. Ps 33:11

The rich suffer want and go hungry,
but those who seek the Lord
  lack no blessing.

Or: 1 Jn 3:2

When the Lord appears,
  we shall be like him,
for we shall see him as he is.

Ant. ad communionem

Divites eguerunt et esurierunt;
quærentes autem Dominum
    non minuentur omni bono.

Vel:

Cum apparuerit Dominus,
    similes ei erimus,
quoniam videbimus eum sicuti est.

Prayer after Communion

We entreat your majesty most
  humbly, O Lord,
that, as you feed us
  with the nourishment
which comes from the most holy
  Body and Blood of your Son,
so you may make us sharers
  of his divine nature.
Who lives and reigns
  for ever and ever.

Post communionem

Maiestatem tuam, Domine,
    suppliciter deprecamur,
ut, sicut nos Corporis
  et Sanguinis sacrosancti
pascis alimento,
ita divinæ naturæ facias
    esse consortes.
Per Christum Dominum nostrum.

21 October

TWENTY-NINTH SUNDAY IN ORDINARY TIME

Entrance Antiphon   Cf. Ps 16:6,8

TO you I call; for you will surely
heed me, O God;
turn your ear to me; hear my words.
Guard me as the apple of your eye;
in the shadow of your wings
    protect me.

Ant. ad introitum

EGO clamavi,
quoniam exaudisti me, Deus;
inclina aurem tuam,
    et exaudi verba mea.
Custodi me, Domine,
    ut pupillam oculi;
sub umbra alarum tuarum
    protege me.

Collect

Almighty ever-living God,
grant that we may always conform
    our will to yours
and serve your majesty in sincerity
    of heart.
Through our Lord Jesus Christ,
    your Son,
who lives and reigns with you
    in the unity of the Holy Spirit,
one God, for ever and ever.

Collecta

Omnipotens sempiterne Deus,
fac nos tibi semper et devotam
    gerere voluntatem,
et maiestati tuæ sincero
    corde servire.
Per Dominum nostrum Iesum
    Christum Filium tuum,
qui tecum vivit et regnat
    in unitate Spiritus Sancti,
Deus, per omnia sæcula sæculorum.

FIRST READING

A reading from the prophet Isaiah   53:10-11
If he offers his life in atonement, he shall see his heirs, he shall have a long life.

The Lord has been pleased to crush his servant with suffering.
If he offers his life in atonement,
he shall see his heirs, he shall have a long life
and through him what the Lord wishes will be done.

His soul's anguish over
he shall see the light and be content.
By his sufferings shall my servant justify many, taking
their faults on himself.

    The word of the Lord.

Responsorial Psalm   Ps 32:4-5,18-20,22. R. v.2

R. **May your love be upon us, O Lord,
as we place all our hope in you.**

The word of the Lord is faithful
and all his works to be trusted.
The Lord loves justice and right
and fills the earth with his love. R.

The Lord looks on those who revere him,
on those who hope in his love,
to rescue their souls from death,
to keep them alive in famine. R.

Our soul is waiting for the Lord.
The Lord is our help and our shield.
May your love be upon us, O Lord,
as we place all our hope in you. R.

SECOND READING

A reading from the letter to the Hebrews   4:14-16

Let us be confident in approaching the throne of grace.

Since in Jesus, the Son of God, we have the supreme high priest who has
gone through to the highest heaven, we must never let go of the faith that
we have professed. For it is not as if we had a high priest who was incapable
of feeling our weaknesses with us; but we have one who has been tempted
in every way that we are, though he is without sin. Let us be confident,
then, in approaching the throne of grace, that we shall have mercy from
him and find grace when we are in need of help.

The word of the Lord.

Gospel Acclamation   Jn 14:6

R. **Alleluia, alleluia!**
I am the Way, the Truth and the Life, says the Lord;
no one can come to the Father except through me.
R. **Alleluia!**

Or: Mk 10:45

R. **Alleluia, alleluia!**
The Son of Man came to save
and to give his life as a ransom for many.
R. **Alleluia!**

GOSPEL

A reading from the holy Gospel according to Mark 10:35-45

The Son of Man came to give his life as a ransom for many.

James and John, the sons of Zebedee, approached Jesus. 'Master,' they said to him 'we want you to do us a favour.' He said to them, 'What is it you want me to do for you?' They said to him, 'Allow us to sit one at your right hand and the other at your left in your glory.' 'You do not know what you are asking' Jesus said to them. 'Can you drink the cup that I must drink, or be baptised with the baptism with which I must be baptised?' They replied, 'We can.' Jesus said to them, 'The cup that I must drink you shall drink, and with the baptism with which I must be baptised you shall be baptised, but as for seats at my right hand or my left, these are not mine to grant; they belong to those to whom they have been allotted.'

When the other ten heard this they began to feel indignant with James and John, so [Jesus called them to him and said to them, 'You know that among the pagans their so-called rulers lord it over them, and their great men make their authority felt. This is not to happen among you. No; anyone who wants to become great among you must be your servant, and anyone who wants to be first among you must be slave to all. For the Son of Man himself did not come to be served but to serve, and to give his life as a ransom for many.'

The Gospel of the Lord.]

Shorter Form, verses 42-45. Read between [ ]

Prayer over the Offerings

Grant us, Lord, we pray,
a sincere respect for your gifts,
that, through the purifying action
   of your grace,
we may be cleansed by the very
   mysteries we serve.
Through Christ our Lord.

Super oblata

Tribue nos, Domine, quæsumus,
donis tuis libera mente servire,
ut, tua purificante nos gratia,
iisdem quibus famulamur
   mysteriis emundemur.
Per Christum Dominum nostrum.

Preface of Sundays in Ordinary Time I-VIII, pp.61-67.

Communion Antiphon Cf. Ps 32:18-19

Behold, the eyes of the Lord
are on those who fear him,
who hope in his merciful love,
to rescue their souls from death,
to keep them alive in famine.

Ant. ad communionem

Ecce oculi Domini super
   timentes eum,
et in eis qui sperant super
   misericordia eius;
ut eruat a morte animas eorum,
   et alat eos in fame.

Or: Mk 10:45 | Vel:

The Son of Man has come | Filius hominis venit,
to give his life as a ransom for many. | ut daret animam suam
                                        | redemptionem pro multis.

Prayer after Communion | Post communionem

Grant, O Lord, we pray, | Fac nos, quæsumus, Domine,
that, benefiting from participation | cælestium rerum
    in heavenly things, | frequentatione proficere,
we may be helped by what you give | ut et temporalibus
    in this present age | beneficiis adiuvemur,
and prepared for the gifts | et erudiamur æternis.
    that are eternal. | Per Christum Dominum nostrum.
Through Christ our Lord. |

28 October

THIRTIETH SUNDAY IN ORDINARY TIME

Entrance Antiphon   Cf. Ps 104:3-4 | Ant. ad introitum

LET the hearts that seek | LÆTETUR cor
the Lord rejoice; | quærentium Dominum.
turn to the Lord and his strength; | Quærite Dominum et confirmamini,
constantly seek his face. | quærite faciem eius semper.

Collect | Collecta

Almighty ever-living God, | Omnipotens sempiterne Deus,
increase our faith, hope and charity, | da nobis fidei,
and make us love | spei et caritatis augmentum,
    what you command, | et, ut mereamur assequi
so that we may merit | quod promittis,
    what you promise. | fac nos amare quod præcipis.
Through our Lord Jesus Christ, | Per Dominum nostrum Iesum
    your Son, | Christum Filium tuum,
who lives and reigns with you | qui tecum vivit et regnat
    in the unity of the Holy Spirit, | in unitate Spiritus Sancti,
one God, for ever and ever. | Deus, per omnia sæcula sæculorum.

FIRST READING

A reading from the prophet Jeremiah   31:7-9

I will comfort the blind and the lame as I lead them back.

The Lord says this:
>   Shout with joy for Jacob!
>   Hail the chief of nations!
>   Proclaim! Praise! Shout:
>   'The Lord has saved his people,
>   the remnant of Israel!'
>   See, I will bring them back
>   from the land of the North
>   and gather them from the far ends of earth;
>   all of them: the blind and the lame,
>   women with child, women in labour:
>   a great company returning here.
>   They had left in tears,
>   I will comfort them as I lead them back;
>   I will guide them to streams of water,
>   by a smooth path where they will not stumble.
>   For I am a father to Israel,
>   and Ephraim is my first-born son.

  The word of the Lord.

Responsorial Psalm   Ps 125. R. v.3

R. **What marvels the Lord worked for us!**
   Indeed we were glad.

   When the Lord delivered Zion from bondage,
   it seemed like a dream.
   Then was our mouth filled with laughter,
   on our lips there were songs. R.

   The heathens themselves said: 'What marvels
   the Lord worked for them!'
   What marvels the Lord worked for us!
   Indeed we were glad. R.

   Deliver us, O Lord, from our bondage
   as streams in dry land.
   Those who are sowing in tears
   will sing when they reap. R.

They go out, they go out, full of tears,
carrying seed for the sowing:
they come back, they come back, full of song,
carrying their sheaves. R.

SECOND READING

A reading from the letter to the Hebrews   5:1-6
You are a priest of the order of Melchizedek, and for ever.

Every high priest has been taken out of mankind and is appointed to act for men in their relations with God, to offer gifts and sacrifices for sins; and so he can sympathise with those who are ignorant or uncertain because he too lives in the limitations of weakness. That is why he has to make sin offerings for himself as well as for the people. No one takes this honour on himself, but each one is called by God, as Aaron was. Nor did Christ give himself the glory of becoming high priest, but he had it from the one who said to him: You are my son, today I have become your father, and in another text: You are a priest of the order of Melchizedek, and for ever.

The word of the Lord.

Gospel Acclamation   Jn 8:12

R. **Alleluia, alleluia!**
I am the light of the world, says the Lord,
anyone who follows me
will have the light of life.
R. **Alleluia!**

Or: Cf. 2 Tm 1:10

R. **Alleluia, alleluia!**
Our Saviour Christ Jesus abolished death,
and he has proclaimed life through the Good News.
R. **Alleluia!**

GOSPEL

A reading from the holy Gospel according to Mark   10:46-52
Master, let me see again.

As Jesus left Jericho with his disciples and a large crowd, Bartimaeus (that is, the son of Timaeus), a blind beggar, was sitting at the side of the road. When he heard that it was Jesus of Nazareth, he began to shout and to say, 'Son of David, Jesus, have pity on me.' And many of them scolded him and told him to keep quiet, but he only shouted all the louder, 'Son of David, have pity on me.' Jesus stopped and said, 'Call him here.' So they called the blind man. 'Courage,' they said 'get up; he is calling you.' So throwing off his cloak, he jumped up and went to Jesus. Then Jesus spoke, 'What do you want me to do for you?' 'Rabbuni,' the blind man said to him 'Master, let me see again.' Jesus said to him, 'Go; your faith has saved you.' And immediately his sight returned and he followed him along the road.

The Gospel of the Lord.

Prayer over the Offerings

Look, we pray, O Lord,
on the offerings we make
   to your majesty,
that whatever is done by us
   in your service
may be directed above all
   to your glory.
Through Christ our Lord.

Super oblata

Respice, quæsumus, Domine,
munera quæ tuæ
   offerimus maiestati,
ut, quod nostro servitio geritur,
ad tuam gloriam potius dirigatur.
Per Christum Dominum nostrum.

Preface of Sundays in Ordinary Time I-VIII, pp.61-67.

Communion Antiphon Cf. Ps 19:6

We will ring out our joy at your
   saving help
and exult in the name of our God.

Ant. ad communionem

Lætabimur in salutari tuo,
et in nomine Dei
   nostri magnificabimur.

Or: Ep 5:2

Christ loved us and gave himself up
   for us,
as a fragrant offering to God.

Vel:

Christus dilexit nos, et tradidit
   semetipsum pro nobis,
oblationem Deo
   in odorem suavitatis.

Prayer after Communion

May your Sacraments, O Lord,
   we pray,
perfect in us what lies within them,
that what we now celebrate in signs
we may one day possess in truth.
Through Christ our Lord.

Post communionem

Perficiant in nobis,
   Domine, quæsumus,
tua sacramenta quod continent,
ut, quæ nunc specie gerimus,
rerum veritate capiamus.
Per Christum Dominum nostrum.

1 November

ALL SAINTS

*Today, with the entire Church, we celebrate the Solemnity of All Saints.
In doing so, we remember not only those who have been proclaimed saints
through the ages, but also our many brothers and sisters who, in a quiet and
unassuming way, lived their Christian life in the fulness of faith and love.
Ours, then, is a celebration of holiness. A holiness that is seen not so much
in great deeds and extraordinary events, but rather in daily fidelity to the
demands of our baptism. A holiness that consists in the love of God and the
love of our brothers and sisters. A love that remains faithful to the point of
self-renunciation and complete devotion to others. Yet if there is one thing
typical of the saints, it is that they are genuinely happy. They found the secret
of authentic happiness, which lies deep within the soul and has its source in
the love of God.*

(Pope Francis)

Solemnity

Entrance Antiphon

L ET us all rejoice in the Lord,
as we celebrate the feast day
in honour of all the Saints,
at whose festival the Angels rejoice
and praise the Son of God.

Ant. ad introitum

G AUDEAMUS omnes in Domino,
diem festum celebrantes
sub honore Sanctorum omnium,
de quorum sollemnitate
gaudent Angeli,
et collaudant Filium Dei.

The Gloria in excelsis (Glory to God in the highest) is said.

Collect	Collecta
Almighty ever-living God,	Omnipotens sempiterne Deus,
by whose gift we venerate in one celebration	qui nos omnium Sanctorum tuorum merita
the merits of all the Saints,	sub una tribuisti celebritate
bestow on us, we pray,	venerari, quæsumus,
through the prayers of so many intercessors,	ut desideratam nobis tuæ propitiationis abundantiam,
an abundance of the reconciliation with you	multiplicatis intercessoribus, largiaris.
for which we earnestly long.	
Through our Lord Jesus Christ, your Son,	Per Dominum nostrum Iesum Christum Filium tuum,
who lives and reigns with you in the unity of the Holy Spirit,	qui tecum vivit et regnat in unitate Spiritus Sancti,
one God, for ever and ever.	Deus, per omnia sæcula sæculorum.

FIRST READING

A reading from the book of the Apocalypse   7:2-4,9-14

I saw a huge number, impossible to count, of people from every nation, race, tribe and language.

I, John, saw another angel rising where the sun rises, carrying the seal of the living God; he called in a powerful voice to the four angels whose duty was to devastate land and sea, 'Wait before you do any damage on land or at sea or to the trees, until we have put the seal on the foreheads of the servants of our God.' Then I heard how many were sealed: a hundred and forty-four thousand, out of all the tribes of Israel.

After that I saw a huge number, impossible to count, of people from every nation, race, tribe and language; they were standing in front of the throne and in front of the Lamb, dressed in white robes and holding palms in their hands. They shouted aloud, 'Victory to our God, who sits on the throne, and to the Lamb!' And all the angels who were standing in a circle round the throne, surrounding the elders and the four animals, prostrated themselves before the throne, and touched the ground with their foreheads, worshipping God with these words: 'Amen. Praise and glory and wisdom and thanksgiving and honour and power and strength to our God for ever and ever. Amen.'

One of the elders then spoke, and asked me, 'Do you know who these people are, dressed in white robes, and where they have come from?' I answered him, 'You can tell me, my Lord.' Then he said, 'These are the people who have been through the great persecution, and they have washed their robes white again in the blood of the Lamb.'

The word of the Lord.

Responsorial Psalm   Ps 23:1-6. R. Cf. v.6

R. **Such are the men who seek your face, O Lord.**

The Lord's is the earth and its fullness,
the world and all its peoples.
It is he who set it on the seas;
on the waters he made it firm. R.

Who shall climb the mountain of the Lord?
Who shall stand in his holy place?
The man with clean hands and pure heart,
who desires not worthless things. R.

He shall receive blessings from the Lord
and reward from the God who saves him.
Such are the men who seek him,
seek the face of the God of Jacob. R.

SECOND READING

A reading from the first letter of John   3:1-3

We shall see God as he really is.

Think of the love that the Father has lavished on us,
by letting us be called God's children;
and that is what we are.
Because the world refused to acknowledge him,
therefore it does not acknowledge us.
My dear people, we are already the children of God
but what we are to be in the future has not yet been revealed,
all we know is, that when it is revealed
we shall be like him
because we shall see him as he really is.
Surely everyone who entertains this hope
must purify himself, must try to be as pure as Christ.

The word of the Lord.

Gospel Acclamation   Mt 11:28

R. **Alleluia, alleluia!**
Come to me, all of you who labour
    and are overburdened,
and I will give you rest, says the Lord.
R. **Alleluia!**

GOSPEL

A reading from the holy Gospel according to Matthew   5:1-12
Rejoice and be glad, for your reward will be great in heaven.

Seeing the crowds, Jesus went up the hill. There he sat down and was joined
by his disciples. Then he began to speak. This is what he taught them:

'How happy are the poor in spirit;
    theirs is the kingdom of heaven.
Happy the gentle:
    they shall have the earth for their heritage.
Happy those who mourn:
    they shall be comforted.
Happy those who hunger and thirst for what is right:
    they shall be satisfied.
Happy the merciful:
    they shall have mercy shown them.
Happy the pure in heart:
    they shall see God.
Happy the peacemakers:
    they shall be called sons of God.
Happy those who are persecuted in the cause of right:
    theirs is the kingdom of heaven.

'Happy are you when people abuse you and persecute you and speak all
kinds of calumny against you on my account. Rejoice and be glad, for your
reward will be great in heaven.'

The Gospel of the Lord.

The Creed is said.

Prayer over the Offerings

May these offerings we bring
   in honour of all the Saints
be pleasing to you, O Lord,
and grant that, just as we believe
   the Saints
to be already assured of immortality,
so we may experience their concern
   for our salvation.
Through Christ our Lord.

Preface: The glory of Jerusalem,
our mother.

It is truly right and just,
   our duty and our salvation,
always and everywhere
   to give you thanks,
Lord, holy Father,
   almighty and eternal God.

For today by your gift we celebrate
   our mother,
the festival of your city,
the heavenly Jerusalem,
   where the great array
   of our brothers and sisters
already gives you eternal praise.

Towards her, we eagerly hasten
   as pilgrims advancing by faith,
rejoicing in the glory bestowed
   upon those exalted members
   of the Church
through whom you give us,
   in our frailty, both strength
   and good example.

And so, we glorify you with the
   multitude of Saints and Angels,
as with one voice of praise
   we acclaim:

Holy, Holy, Holy Lord God of hosts...

Super oblata

Grata tibi sint, Domine, munera,
quæ pro cunctorum offerimus
   honore Sanctorum,
et concede,
ut, quos iam credimus de sua
   immortalitate securos,
sentiamus de nostra salute sollicitos.
Per Christum Dominum nostrum.

Præfatio: De gloria matris
nostræ Ierusalem

Vere dignum et iustum est,
   æquum et salutare,
nos tibi semper et ubique
   gratias agere:
Domine, sancte Pater,
   omnipotens æterne Deus:

Nobis enim hodie civitatem tuam
   quæ mater nostra est,

tribuis celebrare,
cælestique Ierusalem,
ubi iam te in æternum fratrum
   nostrorum corona collaudat.

Ad quam peregrini,
   per fidem accedentes,
alacriter festinamus,
   congaudentes de Ecclesiæ
sublimium glorificatione
   membrorum,
qua simul fragilitati nostræ
   adiumenta et exempla concedis.

Et ideo, cum ipsorum
   Angelorumque frequentia,
una te magnificamus,
   laudis voce clamantes:

Sanctus, Sanctus, Sanctus. . .

Communion Antiphon Mt 5:8-10

Blessed are the clean of heart,
for they shall see God.
Blessed are the peacemakers,
for they shall be called
children of God.
Blessed are they who are persecuted
for the sake of righteousness,
for theirs is the Kingdom of Heaven.

Prayer after Communion

As we adore you, O God, who alone
are holy
and wonderful in all your Saints,
we implore your grace,
so that, coming to perfect holiness
in the fullness of your love,
we may pass from this pilgrim table
to the banquet
of our heavenly homeland.
Through Christ our Lord.

Ant. ad communionem

Beati mundo corde, quoniam ipsi
Deum videbunt;
beati pacifici, quoniam filii
Dei vocabuntur;
beati qui persecutionem patiuntur
propter iustitiam,
quoniam ipsorum
est regnum cælorum.

Post communionem

Mirabilem te, Deus,
et unum Sanctum in omnibus
Sanctis tuis adorantes,
tuam gratiam imploramus,
qua, sanctificationem
in tui amoris plenitudine
consummantes,
ex hac mensa peregrinantium
ad cælestis patriæ
convivium transeamus.
Per Christum Dominum nostrum.

A formula of Solemn Blessing, pp.146-149, may be used.

2 November

THE COMMEMORATION
OF ALL THE FAITHFUL DEPARTED

(ALL SOULS' DAY)

To see God, to be like God: this is our hope. And today we need to think a little about this hope: this hope that accompanies us in life. The first Christians depicted hope with an anchor, as though life were an anchor cast on Heaven's shores and all of us journeying to that shore, clinging to the anchor's rope. This is a beautiful image of hope: to have our hearts anchored there, where our beloved predecessors are, where the Saints are, where Jesus is, where God is. This is the hope that does not disappoint. Hope is a little like leaven that expands our souls. There are difficult moments in life, but with hope the soul goes forward and looks ahead to what awaits us. Today is a day of hope. Our brothers and sisters are in the presence of God and we shall also be there, through the pure grace of the Lord, if we walk along the way of Jesus. Today before evening falls each one of us can think of the twilight of life: "What will my passing away be like?". All of us will experience sundown, all of us! Do we look at it with hope? Today is a day of joy; however it is serene and tranquil joy, a peaceful joy. Let us think about the passing away of so many of our brothers and sisters who have preceded us, let us think about the evening of our life, when it will come. And let us think about our hearts and ask ourselves: "Where is my heart anchored?" If it is not firmly anchored, let us anchor it beyond, on that shore, knowing that hope does not disappoint because the Lord Jesus does not disappoint.

(Pope Francis)

The Masses that follow may be used at the discretion of the celebrant. The readings are found on pp. 606-608.

1

Entrance Antiphon Cf. 1 Th 4:14; 1 Co 15:22	Ant. ad introitum
Just as Jesus died and has risen again, so through Jesus God will bring with him those who have fallen asleep; and as in Adam all die, so also in Christ will all be brought to life.	Sicut Iesus mortuus est et resurrexit, ita et Deus eos qui dormierunt per Iesum adducet cum eo. Et sicut in Adam omnes moriuntur, ita et in Christo omnes vivificabuntur.

The Gloria in excelsis (Glory to God in the highest) is omitted.

Collect

Listen kindly to our prayers, O Lord,
and, as our faith in your Son,
raised from the dead, is deepened,
so may our hope of resurrection
    for your departed servants
also find new strength.
Through our Lord Jesus Christ,
    your Son,
who lives and reigns with you
    in the unity of the Holy Spirit,
one God, for ever and ever.

Collecta

Preces nostras, quæsumus,
    Domine, benignus exaudi,
ut, dum attollitur nostra fides
in Filio tuo a mortuis suscitato,
in famulorum tuorum
    præstolanda resurrectione
spes quoque nostra firmetur.
Per Dominum nostrum Iesum
    Christum Filium tuum,
qui tecum vivit et regnat
    in unitate Spiritus Sancti,
Deus, per omnia sæcula sæculorum.

Prayer over the Offerings

Look favourably on our offerings,
    O Lord,
so that your departed servants
may be taken up into glory
    with your Son,
in whose great mystery of love
    we are all united.
Who lives and reigns
    for ever and ever.

Super oblata

Nostris, Domine,
    propitiare muneribus,
ut famuli tui defuncti assumantur
    in gloriam cum Filio tuo,
cuius magno pietatis
    iungimur sacramento.
Qui vivit et regnat
    in sæcula sæculorum.

Preface for the Dead, pp.74-79.

Communion Antiphon Cf. Jn 11:25-26

I am the Resurrection and the Life,
    says the Lord.
Whoever believes in me, even
    though he dies, will live,
and everyone who lives and believes
    in me will not die for ever.

Ant. ad communionem

Ego sum resurrectio et vita, dicit
    Dominus.
Qui credit in me, etiam si mortuus
    fuerit, vivet;
et omnis, qui vivit et credit in me,
non morietur in æternum.

Prayer after Communion	Post communionem
Grant we pray, O Lord, that your departed servants,	Præsta, quæsumus, Domine, ut famuli tui defuncti
for whom we have celebrated this paschal Sacrament,	in mansionem lucis transeant et pacis,
may pass over to a dwelling place of light and peace.	pro quibus paschale celebravimus sacramentum.
Through Christ our Lord.	Per Christum Dominum nostrum.

A formula of Solemn Blessing, pp.148-151, may be used.

2

Entrance Antiphon Cf. 4 Esdr 2:34-35	Ant. ad introitum
Eternal rest grant unto them, O Lord, and let perpetual light shine upon them.	Requiem æternam dona eis, Domine, et lux perpetua luceat eis.

Collect	Collecta
O God, glory of the faithful and life of the just,	Deus, gloria fidelium et vita iustorum,
by the Death and Resurrection of whose Son	cuius Filii morte et resurrectione redempti sumus,
we have been redeemed,	propitiare famulis tuis defunctis,
look mercifully on your departed servants,	ut, qui resurrectionis nostræ mysterium agnoverunt,
that, just as they professed the mystery of our resurrection,	æternæ beatitudinis gaudia percipere mereantur.
so they may merit to receive the joys of eternal happiness.	Per Dominum nostrum Iesum Christum Filium tuum,
Through our Lord Jesus Christ, your Son,	qui tecum vivit et regnat in unitate Spiritus Sancti,
who lives and reigns with you in the unity of the Holy Spirit, one God, for ever and ever.	Deus, per omnia sæcula sæculorum.

Prayer over the Offerings

Almighty and merciful God,
by means of these
   sacrificial offerings
wash away, we pray,
   in the Blood of Christ,
the sins of your departed servants,
for you purify unceasingly by your
   merciful forgiveness
those you once cleansed in the
   waters of Baptism.
Through Christ our Lord.

Preface for the Dead, pp. 74-79.

Super oblata

Omnipotens et misericors Deus,
his sacrificiis ablue, quæsumus,
   famulos tuos defunctos
a peccatis eorum
   in sanguine Christi,
ut, quos mundasti
   aqua baptismatis,
indesinenter purifices
   indulgentia pietatis.
Per Christum Dominum nostrum.

Communion Antiphon Cf. 4 Esdr 2:35, 34

Let perpetual light shine upon
   them, O Lord,
with your Saints for ever,
   for you are merciful.

Ant. ad communionem

Lux æterna luceat eis, Domine,
cum Sanctis tuis in æternum,
   quia pius es.

Prayer after Communion

Having received the Sacrament of
   your Only Begotten Son,
who was sacrificed for us
   and rose in glory,
we humbly implore you, O Lord,
for your departed servants,
that, cleansed by
   the paschal mysteries,
they may glory in the gift of the
   resurrection to come.
Through Christ our Lord.

Post communionem

Sumpto sacramento Unigeniti tui,
qui pro nobis immolatus
   resurrexit in gloria,
te, Domine, suppliciter exoramus
   pro famulis tuis defunctis,
ut, paschalibus mysteriis mundati,
futuræ resurrectionis
   munere glorientur.
Per Christum Dominum nostrum.

A formula of Solemn Blessing, pp. 148-151, may be used.

3

Entrance Antiphon   Cf. Rm 8:11

God, who raised Jesus from the dead,
will give life also to your
   mortal bodies,
through his Spirit that dwells in you.

Collect

O God, who willed that your Only
   Begotten Son,
having conquered death,
should pass over into the realm
   of heaven,
grant, we pray,
   to your departed servants
that, with the mortality
   of this life overcome,
they may gaze eternally on you,
their Creator and Redeemer.
Through our Lord Jesus Christ,
   your Son,
who lives and reigns with you in
   the unity of the Holy Spirit,
one God, for ever and ever.

Prayer over the Offerings

Receive, Lord, in your kindness,
the sacrificial offering we make
for all your servants who sleep
   in Christ,
that, set free from the bonds
   of death
by this singular sacrifice,
they may merit eternal life.
Through Christ our Lord.

Preface for the Dead, pp.74-79.

Ant. ad introitum

Deus, qui suscitavit Iesum a mortuis,
vivificabit et mortalia
   corpora nostra,
propter inhabitantem Spiritum
   eius in nobis.

Collecta

Deus, qui Unigenitum tuum,
   devicta morte,
ad cælestia transire fecisti,
concede famulis tuis defunctis,
ut, huius vitæ mortalitate devicta,
te conditorem et redemptorem
possint perpetuo contemplari.

Per Dominum nostrum Iesum
   Christum Filium tuum,
qui tecum vivit et regnat
   in unitate Spiritus Sancti,
Deus, per omnia sæcula sæculorum.

Super oblata

Pro omnibus famulis tuis in Christo
   dormientibus
hostiam, Domine, suscipe
   benignus oblatam,
ut, per hoc sacrificium singulare
   vinculis mortis exuti,
vitam mereantur æternam.
Per Christum Dominum nostrum.

Communion Antiphon Cf. Ph 3:20-21

We await a saviour,
    the Lord Jesus Christ,
who will change our mortal bodies,
to conform with his glorified body.

Ant. ad communionem

Salvatorem exspectamus
    Dominum Iesum Christum,
qui reformabit corpus
    humilitatis nostræ,
configuratum corpori claritatis suæ.

Prayer after Communion

Through these sacrificial gifts
which we have received, O Lord,
bestow on your departed servants
    your great mercy
and, to those you have endowed
    with the grace of Baptism,
grant also the fullness of
    eternal joy.
Through Christ our Lord.

Post communionem

Multiplica, Domine,
    his sacrificiis susceptis,
super famulos tuos defunctos
    misericordiam tuam,
et, quibus donasti
    baptismi gratiam,
da eis æternorum
    plenitudinem gaudiorum.
Per Christum Dominum nostrum.

A formula of Solemn Blessing, pp.148-151, may be used.

FIRST READING

A reading from the prophet Isaiah   25:6-9
The Lord will destroy Death for ever.

On this mountain,
the Lord of hosts will prepare for all peoples
a banquet of rich food.
On this mountain he will remove
the mourning veil covering all peoples,
and the shroud enwrapping all nations,
he will destroy Death for ever.
The Lord will wipe away
the tears from every cheek;
he will take away his people's shame
everywhere on earth,
for the Lord has said so.
That day, it will be said: See, this is our God
in whom we hoped for salvation;
the Lord is the one in whom we hoped.
We exult and we rejoice
that he has saved us.

    The word of the Lord.

Responsional Psalm   Ps 26:1,4,7-9,13-14. R. v.1. Alt. R. v.13

R. **The Lord is my light and my help.**

> Or: **I am sure I shall see the Lord's goodness
> in the land of the living.**

The Lord is my light and my help;
whom shall I fear?
The Lord is the stronghold of my life;
before whom shall I shrink? R.

There is one thing I ask of the Lord,
for this I long,
to live in the house of the Lord,
all the days of my life,
to savour the sweetness of the Lord,
to behold his temple. R.

O Lord, hear my voice when I call;
have mercy and answer.
It is your face, O Lord, that I seek;
hide not your face. R.

I am sure I shall see the Lord's goodness
in the land of the living.
Hope in him, hold firm and take heart.
Hope in the Lord! R.

SECOND READING

A reading from the letter of St Paul to the Romans   5:5-11

*Having died to make us righteous, is it likely that he would now fail to save us from
God's anger?*

Hope is not deceptive, because the love of God has been poured into our
hearts by the Holy Spirit which has been given us. We were still helpless
when at his appointed moment Christ died for sinful men. It is not easy
to die even for a good man – though of course for someone really worthy,
a man might be prepared to die – but what proves that God loves us is
that Christ died for us while we were still sinners. Having died to make us
righteous, is it likely that he would now fail to save us from God's anger?
When we were reconciled to God by the death of his Son, we were still
enemies; now that we have been reconciled, surely we may count on being
saved by the life of his Son? Not merely because we have been reconciled

but because we are filled with joyful trust in God, through our Lord Jesus Christ, through whom we have already gained our reconciliation.

The word of the Lord.

R. **Alleluia, alleluia!**
It is my Father's will, says the Lord,
that I should lose nothing
of all that he has given to me,
and that I should raise it up on the last day.
R. **Alleluia!**

GOSPEL

A reading from the holy Gospel according to Mark   15:33-39; 16:1-6
Jesus gave a loud cry and breathed his last.

When the sixth hour came there was darkness over the whole land until the ninth hour. And at the ninth hour Jesus cried out in a loud voice, 'Eloi, Eloi, lama sabachthani?' which means, 'My God, my God, why have you deserted me?' When some of those who stood by heard this, they said, 'Listen, he is calling on Elijah'. Someone ran and soaked a sponge in vinegar and, putting it on a reed, gave it to him to drink saying, 'Wait and see if Elijah will come to take him down'. But Jesus gave a loud cry and breathed his last. And the veil of the Temple was torn in two from top to bottom. The centurion, who was standing in front of him, had seen how he had died, and he said, 'In truth this man was a son of God'.

When the Sabbath was over, Mary of Magdala, Mary the mother of James, and Salome, bought spices with which to go and anoint him. And very early in the morning on the first day of the week they went to the tomb, just as the sun was rising.

They had been saying to one another, 'Who will roll away the stone for us from the entrance to the tomb?' But when they looked they could see that the stone – which was very big – had already been rolled back. On entering the tomb they saw a young man in a white robe seated on the right-hand side, and they were struck with amazement. But he said to them, 'There is no need for alarm. You are looking for Jesus of Nazareth, who was crucified: he has risen, he is not here. See, here is the place where they laid him.'

The Gospel of the Lord.

The Creed is not said.

4 November

THIRTY-FIRST SUNDAY IN ORDINARY TIME

Entrance Antiphon Cf. Ps 37:22-23

FORSAKE me not, O Lord,
my God;
be not far from me!
Make haste and come to my help,
O Lord, my strong salvation!

Ant. ad introitum

NE derelinquas me,
Domine Deus meus,
ne discedas a me;
intende in adiutorium meum,
Domine, virtus salutis meæ.

Collect

Almighty and merciful God,
by whose gift your faithful offer you
right and praiseworthy service,
grant, we pray,
that we may hasten
without stumbling
to receive the things you
have promised.
Through our Lord Jesus Christ,
your Son,
who lives and reigns with you
in the unity of the Holy Spirit,
one God, for ever and ever.

Collecta

Omnipotens et misericors Deus,
de cuius munere venit,
ut tibi a fidelibus tuis digne
et laudabiliter serviatur,
tribue, quæsumus, nobis,
ut ad promissiones tuas sine
offensione curramus.
Per Dominum nostrum Iesum
Christum Filium tuum,
qui tecum vivit et regnat
in unitate Spiritus Sancti,
Deus, per omnia sæcula sæculorum.

FIRST READING

A reading from the book of Deuteronomy   6:2-6

Listen, Israel: You shall love the Lord Your God with all your heart.

Moses said to the people: 'If you fear the Lord your God all the days of your life and if you keep all his laws and commandments which I lay on you, you will have a long life, you and your son and your grandson. Listen then, Israel, keep and observe what will make you prosper and give you great increase, as the Lord God of your fathers has promised you, giving you a land where milk and honey flow.

'Listen, Israel: The Lord our God is the one Lord. You shall love the Lord your God with all your heart, with all your soul, with all your strength. Let these words I urge on you today be written on your heart.'

The word of the Lord.

Responsorial Psalm   Ps 17:2-4,47,51. R. v.2

R. **I love you, Lord, my strength.**

I love you, Lord, my strength,
my rock, my fortress, my saviour.
My God is the rock where I take refuge;
my shield, my mighty help, my stronghold.
The Lord is worthy of all praise:
when I call I am saved from my foes. R.

Long life to the Lord, my rock!
Praised be the God who saves me.
He has given great victories to his king
and shown his love for his anointed. R.

SECOND READING

A reading from the letter to the Hebrews   7:23-28

Because he remains for ever, Christ can never lose his priesthood.

There used to be a great number of priests under the former covenant,
because death put an end to each one of them; but this one, Christ, because
he remains for ever, can never lose his priesthood. It follows, then, that his
power to save is utterly certain, since he is living for ever to intercede for all
who come to God through him.

To suit us, the ideal high priest would have to be holy, innocent and
uncontaminated, beyond the influence of sinners, and raised up above the
heavens; one who would not need to offer sacrifices every day, as the other
high priests do for their own sins and then for those of the people, because
he has done this once and for all by offering himself. The Law appoints
high priests who are men subject to weakness; but the promise on oath,
which came after the Law, appointed the Son who is made perfect for ever.

The word of the Lord.

Gospel Acclamation   Cf. Jn 6:63,68

R. **Alleluia, alleluia!**
Your words are spirit, Lord,
and they are life:
you have the message of eternal life.
R. **Alleluia!**

Or: Jn 14:23

R. **Alleluia, alleluia!**
If anyone loves me he will keep my word,
and my Father will love him,
and we shall come to him.
R. **Alleluia!**

GOSPEL

A reading from the holy Gospel according to Mark   12:28-34
This is the first commandment. The second is like it.

One of the scribes came up to Jesus and put a question to him, 'Which is the first of all the commandments?' Jesus replied, 'This is the first: Listen, Israel, the Lord our God is the one Lord, and you must love the Lord your God with all your heart, with all your soul, with all your mind and with all your strength. The second is this: You must love your neighbour as yourself. There is no commandment greater than these.' The scribe said to him, 'Well spoken, Master; what you have said is true: that he is one and there is no other. To love with all your heart, with all your understanding and strength, and to love your neighbour as yourself, this is far more important than any holocaust or sacrifice.' Jesus, seeing how wisely he had spoken said, 'You are not far from the kingdom of God.' And after that no one dared to question him any more.

The Gospel of the Lord.

Prayer over the Offerings

May these sacrificial offerings,
    O Lord,
become for you a pure oblation,
and for us a holy outpouring
    of your mercy.
Through Christ our Lord.

Super oblata

Fiat hoc sacrificium, Domine,
    oblatio tibi munda,
et nobis misericordiæ tuæ
    sancta largitio.
Per Christum Dominum nostrum.

Preface of Sundays in Ordinary Time I-VIII, pp.61-67.

Communion Antiphon Cf. Ps 15:11

You will show me the path of life,
the fullness of joy in your presence,
    O Lord.

Or: Jn 6:58

Just as the living Father sent me
and I have life because of the Father,
so whoever feeds on me
shall have life because of me,
    says the Lord.

Prayer after Communion

May the working of your power,
    O Lord,
increase in us, we pray,
so that, renewed by these
    heavenly Sacraments,
we may be prepared by your gift
for receiving what they promise.
Through Christ our Lord.

Ant. ad communionem

Notas mihi fecisti vias vitæ,
adimplebis me lætitia
    cum vultu tuo, Domine.

Vel:

Sicut misit me vivens Pater,
    et ego vivo propter Patrem,
et qui manducat me,
    et ipse vivet propter me,
dicit Dominus.

Post communionem

Augeatur in nobis,
    quæsumus, Domine,
tuæ virtutis operatio,
ut, refecti cælestibus sacramentis,
ad eorum promissa capienda tuo
    munere præparemur.
Per Christum Dominum nostrum.

11 November

THIRTY-SECOND SUNDAY IN ORDINARY TIME

Entrance Antiphon   Ps 87:3 | Ant. ad introitum

LET my prayer come
into your presence.
Incline your ear
  to my cry for help, O Lord.

INTRET oratio mea
in conspectu tuo;
inclina aurem tuam
  ad precem meam, Domine.

Collect | Collecta

Almighty and merciful God,
graciously keep from us all adversity,
so that, unhindered in mind
  and body alike,
we may pursue in freedom of heart
the things that are yours.
Through our Lord Jesus Christ,
  your Son,
who lives and reigns with you
  in the unity of the Holy Spirit,
one God, for ever and ever.

Omnipotens et misericors Deus,
universa nobis adversantia
  propitiatus exclude,
ut, mente et corpore pariter expediti,
quæ tua sunt liberis
  mentibus exsequamur.
Per Dominum nostrum Iesum
  Christum Filium tuum,
qui tecum vivit et regnat
  in unitate Spiritus Sancti,
Deus, per omnia sæcula sæculorum.

FIRST READING

A reading from the first book of the Kings   17:10-16

The widow made a little scone from her meal and brought it to Elijah.

Elijah the Prophet went off to Sidon. And when he reached the city gate,
there was a widow gathering sticks; addressing her he said, 'Please bring
a little water in a vessel for me to drink.' She was setting off to bring it
when he called after her. 'Please' he said 'bring me a scrap of bread in your
hand.' 'As the Lord your God lives,' she replied 'I have no baked bread, but
only a handful of meal in a jar and a little oil in a jug; I am just gathering a
stick or two to go and prepare this for myself and my son to eat, and then
we shall die.' But Elijah said to her, 'Do not be afraid, go and do as you
have said; but first make a little scone of it for me and bring it to me, and
then make some for yourself and for your son. For thus the Lord speaks,
the God of Israel:

  "Jar of meal shall not be spent,
  jug of oil shall not be emptied,
  before the day when the Lord sends
  rain on the face of the earth."'

The woman went and did as Elijah told her and they ate the food, she, himself and her son. The jar of meal was not spent nor the jug of oil emptied, just as the Lord had foretold through Elijah.

The word of the Lord.

Responsorial Psalm   Ps 145:7-10. R. v.2

R. **My soul, give praise to the Lord.**
   Or: **Alleluia!**

It is the Lord who keeps faith for ever,
who is just to those who are oppressed.
It is he who gives bread to the hungry,
the Lord, who sets prisoners free. R.

It is the Lord who gives sight to the blind,
who raises up those who are bowed down.
It is the Lord who loves the just,
the Lord, who protects the stranger. R.

The Lord upholds the widow and orphan
but thwarts the path of the wicked.
The Lord will reign for ever,
Zion's God, from age to age. R.

SECOND READING

A reading from the letter to the Hebrews   9:24-28
Christ offers himself only once to take the faults of many on himself.

It is not as though Christ had entered a man-made sanctuary which was only modelled on the real one; but it was heaven itself, so that he could appear in the actual presence of God on our behalf. And he does not have to offer himself again and again, like the high priest going into the sanctuary year after year with the blood that is not his own, or else he would have had to suffer over and over again since the world began. Instead of that, he has made his appearance once and for all, now at the end of the last age, to do away with sin by sacrificing himself. Since men only die once, and after that comes judgement, so Christ, too, offers himself only once to take the faults of many on himself, and when he appears a second time, it will not be to deal with sin but to reward with salvation those who are waiting for him.

The word of the Lord.

Gospel Acclamation   Rv 2:10

R. **Alleluia, alleluia!**
Even if you have to die, says the Lord,
keep faithful, and I will give you
the crown of life.
R. **Alleluia!**

Or: Mt 5:3

R. **Alleluia, alleluia!**
How happy are the poor in spirit;
theirs is the kingdom of heaven.
R. **Alleluia!**

GOSPEL

A reading from the holy Gospel according to Mark   12:38-44
This poor widow has put in more than all.

In his teaching Jesus said, 'Beware of the scribes who like to walk about in
long robes, to be greeted obsequiously in the market squares, to take the
front seats in the synagogues and the places of honour at banquets; these
are the men who swallow the property of widows, while making a show of
lengthy prayers. The more severe will be the sentence they receive.'

[He sat down opposite the treasury and watched the people putting
money into the treasury, and many of the rich put in a great deal. A poor
widow came and put in two small coins, the equivalent of a penny. Then
he called his disciples and said to them, 'I tell you solemnly, this poor
widow has put more in than all who have contributed to the treasury; for
they have all put in money they had over, but she from the little she had
has put in everything she possessed, all she had to live on.'

The Gospel of the Lord.]

Shorter Form, verses 41-44. Read between [ ]

Prayer over the Offerings	Super oblata
Look with favour, we pray, O Lord, upon the sacrificial gifts offered here, that, celebrating in mystery the Passion of your Son, we may honour it with loving devotion. Through Christ our Lord.	Sacrificiis præsentibus, Domine, quæsumus, intende placatus, ut, quod passionis Filii tui mysterio gerimus, pio consequamur affectu. Per Christum Dominum nostrum.

Preface of Sundays in Ordinary Time I-VIII, pp.61-67.

Communion Antiphon   Ps 22:1-2

The Lord is my shepherd;
  there is nothing I shall want.
Fresh and green are the pastures
  where he gives me repose,
near restful waters he leads me.

Or: Lk 24:35

The disciples recognised the Lord
  Jesus in the breaking of bread.

Prayer after Communion

Nourished by this sacred gift,
  O Lord,
we give you thanks and beseech
  your mercy,
that, by the pouring forth
  of your Spirit,
the grace of integrity may endure
in those your heavenly power
  has entered.
Through Christ our Lord.

Ant. ad communionem

Dominus regit me,
  et nihil mihi deerit;
in loco pascuæ ibi me collocavit,
super aquam refectionis
  educavit me.

Vel:

Cognoverunt discipuli Dominum
Iesum in fractione panis.

Post communionem

Gratias tibi, Domine, referimus
  sacro munere vegetati,
tuam clementiam implorantes,
ut, per infusionem Spiritus tui,
in quibus cælestis virtus introivit,
sinceritatis gratia perseveret.
Per Christum Dominum nostrum.

18 November

THIRTY-THIRD SUNDAY IN ORDINARY TIME

Entrance Antiphon Jer 29:11,12,14

THE Lord said: I think thoughts
  of peace and not of affliction.
You will call upon me,
  and I will answer you,
and I will lead back your captives
  from every place.

Ant. ad introitum

DICIT Dominus:
  Ego cogito cogitationes pacis
  et non afflictionis;
invocabitis me, et ego exaudiam vos,
et reducam captivitatem vestram
  de cunctis locis.

Collect	Collecta
Grant us, we pray, O Lord our God, the constant gladness of being devoted to you, for it is full and lasting happiness to serve with constancy the author of all that is good. Through our Lord Jesus Christ, your Son, who lives and reigns with you in the unity of the Holy Spirit, one God, for ever and ever.	Da nobis, quæsumus, Domine Deus noster, in tua semper devotione gaudere, quia perpetua est et plena felicitas, si bonorum omnium iugiter serviamus auctori. Per Dominum nostrum Iesum Christum Filium tuum, qui tecum vivit et regnat in unitate Spiritus Sancti, Deus, per omnia sæcula sæculorum.

FIRST READING

A reading from the prophet Daniel   12:1-3

When that time comes, your own people will be spared.

'At that time Michael will stand up, the great prince who mounts guard over your people. There is going to be a time of great distress, unparalleled since nations first came into existence. When that time comes, your own people will be spared, all those whose names are found written in the Book. Of those who lie sleeping in the dust of the earth many will awake, some to everlasting life, some to shame and everlasting disgrace. The learned will shine as brightly as the vault of heaven, and those who have instructed many in virtue, as bright as stars for all eternity.'

The word of the Lord.

Responsorial Psalm   Ps 15:5,8-11. R. v.1

R. **Preserve me, God, I take refuge in you.**

O Lord, it is you who are my portion and cup;
it is you yourself who are my prize.
I keep the Lord ever in my sight:
since he is at my right hand, I shall stand firm. R.

And so my heart rejoices, my soul is glad;
even my body shall rest in safety.
For you will not leave my soul among the dead,
nor let your beloved know decay. R.

You will show me the path of life,
the fullness of joy in your presence,
at your right hand happiness for ever. R.

SECOND READING

A reading from the letter to the Hebrews   10:11-14,18

By virtue of one single offering, he has achieved the eternal perfection of all whom he is sanctifying.

All the priests stand at their duties every day, offering over and over again the same sacrifices which are quite incapable of taking sins away. Christ, on the other hand, has offered one single sacrifice for sins, and then taken his place for ever, at the right hand of God, where he is now waiting until his enemies are made into a footstool for him. By virtue of that one single offering, he has achieved the eternal perfection of all whom he is sanctifying. When all sins have been forgiven, there can be no more sin offerings.

The word of the Lord.

Gospel Acclamation   Mt 24:42,44

R. **Alleluia, alleluia!**
Stay awake and stand ready,
because you do not know the hour
when the Son of Man is coming.
R. **Alleluia!**

Or: Lk 21:36

R. **Alleluia, alleluia!**
Stay awake, praying at all times
for the strength to stand with confidence
before the Son of Man.
R. **Alleluia!**

GOSPEL

A reading from the holy Gospel according to Mark   13:24-32

He will gather his chosen from the four winds.

Jesus said to his disciples: 'In those days, after the time of distress, the sun will be darkened, the moon will lose its brightness, the stars will come falling from heaven and the powers in the heavens will be shaken. And then they will see the Son of Man coming in the clouds with great power and glory; then too he will send the angels to gather his chosen from the four winds, from the ends of the world to the ends of heaven.

'Take the fig tree as a parable: as soon as its twigs grow supple and its leaves come out, you know that summer is near. So with you when you see these things happening: know that he is near, at the very gates. I tell you solemnly, before this generation has passed away all these things will have taken place. Heaven and earth will pass away, but my words will not pass away.

'But as for that day or hour, nobody knows it, neither the angels of heaven, nor the Son; no one but the Father.'

The Gospel of the Lord.

Prayer over the Offerings	Super oblata
Grant, O Lord, we pray, that what we offer in the sight of your majesty may obtain for us the grace of being devoted to you and gain us the prize of everlasting happiness. Through Christ our Lord.	Concede, quæsumus, Domine, ut oculis tuæ maiestatis munus oblatum et gratiam nobis devotionis obtineat, et effectum beatæ perennitatis acquirat. Per Christum Dominum nostrum.

Preface of Sundays in Ordinary Time I-VIII, pp.61-67.

Communion Antiphon Ps 72:28	Ant. ad communionem
To be near God is my happiness, to place my hope in God the Lord.	Mihi autem adhærere Deo bonum est, ponere in Domino Deo spem meam.

Or: Mk 11:23-24	Vel:
Amen, I say to you: Whatever you ask in prayer, believe that you will receive, and it shall be given to you, says the Lord.	Amen dico vobis, quidquid orantes petitis, credite quia accipietis, et fiet vobis, dicit Dominus.

Prayer after Communion	Post communionem
We have partaken of the gifts of this sacred mystery, humbly imploring, O Lord, that what your Son commanded us to do in memory of him may bring us growth in charity. Through Christ our Lord.	Sumpsimus, Domine, sacri dona mysterii, humiliter deprecantes, ut, quæ in sui commemorationem nos Filius tuus facere præcepit, in nostræ proficiant caritatis augmentum. Per Christum Dominum nostrum.

25 November

OUR LORD JESUS CHRIST, KING OF THE UNIVERSE

Solemnity

Entrance Antiphon Rv 5:12; 1:6	Ant. ad introitum

HOW worthy is the Lamb
who was slain,
to receive power and divinity,
and wisdom and strength
   and honour.
To him belong glory and power
   for ever and ever.

DIGNUS est Agnus,
qui occisus est,
accipere virtutem et divinitatem
et sapientiam et fortitudinem
   et honorem.
Ipsi gloria et imperium
   in sæcula sæculorum.

The Gloria in excelsis (Glory to God in the highest) is said.

Collect	Collecta

Almighty ever-living God,
whose will is to restore all things
in your beloved Son,
   the King of the universe,
grant, we pray,
that the whole creation,
   set free from slavery,
may render your majesty service
and ceaselessly proclaim your praise.
Through our Lord Jesus Christ,
   your Son,
who lives and reigns with you
   in the unity of the Holy Spirit,
one God, for ever and ever.

Omnipotens sempiterne Deus,
qui in dilecto Filio tuo,
   universorum Rege,
omnia instaurare voluisti,
concede propitius,
ut tota creatura, a servitute liberata,
tuæ maiestati deserviat ac te sine
   fine collaudet.
Per Dominum nostrum Iesum
   Christum Filium tuum,
qui tecum vivit et regnat
   in unitate Spiritus Sancti,
Deus, per omnia sæcula sæculorum.

FIRST READING

A reading from the prophet Daniel   7:13-14

His sovereignty is an eternal sovereignty.

I gazed into the visions of the night.
And I saw, coming on the clouds of heaven,
one like a son of man.

He came to the one of great age
and was led into his presence.
On him was conferred sovereignty,
glory and kingship,
and men of all peoples, nations and languages became his servants.
His sovereignty is an eternal sovereignty
which shall never pass away,
nor will his empire ever be destroyed.

   The word of the Lord.

Responsorial Psalm   Ps 92:1-2,5. R. v.1

R. **The Lord is king, with majesty enrobed.**

   The Lord is king, with majesty enrobed;
   the Lord has robed himself with might,
   he has girded himself with power. R.

   The world you made firm, not to be moved;
   your throne has stood firm from of old.
   From all eternity, O Lord, you are. R.

   Truly your decrees are to be trusted.
   Holiness is fitting to your house,
   O Lord, until the end of time. R.

SECOND READING

A reading from the book of the Apocalypse   1:5-8
Ruler of the kings of the earth. . . he made us a line of kings, priests to serve his God.

Jesus Christ is the faithful witness, the First-born from the dead, the Ruler
of the kings of the earth. He loves us and has washed away our sins with
his blood, and made us a line of kings, priests to serve his God and Father;
to him, then, be glory and power for ever and ever. Amen. It is he who
is coming on the clouds; everyone will see him, even those who pierced
him, and all the races of the earth will mourn over him. This is the truth.
Amen. 'I am the Alpha and the Omega' says the Lord God, who is, who
was, and who is to come, the Almighty.

   The word of the Lord.

Gospel Acclamation   Mk 11:9,10
R. **Alleluia, alleluia!**
Blessings on him who comes in the name of the Lord!
Blessings on the coming kingdom of our father David!
R. **Alleluia!**

GOSPEL

A reading from the holy Gospel according to John   18:33-37
It is you who say that I am a king.

'Are you the king of the Jews?' Pilate asked. Jesus replied, 'Do you ask
this of your own accord, or have others spoken to you about me?' Pilate
answered, 'Am I a Jew? It is your own people and the chief priests who have
handed you over to me: what have you done?' Jesus replied, 'Mine is not a
kingdom of this world; if my kingdom were of this world, my men would
have fought to prevent my being surrendered to the Jews. But my kingdom
is not of this kind.' 'So you are a king then?' said Pilate. 'It is you who say
it' answered Jesus. 'Yes, I am a king. I was born for this, I came into the
world for this: to bear witness to the truth; and all who are on the side of
truth listen to my voice.'

The Gospel of the Lord.

The Creed is said.

Prayer over the Offerings

As we offer you, O Lord,
     the sacrifice
by which the human race
     is reconciled to you,
we humbly pray
that your Son himself may bestow
     on all nations
the gifts of unity and peace.
Through Christ our Lord.

Super oblata

Hostiam tibi, Domine,
humanæ reconciliationis
     offerentes,
suppliciter deprecamur,
ut ipse Filius tuus cunctis gentibus
unitatis et pacis dona concedat.
Qui vivit et regnat
     in sæcula sæculorum.

Preface: Christ, King of the Universe. | Præfatio: De Christo universorum Rege.

It is truly right and just,
  our duty and our salvation,
always and everywhere
  to give you thanks,
Lord, holy Father,
  almighty and eternal God.

For you anointed your Only
  Begotten Son,
our Lord Jesus Christ,
  with the oil of gladness
as eternal Priest and King
  of all creation,
so that, by offering himself
  on the altar of the Cross
as a spotless sacrifice
  to bring us peace,
he might accomplish the mysteries
  of human redemption
and, making all created things
  subject to his rule,
he might present to the immensity
  of your majesty
an eternal and universal kingdom,
a kingdom of truth and life,
a kingdom of holiness and grace,
a kingdom of justice, love and peace.

And so, with Angels and Archangels,
with Thrones and Dominions,
and with all the hosts and Powers
  of heaven,
we sing the hymn of your glory,
as without end we acclaim:

Holy, Holy, Holy Lord God of hosts...

Vere dignum et iustum est,
  æquum et salutare,
nos tibi semper
  et ubique gratias agere:
Domine, sancte Pater,
  omnipotens æterne Deus:

Qui Unigenitum Filium tuum,
Dominum nostrum
  Iesum Christum,
Sacerdotem æternum
  et universorum Regem,
oleo exsultationis unxisti:
ut, seipsum in ara crucis
hostiam immaculatam
  et pacificam offerens,
redemptionis humanæ
  sacramenta perageret:
et, suo subiectis imperio
  omnibus creaturis,
æternum et universale regnum
immensæ tuæ traderet maiestati:
regnum veritatis et vitæ;
regnum sanctitatis et gratiæ;
regnum iustitiæ,
  amoris et pacis.

Et ideo cum Angelis et Archangelis,
cum Thronis et Dominationibus,
cumque omni
  militia cælestis exercitus,
hymnum gloriæ tuæ canimus,
sine fine dicentes:

Sanctus, Sanctus, Sanctus . . .

Communion Antiphon Ps 28:10-11

The Lord sits as King for ever.
The Lord will bless his people
   with peace.

Prayer after Communion

Having received the food
   of immortality,
we ask, O Lord,
that, glorying in obedience
to the commands of Christ,
   the King of the universe,
we may live with him eternally
   in his heavenly Kingdom.
Who lives and reigns
   for ever and ever.

Ant. ad communionem

Sedebit Dominus Rex in æternum;
Dominus benedicet populo suo
   in pace.

Post communionem

Immortalitatis alimoniam consecuti,
   quæsumus, Domine,
ut, qui Christi Regis universorum
gloriamur obœdire mandatis,
cum ipso in cælesti regno sine fine
   vivere valeamus.
Qui vivit et regnat
   in sæcula sæculorum.

RITE OF EUCHARISTIC EXPOSITION AND BENEDICTION

The service of Benediction developed during the Middle Ages during the Corpus Christi processions in which the Blessed Sacrament was held up for veneration. The service was subsequently used at other times throughout the year as an opportunity to give thanks for the Mass and adore Christ present under the form of bread.

Today, the Church encourages this rite to be celebrated in the context of a longer period of reading, prayer and reflection.

Exposition

First of all, the minister exposes the Blessed Sacrament while a hymn is sung, during which he incenses the Sacrament. The following or another hymn may be chosen.

O saving Victim, opening wide, The gate of heav'n to man below Our foes press on from every side; Thine aid supply, thy strength bestow.	O salutaris hostia, Quæ cæli pandis ostium; Bella premunt hostilia, Da robur, fer auxilium.
To thy great name be endless praise, Immortal Godhead, One in Three; O grant us endless length of days In our true native land with thee. Amen.	Uni Trinoque Domino Sit sempiterna gloria, Qui vitam sine termino Nobis donet in patria. Amen.

Adoration

A time for silent prayer, readings from Scripture, litanies or other prayers and hymns may be used. On some occasions, the Prayer of the Church might be said or sung.

Of the Glorious Body Telling	Pange Lingua
Of the glorious Body telling, O my tongue, its mysteries sing, And the Blood, all price excelling, Which the world's eternal King, In a noble womb once dwelling Shed for the world's ransoming.	Pange lingua gloriosi Corporis mysterium, Sanguinisque pretiosi, Quem in mundi pretium Fructus ventris generosi, Rex effudit gentium.

Given for us, for us descending,
Of a Virgin to proceed,
Man with man in
    converse blending,
Scattered he the Gospel seed,
Till his sojourn drew to ending,
Which he closed in wondrous deed.

At the last great Supper lying
Circled by his brethren's band,
Meekly with the law complying,
First he finished its command
Then, immortal Food supplying,
Gave himself with his own hand.

Word made Flesh,
    by word he maketh
Very bread his Flesh to be;
Man in wine Christ's Blood
    partaketh,
And if senses fail to see,
Faith alone the true heart waketh
To behold the mystery.

Nobis datus, nobis natus
Ex intacta Virgine,
Et in mundo conversatus,
Sparso verbi semine,
Sui moras incolatus
Miro clausit ordine.

In supremæ nocte cenæ
Recumbens cum fratribus,
Observata lege plene
Cibis in legalibus,
Cibum turbæ duodenæ
Se dat suis manibus

Verbum caro, panem verum
Verbo carnem efficit,
Fitque sanguis Christi merum,
Et, si sensus deficit,
Ad firmandum cor sincerum
Sola fides sufficit.

Sweet Sacrament Divine

Sweet Sacrament divine,
Hid in thine earthly home;
Lo! round thy lowly shrine,
With suppliant hearts we come;
Jesus, to thee our voice we raise
In songs of love and heartfelt praise
Sweet Sacrament divine. (repeat)

Sweet Sacrament of peace,
Dear home of every heart,
Where restless yearnings cease,
And sorrows all depart.
There in thine ear, all trustfully,
We tell our tale of misery,
Sweet Sacrament of peace. (repeat)

Sweet Sacrament of rest,
Ark from the ocean's roar,
Within thy shelter blest
Soon may we reach the shore;
Save us, for still the tempest raves,
Save, lest we sink beneath the waves:
Sweet Sacrament of rest. (repeat)

Sweet Sacrament divine,
Earth's light and jubilee,
In thy far depths doth shine
The Godhead's majesty;
Sweet light, so shine on us, we pray
That earthly joys may fade away:
Sweet Sacrament divine. (repeat)

(Francis Stanfield)

Benediction

Towards the end of the exposition, the priest or deacon goes to the altar, genuflects and kneels. Then this hymn or a suitable alternative is sung, during which the minister incenses the sacrament.

Therefore we, before him bending	Tantum ergo Sacramentum
This great Sacrament revere	Veneremur cernui,
Types and shadows have their ending	Et antiquum documentum
for the newer rite is here	Novo cedat ritui;
Faith, our outward sense befriending	Præstet fides supplementum
Makes the inward vision clear.	Sensuum defectui.
Glory let us give, and blessing	Genitori, Genitoque
To the Father and the Son	Laus et iubilatio.
Honour, might, and praise addressing	Salus, honor, virtus quoque
While eternal ages run	Sit et benedictio;
Ever too his love confessing	Procedenti ab utroque
Who, from both, with both is one.	Compar sit laudatio.
Amen.	Amen.

The minister then says the following prayer (or a suitable alternative)

Let us pray.	Oremus.
Lord Jesus Christ,	Deus, qui nobis sub sacramento mirabili
you gave us the eucharist	
as the memorial of your suffering and death.	passionis tuæ memoriam reliquisti: tribue, quæsumus,
May our worship of this sacrament of your body and blood	ita nos Corporis et Sanguinis tui sacra mysteria venerari,
Help us to experience the salvation you won for us	ut redemptionis tuæ fructum in nobis
and the peace of the kingdom	iugiter sentiamus.
where you live with the Father and the Holy Spirit,	Qui vivis et regnas in sæcula sæculorum.
one God, for ever and ever.	R. Amen.
R. Amen.	

The Priest or Deacon now puts on the humeral veil and blesses the congregation with the Blessed Sacrament.

The Divine Praises formerly said at this point may more properly be included within the period of adoration.

The Divine Praises

Blessed be God.
Blessed be his holy Name.
Blessed be Jesus Christ, true God and true Man.
Blessed be the name of Jesus.
Blessed be his most Sacred Heart.
Blessed be his most Precious Blood.
Blessed be Jesus in the most holy Sacrament of the Altar.
Blessed be the Holy Spirit, the Paraclete.
Blessed be the great Mother of God, Mary, most holy.
Blessed be her holy and Immaculate Conception.
Blessed be her glorious Assumption.
Blessed be the name of Mary, Virgin and Mother.
Blessed be St Joseph, her spouse most chaste.
Blessed be God in his Angels and in his Saints.

Reposition

Immediately after the Blessed Sacrament is reposed in the tabernacle, the following may be sung:

Ant. Let us adore for ever
    the most holy Sacrament.

Ps. O praise the Lord,
    all you nations
Acclaim him, all you peoples
For his mercy is confirmed upon us
and the truth of the Lord
    remains for ever.

Glory be to the Father,
    and to the Son
and to the Holy Spirit
As it was in the beginning, is now
and ever shall be,
    world without end. Amen.

Ant. Let us adore for ever the most
    holy Sacrament.

Ant. Adoremus in æternum
    sanctissimum Sacramentum.

Ps. Laudate Dominum,
    omnes gentes;
laudate eum omnes populi.
Quoniam confirmata est super
    nos misericordia eius;
et veritas Domini manet
    in æternum.

Gloria Patri, et Filio,
    et Spiritui Sancto.
Sicut erat in principio,
    et nunc, et semper,
et in sæcula sæculorum. Amen.

Ant. Adoremus in æternum
    sanctissimum Sacramentum.

An alternative acclamation:

O Sacrament most holy,
    O Sacrament divine!
All praise, and all thanksgiving,
Be every moment thine!